CAMPAIGN AMERICA '96

CAMPAIGN AMERICA '96:

The View
From the Couch

William O'Rourke

Marlowe & Company
New York

Published by
Marlowe & Company
632 Broadway, Seventh Floor
New York NY 10012

Library of Congress Cataloging in Publication Data

O'Rourke, William.
    Campaign America '96 : the view from the couch / William O'Rourke.
        p.   cm.
    Includes bibliographical references.
    ISBN 1-56924-758-7
    1. Presidents—United States—Election—1996.   2. Presidential candidates—United States.   3. United States—Politics and government—1993–   4. Mass media— Political aspects—United States.   5. Voting—United States.   I. Title.
    E888.076   1997
    324.973'0929—dc21   97-13154
                                                                          CIP

ISBN 1-56924-758-7

Manufactured in the United States of America

To Teresa and Joseph

Contents

Contents

My friends, a presidential campaign is more than a contest of candidates, more than a clash of opposing philosophies. It is a mirror held up to America.

—Bob Dole, August 15, 1996, San Diego, California

From Imus in the morning to Koppel late at night, America has become a talk show nation, a boob-tube civilization, a run-at-the-mouth culture in which anyone can say anything at any time as long as they pull some ratings.

—Howard Kurtz, *Hot Air*

We must stop bravely at the surface.

—Leonard Cohen, *Beautiful Losers*

CAMPAIGN AMERICA '96

A Note to the Reader

I do not study TV, I watch it. *Campaign America '96: The View from the Couch* is not meant to be all-encompassing or exhaustive. I did not watch everything, or hear or read everything on the campaign. This book is about how a campaign is consumed, not produced. Consumed by a white American male of Bill Clinton's generation. So I consumed and processed it, absorbing more than most, doubtless, but less than some. It was a campaign designed for consumers—of media. In the tradition of campaign books, from Teddy White to Hunter Thompson's, this might be an unorthodox approach, but I decided to join the great majority and report the 1996 campaign from the point of view most Americans actually experience it.

Television came into my consciousness in 1952. My earliest memories of TV are the Eisenhower and Stevenson Republican and Democratic conventions, which, at age six, I thought were the only things on daytime television.

A lot of commentators forget the import of the clichés of television: television does bring people into our living rooms. People who are invited into our living rooms become our friends, or at least faux intimates. Such folks bask in the intimacy of our surroundings. Everyone notices this, but few deal with the consequences. If Walter Conkrite is Dad, and Johnny Carson is everyone's often-married uncle, and Annette Funicello is all the boys' sweetheart, what does that make us—me? Well, one big happy family.

Television *is* America's great melting pot—not its immigration policy or the living patterns of its citizens. The distance between our "leaders" and the "public" has collapsed. We know them, or we feel we do. The price public figures (and everyone on television becomes a public figure) pay for coming into our living rooms and being either ingratiating or overwrought is the way they become ours to do with what we will. They become our friends, a television circle of intimates. The most extreme form of the overidentification that takes place is stalking. The kind most of us indulge in is just damning overfamiliarity. One becomes closely attached to those whom we look at so intently and for so long.

The effect of watching someone on television is to watch without the fear of him or her noticing as we do it. In "real life" we modulate our reactions when we are in someone's actual presence. But the power relationships are inverted when we watch television. The viewer is powerful. We control the gaze.

Campaign America '96 is also about the America of '96, the elaborate setting of the electoral jewel. What I attempt herein is to put the square peg of the '96 presidential campaign into the round hole of America's everyday culture. I am after history and its context. The form I use is modified diary-narration (with emphasis on the modifications). I follow the campaign month by month, chronicling it as I saw and heard and read about it. I don't work backward in *Campaign America '96,* only forward. What occurs happens in real time: when I learn of it the reader learns of it. There are two or three forays into more typical reportage (off the couch), one coming early in the year, when I found myself at a conference of economists in San Francisco, California, others haphazardly through the year, dictated largely by happenstance.

Over time, themes and individuals began to surface and they started to bend the shape of the narrative. Rush Limbaugh turns up quite a bit, partly because of the hours (noon to three five days a week) his radio show is on. The "liberal" talk show host Diane Rehm I heard quite a lot, too. She may not be known to large sections of the country, but her show provided a platform for a lot of folks who turned up on other radio talk programs elsewhere. There's oblique autobiography throughout, and my generational concerns are evident: the Vietnam War, baby boomers, the economy, O. J., and the media.

Campaign America '96: The View From the Couch

The media are the message here, since 90 percent of what I recount is filtered through them. And the media spin, but the question is: Are they spinnable? I don't think so. You can't spin the media. In the world of blind people, the one-eyed person might be king, but the media are all our eye now and they rule. Patterns of viewing emerge, based on my interest and what is available to me. The expected ones are here: C-SPAN, CNN, PBS, the other networks, including the Christian Broadcasting Network and a number of the outliers of my local cable system. But herein is what I was exposed to (or exposed myself to)—and though I didn't intend to be encyclopedic, I did fall into some nooks and crannies. It's what one person could reasonably take in. (Contrary to what this book may suggest, I do have a life.)

The images of television and film are mute; the people talking say things, but images do not speak. They need to be articulated. One paradox of the age is the more we get to see, the less many are able to say. When we read, we are given the tools (the words) to discuss what we are doing. When we watch, images give us no vocabulary, no tools that allow us to "speak" about what we see. A visual culture needs to be literate or it goes mute.

During the year many things came to mind, among them two literary truisms: the old saw, I didn't have enough time to write you a short letter, so I'm writing you a long one instead, and Matthew Arnold's dictum that journalism is "literature in a hurry." As the contemporary saying goes, I have attempted to control for these two variables. But even this unseemly haste is not without its benefits: one must realize that not all hindsight is twenty-twenty.

And to rearrange one more old chestnut, every campaign gets the book it deserves, and the '96 presidential campaign deserves the one in your hand.

January 15, 1997
South Bend, Indiana

Preface

Bill Clinton is the only president whose hand I have ever shaken. He was Candidate Clinton at the time (early fall '92) and had come to the University of Notre Dame to deliver a speech. Four years earlier, in 1988, Notre Dame's football team had won the national championship and George Bush came to campus and had his photograph taken with Coach Lou Holtz and the victorious squad. That photo ran in a lot of newspapers and, doubtless, got Bush a few votes.

Clinton's visit to Notre Dame was not without controversy. The campaign event was held in the Stepan Center, an ugly geodesic dome in the least picturesque part of Notre Dame's largely bucolic campus. Above the Stepan Center flew an airplane trailing a nylon tail of deprecations about the draft-dodging, pot-smoking, baby-killing candidate.

As one would imagine, the antiabortion forces are sizable at Notre Dame, and they intended to mount some vocal opposition to Clinton's presence. Clinton's advance team and the university's student Democrats (and the local powers that be) had arranged for the audience immediately in front of the stage to be a by-ticket-only section, and the tickets were distributed by the party's faithful to, for the most part, the party's faithful.

One of the well-connected got two tickets and brought me along. The Stepan Center is used to best effect for pep rallies the Friday night before a football game. Filled to its nonrafters, the building provides an impressive setting for whipping up rhetorical frenzy. Anything more intimate, say less than a thousand people, is lost in bad acoustics and dead space. But filled to the gunwales, it can be a rocking place.

Clinton delivered a rousing speech, interrupted hardly at all by the distantly seated protesters. He came on the stage accompanied by local South Bend politicians and the Democratic governor of Indiana, Evan Bayh, and his wife, Susan. Mrs. Bayh looks enough like Tipper Gore that, for a moment, I thought we were getting a twofer. Clinton quickly reminded (or informed) the audience that if elected he would be the first president ever to have graduated from a Catholic university. This met with an equivocal reaction, insofar as it did recall JFK and the fact that he went to Harvard, not Georgetown, as Clinton did, but in the mind of a lot of the students, Notre Dame is the only really Catholic university, since Jesuits have always been seen as a world unto themselves.

It was a successful event for the young candidate, one shown on the national news that night and in newspaper photos the following day, with the Notre Dame seal below and above him, adding a (however begrudging) nonendorsement-endorsement by the largest Catholic university in the country. Clinton wasn't Gipperizied, but he wasn't ostracized either.

After the speech, Clinton left the stage and came down to shake hands with the crowd, the crowd at the front of the stage being the assembled supporters, not the students who were looking to put an embalmed fetus in his outstretched hand.

I found myself moving forward in the tide and managed to be near the front of the rope line when he appeared. Coming from my left, it appeared to be some sort of human earthquake heading your way: the ground was rippling, heaping up and settling back down. Because it was not just one man moving down the line, but three or four moving semi-iattached, two Secret Service people and a campaign person, all Siamesed, bumping up and down. The Secret Service agents were tense, at work, looking at you, beyond you, to the side of you, appraising whether you or anyone near was going to make them earn their pay.

In the middle of this many-men-man was Clinton himself. The first impression I had was the largeness of him close up, since he loomed over the horizon of the rope line. I am not tall, but Clinton seemed taller and bigger than I expected (I once stood next to Muhammad Ali, and he seemed smaller than I had thought him to be), partially because Clinton was the candidate, partially because he was bookended by two beefy guys with guns and fancy electronic gear.

Clinton stuck out his hand and I grabbed it, though he applied most of the pressure. I had been wondering what minimalist speech I could impart to him. (He hadn't stopped the progression yet, no matter what anyone had said.) "Great speech," I said, witlessly, having discarded such prolix substitutes as "You should read my novel about draft evasion," then much in the news—his own draft history, that is, not my 1974 first novel—and other self-serving bits of information. What I almost did say was "Boy, you work hard," which was apparent. He was sweating through a blue shirt and an undershirt. (His dress was like a lot of contemporary corporate chieftains I have met, their underdress being as elaborate and costly as their overdress—no cheap T-shirts next to their expensive skin.)

What was clear on Clinton's flushed red face was that he was enjoying this. The Secret Service men did not look happy. Clinton did. The blob-multi-man moved on. I noticed my hand was still outstretched, but now empty. I also detected another ripple, a smaller up-and-down down the line. Hillary, it appeared, was making this same journey, too.

The Secret Service attached to her were not as large, and one was a woman. I looked at both women, Hillary and the agent. They were moving a bit slower than Clinton's group had been, but the crowd was shifting, some having pulled back, and the rhythm of hands shook per linear foot was dropping fast. The angle from where I stood would only allow me an unseemly lunge toward Mrs. Clinton (perhaps alarming all that heavily armed protection nearby), and then it wasn't clear that she would take my hand, since she wasn't taking all that were offered. So I watched.

She, in contrast, was not big. Two other things stood out: the amount of makeup she had on (doubtless another long day) and the look in her eyes. It was classic doe in the headlights, part fear, part displeasure, part affront. She was not enjoying this at all. The Secret Service woman next to her was all business, from her tightly coiled wired earpiece (not off the shelf from Radio Shack, that bit of equipment), to her clothes, which could have been a uniform, something a navy woman would wear, an outfit made to pass as civvies. A telltale pin was in the lapel, as if beyond the headsets and handmikes and semiautomatic weapons they needed some further insignia.

Soon, they were gone, but I had seen the alpha and the omega of the '92 campaign, the poles of Bill and Hillary Clinton, one loving what he was doing, the other enduring it.

The Nobel Prize–winning poet Czeslaw Milosz once said within my hearing that all the bad things Americans said about Russians were true and all the bad things Russians said about Americans were true. I had concluded by the time of Clinton's visit to Notre Dame that all the bad things said about the Clintons appeared true and all the good things said about the Clintons were true, too.

The Gennifer Flowers flak was helpful during the '92 campaign, insofar as it filled up a lot of space and most of the Arkansas financial back-scratching that had gone on in the past took a backseat to Clinton's chief bimbo eruption. Clinton had been wistfully talked about in 1988 as possible future presidential timber by some Democrats, but then his "women problem" would come up and a sigh of regret would issue forth. And it was often political women who were raising Clinton's name as an up-and-comer. After Gary Hart went under, drowned in his own Caribbean dalliance with Donna Rice, Clinton must have wondered himself, or so I thought.

What I call the Vanessa Williams principle applied, or so I thought: Ms. Williams never would have had those erotic photos taken that appeared in *Penthouse* if she had ever thought she would one day become Miss America. She suffered, as they say, a failure of imagination.

When I got free of the draft in 1969 I realized I could never be president of the United States. Not that I thought I would, but as a typical American (white) boy of the period, that was one of the myths (grow up to be president . . .) that surrounded me, so it passed through and out of my mind. Evidently it didn't pass through Bill Clinton's mind.

But I didn't think I could ever be elected governor of Missouri (where I grew up) either. And it didn't take many years after Clinton's dance around the draft for Clinton to think that he could be elected governor of Arkansas. However chaotic Clinton's family life had been, he and his family never left Arkansas while he grew up, which did leave him rooted somewhere. (And, doubtless, the whole Vanessa Williams principle needs to be revised, since she is probably the most successful ex–ex–Miss America in contemporary history. She has come through smelling like a rose and since I did see the offending photos, I never doubted she wouldn't for a minute.)

But there were other odors in the air during the first and second years of the Clinton administration, the smell of actual fire and brimstone. On February 26, 1993, the World Trade Center was rocked by an explosion. Soot-blackened faces emerged on the television screens of America from the belly and heights of the Twin Towers. Two days later four federal agents were killed raiding a religious compound outside of Waco, Texas, and fire consumed the Branch Davidians on April 19 of the same year.

Two smaller, individual, more localized events in Washington during the fall of '94 supplied their own bad smells. In between (October 3) were scenes from Somalia of American soldiers being dragged through the dusty streets, and then Michael Durrant's interview was taped by his captors and shown worldwide.

Pilot Frank Corder's September 12, 1994, small-plane kamikaze attack on the White House and Francisco Martin Duran using the White House for target practice the next month did seem to fit a larger pattern—a vague, strangely depersonalized, albeit potentially lethal, lashing out.

It was not the man, but the institution, the presidency, the White House itself, *government,* that was under attack. It wasn't the early Clinton presidency, which was a mess, that had set the stage for these attacks. It wasn't the figurative fact of the health care plan going down in flames, it was the real flames that were flaring out across the country that were heating the atmosphere. That both White House incidents were carried out by fairly young male adults linked them to another, more successful, brand of representative violence that had been going on during those months, violence aimed at abortion clinics.

The first two years of the Clinton administration were conducted in this acrid haze. Young males, especially young white males (Paul Hill, Michael Griffin and John Salvi, among others), seemed particularly agitated in '93 and throughout '94, and their impulsive rages were directed not so much at individuals as at abortionists, who are seen as a caste, not individuals, which made it easier for the religious to kill physicians and clinic employees. It's nothing personal.

President Clinton, it was reported, was watching a football game on television while Mr. Duran emptied the clip from his Norinco Sks 7.62-mm semiautomatic rifle (made in China, bought in Colorado) at the side of the White House on October 29, 1994. Watching football on TV is what the greatest proportion of American males do in order to work out fantasies of violence and commonly accumulated frustrations.

My it's-not-personal theory does fly in the face of conventional wisdom—given Bill and Hillary Clinton's complaints (early and late) of all the public venom directed at them personally. But those two White House outbursts did seem to have their impersonal side—and the months before the midterm elections generated a lot of hot air, which got blown about the country at large by various fans of the obliging media.

It is monumentally depressing to note what checked the momentum described above, the event that muted the insistent drumroll of vocal cheerleading for this sort of discontent (G. Gordon Liddy, former plumber, current talk radio host, calling for head shots), which had helped to usher in the Republican "revolution" of November '94 (sanctioned by 34 percent of the electorate who bothered to vote in the off-year election). It was the bombing of the Oklahoma City federal building in April of 1995.

Timothy McVeigh appears to be the nineties version of Lee Harvey Oswald. (The indicted McVeigh fits into the it's-not-personal theory since, it appears, he had no specific individual in mind, just institutions. Oswald at least wanted to kill *someone* specific.) McVeigh apparently was striking out, making a personal statement, like Frank Corder with his kamikaze White House Cessna mission. Had Corder, the lone pilot of Seventeenth Street, loaded explosives onto his plane, what would our present condition be?

The Oklahoma Federal Building bombing of April 19, 1995, served as a national backfire. It didn't necessarily snuff out the flames that had sprung up, but it did tamp them down for a while, though, of course, they are stubborn and can spring up again. But the backfire did allow the Clinton presidency to reorient itself.

The Reagan presidency gained traction after John Hinckley shot Reagan on March 30, 1981; Reagan's budget quickly passed, he was treated more reverentially, his stature rose, not just in the minds of the people, but in the estimation of the media: anyone who almost gives his life for a job seems automatically more serious, and more worthy of regard. And when the federal building was brought down by the bomb-packed Ryder truck, the Clinton presidency began its own rebound.

PROLOGUE

The Prologue Is the Past

★

12/31 I am imagining Dick Clark, one of the eerily unaltered faces of my generation's own psychic Mount Rushmore, standing over the cheering, youthful crowds in New York City's Times Square counting down, not the Top 40, but the final seconds of 1995, while I am sitting, not on my couch in South Bend, Indiana, but in a seat of a multiplex in northern California, down the road a bit from the state capital, Sacramento, watching Oliver Stone's new film, *Nixon*.

It is a fitting enough place to observe the turning of the new year, the new campaign year of 1996. My watch is still set on Times Square time, though I no longer live in New York City, but South Bend is the farthest outpost of eastern standard time. It often feels like an insult of some sort to share the clock in Indiana with Manhattan and Washington and Boston, power capitals all, a Copernican rebuke that adds to the small-town blues of our Rust Belt city, largely deindustrializied, turned into a regional service economy, nostalgic for its once dynamic past, when it was the home of Studebaker, now as defunct as the dinosaurs, models of which are sometimes exhibited, along with cars, in the Studebaker

Museum, occupying a building which housed the flagship car dealership across the street from the vast, and now hollow, factory complex.

But we're not in South Bend, Indiana, now. And President William Jefferson Clinton isn't in Washington, either. The Clintons are in Hilton Head, South Carolina, attending yet another Renaissance Weekend, the yuppie version of California's rich men's enclave, Bohemian Grove. The Renaissance Weekend is an eighties-nineties blend of corporate retreat, high-powered convention, and academic conference. But this particular theater of the California multiplex is a small one. More moviegoers are going to see *Grumpier Old Men, Jumanji,* and the pig film, *Babe.* The audience is, I'm alarmed to see, *elderly.* I, having this month turned fifty, must be near (or below) the average age. The only one I see who is a twenty-something is my brother-in-law's fiancée.

Richard Nixon, of course, could be up on my Mount Rushmore with Dick Clark, though, unlike Clark, Nixon did age: not that much, since, like a lot of men of his generation, he looked old at twenty. And over the years, his wardrobe never really changed; it only became more costly.

During Reagan's first term, I wrote that Reagan would be the first president not to visibly age while in office, because the emotional toll that affects those who occupy the office would not be as arduous for him, since he wasn't, ah, deeply involved, or intellectually troubled, in the job. But Hinckley shot him, and near the end, other medical problems further dimmed his physical aura. But no Lincolnesque angst was ever etched in his face.

In the Sacramento state capitol, portraits of the former governors are displayed. Reagan's was hidden behind a stairway, a rendition close to life-size, done in photo-realist style. That choice seemed most apropos, since Reagan was a creature of film and it was fitting that his image would be reproduced not from life, but from a photograph—as a photograph.

Reagan always appalled me, but when he became president I was old enough to be philosophical about it, whereas when Nixon was in office I was very much in process, not at all fixed, often unemployed, a young man without too many prospects. Nixon seemed to have his hand on the personal tiller of my little boat, whereas I felt largely a spectator when Reagan cruised by on his own *Queen Mary.*

Nixon was the first president I ever voted against. It was the first time I ever voted, having turned twenty-one in 1966. I voted for Hubert Horatio Humphrey. I did not want to *heighten the contradictions,* as it was put back then, by dumping the Hump and not voting. Nixon squeaked in; the election was close, but not quite as close as when Kennedy had defeated Nixon eight years earlier.

Except for Reagan's second term, all the presidents of my day were accidental, or so it seems. Kennedy slipping in with the help of Mayor Richard J. Daley and the pliant river wards; Johnson getting in with the aid of Oswald et alia, then sidestepping Goldwater, despite young Hillary Rodham's Illinois efforts on the Arizona senator's behalf; Nixon being aided by Johnson's abdication, the Democratic Party's implosion and resulting desertions; then Ford (proving beyond a reasonable doubt that *anyone* can be president), thanks to his Warren Commission work (I *am* at an Oliver Stone movie); and then Jimmy Carter, barely elected by a country somewhat shell-shocked by the previous ten years of American history, which included the first resignation of a sitting president; then Reagan, thanks, in part, to the Ayatollah Khomeini, Ted Koppel and the creation of *Nightline,* aka *America Held Hostage,* day 365, not to mention the almost 20 percent interest rates sanctioned by the Federal Reserve, etc.

Despite talk of a constitutional change allowing for a third term, Reagan (FDR in reverse) finally departed into announced Alzheimer's, leaving an open race: Dukakis, the last white man standing in the Democratic primaries, though not standing quite tall enough (oh, Gary Hart); and Bush arrived, having "lied" sufficiently about poor old Bob Dole's record. Bob Dole beat Bush in the Iowa caucuses, leaving New Hampshire a critical race, which Bush won, thereby saddling himself with the wonderful former New Hampshire governor John Sununu, which helped cripple the Bush administration and the upcoming '92 campaign. And then the last banana peel Bush slipped on was Mr. Ross Perot. Enter Bill Clinton, pursued by a bear—or teddy bear, or Gennifer Flowers in a teddy.

Bill Clinton, my accidental president. I have finally gotten used to my doctors being younger than myself, but still recall being shocked when I was at the governor's mansion (Indiana's, not Arkansas') a few years ago and realized Governor Bayh was younger than I was. His wife and my wife (Bayh's age) had gone to UC Berkeley at the same time but hadn't, they quickly discovered, traveled in the same circles. And Bill Clinton is a few months younger than I: I was born in the last month of 1945, so missed out by a few weeks being a bona fide member of the baby boom. My wife was born in 1957, the peak year of the baby boom, so we cover the waterfront.

One of my crank theories regarding Bill Clinton and the '92 election is that he entered the race not expecting to win. There is a good deal of evidence for that assertion. He expected to be nominated. He wanted to be crowned the leading Democratic figure, wanted to walk into the job in '97 after easily vanquishing—whom? Dan Quayle?—but, surprise, surprise, he won. It's Ross Perot, stupid. Not just in the votes Perot skimmed away from Bush, but for how Perot changed the dynamics of the entire race.

The first debate, on October 11, 1992, had been, in my view, the final straw. Perot set Bush wobbling. Clinton had given the first answer and Bush followed, sounding, to me, forceful and dismissive of Clinton. The camera lingered on Clinton's face when Bush concluded, and Clinton looked chastened. Then it was Perot's turn. Ross snapped at Bush, treated him as an annoying underling, the son of the owner who really doesn't run things. Perot trampled over Bush's authority, took it away from him. You're *president of the United States,* Perot seemed to be saying; who cares? From then on Clinton recovered and Bush never did. Had that debate just been Bush and Clinton the verdict likely would not have been "Clinton In Control," as *Time* magazine announced in large bold letters the next week (October 19, 1992) but "Bush Storms On."

Bush helped throughout the campaign, running the dottiest race possible. When the bar-code-scanner flap occurred, Bush's spin doctors couldn't change what seemed painfully obvious to a lot of voters: George Bush didn't go to grocery stores, never had *bought* anything as mundane as food in who knew how many years. Wal-Mart America took offense.

So Clinton won. He was delighted, but surprised—almost, it seemed, stunned. What highlighted his general unpreparedness for me was all the trouble he had selecting an attorney general. He and Hillary are lawyers; they went to Yale Law School. And he doesn't have someone he's personally and politically close to that he can appoint attorney general?! Even if the plan was to make the AG post a figurehead, and have Hillary run the Department of Justice, Bobby Kennedy in drag. Shocking. One can't underestimate the true backwaterness of political life in Arkansas. Clinton couldn't appoint, it now appears, any of the cronies of the Rose law firm to that high a post, since he was obviously aware of their potential indictability. (The qualification of Reagan's AG, Mr. Edwin Meese, it must be remembered, was his not quite indictability—but California isn't the same sort of backwater Arkansas is.) So Zoë Baird emerged from Warren Christopher's Rolodex and the trouble began. Clinton never thought he would win, or he would have given a bit more thought to who might fill a few of those jobs. Everything happened so fast.

Nixon, the film, unleashes such cataracts of recollection. Stone's semihistories are an adolescent's indulgent pimple-lancing, and a therapeutic mess does flow forth. The walls of the multiplex theater are draped with dark brown cloth; there is a drab funeral-parlor atmosphere about the place, and indeed this is, in large part, a viewing, Nixon in a box. It is tempting, as Stone is tempted, to link Nixon to JFK's death, since he profited so much from the coup, but even in Stone's movie the connection is thin. The link begins, according to a wild article first published in *The Realist,* then reprinted in *Rights* (July-August 1991), with Nixon's entry into politics: he read an ad, goes the story, in a Los Angeles newspaper, placed by Preston Bush and others, seeking a candidate for Congress. Preston Bush later played a role, evidently, in arranging the Eisenhower-Nixon ticket. All that, however worrisome, is not the point. The clincher is that *George Bush* played a role in Kennedy's assassination and that is how Nixon profits from it. This, doubtless, is the cloudy Texas connection Stone plays up in his film. All of this orbits around the unexplained memo of J. Edgar Hoover stating that "Mr. George Bush of the CIA" had been briefed on November 23, 1963, about the assassination. The memo appeared in the August 13, 1988, *Nation.* These connections are what set conspiracy theorists' minds ablaze.

I am amused by the beginning of the film, done in black and white, the wacky salesman film the burglars watch, then the Watergate break-in itself, the White House shot through wrought iron, surrounded by roiling storm clouds, part *Citizen Kane,* part a Hammer-produced Dracula film. Lightning crackles and thunder rumbles and Dracula should emerge. Tricky Dick as the living dead. Stone's film mixes styles, a little documentary here, a little domestic comedy there, some *Shane,* a bit of *Viva Las Vegas.* J. Edgar Hoover as one of the boys in the band.

What Stone does capture is the essential pathology of the time. He's a caricaturist who uses film. I've always thought Bob Dole's funniest line was one he uttered inspired by seeing Carter, Ford, and Nixon entering the White House for a ceremonial reunion: "See no evil. Hear no evil. And evil." That sums up the fifties and early sixties for me. Hypocrisy, denial, and evil. The much maligned sixties—the period of "our long national nightmare" (who did write that, Ford's single electric perception?)—did end in August of 1974 with Nixon waving spastically from the door of the presidential helicopter, his V-signs flung out, as if he were trying to shake filth from off his fingers.

See no evil, hear no evil, and evil stopped being the actual version of "All the News That's Fit to Print." Newspapers began in the late sixties and early seventies to anticipate their own version of C-SPAN yet to come: print the documents raw, print transcripts raw, let the public read. It was different. Hitherto, the *New York Times* was playing the role of paterfamilias, instructing the public on what the *Times* thought the public needed to know. The *Times* would know, but there was a gulf between them and us. The *Wall Street Journal* has always known who its audience is, and that is why its journalism is always useful—the editorial page notwithstanding; but the *Times* was in the business of social betterment, old-style paternalism. Guidance, not just information. (See, for example, the *Times* spiking the Bay of Pigs story.) But once it started to print the Daniel Ellsberg–provided documents the rift began to knit. It became, for a while, us and us. My God, the government was suing the *Times*! In solidarity with the people, the *Times* began to acquire empathy. It, too, was being dragged off to court by the same lawbreakers the kids were protesting.

Nixon's exit eventually brought us Jimmy Carter, the greatest failure as American president, in the sense of lost opportunities. What the country was ready for then! Carter could have nationalized the oil companies and received popular support (though he was a corporate mind caught in a peanut farmer's body), but he was paid back for his temerity by out-of-sight inflation and terminal humiliation at the hands of religious Iranians—his kowtowing to the shah had become a pitiful sight.

Midway through *Nixon,* the film, I realize that one reason there are only older people in the audience is that most teenagers wouldn't have a clue about what is going on on the screen: you had to be there, or at least be more than half-informed about the period. Any mall rats wandering in might assume that at any moment Anthony Hopkins's Nixon is going to flay Alexander Haig (Powers Booth) and hang him, batlike, up on the ceiling, Hannibal Lector style.

Stone and the actress (Joan Allen) playing the role do give Pat Nixon more verve than she showed us in life, since her public role was as a symbol of the silent sufferer. Back in 1972, when Nixon the real was still president, I sat in a Harrisburg, Pennsylvania, auditorium and watched a crowd of young people, younger than I (I was twenty-six), high school kids, watch the Checkers speech (reproduced in a documentary) and was amazed then by their laughter: not at what Nixon was saying, but at how he looked. I was five before my parents had a TV and it was a small black and white and I did "grow up" watching it, but these youngsters, hardly a decade younger, were children of a new technology. They laughed at Nixon's shifting eyes, little ticks, all of which were magnified by the large movie screen.

They were laughing at old TV, at the way, in the fifties, most TV shows looked like something put on in the family garage. In a history of television I read twenty years ago (*CBS: Reflections in a Bloodshot Eye*) I was most struck by one thing: those involved in the invention of television were always after color. Black and white just came along first, but they knew color was what the medium had to have, because that's what would sell things, make the world look desirable.

Nothing much looked that desirable on TV in the fifties, certainly not Nixon, or tight-lipped Pat, sitting off to the side on a hard upholstered Republican chair.

I am not a Pollyanna, but things have generally improved: the country is not quite as crazy as it was back then. It isn't "See no evil, hear no evil, and evil" any longer, at least not entirely. Some hypocrisy was removed—forever?—from the culture because of the "sixties." When

James Baker said the Gulf War was about "Jobs, jobs, jobs," I knew we were living in a new time.

That is one reason why when people complain that things have gotten meaner, that there is less civility in "discourse" (such an odd word of our time), that cultural Darwinism is everywhere, that the Republicans want the poor to starve and more citizens housed in jails, I smell not just bloody teeth and claws, but the sweeter fragrances of the sixties. Everyone is coming closer to saying what they mean; there is less hypocrisy and that is why so much said is so blunt and cold. Victory for the sixties, albeit we reap the usual variety of somewhat unintended consequences.

History is often hidden history, but perhaps there is just a wee bit less hidden these days, and what Stone shows us in his film, however fanciful, is what we didn't get to see then—it does remind one of how much was never shown, however many people might have known it at the time.

Stone's film near its end does turn into actual news footage and, who knows, I may be hallucinating, but there is Bob Dole saying the second half of the twentieth century will be "the age of Nixon." And Dole's practically blubbering. And then there's Bill Clinton up on the screen at Nixon's funeral, delivering what sounds like a complimentary eulogy, too. "He gave of himself with intelligence and energy and devotion to duty. . . ." Whoa! Clinton's not dancing on Nixon's grave, but Clinton, our latest accidental president, is currently sharing Nixon's former dance floor, and Clinton himself is now the beleaguered commander in chief. He obviously feels some wild, but appropriate, sympathy for the dead old crook, yet another modern president with less than half the popular vote, another 43 percenter, thanks to that other southern boy, good ol' George Wallace.

ONE

The State of the Union

1/1   On January 1, 1996, what does Campaign America look like? The view from California is foggy this morning, at least from the San Jose area and around Sacramento, San Francisco, Santa Cruz, Monterey, and Carmel—my points of reference. I've been trying to avoid road rage on the highways as I drive around in my rented Nissan, but I don't detect any immediate uprisings among the population as a whole. In fact, things look fairly OK.

Every time I come to California I say the following, since it seems easier to say here than in some parts of the Midwest: How rich this country is! When the Reagan eighties began to strip-mine the surplus value out of this country, it had a thick vein to gouge. The biggest thing manufactured in the eighties (except for the computer and software industry) was the money being produced out of the accounting legerdemain of the junk-bond, arbitrage laborers. Overvalued and undervalued companies were vampirized, and what was extracted was cash. Reagan was the Hollywood president, the corporate commander in chief, so it wasn't strange that his decade was so symbolized by this sort of sucking sound. That's the sucking sound I heard, not Ross Perot's.

William O'Rourke

The rich got richer and the poor got poorer through the eighties and nineties, but driving around California one is impressed with the amount of wealth scattered everywhere. It's the bounty hanging from the trees (oranges in this case), the fruited plains, indeed—the fruited hills and valleys is more to the point. And driving through the fruit basket of the world (the Watsonville area, the valley) and seeing stoop laborers, little clots of dark men and women and children in the fields, backs bent in the narrow rows, is like looking at stopped time. The insidious thought is that there seem to be relatively few of them and they look happy to be employed, exploited, and harassed. Such is trickle-down, where the only thing that trickles down is anxiety about having a job.

Shortly after the Rodney King verdict and the burning of South Central LA, my wife and I and our boy were in California visiting family. We had been invited to a wedding of an old friend in Beverly Hills and since we were in the state, my wife and I (Grandma baby-sitting!) were able to fly down from Sacramento to LAX. We arrived a few hours before the wedding and went to see the Watts Towers, the homespun American version of Gaudi's Barcelona sculptural configurations, built by a man named Rodia between 1942 and 1954. The route took us through the burned-out South Central area.

It was my first time in Los Angeles and I was mildly surprised by the "single-family houses," the neighborhoods of bungalows (though how many were rentals I do not know), the large sky above; and I wondered why, if so much social unrest can ferment so effectively in this sort of mild climate (as well as Florida's), the colder climates are not more racked and ruined. The Watts Towers, stuck at the end of a dry dusty road, adjacent to empty fields and the freeway, turned out to be a smaller, less colorful structure, its twisting surfaces studded with bottle caps, seashells, bits of china and glass, than I had envisioned from photos. We drove back toward Beverly Hills and, not knowing my way around, following signs, ended up on the road most burned out in the rioting. Not homes, but businesses, one after another, and I recalled that the torching was racial, attacks against "foreign" ownership, though in both examples of unrest (California and Florida) the match was a court verdict that was seen as unjust.

Riot as speech. At the wedding I was surprised to see that my friend, the groom, had hired off-duty LA policemen as guards. This was before the Year of O. J., but I do recall them being Mark Fuhrman look-alikes, since the fire-ravaged road reached Beverly Hills, and who knows what sort of intrusion the wedding party feared.

But on this family visit on the eve of Campaign '96 we travel to Half Moon Bay in my father-in-law's RV between Christmas and New Year's and we run into some German tourists who are very upset that Yellowstone and Yosemite—their next would-be destinations—are closed, thanks to the second government shutdown of nonessential government services. Not that I care too much about upsetting German tourists, but the idiocy of yet another congressional shutdown over Christmas is manifest. (The first was November 4–20, the current one began December sixteenth.)

The German tourists may or may not care about balancing our national budget (they sure aren't talking about privatizing their own social security system), but their vacation plans have been spoiled. Americans, those directly, or indirectly affected are getting to experience the first manifestation of the '94 Republican "revolution" (and what the Republicans have wrought are not all those parts of the Contract with America that have been voted on, all for the never-never land of down the road, but gridlock, parks closed, a hodgepodge of government services shut down, the type not much noticed till absent.) The shutdowns are in the long line of management "strikes" that have bothered the American electorate, the nonelite majority. The baseball strike of '94–'95 was an eye-opener. (Carter's reelection hopes, one recalls, were not aided by canceling our country's participation in the Moscow Olympics during his one and only term.)

Cracking down, having their way, was the name of the new Congress's game. The rich folks who own major league baseball teams felt the same way: they're real men, too—even Marge Schott. The authoritarian impulse, following the '94 election, was at loose in the land.

Cutting the NEA, the NEH, and PBS is also symbolic. Authoritarians (remember the good name Jeane Kirkpatrick bestowed on them back in the Reagan era) don't like antiauthoritarian institutions, and giving money to artists is something riddled with antiauthoritarianism. Forget the nitpicking over the pros and cons: it's about control. Ask bad Bud

Selig. The baseball strike was finally "settled" in April of '95—canceled World Series back to back was unthinkable even for the owners.

But Bob Dole has let Newt Gingrich and the class of '94 shut down his Congress (*Newsweek*'s December 26, 1994 cover, "How the Grinchrich Stole Christmas!," certified the popular perception). By the end of '95 Gingrich had imploded: on December 6 the House Committee on Ethics voted to hire an independent counsel to investigate Newt's TV "college course" and other possible violations of tax laws. His initial acceptance of a $4.5 million book advance from Rubert Murdoch seemed not only to be an act of hubris, but plain dumb. And Dole's presidential ambitions will get to reap the population's ire and disgust.

As diversion, Senator D'Amato still makes midnight raids on the Arkansas cemeteries of Whitewater. But what we have been hearing loudly and stridently from the haves the last two years, the Seligs, the Schotts, the Steinbrenners, the Doles, the Gramms, the Gingriches, has been a continual chorus of "Play ball!"—or else.

But Dole and Company, not learning much from the baseball strike, have let the big baseball team in Washington lock out their players— over Christmas!—and the natives are restless—cold (in most of the country), but restless. Even in mild Half Moon Bay—especially the tourists who can't point their RVs in whatever direction they choose and be welcomed.

A '92 campaign button I have reads, "Our Family Values Bill Clinton." It was produced somewhat late in the '92 campaign to counter, comment upon, the Republican Right's values campaign. Given the Bush family, the amount of capital involved, family values couldn't be pushed too hard by the candidate himself (his remark about his grandchild, the brown-blood remark, was Bush himself tangling with the issue); but the Republican Right, which was on the rise and would have its apotheosis in '94, pushed and pushed.

Values campaigning is nothing new. Bush had pushed this in '88, but the values were societal, not personal. Dukakis was not attacked for moral shortcomings, only physical. But, in a case of the sixties generation getting its wish, the old slogan triumphed, and the personal in '92 *became* political and the values attack was personalized.

Clinton may have flown back to Arkansas early in the '92 campaign to fry some brain-damaged death row resident, but he did so just as Gennifer Flowers was blooming in the national media. His death-penalty stance was the sort that would have been embraced by the Republican Right family-values crowd (they love the death penalty), but that was dissolved in the hot attention focused on Ms. Flowers.

So we got the "Our Family Values Bill Clinton" button. That elliptical statement carries its own implied "despite," despite this, despite that, etc.

But we all have families, and in California mine are quite representative of the nuclear (as in weapons, energy) family of the 1990s. I have two sets of in-laws, given that my wife's parents divorced in the sixties and both have since remarried. They are my own personal focus-group yin and yang.

My contention has always been that the "family values" issue is generated out of despair when those who see it violated everywhere see their own families violate it and can't do anything about them, so they want someone to put a stop to it somewhere.

If anyone looks at the American family these days why should it be valued? One of the legacies of the 1960s and 1970s was that they did reduce the amount of hypocrisy allowed in the body public. After a period of revelation, of the unveiling of enough secrets—Pentagon Papers, Watergate, the White House tapes, the Church committee, etc.—it was a little difficult to cling to utter fantasy about what the world looked like. The election of Reagan signaled the change in perspective, the return of wishful thinking. We had Reagan's video view of America (a New Morning, etc.), and, in contrast, Reagan's actual family to contemplate, Ron, Patti, Maureen, Michael. They were Californian, too.

American families are well versed in the peculiar. From the richest to the poorest. Family-value issues are a curiously revisionist utopia, wishing for a perfect world that never was. It is a post–World War II world, the United States being the superpower, the only superpower, women returned (prodded) to the home from the factories, children off to school, Sis a virgin, little Butch on the baseball team, Dad in his chair, reading the paper, chuckling at *Bonanza*.

It was nice while it lasted. And why can't it be again?! the family-values crowd cries.

Well, all American families are typical, but each American family is typical in its own way. When I arrived at my father-in-law's house for Christmas, two books were on his cocktail table: Rush Limbaugh's *The Way Things Are Supposed to Be* and Charles Murray and Richard Herrnstein's *The Bell Curve*.

I, like Bill Clinton, have a Rush Limbaugh problem (and a Charles Murray problem, too). I have never met Mr. Limbaugh, but I have met Murray once. I—what's the word?—enjoy Limbaugh, first being exposed to him via my car radio. He, like George Will at the beginning of his national ascendancy, seemed to be the usual sort of anti-fluoride-in-the-water conservative libertarian, but, over the months I sporadically would hear Limbaugh, through the early nineties, a couple of major differences emerged.

For one, Limbaugh was funny, and he seemed genuinely surprised and pleased to death that famous people were beginning to take him seriously. I recall one radio broadcast early on when Rush couldn't get over the fact that Ted Koppel had either mentioned him kindly or quoted him approvingly (or returned his phone call), and Rush went on about sending Koppel a fax in thanks. I realized back then that you don't often hear so much undisguised happiness on the radio. Rush was, is, one happy guy. He might rant and rave, say all sorts of mean things, but you can't deny that he is happy, happy, happy. He likes his work. Americans respond well to that: they like success and people who really enjoy what they do. A portion of the public responds well to Bill Clinton for the same reason.

Charles Murray doesn't exude that joie de vivre. When I met him in the eighties, shortly after his 1984 abolish-welfare book, *Losing Ground,* appeared, he was decidedly melancholy and, even though he was suc-ceeding, he seemed genuinely depressed about the gloom and doom he saw all about him. His aspect, I thought, was that of a low-level State Department functionary billeted in some second-rate Third World coun-try. I told him that the Reagan administration would soon be calling, and he demurred, saying it hadn't happened yet. I then realized that his most productive role for conservative administrations might well be that of the friend outside, rather than the nonenemy within.

Murray, unhappy and dour as he still appears to be, doesn't inspire a lot of fan-club dittoheads to spread his fame, but he is after slightly harder fish to deep-fry. The talk about IQ that *The Bell Curve,* his 1994 book, generated—Murray has had the good luck to have a dead coauthor—is redolent with stale eugenist odors. They waft over the country whenever there is scarcity and economic fear afoot. In the early twentieth century such discussions were usually yoked to immigrants and immigration (and it is not coincidental that Proposition 187 in California had been penned with the same sour ink that Murray used). It has been pointed out a number of times that Bill Clinton is a product of the baby boom meritocracy, that period my generation of white males (which includes Murray and Limbaugh) so hugely profited from: the Great Society, Sputnik, the boost to education, the growth of jobs, the economy, one where all sorts of people were needed and had opportunities to show their stuff, get to Georgetown, Yale, and other elite institutions from various backwoods, play around in exotic foreign countries like Murray did after college, then go on to get advanced degrees from MIT.

But the more recent generation of white males have been feeling the pinch for some time. Reports reveal that college-educated white women have advanced their income levels, whereas college-educated white males have remained about the same, and white high school dropouts have fallen into the basement since the early seventies. It is not that unusual that when you reach the apotheosis of a phenomenon (Bill Clinton's election in '92 as a triumph of the postwar meritocracy), it signals the end of the phenomenon, not its continuation.

America before LBJ's Great Society, that explosion of mutual human and federal generosity, is now what the conservatives want to conserve; they wish to return to the thirties, forties, fifties, not the sixties, seventies, eighties. Blaming IQ lets you justify anything you care to: abolish general education, reinstate elites. The country needs fewer people to run things, corporations are downsizing: stop looking beyond the Ivy League for your talent. Upward mobility is derailed, why educate the messy masses? It shifts the blame onto the backs (so to speak) of human beings, where only procreation is to blame. Blame IQ and you blame nobody—and everybody: groups, "races"—but there are plenty of individual folks to blame for policies that were put into motion by a number of Republican administrations.

Back in 1970, there were other visionaries like Murray around. Roger

Freeman, a key educational adviser to President Nixon then working for the reelection of Governor Ronald Reagan, warned: "We are in danger of producing an educated proletariat. That's dynamite! We have to be selective on who we allow to go through higher education. If not, we will have a large number of highly trained and unemployed people" (*San Francisco Chronicle,* October 30, 1970). Murray was banging a similar drum except he offered the apologia for the curtailment of affirmative action services.

My father-in-law jokes that Bill Clinton is going to impose a forty-eight-hour cooling-off period for the renting of Ryder trucks. The doorbell rings and a couple who appear to be dressed for a senior prom hand me a copy of *Awake!* (the December 12, 1995 issue). "Schools in Crisis" a cover line screams on top of a photo of two ten-year-olds, one black and one white, pointing a large handgun. Now, no one I know of is walking around passing out free copies of, say, *The Nation* house to house. That brackets one side of the family equation.

When I arrived at my mother-in-law's house on New Year's Eve day, there was a new six-foot TV and the only magazines on her table were copies of *Architectural Digest*, the *Cosmo* of the middle class home owner. The new TV was her husband Nick's, who bought it because he just got a lump-sum resolution of a past worker's comp claim. He is on disability and his monthly check makes the mortgage payment.

My mother-in-law is in a union, works for Democratic candidates locally, and has a lot of '92 Clinton campaign materials hanging in her laundry room.

My in-laws are very typical, as is my own family back in the Midwest. How anyone can think the American public is not sophisticated in the ways of America's family values is beyond me, beyond wishful thinking. The leaders of those who are most vocal on this issue—the Christian Coalition, the Moral Majority, all those organizations which love alliteration—may or may not have fashioned their own 1950s lifestyle (see Jimmy Swaggart's motel forays), but only in the sense that Dad is gone a lot of the time.

1/3 For the first two days of the new year, football occupied most screens in the homes of Campaign America '96. The Fiesta Bowl spectacle, Nebraska versus Florida, on January 2, provided the sight of Lawrence Phillips, the black running back who vigorously assaulted his basketball-playing white former girlfriend (a confluence of two kinds of affirmative action in university sports, a Title IX clash, leading the Nebraska squad to victory and a national championship.

The case of Phillips is one of many in our accelerated culture: in 1996, a young African American football player of exceptional talent can still be a potential star after assaulting a woman, rather than having to keep his nose slightly clean till a long sports career has certified his stardom. Then, and only then, assaulting women might finally upend his stardom. Like O. J.

And, speaking of O. J., I often wondered during 1995 if a retrial of O. J. would help or not help Bill Clinton's reelection chances, since during most of the year I, along with quite a few, thought the most likely outcome of the Simpson murder trial would be a hung jury. My assessment was that a retrial would help, since it would monopolize so much television time that there would be less attention paid to the campaign.

On October 3, 1995, I too watched "live" the reading of the jury's verdict. I was looking at O. J.'s face, and a medley of very complicated emotions was playing across it, however he was trying to suppress them. When the first not guilty was read out, after the split second it took to absorb it, he turned to his left and, fleetingly, the expression on his face seemed to be one of embarrassment.

He quickly recovered, turned back, and mouthed "Thank you" to the jury, and Johnnie Cochran did his Sammy Davis clutching Nixon imitation, hugging Simpson's back, banging it with love pats.

That second of embarrassment will probably be as close as the public will get to a show of contrition on O. J.'s part. If any lesson of the late twentieth century has generally sunk in, it is just say no, just stonewall, just say I didn't do it, and some people will be persuaded.

That there was an instantaneous verdict in the Simpson case pointed out a number of things, but indisputably it showed the jury couldn't wait to get out of there.

During the trial, there was always the great white hope analysis, that the lone white woman on the jury would somehow persuade the majority that O. J. should be convicted. She had turned one jury earlier, we were told often. But what became clear is that she had become a minority figure in many ways and was treated to the same forces O.J. was during his famous life (or life as a famous person). After so many months of being in the intimate company of so many nonwhites, she became an honorary African American, in the same way that O.J. had turned himself into an honorary Caucasian.

One reason why Colin Powell has become white America's most popular African American is that O.J. abdicated the throne that bloody night in Brentwood. And our culture is a bifurcated Noah's ark—there's only room for one of each species.

So I wasn't overly surprised, watching CNN, that when Powell was asked out on his book tour for his reaction to the O.J. verdict, he said, hurrying to a waiting car, that since the jury had found Simpson "innocent," we should respect the jury's verdict. Innocent is not what O.J. was found, of course: not guilty was the verdict, beyond a reasonable doubt, etc. "Not guilty" is a long way from *innocent*. But it is hard to be the chairman of the Joint Chiefs of Staff and always be a stickler for the finer points of law.

During a variety of protests at the Pentagon during the Vietnam War, the Pentagon would often send out an African American officer to deal with the crowd. The public-relations aspects of that were not to be overlooked. How many African American officers were running around the Pentagon in the late sixties and early seventies? But, however few, they were put out in the front lines of publicity. I'm not sure Powell ever got called for that duty, but I'm sure he wouldn't have refused (he was in Washington during that period).

"Will Powell succumb to the call of duty and take the vice presidential spot on the GOP ticket?" is already, in early January, the $64,000 question. But given the usual amnesia that affects the population every four years, one should recall (as does a Powell biography, *Sacred Honor*) that the first time the vice presidency and Powell came up nationally was on the weekend *CBS News with Bob Schieffer* on June 23, 1992, when Bruce Morton offered up the notion of a Clinton-Powell ticket. Evidently, the Bush camp gave it some thought at the time, too, according to Mary Matalin's part of *All's Fair* (see page 205).

So the Powell factor abides. There are many reasons to think he might run. The chief one is that is how he has advanced his entire career: a more powerful man taps him for a job, he complies. It would be easy to see the deal worked out. Dole would be the best match: the age problem becomes less of a problem and also is the carrot for Powell. Dole agrees to be a one-term president (the fact of this is already beginning to dawn on people, the unlikelihood of Dole charging into a second term, much less a first), which would leave Powell on the top of the ticket for Campaign 2000.

Powell would have finally been elected to something, would acquire yet more Oval Office experience, and might stand a chance to be elected on the top of a ticket (though that might seem a part of millennium madness). But this is how Powell has conducted his whole career, pleasing men and moving up.

Campaigning for a couple of months, from late August to the end of October, would not be too arduous and not that exposing. It is easier to say Dole-Powell than, say, Forbes-Powell, Gramm-Powell, Buchanan-Powell, etc.

But the second most likely veep (according to conventional wisdom) would be the governor of New Jersey, Christine Todd Whitman, rich-person buddy of Steve Forbes. It's hard to see Forbes Whitman. Can the country take two silver spoons out of its mouth at the same time? I doubt it. (Though it did with Bush-Quayle and it made the '88 race against Dukakis-Bentsen closer than it might have been, but Quayle never seemed *patrician* the way Whitman does.) The Republicans not only have a problem of who might be the standard bearer, but they also have a ticket problem.

TWO

"It's Not the Deficit, Stupid"

★

1/5 *It's the economy, stupid,* thanks to Carville and Company (though Carville's version lacked the "It's"), became a bumper sticker for the brain after 1992, so I thought it only appropriate to surround myself with economists at the start of Campaign '96. Since I am in California, this proved easy enough to do: the Allied Social Science Association's Annual Meeting for 1996 is being held in San Francisco during the first week of the new year.

The ASSA convention is the meat market of the economics profession, for, as innumerable papers are being delivered in the various rooms of the downtown glittering Hilton and Marriott and Westin hotels, in meeting rooms named so tropically they all begin to take on a tropical-island atmosphere, peopled with washed-up raftloads of shipwrecked economists, so are the actual hotel rooms filled with job seekers, supplicating themselves before interview committees, looking for a first job, a better job, any job.

I am sitting in the Hilton, in the large area in front of the reception desk, waiting for my wife and surveying the crowd. This lobby passes for a pretty good replica of the check-in area one expects at the pearly gates, all shiny columns, glass, mirrors, every reflective surface bright and star-tling.

There are the expected white males, thinner, taller on average than the usual, yet enough women to make the profession seem to support the gains of affirmative action into solidly all-male occupations of the last twenty years: about 10 percent. This is not a feminized profession, yet. There are about an equal number of what I gingerly think of as "for-eigners"—anyone whose first and preferred language is not English. Three Middle Easterners are chatting together in some Arabic tongue which I could no more successfully name than all the varieties of Persian rugs; the Middle Easterners are, at least not tall, but appear friends from different schools (given their name tags). A tall white guy walks past and catches the eye of one of them, who turns and greets him effusively.

"Well, has someone lured you away?" the short man asks the tall.

"Lured me away! I was fired. I'm desperate. I've been out of work for six months. My unemployment benefits are running out. I'll take any-thing. A visiting position, research. Please, if you know of anything . . ."

The tall man digs into his Lands' End briefcase and pulls out a résumé.

"Take this. I have to run to an interview now. It's the only one I have. My age is the biggest problem. Any help you can be I will really appreciate it."

He goes off and the short man turns back to his friends and expresses, in his native language, what I take to be dismay and amusement, though all three seem somewhat sobered by the encounter, and they soon break up and go separate ways.

The taller man was somewhere in his fifties, and before he announced his plight, I would have taken his aspect to have been just harried and tired. An angry white male perhaps, but one with advanced degrees. As he explained his predicament, his shined but well-worn shoes, his blazer, even the part in his hair, seemed to be covered with a Willy Loman sheen of desperation, No Sale ringing up in his eyes.

It isn't the aspect of the economists at the session I attend. SOLD SOLD SOLD radiates from them. Success stories all, like most of the panelists who are delivering papers over the three days. And these folks aren't even delivering papers. The really big boys just get up and talk.

The moderator of the session, in Pacific Suite C, is Robert Eisner, author of *The Misunderstood Economy*. Everyone on the panel knows one other; kisses all around, at least from Ann Markusen, a longtime Friend of Bill (FOB) and director of an institute at Rutgers University. Lots of bonhomie.

"Nothing said here today will drive the stock market down," Eisner says to chuckles. The second government shutdown ended yesterday, but the stock market had nose-dived with talk of yet another one.

Clinton's lockout has worked in its paradoxical way, turning the Republicans into the union bosses and the government employees into the reluctant workers, out on the nonessential picket line. The public is happily confused, given the mixup of roles.

The first panelist is Paul Davidson, of the University of Tennessee, who comments that after you take out defense, the biggest investment item in the federal budget is prisons.

I'm reminded of a visit I made to Washington in the mid-eighties. I sat at a bar around the corner from the Teamsters headquarters, and was accosted by a garrulous fellow who built prisons. He was happy as a clam, having completed a successful visit to Washington, and he couldn't wait to get back to the hinterlands to build more cages. He wanted to take his good cheer out on me.

The second speaker, Lloyd Dumas of the University of Texas-Dallas, laments "public borrowing crowding out private investment" and that the current budget row had "lost touch with any sensible economics." The Republicans were cutting "those programs which encourage investment." He points out that the "private sector is less interested in basic research," that "government needs to fund it or it will be underproduced," and that there is a "crowding-out effect," which has to do with priorities. Germany and Japan, he reminds us, are military-lite, which is one reason why they are doing so well. "Thirty percent," he says, "of U.S. engineers go to the military sector." Our military spending is as much as all the rest of the world's combined. More B2s are in the budget.

Ann Markusen takes the podium. She has the look of a fortyish film noir heroine, but one with overheads, graphs. Markusen is the author of *Dismantling the Cold War Economy* and a college-era girlfriend of Bill Clinton (read all about it in David Maraniss's *First in His Class*). She delivers more non-news news—in the sense that it is known, but not widely disseminated: during the eighties the military budget went up 60 percent: 260 million a year; the peak was 400 million. There was a shift in output from private to public markets. R & D comes from the Feds; 82 percent goes to aerospace. Other industries get very little: occupational skewing results. From 1987 to 1994, the defense budget decreased 29 percent. For every four military personnel on payroll then, there are now three.

"Have you ever heard of the B2's recently?" she asks, excepting, I presume, the earlier mention today. "They're sitting on runways in the southern part of this state. Four of them have crashed—"

"And they've been depreciated," Eisner interjects, and the audience laughs appreciatively.

"Supply-side pressures hold the line on cuts," Markusen says, mentioning the case of Maxine Waters, the Democratic California congresswoman who voted for funding the B2. "She's for deficit reduction, but not for her constituents." Meaning Maxine doesn't want their deficits increased. We're in an arms race against our allies, for the sake of TRW, Hughes, Markusen adds.

Eisner reiterates: if military spending goes down, there will be a reduction in GDP, more unemployment. "If we don't do them"—the good things, converting military spending into equivalent civilian spending, he means—"the economy will get worse," with military cuts.

More gloom and doom comes from the next speaker, a substitute for a no-show. (They all know each other and everything's quite cozy and hard to catch.) Eight billion was in Clinton's budget for conversion, but 70 percent of that has been cut out. The substitute points out that the ratio of children to adults in developed countries is three to one; in undeveloped countries it is twenty-three to one. The UN considers adults anyone over fourteen. "So do you wonder why all these labor-intensive industries are going to those countries?" There are still problems with child labor everywhere: one-fourth of our military outlays (what gets spent) are in developing countries. "The UN Security Council bankrupted Rwanda by selling them arms," he says.

"And they used them," Eisner interjects to general laughter. I wonder who had the machete concession. Oh, we are far from the killing fields in Pacific Suite C.

Murray Weidenbaum, a member of Reagan's Council of Economic Advisers, now takes the podium. "I feel like Daniel in the lion's den," he says. He boasts that he was the only one to criticize a sitting president in his own Economic Report (1982).

"Where were you in eighty-three?" is called out.

"In St. Louis," he says dejectedly, to laughter, alluding to his early departure from government.

In California, when government got out of the way, Weidenbaum claims, there has been a substantial employment turnaround in the entertainment industry. "Disney wasn't in any conversion program," he says triumphantly. Chuckles follow that, though it is hard to believe he considers *The Lion King* and the exporting of pop culture to be our sine qua non of economic salvation. Though I also recall the new Disney store on the corner of the street where our hotel is located—and a Borders Bookstore on top of it.

Weidenbaum says scornfully that it's "hard to take seriously the question if the deficit is being cut too fast or deep." Voucher programs for education were derided earlier, and "the GI Bill was a voucher program." He is not against federal investment, as long as it is "rare"—like for education—but he is against consumption spending. If you "eliminate the deficit there will be more funds for private investment.

"The public's attention will shift from balancing the budget," he says almost wistfully. It is interesting that he feels in this forum somewhat defensive, for he has to argue a bit more personally, rather than just lay down the line for the like-minded.

There should be modest increases in military outlays, he says. Republicans will cut consumption. Recall, he says, "the bigger multiplier is in government military purchases rather than in transfer cuts. You guys aren't short of ideology either," he finishes, not quite stating the obvious.

Eisner rises again. "Teen pregnancy is going up," he begins strangely; "Federal spending is up. The question is, relative to what?

"I'm going to quote myself, the last line of an article in the *Wall Street Journal* I published recently." (November 28, 1995. There are no lights hid under any bushels in this crowd.) "It isn't the deficit, stupid." It's a matter of priorities.

Dumas follows and announces the current conventional wisdom: "Deficit reduction is now the consensus view." He reels off a list—the United States, Russia, China, South Africa—claiming that the external threat level is down and the internal threat level is up in all those countries. There is now a ten-year window of opportunity, he says, meaning, not opportunity as much as a period of last chance. He gives some figures about prison costs: millions for cells, maintenance, courts, an investment for which "we get nothing."

Weidenbaum is up and begins to talk of threats. Not Reagan's Star Wars, but blockades. Weidenbaum's voice both darkens and begins to break up as he says we should focus on the South China Sea. China is pushing around Vietnam, unhappy about Taiwan. "What if they block-ade Taiwan?" he asks. The major victim would be Japan. What would we do to let them get their oil? The Russians might not be a threat—but there still are ICBMs. China is continuing a military buildup. His voice is full of the solemn terror that rationalizes any cost and soothes the military's fears of cuts.

Eisner interjects: "I just spent six days in China, and indeed they are having an economic buildup. What more spending could deter them from is beyond me."

He gets some laughter, but it is not quite as throaty as before.

Weidenbaum comments that the UN military was shown to be a complete bust in the former Yugoslavia.

Dumas counters by saying that the largest export earner is aerospace and that the Disney movie *Toy Story* is a result of the Reagan buildup, the advances in computer technology supported by government R & D, through the military. If you want to invest in population, why cut Medicare? "You're against public housing," he says to Weidenbaum, "except for prisons."

Davidson from Tennessee adds that our biggest recent export was Desert Storm. The problem was that Saddam gave in too quickly, or we would have had a surplus that year.

Ann Markusen says we had an industrial policy in the past—defense. We now need another one.

Dumas offers: since we've expanded the spread of rich and poor, then to cut the poor's services is immoral. No one is for eliminating the military, he says.

I wait for an objection from the audience. None comes.

Eisner returns to the current deficit: we enjoy a Toyota, they (the Japanese) buy Rockefeller Center—and then sell it at a loss. They're the losers. All the politicians are arguing about is what forecast they make, what the deficit will be. They go on about how the CBO's are honest numbers, as if the OMB are dishonest crooks. They're not. "No one can say what the economy will be in 2002," he concludes.

1/6   But today's "Campaign 1996: The Economic Issues" is the trophy session, the one with cameras and the press in attendance. The *New York Times* covered it but left out a couple of words when the reporter quoted Michael Boskin, late of the Bush administration, as he was making a point: "We talk a great deal about balancing the budget by 2002," the *Times*man quotes Boskin, "but nary a peep about how to keep it in balance. We'll need a huge tax increase to pay for Medicare after 2002." What was left out was that after "nary a peep," Boskin said, *"from the press."*

After the Vietnam War, after Watergate (overlapping as they were), it didn't take long to notice that from the end of the 1970s on, the biggest story in the press was the economy. Everyone's chief interest, if you added up column inches, was economic. So by 1992, "It's the economy, stupid" was hardly a revelation. Of course, in 1995, O.J. outstripped it all in TV Land.

I often considered during the O.J. coverage the amount of human capital employed at almost minimum wage (for the lawyers involved) as commentators on TV; it was cable's defining moment, outstripping even the limited version of gavel-to-gavel coverage of the Watergate hearings. Hours and hours of analysis from countless shameless hussies of the bar, both male and female. Whatever scale they were being paid, becoming well known, familiar, would be a good investment in future income (though if they were getting a hundred, two hundred, three hundred an hour, that might be in their hourly ballpark—though lawyers get their gadzillions through percentages, not just wages). It would be salubrious if other events were covered with such enthusiasm.

On the two panels I took note of, there was only one woman. The white-men problem keeps cropping up. There are female economists and black economists, but they haven't been vaulted into the public's consciousness like women and minority attorneys have, thanks to O. J.

I am an OAF, a charter and founding member of OAFS—Older American Fathers Society—and was retrieving my five-year-old from his grandmother and bringing him back to San Francisco to ride the cable cars, so I needed to debrief my wife about this session, which I was unable to attend.

Charles Schultze, late of government, now of the Brookings Institution, moderated the panel of government-academia-complex figures: Michael J. Boskin, late of government, now at Stanford University; Rudiger W. Dornbusch, MIT; Lawrence Summers, Treasury Department; and John B. Taylor, also at Stanford.

Michael Boskin was up first, my wife reports. Boskin was glad Clinton broke two stupid promises and dropped two planks from 1992: national fuel-economy standards and the idea that tough environmental standards would help the economy were really bad ideas. "Voters care if things are going well, but TV really doesn't teach the voters anything," Boskin said. If the media really wanted voters to know about economics, the press wouldn't spend so much time in Washington, it would go to the Silicon Valley.

Mistakes had been made and Nixon made the worst mistakes. He and Wilbur Mills jacked up Social Security benefits by 30 percent, by indexing them for inflation.

Boskin said (without any irony, my wife adds) that Bush did great things while he (Boskin) was in the Bush administration. Gramm-Rudman, for instance. They've been remarkable and enduring. Nineteen eighty-one, eighty-six, he says, we got it moving in the right direction.

"He was like Spiro Agnew going after the press," my wife comments. Boskin had this graph—if I see it one more time I will gag, she says—showing that Medicare is going up, 1 percent of payroll tax now, 4 percent more later. So what? We have to pay 5 percent of payroll tax! Ask the voters if they want a 1 percent rise in payroll tax in order to fix Social Security till 2060. What's that? So little, really. Medicare and Social Security go up as people need them.

Boskin said he is dismayed that Clinton has drawn a single line in the sand on entitlements in the budget negotiations. Clinton won't pass on entitlements. But Clinton is good on trade and Boskin gives him strong marks on NAFTA.

These bilateral trade agreements—you know, where Mickey Kantor goes out to negotiate with Japan—Boskin said they were illiterate economics. This is a jab at Laura D'Andrea Tyson, who became his replacement (and the first woman in the job).

Only Republicans can do strict cost-benefit analysis; Greenspan was off by six months, Boskin said. That got a big laugh from his audience: the economy improved during Clinton's first months, not Bush's last.

Interest rates go down nine to twelve months afterward, and then the economy does better, but Greenspan did it six months before. It turns out that the recession was a lot worse than official numbers showed. These economists always like this. It makes economists feel better; they don't have to care about party coalitions, leadership. They rely on the political business cycle as the sole bit of critical information.

But we should congratulate ourselves, Boskin said. Look, Clinton and Dole would agree that curbing inflation was the most important thing. The *most* important is national savings and the long-term budget deficit. So Boskin praised Clinton; maybe he has a vague hope that he will go back to Washington.

Then the pro-Clinton guy, Rudi Dornbusch, the guy with a million-dollar macro textbook, said we have to thank Boskin for praising Clinton and I will continue to do so. The audience laughed at that. It is very important to remember, Dornbusch said, that the Democrats keep the stock market high and Clinton will continue to do this in his eight-year term. The audience laughed some more.

Now there isn't much of a difference between a reasonable Democrat and a reasonable Republican. We have to give credit where credit is due, Dornbusch said. It is very important that in order to get a perspective on the budget crisis, remember that in the bond market long rates are down. This means that for everyone like Dornbusch, inflation won't eat away the value of their bonds. So he was saying that either people like him can rest assured, *or* he was saying that Clinton has delivered for us top 1 percenters.

Now, Dornbusch said, Laura Tyson believes in open trading—that's another knock against Boskin, who called Tyson's economics illiterate.

In macro trade policies, no president could do better than Clinton, Dornbusch said. But he could think of some really bad ideas on the Republican side.

There is one candidate who is proposing the *gold* standard (that's Forbes, of course, but Dornbusch doesn't say) and that zany idea is much worse than fuel-economy standards.

Buchanan wants to close the economy, like those labor unions and the Green Party, Dornbusch said. But those red guards are a bad risk—especially on these protection issues. What do they stand for? he asked. All we know about them are these crazy ideas.

What could Republicans do that Clinton hasn't already done? No inflation, rising stock market, no recession in sight. Looks like this Ray-Fair blip will happen just in time. (That refers to the political business cycle that Boskin was talking about, the one that really hurt Bush because it came six months too late.)

If GDP goes up the third quarter of the election year, then the incumbent party wins. A Yale economist charted a couple of points on a graph. That's Ray Fair. Most economists wouldn't be famous if the rest of the world didn't have graph phobia. Dornbusch was making all the Republicans in the audience depressed, because they all believe this stuff. Some say it is just the economy and politics doesn't matter. They believe that economics is the only thing that matters. They also believe that Clinton is a Republican. So they do believe that they won't really get to leave the Hoover Institute and go to Washington.

That is what is so interesting about Boskin. Boskin is so bitter about being what radical economists call him—a has-been. That explains his early quip: it was his unconscious wish, about the media going to Silicon Valley to teach people economics. He is at Stanford, in the backyard of Silicon Valley—why don't they come talk to me, he's saying.

Dornbusch said there are really problems in the Clinton administration. Just last Thursday, he said, Robert Reich proposed in the *New York Times* that corporations be given corporate charters if they are nice, and nice means they never lay off redundant workers. That is really stupid, Dornbusch said. Maybe Reich had to say that because he had just come back from the Renaissance Weekend and maybe we can excuse him, because he is labor secretary, but this is unbearably stupid, Dornbusch said. I guess we can be thankful, he said, that all this trash is printed in the *New York Times,* so that it doesn't get in the cabinet room.

So it's the economists, you bright people out there. But outside the luxury hotels are the truly homeless, camping out on the corners, snagging change. Some civic outreach has occurred, though, since I've noticed the past few days that they all have the same kind of sleeping bag (in different states of wear and tear), some uniform handout at one period of general betterment.

I have a conversation on the street with a reporter acquaintance and in reply to my question about how Dole looks these days, she says, "How can anyone tell? He's always wearing so much makeup." She does talk about how Newt Gingrich looked some time back, after an auto accident where he almost lost part of his ear. "It really looked bad, black, but he's there, answering questions on the Capitol's steps."

She says she interviewed Alan Keyes, the ambassador to the UN Economic and Social Council during the Reagan administration and sometime radio talk show host, the one nonwhite male running for president. He is truly from the moon, she says. Her crew went to his house and there was one room he wouldn't let them see: his office. It wasn't a big deal, since we didn't want to see it, she says, but he kept making it a big deal. His private, sacred place. The key to Keyes, I say.

During the evening, we're in a Berkeley, California, bungalow plotting revolution. Just kidding. Two lawyers and two nonlawyers are present. One of the attorneys, Randy Shaw, head of the Tenderloin Housing Clinic, says, "I'm sick of new ideas, bring back old ideas." Shaw has just published *The Activist's Handbook.* He contends there has been no shortage of good ideas, but what has been absent is the ability to have long-standing progressive agendas prevail: like the minimum wage and more social spending on human needs.

Shaw had given a harsh assessment of the Clinton administration's record on the environment, in spite of Al Gore's public persona as Mr. Green Jeans. A garbage incinerator project in West Virginia that Gore said would never fire up if he and Clinton were elected is belching flames (and, one supposes, pollution).

Everyone remarks on the irony of Buchanan being the only candidate rallying workers to his side. The pin-striped populist. The weather is getting worse on the East Coast (Washington, D.C., and Manhattan are awaiting a blizzard), and no one in the house in Berkeley is feeling too sunny, either.

"Forget the new ideas, bring back the old ones," Shaw says again, heading out into the night.

THREE

A Season of Snow Jobs

1/9   The Couch is back home in Indiana. When we left California yesterday, flying out of the San Jose airport, local television crews were accosting travelers, looking for any who were stuck because of the East Coast storms. They hadn't as much luck as they hoped, but finally found one woman who couldn't get back east the day before. She, too, had been at the ASSA meetings in San Francisco. As we boarded our flight to Chicago (not delayed), a lone print journalist showed up on the same errand, his narrow notepad drooping. After making the rounds, he found the stranded traveler, and she obliged with the same story the third time. Everyone's willing to be a candidate, willing to give the same speech over and over.

1/10   There are interesting AP and Scripps-Howard stories in our local paper, the *South Bend Tribune*. In the AP dispatch, there's a list of quotes from other Republican candidates attacking Dole. It brings to mind Mary Matalin's remark in *All's Fair*. Her and James Carville's joint book-memoir on the 1992 campaign, published (rather belatedly for a campaign book) in 1994, had been my transcontinental airplane reading.

"Primary fights are a lot more emotional, corrosive, and painful than general elections" (42).

It is the first time in the last three decades that the Republicans are so closely imitating the Democrats (a paradoxical result, perhaps, of Republicans controlling Congress and Democrats being out of power in the White House) and are having a wide-open primary—at least in the numbers of visible candidates involved.

1996 seems utterly different than the contested Republican primaries of the recent past: Goldwater versus the "moderates" was bruising—but Rockefeller and Nixon, Reagan-Bush, even '88's Bush, Dole, Buchanan, and Pat Robertson? Nineteen ninety-two's Bush-Buchanan was high on contrast, low on definition. The current large field of "viable" Republican candidates (Morry Taylor? Alan Keyes?) and the widened cable coverage crack open the primary debate—at least in how it is reported. If there are only two contrasting viewpoints, the usual full-court press can cover the debate rather bluntly. *Crossfire* writ large. But eight (or more) candidates require sharper distinctions not normally drawn. So the early crammed field—and, most importantly, the absence of any Democratic Party challenge for Clinton—forces open the discussion of Republicans in a particular way: how Forbes differs from Gramm differs from Buchanan differs from Keyes (Morry's differences are, as yet, hardly noticed) differs from Lugar differs from Alexander differs from the presumed front-runner, Dole, etc.

Even the insults traded among the candidates are a bit more particularized. And the chorus effect has been damning Dole. If it was just Buchanan making raspberries at him, Dole wouldn't be that splattered. (Buchanan did damage Bush in '92, but he didn't single-handedly cost him the election. Buchanan may have emboldened Perot, who didn't require much emboldening.) But a full chorus is hounding Dole! That is what the AP article points out—absent, of course, my analysis. The article lists derogatory statements by Alexander ("He [Dole] is not the right man"), Gramm ("Bob Dole lost his nerve"), Keyes ("a Republican leadership [Dole] without the guts to stand for what we really believe in"), Buchanan ("Clinton held firm and Dole moved toward him. That's not leadership").

Lugar remains the nice guy (though "nice" is not the reputation of

Lugar's handpicked Hoosier campaign manager) who is finishing last. Nor is all of Lugar's advertising nice: his terrorism campaign commercials are scarier than LBJ's petal-picking, atomic bomb, anti-Goldwater ad.

The Scripps-Howard report covers Newt Gingrich's it's-my-ball-and-I'm-taking-it-home-with-me style, revealed when he cancels fund-raising appearances with House GOP freshmen who voted against ending the last government shutdown (officially over January 4). Newt finally realized it was a big loser and wanted to display discipline. The three Republicans who got snubbed were two hard-liners from Indiana (yea, Hoosiers!), Representatives John Hostettler and Mark Souder, along with the stapled centerfold of the armed and angry, Helen Chenoweth of Idaho. Gingrich doesn't want anyone out-Newting Newt. *I had to fly in the back of* Air Force One! *No one is nice to me!*

On PBS's *NewsHour* in the evening, there's a discussion among Republican senator Robert Bennett of Utah, Ann Lewis, Paul Gigot, and Elizabeth Drew about the recent discovery of the billing records of the Rose law firm in the White House living quarters. Drew says, with sympathy toward Hillary, "Friends are sad at how these things are handled." She mentions the "naïveté" the Clintons displayed when they "first came to Washington."

Bennett asks, "Why didn't she look at those files?" referring to the woman who "found" them in the book room. "I compare it to Sherlock Holmes's dog that didn't bark," he adds, trotting out a popular-touch erudition.

Ann Lewis offers, "We were grieving," and adds, "I've rarely seen an investigation searching so hard for a problem. . . . These charges have no verb."

Bennett supplies, unless "something else comes forward."

This particular discovery scene in the White House's "book" room is essentially ludicrous, and even Ann Lewis seems hard-pressed to be straight-faced about this episode. Carolyn Huber, the aide who found the records, was a former Rose law firm employee and she recognized them (sitting on a table in the White House living quarters) for what they were, knew there were subpoenas issued asking for documents, yet stuck them in a box and placed them in storage, only to come upon them months later. Carolyn Huber is the Rose Mary Woods of the Clinton administration. I recall the picture of Rose Mary Woods demonstrating how she might have erased the eighteen-and-a-quarter-minute gap: stretched out, contorted, poor Rose Mary on the rack, serving her president.

The most instructive moments in C-SPAN are the ones before the event and after the event, when the videotape keeps, what, spooling? Everyone gets to be a journalist then, since you get to see behind the curtain as well as in front of the curtain. Like most advances in communication, it has educated a lot of people in how news is generated and processed, but it has taken a long while to sink it, saturate the culture.

"I came from Hope, Arkansas, before it became politically expedient," says Lieutenant Governor Mike Huckabee, (R, Arkansas). He's speaking at a Dole rally in Des Moines, Iowa, and, thanks to C-SPAN, I am "there." He calls Dole "a man of principle, not pollsters." He recalls for me the irony of the Clinton nominating convention film (*The Man from Hope*), put together by the Hollywood-connected Arkansas couple, Harry Thomason and Linda Bloodworth-Thomason. (The Clintons' trouble often comes in pairs—see the McDougals, etc.) It was the mythologizing of Clinton's boyhood, as ludicrous in its way as Reagan's own celluloid reality and fantasies, Clinton's contribution to the relatively new genre of the convention bio-video.

Did such films start by honoring dead men? I attempt to recall. Robert Kennedy? While I wonder, the new governor of Mississippi speaks for Dole in Iowa: "I'm the first Republican governor in one hundred eighteen years." Yeah, I think, 118 years of glorious Mississippi history. There must not have been a Democrat backward enough available as competition. The New South leans Republican, or toward David Duke, but Clinton/Gore won a couple of southern states in '92. Those voters are not fairweather former northern and midwestern "Reagan" Democrats, but a different sort altogether. "My inaugural activities begin tomorrow, but I'm in Iowa tonight because Bob Dole must be elected president."

1/11 *NPR* reminds us of Lamar! Alexander's old slogan, regarding Congress, "Cut their pay and send them home," which, after the '94 election, isn't as sweet to his party's ears.

William Safire has caused a stir with his January 8 Hillary column in the *New York Times,* where he labeled Hillary a "congenital liar." Safire's columns do generate news; he can work the phones, is his reputation among journalists. But his job history is emblematic of the changes in the "mainstream" press since the early seventies.

If one wants to date the rise of the right-wing "intellectual," one could do worse than choose the date of Safire's first column for the *New York Times* (April 16, 1973). Other events might be claimed, but they are mainly precedents: the founding of *The National Review* by William Buckley, for instance. But Safire hired by Punch Sulzberger is the date the music died. The others were outliers—Safire was the Trojan horse.

It is always amusing to hear Rush and others attacking and bemoaning the liberal bias of the "mainstream" press. On Rush, before Christmas, a caller said: "Bob Dole didn't mangle his arm fondling Gennifer Flowers." Rush immediately gave the guy a free tie. (One could pause over the ironies of the tributaries having more influence than the "source.") For every left publication on newsstands now, there are a fistful supported by right-wing foundations. If there was an era when the press dictated to a population it was the postwar period, its heyday being the 1950s. *Time* magazine's faults today, for instance, are not the faults it had in the fifties under Luce. It isn't a direct organ of foreign policy, as its owner saw it. During the boom postwar years, magazines rode the wave of general growth and prosperity; they were not, as today, desperately trying to retain market share. So the attack on liberal bias only brings to mind the conservative bias (establishment bias) the world of journalism had kept so inviolate previous to the sixties. In 1974, I taught a journalism course, my first plunge into that end of a classroom, and a journalism text had already been assigned to the class. In it there was a picture of the AP bureau chiefs of a few years before. What a picture! All these white guys in suits—it looked like the fifties, even though the photograph had been taken in the late sixties. Regardless, when Safire was hired on at the *Times* a new nexus was made, epitomized by Safire: from public relations, to government flackery, to editorial respectability.

Sulzberger was practicing a form of affirmative action, letting Safire onto his newly revamped op-ed pages, a small atonement for the sins of the Pentagon Papers. See, we let divergent voices speak. Safire, smarter than most rats, exiting the Nixon administration early, knew when to leave a sinking ship. But it was affirmative action at the *Times*. Someone barely qualified for the job, from an eccentric background (though PR and government quickly became the preferred background for both print and nonprint journalism), a guy who wouldn't "normally" be hired at the *Times*. And he didn't have to take the George Will route, which was to be the conservative you would have over to dinner, the presentable one, the one who didn't look like a geek on bad drugs. Will, after his advancement was secure, shed his conciliatory, civilized tone and became a ranter, surviving everything, even his praise of nuclear power stations that appeared right before Three Mile Island blew. You can see why conservatives have a deep well of hate. It is similar to Clarence Thomas's own brand. I was kept out and now am admitted, but only because I am useful, not really wanted. Lots of stored-up spleen, especially if you have any gift for delusion and self-righteousness.

Safire got his beachhead and he has hung on to it. Again, it's the Harvard principle, one that is associated with government, Hollywood, and the celebrity side of journalism: You only fail upward and you hardly ever get thrown out.

Safire's January 8 column he today describes as being "rescued from obscurity"; it would have been covered by the drifts of the "Blizzard of '96," but for the president taking such pugilistic notice of the columnist calling Clinton's wife "a congenital liar."

I thought it was an odd phrase for this self-appointed language capo, autopedant, and general mercenary scold of grammar foibles to use. And not just because it is a cliché.

As Safire would be the first to point out, *congenital* is the opposite of *hereditary: congenital* means existing prior to or at birth, but not inherited.

Popular usage has confused its meaning, given the association with birth defects, and extended it to inheritance. (Charles Murray take note.) What brought Safire to the phrase, the word, was doubtless much simpler. Every once in a while, all that is at great cost restrained in Safire, all that has been bubbling there since his days in advertising and PR, bursts forth, resulting in such spectacular columns as "Gunga Dean" (wretched poetry mocking merely bad poetry) and "Thataway, Posse Comitatus" (some fig leaf presented to the nascent militia world) that show us where he really lives. It is the puns, the associations of congenital, that attracted him. With balls, for one. With genitals, for all, especially Hillary. The birth associations sucked him in, isolated the femaleness of the charge, since men are, by definition, the victims of congenitalism, not its agents.

Language has lured Safire with its siren song and served up its own revelation of what he really finds objectionable in the first lady.

Nightline. Al D'Amato is on, given the hullabaloo in the media universe over the newly found Whitewater billing record documents. Al keeps calling Ted Koppel "David." Twice. Koppel, at ease and smiling the smile of serene public recognition, a man comfortable with the fact that he is known to all, says, "Someday David Brinkley and I and you will go out for a drink, so you can tell us apart."

The '92 election had at least one meaningful upset (if you don't consider Bush losing an upset): Alfonse D'Amato beat Robert Abrams in the New York Senate race. By now, the Clinton administration and the DNC doubtless regret not putting more resources, more money, into the Abrams campaign. Abrams came close, but close is hollow in our culture. Close is also-ran, see you later, old news. But that Senate race is a precursor to this campaign.

Abrams lost for a variety of reasons (Perot's voters hurt him, too), but the contested primary campaign provided most of them. (Dole is living through his version of this now. Oddly, Clinton wasn't injured by his '92 campaign competitors, but by his own self-inflicted wounds: the draft, Gennifer Flowers.) Abrams announced his candidacy early, when Geraldine Ferraro was still vacillating. The eternally aggrieved Liz Holtzman was also running once again (like Dole, it was her turn and she thought she deserved it), and, significantly, Al D'Amato's colorful stalking horse, Al Sharpton, threw his hat in. The back-channel connections of Sharpton to D'Amato's people would tax the plotting skills of John Le Carré.

Sharpton was there to make Abrams uncomfortable, to remind everyone of Tawana Brawley, to bring the odor of that case back (a young black woman claimed, falsely it became clear, to have been grievously attacked by white law enforcement men), to slice away whatever African American support from Abrams that he could. Just to be there.

When Ferraro announced, Abrams was stuck. Some deal should have been made—here, the efficacy of smoke-filled back rooms is nostalgically evoked—and one or the other could have dropped out. Ambassadorships could be dangled, etc. But the Democratic Party itself had no weight to throw here. It was a free-for-all. As was the primary campaign for the Democratic presidential nomination. The specter of D'Amato remaining the junior senator from New York wasn't frightening enough to instill any party discipline, though what was apparent was that there was a party out there without discipline.

Abrams might have been ahead of D'Amato by twenty-five points in the polls the day after he won the primary, but the power of the incumbency is worth at least that. What Abrams had to spend was also 25 percent of what D'Amato had, and Al was ready with attack ads the day after the primary was over. His campaign strategy seemed to be, pretend my opposition is *me*.

What is clear in 1996 is how vaporous the two-party-system notion is. That has become the conventional wisdom. It appears to be one party, with some superficial differences. When Bill Clinton became a New Democrat, he was staking out the territory where the two parties overlap, and that territory is becoming larger and larger, two amoebas absorbing each other, with only tiny crescents of difference left at either end.

A friend involved with the operating engineers union asked some New York State union officers early in the '92 campaign who they were supporting for senator. My friend expected Abrams to be the answer, but it was D'Amato. He butters our bread, or is the date that brought us, or we owe him, were among the explanations. Senator Pothole, indeed. If the big New York unions were going for Al, where was Abrams's support?

It is not entirely sexist to say Ferraro and Holtzman were in a catfight. Holtzman felt she deserved to be the candidate (she had lost so many times before)—the woman candidate, at least. Abrams stood to the side, along with Sharpton, till late in the campaign. It's not easy to follow a New York State primary race from Indiana, but I did hear one of the last radio debates on the local NPR station, and Abrams finally began to criticize the former Pepsi spokesperson. "Now, Geraldine, you'll have to admit . . ." It was a bad move. He should have remained as Apollonian as Sharpton. In Manhattan, the women's vote was beside itself, but

Abrams managed to narrowly win the primary, the quintessential Pyrrhic victory.

D'Amato had money to spend and was ready to go: immediately he hit Abrams, resurrecting corruption charges made by the New York weekly *The Village Voice* about fund-raising breakfasts Abrams had held in the past. It's hard to be attorney general and raise money from wealthy New Yorkers who wouldn't have potential business with the state. D'Amato had a lot to thank from the *Voice* for its earlier attacks on Abrams throughout the years (power breakfasts for rent are not a pretty sight, and some *Voice* reporters appeared to dislike Abrams intensely). The *Voice* had also attacked D'Amato robustly (though, obviously, ineffectually).

Abrams is possibly the closest thing there is to an honest politician I have seen, but political reporters have to generate some copy even about the good guys. And so the *Voice* can take some credit for making D'Amato's reelection possible—and the nation's dittoheads worry about the "liberal" media!

By the time Ferraro was persuaded to endorse Abrams, her eleventh-hour TV commercial doing so probably cost him more votes than it got him. Ferraro, by all reports (including *The Village Voice*'s of November 17, 1992) looked like a downed pilot giving one of those scripted endorsements of her captors.

Everyone contributes to the health of the country and it does become very personal. Clinton kept being a surprise, a surprise he won the nomination, a surprise he won the election (which wasn't clear till after the convention and Perot's return to the race), so it might not have been a surprise he could not come to Abrams's rescue. But New York's governor, Mario Cuomo, certainly didn't do any favors for Abrams either. There arose an unfortunate triangulation of Italian Americans in Bob Abrams's astrological chart: Cuomo, Ferraro, D'Amato. Abrams used the word "fascist," in connetion with D'Amato and with the help of the *New York Post,* D'Amato turned the word into an attack, not on him, but on all Italians. Even Cuomo chimed in.

Cuomo was lost in a funk of blasted possibility when he realized that he could have been the nominee in 1992 had he not frozen at the critical moment. Early on, he thought, as did most, that Bush would walk into a second term, so he didn't want to risk the bruising he would receive for a losing cause.

But there it was: Clinton might well win. He, Mario, could have won! Lost, ah, lost. Clinton's recorded Mafia/Gennifer Flowers exchange didn't help, I suppose, but it appears the now former New York governor (and he should have realized the day Abrams lost that so would he) has a character trait that restricts what he does for others: he can't stand, it seems, for those directly under him to do better than he. And the thought of Bobby Abrams becoming senator was not one Mario Cuomo could be overly enthusiastic about. Cuomo might do something for the little guy, as long as the little guy doesn't have the nerve to become a bigger guy than Mario.

Since Al D'Amato is conducting the shadow anticampaign, via the Whitewater hearings, all this blood under the bridge has contemporary significance. D'Amato's narrow victory (and his campaign claim—perhaps true, who knows?—that the '92 Senate race would be the last time he would run) has allowed this term to be one of payback and payoff. The hotly accused becomes the solemn accuser.

The former receiver of taxes for the town of Hempstead, Long Island, knows about corruption. It reminds one of Nixon on the Kennedys: why could John get away with things and not I? Tricky Dick thinks.

D'Amato the super patriot never served in the armed forces and like a number of men of his generation is generally pissed off at the generation that came after: sex, drugs, and rock 'n' roll, all of Bill Clinton's youth. The baby boom meritocracy; D'Amato rose the old-fashioned way, paying dues, not winning scholarships to Oxford.

In D'Amato's 1995 autobiography, *Power, Pasta and Politics,* he took note of what cost Abrams the election (other than mounting a poor campaign): the fact that hundreds of thousand voters of New York State did not vote for anyone for senator in the election, because of the bad feelings generated by both the primary and the Senate race itself. D'Amato wrote, "A significant number of liberals were so turned off by Abrams that they voted for Clinton and then did not vote in the Senate race at all. I may not have won liberal Ferraro voters, but Abrams lost many of them. As I learned in Island Park as a young boy, in a close election every vote *and* every *non*-vote counts" (224).

Bill Clinton beware. What is the largest number of people who did not vote for president, even if they went to the polls? It cost Abrams a close election. What could it cost Clinton?

1/12 Clinton and Gore are at the Opryland Hotel, in Nashville, Tennessee, televised by C-SPAN. "Four more years, four more years," the crowd chants. Not the best slogan for Clinton, given its Nixon roots. The prez says: Why is government the smallest since '65? We did not go to Washington to walk away from the problems of the American people . . . because we work with other countries. . . . He goes on about capturing terrorists, seven Cali drug types and praising free trade earlier in the day at a Peterbilt truck plant—a feeling of pride for all Tennessee. "They work together. Winners work together. We want a country where everyone works together."

Clinton's on a stump, campaigning, saying we "didn't have a permanent deficit till twelve years before I came to office." He talks about the debt being interest payments on those twelve years. About poor children, middle-class folks in nursing homes, handicapped children. He derides being accused by Republicans for "pandering to old people." Bull——, he says. There's applause.

It's not just elderly people, he says. We're all in this together. That is the central issue. "I think we're better when we're a team." He talks about "those military people" who are Bosnia bound: "They're a team, you know they'll be successful." He refers to the local football team and the Ohio State–Tennessee game. "We came together—God bless you!" It's the most comfortable I've seen Clinton look recently—he really loves talking to a crowd.

1/13 Legal bills of $1.6 million, $890,000 collected, *NPR* reports. What have those lawyers done that they can bill so much? The Clintons will be bankrupt, a spokesperson implies.

Speaking of bankrupts, Clinton comes up in a discussion today about the working poor. I hear a description of how Governor Bill handled union problems in Arkansas. "Come to room 300," Bill says, so the union folk show up and there are Tyson's PR men and lawyers. Clinton comes in. "You all work it out," he says and leaves. But when Tyson has a problem, Clinton just fixes it.

African American working poor, according to the friend I was chatting with, screen their home phone calls. It often takes talking to two women before you can get to the man you want to reach. The women have to find out who you are, what you want first. Similar to executive secretaries and CEOs. There's very little gift exchange, since all are poor folk. Men over thirty-four, they once had a good job and lost it. Under thirty-four they never had a good job. All have transportation problems. But they don't have $1.6 million in legal bills.

Hillary is talking about Safire's column on NPR's *Weekend Edition,* saying that it had caused her mother some distress, "because being called a congenital liar seemed to reflect badly on her and my late father." She sees it as a DNA problem, too.

1/14 Phil Gramm is on C-SPAN from Cedar Rapids, Iowa. He's holding up a piece of *"Gramm"* campaign plastic. "You're not marrying this bumper sticker . . . it's made out of plastic and you can peel it off." (A C-SPAN retread, the events shown took place on January 4 and 5.) A pretty reporter from an Iowa Channel 2, looking like a smalltown prom queen, is nodding vigorously as Gramm speaks: She's trying to make him go on, a kind of flirtatious face beckoning.

About the people of Iowa, Gramm predicts: "I believe they're going to give me the ball and I won't fumble it."

C-SPAN then shows a medley of campaign advertisements. An anti-Dole Senator Straddle commercial from Gramm. Dole ads: "Stop Hollywood from corrupting our children."

Buchanan: "I'm not afraid to lead."

Lamar: "I'm the only governor running for president."

Forbes has an ad against presidential pensions (now there's an issue!).

Gramm is now in Humboldt, Iowa. Martin Luther King's birthday is coming up, and an antiabortion supporter in the crowd asks a question, with a preface about a current and local news story about five monkeys killed in a fire: "There were monkeys caught in a fire in a zoo. . . . I wouldn't be surprised if there was a national holiday to remember them

... but they are killing children every day. ...." Linking monkeys and MLK, while being so pompously Christian, is not a pretty sight. But Gramm doesn't blink at the implications of the question. I'm prolife, he says. But he keeps talking, oddly, about his second term. "I'm for a flat tax," he says, responding to a question about Forbes. But Gramm wants mortgage deduction and charitable contributions. "I voted against Goals 2000—everyone with an ax to grind got involved. I don't want government to decide what is history." A lot of white folk over fifty make up the crowd. "I want to eliminate the Department of Education, repeal Goals 2000."

A supporter comes up, wearing a large Gramm sticker on his forehead: "You stand out," Gramm says. He turns to the man's wife and says, "I know you're a long-suffering woman. People debate whether I will be president, but no one debates whether she [Mrs. Gramm] is ready to be first lady."

1/16 Rush is pushing the book *A Civil Action,* an account of a long civil liability case, the little guys against large corporations. "One of the best accounts of how the legal system works. . . . It's not that corporations are polluters and they've got to be stopped. . . . Just hope you're never in court." Rush must have had some bad experiences back in the bad old days. His corporate cheerleading doesn't always extend to lawyers.

Rush thinks Bob Kerrey's "plan" on privatizing the Social Security system is "not a bad idea." He quotes a Dole spokesman saying, "Mr. Forbes's idea of hardship is when the butler has a day off." Rush is upset with the Republicans' backbiting. "They're eating their own." He's back to Kerrey. "It's an idea whose time has come." Privatizing SS, that is.

I wonder what Rush would have thought of that back in the bad old days when lawyers were giving him a hard time. He continues to chastise Dole's spokesman. He defends Forbes and attacks people who believe that rich people only act in their self-interest. He doesn't say what they do beyond taking care of their self-interest. He must be thinking of charity (which is often in their self-interest—old clothes to the butler, etc.).

Frontline does a Newt bio. (*Time* had named him "Man of the Year" in its January 1 issue.) Some culled facts from the *docutorial*: Newt was born in Harrisburg, Pennsylvania. Adopted around age four. He has flat feet, is nearsighted. Stepfather, Bob. "Newty" is what his mom calls him. At fifteen he visits Verdun. He's an army brat. Fort Benning, Georgia; Columbus, Ohio. (Mark Shields spoke last fall at Notre Dame and called Newt "Clinton's evil twin.") Same father shuffle as Clinton. No football helmet in high school was big enough. He falls for his twenty-four-year-old high school math teacher. Marries her after his first year of college. Love those sideburns Newt sports at Tulane in the sixties! In '68, he's an organizer for Rockefeller against Nixon. He gets to West Georgia College, where he plots his political future, the Sixth District race. "Mr. Truth" is his nickname. Jack Flynt is his Democratic opponent. Sideburns a bit shorter in '74. Nineteen seventy-six Carter "landslide." Nineteen seventy-eight, wanted to write a novel. Thirteen thousand dollars is raised. Plot is NATO versus Russians. "Learns the ruthless road to power," sayeth *Frontline*. In '78 he runs as a conservative. "Raise hell. Raise hell all the time." Negative campaigning worked. Newt is playing around. Wife composes a campaign letter: "Let our family represent your family." A year later—divorce. New math. Alimony and child support are ordered, but Newt refuses to pay. Marries a thirty-three-year-old. Newt is a C-SPAN creation, sayeth *Frontline*. In 1981 he began the Jim Wright attacks. In '90 Newt's majority whip. He defies Bush on taxes. Forms GOPAC. "Use the same words," Newt advises candidates. Newt's use of tapes is discussed. His "college course" is described, an apparent fund-raising vehicle. The fall of '94. The Contract with America.

A David Frost interview with Bush (March 9, 1991) is aired on PBS. Filmed at Camp David. Tears from Bush about sending people off to die. This wasn't shown till now. I speculate on what its impact would have been and conclude it would have helped Bush, since he did appear so out of touch generally (grocery store scanning machines, etc.), that he would have been in touch with the folk in this display of emotion.

I flip past the channel (TNN) that is always showing the line dancers. A long tradition there. The folk do seem to like regimentation, something learnable and not too free-form: square dance "hoedowns," Shakers' pattern dances, simple ideas rigidly enforced, religious cults, etc.

1/18 Rush is complaining: now we have "deep files." The ghost of Eleanor Roosevelt! He's going on about the files found in the White

House book room. Rush is playing a Carly Simon song ("Clouds in My Coffee"), saying, Pretend you're Mrs. Clinton . . . while she strolls the White House grounds. "You're so vain, you probably think this song is about you. . . ." He recounts his talk to the incoming Republicans after the victory of '94, sponsored by the Heritage Foundation, spectacle I saw on C-SPAN, interesting because it showed how nervous Rush gets around power crowds, unfamiliar people. He's genuinely insecure, which is part of his charm. I warned them, Rush is saying, about the press. The press is liberal. They (some Republican pols) want to impress the press, not the people. He's waiting for that "glorious day when the press finally treats us with respect."

I'm at the mall thinking that the circus has just come to town, given the sideshow proportions of so many of my fellow midwesterners. And I'm still thinking about Rush, the man of the people, which, by definition, means large and overweight.

On CNBC, there's *Rivera Live.* "Hillary in Hot Water" is the show's theme. It's odd seeing her face and caption in the same place and same graphics after seeing O. J.'s there for a year. There's an economic explanation for why O. J. was acquitted. Nicole was what is known in those circles as a "luxury mammal," a person who doesn't produce any money, but just spends it. Whereas O. J. was the big, big earner, a capital fountain, and a lot of people got the benefit of the spray. So in our society, one money machine is allowed to kill one luxury mammal. If Ron Goldman hadn't wandered by, who knows if it would have gone to trial.

1/22   I first heard the Diane Rehm talk radio show when I was visiting Washington, D.C., in 1994. Who is this? I asked my Washington contact. "She's very popular," was the response. It wasn't the voice of Diane Rehm that had caught my attention; it was the voice of Camille Paglia, who was being interviewed, the author of *Sexual Personae,* doing her early Cassius Clay number, "I am the greatest, I am the greatest." Paglia, the bad-girl cultural critic, had become prominent for a variety of reasons, one being that a lot of her "critique" fit nicely with the right-wing Left-bashing antifeminist backlash of the eighties and early nineties.

Their voices were certainly contrasting. Paglia's aggressive and grasping, full of energy, and Rehm's older, measured, soft, slightly censorious.

Then, in 1995, Rehm became syndicated and the local National Public Radio station here in South Bend began airing her show. Bill Bradley is on today, pushing his new memoir. He's talking about the reasons for his departing the Senate, his narrow victory in '90 being one of them. He won by only three points. For an athlete that is victory enough, but for him it is not up to his personal goal, Bradley says. That narrow victory in '90 prefigured the losses of Abrams in '92, Cuomo in '94. Bradley discusses the Rodney King case, says King was hit fifty-six times in two minutes. He tells Rehm: I hit the Senate podium with a pencil fifty-six times.

1/23 Diane Rehm is doing a Crista McCullife memorial *Challenger* explosion show. Reagan's "slipped the surly bonds of earth" speech is recalled. Peggy Noonan's authorship is pointed out. When I heard Reagan say that, I thought it was he that had been watching a lot of late-night TV. When I first moved to Indiana a local TV station used an air force promo as a sign-off (when TV signed off!) at the end of its broadcast day, which recited that poem. When it turned out to be Peggy Noonan, I figured it was she who had been up watching late-night TV.

An older male caller is telling Rush: How they jump on Forbes because he is a millionaire. I voted for my first multimillionaire when I voted for JFK. I liked his message . . . and voted for another, George Bush, and voted against George Bush when I did read his lips. . . .

Rush talks of all the sports stars getting millions. Nobody tells them not to play, Rush says. Rush is protective of millionaires. Though he is now one himself, it's still a valet's protection of his master. I like Forbes's message about the flat tax, Rush says. The caller's a retiree who has an income of thirty-six thousand a year "when everything is squeezed out of the rag." Rush spells it out: The networks, the *New York Times,* the *Washington Post*—they are liberals. Rush is onto sports metaphors, invoking the Super Bowl: What are you going to do if we're down by ten points. It's an eleven-month game. Rush then skips to a New York case, a judge throwing out the confession of a drug courier—$4 million worth of cocaine and heroin. The judge is a Clinton '94 appointee. This is why the presidential race is important, Rush says. He's hot because the AFL-CIO just announced it will spend $35 million to rewin the seventy-four seats lost in '94. Why are they doing this one-note mantra on Steve Forbes being rich? Rush asks. Everyone wants to beat up on Steve Forbes, he says, a guy who's spending his own money. He can't understand it.

When I watched Princess Di's televised interview late last year it brought to mind Hillary and Bill's *60 Minutes* appearance after 1992 Super Bowl. Whatever subtle compromises Hillary Rodham made with herself to go off with her man to Arkansas after life in the fast lane, now echoed back in even larger compromises in order to get out of Arkansas forever. That seemed to be her motto: I'll do anything to get out of Arkansas. Who wouldn't? That might have been her actual pact with the devil.

She was ready to admit more than Bill was. Yes, he's played around and we've worked it out, she conveys to the eager audience. Bill hems and haws, claims he didn't have an "affair" with Gennifer Flowers. A more direct question would have been harder to finesse. He most likely didn't, doesn't, consider what was going on between him and Ms. Flowers an "affair."

But Hillary seemed to be inclined to swerve more toward the truth of the matter. Her statements are lawyerly, but they point in the direction of the facts, rather than away from them, while at the same time not entirely confirming them.

Both spectacles (*60 Minutes* and Princess Di's television interview) do entwine: two women, both near the throne, so to speak, admitting the adultery of their husbands, more or less. In Di's case, her own along the way.

I regret once again Gilda Radner's early death, since she would have been able to lampoon the princess's performance pricelessly. Radner would have been able to capture the tiny medicinal twitches, the pursed lips, the sucked-in cheeks, revealing hilariously the manic cracks under the attempted surface calm in Di's delivery.

But the princess was not trying to hold together a campaign in order to get out of Arkansas. Her purposes were a bit more diffuse: revenge, palace intrigue, self-protection, alimony, cash settlements. But these television confessions by a future king and queen were set in motion by the Clintons' precedent when they were longing to become heads of state.

Prince Charles climbed on after it worked for them, and Princess Di was not to be left out on the side of the road.

In the Ann Landers profile (December 4, 1995) in *The New Yorker,* Landers is quoted saying about Clinton, "I don't think he's fooling around anymore. Nor do I think he will. I read that Hillary threw a lamp at him. I read that. Did you read that? You know something? I think she did." The lamp story is getting a lot of play. The third floor of the White House seemed to be becoming the set of *Dallas* (or Little Rock). Bill's envy of JFK must increase with every passing day, for the amount of slack the press cut Kennedy back then.

(Though one wonders how much Clinton's catting around has been cut back. On December 14, 1995 there was one of those seasonal shows on television, "Christmas in Washington," a night of entertainment with the first family in attendance, full of holiday good cheer, all looking like the fanciest decorated store window, a Christmas party with the president playing host, entertainers belting out show tunes, good family fare. I caught the end of it and Gloria Estefan was singing some heated tune, and the camera cut to Bill watching, and his expression seemed to be announcing, How can I get a date with her? She was the climax of the show and he got up on stage and said a few happy seasonal words, Hillary and Chelsea joined him, and it was over, but as soon as the NBC credits started to roll, he broke away from his family and made a beeline to Ms. Estefan, grabbed her with both hands, and said something to her. He was led back to Hillary and Chelsea and the camera was panning the performers as they were standing there singing along, accepting applause, and when the camera landed on Ms. Estefan's face she had a most alarmed expression playing over her pretty features, and one had to wonder just what he said to her that would generate such an unprofessional reaction from a professional whose job it was at that minute to look glowing and amused.)

But the State of the Union was payback time. Hillary under attack. Hillary twisting slowly, slowly in the wind. So it is up to Bill to publicly praise her, pat her on the back, stand by his woman, show his congenitals. We're in this together, kid, even though your chances of being indicted are far greater than mine.

Much was made of Clinton's first State of the Union address, when

Alan Greenspan was seated next to Hillary—and Tipper Gore. Greenspan was bookended by blondes. Strokes for the bond market, we're friends of the Fed, blared the message.

So it is with some amazement I see who is seated next to Hillary for this one. Elie Wiesel, the author and concentration camp survivor. Chelsea also appears at her side for the first time (wife and mother), but it is Wiesel's appearance which is the more telling symbol. It is not unkind to call Wiesel a symbol of victim as survivor. And his place of honor next to Hillary is a bit much: the message being, You see I'm a victim, too, persecuted by the state, herded into a camp, at the mercy of guards, threatened with extinction, but, however unjust, I will prevail.

All politicians need to be calculating, but one wonders at what point it desists. No point, perhaps. At least not in public, and that is one reason why scandal is so captivating in any society, for it is the only chance people get to see the unscripted, the out-of-control, and those episodes that surface tend to make public figures human.

Bill and Hillary on *60 Minutes* was crisis management, but the veneer of control was thin there and except for the constituency that finds them abhorrent in every way it did make them real to their audience.

1/24 The *NewsHour,* with Jim Lehrer, is doing a postmortem on the State of the Union speech and Dole's following remarks. Clinton's The Era of Big Government Is Over gets a good going-over, but no one calls it a non sequitur. In Dole's case, it is truly postmortem, since he did look like he was raised from the dead, a body double for Christopher Lee, the Dracula actor, looking at home in the mausoleum. We had just been in the great hall of the rich and powerful (how many millionaires were present? The percentage must have been higher per capita than Idaho's), the center of Big Government, full of light and glitter, and then we get the tomb, with dark Bob Dole standing all alone. We're going to have a year of this contrast, or ten months more. Bill Clinton as life, Eros. Bob Dole as death, Thanatos.

Mark Shields points out on the *NewsHour* that "Dole invited the fire and the criticism of his own challengers for the nomination. . . . There was Pat Buchanan out today saying he lacks vision and Lamar Alexander saying the same thing, so he had intraparty sniping and Clinton was free of it. It's a big, big difference the day after."

1/26 On Dan Rather's CBS News, Dole is saying, "We'll name names, share them," the Hollywood names of the no-accounts who are polluting our youth with salacious and violent movies. He sounds like McCarthy naming names.

Republican John Kasich, of Ohio chairman of the House Budget Committee, is being interviewed on the *NewsHour*. He uses the tooth-paste-in-the-tube analogy of H. R. Haldeman, though it seems uncon-scious. How Washington has changed. Kasich makes a crack about the Michael Jackson–Presley marriage being on the rocks. Kasich says he wants to take the power out of this city (Washington). He could leave, I suppose.

1/27 Bill Bradley is on *Meet the Press*. His new memoir, *Time Present, Time Past*, serves as the ticket to the round of radio and television shows. Bradley talks about the Big Brother scrutiny that presidential candidates are exposed to, something he's avoiding.

1/29 Rush is speaking to a woman caller talking about the case of the eccentric du Pont heir who shot a wrestler who was living at his estate. She says because John du Pont is homosexual, the "liberal media isn't going to attack him." Her prejudices are so ugly even Rush rushes her off.

1/30 The news today, my wife comments, about the Feds meeting shouldn't be news. When jobs are created right before the election, the incumbent party wins. Everyone knows that—so why was it any question that a Federal Reserve chair one month before his twelve-year reappoint-ment and nine months before an election wouldn't lower interest rates? A twelve-year reappointment will take Greenspan comfortably into re-tirement.

FOUR

February Blues (and Reds and Whites)

News is advertising. It requires repetition. Any announced fact dies without dissemination. There is almost a uterine aspect to news: said once, twice, a fact is still embryonic. It needs the spatial equivalent of nine months' worth of repetitions. Like some science fiction film, news needs to be fast-multiplying, and, often like the same films, it will finally exhaust its ability to reproduce and split. It dies; the millions of husks blow away in the wind. I live by a river and twice a year some bug equivalents of mayflies appear, filling an intersection with their gossamer fluttering, creating a faintly greenish cloud, a huge bubble of bugs. They are lovely, poignant in the grammar school way of an example of a species that seems to exist only to reproduce and die. For a day (or actually a night) it is captivating. Then they're gone: old news. Andy Warhol's single enduring aphorism, about fifteen minutes of fame, though unexamined, captured this flaring quality. But it requires fifteen minutes on every clock, fifteen minutes of everyone's consciousness.

The Big Lie, in the Goebbels manner, needs repetition, too. Over and over a lie becomes metatruth, however false it might be. It takes on its own role in the culture, goes from lie to myth, and myths are always afforded some respect.

Progressive journalists were not surprised by Watergate, and that hurt them: fresh scandals are usually pursued with more vigor. But if anyone had laid out exactly what occurred the day after it happened, it would not have mattered much. The structure of the "revelations" set in motion the forces that brought Nixon down. It was the drip drip drip aspect, and the fact that the drips were coming from the most influential and establishment newspapers. It was the repetition, the advertising of the Nixon White House—for what it was. And, finally, the tapes. News is not news until it is repeated seven times seventy (at least), and Woodward and Bernstein were the agents of redundancy. After the gridlock of campaign news abates, the media can isolate one issue and pick it apart. The post-election news lull is a dangerous time for a successful politician.

Katherine Graham and Ben Bradlee were not undisposed to the abdication of Nixon, whom they viewed, at the very least, as the chief profiteer from the death of Camelot. Whether they thought that Nixon had a more direct role in Kennedy's death was secondary.

But it took time for the news to become the news. *All the President's Men,* the film of the Woodward/Bernstein book, came out in 1976, not long after Nixon resigned, and I remember how I was struck seeing it then: history barely cold turned into Hollywood artifact. It was stunning. And the precursor. One first shot across the bow in the acceleration of the political culture.

What the Pentagon Papers and Watergate did to realign how the news was presented in the seventies, the O. J. trial did in the nineties. The Pentagon Papers, et alia, brought us transcripts, reports, raw data in the newspaper. O. J. brought us experts in volume. Not commentators, but an era of institutionalizing and professionalizing comment.

There was already a degree of this at large: reporters as experts, economists working for papers, even lawyers. But what happened with O. J. was unprecedented: out of the woodwork came a multitude of attorneys, in every town and village, happy to comment (free advertising if they were on often enough) on the yearlong proceedings. The amount of human capital involved is staggering—especially if those were billable hours: chatting on an on, the pro–O.J. African American attorneys, the perceived Uncle Tom neutral Afro Am attorneys, white attorneys, female attorneys, attorneys everywhere. The O.J. model is now the campaign coverage model.

What had once been on the fringes was now all over the map: in fact, it resembles one of the epidemiological maps much in the news these days, of a virus out of control. One hour here, twenty-four hours everywhere. The attorneys solidified the phenomenon. Those who now transmit the news are no longer observers, but "creatures of the event." And so it is in the campaign: though the political hack/reporter has its public face in the ascendancy of Safire and others, mentioned earlier, it is no longer mere happenstance, but a total condition (and being recognized as such). And when the creatures of the event take over, look out.

The Ayatollah Khomeini helped to restructure American media by giving us *Nightline,* which was, at first, *America Held Hostage,* Day whatever. More than a decade later, O.J. gave us the surplus of freelance attorneys wanting the free advertising of the tube. Cable channels piggyback on courtroom drama. After a generation of explosive growth in the legal profession, it is not odd that the business of lawerying now laps over onto the shores of the popular culture. Nixon prepared the world for John Grisham.

Cable provides space and has a need for material. It is similar to the early days of *Rolling Stone,* which did foster the careers of a number of writers because in its heyday its format allowed—demanded—long articles, something to separate the columns of endless stereo advertisements.

Bob Dole is a generational symbol in unlikely ways—not just World War II versus baby boomers. He represents a whole generation of men who hang on to power for longer than some think advisable: the Lears of their time, hoping for no tragedy (the sacrifice of their daughter, say) to blight their last days.

One could make a list, but let's stop with three: Dole, Lane Kirkland, Fidel Castro. Kirkland wanted to die in office, and Dole and Fidel, too, are hoping for that outcome, it appears. Castro still has a chance to have his reign expire with his last breath (old age–inspired, not CIA–induced), and probably has a better shot at it than Bob Dole does.

The AFL-CIO had its own open election in '95, the first in its long history, resulting in the ouster of Lane Kirkland and the elevation of John Sweeney to the federation's presidency.

To say Lane Kirkland presided over the decline of the labor movement is true, though how causal was his role in the decline can be debated. I was not raised in a union household. As a teenager, I thought unions in Kansas City desirable, but exclusionary (and mobbed up). My high-school mates who got cushy summer jobs (holding flags on highway construction projects) were connected to unions. My Chicago steelworking uncles were in unions. Visiting Chicago relatives always had the atmosphere of a union picnic; men in windbreakers, bratwurst on the barbecue. But Kansas City had a different atmosphere; my father was a manager of a bearing distribution company and unions were kept at arm's length.

One of the unhappiest episodes of the Vietnam War protest era was the scenes of hard hats fighting with antiwar demonstrators: Those generations-at-war photos ran everywhere. The hardline anti-Communist side of American trade unionism let labor appear to the young its personalized enemy (by letting them beat up on their own ungrateful sons and daughters, the lazy kids in college, the place they never got to go). The two "working-class" swans of the right, Mary Matalin and Peggy Noonan, cite their conversions to such scenes, becoming antiunion free enterprisers in the bargain. Those who aided and abetted these scenes (helping Nixon be elected twice) probably didn't care how they were damaging the image of unionism in the minds of a generation. Indeed, that might have been one of their goals.

Even Michael Harrington, author of *The Other America* and an American socialist, who was inclined to try, couldn't heal the rift between the intellectual young and big labor during that period. So the union movement went, more or less, to sleep. It managed to skip a generation, the first wave, the early years of the baby boom, the Vietnam generation; so as unionism declined to the low teens (and even those statistics are inflated, since they include retirees, and there are a lot of them, though they won't last forever), actual jobs disappeared, and the powerful image of unionism, so potent in the fifties, weakened and faded. Lane Kirkland would not have been recognized by many people of my generation, unless they had family in a union, and perhaps not even then.

One of the beefs against Kirkland was just that: that he didn't play the public spokesman role enough for labor. After Hoffa became a *desaparecido*, there was no union figure who had national recognition. Kirkland was more than content to deal with his powerful peers, play golf with senators and not upstage the other federation presidents. Some appreciated Lane not hogging the limelight, not becoming more well known than any one of them.

Kirkland would have been good at more public exposure; I've seen some of his public performances on video (mainly testimonies), and he was impressive. And videogenic. Wry, imposing, quick-witted, worldly, a great public presence for labor, but one fatally underexposed. He disliked the press, liked overmuch men with real power, not countenancing the hollow, but potent, power that the media can wield.

Kirkland never really groomed a successor—Tom Donahue was the titular hopeful. But you're not grooming a successor if you hope to die in office.

And in the AFL-CIO's headquarters on Sixteenth Street in Washington, D.C., floors of offices began to resemble dying strip malls, one office after another left dark, unused, a single one still lit, trying to do what whole departments did in the flush past.

So the country got treated to its own Eugene O'Neill drama, a long night's journey into American democratic unionism. And we watched John Sweeney, a not very videogenic figure from Kirkland's own backyard, marginally younger, emerge. Offers are made to let Kirkland resign, but Kirkland, as befits his ego, wants to be slain, as any real ruler desires.

It's a small world up at the top of the AFL-CIO, and at least Sweeney wants to make the rings of power around him—no matter what their actual effective orbit might be—look more, à la Clinton, like the real world. Some women, some people of color (best if one is both), some guys who aren't near retirement age already.

So we have Sweeney, Richard Trumka, Linda Chavez-Thompson. Kirkland "resigns," spending his last month in office at the AFL-CIO headquarters east, at the Hotel Intercontinental, in Geneva, Switzerland, sipping, as the saying goes in labor circles, chardonnay by the lake.

Campaign America '96: The View From the Couch

Class warfare has many fronts, but every once in a while they bleed together and run from one end of the country to the other. One defining event that awakened and prepared the ground for the current class-warfare battles in the Republican Party was the baseball strike. There are many ways the filthy rich make spectacles of themselves, but only a percentage of that is circuses for the masses: Donald Trump and his blondes, *Lifestyles of the Rich and Famous:* they function like American royalty, our version of the British royals, at least producing some surplus value of entertainment. But the baseball strike was different. The economics of the country affect everyone, and the stagnating phrase "stagnating wages" has finally become conventional wisdom, but it is still difficult to put a face on it (though in '92 it was Bush's face); the baseball strike affected a verticle demographic, gave different sorts of folks (OK, mainly white males, but not all, by any means) cohesion, shared, ah, values. And those who don't care about baseball still saw the same thing.

No World Series. Rich men and Marge taking their balls away. This spectacle raised resentments not yet put to rest. When the government was shut down in late '95 by the Congress's refusal to pass a continuing resolution, the battle for a "balanced" budget was all too familiar.

Though the balanced-budget amendment lost by one vote in the Senate at the end of February 1995, thanks to the Oregon Republican senator, Mark Hatfield, the movement for a de jure balanced budget comes creeping out of the same overworked soil the owners of professional major league teams tilled in their futile quest for a salary cap, the purported cause of the baseball strike. The same "Stop me before I kill again" spirit (echoing the signs appearing on redwood trees after Ronald Reagan accused them many years ago of contributing to deadly air pollution) prevails. The rich men (and women) of baseball couldn't get themselves to stop bidding wars for spectacular players and wanted the players to curb it for them.

Legislators can't solve the deficit, so the reasoning goes, and they call out for a constitutional amendment to do it for them.

You don't need a program to sort out the players: Bob Dole is Bud Selig; Phil Gramm is the sputtering image of George Steinbrenner; and Newt Gingrich, the Speaker of the House, he's my Marge Schott, who cheered on the twenty-seven players who participated in the Cincinnati Reds' exhibition opener (and fired the sixteen who wouldn't) with "You're not wimps out there. You guys are men."

The baseball strike was, in many ways, a parody of labor-management negotiations. There is the unresolved paradox of millionaire workers still being "employees." That the Congress continues to flirt with amendments of easy virtue coyly attached to the skirt of the Constitution (aren't the Republicans the conservatives, who want to limit the Constitution, not extend it?) is more than a bit sinister. Like the Contract with America, the balanced-budget amendment is a marketing ploy, largely symbolic (except for the work program it will make for lawyers down the road).

When the wealthy strike, people get pissed off. They should, after being exposed to over two decades of demonizing the labor movement by the wealthy and making strikes anti-America. They did their PR too well. So when they try their own lockout, there is a cost.

Baseball strike equals-budget-battle shutdown equals Pat Buchanan. The so-called Reagan Democrats are volatile. They've turned once, they can turn again.

Buchanan is not an anomaly on the public stage. That he is a spokesperson for the "Republicans," labeled extreme by Dole et alia, that the vanguard at present is Buchananism, is reflected, mirrored, in other social movements. Louis Farrakhan, for instance.

Farrakhan's "Million Man March" on October 16, 1995 was his own early primary. Holding it in Washington was not a bold move, since Washington already has a sizable number of African American males in it. Regardless of the actual count of those in attendance—four hundred thousand or so—Farrakhan's march was no bolt of original lightning. He was following in the very white footsteps of the Promise Keepers, the all-male, overwhelmingly white society. (Even though when they show up in the press—*USA Today,* for instance—pictures invariably show one or two black males, the ratio is similar to the number of black cheerleaders over the years at Notre Dame and the percentage of black students at our university.)

Buchanan is the beneficiary of a lot of toxic strains in our culture. Like a tumor which thrives on poison, he is fueled by them. If the Republican establishment is looking for extremes, it doesn't have to look far.

The angry white male phenomenon has effectively been institution-alized over the last two decades. The antiabortion (aka Right to Life) movement is a hotbed of angry white males. The Christian Coalition, the latest in the line of *700, 400 Clubs,* Moral Majorities, Swaggart and Bakker, are theme parks of angry white males and their wives and chil-dren. Not to mention the Klan, skinheads, survivalists, etc.

The decline of unionism points out the paradox: The country loves to come together in groups, to identify with common circumstances. Start wherever on the time line: mainstream organized religions lose members and unorthodox religions gain them. Moonies, Scientologists, gurus of various denominations. What are our communal, national experiences? Look to the rates television can charge for commercials. The Super Bowl. Coca-Cola–induced tribal rituals—the summer Olympics to come. Be-yond those it is great disasters. The O. J. trial.

Pat Buchanan has often been named as one of the progenitors of Nixon's enemies list (though it was Nixon who was the master list maker), and when that charge was raised again (on *Face the Nation*) William Safire denied that there even was an enemies list and went on blathering about how he and Buchanan were alliteration mavens, nattering nabobs, just team players giving their all for Dick. The two of them were also angrier then, because Nixon suffered his own paradoxes: elected by a grand margin and simultaneously being derided and disliked by so many people orbiting around Buchanan's and Safire's world.

The Reagan years were interesting in their depiction of the business world in the popular culture. Films like *Wall Street* (1987), about the rise of the arbitragers, portrayed the corporate world in a new light: insofar as the free market's tooth and claw became physical, everyone was screaming at each other. And if conservatives want to banish violence in movies, they should look to boardroom violence: films of the eighties normalized screaming and cursing as business discourse.

As conservatism rose throughout the culture it ushered in its reimag-ing, that of the American businessman. At its furthest point it entailed eroticizing their status. Kissinger's remark, "Power is the ultimate aph-rodisiac," found a material base.

William O'Rourke

The red suspenders, slashes of bloodletting the initiating symbols of the Wall Street warrior, the screaming, the alpha behavior, the law of the jungle, was to Tarzanize the man in the gray flannel suit. The Marlboro Man in mufti. They are now just suits, which is quite close to sluts, a remark full of both insult and envy.

There's a lot of violence in our culture, but in this regard I do tend to believe in trickle-down. Anger without profit is what is still denigrated in our culture. How often does one hear about some sorry murder victim that he or she only had a few dollars to steal and society seems doubly outraged, since the implication is that it can at least understand the killing if the perp made off with, as they say in the boardrooms, "a killing."

Steve Forbes is the least telegenic rich man I have ever seen on television. In person, millionaires invariably look like a million dollars, even when they don't look good. If they are bloated on a life full of vices (say, Ted Kennedy), they've been very expensive vices. Embalmed, perhaps, pickled even, but the brine is the finest vintage, the attendants the most elaborately trained. They look like a million.

But on television Forbes looks bad, sounds bad, and when you watch him on a variety of outlets and he—like most of the others—repeats a few rote lines, his voice is a medley of wrong notes, all sounding cultural chords that one would think would be music to his rivals' ears. Squeaky, high-pitched, upper-crust, all delivered through the most amazing fixed, clenched smile.

Looking at his face, his gimlet eyes behind his I'm-a-genius glasses, the hilly, pocked mounds of his cheeks and jowls, it appears that I am looking at the sins of the father, or, rather, the portrait of Dorian Gray visited upon the vulnerable canvas of his son. His father's visage remained smooth, whatever bizarre lengths he went to in pursuit of his flamboyant indulgence, signifying the *fin* of his *siecle*, squiring (a la Michael Jackson) Elizabeth Taylor, the beard of beards. The era of decadence best embodied by Malcom Forbes Sr. and Roy Cohn and Studio 54 and leather and motorcycles has somewhat sputtered out, leading to *Angels in America,* angels everywhere, a period of cultural afterlife we are all now wandering around in.

It is odd how the rich have to change their names to wander among the people, come out from behind their walls, cloaked in the mufti of regular guy names: Pierre du Pont becomes Pete, Malcolm Stevenson Forbes Jr. becomes Steve. Just as some ethnic groups altered their names to make them less "foreign," the ethnic group of the very, very rich has to modify their "funny" names to be more readily accepted by the masses.

Pat Buchanan, though rich, doesn't have that problem, since his wealthy father had a lot of plain Irish names to dole out. Everyone becomes vaguely Catholic and low-rent Protestant in this name game. Lamar! will be the proof of the pudding. Larry Alexander, perhaps. Lamar! I don't think so.

It is easy to call Forbes *Forbes,* since not everyone has a magazine with the same name in the family, and that is why it rolls so easily off the tongue and the page.

I have been wondering about Forbes's domestic life and I have now discovered his Sabrina (in the *Time* magazine of January 29)—and their five daughters!—via print media, but not in the warm world of the pixel screen. I recall Forbes's mantra on abortion: "I want it to vanish from the culture." I guess. The wishful-thinking world. All that he might want to vanish. Five daughters, a substantial wife. He wants a lot to vanish. The world as he doesn't know it.

A friend I ran into related a Forbes senior story. A young man of distinctive good looks and muscular bearing was riding his motorcycle in lower Manhattan late one night when an older man on another motorcycle pulled up next to him. Eddie, as I'll call him, has been described as "friendly as a puppy," and he struck up a conversation. The two rode along for a while, the older man quite taken with the younger, until Eddie suggested he come along with him to a bar for a drink where he was going to meet his girlfriend. The mention of the girlfriend dampened the interest of the man, Malcolm Forbes, and he rumbled off alone.

But mutual friends put them back in touch and Eddie began to work for Forbes doing a variety of things, ending up in Morocco escorting Elizabeth Taylor around. Forbes kept up his interest in the young man, but after Malcolm's death the family cut off Eddie's work, along with others who they thought were mere playthings of their father. They vanished, too. I want it to vanish from the culture. *Droit de signeur.*

Nearly a year ago, back on February 26, 1995, the political editor of the *San Fransico Chronicle,* Susan Yoachum, did an article headlined "They Shoot Elephants, Don't They?" giving odds on all the potential GOP candidates. She listed one who never entered the race (Lynn Martin), and didn't list the one who is filling up the news: Steve Forbes.

Since Alan Keyes is in the race, it can't just be, for Republicans, a matter of picking the last white man standing. Back in '95, Ms. Yoachum gave Dole's odds of capturing the nomination at two to one.

Buchanan's beer hall oratory at the '92 Republican convention is often cited as one reason Clinton squeaked by and Bush slipped. Though it was fitting that Buchanan bedeviled Bush at the beginning of the election—his New Hampshire showing revealing that Bush was vulnerable (the Democrats got to play the circling buzzards, though it wasn't entirely apparent since their nominee was then nearly road kill himself)—and at the end, spoiling Bush's coronation at the convention.

But Clinton's first term has been providing Buchanan with important balancing issues. The passage of GATT and NAFTA, the continuing flattening of middle-class wages (and, more importantly, the growing awareness of that fact), Clinton's relegating the labor movement to a second-tier girlfriend you could always count on for a date when fancier honeys were unavailable, have given Buchanan issues that help balance his religio-loco rhetoric. He gained some substance, sound bites with bite, more regular-guy sangfroid.

I've spent a lifetime viewing blustering Irish Americans, and Buchanan has his bluster down pat. That his life bears no resemblance to his public vision is not unusual in political life, but he has found a way to deal with it. He laughs at himself. Rush Limbaugh is still capable of the same thing. When Buchanan is with some of his media colleagues, in his noncampaign mode, after some lunatic and aggressive assertion, he will chuckle when he gets his friends to roll their collective eyes in response. But bluster he is. On the campaign trial, looking forward to matching funds and donations from the dementedly generous, he will tighten up: the 1992 Republican convention speech did not contain any ironic, self-deprecating laughter.

Forget Buchanan's draft avoidance, his Mercedes-Benz, his lack of children, his hefty personal wealth, his life of speechwriting and bullshitting; he's a man of the people out there, exploiting his ethnic heritage, the superficial qualities of it written on his visage and build, the look (Buchanan's face *is* Lamar!'s red-and-black checked shirt) of a guy who could work, at least if he had to, presenting the basic schizoid view of America the beautiful in 1992: "My friends, this election is about much more than who gets what. It is about who we are. It is about what we believe. It is about what we stand for as Americans. There is a religious war going on in our country for the soul of America. It is a cultural war, as critical to the kind of nation we will one day be as was the cold war itself. And in that struggle for the soul of America, Clinton and Clinton are on the other side, and George Bush is on our side. And so, we have to come home, and stand beside him."

His '92 convention speech ended with a gothic fantasy about the LA riots, and the picture it described, given all the white faces in the audience, was curdling: Soldiers "had come into LA late on the second day, and they walked up a dark street where the mob had looted and burned every building but one, convalescent home for the aged. The mob was heading in, to ransack and loot the apartments of the terrified old men and women. When the troopers arrived, M16's at the ready, the mob threatened and cursed, but the mob retreated. It had met the one thing that could stop it: force, rooted in justice, backed by courage. . . . And as they took back the streets of LA, block by block, so we must take back our cities, and take back our culture, and take back our country."

FIVE

The Shortest Month

★

2/1 NPR's *All Things Considered* has inquired of the favorite songs of candidates. *ATC* supplies familiar renditions as they are announced. "I Could Have Danced All Night," Julie Andrews trills for Richard Lugar. "My Funny Valentine" is Lamar Alexander's, revealing a hitherto non-red-and-black-check-jacket side: Lamar!, the bistro guy! Dole's is, I think I hear, "You'll Never Walk Alone" and Forbes's is Sousa's version of the "Star-Spangled Banner," which I do not believe; if true, his cultural world is more terrible than I have hitherto thought. From Gramm, there's no response. He might see it as the Rorschach test it is. My speculations make me queasy. Buchanan's is a Patsy Cline tune. Oh, Pat, the Irish sentimentalist, looking for sophistication in all the wrong places. B-1 Bob Dornan's is some air force pep song, "Tip Your Wings" or some such. I didn't catch one from Alan Keyes; perhaps they didn't ask him.

CNN's *Inside Politics* says Forbes was against a balanced-budget amendment as late as September 1995, but now is for it with a tax cut.

Watching *Rivera Live* after the O.J. trial is over is like visiting the formerly popular diner on the state road after the new superhighway has opened up and hard times have set in. Everything's slightly stale, the action has moved on.

In January the stories were the budget, the snow, the State of the Union, the era of big government being over, etc. Dole is down, Forbes is up. Hillary and Whitewater are staying fresh: her book, *It Takes a Village,* is out. But the book of the talk month is *Primary Colors* by Anonymous.

2/4 *The McLaughlin Group* went on the air early in the Reagan ad-ministration and it was part of the general gestalt. Hollywood would be gearing up in the *Wall Street* mode, when the culture of business became, post-Vietnam, the field of battle. During the war those in business felt themselves somewhat restrained, since a lot of them avoided service, but during the eighties the rage-as-style phenomenon took off. It's the David Mamet syndrome: a pampered upper-middle-class kid who never left easy street was, through his plays, depicting a world of screaming dog-eat-dog commerce. The Sutton Place dead-end kid—not that Mamet was from Sutton Place, just some upper-middle-class suburb. Being an artist, Mamet, at least, had the talent to see where things were going.

But one Wall Street figure who best epitomized the era was Jeffery Beck, a fraud yelling "Lock and load" every chance he got, one who, when his bluster as an eighties merger rainmaker was finally spent, the *Wall Street Journal* (January 22, 1990) characterized as "a parable of Wall Street in the 1980s." The *WSJ*'s headline: "Top Deal Maker Leaves a Trail of Deception in Wall Street Rise." (A friend of mine was pre-paring a movie based on Beck's life when his story began to blow sky high.)

After the Vietnam War the vast majority of men who did not serve in the military wanted to display how tough they all really were and the business world got to bear the brunt of the new, displaced fierceness. Hollywood made it easy to track, all those corporate chieftains screaming at each other up on the silver screen.

The McLaughlin Group, led by former Father John, was right at the heart of the zeitgeist (as Eric Alterman demonstrates in his *Sound and Fury,* page 113). To succeed in this culture, you need ability and, more elusively, you need to be truly *of your time.* Father John is that in spades.

One thing I was amused by not long ago was an op-ed piece (August 8, 1994) in the *New York Times* by William Buckley, who went out of the way to remind us that it was John McLaughlin who was on the steps of the Capitol in his priestly regalia defending Nixon till the end. Why Buckley stuck that aside in his piece, I presume, is because he somewhat resents his former Washington correspondent (of Buckley's *National Review*) his great success, success that certainly has eclipsed his old boss's own television show, *Firing Line*. Buckley seems to have a bit of a Mario problem, though not such a virulent case.

Again, in all the campaign's raging against Hollywood (Republicans) and talk radio (Democrats) in '88, '92, and now, for coarsening the "discourse," it is actually the business world and its cultural representations that have coarsened it, and legitimized this coarseness, via the World Wide Wrestling ring atmosphere of the boardroom.

McLaughlin is yet another example of the can't-fail-once-admitted axiom, and of the happy nepotism that goes along with it. One of the hallmarks of the Republican scorn for labor is that they feminized the cabinet position in their administrations. The secretary of labor became a woman's position under Reagan and Bush. That gave them a laugh, a twofer, to downplay labor and to claim they were elevating women. McLaughlin's wife (now ex-wife), Ann, who led the way, had to be excused from her business-school class (she was attempting to get an MBA) when Reagan named her secretary of labor in 1987. Poor Frances Perkins, the last female secretary of labor (1933–44), was turning in her grave. After the graduate-student McLaughlin came Liddy Dole (1989–90), then Lynn Martin (1990–93).

What does it matter? Labor did know what the Reagan and Bush administrations thought of it. Robert Reich, initially, was not too happy about taking the secretary of labor job, given its recent history; and, unfortunately, his stature let the Rushes of the world continue to make fun of him and it. On Rush Limbaugh's television show, when Reich is discussed, the image of him that appears barely peeks above the bottom of the screen. The only part of Reich that is visible is a half-moon of forehead and hair.

But ex-Father McLaughlin is like Buchanan and a few other right-wing celebrities who have risen in the eighties. They have retained a sense of irony and will, at times, laugh at themselves, the hearty ho, ho, ho of the self-directed misanthrope. Those who don't have that ability usually remain parochial and their bitterness and endless spleen are confined to family and friends.

McLaughlin himself seems supremely confident in his role, doubtless a holdover from his Jesuit past: he sits high in the celebrant position, with his fellows arrayed two on his right, two on his left, acolytes at the ready, altar boys and girls set to defer and fetch. The vestments he favors are colored or striped shirts that retain a starched bright white collar, another remnant from his professional cleric days.

Eleanor Clift has to carry the majority female load for the gang and she often has the hangdog look of the perpetually outnumbered. Yes, and Bill Buckley does have cause to worry, since Father John's show does have more influence (certainly notoriety) than *Firing Line—The McLaughlin Group* is more firing squad in execution, which is what the times call for.

Today they're discussing Bill Bradley, Forbes, the primaries. They all think it's Dole's to lose. Today's cast includes Fred Barnes, late of *The New Republic,* now at the Rupert Murdoch–bankrolled *The Weekly Standard;* Clarence Page, the genial African American from the *Chicago Tribune* (genial is important on TV); Tony Snow, identified as a columnist for *USA Today;* and Eleanor Clift, who toils at *Newsweek*. Clift is Hillary's defender against Tony Snow's insistent, but genial, charges: "The D'Amato hearing is a big flop!" she says.

2/5 NPR's *ATC* discusses how the primary candidates use caucus videos. Videos are everywhere and are used for everything. When I was due for an angioplasty, I was shown one, except it turned out to be about a bypass operation, but they showed it to me anyway.

The pope is in Guatemala, part of his visit to Central America. Various reasons for his trip are offered: "Competition from evangelicals," because it was "safer being a Protestant during the eighties." An attempt to "reinvigorate the Catholic Church" among the people.

Throughout the campaign there are a number of issues which are not issues, but need to be noticed, for their lack of coverage if nothing else. Take El Salvador—or all of Central America, for that matter. Big news in the Reagan years, Ollie North and all that. A friend of mine has been going down to El Salvador for the last decade, and I ran into him right after returning from California to the Midwest, which, though cold, was not at that moment as snowbound as the East Coast. I was bragging about being in California, relatively warm for the holidays, and he said he was warmer in El Salvador. How's it going? I asked, and he told me.

Everyone's nostalgic for the war, he said; both sides would like those days to return. Corruption is, as they say, rampant—growling—both sides are stealing every dollar that comes their way. The new bishop is an Opus Dei devotee, formerly in bed with the military, and they are rebuilding the cathedral in the center of San Salvador, to make the rich families who run the show happy. The only thing that seems to keep the economy afloat is the American dollars working El Salvadorans living in the United States send down to their relatives. The Catholic Church's relationship with the society now resembles Cuba before the revolution, insofar as the Catholic Church is back to being the consort of the rich. Poverty is increasing, everything is going to hell.

Things do come and go, off the radar screen, but only NAFTA will bring up things south of the border these days. Luckily, the pope is out campaigning too this year, and today the *New York Times* has a front-page article on the scene in El Salvador on the eve of the pope's visit, part of a tour of Latin America. It runs on a Sunday, doubtless because it's packaged as a religious article.

It covers the same ground that my friend had reported to me last month.

When conservatives rail against the liberal press, what is most often spewing out of their mouths is just straight anti-Semitism. Liberal media means "Jews" to the militia world. But, aside from that, what an article that wouldn't be biased and liberal would tell them is that the pope was visiting his good friend, Archbishop Fernando Saenz Lacalle, an international figure, born in Spain, and a man who had worked directly with the Vatican in the past keeping track of the military, holding down to a few dozen or so the killings of priests and nuns and one former archbishop, Oscar Romero, unfortunately riddled with bullets when he was in church, and Lacalle is now heroically finishing the cathedral in San Salvador and has the support of the business community in the democratic nation of El Salvador, a good place to visit over the Christmas holidays, especially after the cathedral is finished, to get away from the snow on the Capitol steps of Washington.

If the liberal media weren't the liberal media, that's how the pope's visit would be reported, with no bias, just God-fearing American objectivity.

During the presidential campaign there is always new cartography, a new map of the world involved: who can force its way onto the map? This year is *us and them,* and one "them" is the former Yugoslavia. Everywhere else is the margin, terra incognita, unless visited by natural disasters.

The pope is admirable for his stamina, which appears to be a public figure's most necessary attribute. But after Pope John Paul (George, Ringo) suddenly died, the current pope was a harbinger of all the conservative impulses at loose in the land, and the rollback he is effecting in the worldwide Catholic Church is the same as the religious Right is attempting here at home.

On C-SPAN, Buchanan is doing his own brand of anti-Semitism, attacking Wall Street types in the Clinton administration: Robert Rubin, the treasury secretary, "paid back the big banks, Goldman Sachs. . . . They are off the hook. . . . Who's on the hook? . . . Your children . . . It's an outrage. We will cancel NAFTA." And there will be "no bailing out socialist regimes anywhere." He's in Waterloo, Iowa, being Napoleon-like.

Reading the on-site campaign coverage, I think of my father, stateside during World War II, working in a defense plant. The others are out there on the front lines while I'm back at home on the couch. Michael Lewis, at *The New Republic,* is doing the most amusing stuff. He's met Morry Taylor and Lewis knows a character when he happens upon one—and a character he will have all to himself, since no one else will likely care about Morry Taylor, a rich businessman who is floating his own run, Perot with a sense of humor. Lewis owns Taylor now, and I doubt anyone else will be bidding for him. Morry—Morry!—is the bookend of Forbes, blue-collar side, the self-made millionaire who wants to be a candidate and, in America, by God, thanks to the Supreme Court, he can be.

Lewis ends his piece of February 5, 1996, with a vignette of the Republican congressman from California and presidential contender B-1 Bob Dornan having trouble getting on a plane to Chicago from Des Moines, Iowa, after the January 14 debate. Lewis helps him get on after he explains to the counter folks just who B-1 Bob is. (He was not recognized by the airline employees—no National Figure Bob, and not enough C-SPAN viewing by the employees.) Then Lewis writes, "Dornan and I walk together to the end of the concourse. There we are nearly alone with a clear view of a row of private jets across the tarmac. He points to a Lear Jet. I tell him it belongs to Dole." Dornan is upset that Dole hadn't offered him a ride back. But the import of the scene is Lewis's bemusement at being all alone with Dornan, the reporter and the subject, the world paying no attention. Any reporter—any cub reporter—has had this sort of experience, covering a story, discovering that the whole world doesn't seem to care and here you are standing next to one of the players (true, in Dornan's case, a walk-on role), and how easy proximity and access combine.

2/5 On NPR Diane Rehm is doing a polling show. Ignorance, the polls have discovered, is everywhere. Two hundred twenty-six million people are in danger. I hear that Rush listeners are exceptions to the rule. Very informed and very cynical.

Later, Rush is saying Clinton wants more B-2 bombers. Where do they build them? California, Rush answers. Won't please his liberal friends like Al Hunt of the *Wall Street Journal*. To charges that Forbes is buying the election, Rush says Bill Clinton's engaged in the same thing. Labor unions against NAFTA. But are for Bill Clinton. Big Labor. They understand partial victory, Rush explains.

A friend's take on the state of things: The progressive narrative has wound up in the dustbin. The Constitution is a hassle and impertinence to the right wing. Colin Powell is a perfect candidate, since he merges the two parties. My friend toils in advertising in Indianapolis. We talk about our governor. In Indiana there are term limits for the governor and Evan Bayh can't run again. Bayh is a dandy New Democrat. There's a poll in today's *Indianapolis Star/News*. A large percentage of Hoosiers think Bayh's a Republican. Fourteen hundred Hoosiers were polled. Bayh came in second running as a Republican.

I have a couple of other friends who work in advertising and all of them are creating Web sites and attempting to make them profitable. All of advertising is rushing to the World Wide Web: it's a scene from the nineteenth century, a frontier landgrab.

Radio was eclipsed as an acclaimed cultural organ for a couple of decades (sixties and seventies), while television became the personification of all that was wrong with America, but the car culture never abandoned radio, and slowly but surely, it matured. And commutes lengthened. Radio, as the French would say, foregrounds the individual. It is not pictorial, kaleidoscopic, full of sensory information; it's intimate, it's talking in the dark. Television is a lot of things, but it is not a phone call for the mind. And it is not strange that the rise of radio was brought about not by more music (and very little "drama") but by talk. The radio is the public phone, not quite a party line, and once it became "interactive," meaning the audience started calling as well as answering, it took off. The equation was finally closed. Someone talks to me and now I can respond. Top 40 stations had a version of this for a long time. People would call in with requests or dedications. "Play 'Misty' for me."

Radio is more linear, more like "reading"—when one reads, one mind usurps the privacy of another; with radio, one voice usurps, not privacy, but the public consciousness of another mind, often in a private setting, one's car, one's room.

The common wisdom one heard about radio and why, in the old days, it was seen as a spur to the imagination is that the listener has to "imagine" what he or she hears, the idea being that it is exercise for the imagination, regular creative aerobics. Similar to the folktales about how the blind compensate: that hearing becomes more complicated and complex. Well, yes and no.

If you have to "make up" things about the person you hear but do not see, you doubtless are involved in some sort of fantasy. The voice, the voice, ah, the voice in the dark. It is curious to see people in radio journalism emerge on (not graduate to) television. Cokie Roberts is a good example, as are a number of women journalists who began in radio, principally on NPR, and are now on the television screen. Radio is like the baseball of public journalism: you can look strange and still have a career. You can appear nonathletic, like a lot of professional ballplayers do. The unnatural selection of careers in the public eye sorts looks in the usual unfair way. Typical television contracts have clauses about any change in appearance, especially the face, that can be cause for dismissal.

But prominence can overwhelm unnatural selection, and once Cokie Roberts and others (Nina Totenberg, Elizabeth Arnold) became well known, that, along with the fact of their intelligence (which might be the pretty-face liability—see the career of Jessica Savitch), vaulted them through the mask of television aesthetics. Cokie does look strange on TV. Words like "striking" come to mind. Oddly, in this context age helps: maturity softens the standard criteria.

Take Rush on radio and Rush on TV. In the old days Rush might do the weather. Anyway, I do not know what Diane Rehm looks like and her voice is my only brush. Older, well-bred, prim, not the principal of the all-girls school, but the most high-strung teacher. When I hear Diane Rehm, I think conflict resolution.

And I think of Bailey White. Bailey White's little stories on NPR were interesting to me because I was imagining some little old lady, on the verge of senility, still having these quirky notions. NPR's *ATC* over the years has, like everything else, become filled with more conservative commentators, and general folksy types (large animal veterinarians, etc.) are sops to the congressional purse holders. Bailey White fell in my estimation when I learned she was a relatively young woman, nothing like her voice portended.

So, listening to Diane Rehm today, I only have her to imagine, though if I searched it out I might be able to fill in biography and even pictures; but for most people who listen to the radio, she is a voice, not quite grandmotherly, but soothing, one that infiltrates into the mind in ways that television complicates with images, the promise of glamour.

C-SPAN is showing an Iowa evening news show. Those local Iowa TV folks are positively giddy. It's Christmas in February. Everyone in TV Land is happy with the revenue and the attention. Keep those attack ads running. Money, money, money.

2/6 *Nightline.* The Louisiana caucus results are in. Two to one for Buchanan. He gets sixteen delegates. Gramm eight, Keyes a couple. It's bad for Gramm: the religious Right seems to being going for Buchanan. Dole is flying on a corporate plane, saying: "If Bill Clinton thinks he can talk Right and govern Left he's wrong."

A colleague at Notre Dame earlier in the day was talking wistfully about wanting his children to be imbued with his religion, which was, no surprise, Catholicism. I never thought the Catholic Church's traditions would be that precarious, that close to extinction, at least in the minds of the faithful. That was what he implied. The religious Right does act under a sense of imperilment.

Diane Rehm had done this morning a show on "character," the lack of it in young people, the fact it needs to be taught. The conventional wisdom is now starting to crack down on "permissive" child rearing. The tenor of the program shows the general cultural shift to more "conservative" values. "A consensus on this problem" is claimed. Doubtless, it is part of my colleague's sense of fear and defensiveness.

2/7 Rush is claiming that Dole operatives helped Buchanan in Louisiana. Dole would rather face Buchanan than Forbes is Rush's analysis.

2/8 The *Washington Post* reports that Clinton has two insurance policies, which cover law suits of various sorts. Nine hundred thousand dollars in bimbo-eruption insurance has been paid. No more crocodile tears about bankruptcy flow today from the Clintons.

Fiction, these days, seems to be read in motion: planes, trains, buses, subways. Fiction is read while the body is hurtling through space. That is one role it still has in the culture, to transport the mind as the body is literally transported.

The most popular airplane book between Washington and Chicago, a frequent flier tells me, is *Primary Colors*. John Grisham, move over (Grisham is the reigning read-in-motion best-seller).

Before *Primary Colors,* the only novel I thought might have played a visible role in our recent culture was the right-wing cult book, Timothy McVeigh's most influential reading, *The Turner Diaries.* But here was a new novel being talked about everywhere, not just on the few shows that grant authors of fiction some airtime. Ours is an aural-oral-visual culture and the most literate fiction does not translate well into the medium. The great majority of nonfiction is written in a largely oral voice. The history of the teaching of English in the United States can be seen as an attempt to change a predominantly oral culture into a predominantly written culture: speech was oral, memorization was oral, rhymed poetry is oral, radio was low culture, books were high culture. The academy promoted the power of the written over the spoken.

But that all began to change. Television, of course. By the fifties, television began to enter most Americans' lives, by the sixties all their lives, and by the seventies color was dominant and the evolution of the medium was exponential.

The late sixties saw Marshall McLuhan become famous. Hot and cool mediums. The medium is the message. The oral culture was social, and literate culture was antisocial. Oral culture: Hitler's rallies. Literate culture: an individual alone in a room. While I grew up in the 1950s most parents were worried when their sons and daughters spent too much (almost any) time alone in their rooms reading. The anxious, cliché question/command was, "Why don't you go out and play with some friends?" Parents (mothers in the fifties) didn't want their children to be antisocial.

Now, to get a child to read alone in a room would be seen by some as a triumph. Our chiefly aural-oral-visual culture, what we hear, say, and see, is in control. Note newspapers. *USA Today* is a product of adaptation. It is above all visual rather than literate: news that can be looked at more than read.

I *read* it most every day, along with the *New York Times,* and one sour thought is how they are meeting in the middle. *USA Today* used to be joked about in the trade (MacPaper), but it is now the model. The *Times* has adapted: it is now full of graphs, charts, lists of best-selling ("Most Wanted") whatevers (CDs, videos, etc.). And *USA Today,* occasionally, will attempt some actual reporting, investigations even! In 1984, when I was a writing "coach" at the *Columbus Dispatch,* two things were happening. Columbus, Ohio, was becoming a one-newspaper town, completing that trend with the demise of the "Democratic" paper, the *Citi-*

zen-Journal, and the *Dispatch* itself was being changed to resemble *USA Today,* which was the new competition on the block. No story in the *Dispatch* was to jump from the first page. Short stories, in nonfiction, at least, are considered fillers and, most pointedly, captions. The look of old newspapers, early twentieth-century copies of, say, the *New York Times,* were dense with print (the old literate culture taking over), though you would encounter serial headlines, and subheads, before you got to the body of the stories. Now the stories are as long as the column of headlines used to be. Which came first, Web site design or the look of the new-sweeklies' catchy digest pages?

I would date the end of the literate culture to the general introduction of color television in the late sixties and early seventies. Black and white had its own alienating affect: it remained the *other* in many important ways.

The nail in the coffin of the literate culture was the spread of VCRs. One critical aspect of the literate culture is that you control time in the literate culture. You can put this book down and pick it up later. Oral culture allows someone else to control the time. Television had to be watched at the moment or it was gone. But the VCR took away that obstacle of time control and gave it back to the consumer. It also, of course, let people choose to watch whatever they wanted to watch, and what they wanted to watch wasn't always on what used to be called, back in the dim seventies, "free" TV.

The resurgence of radio, of talk radio, is the oral culture reasserting itself. (You can't drive a car and read—or watch TV—though some try. You can, evidently, talk on a phone.) Those expanding commuting hours by car played havoc with the old oral-literate components. Though the literate culture was essentially private and the oral culture public (except in the world of confidences and confession—you see the drift), riding in one's car listening to the radio became a perversion of the norm. The oral was becoming intensely private. It is the condition of listening. No longer the family gathered around the Magnavox, but the alienated commuter stuck in traffic (listening—or on a cell phone).

TV played havoc with the oral-literate conventions, too. Movies were in some ways literate: dream factories. As Cocteau wrote, everyone in the darkened theater has the same dream. The stage, the film, places where you sit in the dark, suspended midway between the private and the public, evoked community suspended.

But television again changes the equation. It is watched in the light (quite often), but it requires the act of separation from the group, even as a group watches it: it is not so much suspension of disbelief as suspension of life at the moment. It moves you from the here and places you in the now, the now of what is "on." Alpha waves, perhaps, but it is the transport out of the community, into the realm of the private. It is the aural-oral-visual at its most potent. The worst of both worlds.

It is quite often the background of lives. It is just *on,* and what issues forth puts us on the magic ship, where we overhear snatches of this or that and they become our stream of consciousness.

It is not odd that the most intimate '92 Clinton campaign book would be a novel. In a world of images and perceptions, where we navigate between fiction and "reality," only a novel travels confidently in those gray zones. Of course, there was Matalin and Carville; their book, *All's Fair,* came out in 1994 and was somewhat sui generis. It wasn't an outsider/insider consciousness, and, however frank in spots, it was cloaked in the self-censoring of professional partisanship: creatures of the event becoming its most successful chroniclers.

No "writer" had climbed aboard the Clinton campaign bandwagon early enough to do an insider/outsider book. The reasons for that are provocative. Why? For the Mario Cuomo reasons, not thinking early enough that Clinton would win—and there is less interest in a campaign book done from the loser's side. Matalin, ironically, has more to tell (insofar as her campaign was far less public), but Carville's *win* was the story.

The '92 campaign did get a film, a "documentary," *The War Room.* That fit the generation, indeed. Print old journalism, film new journalism, video newer still.

Nonetheless, *Primary Colors* served as the insider's/outsider's campaign account. It paraded all the oft-repeated Clinton-world rumors as fictional fact (the candidate's girlfriends, illegitimate children, etc.) and enhanced hardly repeated rumors, making the candidate's wife bisexual, and moving a Vince Foster–like suicide up in time and altering the sex of the individual from male to female.

Sexing an "anonymous" text is always a tricky business, but whoever wrote it has a fey take on women. See, for instance, the description of the FOH Susan Thomases character, Lucille Kaufman, on page 62: "Richard would have despised her even if she weren't dowdy and awful, even if she didn't always wear power suits and running shoes and Gloria Steinem aviators, even if she wasn't always rousting around in her purse for her compact, fussing with her hair, pulling out lipstick and applying it in the most ridiculous manner, squeezing her puckered lips around it, rolling it once, twice, then saying—always—'There!' "

Ridiculous to whom? Someone else who applies lipstick. It could be strange, funny, distasteful, but ridiculous only if you do it, too.

Not just cosmetics, clothes (page 280): "She wore a high-necked, embroidered—red and black on white cotton—Russian-style narodniki blouse; a floor-length black Indian skirt with elaborate creweled flowers in horizontal bands, and a multicolored Andean (or perhaps African) bandanna, which covered her head." It isn't just the entire description, which rolls off our male protagonist's tongue too easily; it is the single term "creweled." Some male writers might have that word so readily at their fingertips, but they (the one or two that do) would probably let you know why it is such an everyday bit of knowledge to them.

And the sex (246): "Everything about sex is banal except the anticipation. The act itself, though undeniably satisfying, is memorable no more than a handful of times in the course of a life—and imperfect more often than not. I can remember every twitch, glance, touch, hint—the way my hair felt—the afternoon Daisy and I first made love in Mammoth Falls." This is more theoretical than experiential, more fussy than forthright.

Most informed opinion says the author is the journalist Joe Klein, but *Primary Colors* doesn't feel like a first novel. (But perhaps Klein has written an unpublished apprentice novel or two.) Mandy Grunwald's sister is a novelist, it might be her, though it is denied. (What would someone do? Say, OK, you guessed right. Anonymous, one presumes, would deny it if asked.) Maybe Nora Ephron, but it would be a little funnier—and have more food in it. (Though the line after the clothes description is Ephronesque: "I thought for a moment that she might be a recent chemotherapy patient. . . .")

Regardless, the author's confidence is impressive, especially making the narrator "black." That is even trickier than making the narrator male if the writer is female. That takes nerve if you are white, or a high comfort factor. And again, I think, no doubt sexistly, that a woman would have less cultural static about doing this sort of persona. If the author is white, this is a more risky cultural business than recycling Clinton scandals.

But what I think is really indisputable is that whoever is the author, s/he was already upper middle class, so the change in bank account wouldn't appear dramatic to those around her or him.

Beyond the question of the author, there is a question of the book—and it owes a lot to Matalin and Carville. Their coauthor, Peter Knobler, would be in a good position to know. Does his wife? Does he have a wife? Does she write fiction?

2/10 Al D'Amato has broken up with Claudia Cohen, says a friend, an ex–New Yorker. (Al had been shopping around a while back for an annulment of his marriage.) Cohen was hurt by her ex-husband, who was dating all these young WASPs, I'm told. "And Claudia looked around to see who was available and who would really be offensive to him. Someone who would really bother her ex. And Al D'Amato was there. Then she finally woke up. And now D'Amato is taking it out on Hillary. She's a surrogate for Claudia—that bitch."

When my son was born one of his first expressions was a horseshoe frown. He looked very peeved, mad, I guess about being expelled from the womb. It's an expression that Clinton uses often; still, at almost fifty, he has the ability to do it. I can't. The face has, supposedly, millions of nerves—or something—for facial expression (this is the sort of odd fact one learns reading childbirth books), and Clinton must have retained them all.

On NBC's evening news I see Phil Gramm. It's almost over for Gramm. His campaign is going nowhere, losing Louisiana wasn't in the cards, his ready-cash friend isn't so ready anymore. Prospects in Iowa are bleak. And I notice how he's starting to look positively Asian. I recall how couples are supposed to begin to resemble each other. Gramm now looks like his wife, Wendy Lee. Before, his smile was one of fated resignation. He could pass for Buddha.

There are reports of the aftermath of the IRA bombing in the Docklands area of East London: two dead, over a hundred wounded. No more cease-fire. Clinton's earlier happy trip to Ulster is shown.

2/11   It still appears likely Dole will "win" the nomination. He should win tomorrow's Iowa caucuses. And there's New Hampshire ahead.

Buchanan is the dark shadow of these elections, not Forbes, glowing as he is like the gold standard. Buchanan won the Louisiana "caucuses," taking them away from Gramm, who had presumably bought it, leaving Buchanan with more delegates than anyone else in the race has—thirteen.

There was a "town hall" broadcast on Friday the ninth—and the specter of TV town halls is peculiar in itself. The microphone-toting emcee and the prescreened questions are hardly "town" at all. "Town" is just a homey marketing name to take the chill off the global village. TV Town. The candidates were all supposed to be there, but it turned out to be a display of the one-percenters. The top four had withdrawn: Dole, Forbes, Buchanan, Gramm. So in Iowa the town was the B-list: Lugar, Keyes, Morry Taylor, B-1 Bob Dornan.

They all had the calmness of those who knew they weren't going to get the job. Only Lugar seemed, at times, ill at ease: only because he was a major leaguer suddenly sent down to the minors. Senators are used to more lofty company, and for him to be no closer to election than Morry Taylor, or Keyes, was something of an affront. But he masked it under his Hoosier good cheer, smiling through the pain.

Was there a vice president sitting up there? Lugar, maybe, or Keyes? No. Why do individuals get into losing campaigns? For the matching funds, for the ability to form nonprofit organizations and have money donated to you. Keyes took over eight thousand dollars a month in salary during his unsuccessful 1992 run for the Senate against Barbara Mikulski in Maryland. And Buchanan's entry smacks of that, too: a job. Jimmy and Tammy Bakker, Jimmy Swaggart, Pat Robertson, and a horde of small-town others have shown that people will send you money if you ask for it. That's what religious broadcasting taught the world. It just takes the proper packaging. Newt learned the lesson. He's the spawn of the audio-and videocassette. I ponder the fact that, since his early twenties, Bill Clinton has been asking people for—and receiving—money. Ostensibly, for "nothing" in return. What does a lifetime of such requests (answered positively, as they have been) do to a person? And the amounts Clinton receives just keep getting bigger and bigger.

2/13 On *The Late Show* with David Letterman: ten ways Bob Dole celebrated his Iowa victory. Number two: Went cruising for chicks with Strom Thurmond. Number four: Before he went to bed he put his teeth in a champagne glass.

C-SPAN is showing a medley of the Pat Buchanan show. Buchanan, who came in second in Iowa, tells us from Manchester, New Hampshire, "I think a tremendous amount of small contributions will be pouring in." 1 800 Go Pat Go. "The cultural war for the soul of America" blah, blah. "The Republican Party is becoming the Buchanan Party." "Even I am coming to believe it," Pat says of his chance of becoming president. "I'm proud I stood up to protect the wages of American workers in two trade agreements." (He means NAFTA and GATT.) He jumps on Treasury Secretary Robert Rubin, a favorite target. "Citibank, Chase, and Goldman Sachs": the policies are "to protect them from suffering the ravages of the marketplace." "Attack ads are responsible for the rising numbers of undecided." "You don't need pollsters, focus groups, consultants making five hundred thousand dollars a year." He says, "Senator Gramm did a magnificent job fighting national health care," and there's no irony in Pat's voice, though it is hoarse. He's losing it. "My trade position is one I believe in." He's asked about Taiwan: "I wouldn't tell them this publicly [that it would lose its World Bank loans, won't sell a single toy in the United States]."

Dole did win the Iowa caucuses and Buchanan, the id of the party, came in second. Watching Buchanan a lot on C-SPAN, one is struck by a number of things, especially how all the reporters call out "Pat, Pat," trying to get his attention. Looking at the other hopefuls on C-SPAN, you don't get such, ah, collegiality. It's not "Bob, Bob," or "Lamar!,

Lamar!," or "Dick, Dick." They all have titles, Senator, Governor, Senator, which are used. But the title that has the most cachet at the end of the twentieth century is the most familiar: Pat, Pat your pal, one of us. Not only well known, but your friend. TV personalities over the years insinuate themselves into all our lives: it's like I've known you . . . all my life.

So it's Pat, since most of the journalists shouting out his name consider him one of them, feel they know him, or, better yet, are likely to work with him. Eisenhower's famous "military-industrial complex" speech highlighted the revolving door between industry, the military, and government figures; but there is also a "media-industry complex" that is beginning to be noticed, even though it has been functioning as smoothly, and for just about as long, as the other one.

One fails upward in both Hollywood and Washington because, like gaining admittance to an Ivy League school, gaining admittance is the highest hurdle. Once you're in, it's hard to flunk out. The turnstile is spinning: look anywhere. Diane Sawyer advancing her career by following Nixon into his period of exile in San Clemente. Rick Hertzberg goes from *The New Yorker* to speechwriter for Carter, working under old buddy James Fallows (and they really did a good job for Carter, helping the peanut farmer to be swiftly unelected). Fallows, in a new book, *Breaking the News*, goes on to criticize the system he has manipulated so well. When I covered the Harrisburg trial Carl Stern was the prosecution's friendliest network reporter and where is he now? State Department spokesperson. Pete Williams, the Bush administration's Pentagon press spokesman, now works for NBC.

This is more than cozy, so Buchanan's covert campaign as a flack journalist/flack candidate—see Safire's career in this regard—is just a bit more focused in its ambition.

2/14 Poor Lamar!. Wandering in the snow on Valentine's Day (no valentine from CNN) in Milford, New Hampshire, fresh from his third place in Iowa and Phil Gramm's departure from the race, he's asked some real-world questions, like what a gallon of milk and a dozen eggs cost. It's a spectacle. Lamar!'s wearing his red-and-black lumberjack shirt and tight O. J. gloves, and, according to CNN (which is rehashing the scene), he ignores the question, then tells an aide to "get the answers right away." The Dole camp couldn't be more pleased (though there is no proof that Bob Dole knows this IQ test answer for being one of the people): "Next time he's [Lamar!] walking across New Hampshire he might want to stop at a supermarket."

CNN replays George Bush in Orlando, Florida, on February 4, 1992, being amazed at the wonderfulness of a price scanner. (Bush actually seems more amazed holding a carton of milk, running it over the glass right side up, thinking the milk's bar code might be on the bottom.) Al Gore is quoted as saying Bush appeared as incredulous as "an ape discovering fire." That incident helped Clinton, who might well have known the price of a gallon of milk (certainly of a Big Mac), having perhaps picked up one on the way over to Gennifer's pad. Arkansas is *of the people*.

But Lamar! and Bush and Forbes (asked if he had ever been personally challenged, since he had inherited his wealth and position, Forbes replied that he was challenged when he had to go off to prep school alone) can't resist reminding the American voters that they live in another world altogether. Clinton, of course, lived in another world altogether in Arkansas, too. Despite the paltry salary the governor received there of thirty-five thousand dollars (presuming, doubtless, that graft would raise it), around eight hundred thousand a year was spent on support services for the first family of Arkansas. Room and board good, pay bad. No wonder the Clintons didn't own a house. Maybe they should have kept the one Hillary had on the godforsaken Whitewater (slow as molasses) bug-infested river.

Dole (on NPR's *All Things Considered*) is saying, "If there's a crisis on the first day of the presidency, who do you want?", meaning, you want a man of experience in the job. It sounds like a reason to vote for Bill Clinton, since he is already in the office, well beyond his first day.

2/15 In the *Chicago Tribune* (section 1, page 11), I read, "If they get up to 60 percent, his people tell me, Bill can start dating again," a joke made (or repeated) by Senator Ernest Hollings (D, S.C.) about Clinton's rising approval ratings. This does conjure up the idea of how loose a second term will be for Clinton—nothing more to run for. 1 800 Go Babes Go.

C-SPAN bucolics: we wander around in the snow with Richard Lugar in New Hampshire. Thankfully, after a lot of heavy breathing, he's in a café for an early-morning breakfast, spreading the syrup of his good cheer on all the hapless diners. Real politicians have a switch in them: they can go from zero to sixty instantly in the charm-projection race. Not that Lugar has an overabundance of charm. Lugar, after making everyone in the café miserable with his good cheer, finally sits down to eat. One of his companions is a guy from Indianapolis who just got in his car the day before and drove to New Hampshire to help the senator. Lugar is meeting him for the first time at breakfast, and they are on their way to becoming fast old friends. The fellow runs a car repair shop in Indianapolis. Lugar presses him for more details, which the fellow is reluctant to divulge. But the senator gets it out of him. What kind of cars? Foreign cars, his new volunteer says, which ends that discussion. I realize I could be having breakfast in New Hampshire with the senator if I had made the drive, he's so far out on the margins of probability. *The New Republic*'s Michael Lewis certainly could be, too, but Lugar is not as entertaining as Morry Taylor.

2/16   On Diane Rehm's program Lamar!'s wealth is taken to task by the *Washington Times*'s Major Garret. He says a $1 investment in the Gannett newspaper in Knoxville turned into $650,000 and Lamar! says, I could have gotten a lot more if I had left it in longer. Steve Roberts (*U.S. News & World Report*), husband of Cokie, says Americans are ambivalent about wealth. They all want to be rich, he says. (I guess Steve wants to be rich, or stay rich.) It's a sign of divine grace, Steve says, chuckling, protesting a bit too much.

Moving off easy wealth, white supremacy, it appears, is being unrobed once again in the Buchanan camp. His campaign's cochair, a Mr. Larry Pratt, of the Gun Owners of America, is mentioned as a liability by Jodie Allen of the *Washington Post,* since Pratt had a habit of showing up at meetings of ultra "conservative" white supremacist and militia groups. She says the GOA makes the NRA look like moderates. Pratt says he's not anti-Semitic in the least and is a member of something called Jews for the Preservation of Firearms Ownership.

The upcoming June election in Russia is raised as "very important." Boris Yeltsin is the great white hope, but he's down in the polls.

A caller asks the reporters why—"Where's the objectivity in all this?"—they are calling Buchanan "Pat." Roberts gives a lame answer that he has known Buchanan since he (Buchanan) worked for Nixon, so he calls him Pat. The discussion moves on.

Rush is on the subject of moral decline. Suggest you look no further than the current occupant of the White House, he says. Pull up to the 7-Eleven in the El Camino with AstroTurf in the back. Condoms, etc. If that's what you think it takes we're in trouble, Rush says about campaign strategy. He's doing damage control as the Republicans seem all at each other's throats. "I got into the price of milk and eggs and I didn't intend to." He goes to Hillary resisting the independent prosecutor. He puts on his Cher "they'll get you babe" parody. "I may be bad, but you're a clown" (Hillary). "Presidents get pardoned, others do hard time" (Bill).

I know you've already done your Lexis/Nexis search to find criticisms, but Phil and I have been friends for years, Dole is saying on the news, apropos of Gramm's leaving the race. Dole is expecting an endorsement from him.

2/18   I see my first campaign bumper sticker: "Labor's Fix for '96: Vote."

On the eve of the New Hampshire primary, it is doubtful that Keyes, Lugar, Dornan, will become news (except for the obituary flare when any one of them drops out). Dole is in the world of antinews, insofar as bad news is the only news where Dole is concerned, the fate of the front-runner. Clinton receives a version of this. (The president is also in New Hampshire, shaking schoolchildren's hands, but unless Clinton misspells *potato,* it won't be played hard.)

Buchanan might be branded a McCarthyite, but he is more a secular Father Charles E. Coughlin, the "radio priest" of the 1930s. McCarthy had been elected to the Senate, from whence his authority flowed, while Coughlin gained his thanks to the Catholic Church and promoted it over the radio. Buchanan gains his authority from television and promotes it as a politician. (The question is, Where does Rush get his "authority" from?) In Buchanan's C-SPAN stunt of rehearsing his "advertisement" in front of the reporters in New Hampshire, Buchanan kept saying, "How's the voice?", not "How's *my* voice?" "The voice" is that third-person asset that stands apart, needs to be protected, is the tool of the trade, the key to Americans' steely hearts.

There's quite a tradition of Catholic demagoguery, and Buchanan is a direct descendant. The anti-Semitism flows from it (Father Coughlin was very direct about that), as do Buchanan's support for the odd Nazi-era naturalized American charged with being a concentration-camp guard (all those good Catholics just doing their country's bidding), his childless paternalism, his 1980s columns about women lacking the necessary ambition to succeed in the rough-and-tumble world of business.

The old verities are nostalgia-gimcracks these days, but Buchanan can get wet eyed about them. He credits his "German and Scotch" ancestry for some of his attributes, attempting to internationalize his DNA, keeping it as Aryan as possible.

So when Buchanan's Florida operative's answering machine first announces her connection to the NAAWP (National Association for the Advancement of White People), then says she hopes you're volunteering to work for Buchanan; when his aide Larry Pratt is "revealed" (the price of the press actually glancing in your direction—though it was a "special interest" group, the Center for Public Integrity, that served it up to reporters in a press release: the press will often only press what has been pressed into its palm) to be the consort of a tasty variety of white supremacist groups; and most wonderfully, when Buchanan in Pratt's defense says Pratt is a member of Jews for Guns (!) and the founder of Guns for America (!)—one hears the thwapping of those black helicopters piloted by one-world traitors (they must be traitors, for how else could God-fearing he-men helicopter pilots be recruited to fly them?) around the head of Buchanan, the bats in all their belfries. White supremacist groups on the Internet have links back to Buchanan's home page: a new category, links by association.

Anticommunism is mutating, but its center is still holding. Paranoia focused is not necessarily a bad thing, at least in comparison to paranoia diffused. Buchanan is the beacon of diffusion. Illegal aliens. Build a fence. The Berlin Wall is down, the Buchanan wall is on order. (Lamar!, not to be outflanked, has called for a new branch of the armed forces to patrol our southern borders. Where are those crazed Canadians sneaking over that long border looking to steal those picking-in-the-fields jobs?) Jail gays. Restrict "free" trade. Protectionism.

It's the last of that list that gives Buchanan his ballast. The populist Democrat Buchanan: anti-NAFTA, GATT. Lambasting CEOs. Goldman Sachs Salomon Brothers (read: elders of Zion). Citibank, Chase, Rubin, etc.

Buchanan the populist is as hollow as Buchanan the anything else. Asked by a New Hampshirite if he would raise the minimum wage, Buchanan says no, no. "All the studies show" (I have here in my hand a list . . .) that when you raise the minimum wage, somebody in the ghetto may get ninety cents more, but hundreds of thousands lose jobs. American business, if it has to pay more, has even more incentive to flee to Mexico, where they are making fifty-eight cents an hour.

The questioner has the wit to ask, given Buchanan's drivel, Then should we lower the minimum wage to create more jobs? The Great Blusterer is momentarily flustered and then says no, he wouldn't lower the minimum wage, just leave it where it is. You don't want to let businessmen be able to tell their employees they must take a dollar less after they've started working.

It's all quite extraordinary. Buchanan, other than his hot-air rhetoric, can't let himself succumb to such a tiny gesture to appease (or appear to be one of) the truly populist. For all practical purposes the minimum wage has been abolished (it is so low). Raising it doesn't lose jobs for the mythical teenagers working at Burger World, since those companies have paid for their exception status a long time ago.

If Buchanan doesn't win in New Hampshire, his boomlet will die down. (He has no incentive to get out, since, like Keyes, running is an income-producing endeavor for him. Morry Taylor might actually be losing some money, since his businesses may need some attention.) But Buchanan is Buchanan's business (a la Calvin Coolidge), and so is Keyes. Lugar needs to return to the Senate, Dole too; and Dornan needs to get back to Congress—he's actually running for two things, the presidency and his congressional seat in Orange Country—to put more amendments in bills to put HIV (which he disconcertingly keeps calling HI) infected military personnel on the street where they belong.

Buchanan is being roughed up by the gang of four on ABC's *This Week with David Brinkley*. The word "Nazi" is brought up a number of times in questions and what is interesting is that that can be done in conversation with a "major" candidate.

"The Dole Campaign is hollow at the core; they don't believe anything," Buchanan offers at the end of the interview after being asked if he is assuring the reelection of Clinton, as it is said he helped elect him in '92 after smearing Bush in New Hampshire.

"Would you support him if he is the candidate?"

"I've said I'd always support the Republican candidate."

"Even if he's hollow at the core. What kind of hypocrisy is that?"

"He's better than Clinton."

"Oh, oh, oh."

In discussion, Sam Donaldson points out that George Will's wife, Mari, is communications director of the Dole campaign.

Will, the Great Communicator's communicator (he was once Reagan's debate coach) and husband of Mari, Dole's communications director, says that as soon as the clutter of candidates comes down to two or three (Dole, Lamar!, and Pat are his choices), there will be "less static" and issues will come to the fore.

On the contrary, the structure of more than a half dozen voices has forced the press to discuss why one is different than the other, and however superficial this exercise has been, it has produced more discernment. When the number goes down, things will get blunter, not more supple.

Wall Street Week's Louis Rukeyser's gives one of his *le roi s'amuse* monologues making fun of the Republicans adopting Democratic economic ideas, "attacking the profit motive." Pat Buchanan seems to be running for the presidency, not of the country, but of "the AFL-CIO"; he is "a Republican delivering Democratic ideas on the economy." And Dole is "demagoguing" that the number of corporate layoffs matches the current record corporate profits; Rukeyser points to a *Wall Street Journal* graph that shows corporate layoffs are down to a low (matching 1990), "down 29 percent from the 1993 peak."

Rukeyser is the Oscar Wilde of the stock-market commentators and doesn't seem to be worried about being laid off, having had his show succeed for over two decades. He is sardonic and above it all, which accurately positions the place of capital over government.

On McLaughlin's show, Father John remarks late, in defense of Buchanan, that he might have the seat bronzed that "Patrick J. Buchanan, one of the founders of this show" sat in.

2/19   Safire in the *Times* thinks it is between Dole and Lamar!. Buchanan, his old buddy, is a sideshow. Safire knows sideshows. But he doesn't seem to know Lamar!.

On *Larry King Live* we have the sight of Lamar! and Mrs. Lamar! Her name, I think I hear, is Honey. She looks a bit older than Lamar!; she's thin, a bit gray.

"Do you want to be first lady?" Larry, the king, asks.

"No!" she says, and Lamar! looks like he has been hit by a two-by-four.

"I want to garden, to play tennis." And then she adds, "Read novels." She has my vote.

2/20   Larry King again. Mary Matalin and Bob Squier (Democratic consultant) square off, or Squier off. Squier's free advice is he would have the Republican Party lean on Lugar for his 5 percent of the vote and dry up Alexander's money and let Dole take it all.

On CNN's *Inside Politics* Dan Quayle says, "New Hampshire is a very unique state." One can always count on Dan to modify an absolute.

Then there's a *U.S. News & World Report* ad. Such a bad ad. A woman's head swelling. *I feel heavier. I must be retaining knowledge.* That should offend a lot of people.

Fat Tuesday news. Mardi Gras. More commentators on all the candidates, like the horde of lawyers on O.J.'s case, inspire "better" coverage, since they do compete with each other—and are forced to give a little more from the inside, something closer to what they think, what they usually save for each other in private: good ol' free enterprise, the market forces at work, etc.

Camille Paglia (in the March 4 *New Republic*) thinks Bill Clinton has buttoned up since he's been in the White House. She's echoing Ann Landers, great minds thinking alike. Clinton evidently, hasn't made a pass at Camille—no encounter with his roving eye, in contrast to her once catching the long-departed Massachusetts senator Ed Brooke's (Hillary's target at her Wellesley graduation speech) roving eye on the Capitol's steps back in '72. (Camille doesn't take note of the fact she's now twenty some years older.) And further proof, she offers, is that Chelsea no longer looks like a war orphan.

On Diane Rehm there's Steve Bell, a financial consultant, saying we're going to have more interventionist government, whoever is elected. "Build that bridge back home," he advises. Canada and Mexico are our two largest export markets, Bell supplies.

And speaking of capitalists, I recall how "capitalists" used to be used in the *New York Times* back early this century as a noun: "Capitalists meet," etc. Its usage dropped out of newspapers by the thirties. "Capitalists" became mainstreamed, no longer a separate group in society— they have done well in covering their tracks.

Rush: "These people have a death wish." He's talking about the Republicans. "And you wonder why I won't get involved." He sells his ties: $159. Buy four and get one free. No Boundaries ties. Subtle wordplay. There's a commercial for Nighthawk carbon-monoxide detectors. Rush has a lot of these low-rent sponsors. On TV he sells his own commemorative beer steins.

2/21   A Diane Rehm caller is not pleased. He calls her station the Government Propaganda Network. He slurs the "Rehm Brigade," etc. He's an attack radio caller.

"Pat on a Roll, Dole in a Hole." A New York *Daily News* headline, given Buchanan's New Hampshire win yesterday and Dole's loss.

I contemplate a Buchanan-Lugar ticket. It has a nice German ring to it. Bang. Bang.

Buchanan keeps the old Democratic rhetoric alive: it's cracked, but it's there. And it is not surprising Buchanan has women running his campaign, his one counter to his published antiwomen positions. He's very comfortable with women doing things for him, especially his sisters. What are Irish American sisters for, but to help their brothers?

Buchanan's Civil War language—"Don't wait for orders. . . . Mount up and ride to the sound of their guns"—is to remind folks what side he's on in the Civil War. His Web site looks like a stop for the Civil War reenactment crowd.

Dole was reading from a script last night in New Hampshire, giving his concession speech; this is a bad sign, is the talk world consensus. Rush often chastises a caller after he's gone. Pretends otherwise. Radio doesn't cause alpha waves.

C-SPAN has William Bennett on Buchanan, playing catch-up: "Once you get over anger, the peasants with pitchforks, ride at the sound of the guns, what do you do? It doesn't get people off welfare. Buchanan is not the true conservative."

2/22 *Morning Edition* on NPR has Dole saying wages are down 5 percent, but corporate profits are up. This is Buchanan's work—he has the Republicans skating on the thin ice of worker discontent. The more of this there is, the sweeter it becomes for Clinton and the Democrats. The theme of economic insecurity is all over the news. The *New York Times,* on the front page of its business section, does a story on the astronomical sums CEOs are getting. Such contrasting stories are the loudest clashing cymbals.

Buchanan was in South Dakota yesterday standing in the restaurant area below Mount Rushmore, the prime picture-taking spot, basking in his New Hampshire win: "Yesterday, I won the first election of my whole life."

2/23 I switch on the Christian Broadcasting Network news and find them lamenting that California's Proposition 187, which, among other things, denies medical care to immigrants, has been "gutted" by the courts.

It's clear that Forbes thinks it's worth 20 million to 30 million inherited dollars to get out from under his father's shadow.

Buchanan's matching funds were more than anyone's in the third and fourth quarters, except for Dole. Buchanan at a Wednesday news conference exulted: $500,000 in small donations landed in our headquarters in McLean.

Speaking of small donations, the *Times* does an article headlined "Donations Drop at Year's End for Clintons' Legal Defense." In the small-world department, William Bennett's brother Bob is defending the prez, and his firm (Skadden, Arps, Slate, Meagher and Flom) has been paid, according to the *Times*, $891,880. Why isn't Bennett a partner? I wonder. Or, why isn't his name part of the firm's name? What do those guys get paid? Nearly $900,000 for Paula Jones–associated work? Jones claims she was summoned to a hotel room in Little Rock by Bill Clinton, and she went, thinking the governor was going to offer her "a job." Evidently, he did, but not the kind of job she had in mind. The hovering Paula Jones case has become the O. J. civil trial of this campaign. Why not just give her all the money Bennett is getting? Obviously, Skadden, Arps lawyers on call have better pay scales than call girls. Or, in Paula's case, young women who come when they are called. What does Bennett bill per hour? This is the scandal. Clinton's legal defense fund has only collected barely a hundred grand. Whitewater-related expenses are now over a million. So the Clintons, it appears, are still faced with "insolvency."

If someone wants to look for an Arkansas scandal involving sweet deals for the Clintons, one should look to whoever it was who wrote those two liability policies for Bill. Who did that risk assessment? Who in Arkansas was more likely to be sued than Bill Clinton? Let's see a picture of that insurance agent.

2/25 Today on NBC's *Face the Nation* Safire concludes the last week has been "a shot in the arm for the Forbes campaign, another body blow for Dole." Safire can't keep from calling Buchanan "Pat."

Listening to Buchanan on the same show trying to defend his not supporting a minimum-wage increase is taking a walk down memory lane with Pat. He recalls how young men would rush out and clean your window at the gas station, how kids would sweep out factories, and all because they were paid twenty-five cents an hour in their "first jobs," learning the job skills that would help them throughout their lives. What is most disturbing about his bath of nostalgia is that Buchanan does want to re-create his youthful world. And why not? That world let him become successful. It's hard to abstract your experience and translate it for generations yet to come. Buchanan won't even try.

2/26   Two Cessnas from Florida were shot out of the sky by the Cuban air force over international waters. On *Larry King Live* Wolf Blitzer, CNN's transnational "foreign correspondent," formerly of the *Jerusalem Post*, reports Forbes's remarks on the downed planes, "It's unfortunate that Clinton for the last months has been making goo-goo eyes at Castro." The pot of goo-goo calling the kettle goo-goo.

On C-SPAN I watch Louis Farrakhan celebrating his return from Libya: "Muslims were a convenient vehicle" in the death of Malcolm X, he says. Now there's a way to make a silk purse out of a sow's ear. Since Muslims killed Malcolm X. A sore spot for Farrakhan. "America is more segregated thirty years after the man [MLK] died and Farrakhan didn't do it." Didn't kill King and didn't segregate America. So much for charges of isolationism. Farrakhan is thoroughly American and thoroughly successful at this time in our history since he has mastered, as have so many, the ability to say confidently whatever nonsense he wishes to say. He's the best spinner I've seen this election year. "When the Doctor [King] became international, when he tied the war in Vietnam with the war on poverty [they—the forces of evil—said] "he had no business meddling in international affairs." Farrakhan does sarcasm better than most, since he appears to enjoy it, administering it not as a slap, but as a caress.

His FOI guards wear uniforms (their hats especially) which make them look like some futuristic train porters. Farrakhan has concluded his eighteen-nation tour of Africa and the Mideast. "You say"—he says this often, rhetorically, since he is speaking to whites, the TV camera, the press. The crowd, too, but it likes it when he taunts the absent audience. He recommends a book, *The Trial of the Octopus*, which sounds like a must read for the militia crowd and he refers often to himself in the third person: "Farrakhan will overthrow the government of your mind." And then he continues his anti-Israel line (I think he does this since he knows he will get some white assent here): "I call the roll of how many senators are honorary members of the Israeli Knesset." He's appalled at the $4.5

billion sent to Israel each year, and denounces the pittance his folks get at home. If you deny us the aid of our black brother "we're going to rise up against you." Mu'ammar al-Gadhafi wants to lay millions on Farrakhan. That gets the biggest response of the evening.

Watching him, I think of coming off the Skyway in Chicago, onto Stony Island Avenue, and going past Farrakhan's mosque, watching services conclude or start, the people dressed, the children in tow, a picture of order and discipline. How people want it, and what a price they will pay for it. Community. I suppose it is no more homogenous than the crowd I was part of with my family in front of St. Francis Xavier's Church in Kansas City in my youth.

Farrakhan has created his own version of the fifties.

Hillary appears on C-SPAN's *Booknotes* show with Brian Lamb, talking about the 1950s, too, her days as a "Goldwater girl." Lamb asks about the controversy (limited) over not naming the person who worked with her on her book, *It Takes a Village.* Maureen Dowd's January 14 *New York Times* op-ed column on the subject began the "controversy." Hillary has an explanation. After listing sixty names of people who "helped" in her acknowledgments, she decided she would miss someone, so she wouldn't name any. "I thanked her," Hillary says, meaning, presumably, in person. But the ghost writer's name (Barbara Feinman) does not pass the lips of the first lady (as it did not when she was on Diane Rehm January 15). Hillary's composed throughout the interview— smooth hair, smooth answers.

2/27 NPR's *Morning Edition* does a Buchanan fallout story on declining wages. *The Nation* runs a Robert Sherrill article (March 11) that lists Alan Greenspan's sins, and also manages to ape Buchanan regarding Robert Rubin, Clinton's second treasury secretary, after Lloyd Bentsen. Sherrill writes that Rubin is "best known for leading Clinton down the primrose path in Mexico to protect the investments of Wall Street pals; and Greenspan."

On Rush there's talk of Farrakhan and his Gadhafi-sponsored Libya trip. A woman caller uses the phrase "people of that persuasion." Black people—not, from my sampling of his callers, a big part of Rush's audience. Rush says "people who should have been outraged weren't" regarding the Million Man March. "He's become an important leader," Rush concludes.

A "former ditto" caller is on the line, not happy with Rush's nonembrace of Buchanan. Rush counters, "I'm as Reaganesque a conservative as I've ever been." Rush is a bit defensive. School uniforms . . . will stop crime? he mocks. To the charge that he is "too liberal" he says: My mind is open. "It's a capitulation—you are allowing the aggressors [the Cubans] to make the rules," he says about the Cubans shooting down two Cessnas, piloted by anti-Castro Cubans living in Florida, ostensibly looking for at-sea refugees and getting ready to leaflet Havana. What we ought to have said to them is "Try this one more time and you won't have an air force." "Oh, for the good ol' days," Rush says, and I wonder what days those were: the mob days in Havana? Fidel injects himself in a campaign year, Rush says—in his look-at-it-from-every-angle thinking—in order to let Bill shoot down a plane and appear tough. "It's weird thinking, I know," Rush confides to his audience.

Yesterday there was a Buchanan shotgun story. Buchanan's symbols are now shotguns and pitchforks—Buchanan, the mob of one. According to the *Los Angeles Times,* Buchanan, after waving it around, pointed the shotgun at a reporter and then his wife pointed it, too. The gun, evidently, was made in Japan.

I'm watching an Arby's commercial: a Clinton look-alike jogging with Secret Service lumbers past McDonald's. "He's not stopping." Jogs into Arby's. Shot of a big order of French fries. It's funny, but also reminds me that this is a view we don't see of Clinton these days, ever since Oklahoma City—no more boy president in baggy shorts.

In all the Clarence Thomas brouhaha, one thing that was never referred to was his leaving the attorney general's office in Missouri and going to work immediately for Monsanto, one of the largest firms in the state, and one the attorney general's office would be, should have been, scrutinizing daily. But that revolving door (regulator to the regulated) didn't bother anyone about Clarence, since it was so much business as usual.

Cokie Roberts on *Nightline* is talking about the Arizona primary, Forbes's victory, his many, many anti-Dole TV ads, and says "as long as Forbes is willing to spend his family's money" he'll be around. And she knows about family money. Hal Bruno had just referred to Forbes, using the words "his money."

2/28 Rush is setting us straight: "Every candidate is committing something to this screwup." "We've got our own house to clean up here," he says. He talks about the Buchanan supporter profile. "Sinister forces are manipulating" events to influence America, Rush maintains. More weird thinking from the Rushster. Rush is happy, though, that the networks are down from 32 million viewers to 25 million in two years.

Monitor News reports $30 million has been spent on Whitewater investigations. Independent prosecutor Kenneth Starr is spending $1 million a month.

2/29 On Diane Rehm a caller heard she would be put in harems for Muslim men. Why would the radio lie? she says to Diane's skepticism.

I go to lunch with Ray Suarez, host of NPR's *Talk of the Nation,* at the LaSalle Grill in downtown South Bend. I and about a hundred other folks, that is, at a benefit for members of the local public radio station, WVPE. I was provided a ticket. The LaSalle Grill is what passes for with-it here in South Bend. Pretty food on big white plates. A roomful of NPR supporters is an unsettling sight. Here are tidbits from Ray, who has the more traditional looks of someone who belongs on radio. When he first proposed his show the response at NPR was, If you let them just talk they might say anything. It turns out that only one out of seven callers are female. They call later in the show after they make up their minds on the subject under discussion. Men just call. In the eighties, improved FM took over rock and AM went to talk. He's funny about his employers. Speaking of the musical interludes that end each story on NPR's news shows, he says that the hairshirts at NPR spend all their time getting just the right music.

No lunch with Rush, though. He's on the subject of Powell, Kemp, Bennett. Rush went to "an exploratory meeting two years ago" for Bill Bennett (a Rush wedding guest). "I don't want to stick my hand out and ask for money," he quotes Bennett as saying. "I don't want to be away from my family." Rush says, "We've got to make the best of what we got." A caller talks about Jack Kemp, Bennett, William Kristol on *The Charlie Rose Show*. He's pissed off at their elitist attitudes. There will be a third party. . . . I can't believe they did that. . . . We have a wealth of good candidates, he says.

Rush on Powell says, "It was when he got out of the race we found out he was a Republican." "Why should Powell be president? . . . It's just image." Rush reacts to the charge that Warren Buffet "made five billion and you [Rush] want him not to pay taxes!" Rush says Buffet only pays himself one hundred thousand a year. They're paper profits, Rush says. Buffet doesn't have it. He doesn't pay taxes now. He may lose it all. "Liberals don't have the slightest idea about this," Rush says, meaning, I suppose, his understanding of entrepreneurial risk-taking and the fact that Warren Buffet may "lose it all."

The *NewsHour* shows us some of yesterday's Republican primary debate in Columbia, South Carolina. Negative ads are the topic. Forbes is asked if they are "hurting the political process." Steve regrets "having spent so much time discussing my opponents." Maybe he meant dissing, or dishing, his opponents. But now, "I've concentrated on getting my message of growth, hope, and opportunity across to the American people, particularly in Delaware and in Arizona."

Dole isn't so sanguine. "Well, I think Steve has been very effective with these negative ads. I saw my favorable ratings go from 80 percent in Iowa down to 50, and he spent about twelve million dollars, I think, just on Bob Dole." It's hard for Bob to say "me." "He's the king of negative advertising. He gets the title without any contest," Dole says about Forbes.

The debate becomes a seminar in advertising. Ads are shown and responses from the candidates are solicited. Dole's anti-Buchanan ad runs. A voice intones: "President Buchanan? He says, Women are simply not endowed by nature with the measure of single-minded ambition and the will to succeed. And he advocates arming South Korea, Japan, and Taiwan with nuclear weapons. He's too extreme, and he can't beat Bill Clinton."

Pat's upset. "Bob, it is a sign of the vapidity and the hollowness of your campaign that in your seventy-two years as majority leader that you're running these kinds of ads—"

"Eleventh year," Dole inserts.

"Thirty-fifth year in Congress, that—"

"You've been in Washington thirty-five years, so . . ."

This is all very amusing. A Lamar! anti-Dole ad is shown: "Bob Dole voted to raise taxes by $320 billion. Alexander supports term limits. Dole opposes term limits. Alexander has fresh, conservative ideas. After 35 years in Washington, Bob Dole is out of ideas."

But Dole might know the price of a gallon of milk. But he might not, too.

A Forbes anti-Lamar! ad is shown. "Running for President, Lamar Alexander collects 295,000 a year from his law firm that lobbies for special interests in Washington."

Steve stands by his ad, and adds, "That was a charitable ad. That ad did not talk about some of those cozy business deals you did as governor, investing one dollar, getting—"

"There you go again, Steve," Lamar! says, attempting to sound Reaganesque. He misses his checked shirt.

Forbes's momentum won't be stopped: "—getting six hundred and twenty thousand dollars in return."

They bicker on. Dole and Buchanan look pleased. Buchanan says, after Dole says, "Time out," "It's my turn, I think. Bob, can you get 'em to yield to me, Bob?"

"I like what they're doing, but," Dole says.

"I'm enjoying this!" Buchanan exults.

Food fight. Food fight. For a moment Buchanan does look like John Belushi.

SIX

The Longest March

★

3/1 Rush is not a happy guy today. "It's been a long week," he laments, and a caller offers "lukewarm dittos," saying Rush might not support any single candidate, but he's certainly "unsupported candidates." And he seems to be "an apologist for Forbes." Rush does like Forbes. Rush, the evolving millionaire, now feels some kinship with the inheriting sort of millionaire, but by way of defense, replies, "I'm for freedom," which is of course true, since Rush is essentially a libertarian in conservative clothing.

New York magazine has published an article (February 26) by a Vassar English professor, Donald Foster, which contends that Joe Klein is the author of *Primary Colors*. *New York* is Klein's old stomping grounds, from where he blossomed into a political commentator. Foster has been working with computers and has done enough matches to convince himself that Klein's the one. He convinces me, especially with a noncomputer bit of textual criticism. Foster quotes from the beginning of the novel, the mulatto narrator saying, "I am small and not so dark," and concludes, with a bit of German (Klein must have gotten a decent enough education at Penn), that it is a private joke because it can be read, "I am *Klein*—and I'm not really black." Klein being "small" in German. That's the sort of cleverness that trumps denials. I realize it's only my, ah, lack of generosity at Klein's good fortune that made me not want to believe he was the author earlier. And that "creweled" business.

3/3 The *New York Times* has started a series, "The Downsizing of America," and the first of seven articles runs today. The graphic the *Times* uses for the series is four "workers" with their heads bowed. More of Buchanan's mischief; he scared folks in '92 with his culture war, and now he's got hold of an issue that really scares people, class war. The *Times* says, "Yet this is not a saga about rampant unemployment, like the Great Depression, but one about an emerging redefinition of employment." Lots of scary facts in the piece. And there are going to be six more! "Workers Fall, Business Rises" is a subhead.

3/4 Rush is trying to rally the troops. He warns that all the Republican self-bashing is making the Democrats happy and "when you have liberals with confidence you have trouble." Bringing Republican disputes to the forefront can be overcome. "It's surmountable," he says, refusing to be pessimistic, but, he adds, "I predicted this," these sour wages of war.

3/5 NPR has an audio tape of Buchanan saying, at a Columbus, Georgia, carpet factory owned by a contributor, "You need to know where a man stands on this issue"—the issue being abortion. Buchanan and his supporters are waging their pitchfork battle, with the cry: We want to get into the Republican country club and use the pool and everything.

Newt votes for Dole in the Georgia primary. "A tepid endorsement," Buchanan calls it.

Then there's a Peter Overby report and we hear Newt going on, about nine out of ten incumbents reelected, that PAC spent less than what *Waterworld* cost, than what the country spends on antacid tablets, *Seinfeld* reruns, all marketplace comparisons. Newt advises, don't be outspent the last week of the campaign. I recall that Bobby Abrams was outspent in the last week of the Senate race by D'Amato.

Minnie Pearl (Sarah Ophelia Cannon), the Grand Old Opry fixture, died yesterday, Monday, the fourth. She wore a price tag hanging from her hat, which made her the country star forerunner of African American athlete style, ball caps with tags dangling.

Lester Thurow ("less than thorough" is his trade nickname) is on Diane Rehm's show. He's saying that America is now in a condition where for the "first time a society [is] dominated by old people." (I think of China. Even its aged rulers die off, eventually. But Thurow doesn't mean rulers.) Males' wages have been falling for twenty-five years, females' wages for fifteen, family incomes since 1989. Thurow says in 1996, we're finally talking about it, thanks to Pat Buchanan. Of Alan Greenspan he says, "Conservative is not the word." The nineties look like the sixties. Greenspan "hasn't caught on to the fact that the world is different." He should be told, "Take your feet off the brakes" since the economy is growing at only 1 percent; 2 percent is enough for Greenspan. No education strategy works in a 2 percent growth environment, Thurow says. Even Ph.D. males' salaries are falling. (The end *is* near.) But that's inevitable, Thurow says, after a twenty-five year war on inflation. He asks if you are a "worker first or a consumer first" when cheaper long-distance calls are touted as a benefit of the moment.

Rush is saying that Buchanan is the average slumlord; he bought five or six retail properties in Maryland for $35,000 or so in the sixties. Assessed value is now $102,000 to $260,000. Mold in the shower is a problem. The answer, Rush says, is Comet cleans the showers. Tenants complaining Pat rents them out for $1,200 to $1,500. Rush has been reading the *Washington Post*. Rush's callers, like Thurow, are interested in economic growth today, too. One asks, since it is Rush's solution: "Grow the economy"—but how? If a guy's forty-five to fifty-five he's out. He's a hard-luck case. Yes, Rush admits, there are individual cases, but nationwide it'll work out. Rush is echoing Stalin's remark, the death of one man is a tragedy, the death of a regiment is a statistic. "It is a crap shoot over which you have control. Retrain yourself," Rush advises. Everyone's an economist today. Look what Buchanan has wrought. "Everybody has to take steps back in his life," Rush muses, talking about himself. He begins to sound like Werner Erhard of EST fame. "Risk is something more people have to have the ability to take. . . . I made twenty-four thousand in 1972. Till 1984 every job I had in that period I lost money," Rush confides. "I know it can be done." A woman caller comes on: "I'm sick of country club Republicans. I'm ready for another party." The culture war/class war is coming home to roost for the GOP.

Rush is freewheeling. Gramm drops out after criticizing Dole and now says Dole's the best. Rush talked, he says, mainly about Perot in '92, regarding NAFTA and GATT. Buchanan was right on those issues then. There was no congressional oversight. Rush is back to Buchanan the slumlord. Rush reminisces about his own run-in with mice running across the floor—the Buchanan properties' problem. Rush sprayed a trash can with Pam and then shook the can. Mice dead. He resents the media trying to characterize Buchanan as a Ron Brown–type slumlord. This is why people don't want to run for president, Rush says petulantly.

The New Hampshire primary's slogan, I discover, is "Always first, always right." Though it was wrong in '92. Senator Paul Tsongas of Massachusetts won the '92 Democratic primary by some nine thousand votes. Lowell, Massachusetts, the senator's home, is near the New Hampshire border. Clinton got a second wind because of his close second, hence "the Comeback Kid." Buchanan won in '96. Is he the Tsongas of this campaign? Though it doesn't appear that Buchanan plans to withdraw soon after his victory like Tsongas did.

Changes in rules after 1968 brought on more primaries (paradoxically making New Hampshire's more prominent by being first), and by 1983 you no longer needed petitions to get on the ballot, but only a filing fee of one thousand dollars. (Which is why there is such a long list of candidates running there [not quite four score], though not even fifteen minutes of fame accrued to most of them.)

On CNN (and C-SPAN) I get to see film of Alan Keyes being hustled, handcuffed behind the back, into an Atlanta, Georgia, patrol car by white officers after being denied entry into a primary debate sponsored by a local TV station, WSB-TV. Lamar!, Pat, and Steve debate; though asked, Dole chose not to come (looking senatorial, proclaiming himself the front-runner by staying away from all the non–office holders). The Keyes footage is not pretty (though the images are familiar) from Atlanta—the city which is looking forward to the summer Olympics. The coppers evidently let Keyes out somewhere near a phone booth and Atlanta's mayor, Bill Campbell, came to pick him up.

The campaign is almost complete, now that we have the scene of a black man in a patrol car. Keyes was also barred from the South Carolina debate. The South only wants the leading contenders, but how Georgia and South Carolina justify Lamar! is a stretch (except that he is white and a former southern governor).

3/6   As goes Hawaii, so goes the nation, or so America's conservatives think, according to the *New York Times*. A Defense of Marriage Act (to counter what it is feared Hawaii will allow: marriage between those of the same sex) is forthcoming from the Senate, and in Sacramento, California, the local pols are mulling over their own version of the Senate bill. No more cold war, but there are gay marriages to scare people. And, speaking of not so gay marriages, my favorite Utah representative, Enid Greene Waldholtz, one of Gingrich's pinups of '94, is reeling under domestic and economic stress and has announced she will not seek reelection. Perhaps she can join one of the anti–gay marriage lobbying groups and collect a paycheck. On the op-ed page, Frank Rich—it is, of course, predictable that in the nineties, political and press analysis comes from a former film and theater critic—does a column on the "alternate" press. He calls attention to a handout he received at the Media and Democracy Congress held in San Francisco. "The handout was a chart, complied by Mark Crispin Miller, a professor of media studies at Johns Hopkins University, and his graduate students. At its top are the names of four huge media conglomerates; Time Warner, General Electric, Disney/Cap Cities and Westinghouse. Underneath, genealogy-style, are the many news and culture outlets they own, from behemoths like NBC down to cable systems, local TV stations and small-town papers such as the Narragansett Times." It strikes me that even the *New York Times* might feel nervous having those "behemoths" breathing down its neck.

Rush is talking to Bob Dole, congratulating him on his big primary wins yesterday, which was Mega Tuesday. Colorado, Connecticut, Georgia, Maine, Maryland, Massachusetts, Rhode Island, and Vermont had primaries, and caucuses were held in five other states. "This is Bob Dole. Everybody knows I'm Bob Dole," Dole says in answer to Rush's question about why Dole refers to himself in the third person. It gets his name out, Bob says, a Dole wisecrack.

Afterward, Rush does a segment about people who were fired and got their careers going again. Earl the logger; a woman who started a "cable" company; a man who's into wholesale auto parts. He's pushing the optimism button hard.

When all else seems to be too downbeat, he goes to "You don't find a sex scandal with Bob Dole" and then runs through the Republican candidates, all apparently upright guys.

There's a labor joke going around, apropos of the forty thousand layoffs at AT&T engineered by Richard Allen, the CEO: What's AT&T stand for? The answer: Allen and Two Temps.

And speaking of downsizing, Lugar and Lamar! are out of the race, but Jack Kemp endorses Steve Forbes, a real beauty-and-the-beast match, made in flat-tax heaven. Forbes calls Kemp "my guru in chief," which sounds more like goo-goo in chief.

PBS's *NewsHour* has "four key Republican players in this campaign" discussing Tuesday's results. It is a reasonable sample, however weird: William Bennett, Vin Weber, Gary Bauer, and the only media nonused tire, Malcolm Wallop (a former senator from Wyoming who didn't get on national TV much back then), identified as the Forbes campaign chairman. Weber is cochair of the Dole campaign, Bennett is national chairman of the late Lamar! show, and Bauer is there representing the other campaign, the grassroots religious Right. Bennett, the only representative of the truly lost, is saying that his man's endorsement of Dole will be a big help. Wallop, who packs less than, is happy with today's Jack Kemp endorsement of Forbes, the "colleague of Bill Bennett," as he calls him. The race is not over, according to the lesser Malcolm in Forbes's world.

Vin Weber (I thought Vin wanted to write a novel when he "retired" from the House) says, "Dole has effectively won the nomination, unless he makes some huge, unexpected error." Which leads me to believe that Vin might think that "unexpected," but not an impossible move on the part of the Bobster. A lot of confidence, there, in the cochair's chair.

Margaret Warner asks Bauer, who functions as Buchanan's person, insofar as most official spokespeople of the Buchanan campaign have been let go because of ties to white supremacist groups, what Buchanan really wants at this point. Bauer replies, "I think he has been very specific about the social issues, the sanctity of human life, a feeling that the party has devoted a lot of rhetoric to those things but really hasn't done much policy-wise. . . . And you know, Margaret, I actually think that Forbes and Buchanan being in the race improves Bob Dole's chances, because it makes him sharpen his message." Bauer has a very in utero look about him.

But Bennett isn't so cheery about Buchanan's role in the campaign. "Will Pat Buchanan stop talking about Bob Dole as the bellhop of the Business Roundtable and these other things? . . . So, if he stays in, is he really going to do Bob Dole any good?" Vin lets lose some vigor: "We're at the whining and nitpicking stage in this campaign. When you talk about economic reform and economic growth, Bob Dole, along with Newt Gingrich, was responsible for forming, and choosing Jack Kemp as the head of, the tax commission that has really set in motion the supply-side reform of the tax code. For this, he gets Jack Kemp endorsing Steve Forbes for president, which I totally don't understand."

Bauer chimes in: "Look, Senator Dole's a great guy, Vin, but when he says in New Hampshire he didn't realize economic issues were going to be a major factor in the New Hampshire campaign—"

"That's not what he said. That's not fair," Vin interrupts.

"Well, whatever he said, it's hard to put a good spin on it," Bauer counters. "He said he didn't realize that trade was going to dominate the New Hampshire primary."

"He said—he said economics," Bauer insists. Margaret Warner stops the exchange. I see what sort of huge, unexpected error Weber is afraid of.

These folks are followed by Shields and Gigot, along with William Kristol, guided in their discussion by Jim Lehrer. Kristol the younger is the son of Irving Kristol, famous neocon of decades past: Kristol is the Steve Forbes of this group of journalists, having won his spurs in the usual places, thanks to Dad, along with mighty service in government as Dan Quayle's "brains" (more failing upward).

Lehrer asks, "Bill Kristol, why was Buchanan not able to build on his, his—on what happened in Iowa, and then most particularly in New Hampshire?"

Kristol replies, "Well, it turned out that he really can't get more than 30 percent of the vote in the Republican primaries across the country.

He's got a tap of support at 30 percent, and it turned out that Bob Dole was able to rally the other 70 percent of the voters increasingly to him. But at the end of the day, one has to say that Bob Dole was lucky in who he ended up with as his two final opponents, and I say this meaning no disrespect to Steve Forbes or Pat Buchanan, but they are two journalists. I say that meaning no disrespect to journalists here in this—this could be very dangerous here, but . . ."

Lehrer says, with mock solemnity, "Let's move right along."

Kristol still is shaking this bone. "You know, I mean, just in a simpleminded way. Neither . . ." Kristol is tongue-tied, as if his brain won't let him say what he really knows.

Shields butts in with a joke: "You're editor and publisher." Meaning not just a mere journalist at *The Weekly Standard*. And the foursome dissolves in laughter. Who's got the cards, who's deal is it? It's boys-night-out time.

Kemp's endorsement of Forbes takes up a good bit of their time remaining, and Lehrer says, "They're close friends. They're also political friends and ideological friends on issues, right, for a long time?" And Paul Gigot supplies, doubtless because this chat has gotten very clubby indeed, "Oh, absolutely. Steve Forbes, in fact, is, I think, involved in financing Empower America, which is Jack Kemp's think tank here in Washington."

The smallest of small worlds at work.

3/7   On Rush there's a hot white male caller sounding off against William Bennett's (of, let us not forget, Empower America) support of Alexander: "Hey, man, you picked a loser. Get lost." Dole's sweep of Super Tuesday is on the people's minds, Dole winning primaries in Massachusetts, Maryland, Maine, Connecticut, and Vermont.

Rush is decrying a Ninth Circuit Court of Appeals suicide decision up in Seattle. The judge, according to Rush, is married to the head of the California ACLU. This leads Rush to Dr. Kevorkian, who Rush says is "in love with death." Kevorkian is a pathologist, so I don't find that strange. My uncle is a pathologist and was one of Kevorkian's first partners, long ago, at the beginning of both their careers in medicine. But they quickly parted company over an incident in their office. An employee had made a mistake and Kevorkian wanted her fired immediately. My uncle was willing to give her another chance. Kevorkian issued an ultimatum: It's either her or me; and the next day Kevorkian left, never to return. My uncle mentioned Kevorkian's wife's family had money. But it also indicated Kevorkian's obvious sense of "above all, I am right."

Rush is continuing on about "assisted suicide practitioners"—or whatever they are to be called, he says—and the corruption of the medical establishment, the likelihood of death centers. Kevorkian oddly helps the Democrats, insofar as every time he pops up and plants another one, he makes people worried not so much about death as about old age and medical care. He's a thorn in the side of the body politic, but not for bumping people off.

A man gets through to Rush. He'd been waiting for an hour and a half, but to him it felt like waiting for Christmas. He's full of emotion. "I felt renewed," he says, getting to speak to his hero. He asks for a picture of Rush. Rush says yes, but it's the "only time I'll do it today."

On CBS's *48 Hours,* there's a roundtable of notables. Arianna Huffington, the Greek wife of the failed California Senate candidate millionaire, Arianna of the Zsa Zsa Gabor voice—what is she doing there? Affirmative action *has* gone too far. Affirmative action for rich wives. Gary Hart, looking absurder than ever (the defrocked-minister aspect has really settled in with age) is there, along with Dan Quayle, boyish as ever. Cornel West is doing his davening (up and down) number. Quite a group. But they only get twenty-second sound bites; if it was on NPR or cable, they would at least get to speak paragraphs.

The networks still resist letting anyone talk too long, which means longer than a sentence or two. This show is not live, it has been edited, and CBS has decided to stick to its entrenched formula. A sentence or two, clip, clip.

3/8   Rush is saying Perot attacked Buchanan in a major way. But he "doesn't want to work with him on a third party."

Rush is attempting to do the opposite of what the *New York Times* is doing with their downsizing series. Rush is doing—success stories! Upbeat yea! Downbeat boo! The *New York Times* series on "Downsizing America" is Pulitzer Prize bait, similar to the *Philadelphia Inquirer* series

"America: What Went Wrong?" of a few years ago. Pulitzers for documenting the obvious, though it's always surprising when you do so.

On HBO's *Dennis Miller Live,* Dennis Miller jokes: Pat Buchanan is going to build a two-hundred-mile wall to keep out illegal immigrants. Pat, Miller says, who do you think is going to build that goddamn wall?

Miller puts me in mind of conspiracy theories: the nonconspiracy view of Oswald and Ruby (lone gunman, no connection) is the true portrait of America—two American types in close proximity without any causality. Conspiracy theorists (Oswald and Ruby as two players in an elaborate game) really want to believe that our country is more sane than that.

3/10 Carville and Matalin are on NBC's *Meet the Press.* Carville wants to subpoena Perot to discover the source of Perot's charge that a "party" was going to provide him a million for dirty tricks. "A felony," says Carville. Well, even Carville can't contain an eagerness to prosecute. He is a lawyer, after all, regardless of his Hunter Thompson-on-baddrugs persona. Thinking of Safire's "congenital" liar crack, it is easy to see Matalin as having a congenital sneer.

There's an AP article on James Stewart's book, *Blood Sport.* Last sentence of the wire copy: "Clinton told Susan McDougal that he loved being governor because of all the female attention it brought."

3/11 Rush says, The next whiner I get I'm going to explode. I'm apologizing in advance. "Even people on my side think I am botching it." A caller says that they should call it the Beijing Republican Party. Is it any different from what Beijing is doing to Taiwan? What they did to Buchanan to twist this whole election around, he exclaims. A large segment of Rush's audience is unhappy with all the attacks on Buchanan.

And Rush is alienating a lot of them. One does have to presume that Buchanan doesn't care if Dole gets elected. Buchanan has confused the class war/culture war aspects of the down-scale end of the Republican Party. The Christian Coalition isn't into class war, just culture war, and its troops are confused.

3/12 Rush is in a tizzy: " 'Dole's a compromiser'—if I hear that one more time!" No more Buchanan-supporter calls, he says to his screener, no "fundamental Buchanan supporters." They want the same things Reich and Gephardt want. Rush is talking about an ABC program last night. Twenty-two million dollars is owed in student debts. Where are the students bellyaching about that? They "have to be told the day of the free lunch is over," Rush says. So, too, "the geezer lobby." Not a soul out there who will do what needs to be done. That leader . . . is not on the scene. Social Security was bad enough at the beginning, but this! A four-year-old gets Social Security from her dead father; she's the product of artificial insemination after his death. You find where this was in the original Social Security idea, Rush says, baffled.

3/13   Rush reports a "Battleground" poll: Dole and Clinton are separated by 8 percentage points, 41 to 49. This poll was more accurate on Bush-Clinton, he says. The survey has not changed in the last one and a half years. It differs from other polls, which have 58 percent for Clinton.

Rush is mispronouncing the word prophylactics, talking about a town near Richmond, Virginia, that's getting new business—a Trojan condom factory. Pro-fol-laugh-ti-size. "Buchanan has less support than he had in ninety-two." A woman caller says: Powell is not that far off the reservation. "What is the difference between Whitewater and Watergate?" Rush asks; then he answers, "The whole Republican Party didn't get involved in the cover-up of Watergate. The whole Democratic Party is involved in the cover-up of Whitewater. They're filibustering in Congress."

Rush tells story of when he first was in New York City. He was anonymous. It was a different world. A friend took him to the Rainbow Room for a Ms. Foundation ceremony. It was full of the glitterati of the liberal intelligentsia congratulating themselves on electing the city's first African American mayor. "This was painful," Rush says. Phil Donahue was in the elevator staring at Rush. "What is he doing here!" Donahue exclaimed.

Rush plays a song. General David Dinkins where are you? Dinkins was saying the town was "a gorgeous mosaic," but when introduced to Rush he froze, then frowned—"I saw what David Dinkins's value was to this liberal town . . . that he was black . . . it made them feel better."

Rush has flop-sweat problems. These two weeks or so (all of early March) of declining dittos are attributable to the last few years of his high living, being married by Clarence Thomas, etc., all of which is seen as a defection to the swells by the large part of his audience galvanized by Buchanan. And Rush is still insecure enough to show his ill ease. He had a face full of flop sweat when he was in front of the new '94 congressional officeholders he helped to elect, looking like Madonna being amateurish in her Oscar-performance Marilyn Monroe number, revealing herself to be Not Ready for Prime Time, except that prime time has descended to them. Madonna performing in front of the entertainment world's stars is similar to Rush giving advice to the newly elected Congress members.

Since Rush has been rehashing Cuba shooting down the two Cessnas over international waters, the idea that Juan Pablo Roque, the Cuban pilot "defector" involved in the anti-Castro group that organized the flight (and now labeled a double agent: working for the FBI, but actually still working for the Cubans), is a triple agent (really working for the CIA) becomes more plausible—he got the Cubans to shoot down the planes so that Clinton would toe the anti-Castro line. Juan showed up on CNN attacking Brothers to the Rescue, his former compatriots' anti-Castro organization.

On PBS's *NewsHour,* Pat Buchanan is being interviewed. Pat seems to adjust better than most to whatever the media environment happens to be. He's on PBS, so his demeanor becomes softened, his voice less strident. "Hi, Margaret," he says to Margaret Warner, who will be lobbing the questions to him. It's Pat, your old pal and colleague.

"Thanks for being with us," Margaret says, and asks about his thoughts on Steve Forbes leaving the race.

Pat says, "I think it will turn it into—" and then he offers, "Incidentally, we're getting some feedback in that earpiece." He's at home with the hardware. Then he continues, "I think it will turn it into a Pat Buchanan–Bob Dole race, which I felt it was from the beginning, a battle for the heart and soul of the Republican Party. . . . We're going to stay right to the convention," he announces.

Margaret, earnest, dark haired, the good student, says, "Now, you are losing 75 to 80 percent of the Republican vote in all of these primaries." Buchanan murmurs, and she continues, "I mean, how is this battle for the heart and soul of the party?" Good for Margaret.

Buchanan is a bit flustered, stops and starts, saying, "Well, you, if you're here, look at the polls, I think something like 55 percent of the Republicans say they do not believe Bob Dole has ideas, and an equal number do not know where he's going to take the party." By the time Dole wins the nomination he will look like he did after World War II was over: damaged, crippled, in need of lots of rehabilitation.

Margaret wants to know if Buchanan will support Dole.

"Well, we're not setting conditions right now, Margaret. What we're doing is right now we are moving toward a situation where I will have far more votes going into San Diego than I had going into Houston, and that was three million votes . . . I said I will go all the way to San Diego. I will stand up there for life, I will stand up for the working men and women who are losing their jobs, I will fight these unfair trade deals that are sending your jobs overseas, I will try to make this party more responsive to the people who walked out in 1992 and went for Ross Perot."

He goes on to say that he will most likely be locked out of the convention. "I cannot believe that they can tell the nation why they denied a prime-time speaking place to a candidate who ran a fair campaign on issues and ran second and collected millions of votes and defeated individuals like Senator Gramm with more money and Mr. Alexander and Mr. Forbes. I don't know how they're going to make that case, but look, if that's what they want to do, I don't know how they can call themselves the party of ideas."

Buchanan's main idea seems to be wanting to be renewed for his second prime-time speaking slot, like any TV person would want. He doesn't want to be canceled. He knows it would hurt his ratings everywhere.

Then we have Shields and Gigot (Amos and Andy, Jerry and Dean, Archie and Meathead) discussing the state of the campaign. Elizabeth Farnsworth is keeping them apart. Women do a lot of moderating in television. She is blond, a bit more ameliorating than Margaret Warner; her voice doesn't go up into high registers as Warner's is tempted to do. Mark Shields, the former political op, now pundit, says, "Pat Buchanan's

implicit argument is Bob Dole is yesterday, our movement is tomorrow,"
and that "the Democratic incumbent" will be making the same sort of
argument. Paul Gigot has become the *Wall Street Journal*'s human face.
He says, "This is a race between Bob Dole and Bob Dole. I mean, Pat
Buchanan isn't going to win it." Farnsworth asks, "Why do you think
Steve Forbes is pulling out?" Gigot thinks Forbes is unwilling to spend
ten million in California, especially if he can't win the nomination.
Forbes, the skinflint. Shields is a bit more philosophical. He thinks, "For
Steve Forbes, it's doubly difficult, because he had the . . . exhilaration.
He had the adrenaline high of winning. He won in Arizona." And prob-
ably lost that state for Dole in November, I think. "And I think it's a
time to be gentle with people who are leaving and you realize you're not
going to rekindle and recapture what you had."

Yeah, national obscurity and living in the shadow of his old man,
that's what he's not going to recapture. Shields is more vulnerable to
sentiment than Gigot. He says Forbes "put the growth agenda, the tax-
cutting, Reaganite optimistic message back in the Republican Party . . .
That's the vacuum he sought to fill, and really, if Bob Dole now wants
to take that message, he can take that once Forbes leaves the race and
run with it himself, some version of it, not the pure flat tax necessarily,
but some version of it, and use it as an antidote to Pat Buchanan and
frankly, against Bill Clinton in November."

Farnsworth quotes Buchanan saying, "Our agenda is the agenda driving the nation and the party," and Gigot agrees, saying Buchanan's "going to prevent any change in the platform on abortion at the Republican
convention, but I think that as regards to trade protection, for example,
and the trade issue, I think that's been repudiated in the primaries. That's
not driving anybody, and as regards his economic diagnosis, the anxiety
that people feel, he's put that on the table, but the solutions, that debate
has still to be fought out in years to come." Thus sayeth the *Wall Street
Journal.*

"I think," Shields says, "that Pat Buchanan deserves enormous credit
in an underfinanced campaign,"—yeah, I'd liked to see what his spin-
off, nonprofit companies have brought in—"an overlooked *[!]* campaign,
a much disparaged campaign. He has put front and center the economic
anxiety and the question of corporations that are consistently putting

profits before people, and I think Pat Buchanan has made that case, he's made it compellingly, and others are parroting what he said."

3/14   Forbes officially retires from the race. Sixteen children were killed at school yesterday in Dunblane, Scotland, by a man with hand-guns, identified as Thomas Hamilton, forty-three, an "avid gun enthu-siast." The NRA and Buchanan will not be raising their rifles quite so high today.

As we of the television audience all went to law school during the O. J. trial, we're in for political science and history classes, too. On the *NewsHour* tonight, we have their team of experts, ready to discuss the history of the Republican Party. Michael Beschloss, Doris Kearns Good-win, and Haynes Johnson are the regulars. They're joined tonight by a political scientist, James Reichley. Johnson quotes Bill Clinton, wondering "if the Democratic Party wasn't going the way of the Whigs, and you could make a case. There is no Democratic Party. There are five Dem-ocratic Parties. The Republican Party has been more unified, but it—you're seeing the fissures within itself, so I think the whole idea of the political parties in the country, which have been stabilizing, important, giving ideology, consensus, for both, we've been very lucky to have a stable government, for all this period of time, is now up for grabs, and I think the public reflects that. There's new interparty movement, third-party movement, it's all there." Beschloss agrees, and so does Ms. Good-win. They all think, though, that Dole can "unite" the Republican Party. Professor Reichley says about Dole, "He brings together, one might say, the Eisenhower and the Taft traditions in the Republican Party, which is a pretty powerful force among Republicans." National Educational Television (as it used to be called) at its finest. I don't think the professor will be back.

3/15   When Forbes threw his support to Dole yesterday, Bob didn't catch it so gracefully, according to the *New York Times,* which quotes Dole saying, "He was bashing me. I don't have to worry about that for a while." Losing Arizona and all those attack ads really got to him.

3/17 On C-SPAN I see the Friday the fifteenth, (aired on the seventeenth) remarks of Senator Carl Levin, Democrat from Michigan: Gingrich wanted his way on big-budget entitlement issues. It was irresponsible and it fouled up education, Pell grants, Title I hirings, student loans, loan programs. And we are still dithering around with an end of March continuing resolution. These are irresponsible tactics on the part of Gingrich, Levin says. Restoration of educational cuts is a big victory for us. Most people didn't even know the cuts were made.

3/18 Buchanan is on NPR's *Morning Edition,* saying he thinks the GOP might reconsider the striker replacement law (after I saw him saying no to reconsideration Sunday on *This Week with David Brinkley*). "I've been talking with these guys." Buchanan is testing the waters of conversion. Still too hot.

On the *New York Times*'s op-ed page there's a Reed Irvine, Accuracy in Media ad on Vince Foster, "No Bullet, No Bone, No Brains, No Blood" (but plenty of alliteration), and a sketch of a man seen near Foster's car that resembles one of the Cuban types last seen on the Grassy Knoll. Reed wants to know why the *New York Times* hasn't been more on the case, and Senator D'Amato, too, for that matter. By coincidence (in a world where there is no coincidence) there's a story on page B12 of a policeman's suicide at a concert; he shot himself in the head and the bullet wounded two women behind him. It isn't clear from the article if the bullet was recovered. The ad cost Reed $19,825.

On Rush we have Tony Snow as a substitute host. He's talking to a guy from the Battleground poll. "Americans like gridlock," the pollster says. Fifty-seven percent think any deal Republicans and Democrats make would be bad for them. Only seniors and minorities disagree. The Million Man March is discussed. He was there with his godson. It was a "sense of empowerment for those people."

The discussion goes over to Democratic strategies to cover up Whitewater. But then there is an Oliver Stone minute, a fake commercial. Vince Foster . . . the film. An appearance by Lenin's body as Vince Foster's corpse. Anyone over the age of thirteen who believes a minute of it will not be admitted.

On CNN, Bernie Shaw, famous for being under the bed in Baghdad, is interviewing James Stewart, the author of *Blood Sport,* which has replaced *Primary Colors* as the Book of the Talk Month. *Time* magazine (March 18) is out with an excerpt. *Time* and its covers. It got all sorts of flak about its too dark O. J. cover and its editor hemmed and hawed about that, but must have concluded the publicity is worth the disapprobation (money talks), so *Time* has continued the arty, touched-up, editorial covers. This one has Hillary wearing black, with desperate noir shadows playing across her face, and the capital letter M of TIME is centered on her forehead, giving her two cute red horns. Way to go, art director. I suppose his/her salary has been going up since the controversies began.

Bernie Shaw says, "A majority of Americans say 'enough already' when it comes to extending the Senate's investigation into Whitewater. According to the same *USA Today*/Gallup poll, more than half those surveyed also dismiss any link between the Whitewater allegations and President Clinton's ability to serve in office . . . You say whether specific laws were broken should not obscure the broader issues that make Whitewater an important story. What are some of those broader issues?"

Stewart replies, "I think probably the most important is the character and integrity of the president and the first lady." Stewart has a snappish voice shot through with an I-wouldn't-be-caught-dead-in-the-bars-you-go-to tone. Formerly the front-page editor of the *Wall Street Journal,* his earlier Wall Street book, *Den of Thieves,* equipped him to wade through the slow-moving, bug-infested Whitewater matter. Visually, there's something about Stewart that makes him appear a mean Bill Moyers.

Shaw asks, "Former *New York Times* reporter Jeff Gerth was trying to get to the bottom of how Mrs. Clinton was so successful in the highly volatile commodities market—successful to the point of making virtually one hundred thousand dollars in profit. He was told by a White House person that she read the *Wall Street Journal,* had done her research. He later found out this was not so, went back to this person and said—to that person—why did you tell me this story. And then in your book, you quote him as saying, 'The first instinct from everybody from Arkansas is to lie.' Now, is that a fair assessment, or an exaggeration?"

"Well, I'm simply quoting a White House official saying that. First of all, I think he meant the people from Arkansas in the White House. And it's an exaggeration, of course, but nevertheless, there is a pattern, both on the part of the Clintons and people around them, of having a knee-jerk reaction to questions, to say something that will make them seem better and what the public would want to hear."

The public is hearing the pitter-patter of the countercampaign.

On C-SPAN, Buchanan is being asked, "What are you going to be doing four years from now?" "That's a good question. . . . I'm not sure what we'll be doing . . . except when we come down out of the hills in August . . . we're taking this week by week. . . . I don't know what's happening."

John Salvi, a less flamboyant nutcase than the Long Island Railroad shooter, was convicted in Dedham, Massachusetts, of murdering two abortion clinics' workers. It's hard to separate any trials from this campaign, since the odor of the courthouse hovers over all the proceedings. Salvi made a fittingly strange remark: "I am against abortion and pro–welfare state and pro–Catholic labor union." Is that a Reagan Democrat, or what? Salvi, a tiny twenty-four-year-old, looks like some cartoon character, insofar as he is wearing a white shirt with a collar about five sizes too big for him, so it appears that his head has recently shrunk, which is what his parents think he needs, some severe professional shrinking. In his dark jacket's pocket there's one of those saw-tooth fake handkerchiefs. The Long Island Railroad killer wanted to shoot white folks, it appeared, but Salvi had a bit more focused target, employees of abortion centers, which shows a narrower degree of lunacy.

3/20 Half of Diane Rehm's postprimary political roundup show (the Midwest is heard from: Wisconsin, Illinois, Michigan, Ohio) is spent discussing abortion, as are all the calls. The Salvi verdict effect. Future Supreme Court appointments will be at play—Rehnquist and O'Connor are the likely retirees, Norman Orstein says. Ten percent of the people are against all abortions; 10 percent favor no restrictions, says Orstein. In the second hour we get James Stewart and *Blood Sport*. Stewart doesn't seem to notice the irony of him participating in the blood sport he decries. But his is a story of sex and death. Bill is the sex and Hillary is death (money).

I watch our local Christian TV person, Bob Enyart. Bob Dole would rather spend time with homosexuals than Christians, Enyart's saying. Even he isn't keen on Dole. The Bible hasn't solved any public policy question, Enyart says scornfully, claiming to quote Dole. Well, Enyart says, if Dole doesn't take the time to read the Bible . . .

. On a non-Christian channel a Polaroid commercial comes on. A phone call interrupts a meeting, people (all twenty-and thirty-somethings) looked pissed, annoyed. "Have you looked in your briefcase yet?" a woman's voice says. The wife. Guy finds a Polaroid photograph. He's gaga. "I'll be home in ten minutes." Polaroid's business must be bad to push naughty pictures—because video has cut into their business?

3/21 On NPR's *Morning Edition,* I again hear Donna Rice Hughes speaking for Internet censorship. She continues to be dismayed at what children get to see. Pictures of her and Gary Hart down in the Caribbean, doubtless.

On Rush, Tony Snow is talking about James Stewart's book. What began as a puff piece turned into a devastating indictment of the Clintons, Tony says. The White House is stonewalling. He reads a Gennifer Flowers/troopers section. And scenes of fights, which Snow has accompanied by breaking glass, screams, sound effects, etc. Also travel-office sections. Tony praises Maureen Dowd for her good work on the *Time*'s op-ed page. Stewart and his book are getting close to total saturation.

On C-SPAN I'm watching Don Imus at the Radio and Television Correspondents Dinner with the Clintons. This is one of the many unintended consequences of C-SPAN, a peek into the ceremonial amusements of the well-placed and the powerful. They are used to these events being "private," not broadcast nationwide, but habit has let them be less guarded than they might ordinarily be. C-SPAN still operates in a strange gray world between public and private. Newt has been up making jokes, some funny, and then the president delivers a few, even more amusing bon mots. He does presidential bumper stickers, has the visuals prepared: "If you can read this, I've lost my motorcade." I wonder who the principal joke writer is for the White House. Clinton is very comfortable in his delivery as he lightly needles his audience. The large room's ceiling is blue and it sports slightly science fiction–like starlights. Clinton says about the Republican family tax cut, "They have targeted theirs at the Forbes family in New Jersey." The camera shows Forbes chuckling. Oh, what a kidder; it's only five hundred dollars per child. "Next time I address the national public," the prez says he has been advised, "I should run the lottery-ticket winners underneath."

But Imus, of the three, is the only one who wrote his own remarks, and I wonder whose idea it was to invite him. Clinton had referred to his being on Imus's radio show, and that Imus took credit for electing him. "Well, what have you done for me lately?" is Clinton's joke and challenge. This has been "a good news evening for me," Clinton says. We shall see.

Imus shambles on. He fumbles at the lectern with some papers and starts making jokes about these materials not being his, someone must have just left them here, but who would leave important papers lying around and he looks to his left at Hillary. She smiles and there is laughter throughout the crowd.

Imus reads the purported papers: "S. McDougal called again. I told her both were in the mail. Ha. Ha. Jesus, she looked stupid in those tank tops."

Looking at Imus one thinks of a bad night at Plato's Retreat, the Manhattan sex club of the 1970s. He goes on: "You know, I think it would be fair to say that back when the Clintons took office, if we had placed them all in a lineup—well, not a lineup—if we were to have speculated on which member of the first family would be the first to be indicted—I meant to receive a subpoena—everybody in this room would have picked Roger." There is more laughter, but it is checked by a slight breeze of caution, danger in the air. "I mean, been there, done that. Well, in the past three years, Socks the cat has been in more jams than Roger. Roger has been a saint. The cat has peed on national treasures. Roger hasn't. Socks has thrown up hair balls. Roger hasn't. Socks got his girlfriend pregnant and had—well, no, that was Roger."

Both Clintons are looking at him in severe profile now, since that position reveals less of their expression than full front. The profile doesn't betray complicated emotions.

Imus goes on, after greeting his audience once again ("Radio and TV scum"): "And, as you know, nearly every incident in the lives of the first

William O'Rourke

family has been made worse by some creep in the media, by each and every person in this room—the radio and television correspondents." Ah, Imus, the truth teller. Unlike Newt and Bill, his humor isn't bathed in exaggeration and irony. "Even innocuous incidents. For example, when Cal Ripken broke Lou Gehrig's consecutive-game record, the president was at Camden Yards, doing play-by-play on the radio with Jon Miller. Bobby Bonilla hit a double, and we all heard the president, in his obvious excitement, holler, 'Go Baby!' And I remember commenting at the time, 'I bet that's not the first time he's said that.' Remember the AstroTurf and the pickup?" Yes, I do—the El Camino. There is laughter, but it is, as they say, nervous, uneasy. The experience is somewhat like watching the Rodney King tape, or, rather, like watching *live* the Rodney King beating, since this is a real-time event.

"Imagine if back in 1978, Mrs. Clinton had not said to Mr. Clinton, 'Honey, Jim and Susan are here and they've got some riverfront land for these great vacation homes and maybe we can make some serious money.' And he said, 'God, I love this Reaganomics!', which reminds me: In light of the controversy that surrounded publication of Mrs. Clinton's book, perhaps Anonymous should have written *It Takes a Village*. And then there's Senator D'Amato's book, *It Takes a Village Idiot*. The senator suggests that the Clintons hung around with unsavory characters in Little Rock. What the hell is he talking about? All of his friends have bodies in the trunks of their cars."

The camera cuts to Newt Gingrich. His mouth is opening. He's gasping. Mary McGrory does appear to be an Elton John look-alike. But Mike Wallace is laughing. Well, Imus is giving it to both sides, and he hasn't said anything really terrible—no Paula Jones jokes here, a nod to good taste, since this is a banquet roast. I wonder what anyone thought he would say.

"Do you remember the infamous curbside-shooting photography from the Vietnam War?" Oh, yes, most everyone in the room and a lot of Television Land would remember that: a hangun shot to the head of a Vietcong suspect, a stream of blood spurting from the skull. "Well, I'm watching the *CBS Evening News* one night with Dan Rather and Connie Chung. Things are not going well and I'm thinking, 'We're a couple of nights away from another hideous photograph.' "

128

He's on to his audience, which must be a relief to the Clintons, but their profiles are still rigid, two his-and-her bookends, with Imus as the book.

Dan Rather is laughing, too. He knows laughter is best. From Rather to Brokaw, Imus goes, "By the way, nobody wants us out of Bosnia more than Tom does, simply so he doesn't have to try to pronounce Slobodan Milosevic." Imus has trouble with that infamous name. "Brian Williams is standing in front of the White House thinking, 'I'm two Serb war criminals' names away from having Tom's job.' And then there's Peter Jennings, who we are told more Americans get their news from than anyone else, and a man who freely admits that he cannot resist women. So, I'm thinking, here's Peter Jennings, sitting there each evening—elegant, erudite, refined—and I'm wondering, 'What's under his desk?' I mean, besides an intern."

C-SPAN continues to drift around the audience and with men being the butt of almost all the jokes, I notice a lot more women than men are laughing, though Chuck Robb is laughing at the Jennings/intern remark, looking at Peter Arnett, who doesn't appear quite as amused. Chuck, the politician, likes to have someone else's, some journalist's sexual ox gored, though he's not spared. Spread the blame. But this is definitely a theater of cruelty moment for the crowd. Sam Donaldson's toupee gets tousled. But Donaldson laughs.

"Bernard Shaw and Judy Woodruff round out our network news anchors, and deserve mention only to recognize that Bernie has a greater nut potential than even Dan Rather. If not for CNN, Bernard Shaw is at the post office, marching somebody around at the end of a wire coat hanger and a shotgun."

Will he leave no stone unturned? Appears not.

"Rush may not, as Al Franken suggests, be a big fat idiot, but I'm sick of him." Not my Rush, my main man! "The radio show, the television show, the stupid books, and now men's ties. Bold, vibrant, colorful, and all designed to look great with a brown shirt. What a surprise that Rush is selling something that goes around a person's neck! And Rush didn't date in high school? You're kidding. You mean the varsity cheerleaders weren't falling all over a fat, pig-eyed schmo who looks like a cross between Red Dog and one of those Budweiser frogs? He should be on a beach somewhere in a pair of Bermuda shorts, a Hawaiian shirt, white socks, sandals, holding a metal detector. He couldn't get a date in high school? Maybe they should have had his senior prom at Sea World."

Rush doesn't appear to be in the audience—at least the camera's eye doesn't find him.

"I was in Las Vegas when the news broke that Senator Gramm had financed a porno movie. It was better than having Ed McMahon hand me a check for ten million. The only better news would have been had Senator Gramm actually appeared in a movie. Gramm was fond of saying he was too ugly to be president. Well, that was not his problem. I know he has a Ph.D. in economics, but you can't sound like you just walked out of the woods in *Deliverance* and not scare people."

When Imus finishes, he does get some applause, but the people on the dais stand up quickly and the Clintons leave the stage without acknowledging him, and he seems to be treated by all nearby as an instant pariah.

The Clintons brought this on themselves, like Whitewater, like so much else. It was like a bad high school production of Eugene Ionesco, a play set in hell where they're all trapped in a room and who has the key?

Except for Hillary (and Imus's criticism of her was very mild), Imus only took after the men (Robb, Warner, Gramm, the news guys), which was a show of gallantry for the old, ravaged Lothario.

3/25 Rush is back attacking Perot. "This man is deranged." Sixteen percent still support Perot in the polls. "It's astounding." "Nader doesn't have enough money to make an impact." "Perot-istas waiting to call," he complains. "Bill Clinton is the enemy." He returns to the story of Judge Baer, the Manhattan federal judge who suppressed evidence and a confession from a cocaine bust and said the sight of blacks running away from the police was not necessarily suspicious. Rush would get rid of him, but the judge's family, Rush has learned, are dittoheads. He attacks the prez's press secretary, Mike McCurry; how do we get him to stay on the job? Rush wonders.

Rush gives his take on Imus. "Tasteless." Oh, Rush! I don't want to have to resort to tastelessness, he says. "He only lies about me," Rush states. Stars and important people, Rush says, "by going on the show"—

Imus's show—end up "legitimizing the show." Certain adjustments you have to make. Radio—the sense of hearing. You are using more senses, he says. On the press, Rush says, "They don't care when other people are skewered." Bill Clinton makes Don Imus possible. Clinton told autoworkers about the AstroTurf in the El Camino. Most of what Imus said was true. But, Rush repeats, he lies about me.

Rush is then on to Winnie Mandela beating up Nelson. A worse thing happened to her—his getting out of prison. Sony is Americans' favorite brand. Harris poll. Followed by GE.

Perot is the subject. There's an NBC-WSJ Peter Hart poll. Six out of seven current Perot supporters prefer Clinton to Dole.

That gay marriage is a "San Francisco innovation" is attributed to Rush, in a Friday quote in the *San Francisco Chronicle*. And I was not even here on Friday! Rush complains.

Rush reports that ACORN—a group advocating raising the minimum wage—sued to pay less than the minimum wage to their organizers, so they know what it is like being poor.

Later in the evening on the Oscars (ABC), Robin Williams is wearing insect-wing glasses. An Oscar is given honoring Chuck Jones, the cartoonist/director. Jokes: Forbes is Marion the Martian, Buchanan is Foghorn Leghorn, Gramm is Elmer Fudd. If we could only animate Bob Dole, we'd have an interesting election.

Whoopi Goldberg says the Oscars are younger than Bob Dole (the Oscars are sixty-eight). She gives a funny ribbon monologue (Rush did one on TV a couple of years ago). So many colors, so many potential causes. The little looped ribbon, an infinity symbol sliced open at one end, is now used for a near infinite-spectrum of death-inducing conditions.

Braveheart wins best picture. It's Buchanan's favorite movie. He probably likes the evisceration at the end.

Fashion trend: the celebrity males are wearing colored vests. *Braveheart*'s Mel Gibson is in some reddish Tartan family rag, but most wear the color of foreign money—deutsche marks, francs, etc.

3/26 NPR reviews Whoopi's Oscars ribbon jokes, mentions Jesse Jackson was demonstrating against the lack of adequate black representation in Hollywood at ABC's studios in Burbank, with only 75 protesters.

Lamar! is on with Diane Rehm. He's unburdened himself of his story as a loser in the March 25 issue of *The Weekly Standard*. Like the O.J. juror, Michael Knox, knocked off the jury and quickly publishing a book. Christopher Darden's *In Contempt* (of what? I ask) is reviewed in today's *New York Times*. Darden is the failed O.J. prosecutor, but he's failing upward, as does anyone who appears on national television for a year.

Diane Rehm asks Lamar!: "What would you have done differently?" Not worn that goddamn shirt, I hope—vainly—he would say. "If I was better schooled in how to counteract" negative advertising, he does say, meaning he would have liked to have had better negative ads than his opposition had.

Lamar! raised $18 million in '95. Thirty-five percent of that went to the cost of raising the money. Ten percent went to comply with laws. He had $5.5 million left. Not enough to run for mayor of LA, he says. Oh, well, it'll pay a few bills, I think. The campaign needs more money. Forbes's money had even more effect, since he has no money-raising costs, Lamar! says ruefully.

A woman caller says, wearily, There's been "so much backbiting . . . like little boys." Though she doesn't want to turn off the radio.

A male caller asks: "Why don't we hear about Dole leaving his wife and teenage daughter for a younger woman?" Diane, recognizing his voice, interjects something about the one-call-a-month rule.

Lamar! says about the Dole first marriage: I don't want to comment on that.

Rush says the "media shamelessly sucks up to these people." Meaning the Clintons. In today's newspapers (he's describing Hillary's photos with troops abroad), remember Mrs. Clinton's "No military uniforms in the White House?" I find this obscene, folks, Rush says. Whitewater heats up . . . and you use the military as props. To raise morale? This is strictly for the photo op. Rush recalls the D-day incident, on the beach, when Clinton stooped to turn stones into a cross—there were no stones on the beach, Rush says. They were put there by aides. Oh say can you see it's all a show.

Perot's got no ideas, Rush says. It's true lunacy. You can't tell a whit's difference between the two parties.

On John Sweeney and the AFL-CIO's millions for voter education,

Rush says: It's not about R & D. It's about Democrats. The AFL-CIO is raising dues fifteen cents a month for a $35 million fund. Haley Barbour wants proportional funds.

A woman caller identifies herself as an army brat whose dad did three tours in Vietnam; she's anti-Hillary. Rush says: "No first lady since Mary Todd Lincoln has had such high negative ratings." A conservative believes in conquering the things that get in our way; liberals believe it is government, Rush tells us.

3/28   Today Rush is going on about a book, *Our Stolen Future,* that raises the specter of pollution causing penises to shrink. "I'd rather be extinct," Rush says. Al Gore did the introduction for the book.

On the *NewsHour,* we have the appropriately named Senator Don Nickles (R-Okla.) and Senator Ted Kennedy (D-Mass.) debating a raise in the minimum wage. Kennedy is for it. Nickles argues against: "Why not raise it to ten dollars an hour?" Kennedy doesn't make any reply to his one ludicrous argument. The other is if you raise it, people will lose those first jobs. (Nickles claims he was a janitor, and it appears he still is, cleaning up for the Republican rich.) Kennedy points out that Nickles's minimum wage, back then, was worth more than now. "When Don was working for the minimum wage, it had the value in today's purchasing power of $6.17. Now at $4.25"—Oklahoma's current "minimum" wage—"that's exactly what it was, $1.25 an hour," Kennedy says over Nickles's "No. No. No." "That makes the point. We want to go up to $5.15. I think Don was worth that at that particular time. Beyond that, we're not looking for a maximum wage, we're talking about minimum wage, not a maximum wage, not a medium wage."

Lehrer wants to know about Nickles's claim that jobs will be eliminated.

"Well, we've heard that. Seven times since the end of World War II we've raised it, and that hasn't been the case . . . We've got twelve studies. We'll debate that . . . We're talking about people that do so much of the difficult, hard work of our society. We have seen the United States Senate raise its salary three times since 1991. We've raised ours by thirty thousand dollars, and still we have senators out there that don't even permit a livable wage for hardworking people."

"Senator Nickles," Lehrer says, trying not to sound accusatory.

"Jim, I very much want people on the low-income scale to be able to climb the economic ladder, but what we do by increasing minimum wage, we say if for some reason you can't make $5.15 or something, you can't have a job. And I think that's grossly unfair, and the people it really hurts are people, maybe they're trying to get their first job, they're trying to learn a skill, they're trying to get going, and, and to say, well, wait a minute, it's against the federal law for you to have it, if it pays less than that is serious."

Nickles's face has a prairie look to it, bland, with smooth flaxen hair. (Kennedy looks like old non-Saint Nick.) Though the Republicans are doing the bidding of small business, their stance against raising the minimum wage won't go down with the public, who are choking on news of downsizing, skyrocketing CEO salaries, the rich getting richer and the poor getting poorer. It's a losing issue for them, akin to shutting down the government for the holidays.

Nickles tries to blame it on the AFL-CIO and election year "politics," but people who work know why their employers try to keep their wages as low as possible.

On *Nightline,* we have Farmer Stanton, a neighbor to the Just Us crowd in Montana, telling his side of the neighborhood dispute, the "Freemen" holed up in the spread next to his. And Koppel trots out some Montana sheriff, the embodiment of the virtuous western lawman. Both men are standard American gothic. But the much touted Montana sheriff blames "politicians" for some of Montana's problems, as do the Freemen.

3/29   Rush tells a Hillary joke. "How was the book tour?" "I'm sorry, I don't remember." Then he plays his song parody: "Try to remember." You can do a lot of rhymes with gender in that song. "And my mind in a blender."

SEVEN

The Cruelest Month

★

4/1 I hear the Capitol Steps comedy group on NPR, an April Fools' show: Clinton and Dole: dense and some senility. (A Jane Austen campaign joke.)

There's attempted humor everywhere: on Rush, Perot parodies stream forth in a Perotvian voice: "Secret decoder rings for the Freemen of Montana." Rush does a turn on a homeless story from Santa Cruz, California—they are bused to parks! Rush says, incredulous. "Homeless movement alive and well," he assures us. "You've been April fooled every day of the Clinton administration," he says, in timely fashion. AT&T is supporting nine foreign Olympic teams, Rush says, revealing corporate nationalist hypocrisy. We get more of the Montana Freeman decoding messages from Perot's Dallas headquarters. A caller comments, regarding the Clinton administration: Cream may rise but scum floats. Another caller identifies himself: I am a worship leader in my church. He talks effusively of Rush's neckties. Rush complains that the Gridiron Club dinner plagiarized his "Try to Remember" Hillary/Bill parody. "Mind in a Blender." He's been playing it for a month or so. He reports that at 4:04 P.M. last Friday a blonde wearing a black velvet outfit and white go-go boots was seen (according to the *Washington Times*) entering the West Wing of the White House. The marines saluted. Who is she? Rush is mesmerized by the vision. Hillary is in Bosnia, Turkey, Greece, "wherever she is," he informs us.

4/2 Morning news: Baseball has more problems. On Opening Day an umpire (John McSherry) dropped dead in the first inning of a game. (In Cincinnati: I presume Marge wanted to *play ball* anyway.) But federal judge Harold Baer reverses himself and says all that cocaine can be evidence in the New York case that has provoked Rush and so many others. The Montana Freemen are continuing their holdout. The Freemen are adopting noncooperation tactics. What if you gave a war and nobody came? So much of the eighties and nineties has been a mockery of Left rhetoric and union tactics: You can't fire everybody. Oh, yes you can: PATCO, the *Detroit News* strike.

Diane Rehm's show is talking about judges. Republican judges. The one who fired Fiske, Special Prosecutor Starr's predecessor, overturned the convictions of Ollie North, Admiral Poindexter, and Al D'Amato's brother, a real hat trick.

Rush is speaking against raising the minimum wage. Godfather Pizza will have to charge more for its pizzas. Clinton raises your prices twenty-five cents. Sheila, a Portland, Oregon, restaurant owner, is on the line: We won't give them (her employees) raises as quickly, she says. Her employees are seventeen and eighteen—these are kids who can barely drive and can't read or write, Sheila confides to Rush's radio audience. Rush says the minimum wage is a class-envy problem. (Sheila seems to have her own view of her employees' class.) Last year in *Time* magazine, Rush says, Bill Clinton said it was the wrong way to raise low-income workers' wages. Rush speaks against Christian bashing. Dole is pictured on a cross in a *Los Angles Times* cartoon, the Christian Coalition written across a crown of thorns. "Try it with any other religion," Rush says darkly. He's onto the AFL-CIO dues issue. "Your guy is Buchanan." The AFL-CIO is loyal to the Democratic Party. "It was the government employees who stood by" and let the government shutdown happen, he says, quoting a *Washington Times* weekly edition article. The federal employees union launched a "whatever it takes to defeat the Republicans" PR campaign. "These people caused the shutdowns," Rush says. The shutdown was a ploy, it was a plan. "Internal documents" reveal all. Seven hundred thousand government employees mentioned in an August 8 document. Contingency plans for layoffs. It urged Clinton to stand fast. He cuts to a commercial for his favorite brand of salsa. Rush is forty-five years old. Rush's generation has gone from ketchup to salsa, as the local Key Bank ad notes.

4/3 On Rush, a female caller is complaining about a *New York Times* story yesterday about Dole, in Florida, getting a table while "a starving American family," Rush supplies, had to wait two and a half hours. The woman says, You wonder about their brain power, if they can't see why someone who is a presidential contender should get a table immediately.

David Hale and the Arkansas Whitewater trial of Governor Jim Guy Tucker is the topic. Hale is Prosecutor Starr's star witness. Rush says the mainstream media say Hale's a liar, a liar, a liar. The *New York Times,* ABC, CNN, Rush says, all of them. Rush uses such presumptions as proof of the mainstream media's liberal bias.

An El Salvador interlude: a friend reports the social fabric is breaking down. The rich spend their time shopping in many-storied indoor malls, nannies watching kids while matrons shop till they drop. There are murders of various sorts. Free-enterprise killing, rather than state killing. Though there is some of that. Veterans protesting. The police shotgunned a guy and the film of it was shown over and over on TV. The man was a government army veteran, not a rebel vet. The bishop supports the police, says it's hard to keep order. The new bishop is the former chaplain of the National Guard; high black boots, uniform, cross on his chest. Money coming from the States in drips and drops. If it was from the IMF, they could build factories; as it is, it just keeps people (and the economy) limping along.

4/4 On NPR's *Morning Edition* there's news of commerce secretary Ron Brown's death, the Unabomber, and religious pieces because of Easter. Brown and thirty-four others on a tour to promote U.S. business were killed when a military transport crashed into a mountain near an airport in Croatia. Nina Totenberg talks about the Unabomber, the "her-mit on the hill," as his neighbors called him—see *Columbia Journalism Review*'s article on plagiarism (July/August '95). Totenberg, like Ruth Shalit and others, has had her brush with that problem. It's clear that the FBI should have been looking for every Harvard grad living like a recluse, for anyone who doesn't contribute to the big H's alumni fund, every Ph.D. living alone in Montana.

There's a BBC report about a novel Shroud of Turin theory: it was caused by a nuclear explosion. There's a brown imprint of a man on the shroud. More Easter-related stories follow.

The Charles Keating state trial verdict has been overturned. Lance Ito was the judge in the state trial. Improper jury instructions. Way to go Lance! And the judge who overturned Lance's decision did the Rodney King trial, and was criticized for light sentences for white cops. Keating is still in jail (four years so far) on federal charges.

Rush: Last week the Republicans wanted to close the Commerce Department. If there's still a desire to close the Commerce Department, say, since Ron Brown was "the greatest commerce secretary ever," Rush says, quoting remarks of a Brown acquaintance after his sudden death, let's close it with "honor, dignity" in Brown's honor. Rush is objecting to all the folks calling Brown the "greatest," etc.

Then it's Ted Kennedy, the minimum wage. Kennedy talks about "working families," as if he knows anything about them, Rush says indignantly. "If you can find anyone who's worked at minimum wage for thirty-five years, produce them," he challenges his audience. And they fault Bob Dole for the raise in salary he's gotten, Rush says. There are 110,360,000 people employed. Sixteen million are in unions. Four million receive minimum wage. And they make up 18.2 percent of the workforce. "These are working families," Rush reminds us. "Attempting to divide this country with class warfare," Rush says; "this bugs me, folks." Especially "attacking achievement." He sniffs at the idea of a third party. "The lock-and-loaded crew."

The more I listen to Rush the more I think Imus was being kind to Clinton. Imus must be surprised (though pleased) at all the self-righteous attacks flying in his direction. On the subject of Bill and Hillary, he was actually quite . . . delicate; it was his radio and television colleagues he was hardest on, ready to blurt out all their secrets.

Campaign America '96: The View From the Couch

A caller says Rush (on TV) supported the recent beating of the immigrants that got videotaped in California. (A pickup truck full of people fled, and when it finally stopped, the upset cops beat the folks in the truck's cab, one of them a woman.) They got a blank check, the caller says, and lists the cost to taxpayers over such suits: $1 million in Minnesota, $5 million to Rodney King. Rush says: "It's going to set the stage for some antiimmigration demagoguery."

Then, on the Unabomber, Rush instructs, I want everyone on this program to refer to him as "that left-wing nut Unabomber."

It strikes me that Rush and L. Ron Hubbard have a lot in common—their books, their middlebrowness, etc.—but Rush isn't a real fanatic, though he's trying to talk himself into it.

On the phone I discuss campaign press coverage with an East Coast reporter: the big thrill for a lot of print reporters is getting to stand close to Tabitha Soren, MTV's newsperson. Check out the happy faces in last week's *TV Guide*.

The print people are complaining about the appalling amount of TV people; it's almost impossible for a print reporter to work—every bozo TV station sends their guy for some short bit of video. It's been getting worse since 1988 to 1992 and now is peaking in '96.

It's a pity about Dole, "his failure to connect" groups are wired up, not randomly selected. World War II falls into a netherworld. It isn't yet history, people are still alive, but it has none of the immediacy of Vietnam, the visceral quality. Dole and Bush have the same rhetorical style, are very similar overall. What do they believe in? What they believed at nineteen. They took it for granted "to get the job done and come home." Having a vision (see drugs, etc.) is embedded in Clinton's generation, not Dole's. Their competence, the competence of the generation—for all his flaws, that is what Dole can do. Competence. Getting bills passed, etc. Bush was the same way: "The submarine picked me up out of the sea." Liddy Dole should hold up Dole's arm: "Isn't this enough!?"

Bob Kerrey's leg wasn't, I suggest. Some press people who voted for Clinton in '92 will vote for Dole. Even a Boston Democrat. The Democrats have had a series of state governors (Carter to '88's Dukakis to Bill Clinton) taking them to the middle. Republican governor/presidents take them elsewhere. Some reporters have come to hate Clinton. They can't stand to hear him so willing to lie to whatever audience he is with to gain their approval. Competence. Clinton's lack of it. Running the White House. The World War II generation's habit of living in modest houses. Of course, that generation doesn't have an answer. But Clinton *needs* an answer, since his life didn't prove it, provide one, exemplify it, as Dole's generation's did.

I learn, regarding *Primary Colors,* that Joe Klein ghost wrote an Oleg Cassini autobiography in the eighties. That explains the "creweled" business, all the fashion talk. In Washington, no one writes their own books, my friend says. Why do they think Stephanopoulos could have written *Primary Colors?* Politicians just lie to reporters. Dole often comes closer to the truth. But my friend is voting for Clinton, to atone for voting for Anderson in the Carter/Reagan election.

I think that Prosecutor Starr will say, now that he is defending tobacco companies, if you're a lawyer you have to work for tobacco companies, just as Hillary said in '92 that if you're a lawyer, you have to work for banks.

I've been watching Peggy Noonan's TV show on lofty subjects, goodness, etc., à la Bill Moyers, on PBS. Noonan attempts to appear reflective in the cutaways, instead of looking just generally pissed off, skeptical, and flummoxed, her usual expressions. Coincidentally, a priest told me a joke today. What's the symptom of Irish Alzheimer's? Answer: You can't remember anything except your grudges.

4/5 On Diane Rehm, Morton Kondracke is saying reporters are citizens first, reporters second—don't even begin to apologize, he finishes, talking about how CBS, because it was about to break the Unabomber story, "pushed" the FBI to take the Unabomber prematurely.

Rush says the Unabomber was crushed by computers. He (allegedly Theodore Kaczynski) was, according to Rush, an associate professor at UC Berkeley. He thought he was on top of the world. Then computers came along. He had worked out his math problems in his head, on paper. (I'm following Rush's logic.) Point is, he became obsolete, according to Rush. Computers—kaboom!

Rush does a Montana Tourist Board spoof, honoring the Freeman. "If you're the nutcase leader . . . come on in . . . to Montana."

All of Rush's attacks have put me in mind of all the ceremony attendant upon Ron Brown's death and then back to the Oklahoma City bombing, how that national mourning helped purify Clinton. The death president. Clinton's crucible. Mourning Becomes Him.

Back to Rush. He calls the mainstream media IRT: Instant Response Team. He's talking about how fraudulent Democratic ads are. Everything in the Willie Horton ad was true, he says. He talks about a CNN report: Brooks Jackson on ads. Are the Medicare cuts final? Eighty-five million dollars under Republicans, 59 million under Clinton. Rush claims 20 million listeners. Rush reads excerpts from a recent P. J. O'Rourke (no relation, as the saying goes) *Rolling Stone* article (April 18). It is an attack on Buchanan, since Pat is "a big government guy." Rush finds it somewhat extreme, uncomfortable with P. J.'s imputation of anti-Semitism to Buchanan. ("Somebody, probably with a *stein* on the end of his name, must be hoarding the cash.") Rush doesn't seem to catch the article's tone. P. J. wants to expel Buchanan from the party because "conservatism means belief in the free market." Not just beer-hall anti-Semitism.

4/6 I catch a rebroadcast of March 30, 1996, on C-SPAN. It's a roast of Carville. Matalin is there, Stephanopoulos, etc. It's really weird, C-SPAN doing its Peeping Tom number. The event is held at Carville's alma mater, I think, LSU. Carville is always claiming to be a man of the people, which, I suppose, he is, as long as the people come from a town (however small) that's named after your family. Being a lawyer and a marine usually takes you a wee bit away from being one of the people, but in the South, who knows? He does have a Lee Atwood streak in him (a frat boy raking an electric guitar), which is doubtless what caught Miss Matalin's eye, since Atwood seems to have been an unresolved romantic star in her cosmology. Good old boys with law degrees, just what the world needs more of. But Carville appears plastered and invites a woman up to the stage, an old girlfriend who has been recently battling cancer. This affair seems to be a benefit for a medical school. So we have the spectacle of Matalin and Carville's old girlfriend (not looking that old) bookending him, and Carville wearing a silly drink-enhanced grin, looking like one happy fella, his past and his present both under an arm.

Finishing up, he wants everyone to sing "God Bless America," Kate Smith style, and neither Matalin nor the girlfriend wants to, but because he's the guest of honor he leads a sodden rendition of the tune, sung with great reluctance by those assembled. Weirdness.

4/7 It's Easter and the *New York Times*'s "Week in Review" section has a Ron Brown article, where he's described as coming "from the middle class." His father managed a famous Harlem hotel. It's still hard to admit, it appears, that individuals who are more than "middle" class get ahead in the world. Everyone wants to have bootstraps, be of the people. Brown, Carville, just regular guys. Clinton, at least, has strains of class ambiguity, but growing up in Hot Springs everyone was, by association, a member of the leisure class.

The *Chicago Tribune* runs a lot of Easter material, including a story on Guatemala, Nicaragua, and El Salvador. Catholic Central America gets only seasonal play now. The article concludes that the only ones benefiting from the World Bank's policies in El Salvador are "the Salvadoran rich."

On *This Week with David Brinkley* there was a Merrill Lynch commercial singing the praises of privatization in foreign countries. These ads are propaganda first, sales second.

4/8 *Nightline* does a show on Serb atrocities in the former Yugoslavia. Liberalism is limping along because of the toll of this new version of war in the Balkans—atrocities of all sorts. After Communism's fall we have the domino theory really at work, and its ugliness has made everyone despair of human beings' capacity for betterment. A recent issue of *Lingua Franca* (March/April) did an article on a former Nazi (Hans Schneider) who became a famous scholar—which comes to mind because the author of the "bad German" book (*Hitler's Willing Executioners*) will appear on Diane Rehm tomorrow and was being advertised today. I kept wondering who thought the typical German wasn't culpable in the conduct of the Holocaust. Then in the evening, the TV parades shows like *COPS, Unsolved Mysteries,* etc., which continues to generate an atmosphere of constant crime—realism/conservatism—better than Hoover's G-men shows.

Bill Maher, the comedian, is on with Charlie Rose talking about Imus—"Not before a married couple," he says, of Imus's jokes. Even Maher is taking on the role of genteel Imus critic. Thinking again of the Imus speech, I recall that the last time I saw Roger Clinton was a shot of him among the swells at the *Barbra Streisand Live* broadcast.

Charlie Rose also interviews Larry King, who slips into momentary candor: King says he doesn't want to know any more than his audience. (Rose had asked if he reads the books of guests or otherwise prepares.) "Why prepare if you don't have to?" Both TV interviewers share a non-private, private laugh.

Buchanan more and more looks like Peter Boyle, the actor who played Frankenstein in the Mel Brooks film, especially in profile and the back of his head.

I catch Garrison Keillor's (the show originally aired on the fifth) opening monologue defending the Clintons: 25 million spent on Whitewater committees, "which showed that the Clintons weren't very good at making money." Keillor is the Will Rogers of the late twentieth century.

4/9 Diane Rehm has on Daniel Goldhagen, the author of the "bad Germans" book, *Hitler's Willing Executioners*. All of this seems somewhat inoculating, an antidote to Buchanan and the Freemen.

Rush is saying Berkeley, California, caused the Unabomber. That's what they say about right-wing organizations, he says. That talk radio causes hate crimes. That he had caused Oklahoma City. A caller objects to how Rush uses the word "union": "union" is a dirty word, he says, the way Rush says it. Rush says he means union management luxuriating in Bal Harbour. I am a union member, he says, then adds, everyone should be in a right-to-work state.

Al Sharpton has published his autobiography (with Tony Walton, whom I knew when he was a student at Notre Dame), *Go and Tell the Pharaoh*. One provocative thing is that Sharpton is only forty-one and that Al D'Amato, the chief benefactor of Sharpton's run for senator in the '92 New York Democratic primary, is hardly mentioned. The Tawana Brawley case that will forever be linked with Sharpton was one of the forerunners of the O.J. case. Tawana Brawley's lurid story of abduction and rape was disbelieved by whites, whereas many blacks chose not to disbelieve it (or the rough outlines of it), as the O. J. jury decided not to believe the prosecution's lurid story of O. J.'s killing his wife and Ron Goldman, or not believe it in the way the law requires. (The largely African American female O. J. jury seemed to side with white male economists and take the "luxury mammal" route and give O. J. his one freebie, plus one low-earner white male.) The luridness in both cases helped. O. J. never appeared to live in a lurid world; the history of rape and imprisonment of black women by law-enforcement types was sufficiently lurid to lend credence to Brawley's tale—with a little help from her friends, in this case, Al Sharpton.

Leslie Abramson, the Menendez brothers' attorney, is back in the news, not just on the news, since a shrink says he edited his notes of interviews with the murderous boys at her request. Abramson and Sharpton, and others, are lion-tamer celebrities: put your head in the mouth of the most sensational lion you can find and you get to boast about it. The more lurid (see above) the associations, the better.

Dick Wolf, the television producer, might have been after two half-hour programs when he created *Law & Order,* NBC's long-running show, but it caught on as a one-hour, since the public is interested these days in the inside as well as the outside. Exposure passes for depth in our culture. *Court TV*, etc., profited from O. J. and O. J. continues to be a capital generator, though not so much for himself these days. Most everything is on TV now and that is why debates about having executions shown have moved toward the margin of the possible, if not the probable—Ruby shooting Oswald was one of the earliest snuff films, live for TV. The only videotaping at Harrisburg in '72 during the conspiracy trial that was going on, beyond the snippets of news spots, was the FBI/CIA/NSA videotaping the various protests and crowds. There was a tall guy in a brown suit and cowboy boots who looked comically like your intelligence-service adventurer wielding a camcorder.

Rush says he's responsible for 80 percent of the discussions on on-line services. The Unabomber news provides Rush with spin-offs. Environmental wackos are anticapitalist, anti-American, neocommunist. An *Earth First!* publication read by the Unabomber is called by the *Washington Post* an "outspoken environmental" journal. Rush objects to outspoken. It shows bias. *He's* never referred to as "outspoken." Here we have Earth First! being responsible for the Unabomber picking out a victim, he says. "If it was a right wing—it would be an attack on the right wing."

Dittos from a caller: I could say that I'm your friend, I've tuned in since '84. You "cause me to think," but I'm not such a clear thinker, he says.

The Montana tourism spoof plays again. "Charlie Manson, Ted Bundy, Jimmy Hoffa, and those who couldn't follow a law if you wrote it yourself come on in to Montana—and we'll find you soon." Buy more Loreado and Lefty salsa. Rush says the Clintons approved *Primary Colors*. Rush's second book sold 2 million in six weeks, but was left off some best-seller lists. "A big mystery," best-seller lists, Rush says.

A woman caller suggests Rush endow a chair in memory of his newly dead grandfather. Rush seems stunned, never having considered it. Rush gives a reason to vote for Clinton: "He handles death in his administration well." He refers to a Richard Cohen column in the *Washington Post*. Clinton seems more a "custodial figure" with all the dead around him, according to Cohen. Clinton "should have a bucket and a mop; no offense to janitors," Rush says. They are slouching toward my Mourning Becomes Him notion.

4/10 Rush is talking about Dan Rostenkowski, the ex-congressman. His picture is in the *Washington Post*. He looks like a "Web Hubbell clone," Rush says. Robert Bennett got him a six-month deal and Rostenkowski fired him, Rush says. Now he's got seventeen months, two counts, one hundred grand. These are the guys raising your taxes, Rush says.

Speaking of photos of Rostenkowski, my favorite was one I saw about ten years ago of Dan on a mob-linked golf course out in the Southwest. Democrats at play in the fields of the Mafia.

Rush is back on the minimum wage, just an entry-level, no-skill wage. He's still going on about Clinton wanting to raise Godfather Pizza prices twenty-five cents.

Does Rush have stock in Godfather Pizza? I wonder. Don't you think they would have raised the price if they could have? One of the things that hasn't gone up in price is a lot of prole fast food, because of burger wars and price point limits and oversupply. And the price of beer. There's very cheap beer and now very expensive beer, to serve the diverging markets. If Buchanan wants a pitchfork brigade, just let the price of beer, burgers, and pizza really rise. You can't lease a cheeseburger, rent-to-own French fries.

4/12   On Diane Rehm the talk is about Justice Scalia's speech in Jackson, Mississippi, about religion and cultural decline. Scalia sees disrespect for religion everywhere. Jack Nelson says there's no contempt for religion among journalists that he has detected, Scalia's comments notwithstanding. Scalia led clergy in giving public schools prayers, Nelson says. A Baptist church caller says there is no "Christian antidefamation league." The media are not against religion as much as they push some religions. Jews, the caller means. The caller is explicit about one thing: The media are against "Christians." He claims "your panelists seem to miss the point."

Christianity is the majority religion, Rehm's woman reporter guest says.

Nelson says, apropos the state funeral for Ron Brown: Republicans didn't show any respect for Brown's death. No leading Republicans were there, he notes, except for a couple of moderates. Bill Clinton called it "an interminable week." Clinton is "extremely sincere, extraordinary." Of some 18,000 stories, only 265 dealt with religion, says a caller, the conservative activist Brent Bozell of the organization Media Watch.

They move on to another somehow pertinent event, another plane death—not the military going down in bad weather at an ill-equipped Croatian airport, which killed Brown, but the crash of the seven-year-old girl pilot, Jessica Debroff, she of the pink "Women Fly" cap. Jack pronounces the comments of Jessica's mother "weird." I don't want my children to die, he says. Debroff's mother is reported saying, "She died in joy, what more could you ask?" I don't understand, Jack says. Well, a lot of people profess to understand. Whatever it shows about our contemporary culture, it certainly is in the long American tradition of the freakish hero, from Lucky Lindy to whomever gets shot out of a cannon. Since age and precocity and genius are linked, the bar continues to be lowered. Younger kids in medical schools, younger kids behind a plane's controls. Mom and Dad are a newer version of stage parents, where all the world is a stage. It's our present-day niche-ification and it points out that the niche you might fill is a grave.

A male caller wants to return to a more adult-oriented death: Bill Clinton has politicized Ron Brown's funeral, it is claimed. Doubtless a Rush listener. A woman caller defends Justice Scalia, saying she doesn't like the "tone" of the remarks made by the journalists.

Rush, later, says liberals can't afford to be themselves. Only the Unabomber can be himself.

Some "acting performance," he says, characterizing Clinton's demeanor at the Ron Brown ceremony. He's been showing a news clip on his TV show of the instant tears Clinton produces, he says. They don't think it's news, Rush says, about the larger media, which won't rerun it. How great Clinton is when people die. Rush says Clinton has agreed to appear in a film. Clinton's "too busy to testify in Arkansas, too busy to deal with Paula Jones's suit, but not too busy to be in a movie." Imagine if Reagan did this? he asks, as if Reagan appearing in a film would be strange. Rush saying he was blamed for Oklahoma City by Clinton— Clnton backtracked, but the damage was done.

Rush is pro–Mary Matalin. "Mrs. Carville." You don't hear "Mr. Matalin," he says. There's talk of her coming on to the Dole campaign. Rush says Dole will get eighty hours a week for free if she does.

Rush continues to be happy, and why wouldn't he be? Overachievers often are. "Big Fat Idiots," as the Franken book's title calls him (in the singular), and Imus repeated in his Radio and Television Correspondents speech, who finally wildly succeed have reason to be happy. What Rush retains—part, if not all, of his charm—is a con man's genuine enthusiasm about his success. If I can, anybody can! He believes it. I don't doubt him. You see it emanating from most of the infomercial get-rich hustlers on television, but since they themselves are not entirely convinced (they *pay* to be on TV), they are not as convincing as Rush. He's paid to proclaim on the Excellence in Broadcasting Network. (Rush, if nothing else, has seen the fiery finger writing on the wall of the late twentieth century: *You are what you say you are,* so it's the "Excellence in Broadcasting Network.")

Rush on TV is more of a problem. The *Frontline* tele-bio on him showed tape of the audience rebellion on his brief appearance as a late-night network television talk person. Hostile audience questions undid him and there was the extraordinary scene of him sitting in front of empty studio seats explaining why they had been cleared. So his television-show audience is screened, as is the radio show's. You can disappear people on radio with a touch of a button, but a TV audience just sits there. Rush, it appears, often finishes dressing down people as if they're still on the phone, but they've already been cut off. Talk radio, with its delays and cutoffs, does allow you to control your universe.

And if you screen your TV audience, limit it to supporters and fans, dittoheads, it's a more comfortable world. Sort of like the Hugh Hefner late-night TV show of long ago, Hugh in a bathrobe or whatever (as Bob Dole would say), welcoming you to his pad for his hip televised party. Hey, there's Sammy!

But restricting admittees does produce odd audiences, because you are giving the viewers a weird demographic slice. So when I used to watch Rush's show when it appeared locally late in the evening (and these days much less, since it appears at 5 A.M.), I stare at his small studio audience and am amazed. If I had heeded my mother's most often given bit of advice—If you can't say something nice about somebody, don't say anything at all—I never would have picked up a pen. And looking at the Limbaugh television audience does tax my niceness governor.

Rush is in the great American tradition of middlebrow heroes. He's George Babbitt with an attitude. He gives aid and comfort to the nonelite, a rather large group out there. Validation. You need successes to do that. *I think like you do and I'm a millionaire.* It's reassuring.

And you see the nonelite in his television-studio audience. The clothes they wear, the colors they choose, their look! It wouldn't be so obvious if Rush let in more of a cross section. But if you get your crowd, things stand out. When I went to my first MLA conference, I was shocked to be in the midst of my demographic group. If tweed were an endangered species, we'd all have been under arrest. I had never been among so many of my "peers," my crowd. Frightening. Well, Rush's TV crowd is scary, too.

They are not unattractive Americans, but not particularly attractive, either. Given Rush's girth and visage, good looks is not a prerequisite for dittoheads. Again, it's not odd unless you gather a whole lot of this one type together.

Traveling across the country, we once ended up at a Holiday Inn, and late at night I saw identical twins in the hallway. I didn't think it strange; the next morning my wife, son, and I discovered we had stumbled upon an identical twins convention, in Twinburg, Ohio, no less, and we were the decided minority. (Ours was a room with one double bed, obviously left untaken by budget-minded twins—this was just a sibling gathering, no spouses in attendance.)

Seeing a couple hundred identical twins (in really distinctive matching clothing to boot) is a disorienting experience. Watching Rush's audience creates the same feeling.

Because they are neither bad-looking nor good-looking, one studies the faces for the reason why. The features aren't quite right, or completely harmonious; something is off about the shape of the face, the eyes are small when the nose is shapely, or the mouth is pinched if the brow is noble. Just regular folks, in their dressed-up-for-church look, though the color spectrum isn't earth tones.

What the audience looks like, I finally see, is a collection of clone experiments gone a little awry. Everybody is off standard just a bit; one thing was developed a bit more or less than it should have been, or was taken out too soon, or left in too late.

It is the great middle, in a way, neither ugly nor beautiful, neither dumb nor brilliant, neither fleet nor halt, just Rush's audience, giving their hero standing ovations, day after day, night after night. I will have to rise and shine to see the clip of Clinton laughing then crying he's talking about.

Fresh Air, on NPR, with Terri Gross, repeats a Richard Ford interview of last year. Ford has just won the Pulitzer Prize for his novel, *Independence Day*. It appears a Ford relative managed a Little Rock hotel and Ford comments on the general "licentiousness" of the place. He'd find the governor (not Bill!) where he shouldn't be, the head of the state troopers, as he delivered room service. Ford's father died at sixteen. He has no kids. He was a shoplifter. The interview, strangely, makes no mention at all of Clinton, though their Arkansas connection isn't that common.

Steve Forbes is on *Saturday Night Live*. The comedy of the Steve Forbes candidacy that was implicit now becomes explicit. The only skit with any imagination is Forbes's impersonation of a blue-collar roofer. Forbes is into it more than the other skits. Perhaps it is the blue-collar drag (wig, a headband, etc.) that loosens him up. Upper-class high jinks in the theater (blue bloods in women's clothes), or he's used to going to masked balls like his dad. In the last skit of the show, Forbes makes the remark, "Isn't it bizarre? Yes, three weeks ago I was running for president, now I'm on TV talking to a guy in a bug suit."

Trouble is, it isn't bizarre.

4/14 The *New York Times Book Review* is featuring affirmative action, which brings up the subject of Clarence Thomas, though he's not mentioned in Paul Berman's review of the three books under inspection: *In Defense of Affirmative Action*, by Barbara Bergmann, *Ending Affirmative Action*, by Terry Eastland, *The Affirmative Action Fraud*, by Clint Bolick. You can tell these books by their titles. Those who wish to end affirmative action are always shy about whether there were reasons to start it. Conservatives who think these times are bad look to the good old days for solace; I suppose how one comes down on this question matters: are we better off today than we were forty years ago, meaning, Is America healthier? The answer is a tentative yes. Our lip service is better, even if injustices persist. As physicians say, we no longer have the disease, we have the cure.

Justice Thomas, it appears, thinks affirmative action is insulting to blacks, and he's right—blacks like him who have risen above reason like himself. Such a rapid rise sows self-doubt. It should. Thomas now wants to abolish the laws that let him become a Supreme Court justice, preferential treatment. All things being equal, he would have been some mediocre lawyer somewhere doing good, or ill, however it fell out. Instead, he rose as a right-wing Republican of his race. There are a lot of mediocre lawyers like himself, but he gets to be on the Supreme Court. But a number of white mediocrities have risen (at least to nomination): the Carswell and Haynsworth flap of Nixon's era. Genius is often hard to hold back. It is in the arena of the so-so that the most injustices are noticed. So and so gets published and promoted and a dozen other writers can rightly claim they are as good, but overlooked. Affirmative action is inflation, American dollars after World War II. Thomas is a prime example, and it might add to his self-loathing, but he has an excess of that already, it appears. I profited from affirmative action, as did a lot of my generation, especially Bill Clinton. It opened up the world and let some white boys without the proper class backgrounds slip through, too.

And, on affirmative action, Mary Matalin has withdrawn from her possible service to the Dole campaign: too much flak coming from the too faithful.

One lasting result of the O. J. trial is that we now can see a lot of black lawyers on TV. The chief result of the Vietnam War is the large Vietnamese immigrant population in the United States.

George Will, on *This Week with David Brinkley*, is speaking out against raising the minimum wage. Why not raise it to ten dollars an hour? Who's he parroting? Rush? A GOP fax? Senator Nickles?

4/15   I've come to hear P. J. O'Rourke, the best-selling *National Lampoon* alum, and Michael Moore, the filmmaker, famous for *Roger & Me*, debate the state of the union, under the auspices of Notre Dame's student union. P. J. and I have never crossed paths, though we had mutual friends in New York City when he was an editor at the *National Lampoon* and I was a starving artist living in Greenwich Village. I had published two books, but was leading an economically immature existence, to say the least. So in the early seventies I was, briefly, the literary O'Rourke, but I was not particularly surprised, from what I had heard about P. J., to watch his rise in the world. It more or less coincided with the Reagan eighties. P. J. went to the top and I went to . . . South Bend, Indiana. To the University of Notre Dame. I had always thought my life reflected the upheavals of my generation, so I had persuaded myself, when I accepted the job, that it wasn't so odd, at the beginning of the Reagan era, to go out to the start of it all, so to speak, the launching site of the Gipper.

But P. J. was obviously not as delusional as I was and saw which side his bread was buttered on, and he joined, if he didn't help spearhead, the Right's "intellectual" ascendancy.

Or, at least, the Greed Decade's acquisitional impulses. The literary world is not famously empty of such impulses. But, like with most best-selling authors, you have to tell the culture what it wants to hear if you want it to listen, and P. J. caught the right tone. He, in a number of ways, took the baton from the older Tom Wolfe, a conservative mind in a dandy's clothing.

So when P. J. finally arrived on stage, I couldn't help but note that P. J. does for the preppie-yuppie blue blazer and khaki pants what Tom Wolfe did for the white suit: he has certified it as the costume of the new aesthete, eighties-nineties style.

The show is supposed to start at 7:30, but the stage is empty and the building isn't full either. The crowd is smaller than I had expected, and there appear to be a lot of non–Notre Damers in attendance, high-school kids and townies.

Word finally comes that we are waiting on Moore. He is late. But his plane (not *his* plane, I presume) has landed and he will be here soon. They will bring on P. J. first and let him start. A high schooler says to a friend, "He's the one we've come to hear, anyway."

P. J. will give his opening statement, we're told. But nothing happens for another ten minutes. There is a "backstage" commotion and the stage fills up. It's 8:10 and both of them appear.

Moore is in a costume also, the working-class-whatever look—baggy pants, something that looks like a sweatshirt, and his trademark baseball cap, this time one with an MTV (yea, Tabitha!) logo on it. People who become public figures usually have signature outfits; it reinforces brand identification, and both P. J. and Moore are name brands—at least to a small demographic slice, some of them long cooling their heels here in the Stepan Center.

One thing is obvious from their opening statements: P. J. is well pre-pared. His text has been worked out. (He begins: "I am myself a child of the sixties; it was a decade without quality control.") Moore is just winging it. Unfortunately, this reflects their clothing. P. J. is tightly put together, whereas Moore is way beyond relaxed.

P. J. tells us, "This is actually an optimistic moment in history. . . . We no longer live in grave danger of atomic war . . . that would annihilate humanity and otherwise upset everyone's weekend plans. . . . The Soviet Union has fallen apart. . . . It's nothing but a space on the map full of quarreling nationalities with too many Ks and Zs in their names, armed Scrabble contestants. . . . The other great malevolent regime, Red China, has decided on conquest of the world flip-flop market, its form of global domination. . . . Things are better now than since mankind has been keeping track of things. . . . Life is better than it ever has been. . . . Think about King Arthur's dentist. . . . We should be enjoying ourselves and we are not. . . . I hear America whining."

It's Moore's turn: "Anyways, I'm going to whine for about ten minutes here." Clapping. "Last night my parents called me from Flint to tell me . . . GM announced it was going to close another factory in Flint, another three thousand people out of work. . . . How can a company that made seven billion in profits last year close a factory and throw three thousand people out of work? The bottom line . . . business exists to please their shareholders. . . . A few years ago they made three billion, then four, then five. . . . How much money is enough? Is it ever enough? If you're Robert Allen, the chairman at AT&T, and you announce you will eliminate forty thousand jobs, Wall Street likes that. He personally became five million dollars richer forty-eight hours after making that announcement. Should it be legal for General Motors to close a factory in Flint and move it to Mexico? Why don't we say it's legal for General Motors to sell crack? . . . You could show a nice healthy return to your investors if you sell crack. Why is it illegal? . . . As a society we have decided it is immoral. It destroys inner cities, it is not good to have a population on crack. We don't want crack houses on our street. We make it illegal. Why do we allow a corporation to close down a factory and destroy a town and destroy the lives of tens of thousands of people? Why isn't that illegal? . . . Why aren't we up in arms about that? After twelve years of Reagan and Bush, people have had a pretty rough go of it. . . . We are, what, three miles from Michigan, the state which has fifty militia groups, the most militia groups anywhere in the country. . . . It is pretty easy to manipulate people who are hurting . . . and to offer simple solutions, . . . and it is the miserable failure of the Left that they don't have a single answer for the people who live in the Flint, Michigans, of America. . . . I hate liberals, they're whiners, weenies, . . . they have done more to hold up progress more than any conservative group in this country. . . . They want to vote for someone who believes in what they are saying. . . . What does Evan Bayh believe in? . . . Everyone knows who Bob Dole is, the Republican leader. Can you tell me who is the Democratic leader for our side, the liberals, in the Congress? A third of the crowd. Tom Daschle, there's a name for you. . . . The good news is that Americans didn't vote in ninety-four. . . . Sixty percent of them didn't show up at the polls. . . . Gingrich, and the Gingrich Republicans, got in with 21 percent of the vote and it's a 'landslide'—it's not a landslide, it's a cult. . . . The real whiners are corporate America, they are the biggest whiners, the biggest welfare mothers we have in this society. Alabama comes up with two hundred million dollars in tax incentives so Mercedes, one of the richest companies in the world, can build a factory there. . . . That's welfare, though it's not how we see welfare. If Clinton had balls, I'd feel like a man. . . . I'd like Bob Dole to take that pen out of his hand. . . . We live in a more enlightened time. . . . You don't have to have a prop there. . . . We are proud of what you did in World War II. . . . We love you for it. . . . If you feel like you need a prop, why a pen, Bob, you are not a writer. . . . You want to repeal the ban on assault weapons, a more appropriate prop would be an Uzi, Bob, an Uzi. . . . You'll support a constitutional amendment banning abortions, a coat hanger, Bob, a coat hanger."

P.J.'s opening address was nearly a half hour long, Moore spoke for about ten minutes, but what is manifestly apparent is the familiar distinction between optimism and pessimism their opening statements highlighted. At the heart of that conflict is action and inaction. P.J., like Rush, is on the winning side, whereas Moore is on the losing side. P.J. has the fresh energy of going forward; Moore is expending energy on holding back.

There's another critical difference between P.J. and Moore. P.J. is in the grand tradition of American reinvention and Moore is locked into the traditional (who is the conservative then?): Moore doggedly holds on to who he is (and was) and that often looks more charming when you're young than old (picture, say, Mick Jagger hoping around a stage in his sixties in the same outfits he wore in his twenties). But P.J. has reinvented himself, as a lot of American strivers have over the decades; it bespeaks ambition and a sense of self as something to both improve and leave behind. It's one version of the immigrant dream: I want to be somebody, often somebody different. It's not that Moore didn't, doesn't, want to be somebody, but he doesn't want to have to change to be it; it's a stubbornness to be acknowledged as worthy—early—for what you are, however fat and sloppy that might be. But P. J. acquired taste. When he was at the *National Lampoon*, I took for granted he went to Harvard, since that is where the *Lampoon* originated. Another rich kid moving up and on. But, I soon found out that P. J. wasn't from Harvard, but some third-rate school, and that he didn't come from wealth, or have any pedigree guaranteeing a fast entrance onto easy street. In his opening statement, he described himself as a young man: "Back in the 1960s, I expected permanent Woodstock, a whole lifetime sitting in the mud, smoking Mexican ditch weed, listening to amplifier feedback, and pawing a Long Island orthodontist's daughter who thought she was a witch. Show me somebody with expectations lower than that. Are we disheartened about the breakup of the family? Nobody who ever met my family is."

A number of public intellectuals have made the voyage from conservatism to, ah, liberalism. Garry Wills, for one, from *The National Review* to the *New York Review of Books;* Michael Lind, author of *The Next American Nation*, a former rising star of the Right, is a younger generation example. The trip went the other way, too; these days there might be even more on that road (its entrances are backed up). P. J. got on that road before the crush began. He saw himself as a ridiculous fellow and he intended to leave that behind, and he has.

During the question-and-answer period, Moore recounted a question a cabdriver—one with two degrees, Moore says, who was downsized a couple of times—had asked him: "Why is it that the United States Congress has spent a year and a half and millions of dollars investigating what happened to seven jobs in the White House travel office when tens of millions of Americans have lost their jobs in the last five years and there is no investigation, no outcry because of that?"

While reading one prepared question, the moderator made a malapropism: "working clash" instead of "working class." That it was, some working clash. Moore said, "I voted for Clinton but had my ten-year-old pull the lever—I didn't want blood on my hands. I don't see much difference between the parties. I call them Republicrats. People don't vote since they don't have choices."

P. J. rejoined: "Twenty percent got in their cars and voted for a certified fruitcake." That, of course, was Ross Perot. "White America is willing to vote for Colin Powell," he says, offering the opinion that Americans have pushed through their racism. That jogs my memory again and it occurs to me that P. J. is married to (or at least was once, if not still, married to) a famous African American entertainer's daughter. I try to imagine Michael Moore's relatives' reactions if Moore married a young black woman, however high up in society she might be. Here is a difference between those who aspire to be rich, successful, and still dyed-in-the-wool old-line Democrats with working-class pretensions. Intermarriage, oy vay.

Around the question of affirmative action, Moore offers a critique of the current backlash, the sort where people complain that blacks are getting all the jobs: "What are you saying? That it's really great being black in America?" I expect some uneasiness on the part of P. J., but he retains his headmaster's stiff stance and doesn't venture any biography on this point. About the retired general and new Republican, Moore says, "People don't like Colin Powell—he's black."

To Moore's repeated expressions of exasperation about the low rate of voter participation, P. J. replies, "Stop the vote. I'd like only thirty percent to vote. Twenty percent; they're the only ones who know what is going on. According to Mr. Moore everyone is out of work. In Nicaragua and Cuba, everybody would come out to vote."

Moore muses: "I'm Catholic and overweight." He takes time to compliment P. J. Things are definitely winding down, but we have to leave because our baby-sitter turns back into a pumpkin if we are not home by nine o'clock. Starting forty minutes late cut into our allotted time, so I couldn't ask them a question. I wouldn't have, anyway, but the only one I considered (given that today is the deadline for filing federal income tax) was: What is your effective tax rate? I expected it to be around 22–26 percent, the usual flat tax most Americans pay.

The two of them tonight split a twenty-five-thousand-dollar fee.

4/16   G. Gordon Liddy, I hear quoted, said he wouldn't turn in his brother like the (alleged) Unabomber's did . . . violates the taboo of turning in family. (Good thing Liddy didn't go to Harvard, or he'd be holed up in a Montana shack, too.)

Rush is going on—as is everyone—about the Unabomber. Rush starts to read the FBI's list of seven hundred things it inventoried in the Unabomber's ten-by-twelve-foot cabin.

4/17   Diane Rehm has Morris Dees on today. He's on *Fresh Air*, too. OK, it's near the Oklahoma City bombing anniversary. More seasonal stories. How many pictures have I seen in the *Times* of preparations for the Thanksgiving Day parade? Every year the same story. Morris's book on "white" wing fanatics is *Gathering Storm*. A report his organization did is called *False Patriots*.

Rush asks, Why didn't Bill Clinton want to raise the minimum wage two or three years ago? (The *New York Times* front page of June 3, 1993, says Clinton didn't want to antagonize "conservatives and business executives while the President's budget hangs in the balance.") Rush reads a Michael Kramer, *Time* magazine, Clinton quote about raising the minimum wage not being a good way to raise wages. I'd like to take a camera out and ask the man in the street, Rush says. I wonder why Rush doesn't see this is a losing issue by now, another version of shutting down the government. Raising the minimum wage now just raises it to what Bush raised it to the last time it was raised. The minimum wage was abolished long ago.

Liddy Dole is on *Nightline* alone.

The Imus story still has legs. You can imagine Liddy's reaction. I try to imagine—Don Rickles, perhaps?—saying, with Jacqueline and JFK sitting on a banquet-room dais, "The president and Angie Dickinson really gave the backseat of the presidential limousine a workout."

A Dole/Liddy wedding picture is shown, the young Liddy Dole looking like Mary Matalin. Hillary is a mom, but Liddy, no.

Escaping the first nurse, I read Garry Wills's April 18 *New York Review of Books* article on "The Clinton Scandals."

Overall, at first blush, one would think that Susan Thomases approached the wrong writer. She should have skipped the Pulitzer Prize winner James B. Stewart, author of *Blood Sport*, and gone straight to the

Pulitzer Prize winner Garry Wills, since his view of the Clintons is the more sympathetic.

I've heard Stewart on Diane Rehm, *Nightline, Fresh Air*, etc. (and seen him on CNN, C-SPAN, the networks), but I don't think I will necessarily hear Garry Wills do the circuit, taking the literate word out to the oral world. There isn't anything to sell—except for the newsstand copies of the *New York Review*. And having a product, a book, to sell is usually the implicit contract of mutual publicity. There is something "commercial" in all these interview shows, even those on NPR. The audience is consumers and it needs something to consume.

But who knows? During a campaign year everything in public is at play, so Wills's review-essay might be taken up. I'm taking it up.

The first paragraph implies, but doesn't state, that Garry was at a White House dinner honoring Thomas Jefferson (a book subject for him) in 1994, sitting at a table with, or very nearby, "Ms." (his honorary salutation) Clinton. (I don't think this event was on C-SPAN, alas.) He quotes her saying (either as the party broke up, people rising from the table, or, less likely, from a podium), after she has learned that the historian C. Vann Woodward was born in Arkansas, along with the writer Maya Angelou, who the first Ms. already knew was from Arkansas, "See what good folk come from Arkansas? Why is it the press can find only the same few scumbags there?"

Wills comments, "Why did the Clintons deal with the 'scumbags' being questioned by the press? I assume that Ms. Clinton had in mind not only such colorful Arkansans as Gennifer Flowers and Paula Jones but others, like James and Susan McDougal or David Hale, who have given the Clintons as much grief as any erupting bimbos." Though Hale has been giving the present governor, Jim Guy Tucker, the most grief these days.

What Garry doesn't comment on is the hostility of Hillary's remark and the low-rent locution—scumbags—Ms. Clinton spits out. The lady of the house emptying the chamber pot out the window from a very high floor.

This does hark back to Hillary in her I'll-do-anything-to-get-out-of-Arkansas mode. (Currently, in the circles that purport to care, the chat is how long the Clintons will stay married if he loses, to whether Hillary will ever set foot in Arkansas again, or, rather, ever live there again. One thinks not, to the latter; the guesses run to after Chelsea graduates from college, the former.)

Garry Wills knows well the pricey suburbs of Chicago and so does Ms. Clinton, and he makes proper sport with the "Dogpatch Connections" of Hillary's adopted state. He mentions when he first heard of Whitewater, in the 1992 campaign, "when Hillary Rodham Clinton took me to her husband's campaign headquarters," along with the historian Diane Blair. Ms. Clinton had been telling him funny stories about life in Fayetteville. Yokel central, doubtless. Wills evokes Al Capp's *Li'l Abner* comic strip.

Chicago is to Fayetteville as Paris is to Peoria. The University of Chicago, say, and the University of Arkansas (in Fayetteville) share one thing in common (the first word), but it is easy to imagine the delight of the dishing the backwoods afforded Ms. Clinton and Garry. But there's always the sorry irony for Ms. Clinton that her husband has a deep DNA strain of yokel in him, too, which comes out of remission quite often, most often in connection with beguiling ladies; but the most sophisticated guy can be turned into a yokel when kissed by a country princess (say, JFK and Judith Exner, the Las Vegas–Mafia gal).

But, enjoyable yucks all around. This is a version of ethnic humor, shared by the same ethnics. In this case, two western Chicago suburban ethnics.

In the dueling Pulitzer Prizes contest (history versus current affairs), Garry scores some points on Stewart.

It's not, Who do you love? but Who do you believe?

Wills makes the case that McDougal was hardly an intimate of the Clintons, almost not a friend. But one wonders at the nature of casual wedding-going such barely friends indulged in (though the Clintons also went to Lani Guinier's wedding). So "Make us some money, James" seems to be the extent of it. Wills also discusses Hillary's cattle-futures windfall, and takes the tack that the knowledgeable (too knowledgeable) trader, Robert L. "Red" Bone, was doing this as a favor to Jim Blair, not that he was doing it for some quid pro quo from the governor.

But what dogs the question is as quickly as the Clintons were lured into these two get-rich-quick schemes, were there no others, only these two? If so little time was spent on either, a fact Wills painstakingly presents—Hillary's "passive" attitude—weren't there equal amounts of almost no time to be spent pursuing other moneymaking schemes? It's odd that the Clintons' two speculative ventures—Whitewater and mad cow futures—seem to be their only ventures. Such pikerdom as compared to, say, Lamar!.

Stewart does rely overmuch on the manic-depressive in disco clothes, James McDougal (sexual harasser, college prof without portfolio, who makes off with his nineteen-year-old student) and David Hale, of the Nathan sort of fame, the man who handed out Susan McDougal's SBA loan (her tank-topness [her femaleness] was her qualifying asset).

Kenneth Starr, no ethical hairsplitter, will have his chance to parse Wills's readings of the record. Starr is every small-town hustler's worst nightmare. The Clinton presidency is seen by many as a Faustian bargain, but the burghers of Arkansas' antic hamlets are already reaping its dire rewards. I get to be president, you get to be indicted. The operatic proportions (and fates) of the Clinton core of the Rose law firm—Webster Hubbell, Vince Foster, and Hillary—is startling enough to chill any observer: Hubbell in jail, Foster in the ground, and Hillary . . . Hillary twisting slowly, slowly in the wind.

Imus's joke, "Which of the Clintons would first be indicted?", Roger being the punch line, Hillary being the joke, is graveyard humor vis-a-vis the Rose law firm. Foster and Hubbell are identified by Wills and others as Bill's boyhood friends, and Bill has cost them dearly. Clinton is long used to losing the men in his life, but not the women, which is why he is so sentimental, even to the much maligned Gennifer Flowers. He is sweet to her in his last (recorded!) phone call. Which prompted the episode in *Primary Colors* when the Hillary character slaps the Bill character after she learns the doxy has her man on tape.

What must have been Hillary's reaction when she learned that in real life? Anyone speculating back then, as I was, would have imagined something similar.

And in Wills's most sympathetic brief, even he can't resist the irony of pointing out that Hillary's estrangement from Foster was increased by his not replacing the Secret Service agents at the White House early on, thereby confirming the "leaked" throwing-the-lamp story. The Clintons do have an awkward way of confirming the unconfirmable. As Wills says, "How could she know the source if the story was untrue?"

4/18   Rush says the election is over, according to Christopher Dodd and the DNC's enthusiastic assessment. "Dodd says these elections are over." Everything I say today will be directed at regaining power in 2000, Rush says. He discusses a Mary McGrory column, lampooning her take on Clinton. "His boldness in seeking the White House with the baggage he is carrying becomes more breathtaking when all reviewed again," he reads. "Thank you, Miss McGrory." He's back to the minimum wage: Four twenty-five an hour, five twenty-five—that's going to make a big difference, Rush says scornfully. Let them look at what you're taking from their check. (Rush doesn't seem to know about the earned income tax credit.) You're having what you're earning confiscated from you, he says. Rush's roots as an early antitax, anti-IRS ranter poke up through the drifts of his new prosperity.

I catch some of a Lyndon LaRouche half-hour of paid political advertisement on our local CBS outlet. Rush didn't go down Lyndon's road, however much their ideological paths might overlap. And nothing Margaret Thatcher (a favorite villain of LaRouche) does (or did) would surprise me. I'm glad to see ex-cons like LaRouche rehabilitating themselves. But he doesn't look friendly. More like the uncle with incest on the brain.

4/19   I catch Rush's 5:00 A.M. television show. The audience is full of precisely groomed, but out-of-kilter college kids wearing school spirit sweatshirts: Holy Cross, Syracuse. Rush runs the Clinton "instant tears" Ron Brown funeral video. Clinton is walking outside with someone near parked vehicles. It's not clear if it is before or after the service, but it appears to be afterwards. This is not a ceremonial entrance, but an exit away from crowds. Clinton seems to be enjoying some remark. And then he catches out of the corner of his eye the camera pointed in his direction. His face absorbs the fact that he is being filmed and takes on an expression of sorrow. His finger arrives at his eye and he wipes away a tear. The sequence is hardly five seconds long. What seems incriminating is the subtle recognition Clinton shows (or doesn't show) when he spots the camera. His veiled realization has a professional shoplifter's practiced nonchalance about it.

4/20 On public radio I hear some of the *Whad'Ya Know?* show with Michael Feldman. He does a funny bit on on-line chat talk. He and his callers are hooked up with each other and are typing and reading aloud what they are typing to each other. It points out the ridiculous thing about such "chat": it wants to take the social out of the oral. Literacy, at that level (off the cuff), is low oral in content, but still attempts to retain the privacy of the literate—and control of time. (I'm talking to you, but you can't see me—or get me.)

4/21 McLaughlin says on his show that the old ideas of the Democrats have been pushed aside, and the new ideas of the Republicans have come to the fore. It's been "an intellectual rout."

Christopher Hitchens in May's *Vanity Fair* notes the TV use of John Gillespie Magee's sonnet ("slipped the surly bonds of earth") à la Peggy Noonan's *Challenger* speech, but he says he had to look for it. (Great minds, etc.—it was used at the end of the day on Washington's Channel 9, doubtless a favorite channel of Ms. Noonan.)

4/21 *Dennis Miller Live* has on Arlen Specter, who actually manages to be funny in his defense of his single-bullet theory. I suppose if all former presidential candidates get on comedy shows, Morry Taylor can't be far behind.

In today's *New York Times*, there's a picture of Clinton smiling his special smile at a group of pretty Russian girls.

4/22 C-SPAN does a GOPAC dinner. Gingrich is saying, "Bob Dole won't feel your pain, because he won't cause your pain." Dole is not so bad, Gingrich tries to convince the crowd. He gives a litany of losers who won. "No new taxes" won it for Bush first time around. Newt does a lot of union bashing. Three thousand scholarships for D.C. students, $9,400 for public schools per student. But it was blocked by the Democrats. "Single most tragic thing I've seen in Congress," Gingrich says, never afraid of hyperbole.

4/23 On *NPR News*, William Bennett calls on Dole to step down as Senate Majority leader and focus on the differences between himself and Clinton. Bennett says that the campaign has been "incoherent and dispassionate."

On Diane Rehm the talk is about presidential character. Charles Krauthammer, a shrink in "remission," dissents on Clinton growing into the office. Krauthammer says you want a magnificent bastard as president. He needs to send soldiers to kill and be killed. You need a certain ruthlessness. (Like any boss. If you want to be an academic department's chair, the first test you need to pass is your willingness to fire someone. This bloodletting is the initiation rite of all business.) Krauthammer is not sure we want it next door. But we do have it next door.

In the afternoon, Rush says piously, I've never seen nude dancing, except when it has been thrust upon me in a movie where I didn't know it was coming. "Would you want to live next door to these clubs?" Bachelor parties, though, Rush says, that's another question.

4/24 *Nightline* does a negative Kenneth Starr show. He defends tobacco companies, he wants to run for office, he's a Republican Zealot, etc.

4/25 Rush says that liberal groups are holding seminars on how to disrupt conservative talk radio hosts, that there's "a coordinated campaign" out there. This silly concept that I make things up, lie, Rush says. On the Kennedy/Kassebaum health bill, he says there are "no caps on premiums" and young people will be dropping out like flies. It's an invitation to raise premiums. It's an invitation to the government to get more involved. "More auction news": Jeffrey Dahmer's stuff will be auctioned to help families of victims. Sledgehammer, hatchet, hypodermic needle. Rush says he can't wait to see who shows up. Good Lord, ladies and gentlemen.

"It troubles me all the whining and sobbing in this country they can dredge up," Rush says, acknowledging the avalanche of bad news the campaign has helped put on the front pages of the "mainstream" media. "The jobs are there for qualified people," he says, still beating the minimum wage. He quotes from a "Robert Reich 1993 memo: most minimum wage workers are not poor."

Yesterday's news: Palestinians vote to drop destruction of Israel from their charter.

4/26   On NPR's *Morning Edition* Russell Roberts, of the Olin School of Business, is anti-minimum-wage hike. The only way to raise the minimum wage is "to raise skills." He takes the Rush line—or vice versa. A *New Republic* editor, who is pro–minimum wage, sort of, follows. He says $5.15 holds back the pitchfork peasants crowd. Six dollars an hour is half the average wage of supervisory work, he points out.

Newt is on *The Tonight Show* with Jay Leno. With newts. And a Sicilian donkey. Newt is trying to humanize himself. He tells a story about trying to get to a zoo in his hometown when he was a little kid. I was, Newt confides, "sent home in a cab . . . or I suppose it was a bus." Or whatever.

4/29   Rush says Clinton's "talking about his testimony being downloaded" via satellite transmission. "The decoding capabilities" interest Rush. The testimony ruined Clinton's Sunday golf outing. The minimum wage is now $4.25; enact a 90-cent-an-hour raise, Rush says: "Either sign off on it and put it behind us, or make a principled stand." Rush sounds like he's coming around, or has been told to come around. Though we should say we're against the minimum wage because "it hurts the poor," eliminating entry-level jobs, Rush says.

On C-SPAN, I see a Tom Daschle press conference. He sits at the head of a substantial table (the boss) and reporters (the employees) sit around 'it. For the remainder of the year our program is built around the word "security"—job security, wage security, he says. They certainly want to be on message. "Families First" is the new alliterative slogan and message of the administration for the rest of the year.

David Letterman does O.J. jokes about O.J.'s upcoming trip to London. "I can't find my bloody socks." O.J.'s off to the Oxford debating society. "What, Jack the Ripper wasn't available?"

4/30 Rush: A caller turned conservative, she says, because of friends giving her a hard time over Pampers. (Ruins the environment, won't degrade, fills the dumps.) Welcome to the club! Rush says. (Hypocrisy of liberals allegedly their greatest sin.) "I believe markets work."

He reruns an audio tape of Hillary's Emily's List appearance Friday on C-SPAN where she complains about "demonizing opponents." Rush says stereotypes of conservatives are: sexists, racists, bigots, homophobes, pro–big business, anti-little guy. "Hard to overcome," Rush says, lost in the injustice of it all.

EIGHT

May Flowers

★

5/1 Diane Rehm has Tipper Gore on, talking up mental health: it needs to have "parity" with other diseases, vis-à-vis insurance claims. Lots of the depressed are calling in. Diane mentions a "Where's Tipper?" article, its point being she's been under wraps. Here she is, Diane says.

Rush says "Make everyone as miserable as I am!" is the liberal doctrine; the way to do that? Tax the rich! Let no one do better next year than this year. That's how we'll make things fair. Rush says some Brit shrink thinks poets are crazier than most people, but are less likely to kill themselves. Unlike Tipper, he's not for mental illness health-insurance parity. "Are we all supposed to become poets now?" he asks. Don't tell me that—I've seen, Rush says, searching for a poet's name; he finally says: Jesse Jackson is the poet laureate.

I'm now thinking of Rush as Ayn Rand. There is sort of a physical resemblance.

5/3 Diane Rehm is talking about gas prices, because of the Republican tax-repeal talk, which Dole is campaigning for in Congress. A caller identifies himself as lower middle class, an average working Joe, and says,

"If gas went up to five dollars I'd be better off unemployed," Rush-like. Doyle McManus, a Rehm regular from *The Los Angeles Times*, points out it wouldn't go up all at once. A caller named Jeff says the gas tax is regressive. What is the limit of taxation? He's plaintive, aggressive. Disincentives are described, and the long lines of 1973–74; there was a 25 percent jump in prices and still you couldn't find any. An attempt to wean us off the dependency on Middle Eastern oil—it is a regressive tax.

William Colby, former head of the CIA, disappeared while out canoeing in Maryland's Wicomico River a few days earlier and his body has not yet been found. Seems like a "spy novel" is the consensus. "The problem of an older man married to a successful, busy, young woman . . . jetting around on her business interests," one of Diane's guests offers.

Jodie Allen of the new, soon-to-be (on-line) *Slate* magazine, a Microsoft product, says: Clinton caved in on this (the Helms-Burton Cuba bill), pandering to the Cuban exile community in Miami. It's a very bad act, electioneering.

The D'Amato defection from the party line—on environment, education—is commented on. He's been reading some polls in New York is the judgment.

The New Yorker (April 29 and May 6) is an all-black issue, more or less. (Coverage of groups is hooked on dates—the news is a color spectrum of commemorations, the Irish on St. Patrick's Day, etc.) In Jeffrey Rosen's article on Clarence Thomas, he quotes Thomas, telling an audience of students at Tuskegee, "I'm coming back today on a mission of love. I am no better than you-all. I'm no smarter than you-all. I'm no more talented than you-all. I've never been No. 1 in my class. . . . I'm no brighter than you-all." It doesn't appear that he told the students (though why he supposes they think he's smarter, etc., than they are is a question) that he gets to sit on the Supreme Court because of the expedience of a Republican president who wanted to appear to be practicing affirmative action and who tapped one of the few Republican faithful who qualified.

In the same issue, David Remnick's profile of W. J. Wilson shares my impressions of Chicago in the fifties. Wilson says about Charles Murray (*Losing Ground, The Bell Curve*), "I think a lot of Charles Murray's conclusions are ideologically driven and he doesn't let facts get in the ways of his beliefs. . . . I think he's dishonest. He plays to the conservative fears, and I think he knows better. A lot of what he says he doesn't really believe, but it's conservatively popular." When Murray was profiled in the *New York Times Magazine* on October 9, 1994, the news there for me was how extensive his proposal was for *Losing Ground,* how Murray pushed hard that his ending welfare book would get a big audience because it would be controversial and bring comfort to a "huge number" of "closet racists." Murray, the effete hustler.

5/4 On Comic Relief's *American Comedy Festival* on ABC, a black comic says: The life expectancy of a black man is sixty-five. Why am I paying Social Security? He gets a big laugh. That actuarial bad news is finally sinking in, it appears.

A different male comic impersonates Clinton while an actress begins a question. "First I want to apologize for not being vertical."

5/5 On *Face the Nation,* Newt is inveighing against partial-birth abortions, the newest bloody banner being waved. "How can we override the partial-birth veto?" is his concern.

The Republicans are trying to make abortion the Willie Horton for '96, though they seem to keep forgetting that the ultimate target for such attacks is women, and the gap there will only get wider. The Democratic slogan, "Families First," places itself in an imaginary postabortion universe. Families are after the fact, abortions before the fact: families come first, a woman's decision comes first, that which already exists [families] comes first, where it wants to be. Unlike Steve Forbes the Democrats' language made abortion disappear. The Republicans are still in the abortion world and women hear them, but not sympathetically.

Newt disavows D'Amato's soft remarks on Imus (strange, or not-so-strange, bedfellows there, Al and Don). Then Newt defends himself against D'Amato's charge (that Dole is hurt by Gingrich), saying, "He's wrong," and, moving on to the Republican defections on the minimum wage, he says we've "got to have offsets for small businesses" if the minimum wage is to be raised. Make it part of the welfare-reform bill. Newt says the "gas tax goes to pay for the welfare state," not the highway fund, and that's why he wants these pennies repealed.

It's "absolutely destructive for an American president" to lie about Medicare, Newt says. The American people are "deliberately misinformed by Clinton." Sixty million dollars is being spent on false advertisements. Newt takes the same line as Rush. The Clinton administration was AWOL on the drug issue for three years, Newt says.

Newt has a good political face, the stuff of eighteenth-century etchings. It would make Hogarth happy to work with the jolly corruption of Newt's plump cheeks and jowls.

5/6 There's a *New York Times* article on D'Amato, which cleans up a Dick Armey remark Armey made on yesterday's *Meet the Press*. The *Times* quotes Armey saying, "D'Amato's 'mama apparently didn't teach him not to bite the hand that feeds him.' " What Armey actually said, as he was forming the cliché in his brain, was, D'Amato's mama "didn't teach him to feed"—and then he realized his mistake and continued— "bite the hand," etc. Armey had it right the first time. D'Amato's mama did teach him to feed the hand that could bite him. (See my earlier remarks on D'Amato's '92 Senate race victory, his opportune feeding of unions.) Armey blames D'Amato's fears for his upcoming '98 election for his less than fraternal conduct (looks like '92 wasn't "the last race").

I hear on NPR's *Morning Edition* that William Colby's body apparently has been found; well, not quite found—it washed up on the riverbank after nine days and someone stumbled on it. End of spy novel? Seventy-six thousand dollars has been bid for a round of golf with President Clinton at a fund-raiser for Chelsea's school, Sidwell Friends, everyone catching auction fever, à la the Jackie O extravaganza, the selling of Camelot's Trinkets. There's more on the gas-tax flap. A tax few were complaining about, given that out here, gas is less than $1.25 a gallon. The Republicans want to start some other "populist" conversation, since they are getting killed on the minimum wage. The last thing on the mind of Americans was that 4.3-cent gas tax. But the Republicans have succeeded in moving the conversation off the minimum wage onto taxes.

I watch an HBO docutainment (*Priestly Sins: Sex and the Church*) on sexually harassing priests. After World War II, men in groups, separate from women, seemed so ordinary. It was a holdover from the war. Society was largely divided by gender then—married men gathered in groups, wives taking care of kids at picnics, etc. It took the sixties to start to make men in groups look strange. No one noticed the Senate, the Associated Press, the boardrooms of America. The women's movement, primarily, and, paradoxically, gay rights, finally made men in groups strange (or something to examine)—so video of men on an altar hugging, now looks peculiar or suspect, but for decades after World War II it did not.

In *George* (June-July), Robert Sam Anson has a profile on Bob Woodward. It appears he's going to publish a campaign book (called *The Race*) *during the summer*. Oh, joy. Anson quotes Woodward saying, "The idea is simple. . . . You collect information and present it to people while they're interested—before they vote." It's not that simple: Woodward doesn't want to record history, he wants to *change* history, as Anson says. (Woodward also assumes he can sell more books early rather than late.) Watergate gave Woodward a taste of that and he's never gotten over it. Woodward's many books are policy papers which get things to happen. His is an establishment view of how the world should work (and be). It puts a twist on Renata Adler's December 16, 1979 *New York Times Book Review* criticism of *The Brethren*'s unidentified sources: "It suppresses a major element of every investigative story: Who wanted it known?" Woodward has always been the oddest kind of "investigative" reporter—an ardent supporter of the status quo.

But in the '96 race, Woodward is also, more pertinently, following the O.J. model: publishing a book on the campaign before the campaign is over, just like Michael Knox, the removed O.J. juror, published his "diary" before the trial was concluded.

Rush is back on the gas-tax repeal. And more on Hillary's Emily's List talk. And on "push" polls (leading questions with loaded information disguised as innocent inquiry), "where they slander their opponents," Rush explains. Lawton Chiles, the Democratic Florida governor, started it, according to Rush. The NRA is "putting brochures . . . into every church pew they can reach." How about Jesse? the AFL-CIO? There will be a concerted effort to "confuse people, drive people away from the polls. . . . We win if people feel they have a stake in the future," Rush says. "If you've got no vision to make the world a better place for yourself and your children then you go negative." Lots of Democrats, Rush points out, are saying "mean-spirited" things. Ads and remarks are aired. Gephardt is saying, "Republicans are taking the food out of the mouths of middle-class children." "Draconian cuts . . . Robin Hood in reverse . . . our children are being left the crumbs of Gingrich's revolution." Rush says rhetorically: "Mrs. Clinton . . . they have no vision."

He plays part of a Medicare commercial: "tax breaks for the rich." "You bet we will remember," he says, meaning remember all this calumny. Democrats say "GOP" means "Get Our People." "They're coming for our children."

Al Gore claims, Rush says, Republicans raise money from "the extra chromosome right wing." Rush says Gore's making fun of people with Down's syndrome. "That's an insult to Down's syndrome." Though it is clear enough that Gore's reference is to extra Y male criminal types. Rush says about Hillary: "My guess is the Emily's List speech is one of her last public events. . . . She'll go back to making cookies."

Judy Woodruff is interviewing Ralph Reed on CNN. "Bay Buchanan says you've raised the white flag of surrender," Judy says. "You mean, on the abortion plank?" Ralph says, all confused innocence. "Yes," Judy says. Ralph says he has spoken with Bay (kept her at bay, I suppose) and "sometimes these things get confused when they move through a media filter."

Yes, I contemplate that. Everything means what I say it means right now and right now is always moving forward.

Ralph goes on: "What I have said very simply, Judy—so there's no ambiguity—it is the official position of the Christian Coalition that there can be no retreat. No backpedaling. No watering down. No signal of equivocation sent at the Republican convention in dabbling with the pro-life plank. We think that plank needs to remain unequivocally, unambiguously and eloquently pro-life. What we have said is we do not object to inserting, for example, a sentence that condemns Bill Clinton's veto of the partial-birth abortion ban, a veto that's been condemned by Pope John Paul the second and Billy Graham. We think that could strengthen the plank. It's a change, but it's not a material, substantive or fanatic change."

Ralph slips and slides over what he will or will not allow, or if the platform will specifically include language calling for a human-life amendment. Ralph wants to put a lot through the media filter so it can be distorted in whatever way is helpful to the cause.

Mack McLarty, demoted White House chief of staff and oldest FOB, is on C-SPAN, giving a speech at a Free Trade Agreement and the Americas conference. Boy, he looks bad. Well, at least he hasn't committed suicide. Mack quotes Dayton Hudson and Henry Ford and other business giants. The business of America is business, as Calvin Coolidge said and Mack demonstrates.

5/7 There's a small article in the *New York Times* (A14) saying that Stanley Hill, director of New York City's largest municipal employees union, "stunned everyone" by praising Mayor Giuliani and Senator D'Amato at a meeting of labor leaders and congressional Democrats. If I am not stunned, why are they stunned? Someone at the *Times* is pulling our leg.

Colby's obituary runs. Only being a Catholic spoils the WASP privilege biography (Princeton, OSS, etc.). William Sloane Coffin Jr. once jokingly told me that the CIA used to send their Catholics to South and Central America and their best men (the Protestants) elsewhere (the Middle East[!], especially), but Colby was posted to Stockholm, Rome, and Saigon. He ran Operation Phoenix in Vietnam, which had a lot of people killed (upper-upper-class Americans killing downscale peasants, but Colby never lost his good manners), and, failing upward, he became head of the CIA in 1973. The end of his life was equally bizarre, insofar as the *Times* reports he was "marketing a computer CD-ROM game about espionage and counterterrorism he created with Oleg Kalugin, a former top Soviet intelligence officer."

When I vote (today are held the Indiana, North Carolina, and District of Columbia primaries, all superfluous events nationally), there is an old lady in a voting booth. The large lever is stuck; she can't open the curtain, record her votes. Other old ladies, sitting on folding chairs, make comments on how she must have broken it. The lady sticks her head out each time a critical remark is made: Well, if you know how it broke, why don't you come over here and fix it? She emerges and says it three times.

Who are these people on the ballot? I wonder, gazing at all the unfamiliar local school board, state, and county races. All politics isn't local, if you don't know who these folks are.

Rush is claiming to be on a real radio station and to be a real host. Six hundred fifty-plus stations, not a meager seventy stations, like some other talk shows (Diane Rehm? Cuomo?). Rush claims 20 million listeners. But the Democrats are united. "Who knows what we're motivated by?" Rush wonders. About the Democrats, we're letting them get it.

Maybe in Bob Woodward's new book there will be a canoe-side interview with William Colby.

5/8 Diane Rehm mentions the decline of cursive writing—blamed on computers (all those two-year-olds at a keyboard). The subject is in today's *New York Times* (M. Tabor article). A caller says the 4.3-cent gas-tax repeal would be "a strike against government spending." He's the first antitax person (after seven protax). The caller says, "As a small business owner . . . I don't want to loan them any more money."

Rush is something of the penny-dreadful serial: if you miss a show, some caller, or Rush himself, will refer to an earlier one and catch you up on the week's "plot."

David Brooks, an editor at *The Weekly Standard,* on NPR's *All Things Considered* does a funny piece about Dole not being old enough to be president. In ten or fifteen years, give him another chance at it. Reagan appeared "disengaged." You knew he was going to have a good term when he didn't recognize a member of his cabinet in '82 (his HUD secretary.) Reagan doesn't remember the small things, only the large things. Bush might have been too young, playing speed-up golf (thirty-six holes) in the morning and volleyball with twenty-two-year-olds all afternoon. (Also in his cigarette boat—shades of Bush's Cuba running "oil" youth.) Clinton goes to Martha's Vineyard, plays thirty-six holes of golf, has four meals with Hollywood stars. Golf courses have eighteen holes. Anyone who needs to play thirty-six holes of golf has too much time on his hands.

Steve Forbes is now on *The Tonight Show*. Steve says he "never got beyond being an extra in second-grade plays," though "we did beat Roseanne and Senator Dole" in the ratings, he boasts about his *Saturday*

Night Live appearance. "I think they did the wig better than Ted Koppel does his," he says about his blue-collar long hair. Jay Leno does his "dig" gesture—twist-in-the-knife movements. Forbes turns up in between the actor Charlie Sheen (of Heidi Fleiss fame) and a sadomasochistic woman magician whose act has her gored on an industrial-size corkscrew. She seems to have surgically enhanced breasts. After her act, Jay says to her, "I see why you're linked to Charlie Sheen."

5/9   Rush is going on about the video clip of Clinton laughing and then crying in one step that Rush's still playing on his TV show. He talks about Newt saying, regarding Medicare, on Tuesday, "How can you say it is a cut when it is a twenty-five-hundred-dollar increase?" Rush contends the press judges Clinton as a talk-show host, but not Rush, "since I grew up under Dwight D. Eisenhower." Rush gives poll data: 89 percent of the Washington press voted for Clinton; 60 percent are liberal, 7 percent are conservative. At Wednesday's press conference, Clinton is asked about a recent Democratic attack ad, Rush says. Wolf Blitzer asked about projected Republican cuts. Clinton said, according to Rush, "Let me say this, are you prepared to stop it?" Clinton says, meaning the language of "cuts." "We all learned to use it from the press." Rush says, "They're reductions in rates of growth." After some comic splicing of various sound bites, two of Bill and one of Hillary, Rush says, two out of three Clintons agree they're not cuts, but reductions in the rate of growth.

The 89 percent voting for Clinton—if that's true, then we have a problem, Wolf Blitzer said, according to Rush. Twenty-five hundred dollars per senior citizen over seven years (three hundred dollars a year), Rush says, is the Medicare "cut," hardly worth talking about.

Rush is now on to Robin Williams talking at a soft money fund-raising function for Democrats. Twelve million dollars for two days of fundraising. A record? About Bob Dole, Robin Williams said: "Don't operate heavy machinery while listening to this man." Rush says Maya Angelou is hypocritical. He goes on about the money she's made—"even in the brothel she used to run." They bash people who don't have as much money as they do, he complains.

Rush says on C-SPAN, "Brian Lamb has taught them how to be dull."

The "anchorpeople" can't show emotion. "I couldn't do it," Rush says. The C-SPAN folks, I consider, are the new Buckingham Palace guard figures, known for their impassiveness.

Here's a Notre Dame press release remarking on Catholic voters: David Leege, professor of government, says Catholics, who once were solid supporters of the Democratic Party, now can be divided into three distinct groups: the New Deal generation, which remains committed to the Democrats; the fifty-to seventy-year-olds, about 40 percent of whom have shifted to the Republican Party; and the baby boomers, most of whom are moving to the GOP. The latter group "has swallowed the American dream," Leege says, "and they want to make it big, so it doesn't really matter what their parents or grandparents were. They're truly Americans and they've studied at Notre Dame and other places. They've got good degrees, good jobs and they're very attracted GOP-wards. Social issues (such as abortion or school prayer) are quite secondary." From the horse's mouth, so to speak.

5/10   Driving home from dropping off my five-year-old at kindergarten, I hear on NPR's *Morning Edition* an Alabama state senator going on about how slavery wasn't so bad, how southerners were much nicer than northerners to their blacks. Ah, it's 1996 and *do you know where your state senators are?*

The Progressive Economists Network bulletin board (Pen-1) posted, via the Internet, Princeton economist David Card's response to those who criticized his work showing the minimum wage could increase the number of jobs, not cause employers to lay off workers. His study has been cited often by the pro-raise-the-minimum-wage side. Card said he "never takes a position on subjects he does research on." That's what we need, more disinterested economists. A man with convictions, a true scientist with a condo in the Ivory Tower. Unlike Charles Murray.

Clinton's videotaped Arkansas trial testimony is reported in the *New York Times*. The headlines: "Clinton, on Tape, Denies Role in Whitewater Loan. President Patient and Bristling in His Testimony." In Clinton's testimony he uses the word "never" a lot. He never asked Hale to make a loan to the McDougals, or Jim Guy Tucker. Also, there's an op-ed piece headlined "What Do Angry Women Want?" written by Mary

Beth Cahill, the executive director of Emily's List, the fund-raising group. Emily's List did a poll, she says, and even Catholic women supported Clinton over Dole by double digits, among professional women and "suburban women." Women without college degrees have more "volatility," and are likely to not vote, or vote for Perot. Their support of Democrats is "shallow."

Rush is going on about a Harris poll. Who's more trust (ed), or trustworthy: 45 percent Clinton, 36 percent Dole. More character: 50 percent Clinton, 42 percent Dole. Rush talks about the Emily's List woman's column in the *Times*. Angry white women are the "uneducated women," Rush says sarcastically. Emily's List is worried about losing uneducated women, which shows a lack of confidence in "you women."

Three liberal columnists said taxes aren't too high, Rush says. Look at how much the rich spent on the Jackie O auction (lots), is their point. "It's none of their damn business what they spend their money on," Rush says. Even if Clinton wins we've got to retain the House. The conservative wing of the Republicans should lead that charge. Rush says, I expect it to be a fifty-fifty election.

Rush, it appears, expects Clinton to win. "We're taking it on the chin."

That Alabama state senator (on the NPR report earlier) also blamed all his trouble on "the liberal media."

The three networks in the last ten years have lost viewers, Rush exults; once a 37 share (32 million lost viewers), now low 20s.

5/11 C-SPAN shows a conference, the state of the gay and lesbian movement, lots of tightly dressed guys and gals, lots of expensive short haircuts. Melinda Paras, of the National Gay and Lesbian Task Force, says who is appointed to the Supreme Court is the most important thing about the election. "We will be thinking about that Supreme Court appointment" when we're going into the booth. The chief reason offered to vote for Clinton is to "protect" the Supreme Court.

A ValuJet DC-9 went down in the Everglades, killing everyone aboard, over a hundred people.

Would people get on a plane called "Cheapflight" or "Sav-A-Buck

Air"? my wife asks. There's going to be two tiers of flying, one for the rich, which will be safe, and one for the not rich, where you will take your chances.

5/12   On *Meet the Press* we have Pat Buchanan saying he'll be conducting "sunrise services" at San Diego.

It's clear now that finally D'Amato is emerging as a "national" figure for the first time—the presidential campaign is doing that for him, even more than his Whitewater hearings. And Republicans are paying the price, since he plays so badly outside of New York City's ethnic enclaves, which have more empathy for ethnics (and familiar politicians). New Yorkers have gotten used to him—but not the rest of the United States.

As I flip through the Sunday news programs I encounter O.J. in a bit part performance of some time ago. "You're not taking our jobs— you're going to die," a redneck says. O.J., wearing a tuxedo, knocks him down.

The McLaughlin Group has the same "misleading" ads done up by Rush last week.

The Sunday *Capital Gang*, CNN, has on James Warren, from the *Chicago Tribune,* who looks like a hip minister, and Howard Fineman, from *Newsweek.* Jurors in Little Rock, voters in Russia, and Communists in China—all could hurt Bill Clinton being reelected, Fineman offers. A major scandal and foreign policy crisis perhaps. Juan Williams from the *Washington Post* and Mona Charen, the syndicated columnist and former Reagan administration official, fill out the gang.

Mona has a distinctly dominatrix look and aspect: moan with Mona, hurt me, hurt me. Her slightly cross-dressing style is crisp and her short black hair is razor cut. She has an equivocal gleam in her eye, especially when she says something that stings.

A Clarence Thomas commencement address—"Be a hero and not a victim"—is played. Clarence can't leave it alone. The *Capital Gang*'s moderator looks under his coffee mug: "Made in China," he reads. Earlier in the year everything my family bought in one week was made in China: toys, clothes, and a computer. A contribution to the progressive New Party produced a premium that arrived during the week, a coffee mug proclaiming: Rock the Boat! New Party. A Real Democracy, A Fair Economy, A New Party. On the bottom of the mug a tag announced Made in China.

Crossfire Sunday. Lynne Cheney is on the Right. The gender gap is the topic. Lynn Martin (the former labor secretary) is the guest. Dole filibustered twice on family leave; 60 percent of women are on minimum wage. Martin: They want to make more than the minimum wage.

Joan Calambokides, from the International Masonry Institute, hardly says anything, though she's supposed to provide the Left perspective. Joan is a former White House political director, now working for a union. She smiles a lot, cites a *Ladies Home Journal*/League of Women Voters poll, 51 percent to 42 percent want government to help create jobs.

Martin says women are more dependent on government.

Bob Beckel's on the Left. What is poor old Bob Dole going to do to get this gap down?

Calambokides finally uses the union slogan: America needs a raise.

Cheney: America needs a tax cut.

Martin: I differ with Lynne Cheney.

Cheney: I'm pro-life.

Martin: I don't think women have complete equality in the workplace.

5/13 Diane Rehm has kept up the parade of nonfiction authors. Today's book discussed: *Dirty Little Secrets*, by Larry Sabato and Glenn Simpson. About, surprise, "The Persistence of Corruption in American Politics."

The authors of literate fiction, with rare exception, do not enter the oral culture easily, since what is good about the writing resists paraphrase, which is one reason fiction is largely irrelevant in the oral culture, since so little of it is transmitted that way. Nonfiction is still "information," and most writers can restate what they've written with little damage to their prose.

A caller says: There were "real crimes committed" by the "Nixon and Kissinger cabal" and Watergate was merely a diversion. Like corporate crime, the CONINTEL program.

Rush is talking about Safire's column in the *New York Times* today, which mentions Clinton's large poll lead (25 points), and says "liberal"

James Carville is out, and "centrist" Dick Morris is in. Safire warns the White House against "the danger of complacency." Then, Rush says: as for D'Amato, I for the life of me don't know what's going on. There's something here that doesn't meet the eye.

"There's a clear effort here to undermine Newt Gingrich," Rush warns. A caller says Clinton has been "politicizing the plane crash" in Florida. Snakes and alligators are complicating the salvage operation. The ValuJet pilot was a woman, Candalyn Kubeck, the first woman commercial airline pilot to be killed. Rush says arrogant condescension is part and parcel of being a liberal.

On *Rivera Live,* Geraldo is talking about O.J.'s Oxford Union debating society appearance tomorrow. He shows some of the Brit TV show *Richard & Judy,* which has O.J. on. They are the *Regis and Kathy Lee* of the UK. Richard is known as "Pinch" since he was charged with shoplifting once.

5/14 A Washington insider, at breakfast, says Clinton's PR man has taught him (Clinton) how to immunize himself—to talk about the problems before the opposition does, thereby immunizing himself. Then the negatives work against the opponent since the people are sick of hearing about it (antibodies, etc.). Or whatever. As Bob Dole would say.

On NPR's *Morning Edition,* the Montana Freemen are sounding more and more like the Progressive Labor Party. (It's the Pat Buchanan effect.) "Agencies with long important-sounding names . . . with stolen drug money behind them" are the Freemen's current bête noire. Maybe their satellite has been beaming down Lyndon LaRouche's infomercials.

In *USA Today,* there's an article about a Richard Speck video that is making the rounds. The Ripley's Believe It or Not problem is in full flower again. Home video–style, drug-enhanced prison porn, with Speck looking real bad.

Rush is again on Bill Clinton laughing at the Ron Brown service. Clinton realizes the camera is on, starts crying. Rush shows this tape on TV every night, he gushes. Then Rush becomes Willy Loman: You all know how I feel about small business owners "burning the midnight oil."

Rush says Clinton's eyebrows raise when he "lies" (a caller made that observation couple of days ago). A new caller says she saw a sketch by a courtroom artist (of Clinton's video-taped testimony) with Clinton's eyebrows elevated. Chuckles all around.

5/15 There's a picture of Newt's gay sister, Candace, in the *New York Times* (A10). Family members are coming out of the woodwork everywhere; it is impossible to exaggerate how bizarre the majority of American families are. Everyone knows that. What is the fear? Who are "they" (the Christian Coalition, etc.) trying to protect? Images of pedophiles and serial killers dance in people's brains. That's where the line is drawn. Last week's HBO priest-bashing show didn't make the point, but I will: Married priests won't cut down on any of the abuses—not the flamboyant ones; there are philandering husbands, married pedophiles, serial-killing dads.

In the *Times*'s Political Briefs (A10), "A harrowing factoid": 40 percent of people aged eighteen to twenty-nine "regularly or sometimes learn" about the campaign from "Letterman or Leno." Also in the *Times,* there is an article (A13) about a Hathaway shirts plant being closed in Maine and the CEO of the parent company (the Warnaco Group) being paid $10 million a year. The net income of the company last year was $46.5 million—she (yes, a she!—Linda Wachner) got about 25 percent of the year's income. Women working in the Maine plant were making around $7 an hour. If anything has soaked in over the year it is this sort of thing.

Diane Rehm has Senator Carol Moseley-Braun (D-Ill.) on and she is speaking on her new pension bill, but she doesn't know the number of the bill, which throws into doubt the close work she's been doing on it. Moseley-Braun is the Terry McMillan of the Senate (McMillan's new Jamaica vacation novel, *How Stella Got Her Groove Back,* is reviewed this week in the *Times Book Review,* and most everywhere else)—I've got money, girl, and I can spend it with the best of them!

On *Fresh Air* Terri Gross has Chinese American author Jan Wong, talking about her memoir *Red China Blues: My Long March from Mao to Now.* She says, innocently it appears, "We were middle class . . . my father made his first million by forty." Dad owned restaurants. She appears to be an example of the conversion experience, have your cake and eat it, too. I made mistakes, she says. I "snitched on students." These are Tiananmen Square types of students. "They were irritating. . . . They didn't deserve to die, of course."

On *Talk of the Nation,* Ray Suarez interviews Elizabeth Drew, the *New Yorker* journalist. Dole is resigning from the Senate, not just from his "duties" as majority leader, as the *Times* has it today. The only downside, I see, is that it will remind people of how old he is: Dole can rest—it's too much work, running the Senate and campaigning. Picture Dole coming back to the Senate after the election. Upside, Dole seems serious, burst of publicity, gets out of the tar pit of Congress, saves what's left of his strength.

Rush is trying to find Clinton's hundred thousand new cops—he's looking for the "real" number. Free ties are offered.

Nightline runs tape of Bob Dole's resignation speech: "So today I announce that I will forego the privileges, not only the office of the majority leader, but of the United States Senate itself, and I will then stand before you without office or authority, a private citizen, a Kansan, an American, just a man." Dole looks pained, but not as much as those around him.

Nightline has shown photographs of Dole during the day comforting his staff, a good many of whom will be looking for work soon. There is no taking the air of concession out of the speech; he's quitting the Senate and the text of relinquishment creates its own echoes of what he might be obliged to say come November 5: I will stand before you without office or authority.

Koppel interviews Newt Gingrich and says, "We were talking during the break about the fact that Mark Helprin, who is both a novelist and sometimes a columnist for *The Wall Street Journal,* worked with him on the speech. . . ."

Fiction rears its head. Newt says Bob Dole is "a serious person" and Helprin is "a very serious writer" and he "may have helped fit what Dole's trying to communicate."

Helped fit. As I wonder about Newt's use of language, I marvel that Mark Helprin thinks he has found a character in Bob Dole.

5/16 Rush is on Clinton as commander in chief and his claim that "active duty in the armed services of the United States . . . ," which is contained in Bob Bennett's latest Paula Jones legal pleadings, allows Clinton to avoid civil suits while he's president. Rush says it's being used so Clinton can't be brought to justice now in re Paula Jones. Rush chuckles. The first hour of this show, Rush says, goes to the Armed Forces network. They'll get a laugh out of this, is the point.

He moves to Richard Speck—did you see the video of Richard Speck? Rush asks. He says Speck obviously has had breast enlargement. A 36D, he guesses. Rush is a big-boobs guy.

Congress in '82 only got a 14 percent approval rating from the people, now it's 30 percent, Rush says, claiming that Republican Congress is winning support. "This country is moving to the rich," Rush says, which I presume is a malapropism. The right? "Most people have good manners," Rush says, though not the Democrats. "The net effect is a minus," Rush concludes, about saying bad things about Dole's resignation. He's back on Maya Angelou: 4.3 million jobs a year? Rush says skeptically about Clinton administration claims. "When she ran the brothel, are those the kinds of jobs we want created in America?" Don't CEOs do more for the country than Maya Angelou? he asks. "If you're bashing rich people, I don't like you exempting anyone." In a bashing turn, he says, "There's too little spanking going on in the U.S. these days." "The discipline born of love," he calls it, referring to a news story about a man being faced with up to twenty years for spanking his stepdaughter. Rush laments and acknowledges, I get the letters claiming, "I have forsaken my cultural roots and all I'm concerned about is money."

5/18   Clarence Thomas is on C-SPAN. He says he has to do what the law dictates, not make law. He doesn't seem to realize that's what the Supreme Court does. It's the Constitution he's protecting, not the laws. It's clear Clarence sees himself doing what some "other" force needs, or wants done. He's just doing what he's told.

5/19   Dick Armey is on the new *Fox News* Sunday show. And who is the moderator? Formerly with Bush's '92 reelection campaign, another creature of the event, Mr. Tony Snow.

Meet the Press. Mississippian Trent Lott and Democrat Daschle are on; the talk is about the two Mississippians up for Dole's job, one being Lott. Richard Ben Cramer, author of *What It Takes,* talks about Dole. Cramer has a lot of affection for Dole. There's film of the governor of Massachusetts and current Senate candidate, William Weld, collapsing at a college graduation ceremony, and I think, John Kerry has just won the Massachusetts Senate race. I have the collapsing-on-film principle, which makes you a sure loser. Bush throwing up on Japanese dignitaries and falling under the table (President Quayle!), Carter being held up by Secret Service men woozy from jogging, now Weld going under. It's the kiss of death when a candidate collapses, passes out, on television.

That's why Dole quit the Senate, so they wouldn't get him collapsing on film. It would be the end. "Cokie's Senate," is remarked. Everyone laughs. Other less happy topics: the ValuJet crash, Admiral Jeremy Boorda's suicide on May 16.

On *Face the Nation* Chris Dodd, William Bennett, and Republican governor Stephen Merrill of New Hampshire are talking about same-sex marriage. Let them all get married. Dodd and Bennett would make an attractive couple.

William Buckley on *Firing Line* interviews Lester Thurow on his new book, *The Future of Capitalism.* Thurow is also in the *New York Times Magazine* today. His nickname might be "less than thorough," but he's been more than thorough regarding media exposure. I have parents in their eighties and children in their twenties, Thurow says. "I don't want to make my parents rich and my children poor." Has he done either? I don't think so. I pointed out in my book, Thurow says, that Bismarck invented the retirement age of sixty-five when the average life span was forty-seven, which is like saying we can retire at ninety-five. Thurow doesn't point out that others have pointed that out, too.

On *Washington Week in Review* Jack Nelson talks about his fellow Southerner Trent Lott, who appears to be the best bet to become the new majority leader.

I consider the psychological effect of never considering what Vietnam would have looked like if we had won. Imaginatively impossible. Dole leaving the Senate majority-leader job leaves it to the two weirdos from Mississippi, one of the most backward states of the Union. Whatever the outcome, it will look bad to the nation to see in high relief the southern

Republican crowd in control of the Senate—and the House. The midwestern Dole had provided a veil to disguise what was going on. That veil has dropped.

At a party I talk about the Democratic convention of '92, with a friend who was there. He said there were no debates about votes, but those over what went out on the satellite feeds were vicious. Clinton was great at working the crowd, but it didn't come across on the tape. And for one who believes the truth is on the tape, he says, that was disturbing. The people who were for Clinton were *really* for him; they just had difficulty convincing others, he says.

"For a guy everyone hated ten months ago why is Clinton so beloved now?" my friend asks.

I say that the reason why shows up in the Clinton/Imus flap. It is interesting why the press responded as it did, treating Clinton so gently, Imus so roughly—it is the same as when they stopped treating Reagan as a clown, in the summer of '80: it was apparent Reagan would win. The same with Clinton. The dignity of the office has finally taken hold. Clinton biting his lower lip, all the death business, the gravity of the presidency, the press wanting it to be so. So that is why Imus seemed so out of place—because that respect for power had taken over. A new line had been drawn. Clinton had been president long enough so that he was now The President.

We move to the downside of Dole's quitting: see Trent Lott. Headline: 72-year-old Senator Resigns. No news there. Dole needs to rest. Not like Strom Thurmond, who uses the Senate like the world's classiest old-age home, Dole actually works. I bring up William Weld's collapsing. Republicans don't want film of that happening to Dole. He might now get through the election. "That's a condescending, patronizing view of this seventy-two-year-old man," my friend says.

Anonymous has an article in the *Times Book Review,* becoming less anonymous. There have been a number of president films, *Dave,* with Kevin Kline, *The American President,* with Michael Douglas, others. The Douglas film has gotten a lot of play because the first lady is dead, the country's id wish fulfilled.

I watch David Letterman and agree with the dumbing down of the

America crowd. I just differ on who arranged it. When I was in college in Missouri, Dick Cavett had a morning television show, which I'd watch after an early French class. Cavett had a wit that was modeled on the sophisticated New York City dweller of previous generations, droll and erudite, dry wit and dry martinis. Letterman, an alum of Ball State University in Muncie, Indiana, pasted a different generation's wit onto the common consciousness: stupid pet tricks versus opera-going bon mots. I went to Ball State earlier in the week to record a radio show at its station, WBST, and the young woman working there, in answer to my question (So, this is where David Letterman began his career?), said, yes. Though Dave got fired from the station, she understood, since he made fun of classical music, which WBST played a lot of. Ah, the old days. Most of America's popular consciousness comes from the Midwest, but Cavett's generation wanted to escape it, to emulate the East Coast's version, and Letterman wanted to lambast both. Now, the newer generation wants to emulate stupid pet tricks.

Randy Weaver is on CBS. Ruby Ridge, the 1992 confrontation in Idaho, is rehashed through the medium of a TV movie. Weaver's boy is killed, his wife is killed by an FBI sharpshooter. The eleven day stand-off began with the death of a U.S. marshal. The domestic equivalent of Vietnam, too much technology and too little common sense on everyone's part, but the Montana Freemen are getting the post–Ruby Ridge, post-Waco, kinder, gentler treatment. The tax-avoiding Freemen spend their time picking up news reports on themselves with their satellite TV. Back to the land with backyard satellite dishes. My local CBS news after the movie aired does some nearby Indiana militia people and interviews the owner of a gun store. "Free men own guns," a portly guy says, slaves don't. We're not against the country, "we're against a tyrannical interpretation of the Constitution."

The White House has been planning the second term. Two years for Clinton to be a great president. Third year for Gore to win in 2000. Gore has none of Clinton's negatives, but also has none of his "warmth." Unions are handling local elections.

Tim Russert's show is on CNBC. Jack Germond thinks it's John McCain for veep. Two war heroes, why not? Me, too. Clinton and Gore,

Germond says, have the "same background"! He means southern, I suppose. Jules Witcover, of the *Baltimore Sun,* and coauthor with Germond of a '92 campaign book, *Mad as Hell,* is on, too.

5/20 The *New York Times* does an article on Tailhook and Admiral Boorda's suicide (he was buried yesterday). The *Times* reports that Boorda "had talked of how the 'thing that's killing the Navy is computers, because all a journalist has to do is hit a button on a computer and up on the screen comes the whole litany of Tailhook and it all gets repeated' with each new Navy scandal."

I saw on the news Clinton being given a note at a public event about Boorda's suicide the day it occurred and his shocked reaction. Then it was formally announced. More mourning becomes Clinton. When there's so much death around, Clinton's vitality shines forth even brighter. It's not just Dole in the Thanatos versus Eros contest, it's Clinton versus the world.

On Diane Rehm a caller says: Boorda didn't have the right character. The caller is anti-Clinton and sees a link. Boorda was not moral, had weakness of character. "A stalking horse," the caller says. Something else is going on; it was only an excuse saying a magazine (*Newsweek*) hounded him.

It's always good to hear a real conspiracy type finding evil everywhere, especially since he is so "moral."

More callers are blaming *Newsweek,* which had set up an interview with Boorda that day, to talk about his medals and other topics. This scapegoating seems necessary for those who want answers.

5/21 Rush is going on about the postmodern parody reported in the *New York Times* today, the *Social Text* (46-47) article fraud, the *Lingua Franca* piece of May/June 1996 on why the author, Alan Sokal, did it. "Now only an effete intellectual snob would pretend to understand that," Rush says after reading a bit of the parody, which posed as a nonparody. He's back on spanking again: "discipline born through love." "I was spanked," Rush says, "and on several occasions I had to go out and cut the branch." His hero, Rouben Greenberg, a police chief, brings parents down to the police station so they can spank their children in front of

witnesses. Rush has stepchildren, fifteen and seventeen, he says, in response to a caller's question. Spanking. "There's a way it can be done.
. . . "I'm living proof." Yeah, that's right.

Tabitha Soren, MTV's reporter, is on NPR's *The Campaign Connection*, produced by WBUR and hosted by Christopher Lydon. Tabitha,
unlike Rush, knows what the earned income tax credit is. Lydon plays a
tape of her Dole interview, Do you have gays working for you? Dole
hems and haws. And to Soren's assertion that Jane Roe, of *Roe v. Wade*,
is now against . . . anything but first trimester, Bill Clinton replies: She's
been through a lot of changes, a religious conversion. Tabitha reports:
Eighteen-to-twenty-nine-year-olds' rate of unemployment is double the
national average.

Given the talk about the young, I offer my commencement address:
The good news for the class of '96 is that the minimum wage is going
up.

I watch the *700 Club*. There's a black guy "host." I want to file a
suit, gender discrimination, he says; I wanted to be a cheerleader, but
they didn't want me to. Pat Robertson does an ex–Dallas Cowboy cheerleader inspirational story, one who is now born again. Her marriage fell
apart, and she met a Christian man. Even though she tried to make the
friendship platonic, she . . . started a divorce and pregnant with her husband's baby . . . moved to LA. "What was bad got worse," she says.
Boyfriend refuses to marry her. Robertson slips, and says, "costs to be
prayed," instead of costs to be paid.

And, regarding slips, on Charles Grodin's show on CNBC, Ollie
North says, we have an "intentive" (attentive? inattentive?) electorate.

In the May 27 *Time* Calvin Trillin column, Trillin writes, about Dole's
resignation, "He campaigned without his tie—although not, it should be
said, without his cuff links." The cuff-links thing was mentioned on Richard Ben Cramer's *Meet the Press* appearance, and Cramer objected,
saying Dole wears cuff links because of his war injury, though as he said
it, something else was being said on top of it, and the point about Dole's
not being able to manipulate buttons was muffled. In his piece, Trillin
brings up an article in the *Washington Post* by Jay Mathews about the
effect of tallness in politics. Tall wins more than short in the modern era.
Dukakis's race is recalled by Trillin, but he doesn't mention the most

damning effect of shortness in a politician (beyond looking funny in a
tank wearing a large helmet), which is that it heightens ethnicity. Tallness
can be deracinating, diluting one's ethnic background. Anyway, it helps.

Speaking of short and ethnic, Justice Scalia's language in his dissent
on striking down the Colorado anti–gay rights law reflected his speech
made earlier to a religious group (the ardor of which was fueled by this
decision, I suppose). It's all over the news and in the *New York Times*
today. Accusing his colleagues of taking sides in a "culture war," Scalia
gets to echo Buchanan and things German. His dissent begins: "The
Court has mistaken a Kulturkampf for a fit of spite." Why the German?
one wonders, with all its unhappy allusions. Who are the Nazis in this
case? He also makes another telling point: "This Court has no business
imposing upon all Americans the resolution favored by the elite class
from which the members of this institution are selected, pronouncing that
'animosity' toward homosexuality, ante, is evil." The elite class: him?
Thomas? That they favor? Scalia may hate his colleagues and want to
appear part of the pitchfork brigade, but he is confused, pointing the
finger in his own hall of mirrors. Scalia, Thomas, and Rehnquist all
dissent; what a threesome, what an allegorical triptych.

Mark Helprin and Peggy Noonan are in the same *Time* magazine as
Trillin. Two speechwriters, one new, one old. *Time* says Helprin
"avoided" the draft in the Vietnam War, but "apparently" served a year
in the Israeli armed forces. Peggy Noonan in a faux memo to Bob Dole
supplies some peppy encouragement, in her patented Republican vale-
dictorian style, the master of high school commencement prose. Noonan
and Matalin are two ethnic captures of the Republican Right, both lured
by bitterness.

I have a conversation with a friend who is not on Scalia's side in the
Colorado decision. He tells me, "I had a dream about Bob Dole. . . . you
know Barak, the foreign minister in the Israeli cabinet? He assassinated
two people." (Doubtless, Mark Helprin knows him, I think.) "He wore
a dress to sneak into an apartment building; I dreamed Bob Dole wore
a dress and won the election."

"Strange, but not that strange," I say. "Two months ago you would
have said that Dole quitting the Senate was as likely as Dole wearing a
dress. . . . Maybe it's prophetic. What sort of dress was it? Fashionable?"

"It was a sundress with polka dots."

"A Kansas dress," I say.

5/22 The back page of the "Business Day" section of the *New York Times* sports a *Wall Street Journal* ad that reprints Mark Helprin: "This is the article that caused the candidate to ask the author to write the speech that announced the decision that changed the campaign," the ad copy reads. Here we can read Helprin in a non-Kansan mode: "Before the moon disappeared on election night 1994, one could hear an echo of triumphalism such as had not been heard since the biblically corrupt outpourings of unchecked pride that followed the apotheosis of Bill Clinton." In this era of speedup, the speechwriter is getting as much play as the speech. Dole has admitted that Helprin worked on the speech, and it appears that only Hillary is holding on to the claim that she writes what is written for her (as she did on C-SPAN), which is the best thing to claim under the circumstances. One oddity about Dole's resignation speech was that the cadences were all wrong. They resembled his short, elliptical remarks, but since Helprin's sentences were full sentences, linked together, they sounded decidedly unBob like. It was the theme-park version of Dole, with the software upgraded.

The deaths on Mount Everest are getting a lot of play. Men and women against nature (but accompanied by Sherpas.) The post-Vietnam generation is given over to a lot of "high-risk" adventure, since there were no society-based and sanctioned death-defying activities provided for them, no Vietnam to assuage the risk impulse, at a critical age.

Hillary, it should be clear to every human in the country, deflects heat from Bill—like alum in a water-treatment plant. If they weren't attacking her, the vacuum would suck in Bill. She halves the attacks. The GOP should realize that all its Hillary hating saves her man.

5/23 Maureen Dowd in the *New York Times* does an irate turn. To paraphrase, she's so curt when she's mad. She brings up Paula Jones and the Soldiers and Sailors Civil Relief Act claim on the part of lawyer Bennett. She concludes, "So Bill Clinton is in the Army. He's against gay marriage. His adviser did work for an alleged rapist. He moves from the left wing to the right wing because what he really believes in is the

West Wing." Or, as my wife says, when I read the column to her, what
you need to be is "upwing." The *Times* is upwing, too, giving over a lot
of letter space to responses to Alan Sokal's *Social Text* spoof. I've often
consider what would happen to a lot of recherche academic critics if they
were forbidden to use twelve words, such as "foreground," "contextual-
ize," etc.

Montel Williams has HUD Secretary Henry Cisneros on his show with
an audience of HUD housing women, large women, one robbed while
giving birth. Bill Clinton's one strike and you're out of public housing is
criticized. "It won't be that strict," Cisneros claims. One of the few black
men present complains he was rousted by cops and his seventy-nine-
dollar sweatshirt got a new neckline, and he denies he did anything,
though he was charged with "disorderly conduct." Hard times in public
housing.

5/24 On Diane Rehm Paul Gigot says the Supreme Court is saying
they're bigots out there in Colorado (its antigay amendment has been
struck down by the Supreme Court). Gigot says he wouldn't have voted
for the referendum, but he's worried that the Court has overruled the
53 percent who voted for it. A state's rights have been traduced. Scalia,
of course, voted to sustain the Colorado amendment. Will the courts let
legislatures settle these matters? Gigot asks wistfully, bringing up California's Civil Rights Initiative, which will be on the November ballot.
Gigot wouldn't vote for such things, but he defends their right to be law.
In the oral culture you can always say more things, take more positions.
It's not as easy to be pinned down. In the Rodney King trial the defense
lawyers attempted to interpret what the videotape actually contained.

Dole's speech in Philadelphia in front of the Catholic Press Association
is commented on: Dole fumbling, not going easily from TelePrompTer
to speech. He's not a video-age guy.

On CNN, Clinton, after a visit to the National Geographic Society, I
learn, thinks the fifteen-year-old ancient mummy in the news is good-
looking. You know, if I were a single man I might ask that mummy out,
he says. Bill's got his own version of White House cabin fever.

5/25 On C-SPAN Ranesh Ponnuru, of *The National Review,* says Clinton was "making a pass at a five-hundred-year-old mummy."

A friend has some El Salvador media: an ad supplement for a veterinarian clinic. Where to take your Dobermans and German shepherds. Pictures of the latest surgical equipment and diagnostic machines. The names of the fourteen ruling families all over the supplement. We both conclude El Salvador is a country without irony.

Jack Kemp is on the *Capital Gang,* talking gingerly against gay marriage. I think back to '86, when Kemp was first talked about as a presidential contender, and the rumors surfacing then about too much hand holding in the huddle. He had been asked about it on the *Today* show in '86 and Kemp offered he had never committed a homosexual act. But none of that is resurrected now. He's just against same-sex marriage.

5/27 Memorial Day finds Dole before veterans, thanking families (those who were there in 1940–45!). Clinton beat Bush the warrior, why wouldn't he beat Dole? Isn't being president worth half the votes Perot got?

Hillary wants to adopt a child, according to *Time*'s June 3 issue, and Bill wants to date five-hundred-year-old dead fifteen-year-olds. Here we have two competing fantasies at opposite ends of some desperate spectrum.

Diane Rehm rebroadcasts last year's Admiral Boorda interview. Everything said by the admiral is now bathed in mortal irony. The Clinton suicide watch.

5/28 I watch a show on PBS's *POV* about the successful Rhode Island congressional campaign of Patrick Kennedy. Payback for Palm Beach. Patrick's Republican opponent, Kevin Vigilante, admitted smoking marijuana. What was I supposed to do, Vigilante asks an adviser over the phone, lie? The man on the other end who hears this groans.

The Whitewater verdicts are in (convictions all around) and *Nightline* is on the case. The McDougals and the sitting governor, guilty. When I was young everything I knew or associated with Arkansas was salacious. Even a postcard from Hot Springs! Its serrated edge itself was stimulating. It was always a picture of a hotel. Arkansas is where you went for underage marriage. All of Arkansas seemed to me at around age twelve to be damp with sex.

Public versus private wealth is actually one of the unarticulated themes of the campaign. There are stories on how run-down the national parks are. The folk are noticing the rich get richer. The folk see the national treasures diminish while private wealth soars, public wealth dips. Christian Coalition types might even be taking note. But they don't tend to vote their pocketbooks. Puritanism in part, but it's also their church is their public wealth, picnics, etc. The June *Sunset* magazine, a favorite of retirees and RVers, does a story on poor federal parks, and there's a short piece on CBS news.

5/29 Diane Rehm does Whitewater trial reaction, money through banks through SBA loans and for their own use. A conspiracy charge. The FBI is good at stings and targeting people. If the Starr show moved into any town with a failed S and L (which is most any town), there would have been more McDougals flapping in the legal winds. Starr has spent more than the $3 million the case involved.

Rush: How many dead people do you know? How many do you know who are in prison? "What do all these people," he asks—Jim Guy Tucker, James and Susan McDougal, Web Hubbell, Fitzhugh, Palmer, indicted—"what do all these people have in common?" William Jefferson Clinton. The White House says Clinton doesn't have anything to do with this. "Really?" Rush says, trying to resist gloating. "You have to marvel at the number of people around the president . . . who are dropping," he says. "Starr is vindicated." He taunts Clinton's "partners of the press, guilty, guilty, guilty."

5/30 Rush answers a caller's question: I wasn't drafted, I didn't volunteer. He says no more. He does a "Hillary Clinton update" song, in reference to the adopt-a-baby business: "You're Having My Baby."

Netanyahu will beat Peres, it appears, for prime minister of Israel.

5/31 In a *New York Times* article about reactions to the Whitewater verdicts, a woman Dole supporter parrots Rush of the day before. ("Look, how many people do you know who've been indicted or convicted. I don't know any. I don't know people who've been indicted.") It's obvious Rush provides the talking points for the hoi polloi.

NINE

June/Spoon/Moon

6/3 Ralph Reed is on Charlie Rose. Look who's coming to dinner. Rose asks Reed what single promise he would extract from Dole, if he could extract just one. Reed ponders, well aware of his liberal, upscale Charlie Rose audience. The single promise, Reed intones, would be that Dole appoint a "strict constructionist" to the Supreme Court. And Reed thinks Dole should do a tax cut Clinton could not match. What figure would that be? I wonder. End the capital-gains tax? Ralph also has a book he's promoting, *Active Faith*. Reed's overall aspect is bland enough that he does pick up the coloration of whatever flora he's around. "Whatever Pat Robertson says, Ralph Reed believes," Reed says as Rose tries to lure Reed out of his I'm-just-one-of-the-guys shell. Reed says that the Left has a conspiracy theory: that he is the moderate voice for a hidden agenda. He gives Rose a look of disbelief. "Which is ridiculous," Reed says, meaning the agenda isn't hidden. He smiles his boyish look, which overall resembles one of those sad photographs of a 1930s youth that are produced of the just-exposed elderly SS war criminal. Reed has an odd smile: it snaps open, like a bear trap in reverse, revealing a lot of sharp teeth.

On NBC's *Late Night* show, Conan O'Brien claims Dole's résumé goes back to the seventeenth century. "Sea captain," O'Brien announces, as if reading. "He's old, old."

The couch has returned briefly to California. My brother-in-law was married near a pond in the Santa Cruz mountains. On our way to Steinbeck's Monterey we pass Fort Ord, a friend of mine's last stop stateside before he shipped off to Vietnam in 1968. A lot of the low mustard-colored buildings are shut, empty. They dot the hillside acreage here in this lovely spot near the sea. I imagine Fort Ord when it was teeming with young, expectant men. It is now becoming a branch of the University of California university system. These military holdings have acted, until now, as bulwarks against commercial developers. Perhaps someday Fort Ord University can be an old-folks community for baby boomers. The economy still looks pretty good out here, at least on the Coast.

But, there's fog and and an atmosphere of unfinished business: O.J. is still wandering in California's mist, civil trial preparations are ongoing, and I conclude O.J., all in all, is another public-relations blow for the GOP, the spectacle of yet another rich guy getting off.

6/7 The *San Francisco Chronicle* has a front-page headline: "Study of Monkeys Suggests Oral Sex Isn't Safe." Monkeys are "easily infected" with an AIDS-like virus through the mouth. More bad news in Dole's last days in the Senate: the balanced-budget amendment lost by two votes. Conservatives certainly want to amend rather than conserve. And D'Amato made some quick money ($37,125 in a one-day transaction, according to the story [A3]) in a special deal with a "Lake Success," New York, brokerage house. Al just can't suppress his instincts, but he still wants to get David Hale to testify before his Senate Whitewater committee before it expires next week. A "series of errors" is blamed for the Ron Brown crash near Dubrovnik (A3). (I'm reading this on a plane flying back to Indiana.) There's a picture of Ted Kennedy praying at the grave of his brother Robert, whose death anniversary was yesterday (A4). There's also a piece on the pay of special prosecutors (A2): "The four continuing probes of Clinton Administration officials have cost about $17 million so far, with about $2.2 million spent on salaries and benefits for independent counsel attorneys and support staff from April to September 1995 alone." Keep that employment up! Raise the minimum wage of lawyers!

The *Wall Street Journal* has a "Washington Wire" paragraph saying there are clashes between Clinton's economic team and Dick Morris, who's pushing, evidently, for a capital-gains tax cut (one that Dole can't match, perhaps?).

James Carville is in the "Life" section of *USA Today,* saying it would be "exciting" if the Clintons adopted a child. There's a nondenial denial for you. Can't dispute that. Carville's book, *We're Right, They're Wrong,* is out, and the timing lets him make campaign appearances for free— like Hillary, the Doles, Reed, etc., the slew of public figures who use books as personal advertising vehicles, rather than as entities in themselves. Carville has got the media wired. He's the *Playboy* interview for July. The book sports his cover photo, though aides supplied most of the text. He admits that if he was the sort of person "who put justice above ego, Lowell [Weiss's] name would be on the cover of this book with mine."

Dole is testing some abortion "tolerance," but the left hand knows what the right hand is doing in the GOP. Mary Matalin, in her and Carville's book on the '92 campaign, *All's Fair,* wrote: "But word got out that we were supposedly backing off the pro-life position, and the ground troops of the pro-life movement went absolutely nuts. They drew a line in the sand" (293). This time, Dole's tolerance plea is written in preamble sand, the pro-life plank in concrete.

6/8 Michael Feldman's *Whad'Ya Know?* show opens with a gag: "Mr. Perot, party of one, your table is ready, Mr. Perot, party of one."

6/9 On *Face the Nation,* William Weld takes the liberal Republican abortion position. Ralph Reed declares Dole's position (tolerance in the back of the bus) "a major victory" for our group. Reed is doing yeoman PR work for Dole. A "pro-life, pro-family, pro-term limits" veep choice is necessary, Reed says, if Dole wants to win. No line in the sand, that.

That Ralph Reed is spokesperson is completely credible when one considers the alternatives: Jerry Falwell or Reed's mentor, Pat Robertson.

Couldn't put any of them forward. It requires the new generation, by necessity.

On *Firing Line,* Naomi Wolf expounds on abortion, taking the position she did in her October 16, 1995, *New Republic* article, "Our Bodies, Our Souls: What the Pro-Choice Movement Must Learn to Say," which is similar to James Fallows's fame-making, I-feel-guilty-for-not-serving article, "What Did You Do in the Class War, Daddy?" in the *Washington Monthly* (August, 1975) at the end of the Vietnam War. (Fallows's recent book attacking journalists for his own sins is the more mature version of his old attack on his fellow draft dodgers for not feeling more guilty about getting free of the draft.) Wolf is part of the common-ground movement and, when it comes to abortion, there's not much common ground. The poll percentage numbers in favor of "choice" haven't shifted over the years, even less than the candidate numbers thus far in this campaign.

There's an ad on PBS that boasts: 90 million without cable TV—but are those millions watching PBS? I doubt it.

On *The McLaughlin Group,* Clarence Thomas (there's been some flap over an invitation for Thomas to speak at a school that has been withdrawn) is praised and McLaughlin said the invitation came about when Thomas visited for one and a half hours with these schoolkids in Washington. I wonder why does a Supreme Court justice have so much free time?

C-SPAN shows a broadcast from Friday. Media campaign consultants talk about the Internet. They are not enthusiastic. It's "a gimmick," it's "passive media"—"the only ones who look at it are your enemies and your friends." Not the uncommitted voters you want. Alex Castellanos, who worked for Phil Gramm (and, I presume, is looking for work), brings up the poll about "Who would you like to baby-sit?" and says, if it was asked who would you want to baby-sit your teenage daughters . . .

The Internet: it is the worst of all worlds, the best of all worlds, the end of all worlds, etc. Its biggest drawback is that the Internet is in real time, so it's a time saver that doesn't save you any time. It *is* the modern library of the twenty-first century, where all reference material is "accessible." Web surfing seems to be an enthusiasm (especially its chat groups) of the largely male nerd-world, Tolkien-heads, Dungeon and Dragon devotees, Trekkies, obsessive types. The constant downloading of porn is

similar to when I was a young teenager and discovered the art repro-
ductions in the *Encyclopaedia Britannica*. Bare breasts! Now, of course,
everything is bared and those who want to bar are out there, too. It
doesn't take a Unabomber to see where the wind is blowing.

One thing I discovered on the Internet is that from any Web site you
are six clicks away from an anti-Semitic screed. Of the primary candidates, Forbes's Web site was the most spiffy, which wasn't a surprise,
given that he owns a magazine and has a lot of graphic designers at his
beck and call.

D'Amato's questionable stock profits were the swan song of his Whitewater hearings. Now he's moving on to the White House FBI personnel
files flap.

6/10   The *NewsHour* has Dick Lamm, former governor of Colorado,
who is running to be the Reform/Perot Party presidential candidate,
saying, "The Social Security system is obsolete and should be scrapped."
He's sixty years old and has his retirement all worked out.

On NPR's *ATC,* we learn the Tutsis and Hutus don't like each other,
the same trenchant point Thomas L. Friedman made Friday on *Washington Week in Review* about Serbs and Croats and their immediate
neighbors: they don't want to live next to Muslims. They just don't like
each other, etc. Now we know the reason for conflict in the late twentieth
century. The majority are Hutus, 85 percent, but the ruling class is Tutsis, in Burundi, one of Rwanda's neighbors.

Clarence Thomas: his equation is, if affirmative action put the likes of
me on the Supreme Court, it should be abolished. Proof of the pudding.
That affirmative action helped "elite" blacks more than the common folk
is now used as an argument against it. It made them like dollars in
Europe after World War II. The inflationary value was very high. The
top could write their own ticket. And they would take advantage of the
historic moment. Below, everyone else has to struggle along, though only
Republicans believe things were better in the Jim Crow days.

6/11   A Diane Rehm caller from Washington had seen her somewhere, and supplies: "And you're also pretty." The talk is about burning
churches. And Clinton taking the photo-op lead denouncing them. Pat

Buchanan should be telling them, not the president, Diane says. An anti-Clinton caller named John holds that Clinton politicized the church burnings: "He's the one who is cavalierly lying." "Cavalierly" is Diane's word, used earlier, thrown back at her. And a very Diane word it is.

Ron Noble, former Justice Department and Treasury person, is her guest. He thinks the southern church burnings have come about because of like-minded types doing similar things and not a legal conspiracy. The Internet hooks together right-wing groups: you know what our purposes are is their message and so it is a shared view, but not direct conspiracy. "More than a copycat," Noble calls it. A caller asks darkly: Who gains from this? (The burning of the churches.) Enemies of our nation gain. His analysis is of the wild conspiracy theorist stripe—liberals are burning churches to make good white Americans look bad.

A counsel for the National Council of Churches comes on and takes a more generally pessimistic (but realistic) view. He says the press links O. J. and the Million Man March, and produces a presidential campaign with issues that are all colored: welfare, crime, immigration. He sees the campaign (especially from the Republican side) as largely antiblack, anti–people of color, since all the issues are colored: crime, welfare, immigration.

A black guy from South Bend(!) calls in and asks about all the blacks that have been killed, Fred Hampton, etc., how the government infiltrated black groups. Why? he asks rhetorically.

The Internet phenomenon is returned to and the fact that it is the easiest way to link up crazies. Nothing previous gave disparate people such a private/public way to link up. Ads would be too public—so you get individuals turning into groups because the Internet can be sampled "privately." It is a new kind of voyeurism. The dream of being at one's own funeral, just watching what people think, say, and not being seen. Chat groups can take on a lifeboat atmosphere: the ship of community has gone down and disparate passengers are thrown together, bonded by electronic catastrophe. They're all caught in the web, governed by cyberspace fate.

E-mail is the most rhetorical of communication devices since it is not well considered. You get stream of consciousness, and a version not yet sufficiently inhibited. (True of all new modes of communication: for a while they're freewheeling, till conventions take root.) E-mail mates telegram and postcard style with post it notes and phone conversation. Speed overtakes rhetoric. There's a whole book of Reagan/Bush White House E-mail, called just that, *White House E-mail*, full of embarrassing revelations. It's the generation after taping.

"It's formatted to fit your TV screen," as videos will announce. Formatted for the new context, a new consciousness. We are all being formatted.

6/12 NPR *Morning Edition* has news about an old MOVE lawsuit, finally coming to a conclusion, so *ME* covers some of that case. I was amazed watching the Philadelphia air force drop its bomb. One result was a federal law concerning "unreasonable force." (Though it is often law enforcement which often ends sieges with fire.) Though not the Freemen; they are to "surrender" after eighty-one days. Oh, Montana.

A black comic, James Hanna, on *Def Comedy Jam,* does a black *Jeopardy* parody. Question: What can forty dollars get you sixty-five dollars' worth of? Answer: Food stamps. How you can tell if you're ghetto? If your grandmother is younger than forty years old, you're ghetto. If you keep your money and valuables in a purple Crown Royal bag, you're ghetto. Lots of laughter from the black audience.

6/14 The *New York Times* reports that Arizona governor Fife Symington has been indicted for making false statements to savings and loan officers when he went looking for loans to shore up his real estate shenanigans. I wonder if every sitting governor is indictable. One more down. How many to go?

On the *NewsHour,* Shields and Gigot are chatting with Jim Lehrer about the White House's use of FBI files. Shields says, "I think the demarcation point for Bill Clinton's administration and its political vulnerability is January 20, 1993, forward. I really don't think that the stuff before that, the—sort of the Arkansas stuff is really going to stick with 'em, but this is on his watch. This is during his presidency, and I think this is—this is one that he has to explain." Gigot gives Clinton a drubbing: "He basically said these are these people, these rogue people working, you know, doing this, and, and there's a problem that this White

House has had all along, Jim, which is that with the General Counsel's Office, which is sort of the ethics headquarters of any White House, it gives the impression sometimes that it's being run by Johnnie Cochran." More O. J.-ification of the campaign. "I mean, everything is spin," says Gigot, who ought to know. "Let's claim executive privilege," he says, imagining the White House's attitude, "and then we'll dribble out the documents and dismiss facts."

There is a history of the Clintons wanting to amass files on folks. Roger Morris's new book, *Partners in Power,* is out, another of the precampaign campaign books, and it covers a lot of familiar ground, but with a different emphasis: the Clintons are yuppies overall. Morris concentrates on money, hence *power* (though the Clintons do seem to have accurately surfed their—my—generation's wave, they were antiwar, but never anticapital). A lifelong habit of keeping index-card lists of people one's met reveals a penchant for knowing personal information. (The boss needs to know the names of his employees' children.) In Morris's book there are a couple of examples: one about when Clinton had some competition for governor from Steve Clark, an Arkansas attorney general. Morris writes, "The governor had been anxious about Clark's poll numbers. Clinton pressed for 'somebody to take him down,' as Dickey remembered him saying. 'What can we get that's real good?' Clinton had asked. Records had been checked, calls made, the first tips given in a trail Clark obligingly provided by his own abuses, and a last local obstacle was eliminated" (458).

And personal research was used as a dam against the bimbo revelations flow. Morris writes, " 'Where's the info on Gennifer?' Hillary Clinton had asked Little Rock from a pay phone on the campaign trail when the story broke" (466).

Index cards will eventually lead to FBI files, if it is an obsessive habit. And any lawyer will tell you, you can never know too much. The sympathetic interpretation I hear for summoning all the FBI personnel files is that they were attempting to find a standard of questionable conduct that would be used to compare the folks the Clinton administration wanted to pass through to what had passed through in the past. You had drug use, we have drug use, etc.

Dole's "tolerance" plank becomes the *NewsHour*'s topic. Lehrer says,

"Let's refresh people's memory. What we're talking about here is his insistence that in the party platform plan"—he means "plank"—"on abortion there be a tolerance clause at the top. We're all pro-life but we understand those who don't agree with us, essentially that."

Gigot says, about Dole, "Last week, it looked to be a home run. He had it all settled. The Right and the Left were all pretty happy with it because it was going to be in the preamble?. . . . And then Bob Dole basically on his own comes out and says, you know, I want it in that abortion plank, and the whole—calm waters start roiling again." Shields comments, "I don't know what he did this week, other than guarantee he's going to have a floor fight in San Diego."

Then it's burning churches. Lehrer says, "The president took a hit from Dick Armey, the House leader, for going to this black church that had been burned in South Carolina. Armey suggested it was politics, and he said the president went there for a photo op."

Shields calls Armey's remarks "reprehensible and stupid," and recalls Reagan in '82 going to visit a family who had a cross burned on its lawn. More glorious moments of the presidency all around, comforting the afflicted, etc.

Movies of the moment are *The Rock,* a Sean Connery adventure, Sean as the Unabomber grown old asked to come out of retirement in prison and make one more bomb to be sent to . . . only kidding. It's Alcatraz, missiles, San Francisco in peril, rebel military, unhappy about POWs, etc. As various people have noticed, you can root for the bad guys, the good guys, any of the guys. It's a very guy movie. *Independence Day,* the movie, is getting a lot of promotion. The paperback of Richard Ford's novel of the same name was on *USA Today*'s best-seller list yesterday, number 36. Maybe buyers think it is the movie novelization. Any page now the Martians will be showing up, they think.

6/16 On *Meet the Press,* our host ends the show talking against *Independence Day*. (The campaign is really taking a backseat these days.) When the Capitol dome was disintegrated, Bob Schieffer says, I winced and turned my eyes, as if away from dead bodies at an accident scene.

On *Face the Nation,* William Bennett brings up the ninety minutes Thomas spent in his office with the schoolkids who invited him to speak.

Thomas does his deep thinking quickly, so he has a lot of time to entertain visitors to the Court. The revoked invitation appears to have been unrevoked.

Firing Line has Alan Dershowitz saying, "I believe we should cooperate with crime—" His slip gets laughs from panelists, Tony Lewis and other stalwarts. They're talking about "crime prevention," and Buckley is constantly looking disgustedly dismayed. Dershowitz is doing his brightest kid in the yeshiva number, appearing impossibly smug.

6/17 The *Washington Post* has an article in its June 3–9 weekly edition about the deregulation of airlines. Used jets ValuJet bought cost $6 million, whereas United Airlines and Southwest paid around $30 million. ValuJet's copilots, almost anyone who would go to a school, evidently, were paid $25,000 and incentives. More fruits of deregulation.

Timothy McVeigh keeps reminding me of Lee Harvey Oswald. McVeigh grants a videotaped interview with his lawyer and acts as I imagined Lee Harvey would have, if Oswald had gotten a chance to do the same. I'm a cool cat, yes I am.

On Diane Rehm we have Dick Lamm of the Reform Party. "I hope the Reform Party comes along and eclipses the other political parties," he says, paraphrasing Perot. "I am generally a free trader," he says.

Lamm quotes Richard Hofstadter on third parties, they should "sting like a bee and die." "We could do much better than the gridlock and stalemate that is going on in Congress now," he says.

Bumper stickers which catch my eye: "Perot." "Fed Up with the Fed, Abolish the Federal Reserve." "Defeat the Dope-smoking Draft-dodging . . ."

Rivera Live. After an O. J. Bronco ride reprise, Geraldo reports on polls that show Clinton leads from 6 to 22 points. Then we get the Arkansas trial, the Whitewater report, Hillary's letter, in lieu of testifying, to D'Amato's committee about who hired whom: Craig Livingstone? Don't know him.

Our answering machine gets a recorded message from the police for my wife, the block captain. A robbery in our neighborhood. What was stolen? U.S. currency, miscellaneous identification, food stamps. The usual haul is the VCR, the television set.

6/18 Diane Rehm has open phones today. Nutcases seem to predominate. Ken, the feisty editor of, I think, *CounterPunch,* gets through again to heap some scorn on Diane: I'm glad to hear you read the *New York Times, Washington Post, Wall Street Journal,* the inside-the-Beltway power elite, corporate lackey, etc. Thanks, Ken, she says.

There's economic diarrhea from both ends—surplus capital taken out of industry, housing inflated. Both generated cash based on no production and left the body dehydrated.

Rush is playing "Having My Baby" again: wouldn't have happened two weeks ago (his spirits are up, his criticism of Clinton reinvigorated). A caller says the president should get a divorce, end his Hillary problems.

Rush is now playing "They'll Get You Babe," his takeoff on the old Sonny and Cher hit. "I may be bad, but you're a clown. . . ." "Presidents get pardoned and others do the hard time." "They'll get you for Travelgate, Paula Jones, I just can't wait." Then Rush is on to his "Try to Remember" parody. "I don't remember that big money lender."

USA Today has two news flashes today: Clarence Thomas "converts" to Catholicism and the Catholic author Mary Gordon has discovered her essential Judaism. Win one, lose one.

6/19 In the *New York Times* there's a review of a campaign documentary of the '94 Senate race in Virginia, starring Oliver North and Charles Robb. The only "victories" Democrats took comfort in in '94 were Robb's over Ollie North and Dianne Feinstein's defeat of the millionaire California carpetbagger Michael Huffington, Arianna's husband. Mark Goodin, North's "campaign strategist," is quoted from the film, saying, "So we provide daily entertainment. What we are not providing is serious solutions to what's going on in the country. Not us, not Chuck, not Clinton, not Bush. Not anybody."

Janet Maslin's review puts me in mind of the dumbing-down question again, and one of the hidden causes of that was the Vietnam War. A portion of Dole's World War II generation became international. Dole left Kansas and discovered: It's not Kansas anymore. Washington. Europe. Whereas my generation only had the backwater of Vietnam to go to, not an encounter with Europe, Western civilization, etc. Not that the Vietnamese don't have a glorious civilization, but GIs in Vietnam remained as much as possible in a cocoon of Americana, music, drugs, beer.

On Diane Rehm a caller (!) brings up Garry Wills's *New York Review* article on Whitewater, which reviewed *Blood Sport*. Its author, James Stewart, is Diane's guest. He responds, but never mentions Wills's name or criticisms.

The Clintons have generated more books than Bush, Reagan, and Carter combined. You need to go back to Nixon, and his haul was over a lifetime, not a mere three years in office. But it is odd how *Partners in Power,* the Roger Morris book, is getting treated. As one political wife once told another, the bimbos get better looking as your husband goes upward in political office, from local to national. In fact they go from being bimbos to being accomplished women. And the books, and authors and publishers, get more respectable and exude higher status, too. But, though Morris is highly respectable and his publisher, Henry Holt, is not some weird right-wing press, he's being afforded ten-foot-pole attention. According to the trade magazine *Publisher's Weekly* (June 24), Morris was knocked off *60 Minutes* and the front page of the *Washington Post*'s book review.

Rush ends his program with more talk of Hillary, what she feels when she visits "mansions"—that they should be turned into public housing, what did the people do to deserve this, that she would have one one day. A bit of projection from the Rushmeister.

I'm on the phone with a reporter friend. One subject is the Unabomber. "How close those impulses are to rationality," my friend says. We discuss the differences between Dole's generation and Clinton's. The Unabomber managed to construct and remain in a vacuum of his generation.

We talk about Dole's Mark Helprin speech, Dole's tears. Dole's crying more these days. Which I ascribe to age. Yet his resignation speech was full of different rhythms, Dole the blues singer trying out folk tunes. But it contained genuine emotion. Sorrowful, tragic, a noble gesture—quitting the Senate for the possibility of becoming president—since it will likely go unrewarded.

On the Massachusetts Senate race front, William Weld, it appears, is what you would might call an unapologetic drinker. John Kerry bought a twenty-thousand-dollar motorcycle, but made no charitable contributions. Consultants' judgment of Kerry: he will do anything to get elected and will do what he is told. Ditto Clinton. If McCain is the veep choice, it would give the Republicans double-barreled war heroes. The best ticket for them, I think.

Later, I have lunch with another friend, a former Vietnam-era jailed draft resister. We talk about Roger Morris's book, Morris's speculation that Clinton was a CIA asset when he was at Oxford. We talk about an actual CIA asset, a former NSA president, who created the boom for Ansel Adams photographs. He used his Washington contacts to promote Adams quite successfully. Clinton only looked antiwar (that beard!) when he was in England. SDS types were also the BMOC sorts, which is one of the things made clear in Todd Gitlin's book, *The Sixties*.

6/20   Rush opines it's 40 percent for Clinton, 40 against; it's the 20 percent left they need to get. What should the Dole campaign do? It should heed my advice, Rush says. Tie the character issue to personal leadership. Clinton says we are going to starve your children and we say we're going to increase the amount of aid. Who do you believe?

I muse with a friend over the fact that the phrase "policy wonk" and Clinton came up at the same time. "Nerds are to being as wonks are to becoming," my friend, a sociologist, remarks.

6/21   It remains the mirror image of Bush being up by so much in '90 and then down near the election. Whereas Clinton was down so much in '94 and is now up.

On last Sunday's talk shows, the mantra coming from the Democrats was twenty weeks, twenty weeks. Like the home stretch, hoping their front-running horse doesn't break his leg in the last twenty yards.

On NPR's *All Things Considered,* Dole is claiming all the places he's "lived": Fort Benning, Georgia; Brooklyn College—where he studied after joining the military; in Miami, from where he once called his parents. All because of the army. It's more evidence how World War II made GIs more cosmopolitan, less parochial, even in the States, much less abroad.

Ellen Willis in *The Village Voice* (June 25) does a sharp article on

Sokal's *Social Text* hoax. She writes, "Conservatives have done a good job of fomenting hostility toward the professoriat. As they (accurately) see it, the university is an irritating obstacle to the cultural counterrevolution. Protected by tenure, too many academics remain stubbornly liberal. . . . Even as the right's rhetoric invokes the noble heritage of the liberal arts and sciences against 'politicize nonsense,' its professor-bashing agenda incites and exploits the anti-intellectual currents endemic to American culture." Her personal connections to *Social Text* (living with the founder, friend of the editor) gives her an interesting frankness. Also Arkansas' own Gene Lyons in July *Harper's* jumps on *Blood Sport*. Lyons is committed to the see-no-evil side of this controversy. His "forthcoming" book is to be called *Fools for Scandal: How the Media Invented Whitewater*. State pride at work! I certainly think Jim McDougal invented himself. Lyons's point (or what irritates him the most) appears to be that "the purely commercial aspects of *Blood Sport* exceed by several times those of the Whitewater real estate venture that gave its name to the official Washington 'scandal.' Had Whitewater gone exactly according to plan, the Clintons and their fellow investors Jim and Susan McDougal would have anticipated net profits of $47,500 each—rather less, I daresay, than Simon & Schuster is spending to promote Stewart's book."

Rush on the Republican Congress: "They bit off more then they could chew. . . . Maybe they went too fast." Caller: "Clinton lies so much he had to have a growth removed from his nose recently."

6/23 On *Meet the Press*, we have mayors, including Steve Goldsmith of Indianapolis, the Republican who is running for governor. Goldsmith is getting some national play, since he has sold himself as a darling of privatization, though some of his hometown Marion County Republicans can't stand him. Their thought is he's trying to get out of the mayor of Indianapolis's job before the crows start coming home to roost. After the mayors, William Safire shows he is really upset about Filegate. Woodward's book, formerly *The Race,* is now called *The Choice.* (I figure the folks at Simon & Schuster didn't think the campaign was much of a race.) The "news" of the book—the *Washington Post*'s front-page story— is Hillary holding conversations with Eleanor Roosevelt and Mahatma Gandhi with help from a spiritual adviser. In the tradition of Nancy

Reagan—*Fox News Sunday* takes that tact. Tony Coelho, the Wall Street operative and former congressman, who often needed defending himself when he resigned from Congress in 1989, defends Hillary.

The Choice will be the book of the talk month.

Safire says on *Meet the Press* that the scandal resides in the White House counsel's office. But I wonder how bad could the files be, since all these folks had been "cleared"?

Sherman's March ends in the Atlanta Olympics, a friend remarks. The Disney-fication of history continues, thanks, this time, to Coke.

6/24 The 1982 *Atlantic Monthly* broken-window theory of James Q. Wilson is on NPR's *Morning Edition,* which describes a car experiment, watching it be disassembled after it shows one small bit of breakage. The metaphor of plague, epidemics, as the model for social problems is taking hold throughout the land.

In *All's Fair,* Carville complains that the *New York Times* didn't cover Gennifer Flowers, but "they'd run seven draft articles in one issue" (432)—but that's because the *Times*'s senior editors had so much experience chasing women around their desks. Some of that turns up in Henry Louis Gates's story (June 17) about Anatole Broyard in *The New Yorker*.

Ms. Clinton's psychic story is all over. It's on *Chicago Tonight,* Hillary's hometown and '68 revisited this year (the Democratic convention site.) *Chicago Tonight*'s set has the look, atmosphere of an upscale steak house. I expect to see stiff drinks on the table. Hog butcher to the world, etc. Even the women on the program look to be serious drinker types. Hillary isn't to be compared to Nancy Reagan in the psychic business, but to Nixon, wandering the halls, breaking under the stress, talking to the portraits. It's the pressure, stupid.

CNN's *Inside Politics* reports, according to a survey, there've been 175 Dole jokes and 101 Clinton jokes since the California primary.

O.J. does appear to be a tragic figure wandering the public stage, insofar as that in Greek tragedies the dead are often seen as props, lying about unpleasantly for the protagonist to step over, all the while moaning and groaning about his fate.

Newt Gingrich is on *Larry King Live* (CNN)—Newt seems resurrected, a little rested, thinner. I wonder if he does have a prosthetic ear (the left one?).

Somewhere in Kentucky Dole says milk and tobacco are both harmful. (Would he say that in Wisconsin?)

Gingrich is beating the Medicare drum, defending the noncuts, saying the increment raise was around three hundred dollars a person, and, as an aside, saying he "was at a candidate school today."

On C-SPAN, David Maraniss and Richard Ben Cramer are talking about their books, the Bill Clinton bio and Cramer's painstaking look at the '88 campaign. Cramer tells about Dole humming a song from a campaign video to cheer someone up. Cramer says, "For Dole . . . a political setback isn't the worst day of his life, it isn't one of the worst one hundred." That's what Cramer likes about Dole. (Cramer always comes back to personal sacrifice, which isn't part of Clinton's makeup.)

Raining on Bob Woodward's parade is a *Gentlemen's Quarterly* article (June) about Janet Cooke, late of the Pulitzer Prize and the *Washington Post,* the Vanessa Williams of journalism. Her story of a child needle addict was a fake. Now you see it, now you don't. (Though a brother-in-law of mine, when he was interning at Johns Hopkins, told me of dead children arriving in the ER with needles dangling from their arms, junkie parents having overdosed them in an attempt to keep them quiet.)

6/25 On Diane Rehm Filegate is discussed. Joseph diGenova, a former special prosecutor and O. J. regular from *Rivera Live* is discussing the pitfalls of the special prosecutor's office. He cleared the Bush people involved in the "Clinton passport scandal." O. J. has been the farm club for this year's crop of political commentators.

Nancy Friday follows, discussing her new book on beauty. The subject winds its sinewy way to artifical insemination and sperm banks. Friday tells us: "No one wants the sperm of a short man." And one wonders why Dukakis lost. (When it comes to sperm, I consider Nancy Friday an expert.) I try to imagine Bill Clinton at, say, five-six. No way.

In the July 1 *Newsweek*'s excerpt of the Woodward book, just out, Woodward takes credit (obliquely) for the budget agreement, because he told Dole that Bill Clinton resented Dole's harsh criticism, his call for an independent Whitewater special prosecutor, on the day Clinton's mom died. Dole realized his error and he and Clinton kissed and made up. The result was the latest budget agreement. Bob Woodward saves the nation again!

Last weekend the conventional wisdom on TV solidified. It's Clinton versus Clinton. Dole has vanished from the race, dropped by both parties by and large.

Rush is on to class-envy stuff—it works, he says. For those without "legitimate dreams," who can never see themselves making a hundred thousand dollars. An overly enthusiastic caller gets him to demur on "this New Age stuff. . . . I'm opposed to this self-help stuff. Not all of it mind you; *The Seven Habits of Highly Effective People*" is good, he says. Rush doesn't want to be in the "self-help" camp. He's an intellectual. The Supreme Court has agreed to hear Clinton's request to delay the Paula Jones suit. So no arguments till late fall and no trial, regardless of the outcome, until after the election. Clarence Thomas will hear the oral arguments: Paula meet Anita. The Soldiers and Sailors Civil Relief Act is not the cause, says lawyer Bennett.

The Weekly Standard runs an article on Deepak Chopra (July 1) by Matt Labash. As the Maharishi is to Chopra, Pat Robertson is to Ralph Reed. It's a good article, done before the Hillary flap. It reminds me of the telechurch phenomenon, how fundamentalists led the way using TV and video to raise money (perhaps Jerry Lewis was the avatar, but they got out of the marathon notion). EST didn't last long enough to get onto TV, but this is what the politicians noticed, especially Newt: TV and video aimed at niche audiences to raise funds, both directly (through sales and pitches) and indirectly (fund-raising later, after the marks are softened up).

I catch the end of an *Oprah* show. Oprah pulls Koppel's hair to counter toupee calumny. Ted doesn't say anything. Whatever it is (hair?), it stays on his head. Oprah says, "There!" Maybe it's a weave, I think. Howdy Doody grown up, which is why my generation responds to Koppel's look.

And speaking of looks, I catch Craig Livingstone testifying in congress about how he was hired. Craig claims he never met Vince Foster. Who did he write a thank-you note for getting the job? he is asked. Craig can't pin down who brought him into the White House's orbit. Bar bouncer will now always precede his name, and he looks it. Big, bulky, someone who immediately rumples. Testifying, Craig has the caved-in look about the mouth of a man who's lost his dentures.

On *Nightline* we learn the Saudis have gotten poorer since the Gulf War, according to a *New York Times* reporter, Judith Miller, author of a book on the Middle East. The topic is the terrorist truck explosion near U.S. military living quarters on a base in Saudi Arabia. Shades of Oklahoma City, a building with a façade ripped off. Nineteen American military people were killed today. How did the truck get inside the base? No one asks that question.

6/26 The Supreme Court gelds the Virginia Military Institute. Justice Clarence Thomas's son goes there (where else?), so he didn't deliberate. Scalia the only no vote (7 to 1), Scalia says it "would ruin the school." Go, Scalia, go.

Rush: I don't come here every day to engineer the demise of President Clinton. There are some Republicans who don't believe Nixon did anything wrong. A not too bright caller asks: I can't believe it, how do you motivate yourself?

6/27 Maureen Dowd does another curt-when-I'm-mad column in the *New York Times*: "Bill Clinton is the only president who is still social climbing."

My wife objects when I read her Dowd's column. No, she says. It's Robert Rubin who is president; he's on top of the social heap. He gets to decide who has millions to spend. What does Clinton get to do? He gets Megan's Law.

Diane Rehm is on the VMI case. Then we get the editor of the *New England Journal of Medicine* on breast cancer. She makes the point that silicone was first introduced in Japan to make prostitutes more desirable to American GIs. Another triumph of the war/progress/medicine equation.

Rush has got a call from someone who was at the Filegate hearings yesterday. Rush says, surprised, "You were in the room?" Yes, the caller says, and, somewhat abashedly, I'm one of the 3 percent of the press who is conservative. You know what I would have done, if I was Livingstone, the caller says; I would have told Lantos to come down and take off the gloves and settle it right there, if he would have said those things to me. Rush says Livingstone was already beaten down. The caller persists, wanting to go mano a mano with Tom Lantos (D-Cal.). Then he asks Rush, What's Lantos's claim to fame? The Holocaust. That he says he survived the Holocaust? Rush rattles some papers. I have his bio here. He was born in Budapest. . . . The caller interrupts, restating the physical approach. Rush says, You want them to duke it out, and then goes to the tape and plays Lantos's remarks: "I am pleased you submitted your resignation. You should have done that earlier? . . . With an infinitely more distinguished public record than yours, Admiral Boorda committed suicide when he may have committed a minor mistake? . . . You should have done this a long time ago."

Then Rush says, the Park police have mounted extra surveillance at Mount Morrissey Park (the Vincent Foster suicide site.)

Bob Dole tells Peter Jennings on ABC, apropos of nicotine, that "some people who've tried it can quit easily, others don't quit, so I guess it's addictive to some and not to others." Some Kansan common sense. What Bob needs is some Washington uncommon sense.

I watch Bob Woodward with Gergen on the *NewsHour*. David Gergen, creature of the event par excellence, asks for a Hillary/Liddy comparison. Woodward replies, "I think Elizabeth Dole is a great lawyer, and she is her husband's lawyer. . . . She wrote him a memo, here are the downsides, and then when he said, No, this is what I want to do, uh, she wrote him a note saying, 'Trust God with the outcome.'" "Right," Gergen interjects. "Not something I would expect Hillary Clinton to write to Bill Clinton."

Then there's Jean Houston on *Larry King Live*. She's the New Age figure, Hillary's "guru," who Woodward has made temporarily famous. She looks like an upper-class woman out of the arts and crafts school. Where's Mary Lee Bateson? King wonders, another Hillary adviser, Margaret Mead's daughter. She dropped out, Houston says. Bateson's hiding out at an "art colony." Not King's unspoken point. Houston is the weird news person, Bateson isn't. She fudges the source of her Ph.D here—inflated résumés, including hers, are in the news, thanks to Craig

Livingstone—by mentioning both Columbia and "Union" (Union Theological Seminary).

On my local news: Jeffrey Dahmer's kitchen utensils sold for four hundred thousand dollars to a private business group, which destroyed them. Jackie O and Jeffrey are the big auction stories of the year.

Shaquille O'Neal is on *Letterman* talking about his new film, *Kazam*, where he plays a five-thousand-year-old genie with an attitude. Letterman says: Just like Bob Dole. Shaquille puts on a shocked face and gestures I didn't say that.

6/28   I catch a *USA Today* poll of two days ago on who wants to be president: a small number of young people, less than 20 percent, would. The exposure.

At the I Can't Believe It's Yogurt my family goes to, on the manager's door, there's a clipped article from June's *Restaurant News* titled "Why the Minimum Wage Is Bad for Us All." Fewer employees, etc. This bit of journalism is for the edification of the teenagers behind the counter, I suppose.

6/29   Dole's campaign is going up in smoke. It's not nicotine that's doing him in, but the tar-baby aspect. His campaign keeps compounding his troubles. The *New York Times* reports that Dole's people sent a letter to C. Everett Koop, making Dole's uncertainties news once again. Headline: "Dole Re-Asserts His Doubts That Tobacco Is Addictive." Koop had said he was "baffled" by Dole's earlier remarks. Tobacco is becoming Willie Horton? (This campaign is one, two, three, many Willie Hortons.)

I catch on C-SPAN John Frohnmayer, former head of the NEA, giving a speech on "Censorship and the Arts" in Santa Clara, California. Oh, John. The near demise of the NEA is a Triumph of the Republican Right. He's talking about Internet censorship and the communications bill in Congress; he didn't know this and that aspect of it when it was passed, etc. Forty million use the Internet worldwide. Soon it will be 200 million. I always overestimate what the typical lawyer knows.

6/30 Pages in the Sunday *New York Times* are filled with Jack Joyce, the Aldrich book, Whitewater, a bad day for Clinton. Joyce, serving what might be his last term as the president of the bricklayers union, has come out against Clinton because of his veto of the partial-birth abortion bill. No more union solidarity. Joyce wasn't part of the Sweeney camp and was unhappy that Kirkland was pushed out. Joyce appreciated the fact that Kirkland didn't hog the limelight, treated every union president as important as another.

On CBS, I watch Clinton at the Elgin Air Force Base, in Florida, giving a eulogy for the servicepeople killed in Saudi Arabia. Clinton's face is strangely dark, with bright sun behind, not studio lit. "They have come home. . . . May God bless their families. . . . May God bless their mission for which they gave their last full measure of devotion."

Next, a military man leans forward, and the officer is not in the dark.

Clinton is never comfortable in these military settings, the one place where he can't claim familiarity. And it's a big place for a president to be a stranger.

It's clear that Anthony Marceca, Livingstone's confederate, is the Tony Ulasewicz (of Watergate fame) of the FBI files mess.

Gary Aldrich is on *This Week with David Brinkley*. His *Unlimited Access* is the "bad" book of the moment on Clinton, whereas Woodward's *The Choice* is the "good" book. The Regnery publishing firm has been to the Clinton campaign what Dove Books was to the O. J. trial. In the publishing pecking order, Regnery is above some right-wing presses (of the Klan sort) but beneath the megacorporate respectability that Simon & Schuster wields. It's a status-and-money show. But Aldrich is the FBI agent "inside the Clinton White House" who is telling all. And then some. Aldrich claims he's trying to prevent and expose "the victimization of the FBI." Boo-hoo. The Secret Service and FBI, it's clear, got out of the habit of protecting randy presidents. This points to twelve years of Reagan and Bush—even Carter—not being notorious catter-arounders. And most of the generation that protected Kennedy are retired. George Will, doing his Nixon-in-China number (even though my wife works for Dole I ask tough questions), queries Aldrich about his most "sensational" charge, about Clinton sneaking out without Secret Service protection to rendezvous at the Marriott. (But I find all the information in the book happily sensational—dull in parts, but sensational—especially Aldrich's fussiness about what people wear and how they eat. Hoover's dress codes live on in the soul of the FBI! And Aldrich has a lot of Livingstone material, fortuitously.) Will says he spoke with Aldrich's source (David Brock, of Anita Hill fame), who denies the Marriott story, saying it was just rumor. Aldrich hems and haws. The story is too much right out of the movie *Dave* to be entirely credible: Bill under a blanket, Bruce Lindsey or someone at the wheel. But who cares? Woodward has Hillary talking to Eleanor and that doesn't make Bob a laughingstock (because it's true?), whereas Aldrich's overall portrait is discredited because of unsubstantiated rumors. (Like the O. J. jury, the idea is that you can discount everything if you believe there's a lie in the woodpile.) George Stephanopoulos is on the show, there to attack Aldrich. He does. But George leaves himself open for other questions, and he is asked who hired Craig Livingstone. George says Vince Foster hired him.

I catch a C-SPAN broadcast from Friday at the Washington, D.C., Omni Shoreman Hotel, the College Republican National Committee. Morton Blackwell, "the Leadership Institute" president, says, I wanted to tell Ollie [North] that "College Republicans are the most conservative of all Republican auxiliaries." Ollie North is the confab's featured speaker. Blackwell was once on the White House staff (outreach group for Central America), he tells us, and there were two great communicators in that administration, Ronald Reagan and Ollie North. "When many thought Iran-Contra hearings were going to cripple the Reagan administration . . . Ollie North went on for days over the head of the liberal media." Ollie gets a standing ovation. I hope you will be able to return to your college campuses without being accosted by Bill Clinton on one of his midnight soirées, Ollie says semi-sensibly, well versed in the Aldrich story. He pushes *Unlimited Access* as must reading for the young crowd. And he takes credit for putting Aldrich in touch with its publisher, his, he says. (It's Buchanan's, too.)

Ollie says Hillary's hearing other voices. "Quit now!" LBJ told her talking to Hillary, à la Eleanor. Ollie makes jokes: calls the local paper the Washington *Compost*. Says Dan Rather is often rather wrong. And now that he's got his audience loosened up, he says, I want to tell you what your economics prof, or sociologist, one of the bearded wonders who joined Bill Clinton in protest of the Vietnam War, won't tell you: profit is not a four-letter word. He refers to the "Jane Fonda Network." CNN. I laugh at that one.

Next, C-SPAN does Dole with the Texas VFW at the Hyatt Regency. The self-sacrifice motif. Not in Clinton. Has he had much, any? Dole has on a brown suit, a little campaign hat perched on his head. He looks old, is old. The Seventy-sixth Annual Convention Department of the Texas VFW in Dallas. This is what America is all about . . . you are the real America, Dole says. People who have made sacrifices.

Liddy is wearing a yellow outfit.

Then we get Gore talking to the College Democrats of America. Thank you for all of your work . . . especially in the future . . . smiles . . . especially in the future of the coming months. Gore talks about the books in the White House library and mentions *Where He Stands: the Life and Convictions of Spiro T. Agnew,* foreword by Richard Nixon. There are laughs at *convictions.* This is a real book, Gore says, published by Hawthorne. Al's moved by history.

TEN

Independence Month

★

7/1 NPR's *Morning Edition* reports a League of Women Voters survey full of curious numbers: 58 percent of older people vote, one-third of liberals vote, one-half of conservatives. Both people who vote and who don't vote are interviewed. (The Libertarian candidate, Harry Browne, didn't vote for a couple of decades.) A black man says he doesn't vote anymore—his last vote was for Jesse.

Bob Woodward is on Diane Rehm. He won't admit that any crass marketing aspects played a role in choosing the Hillary-talking-to-Eleanor story to kick off the publication of his book, the first "news" story on the front page of the *Washington Post*.

"How is it sensationalizing?" he asks, wounded at the thought, the imputation of Rehm's question. When asked who made the decision to put it on the front page, he replies the "editors," passing the buck (but not all the bucks). And he's not an editor? "Ultimately it was theirs." Woodward poses as the self-made naïf, the innocent boy. That he can't bring himself to be personally self-critical seems almost pathological. Woodward brings up Kissinger and Nixon praying together, but not in connection with Hillary's discussions with Eleanor, only that those pages were considered a "sensational" aspect of *The Final Days*. Callers accuse him of sensationalizing. Woodward stonewalls. Most of the calls are hostile.

7/2   Rush: yesterday Rush was musing on generational matters. Rush feels like he's in high school. No hard knocks, he says of Clinton. Is Clinton first of a line, or the end? he wonders. Today he's onto the "Clinton cult." People would excuse Clinton if he ran over a blind man on Independence Avenue, Rush says.

There's an *American Spectator* commercial on Rush: Who is the twenty-five-year-old blonde coming into the White House in the afternoon? It's referring to the *Spectator*'s article (May), "Who is Cousin Catherine Cornelius?", a mixture of Travelgate and Ozarkian hanky-panky with kissing cousins.

It's followed by a "fake" commercial, but these days, it's hard to tell: "Vince Foster, the film, coming to a theater near you. 'There's no blood!' "

A woman caller, who describes herself as a self-taught philosophy student, attacks Paul de Man—fine with me (see David Lehman's 1992 *Signs of the Times*)—saying de Man's whole philosophy "turn [s] reality on its head," and informs us darkly that Clinton was at Yale with Paul de Man.

The wildness of the fifties and sixties generation that Clinton saw growing up in Hot Springs comes to mind more than Belgian deconstructionists' self-serving philosophies. Fifties cocktail parties in the sixties progressed to wife swapping, but first you needed wives to swap (one tends to forget that) and to have cocktail parties you needed homes (something the young of the sixties lacked). These were harbingers of the sixties generation. But the sixties generation had no jobs, no homes, and that's what upset the applecart. The Aldrich book brings this up, since he spends a lot of time attacking Clinton's generation—though he seems most offended about the current younger generation, the Xers. Certain kinds of hedonism were OK in the fifties and sixties. After you have a job, a wife, a house, and dress right.

There was a big difference between beats (Lenny Bruce in white shirt and narrow tie) and hippies (no ties, no job). When wives went to work, there was a change: no more rotating weekend cocktail parties.

Dole continues to foul up on smoking (he was snappish to Katie Couric on the *Today* show) and now he lacks the comforting camouflage of the Senate.

7/3 Dole is down, doing his grumpy old man routine on *Regis & Kathy Lee* and on *Today*. The Doles have reissued their joint 1988 autobiography (predating Matalin and Carville), *Unlimited Partners*. Shades of *Unlimited Access*. The *New York Times* reports that Craig Livingstone's claim to fame was "supervision" of Chicken George at Bush rallies. On his résumé Livingstone called it "Senior Consultant to Counter-Event Operations, Clinton-Gore 92." How to Pad a Résumé 101. The *Times* takes note of the obvious contradiction between Stephanopoulos and Livingstone on Vince Foster's role in hiring. It's in *USA Today*, too. *USA Today* also has an op-ed editorial by Gary Aldrich.

A Diane Rehm caller speaks of the "Big Brother" project, keeping data on two hundred thousand people who have come in contact with the White House. It's yet another extension of Bill's little white index cards: Roger Morris's book has Bill in England, writing down names of people he just met, delaying his departure for a pub.

The yuppies-from-hell aspect of Roger Morris's book is foreshadowed by an "innocent" remark by Carville in *All's Fair*. He writes, "Hillary is like me: She really likes room service. I don't know if it's all about rising from humble beginnings, but I think there is something really fun and decadent about room service, and so does she." He seems to be even more delusional about Hillary's "humble beginnings" than about his own.

Books do step on one another—in 1947 Malcolm Lowry was in despair over the popular success of *The Lost Weekend,* when it came out a couple of years earlier than his overlooked *Under the Volcano*. Things moved more slowly then. Woodward, Morris, Aldrich are climbing all over each other. The three books on Clinton cover the spectrum: warm, medium, and hot.

There's a letter in the July-August *Mother Jones* attacking Dole's war record: "The Dole home page on the World Wide Web says: 'In 1942 at the age of 19, Bob Dole answered the call to serve his country by joining the Army to fight World War II. He became a second lieutenant in the Army's 10th Mountain Division, and in the spring of 1943, found himself in the hills of Italy fighting the Nazi Germans.' In December of 1942, Bob Dole signed up for the Army Reserve, a maneuver that allowed him to complete his sophomore year at the University of Kansas. In the Spring of 1943, Bob Dole was still happily ensconced at his frat house at KU. After his 1943 induction, he attended a variety of stateside military training that kept him from duty overseas until late December 1944. He didn't join the 10th Mountain Division until February 1945— at the advanced age of 21 years plus 7 months. On April 14 he was grievously wounded. Sixteen days later, Adolf Hitler and Eva Braun died in a double suicide. As a typical World War II combat veteran who signed up and faced the enemy while still 18, I think it's a travesty to see the press swallow the Dole service story hook, line, and sinker. Peter G. Weinberg, Former Cpl., 503 Parachute Combat Team, Stamford, Conn."

I don't think that fish will fly. Dole's injuries make him eager enough.

It's hard to recall how the women's movement was just starting in the late sixties and Hillary was part of that transitional generation. If she hadn't married Clinton in 1975, but had waited, she wouldn't have been out of step. Hillary wasn't at the leading edge in the sexual politics sweep-stakes.

I'm talking with a friend about World War II vets. Our discussion is brought on by the *Mother Jones* letter questioning Dole's eagerness for service. Dole was in the ASTPR, an army specialized training program. The novelist William Wharton's book, *A Midnight Clear,* covers this ground. But Dole was not George Bush, deeply eager to get into the action. Dole had more the platoon mentality: Even though the captain is bad, I'm loyal. Two guys died trying to save Dole. But his political history is terrible. It covers the years Americans want to forget.

Why Dole is such a bad campaigner: He's out of practice. Dole doesn't have to run for office! For thirty years! Who's going to tell him how to run in Kansas? Until now he hasn't been a truly national figure. The proof: Dole's rhetorical style hasn't been parodied till now. Eros and

Thanatos, vitality versus death, sex versus unsex. Liddy, the first nurse (and if Dole should win, the title "first nurse" would become very personal), not quitting the Red Cross shows that she thinks Dole's running is likely doomed. I've hitched my star to the wrong wagon. That's her look in recent pictures. She expected to retire as head of the Red Cross. She expected Dole to retire as majority leader. Dole equals duty.

On PBS, there's a White House gala performance, with Linda Ronstadt, an old favorite of mine (until she said she was turned on by men "in suits"), looking real bad, singing "Poor Pitiful Me," with three-African-American backup singers and a completely white band. "He was a credit to his gender." Bill Clinton is clapping along. *In Performance at the White House,* with Linda Ronstadt and Aaron Neville, a big black guy who sings in a high falsetto voice: you're no good, baby you're no good. I'm looking around the room for that big white guy, Craig Livingstone. Ronstadt and Neville do a duet. "If something is wrong with my baby, something is wrong with me." Bill is singing along, holding hands with Hillary. He then gets up and makes a speech, quotes T. S. Eliot, in reference to Ronstadt; "You are the music while the music lasts." You take us back, you "embody" . . . Embody, not quite the word, given Ronstadt's present size.

7/4 The *NewsHour,* in the spirit of Independence Day, has its think-tank talk ("panel of historians") about the FBI files and their use in the past. Most of the discussion is about J. Edgar Hoover. Surprise! It's tragedy/farce time. Doris Kearns Goodwin relates tales of sitting around at night with Lyndon Baines Johnson and LBJ saying " 'look at this Teddy [White] wise guy, I know that he's a Communist Sympathizer, look at Joe Kraft. Last night, Dobrynin, the Soviet ambassador, was at his house, and that's why he's writing this antibombing column.' He also had FBI reports done on George Hamilton, who was dating Linda Byrd, his daughter." Terry Eastland, who is identified as a former Reagan Justice Department official, attempts to link Livingstone's files to the days of Nixon's larger schemes, like the Houston plan. "It was searches—it would have called for infiltration of a number of groups and yet this was, in fact, rejected by the FBI to rectify it by Hoover at the time. He thought that this was completely unconstitutional. Nonetheless, these were done in the Nixon years. I think what Bill Clinton has unavailable to him is quite striking. He doesn't have a national security rationale as to what he's been doing. He's, of course, not even tried to invoke one." It's nice to see someone speaking up for J. Edgar Hoover as a defender of the Constitution. Even loathsomeness has its protectors. Michael Beschloss says, "You know, every president worried about the kind of files that Hoover had, and it was also, oddly enough, a tool of the imperial press— we talk a lot on this panel about presidential power. One area of this that was really unseen by the American people during all this period was that presidents really had the power and they used it to use the FBI and in some cases the Internal Revenue Service to harass political opponents." Later, Haynes Johnson supplies, "Let me give you an example. I remember when I was writing on civil rights in the sixties, I had to go places like Birmingham or in Selma, places like that, came back one day, the FBI office, and there the top guy to Hoover had all the files on Martin Luther King. They had 'em open, and he left the room. There were the files on King."

"Sitting there?" Margaret Warner asks.

"Sitting there alone now. I'm in this room. There are the files. Now I looked."

I imagine Clinton, if anything, in the LBJ mode, storing away information, "secrets," as tidbits of hidden power, dark histories to counterbalance his own.

Capitol Steps comedy on NPR: Pat Buchanan will be represented by two constituencies. "One, white guys who watch him set everyone straight on *Crossfire,* and, two, straight guys in white who set crosses on fire and watch." They do parody songs: "The Right Wing Strikes Again" and "Stand by Your Klan." ". . . he's just got a tan, Farrakhan."

7/5 NPR *Morning Edition* does another voting story (it's a series). There is no voting-registration drive by the Democratic Party, but it says it still has time to do one if they wish to. That was Jesse's job, voter registration, but both parties (à la P.J. O'Rourke) don't want "people" to vote.

WNYC-TV, in New York, is now WBIS-TV, gone public to private for $207 million, provided by ITT and the Dow Jones Company.

Thinking about affirmative action and opportunity, or getting jobs you're not necessary trained for: I first started to teach journalism without ever having had a journalism class, but I had written a book; it was a new turn on the old saw, if you can do, you can teach. . . .

The New Republic of July 15 and 22 has run a nonnews news article on Phil Gramm, which was among the strangest. A long article about how Gramm *isn't* a Klan member.

A Diane Rehm rebroadcast from April. Haynes Johnson and David Broder are talking about their book, *The System.* Johnson says, When our new book was published, two million more people did not have health care than when the health care plan failed. Clinton's health care "bus caravan had organized opposition all the way through." Broder adds, they (private interest groups) had more operatives in the grass roots than either the Democrats or Republicans.

I still think there's too much time spent on Whitewater and not enough on whoever wrote the bimbo insurance for Clinton. Talk about a sweetheart deal.

On C-SPAN: "The Internet has grown from the edges, not the center," says John Perry Barlow, the Electronic Freedom Foundation cofounder. The Internet started with 9 percent women and has increased. Gender gaps everywhere. This is a forum called "Technology and The Presidential Campaign." It's at the Kennedy School of Government, and JFK Jr. is the host-moderator, sounding (and looking) really bored. He appears to be doing the family a favor, none too graciously. John Kenneth Galbraith and Uncle Ted are in the audience. Here's a case where the front row of the audience would have made a more interesting panel.

Sander Vanocur, though, is on the panel. He says TV was not important in 1960 campaign, except for the Nixon-Kennedy debates. Even during the Kennedy term, he says, it was radio that was important, not stand-ups in front of the White House.

From the Republican National Committee, we have Lisa McCormack. She says the GOP TV is state-of-the-art, with its own television studio and its own show, *Rising Tide.* Edited events are sent out to other TV studios, fax networks, wire, forty-thousand-plus list of media contacts. (Not me, alas.) They can do "secure" teleconferences. "No one has to go anywhere," she says. GOP TV will broadcast the Republican convention. "Everyone" in the GOP will be "singing off the same song sheet."

Lisa brings up that 89 percent of the "press" voted for Clinton. But she has a Monday briefing that goes out to three thousand. It has seven pages, one page talking points, suggested letters to the editor. A chain letter, a fax "tree." She gives their Internet address: www.rnc.org mainstreet.info@rnc.org

John Perry Barlow says the Internet is not mass communication; it won't have much effect on elections, but will erode the presidency. They (folks on the Internet) are not the voters. Voters are television based, older.

A student comments from the audience: Governor Weld is trying to recover spiritually, politically, and physically from his fainting spell. . . .

"Affect has no effect on the Internet."

Ms. McCormack is back: 60 percent of households with incomes of forty thousand dollars or more have PCs.

Kiki Moore, the Democratic National Committee communications director, chimes in: "Those are her voters."

In '92 Gary Smitten, producer of musicals, ran the '92 Democratic convention; Bill Clinton put it into his hands, Sander Vanocur says.

JFK Jr. is asked about putting pictures of women on the cover of *George,* his magazine. Only 8 percent of political magazines have such photos on the cover, but 80 percent of the others do. Is *George* trying to "harvest attention"? Yes, it is.

Vanocur says, "Familiarity breeds contempt"—how can our elected officials maintain aesthetic distance? he wonders. Lisa defends JFK Jr., says *George*'s art is "fun." Looking for a date? I have now pinned down the Republican woman look—it's a band uniform, vaguely German military tunic style, most often red. Lisa's right in step, seventy-six trombones.

John Perry Barlow says the Internet is now 37 percent female. Our leaders are in data shock. It's a social space. You have to have a reason to come on-line. People who can handle the information flow. The government is fibrillating.

Kiki, the Democrat, says: "We never will win the war of who has the most famous and influential radio talk show hosts."

Should I tell Rush?

From Wimbledon, some tennis news. Bud Collins is reporting on tennis for NPR's *All Things Considered* and for the *Boston Globe*. It's been interesting (the tournament), Collins says, to write about. Whereas my bosses at NBC aren't too happy with the departure of Sampras and Agassi.

That's the difference between print and TV, between ideas and notoriety, between words and pictures.

Is ours the "Not Ready for Prime Time Generation"? David Letterman—one bit of evidence it is—does his Top 10: How Bob Dole celebrated the Fourth of July: number 6: smoked a joint and nailed a campaign worker. No, that's how President Clinton spent the holiday. Number 7: hid Easter eggs, got confused. Number 8: marched in a parade wearing a Joe Camel outfit. Number 1: same as always, kegs and babes.

Jay Leno is onto Clinton's school-uniform initiative, doubtless a Dick Morris idea. Jay shows, for boys, a picture of a guy in a cardigan; for the girls, a woman in a bra, panty, garters, and stockings.

Yeltsin spent his birthday in his usual fashion, with his face down in his cake, Jay jokes.

I hear from a dissenter in academia on talk radio: It's like being at a bad party. They announce, they don't have a conversation. We're onto Rush. He lets his people talk, like we let students talk. We're being paid for an hour and a half and if they want to fill it, that's fine with us.

There's a June 26 *Sports Illustrated* article on a high school basketball player, convicted of assaulting a sixteen-year-old, getting a basketball scholarship. If Bill's in the White House and Newt's in Congress, this guy can go on to higher education.

7/6 Kevorkian nets another (*New York Times,* page 7).

7/7 On *Fox News Sunday* we have Rich Trumka and Haley Barbour. Trumka is labor's most effective spokesman, since he appears to be enjoying himself and will brook no guff. My wife says, passing by, Trumka's for three-quarters of the Republican agenda, if you can sum up the Republican agenda in four words as "cut capital-gains taxes." He's for three of those four words. He wants to *cut* their *capital gains*. The class issues are used to counter the millions the Republicans have to spend, $70 million, and they have to talk about minimum wage and Medicare, whereas they wanted to talk about term limits and family values. Labor has leveraged $100 million, at least, to talk about what is a fair wage and a fair rate of profit. This transforming campaign is focused on class issues. Now union members have to vote their wages, not their rifles and their abortion rights.

Susan Molinari (R-N.Y.) is "on message." All the single voices like multiplexes now showing the same film on many screens. Campaign news does drive out other news, but not all.

The last few weeks have been given over to the first lady/first nurse sweepstakes, Hillary versus Liddy. In the Roger Morris book (and elsewhere), it's clear that because Bill's first race was for Congress, Hillary at first expected to go back to Washington soon.

Face the Nation does an author day. Richard Reeves (*Running in Place: How Bill Clinton Disappointed America*) makes the point of Hillary being a lightning rod for criticism, sparing Bill. That notion has moved into the overcrowded camp of conventional wisdom. Clinton's disastrous first two years, then change, recovery, being similar to losing the governorship and then regaining it, has also hardened into conventional wisdom.

7/8   Speaking to a caller, Diane Rehm says, "I made the decision to keep off two authors"—one being Gary Aldrich, the other unnamed, presumably Roger Morris. That publisher (Morris's) called and called. "I thought it was rumor and innuendo," Diane says of the book's contents. Morris's book, it appears, has been successfully blackballed, at least in the genteel world.

After reading *The Choice,* one thing is clear, though not a thing that has been discussed concerning the book: Bill Clinton, with one obvious exception, only listens to men. Men make up his decision-making world. In the world these days, you can find two kinds of men: Athens types and Sparta types. Some men enter the harem professions (largely Athens men), other men male-dominated professions (Sparta males). Doctors are most often found in harem professions, where a single male is surrounded by many women employees (doctors and dentists, small businesses, retail worlds, a lot of publishing), but Sparta guys want men around them. Women are only good for one (or two) things. The Military, VMI, etc., but other professions, too. Law used to be a Sparta profession (with a harem annex). The most heated affirmative action battles are being fought in formerly Sparta encampments. The "glass ceiling" is a holdout of the Sparta male. Clinton is a bit of both, but when it comes to governing it's a male universe for Bill. It's the Bubba side, the Sparta side. In *The Choice,* Woodward quotes Mike McCurry (the former PR guy who took over Dee Dee Myers's press job—Bill's Bubba/Sparta side surfacing): "Taking all the Republican issues off the table sounded well and good, but if it worked the Republicans would be issueless. . . . 'They can only win by doing the single most dangerous thing for Clinton,' McCurry said, 'which is to totally destroy him as a human being' " (210). McCurry, doubtless, was doing some PR for himself with Woodward. He says it was the Morris strategy, but this "immunization" strategy has many fathers. But the conservatives' attack on Clinton's character, his philandering, only plays up Clinton's vitality versus Dole's weariness, Eros versus Thanatos.

In the Woodward world of bland rhetorical questions and stilted dialogue, all his historical figures end up talking like bad actors. Reading Woodward often reproduces the feeling one has viewing a high school production of, say, Sophocles' *Antigone.*

These days fifteen minutes of fame are not enough—inflation is everywhere. Reverence for the rich has been back since the eighties, but the nineties are taking notice of the growing poor, the stagnating middle class, and the continually skyrocketing rich, which is taking a bit of the bloom off that rose. But the Clinton administration is still holding on to that reverence. "Corporate" is now an adjective that means "money is no object."

The profession of people paid to say the incredible as plausibly as possible is still growing. Forget six degrees of separation, everyone has a Bill Clinton story.

In the price versus service wars, Southwest Airlines is offering twenty-five dollar fares; even the public wonders what you get for such a cheap ride. Only when the government gives you luxury for little do you feel comfortable, since you know it's subsidized.

The Christian Right are neoutopians. The antiabortion stance is neoutopian. The right wing continues to make connections between the "killings" of Lincoln and Kennedy assassination associates and Clinton's list of dead. (See Morris, 314–15.) Wanting the world to make sense, grand conspiracies. If Hillary is "growing" in office, is Bill? At times, it appears the road-show company of *Macbeth* has pulled into 1600 Pennsylvania Avenue, Lady Hillary and King Bill haunting the corridors.

I thought the country would get a president of my generation sooner or later, when it had to, not when one became old enough for the job.

Rush is on Kevorkian. Get a gun permit. I thought you wanted to study death.

I finally catch *Independence Day*. It is a nineties version of the fifties' *The Day the Earth Stood Still*. The latter was for an earth still recoiling from World War II; *Independence Day* is for a world seemingly itching for a world war, nurturing the fantasy that a decisive conflagration would make things better. The world moving from pacifism (after World War II) to violence (twenty years after Vietnam), wanting what you don't have. Large wars are often spaced twenty years apart in order to let a new generation grow old enough to slaughter. *The Day the Earth Stood Still* was for a nation hoping to be out from under the threat of atomic destruction and *Independence Day [ID4]* is for one looking for someone to blame for their discontent and getting to fix them good. The *ID4* Clinton connection is that the first lady dies, like in *The American President,* though later in the story.

In the film *Independence Day, The McLaughlin Group*—Father John, Kondracke, Eleanor Clift—are seen blabbing away about the fake president. Art, life, whatever.

The August *Esquire* is an old-folks reunion, Norman Mailer on Buchanan, Jimmy Breslin on his aneurysm. There's something quite similar about both articles—pounding blood themes.

Nightline: America's political consultants have saved Russia for Boris Yeltsin. They employed "truth squads," like Craig Livingstone, ran negative campaigns, dealt with Yeltsin's daughter Tatiana, the Bay Buchanan of Moscow. Ten Days That Shook the World littered with PR memos and focus groups and finger-sweat response graphs.

The consultants say it's easy to trivialize the minutiae of the campaign. Dick Dressner intones, "Let's not forget what's at stake here." Thirty-two percent of Russians favored Stalin, the consultants discovered. A cap (amount) similar to those who favor Buchanan here at home, though they don't make that point. The consultants are tied to Bill Clinton and "the governor of California." Cokie Roberts says, "The image is the message." The consultants are even quicker than Mark Helprin at taking credit for Yeltsin's "victory."

Final Justice, Unsolved Mysteries, all these true-crime shows on late at night. Reality TV. Edited versions of a violent C-SPAN world.

Chicago Tonight talks about campaign, the provinces are heard from. All the critical Clinton books are creating dust in the eye, but "nothing could be better for us than the good news of the economy," says the Democratic representative.

7/9 Rush: "It's the essence of hypocrisy." Rush is describing Anthony Marceca suing two people in Texas for "defamation of character" because of info Tony discovered in his FBI file. Rush's info comes from a Scripps-Howard story in the *Houston Chronicle,* about Marceca's congressional testimony about how his file "inadvertently" was exposed and he read it.

7/10 Ross is on with Larry King. C-SPAN may have created Newt, but Larry King has been hard at work on Ross. King asks: Will you be on the ballot in all fifty states? Yes, Ross says, oh, absolutely. Then King asks, Do you want people to vote for you? Ross plays coy. I want people to understand the issues. King presses. If you get the nomination, you will run? If the people want me to, certainly, Ross says, all humbleness. King asks: What do you think of Governor Lamm? Perot says, He's a fine man. King says, He said he would not consider being a vice presidential nominee on your party. Well, that's his decision, Ross says, a bit curt. Ross describes the nomination process of the Reform Party: In the nomination process, every person will have a ballot that cannot be forged or duplicated. It will be mailed to their home. They can watch this on

C-SPAN, they can go to a local auditorium if they want to put together a group in their community, we will satellite it across the country. C-SPAN will be showing it live.

Ross has seen the future and it is satellites.

7/11 A conversation by the Coke machine: "I'm studying commedia dell'arte," a friend tells me. We talk about its possible connection to the campaign. "Pantaloon is, of course, Dole, Harlequin is Clinton, and Perot—is Pierrot." What's happening? Dole is going up in smoke. Lamm is being led to the slaughter.

But it makes sense: Pantaloon is a merchant, serious, rarely consciously comic, prone to long tirades and good advice. Harlequin, of course, is most often described as a capricious swain, amoral without being vicious. Pierrot is simpleminded and honest, a victim of pranks. That about sums it up.

7/12 Rush is talking with a gay Republican who is aghast at leather, chains, etc. Rush sounds intrigued, not with leather, but with this conservative gay. Rush says "gay groups," Hollywood, etc., are second in contributions to Clinton, right after the National Trial Lawyers Association.

CNN's *Inside Politics* does a piece on an inaccurate GOP tax ad against Clinton. They break for a commercial and the same commercial runs as a *commercial*. Later, they discuss the flap over Dole not going to the NAACP convention. Dole says he was "set up" by Kweisi Mfume—he's "very liberal." Dole is now dealing with another tar (though not nicotine) baby. Dole calls the NAACP the NAAC.

Jay Leno refers to the trouble the Greek basketball team had on the plane from Greece to the States. They wouldn't stop smoking. "Sounds like the Bob Dole Dream Team," Jay says, and then cites a UN study that the population will swell to nine billion, and, Jay says, not one of them a Richard (Dick) Lamm supporter.

There's no big laugh for that joke. Leno mutters that they (the audience) don't know who he is. He (Lamm) doesn't know who he is.

I switch over to the Christian News network. D'Amato is speaking against ATM machine charges. "They are getting a free lunch." It's the network's new show, *The American Times*. It tries to make its news look like all the "regular" news, and it almost succeeds (except for the antennae coming out of their heads).

Sunday the real Dream Team plays Greece in Indianapolis. Steve Largent, the ex-footballer (R-Okla.), is on C-SPAN, speaking against gay marriage. Marriage "needs to be protected, promoted, and preserved." Hike, hike.

Back to the Christian channel, where Gloria Copeland is speaking on the benefits of tithing (especially to her).

Back to C-SPAN, which is showing some of the debate in Congress on the anti-same-sex marriage bill. The vote's around 342 for, 67 against.

7/13   John Chancellor, the television reporter and personality, died; it turns out, he worked for government, too.

Dole goes to the All-Star Game. On the *Capital Gang,* there's a shot of Dole signing an autograph, seated, for a little skinny black kid. Bob Novak says, "His handlers say it's harder and harder to defend his [Dole's] record as a presidential candidate." About Dole's quote that he's looking for an audience he can relate to (unlike the NAACP), one suggestion is "accident-prone veterans of foreign wars."

"He blew it," Kate O'Beirne, of *The National Review,* says. Novak says this is "the worst possible outcome."

Al Hunt says Dick Lamm would make "an interesting candidate."

Christopher Dodd (D-Conn.) makes the crack "Dead Man Talking" about Dick Lamm.

Gayle Wilson (the wife of Pete, the California governor) is on C-SPAN, talking about teenage pregnancy: in 1960, it was one in twenty-five; in 1995, one in three babies were born to teenage mothers. She gives her portrait of the fifties. Leave it to Beaver. "I want to emphasize that 80 percent of out of wedlock childbirths are not to teenagers." But she says that fifteen minutes into her talk. Two thirds of fathers of teenage births are adults.

All the talk about young people makes no sense, my wife says, wandering by. Six percent of teens are having the kids. The right wing always uses the specter of teenage pregnancy to divert attention, but it is a problem. And I agree with everything she (Mrs. Wilson) is saying, my wife says, exiting the room.

7/14 *Fox News Sunday.* Judge Robert Bork calls Clinton "a serial adulterer and draft dodger." He's still mad about not being confirmed for the Supreme Court. "Borked" is now a verb, meaning "ganging up on someone by revealing his or her public record" (only when the ganging up is successful, though). "You can't separate private character from public." What about Clarence Thomas? I wonder.

Mark Shields defends all the draft dodgers on Capitol Hill. He's being ironic. Bork says, "Best thing for Dole is that he will run out of issues he can foul up."

There's the "Rumor of the Week" on *Fox*, "Outrage of the Week" on *Capital Gang*, "Prediction of the Week" on *McLaughlin*. Newt on *This Week with David Brinkley* says, "Falsehoods [are] the moral equivalent of truth," regarding the Democrats' charge of "cuts" in Medicare.

George Will often has the look of the just-offended man, an expression which is the equivalent of the exclamation "Well, I dare!" He says about Dole: "All he's produced is buyer's remorse in the Republican Party." Bad week for Dole: tobacco (milk), NAACP, assault weapons, abortion-tolerance plank shot down, talk of "revolution" at the convention. How did Dole become the nominee? they wonder. Cookie says, "We did go through primaries." But they are forgotten, indeed.

Firing Line is at the Levy Institute, the liberal think tank at Bard College. Bifurcation of the economy is the subject. They're all white guys. Eight of them! It seems to be the world of clerks, like the Supreme Court of the 1950s. But it is William Buckley's court and he doesn't blush to have nothing but white guys surrounding him. The younger folks who work for the powerful are always a sight: bright, eager, ready to please.

Ross Perot has made twenty-two appearances on *Larry King Live*. The Brit wit Christopher Hitchens is on *The McLaughlin Group*, tie askew. McLaughlin asks, "Is this election over?" Not if the stock market crashes and there are enough foreign problems. Christopher Hitchens says Dole "thinks it a triumph to be photographed with Ron Reagan, both looking like a wax museum."

Mary Matalin on *Meet the Press* was praising "the commonsense conservative agenda," echoing a Republican ad. She's on message.

7/15 Dole is on *Larry King Live*. Liddy is with him. Buchanan raised issues that I agree with, Dole says, abandoning words left and right, "people worried about their jobs . . . and trade. Two issues I agree with."

Susan Molinari is to be the keynote speaker at the convention. She's got "vibrancy." "I've watched you," Dole says, desperate for women. Susan's on the phone from a restaurant, her two-month-old baby home with grandmother. It's real teenage excitement tonight: the quarterback has called for a prom date. Ooooohhh! Susan says this invitation puts him (Dole) right up there with her father and husband.

Dole makes a joke about all the mistakes he's made in last two weeks. King asks, Would you ever lie? Change your mind? Dole makes a joke. Liddy tries to reign him in. She does seem like Dole's nurse here, an unfortunate by-product of marrying a younger woman when you reach a certain age.

Nightline. When the Cokie Roberts story is done, she should be played by Sigourney Weaver at her most uptight. Lewis Lapham, editor of *Harper's,* says we are a conservative country. *The Progressive* editor, Matthew Rothschild, is there, too. Republican and Democrats together. Frank Luntz, a Republican on message, says Bill Clinton's idea of education is closed-captioning *Baywatch*. Frank hits on the economic insecurity of the people. He sounds like a Democrat, but. . . .

Bill Clinton does an interview for MSNBC's "first" day. Looking back on his three-plus years, he says, "No one is prepared for all the pressures of the presidency." Clinton is keeping Bill Gates happy.

Will the most popular children's names twenty years from now be "WWW" and "Dot Com"? WWW will be the boy's name, Dot Com the girl's.

7/16 Diane Rehm has the National Park Service's head on. A caller, RFK Jr., no relation, a lawyer, asks about privatizing federal parks. The head hems and haws.

Then the Libertarian Party candidate, Harry Browne, sixty-three, explains why he didn't vote from 1964 to 1994. "I'm not a joiner by personality. . . . I didn't see any point." Then he adds, "Government doesn't work." Diane gets testy with him about abolishing the Food and Drug Administration.

Rush announces his TV show is going off the air. "It's on a curve heading in the wrong direction." Weird times, weird stations, etc. After watching Dole and Liddy on *Larry King Live,* a caller says, "Short of Bill and Hillary being taken out of the White House in handcuffs, he [Dole] will get only 35 percent of the vote. I will vote for the little guy in Texas," he says. Rush says, Oh, oh, oh, ho. The caller's a Republican—he voted for only two Democrats, Rizzo and Casey; he wanted Buchanan. An older guy, he bets Perot will get more votes than Dole. Rush says: We don't need this depth of negativism. Then he says the market went down yesterday because of my announcement I wasn't going to do the TV show, but it's bouncing back today because I said today it was my decision, what I wanted. He goes on about MSNBC. Jim Guy Tucker, Arkansas. Doesn't that state look like a banana republic? he says. Who's in charge there? The Cali cartel. There are tentacles that reach all the way back to the White House. Rush must be reading the Roger Morris book.

7/17   Diane Rehm is "mature, attractive, chic," according to the frisky novelist Patricia Cornwell's expert assessment. She just got $24 million for novels number nine, ten, and eleven; Cornwell does have a foundation, the favorite tax shelter for the high-minded.

Diane then has on a number of gay spokespersons: David Mixner, the former Clinton friend; Richard Tafel, a guy from the Log Cabin Group, a gay Republican organization; and a woman, Cilind Lake, all speaking on gay issues in the campaign. The last caller is an old man, who exclaims, "They're after our children," and accuses Diane of promoting "mutual masturbation" on the air. I presume he's straight, so he stands a better chance of being a pedophile, statistically, one of Diane's guests offers in rebuttal.

Joe Klein, the *Washington Post* reveals, is Anonymous, though *New York* did a good job revealing it in February. Handwriting on a manuscript did Klein in. I guess it's the difference between informed speculation and physical "proof." And Eleanor Clift speaks up for *Newsweek,* saying they didn't compromise themselves (!). Its editor, Maynard Parker, knew Klein was Anonymous, but kept the secret to himself and let *Newsweek* print false leads. Then there's more thunder and lightning outside, and my radio station goes out in the storm.

Rush: Joe Klein, this is hilarious, the way it's handled.

Then Rush goes on about MSNBC and TWA 800, a 747 that exploded shortly after take off yesterday, barely beyond the coast of Long Island. Hundreds dead.

People who don't know anything, except what they read from a TelePrompTer and there are no details, Rush says, is a prescription for disaster. Yes, unscreened "news" pouring in, then being repeated on the air, a lot like talk radio. Rush said yesterday that he wasn't a member of the "news" media, but a member of the "new" media.

Later, flipping channels, I catch a bit of Martha Stewart and I attempt to divine her appeal. Her gardening outfits (short khaki shorts, blue unbuttoned work shirt) are, in many ways, the eighties-nineties version of a French maid costume so loved by early-twentieth-century pornographers. And those expensive shoes! That fine leather, that shade of brown! To garden in. She's "wholesomeness" fetishized. I recall *Esquire* running a couple of years ago a picture of an attractive blond mom, Martha Stewart type with yellow rubber gloves on up to her elbows and a bathroom brush, kneeling, embracing, her toilet. Same sort of fetish shot, the heart of Martha Stewart's appeal: it crosses a lot of hot wires, and you do get a shock.

I talk with a friend about the Bob Dole and Katie Couric flap. Dole didn't use the word "brainwash" first in the Katie Couric interview. He only responded to Katie Couric's question. It's an important distinction. Not that I am defending Dole's lunacy, my friend says. And what is the secret of Katie Couric's appeal? A lot of mouth, spacious, active, but thin lips.

On *Rivera Live,* Donna Rice Hughes, Gary Hart's former monkey business, in on the phone. Geraldo asks: Donna, are you born again, in a sense? Donna: I did want the negative experience I had to count for something, and now I have the opportunity to utilize a platform to get a message out. (She's speaking publicly against the smut on the Internet.) She says she's not talked to Hart in eight years.

7/18   There's a tale of two local construction projects: one is the Notre Dame Stadium, which is being enlarged to the tune of $50 million. What is amazing is that it appears about six guys are putting it (large sections of preformed concrete) together. The crane operator and a couple of steelworkers are fitting the giant puzzle pieces into place. It's the modern economy at work. I wonder what capital-intensive machinery formed these large sections of walls, seats, ramps, etc., and where those machines were made. When Knute Rockne built the original stadium, hundreds of men were employed. Here it's about six (though more men are working, reworking, the inside of the original stadium). The ringing of the entire stadium was just finished. An American flag flies where the last two sections were joined. I now no longer wonder why ancient cultures would spend so much of their society's capital on a totemic monument (pyramids, Easter Island, Stonehenge). The football stadium is used six times a year. Cathedrals, at least, get used every Sunday and other days, too.

The other construction project is the redoing of the large mall on the outskirts of the city, making it bigger and more spiffy. Malls and stadiums. In most towns, sport complexes and nearby homeless shelters are the most prevalent new construction. Downtown, South Bend is building a new bankruptcy court building. It's made of preformed slabs, too.

I talk with a Hollywood friend about a mutual acquaintance, a former Joe Klein inamorata, who told her husband that some of the things the narrator of *Primary Colors* said in bed were the same things Klein had said to her in bed. Klein's a famous tightwad, my friend reports—and he heard Klein let his wife redo their kitchen.

There's no enthusiasm for Clinton in Hollywood this time around, no one volunteering down at Democratic headquarters. Yeah, I'll vote for him—what's his name? my friend asks. You could have been Anonymous, I say. I write for TV, he replies, that's the same thing as being anonymous.

It's the anniversary of Ted Kennedy and Mary Jo Kopechne. The TWA 800 explosion has muted the Joe Klein publicity—as well as Clinton's own Whitewater trial testimony. The moon walk in 1969 had muted the publicity of Kennedy drowning Mary Jo.

Pete Williams, former-Pentagon spokesperson of Bush administration fame, on MSNBC offers the rumor of a missile, friendly fire, shooting down TWA 800. Williams is used to military sources.

7/19 Rush thinks there is room for a TV network all-news (cable) station that practices "old-fashioned journalism." What's that, holding a newspaper up to the screen? A caller brought the subject up. Rush recounts talking with his brother, dismayed at all the news—everything is going to be covered, "wall to wall," and is dismayed at overproduction, which seems at odds with all his free-enterprising. "If they cover it differently" how many do we need? "They all cover the news the same." There are rumors about Fox taking on Rush. There's a lot of talk about Dole stepping down as the nominee. Caller: "A great American, but he should step aside." More talk about TWA 800 shot down with a Stinger missile.

Gene Lyons reviews Roger Morris's *Partners in Power: The Clintons and Their America* in the August 8 *New York Review of Books*. His two main points: the troopers are unreliable and the Pillsbury report tells a different story about Whitewater and the McDougals' involvement. The drug-dealer Lasater/Bill Clinton connection, friendship, in the book is downplayed by Lyons. The Arkansas state trooper was not on the Bobby Seal drug flight, according to Lyons. What the review doesn't discuss is Morris's critique of money and local government—it brings to my mind Clinton's testimony, released today, about not penalizing contributors to the governor by allowing them to be appointed to state positions. That's the way it works. I expect a rebuttal letter from Morris, which should be interesting (though I saw none from James Stewart (*Blood Sport*) about the negative Garry Wills review; success need not speak to criticism, only the unsuccessful squawk).

The *NewsHour* has Mark Shields and, for a vacationing Paul Gigot, Kate O'Beirne of *The National Review,* a trusty female conservative talking head who shows up elsewhere. Now the right-wing networks are feeding the left-wing networks. It's a two-way street. Jim Lehrer says, with not-so-dry sarcasm, "I want to move on to a key issue of our time. Joe Klein, political editor of *Newsweek* magazine, confessed this week that he was, in fact, Anonymous and he wrote the book *Primary Colors*. There have been angry editorials in the *New York Times* and many other newspapers about this. Are you as outraged as others about Joe Klein?"

Shields said Klein lied to him, and seems disapproving, saying, "Jim, you can't accuse Bill Clinton or Bob Dole or Ross Perot of fibbing and lying and be indifferent to lying in your own profession. I mean, that's the minimum standard of what I see, of what political journalism ought to be." But Kate O'Beirne differs. "I've got to say, Jim, I really don't understand the all but hysterical reaction to the Joe Klein flap. No, I don't put Mark in the hysterical camp. I put him in the thoughtful, reasoned camp. There's a whole lot of the media self-absorption in this story. I don't know that most Americans are. . . . There's no point in putting "Anonymous" on a title if the first time Mark Shields bumps into you, you're going to say, Yeah, okay, it was me. So you knew whoever did it was prepared to say it wasn't me, and separate that from their truthfulness as a journalist, which I think is possible." She makes one final point about the press's parlor game speculating about who wrote *Primary Colors*: "In the course of speculating, it became apparent to the general public that a whole lot of people in the media have very cozy relationships with people in campaigns, and that bothers them far more than the Joe Klein flap." Yes, Katie bar the door.

Clinton is at the Olympics. The only head of state I can recall being at, and linked to, an Olympics is Hitler at the eleventh Olympiad. Hillary is in glasses, the "Ode to Joy" is played, Evander Holyfield and a Greek woman run with the torch, which has been crossing the country—another fund-raising, publicity-generating stunt—and Muhammad Ali, left arm shaking, holds a flame to a fuse (almost getting burned, it appears) that travels up like a Stinger missile to a calla-lily-shaped cauldron, and a large flame fills the night sky, my television screen.

Bill looks moved. Hillary is now without glasses. "The Power of the Dream" is sung by a French Canadian singer, Celine Dion, a thin blonde with a slight country-and-western twang, who grimaces quite a bit for effect. There's lots of African American presence. The opera star Jessye Norman sings: she can really open her mouth. At times, it almost swallows her face.

There are fireworks. The sky looks like Beirut, Baghdad, TWA 800. . . .

A tribute to Martin Luther King Jr. follows, and tears form in Bill Clinton's eyes.

NBC paid $460 million for rights to the Olympics, the local affiliate here announces.

Bob Enyart Live, our local religious TV talk show scourge, is expounding on sexual morality and divorce. Are you loose from a wife? Loose means divorce, he says: 1 Corinthians, chapter 7, verses 26–28. The guy is the obsessive sort who demands you accept his dumb point, the secret clue everyone has overlooked. Enyart sports a small, bushy, Hitler-style moustache, which will doubtless inhibit his rise in TV land. Even Rush lacks that sort of hirsute chutzpah.

7/20 Michael Feldman, on *Whad'Ya Know?* jokes that the Dole campaign has applied for federal disaster relief. And Liddy Dole is running independently for first lady. Bill and Hillary Clinton are not speaking at the upcoming Democratic convention, but they will give taped depositions. The author of *Primary Colors* has been revealed. It is Richard Scarry, which explains why the Bill Clinton character is portrayed as a walking worm. (Thanks to my five-year-old, I get the joke.) Bob Dole is the quintessential male because men don't have to talk, they communicate best when they snarl.

7/21 The *New York Times* has an article about "the Yellow Oval Room" group. "The President's Brain Trust," a headline calls the bunch, which gathers to discuss the "re-election of President Clinton." The *Times* has a diagram, pictures of where everyone sits. Of the twenty-three people identified, only three are female: Evelyn Lieberman, deputy White House chief of staff; Ann Lewis, deputy manager of the Clinton/Gore campaign, sister of Barney Frank; and Maggie Williams, first lady's chief of staff. Maggie is there, doubtless, as Hillary's eyes and ears. The third-ranked person on the list is Dick Morris, "chief outside strategist." Sparta males gather with a bit of female decor.

On *The McLaughlin Group,* Father John is talking about airline safety: "It affects the bottom line. . . . It shouldn't be in the hands of the airlines, it should be in the hands of the federal government." He doesn't seem to notice the contradiction in his ideology. But he does fly a lot, I presume. They run a tape of quotes on how bad the Dole campaign is. Is the Dole campaign finally on the upswing? he asks. We see *Larry King Live,* Susan Molinari, Colin Powell, attacks on unions, the NEA, education, speech. Drug use. Mike McCurry, stumbling over his marijuana past, says it did not prohibit him "from service . . . from serving in the White House." Eleanor Clift predicts, "You will not see Bob Dole and Liddy Dole interviewed together during the campaign again." Happy Birthday Bob Dole. Bye-bye.

7/22   Today is Dole's birthday. Joyce Carol Oates does an op-ed piece in the *New York Times* on Joe Klein and the idea of "Anonymous"—hoax? parody? satire? outright deception?—without mentioning that she had attempted to publish a novel under a pseudonym (à la Doris Lessing) to see how it would be treated without the cachet of her famous name attached to it, but the "hoax" was discovered before she could conduct her experiment (the novel appeared unmasked).

Diane Rehm devotes part of her show to the welfare bill, which ends the Federal commitment to AFDC, replacing it with block grants to the states. This is the State of the Union's "era of Big Government is over" rhetoric personalized. The race to the bottom comes up: Block grants going to the states, welfare reform as a budget-cutting device.

Senator Moynihan is on CNN's *Evans and Novak,* and he's against the bill, too. Moynihan hands are roving around and he says that all of this should be remembered in the future, when these cut-off-welfare kids are a threat to themselves and a danger to others.

Heroin use is reported up 1.2 percent among high school seniors, and the crack market has "matured."

Clinton called last week for distributing cellular phones to community watch groups as a crime-fighting device. This seems a bit sci-fi (though beepers are a staple of the lower-middle-class subculture). Roger Morris supplies a slightly different motivation in his book. He writes that Hillary guaranteed a $60,000 loan in the purchase of a cellular phone franchise in Little Rock and "received $45,998 on her original $2,014 investment" (447). So the Clintons know cellular phones.

Bill also wants to use the Internet to crack down on fathers who avoid child-support payments—seems he is out-Newting Newt's advice from the Tofflers.

Dole would be the oldest man "inaugurated" as president.

On Diane Rehm, Elliot Richardson tells us he had bad dreams about seeing Richard Nixon again. But he did finally see Nixon again at the Chinese embassy. He said to Nixon that he "always affirmed your leadership in foreign policy." And Nixon replied, "Never mind all that," meaning their past history together. "Flaws impelled him to prove he was better than the good-looking guys with the cars, girls," Richardson said. He uses a fish metaphor: Watergate was a trophy fish; Iran-Contra looked like something, but got off the hook. Whitewater would have been thrown back. He's discussing his new memoir, *Reflections of a Radical Moderate*.

Richardson says that the news business has to sell time and space. It's not regulated, is very competitive, and will settle for small corruption, things that wouldn't have been thought of as corruption twenty or thirty years ago, like getting an appointment for a "campaign contribution." He brings up Daniel Webster being paid for speeches on the floor of Congress. Richardson not firing Archibald Cox at Nixon's order on October 20, 1973 was his finest moment—and Robert Bork's, the man who did fire Cox, seamiest.

Asked for his candidate in this campaign, Richardson says, hesitantly, "I'm a Republican. . . . As to this particular campaign . . . I'm still waiting."

Rush says Dole has hired Billy Dale, the fired travel-office guy. Dole should go down to Arkansas, to the Mena airport (site of drug running and Contra arms transfers, big in Morris's book) and give an antidrug speech, educate the public about Mena. He should be "dropping bails of hay."

Rush calls MSNBC the PMS-NBC network. It's Rush's women problem. Rush goes on: Dole should hold a press conference in the Paula Jones hotel room, have a naked woman run by.

Rush moves to the new Nixon book excerpts in *The New Yorker,* by a young scribe named Monica Crowley (Diane Sawyer the second). He reads Nixon quotes about Bill Clinton: "He didn't want to get his ass shot off. . . . He's a fraud." On Hillary: "She wanted to impeach me!" "The kid [Chelsea] ran right to him." "Hillary is ice cold, you can see it in her eyes." A Nixon day: nobody high-up from the Clinton administration appearing at his wife's funeral really upset him.

Bob Dole, Rush repeats, think about that Mena campaign appearance dropping bails of hay.

Then Rush says, correction here, Dole "offered the job to Billy Dale . . . not yet accepted."

Rush comments on Clinton's crying after the MLK tribute at the opening of the Olympics; no one else was in tears, he claims, not Hillary. Clinton can cry "on demand." Rush mentions again his clip of Clinton crying at Ron Brown's funeral. Rush is onto "conflict resolution." It produces weenies, he says. Got to be tough. He knows about teamwork. Dodge ball, he says. Even a caller demurs. High school football, Rush claims. Can you imagine?

On C-SPAN, Kathleen Hall Jameison, of the Annenberg School of Communications, says Republicans use the words "man" and "men" more (and number is going up), and Democrats use "woman" and "women" more.

Then we get Michael Medved, at the Young America Foundation, talking about Trash TV, R-rated, NC 17, stuff; he worries that Christians and Jews get to see them—but he gets to see them, since he is a movie reviewer. *I can handle it, but none other.*

Then "Dr." Ralph Reed recommends Medved's book and his (Medved's) wife's book with Dan Quayle. Did Dan need a little help with *The American Family*? "We need someone in the White House who shares mainstream values." Reed says he was in the college Young Republicans, supporting Ronald Reagan and Jack Kemp. Academia is still where liberals have cultural influence (yea!). Reed talks about this being the last election of the decade, century, millennium. He sounds apocalyptical. He talks about the 1900 election: within a few years of that election, McKinley was dead, Theodore Roosevelt was president, and in twenty years we were a military power. The question of '96? "Who is the best to raise our young?"

Is it government?

Or family?

The Left believes it is government; we believe it is the family . . . and the faith community. It will be about the coarsening of our culture, an illness that ails America's soul. In the words of Ronald Reagan, the government is not the solution, it is the problem, Reed tells us. Shades of Eldridge Cleaver. Where was Ralph on the minimum wage?

Dole should promise "dramatic and sweeping tax relief for American families." We have subsidized "people who break up and have children out of wedlock."

Graduate from high school, get a job and keep it, don't have children till you're married, he advises.

They have homeless shelters throughout the Midwest, Reed says—and new sports complexes!—and they (the folks in the shelters) are reformed spiritually. If the Left could protest that a ground war in Vietnam was a failure, they could protest that the war on poverty was a failure. No program can be devised by the Right. A spiritual conversion is needed. The Holy See and Billy Graham condemned partial-birth abortion. In the '94 election the polls showed by 52 to 48—56 to 44 of mass goers (4 or more a week)—the Catholic majority went to Republicans, he says. Catholics are the jump ball of American politics. He brings up a Tennessee case and says you can't write an essay about God in this country but you can write about Charles Manson. We're an issues organization, he says, giving two examples, tobacco and gambling, claiming the CC is against them (I'll give you 5 to 4 odds on that). But in any event, he says, now that his disclaimers are over, he's back to evangelicals, Catholics, observant Jews, all should form a new coalition. A spiritual and moral renewal. He quotes John Winthrop's words, a "shining city on the hill," and finishes, God bless you.

A woman asks a question on fetuses frozen after abortion so they can be brought back to a life and relieve guilt. (This must be an audience of true believers.) Reed, feeling comfortable, says there's cancer ahead for women who have had abortions, but cancer does not happen with miscarriages. It's a women's health issue, he says.

What children need is face-to-face interaction with parents and ministers, three thousand hours over a lifetime. I wonder how many hours of face-to-face Ralph has gotten in this week, today. He says, I have a seven-, five-, and three-year-old; I took them to *The Hunchback of Notre Dame* (which is the most violent Disney cartoon yet, according to critics; I haven't taken my five-year-old to it). Ralph's idea of face to face with the kids is two hours in a dark movie theater. But, Ralph says, I wouldn't take them to Disney World. Because of Disney's pro-gays policies, etc.

7/23 Diane Rehm does open phones on Deborah Tannen's article, "I'm Sorry, I Won't Apologize," in last Sunday's *New York Times* magazine. Will Joe Klein apologize? Does anybody? A male caller, forty-six, says he never heard a woman apologize. He says Clinton hasn't released his medical records. He makes a crack about Hillary's one-hundred-thousand-dollar futures wins. "Cheap shot, cheap shot," Diane says. He says hers is a subsidized network, and should be, adding, "I won't apologize for that." "I can see why you never heard an apology from a woman," Diane says, which is the first time I heard her insult a caller.

"What are his children going to think of him?" a woman caller says about Joe Klein.

All this exposure (of the Clintons' life), a twist on the emperor's new clothes, naked in public, but who cares? As in contemporary architecture, the inside is now on the outside. Air ducts, pipes, plumbing, electrical work, beams, all in bright, vibrant colors. Think of the Pompidou Center. The new Clinton White House.

Yes, appearance does matter. It isn't just what you know, but who you know. In the Woodward book, the "séance" gets all the play; in the Aldrich book, Clinton under a blanket gets the play, not the other things, most of which are likely true.

Tom Ridge, governor of Pennsylvania, starts up executions, wants to kill Mumia Abu-Jamal, the author of *Live From Death Row*, the subject of an HBO film. Ridge is another possible veep choice. Jamal is the cabdriver-journalist convicted of killing a cop named Faulkner. About the critical moments of the deadly event, Abu-Jamal remains uncommunicative on HBO.

60 Minutes does white-collar crime; all the other shows are downscale.

There's very little "liberal" alternative news on TV (*The Nation*, etc.). It's PBS or nothing—so nothing it is.

Jay Leno tonight only gets his monologue; his show is truncated because of the Olympics. Leno says Bob Dole visited "some of his boyhood haunts"—and there's a picture shown of a camel approaching a pyramid. That's the alternative news; it all comes from comics.

7/24 NPR *Morning Edition* news has a Clinton visit to a high school where he is commended for tears in his eye during the Martin Luther King tribute at the Olympics. Clinton wants a better world for our children. Haley Barbour is quoted: Clinton has perfected the art of crying out of one eye. Barbour and Rush are looped. But, Barbour says, Clinton's gift of empathy serves him well.

Diane Rehm does a show with the author of *Radio Priest: Charles Coughlin, the Father of Hate Radio*. Donald Warren is a bit reluctant to tie too much of the past to the present, even though his book begins: "In the wake of the April 19, 1995, Oklahoma City bombing, the existence of a powerful hate movement—primed by paranoid fears of government control, fed and fostered by talk radio—was suddenly and frighteningly catapulted to national consciousness" (1).

Rush is exulting: no feminist principle was on display last night. He's talking about the women's gymnastic team at the Olympics. No one tried to marry the coach and take over, he says. They got no points for entitlements.

On Newt and the fact Newt didn't say Medicare would wither on the vine, Rush plays Newt, saying that we believe the Health Care Financing Administration bureaucracy's centralized command will wither on the vine since people will leave it. Rush quotes from the Clinton/Gore tome, *Putting People First*, page 21: We will scrap the Health Care Financing Administration. Rush points out that in December '94, Newt on *Meet the Press* said one quarter of the White House staff have used drugs in the last four or five years. Leon Panetta called it a reckless charge, just basically smear; if you're Speaker of the House words matter. Rush says Newt is vindicated, with all that has come out on staff drug use. Rush moves on to, "Joe Klein will now retreat to the woods to pause and reflect." What does that mean? He has to be *really* sorry.

What will Clinton do? A middle-class tax cut. "He'll put the capital-gains cut in there," he'll co-opt the Republican proposal. He blames, credits, Dick Morris. "Mark my words," it will contain some capital-gains alterations, Rush says.

Then we get more sad ads. A Reading Genius commercial, lock it into your memory. Rush's ads are the truest mirror of his audience.

There's an eighteen or nineteen upper limit "of age," Rush says, in women's gymnastics.

More sad ads. Propomex, "natural choice for prostate health."

7/26   Rush is on Janet "Waco" Reno. And Joe Klein. Klein, I see, is now reaping what he feared would be sowed: news about him and no talk about the book. Even Rush says no one is talking about the book, which, Rush says, was praised by members of the administration "as true." He pushes the Aldrich book. Rush says he's the majority maker and truth detector all in one adorable bundle.

On *Washington Week in Review,* we learn Lou Gehrig, John Wayne, and Glen Miller are Bob Dole's favorites. "All dead," it's pointed out. Dole, at the Rock 'n' Roll Hall of Fame, was asked who was his favorite rock 'n' roller. Dole replied, "We didn't visit that part of the museum."

7/27   C-SPAN rebroadcasts the president at the White House Corre-spondents dinner (May 21). Clinton jokes, "Joe Klein introduces every-one at the *Newsweek* table to his imaginary friend, who he identifies as Anonymous." So Clinton knew in May, at least (or he too believed *New York's* article). Clinton cites the baby-sitting poll. Whom do you trust to select the toppings? Dr. Ruth is shown in the audience. Now why did the camera pick her?

Al Franken does a turn at the podium. He says Don Imus is "a putz." Franken imagines Imus on radio in 1944: for those of you listening on radio, the president is a cripple.

7/28   *Fox News Sunday* changes "Rumor of the Week" to "Inside Sources." Presto, chango.

7/29   Woodward's *The Choice* is done in his patented Joe Friday style (just the facts, ma'am), and when Woodward risks a simile, the reader gets something as flat as, "Even on the phone [Dick] Morris conveyed his intensity, his voice like a spring about to pop in your ear" (18). Clinton's "governing" throughout Woodward's account has a decidedly Reaganesque aspect. What Reagan knew internally through his Hollywood training, Clinton has to import from his consultants. Any statements replicated universally (via TV and radio and Internet) become commonplaces overnight.

Some think Joe Klein will be sent to an Elba of political reporters, a university perhaps, but not I. He's a big enough success that he will not fall from the celebrity orbit. And he won't have financial problems unless he really invests his loot badly. Being Anonymous helped hobble criticism of the novel in our politically correct time. Was the author a woman? man? black? It limited what people dared to conjecture.

Rush says: Isn't it strange that FBI agents lose credibility since they have so much reporting from Atlanta, and they lose it when they work in the White House? He's talking about a bomb that has gone off in Atlanta in the Olympic park and its aftermath. The FBI is on the case. "It's amazing if you're in law enforcement and work for the Clintons how much credibility you lose. It's the E-Bubba virus."

Rush won't be going to the Republican convention. Too inconvenient. Like going to the movies. The King is not amused.

Another sad ad: 800-Get-a-Bed. Comfort air mattress. "Select comfort sleep system . . . air mattress . . . it is amazing."

Rush: A caller says he thinks Clinton didn't expect to win in '92. And that he hasn't heard anyone say that (he hasn't talked to me). He adds a sinister reason: Clinton wanting to be positioned for '96 and thereby having enough time to bury his problems, Whitewater, Paula Jones, etc.

Rush says, so what? He doesn't take the bait. "I have trouble with 'ifs.' "

Commercials are said to be mainly about both ends of the alimentary canal. Is there a cat food that "maintains a cat's urinary track" health? Yes, it appears there is. If you watch a lot of TV you watch a lot of commercials.

7/30   Diane Rehm is discussing the gender gap. One caller likes Dole but will vote for Clinton because the Republican Congress "is crazy."

It's clear that Buchanan should have run as a Democrat if he had really wanted to make trouble.

Rush is upset that former White House staffer Lisa Caputo has taken a job at CBS. "Don't tell me there isn't a liberal bias" in the media, he says. She's Hillary Clinton's press secretary, doing the same job for Bill Clinton, saying Clinton created 10 million jobs. That's most of the jobs in the United States, Rush says. Andrew Young is complaining about too few jobs. Why? Rush wonders.

Kevorkian, "Dr. Death," Rush asks rhetorically, Do you think Christ died a "dignified death"? A *Wall Street Journal* article brings up Kevorkian's pathology past.

Clinton's campaign, it's clear, has become a New Mourning campaign, à la Reagan's New Morning.

Roger Clinton surfaces on Charles Grodin's show on CNBC. Roger has a new CD out. "Nothing Good Comes Easy" has only two original songs, one being the title cut, written for his mom. One of the lessons she taught him. "Remember my mother's teachings . . . and my brother's example." They intend to christen his new baby in the White House. But he didn't get married there.

A CNBC newsbreak announces Richard Jewell, who "found" the bomb at the Olympic Park, is a prime suspect. A wanna-be cop, former sheriff's deputy, single, loner, fat, white male, lives with his mother. (How do you spell P-R-O-F-I-L-E?)

The Christian Coalition is being sued by the Federal Election Commission for abusing its no-politics policies.

On CNBC's *America After Hours,* Mike Jerrick tells us about "the case against Richard Jewell." We're moving at rapid speed, though Jewell is not charged officially. CNBC shows a clip of a Katie Couric interview on the *Today* show with Jewell. He wears a kind of out-of-control, gelled flattop. In the '84 Olympics, an LAPD person planted a fake pipe bomb, we are reminded. In reply to Couric saying he might be a hero, Jewell says, "No ma'am, I was in the right place at the right time and used my training." If Jewell did it, he's as good as O.J. at keeping a straight face.

7/31 On Diane Rehm we have Michael Lind on, talking about his new book, *Up from Conservatism: Why the Right Is Wrong for America.* Buchanan is Wallace. The Republicans are "covering up the fact that southerners are the leaders of Republicans by parading Susan Molinari" at their convention. Neoconservatives moved to the right without giving up their commitment to the civil rights revolution. Lind didn't realize the far Right was infiltrating "the grass roots." It "took me by surprise." Surprise, surprise. He speaks about "this hoax about the rising illegitimacy rate." Four-fifths of the increase in the statistics is because the upper-income blacks have fewer kids. "Conservatives have dominated the media." Lind's review of Pat Robertson's book *The New World Order* in the February 2, 1995 *New York Review of Books*, which raised the specter of anti-Semitism, was a big turning point for him. A caller says: I've heard this individual speak before . . . I'm a moderate Republican. Why is he surprised about the Christian Coalition taking over state organizations. "I plead guilty," Lind says about not paying attention. "The southernization of the Right." He says only men call Rush. No, I know there are angry white women callers, too.

A Rehm caller refers to the Civil War as the "War of Northern Aggression." Lind says, "Alienating the middle fueled the Reform Party." Swing votes are the blue-collar workers. Pat Robertson is a crackpot, as is his book, *New World Order,* where he brings up the "international two-hundred-year-old conspiracy." Lind says he was attacked and "I'm not Jewish . . . I'm a Methodist; it was picked up as Jews versus Christians."

I think there won't be any No New Dole in this campaign because there's hardly any Dole left.

There's an ad on Rush for the Army National Guard. "What I like is working with heavy artillery; what I dislike is being away from home." Sounds of a baby crying. "Now I'm back with the artillery I love."

Is this parody, or farce?

The *A&E* network reran Rush's biography last night and a female caller says it was "really an inspiration." A "liberal" caller complains Rush doesn't debate. Rush says he has: Gore versus Rush on *Nightline* with seven others, on Clinton health care. "Why should I join the fray?"

he asks. "I'm in it for the confiscatory advertising rates," he says in his winning way. "I can speak the truth."

Nightline: the end of welfare as we know it. The safety net is rent.

Our Indiana congressman, Democrat Tim Roemer, on local news earlier, said, "We have to get off the dime" on welfare. He's backing the bill and Bill.

The oddity is that the one bit of conventional wisdom that has soaked in during the last ten years is that the rich have gotten richer and the poor poorer. Now the welfare bill promises to make the poor poorer, too. That should create some dissonance.

But Clinton doesn't seem to worry about losing Democrats, like he's not worried about gays: where do they go? Lack of enthusiasm is across the land for Clinton.

Clinton says welfare was meant to be "a second chance rather than a way of life," and he's ending sixty years of commitment. "One half of teenage mothers go on welfare within one year." Sixty-seven cents (the cent sign has left typewriter/computer keyboards, a sign of our inflationary times) per meal on food stamps is the allotment. The cabinet is falling in line. Donna Shalala says it's OK with her. She'll be back, I suppose. A woman interviewed at a North Carolina barbecue place says: "If they're not working it just continues to breed and their children learn it." Moynihan calls the bill the most brutal piece of legislation and public policy since Reconstruction.

On C-SPAN, we get a preview of the Republican National Convention. Paul Manafort, the Dole for President convention manager, gives a press conference outlining the upcoming convention. The theme will be "Restoring the American Dream. That's what this convention should be all about." They did their research. "We recognize that things weren't working" for certain American families. The convention will be pitched at, be for "that 20 percent of swing vote," for whom the American Dream has faded or abated, who believe "life will no longer be better for their children."

When the GOP talks about couples or children, it is talking about women. C-SPAN calls this the Republican National Convention Preview. Manafort wears a light blue tie with white flowerlike bursts. He has dark hair. Behind him is a golden Washington seal. His head appears to be in the middle of a platter. At the end of the four days, "We will have told the Dole story, the Dole agenda." "They don't know now who their nominee is," he remarks about Republicans. Isn't it a little late? Manafort thinks the convention will do it. He is questioned about the sort of research and focus groups they used to identify the themes and the constituency they are after—younger families, lower middle class, those for whom the American Dream has faded, Reagan Democrats redux. "We've talked to people," he says, and when pressed by a woman's voice, he pauses, and I watch his face decide these are questions he doesn't want to answer. He finally says, "We've gone through the traditional resources of research, survey-group research, focus-group research," but it's obvious he doesn't want to talk about it.

"We're not going to get into that today." The woman asks again. He says, "It's not relevant to what we are talking about today." He realizes he doesn't have to answer. "Thank you," he says dismissively.

ELEVEN

The Conventions of August

★

Life on Mars, Part 1

8/1   The couch moves west to Kansas City for a family visit. Congress is out tomorrow on its August recess, so I, too, am going to be with my constituents: some people-in-the-street, focus-group time with immediate family, three brothers and four sisters, two parents, all now back home in Kansas City. Or in the residential districts of Kansas City, Missouri, a good many of which are actually in Kansas, Bob Dole's backyard, since the state line abuts the large Missouri metropolis itself. I used to think of Kansas City as a cow town, but after moving out of New York City and living in South Hadley, Massachusetts, and now South Bend, Indiana, I think of Kansas City as a sophisticated cosmopolitan center. The city is all atwitter, now that the homeboy filmmaker Robert Altman has come and gone, because his new film, *Kansas City,* is about to open nationally. I expect another Altmanesque fantasy, along the lines of *Short Cuts,* where Altman refashioned the class lines of the short-story writer Raymond Carver.

Kansas City (not the jazz, Twelfth and Vine, world of yore) appears to have a lot of money and it certainly has a love affair with residential real estate. I'm not back long before I'm reminded of why as a teenager I couldn't wait to depart—money and looks count a lot in this town, though money still leads the way. The only benefit of having brains in the midwest is if they happened to have acquired any money for you. An idea without a bank account attached is a pretty weightless thing here, not that that is so uncommon in the rest of the country.

But it used to be a reason for some of its young to get out of the Midwest, at least its writers (Lewis, Dreiser, Anderson, Hemingway, etc.), and head for the East Coast, where having an idea or two could be stretched a bit farther on the streets of Manhattan.

Riding in from the airport with my father I discover he isn't yet sure whom he is going to vote for, though a number of months ago he said he wouldn't vote for Bob Dole. My father—in contrast to what the Republican convention manager, Paul Manafort, thinks is the situation of millions of Americans—knows Bob Dole. But my father hasn't made up his mind. This is important since he is my one-person focus group, since he has always voted for the winner in presidential elections. His record is perfect. Memo to Clinton: The race is tightening up.

It does enter my mind, that my father is not the avatar of the American psyche as I always presumed, as much as someone who likes to be on the winning side. And what he is perfect at, as he enters the polling booth, is casting a vote for the man most likely to win.

8/2 On PBS's *NewsHour* I hear (not see—it's hard to watch TV visiting family) Aidid of Somalia fame being called a "warlord." It brings to mind all the language controversy. Is Colin Powell a warlord? Or was LBJ a warlord? Somalia is such a godforsaken country and the news from there (and practically the whole of Africa) the last two decades has reinforced any stereotype the American public wishes to indulge in. The only "good" thing about Bosnia (and Northern Ireland) is that it reminds folks here in the states that white people are as likely to be as barbaric as anyone else.

Aidid is dead. I caught a bit of CBS's coverage earlier. I'll check the papers tomorrow. I do see Robert Oakley, former special envoy to Somalia, being interviewed. The United States and the United Nations made a "misjudgment" there, like in Lebanon ten years earlier. He reminds us that it was only ten days after the events in Mogadishu that the USS *Harlan County* went unloaded in Haiti. More pitiful-giant memories. Oakley's advice is that the outside world should watch rather than intervene.

I get to watch the *NewsHour* report on TWA 800. Disasters often accidentally focus attention on Americans *at work*. Here's a lot of people doing a lot of different things, most highly skilled, and most requiring large outlays of physical effort. We all know Americans work, but we do not actually see that work much on television, except in these catastrophes, especially this one, notable for its ongoingness. Like a miniature Vietnam War, TWA 800 goes on and on. Divers go down, bodies and debris come up. Anything on television consistently for more than two weeks seems to have been going on forever.

Like the Olympics. But there is light at the end of that tunnel.

8/3   I do not harass my family for their views on the '96 election, but during the visit I pick up some information. A sister-in-law, very corporate in outlook, though she was just let go by the company she has worked for for the last six years (her job, for now two successive corporations, was to fire people, and when she fired all there were to be fired she was let go herself), had voted for Perot in '92 but is unsure this year.

Some of my family, those more ardently Catholic than others, are anti-Clinton, with pro-life objections leading the way. A brother-in-law offers the opinion that Bob Dole will not be on the ticket come the end of the month. I am one of eight brothers and sisters and none of them are active politically. From my rough tally of just my siblings, the vote would be 4 Dole, 4 Clinton. The count gets a little stranger when wives and husbands are taken into account.

My corporate sister-in-law, the one who voted for Perot in '92, may be leaning toward Clinton, but doesn't say for certain. But she does talk about a phenomenon that might be making her lean his way. Since she now has more time on her hands she has been going to bookstores, and has noticed the new meeting place for people is (not that she was looking to meet anyone—she is married to my brother) the philosophy or New Age section of Barnes & Noble, on the Plaza, the swank shopping district of Kansas City. "You're either Western or Eastern philosophy," she remarks.

Evidently, the second floor of Barnes & Noble is crawling with corporate types in their forties and fifties who seem to be reevaluating their lives and seeking out the higher sort of self-help books (no big typefaces and boxed lists of numbered rules to live by) to aid them in their reassessment. She agrees it might have something to do with a new insecurity sweeping the corporate world, layoffs, downsizing, the fading of paternalism, etc. But, if you're looking for someone to meet, that's the place. The coffee concession is on the same floor.

Kansas City is the heart of America, more or less, so I consult the *Kansas City Star,* once (in my youth) an independent paper, now owned by Capital Cities/ABC, Incorporated, or, more recognizably, the Disney company. Mickey Mouse rules! There's an article today on Dole's poll ratings as a favorite son in Kansas: "Pitted head-to-head against Clinton Dole leads 48 percent to 39 percent, with 13 percent undecided. Throw Texan Ross Perot into the mix and Dole's share drops to 45 percent." The subhead makes the article's point: "Kansan's lead over Clinton should be bigger in his home state, analysts say."

Other pertinent news is the acquittal in Little Rock of Clinton's Arkansas campaign cronies, reported in yesterday's Star. It's subhead announces: "Whitewater prosecutor has first loss in case alleging fund misuse." "It's politics," juror Mary Zinamon is quoted saying. "You normally appoint people to commissions who are your supporters." Seven counts of the indictment went deadlocked; four, including the two involving Clinton's adviser, Bruce Lindsey, won acquittals. That must have been what E. J. Dionne was referring to yesterday on the *NewsHour,* when I heard him say that the "White House is enormously relieved."

In Mogadishu, Somalia, Mohammed Farah Aidid's (I've seen it spelled "Aideed") death was confirmed. The military's ill-prepared search for him in the fall of '93 resulted in the often played scenes of dead Americans being pulled through Mogadishu's dusty streets. Then there was the hostage tape news clips, all of which added to Clinton's first-year woes. This episode *was* the Vietnam syndrome, insofar as it showed the same pictures of a godforsaken Third World country beating back an attack by a First World power, the Stone Age triumphing over the Electronic Age. The Powell doctrine (enormous force at the ready) didn't seem to matter to the officers who sent in their helicopter gunships to locate the now dead Aidid.

There's a newspaper report on a Pew poll: mention Dole, the first thing people say is "old." Another snatch of dialogue I remember from last night's *NewsHour*: the guy from Pew was there and he said what they were recording is "not populism, but popularism."

My parents were watching *Wheel of Fortune* and a Democratic ad came on: Clinton in color, Dole and Gingrich in black and white, till the very end: "the real Bob Dole" appears in color. Republicans (making use of the Gingrich quote) call Dole "the Tax Collector for the Welfare State," $900 million in higher taxes, a voice intones. Perhaps this does affect the Kansas poll. It is clear that the *Wheel of Fortune* audience is the audience the Democrats want to reach, hoping to maintain their own lucky spin. My dad says such ads having been running for a year or more.

My father and mother are retired and live on Social Security, and a small income from a severance pension package my father received when he left the company (sold in his last working years to a large corporation) that he worked for all his married life.

His economist daughter-in-law, my wife, does pensions, so at this point, the subject of retirement is poignant, but they did their pension preparation the old-fashioned way, by having eight children, most of whom are solvent, though none are rich, and are prepared to be their safety net. My parents sold the last house they owned and a small house on the Lake of the Ozarks, paid off debts with what equity was there, along with part of the settlement package, and now live in a house rented to them by one of my fairly well-off brothers. My parents have downsized quite a bit, but it allows them to get along. (They shop at the large discount stores on senior discount day, bringing along other coupons to shave the prices.) We children are not worried if inheritance taxes rise or fall.

My father spends time golfing on the municipal courses and to support that habit has taken on a job with the Disney corporation, or Capital Cities/ABC, and has a delivery route for advertising supplements from the *Kansas City Star*, which are distributed free to the homes that don't take the *Star,* the region's primary newspaper. (Much to the *Star's* distress, these homes are the majority.) This brings home a number of things. One is that even in the middle-class residential district of Kansas that is the Kansas City suburb they live in, only 30 percent take the town's biggest newspaper. So the advertising is given away free. I suppose someday the newspaper itself may have to be given away "free" (as *The Village Voice* in New York City recently had to do to raise its circulation to please advertisers). And, too, my father is happy to get the fifty dollars a week he clears for his two days of labor—along with a free subscription to the paper—though it is the work of twelve year olds. Have you had your fast-food hamburger handed to you by a retiree lately? He likes the bonhomie he encounters (and instills) in the warehouse crew where he assembles with the coworkers when he picks up his weekly supply of supplements (which he has to stuff into those protective plastic sleeves), shades of when he managed a company that had its own warehouse. His work was a large part of his social life. And in such ways do all families make accommodations with the economy.

8/5 The couch is back home in Indiana. On *Larry King Live,* there's Lamm and his running-mate-to-be, a California congressman with an unpronounceable last name, Zschau. Lamm says, oddly quoting the Weather Underground, "There might be a prairie fire and we'd be the spark." They appear to be the new dumb and dumber duo, replacing Forbes and Kemp, Forbes being harder to look at and listen to, especially when his high-octane smugness kicks in.

Then we get Ralph Reed, on Dole dropping part of the tolerance plank. "I don't think it is a victory just for our organization," Reed tells us. "Let me make it perfectly clear," he says, quoting Nixon. King asks about a donation to defeat Clinton, causing trouble with the feds. "We believe he [the donor] was recontacted. . . . Unfortunately he is deceased." Ralph's head is jiggling around, a robot about to blow a fuse. It always taxes Ralph's disingenuity when he is asked about being an arm of the Republican campaign. "We aren't a tax-exempt organization." "We chose not to do it." (After their application was turned down.) "The same as United We Stand and the labor unions."

Greta Van Susteren comes on during a commercial break, doing a promo for her show, *Burden of Proof*. She is another lawyer–talk person from the O. J. employment agency. Greta is the one who always speaks looking as if she's just been handed some really bad personal news.

8/6 Diane Rehm does a show on Perot, with Gerold Posner, among others, on board. Posner, the author of *Case Closed,* a book on the JFK assassination, has just published a book on Perot. No one asks Posner if Perot shot Kennedy. The author Susan Isaacs comes on next, talks about her meteoric (though late) career as a novelist. She has just received some small nation's GNP–type contract, many millions. Isaacs talks about her early life: "I was ironing my husband's shirts." Diane says, "That's the same job I had, though I was married ten years earlier." No one asks if Isaacs shot Kennedy.

David Letterman cracks wise: "Dole wants to cut five hundred million in taxes and balance the budget by 2002. It's now official. He's senile."

That Dole will advance large tax cuts has been filtering through the news, the crude chunks getting caught by even the coarsest screens.

On *Talk of the Nation*, earlier in the day, Ray Suarez did a pick-your-Republican-veep contest. One caller suggests John McCain, whom I think will be the pick if Dole intends to put the draft dodger, pot-smoking, character issue first. Two warrior symbols, no language required. But if this "no taxes" thing is the flag, McCain becomes less likely. Jack Kemp's name is being mentioned, hoisted up the veep sweepstakes pole, though just last weekend there was no mention of him. But the caller likes McCain and he gives a reason: A Dole-McCain ticket, he contends, "would finally put to rest" the division over Vietnam in the country. If Clinton wins, the country would have finally settled the pain, confronted it, and closed that chapter. It would be, more than the election in '92, the referendum on the war. "It would be Dole's legacy," the caller says.

On C-SPAN Dole speaks to the platform committee via satellite. ("If only we will turn loose the American people, turn loose the American people. We are the party of change. . . . I trust the American people. . . . President Clinton trusts the government. . . . We care about those who work day after day just to make ends meet. . . . Welfare is sometimes necessary, the government safety net is sometime necessary. . . . Thank you very much and God Bless America." And we get a tour of the San

Diego hall where the convention will be held. It is usually used for trade shows, obviously fitting, since we will be getting a trade show. It's a rectangle, rather small, and they're putting in a lot of angles. C-SPAN interviews David Albert, design and construction director. He's asked about the cost involved, but says, "I'm not going to get into that with you." Later, C-SPAN flashes a table; there are 260 technicians, 8,000 man-hours. You can do the math. Don't forget materials.

8/8 In the *New York Times Book Review* of last Sunday, there is a review of Patricia Ireland's autobiography, *What Women Want*. It mentions Phyllis Schlafly. About thirteen years ago I was in a Michigan antique shop and came across a book by her, more a pamphlet, cheaply published. So outré the volume looked, it was practically samizdat. Its nonelite aspects dominated, since this sort of publishing did seem utterly out of the—not the mainstream, but out of the flow itself. These were springs, it seemed, that bubbled up into, at most, ponds and fed only those who gathered at their edges. The "avant-garde"—poets, marginal literary figures—could be a tributary that would with wild luck flow into regular publishing eventually, but this sort was another system, different hydraulics altogether.

The small white pulp book I held in my hand was the true counterculture of the sixties, not the one I was a part of, or aspired to. Mine was rapidly converted into the culture. This chapbook was from another counterworld, of fundamentalism and the marginal white folk culture, and they knew it, too. And they weren't happy about that, taking, as the "avant-garde" used to, pride in their marginalization. They were not the "elite." When the term "elite" is used, this is what they are referring to, the dominant culture, which their fundamental hickness has shut them out of. It's why they hate the "liberal media"—it is not that they are so dumb that they don't realize that the people that control the great corporations don't share their view of Darwinian capitalism, but that their culture and its organs are so alien to those sorts of free marketers, as alien as theirs is to them. They understand they won't be let into Yale, or Princeton, or be well regarded by the other mandarin institutions of that world.

That's how it used to be. And thirteen years ago I was still looking into the past. A change had been under way. My counterculture lasted about five years before it was subsumed. This counterculture just took longer to become the equal to it. They have profited from the "dumbing down" they decry. Now their views of "evolution" will be treated with due seriousness, and Newt Gingrich's former academic colleague can suggest giving equal time to the Nazi point of view and only after enough caterwauling lose her appointment as historian to the Congress. Small-town, small-college professors stand now as equals ("no standards!") to any from hated Harvard.

The culture war hasn't been accurately described. It's not an arena of sex, drugs, and rock 'n' roll. Nor about any standard virtues and vices, drugs and deviance, etc., which cut across all of humanity. The battle is waged by the formerly excluded who now want to be not merely included, but to be elevated over what they want eliminated.

Poor William Buckley does not represent them (and he certainly isn't responsible for them), but they do have surrogates—Charles Murray, William Bennett, and the other spawn from right-wing "think" tanks. They do lag behind, like the Wizard of No-Oz.

Yesterday's Frank Rich *New York Times* column does a skimming of the new Ed Rollins autobiography, *Bare Knuckles and Back Rooms,* and quotes some of Ed's unflattering remarks about Arianna Huffington. Maybe, given her upcoming appearances on *Comedy Central,* Arianna does want to be both Gabor sisters rolled into one. She might be truly laughable (*Comedy Central* notwithstanding), but she paved the way for Mr. Gold Standard Forbes, since Huffington's husband went out of his way to attempt to buy an election to the Senate in California with his own money. (What was he to do, Arianna huffed, buy a second-rate Picasso with it instead?) And, look, Steve Forbes, late of *Saturday Night Live,* is not entirely a joke these days, no longer being the son in the deep shadows, but *the* famous Forbes, which was certainly worth a paltry thirty million. Hillary got out of Arkansas forever and Steve became the famous Forbes. Who says there's no justice on this earth?

In today's *New York Times,* there's a picture of Clinton with some female Olympians (A11). It's a crowd shot, Clinton in the middle with Hillary and Chelsea. He stands out, because of his age and gender. It does sum up why Clinton is president. He loves it. His head is back, his smile is contagious. He wanted it more than Bush or Perot, more than anyone around. Bush and Perot had other things to do with their lives. Bill needed a house, to meet important and wealthy people. Bush and Perot already had both. I doubt if Clinton has a rival for that public pleasure: are you supposed to love it so much, to reveal your joy at being president that nakedly?

Phyllis Schlafly was on Ray Suarez's show yesterday. I heard her, too, but I defer to my wife, who reports, "She was really good. She doesn't engage with the other guests. She talks as if she's just right. Partial-birth abortions, she says were created by doctors and the AMA for the convenience of the mother.' " Pausing, she says, "I know two women who had to deliver dead babies." She turns away at the thought. "Schlafly said, 'We help Bob Dole.' The representative from Women Republicans for Choice acknowledged it. They work harder since they are fanatics. Schlafly pointed out that her wing of the Republican party participate in the most democratic process. They are voted on, and voted on again and again, in order to get on the platform committee. Schlafly, she's good. Partial–birth abortions! What's that! Less than one percent?"

Ed Rollins, of don't-get-out-the-vote fame (engineering Christine Todd Whitman's governor race victory in New Jersey), is on Diane Rehm, pushing his new autobiography. Talking, he's a little gentler on the Huffingtons and others than he is in print. He does speak about meeting the man who arranged, Rollins says, a ten-million-dollar contribution from Ferdinand Marcos for Ronald Reagan's campaign. Why this is shocking surprises me; when the plunder is so astronomical, it gets spread around. Consider Mrs. Marcos's shoes. Ten million might be a new federal election cap maximum in the not too distant future, especially for long-term dictatorial rulers. An article in the December 1976 *Atlantic* by Renata Adler, "Searching for the Real Nixon Scandal," speculated that Nixon's actual impeachable crime was that he was being bribed by the South Vietnamese to prolong the war and foreign contributions were arranged for him by international money-raisers.

8/9 I run into a friend who read all three volumes of congressional hearings on the 1935 Fair Labor Standards Act, which created the minimum wage. There was no mention of fears of the minimum wage causing unemployment. Back then, business wanted the minimum wage, since it covered mostly manufacturing. Very few workers who were covered by the minimum-wage law made less than it, so it wouldn't have much effect. Business wanted protection from "chiselers," as they were called in those days, rogues in the business world. Minimum wage and food stamps were separated out to get around the Supreme Court after it declared the National Recovery Administration unconstitutional. As the number of people who were covered by the minimum wage went up after 1968, the benefit itself went down. Of the 20 percent or so who are covered, very few make less. Enlightened capitalists have lost their war (though they won their battles in the sixties), chiselers have won. The chiselers now set sail for other countries.

Today, Dole visited the Eisenhower Museum in Abilene, Kansas. No mention was made of the Greyhound Hall of Fame, which is directly across the highway. The liberal media strike again, not showing something of real interest to the people.

Rush comments on his show that Kemp "has Kennedy hair." Rush says people want to vote for Kemp but that "Kemp never ran for anything." Rush seems not to remember the '88 primaries or Kemp's time in congress. Rush also says, still thin-skinned, that he doesn't create "mind-numbing" robots, but merely "validates" his listeners' views.

There's an ad for the new Trump Casino near Gary, Indiana, that has recently opened. The ad buyers think Rush's listeners hereabouts are their sort of crowd.

A woman caller is irate about "Jock" Kemp, that he will "only appeal to jockstraps," and is "a mascu-nazi." She's not a Clinton supporter— would have liked to have Forbes. Rush tries to placate her, though she is obviously a resident of the GOP gender gap.

Rivera Live replays an anniversary show of the Brentwood killings. There are the Goldman father and sister again, crying, tears, Geraldo quivering.

I'm reminded of earlier in the day when I was exercising in the faculty/staff weight room and watching *CNN Headline News;* I was amazed at the new commercial that has been running: 1-800-US Search. Two guys will find anybody in the States for a fee. We are living in a country of the lost.

They show a clip on *Rivera Live* of Dr. Henry Lee, one of my choices for chief egregious villain of the O. J. trial, someone going way out of the way for one's employer. "Not a short struggle," the clip has Dr. Lee saying about the death of Ron Goldman—doubtless, to heighten the grief of the Goldmans for this particular show. But it recalls Dr. Lee's testimony, his claim that the killings could have taken a long time, much too long, the implication being, for O. J. to have done them. I remember Dr. Lee said it could have taken ten minutes to kill Goldman. The prosecution did nothing with that. Ask Dr. Lee, I was instructing the tube, if he knows how many minutes a round takes in a professional boxing match? Or tell Judge Lance Ito that the courtroom will now remain silent for ten minutes to gauge how long ten minutes is.

8/10 Michael Feldman's radio show, *Whad'Ya Know?*, is on. Feldman reports on the Dole five-hundred-dollar tax credit for each child. Feldman comments that Bill Clinton is offering five dollars for each act of purely recreational sex. Feldman also adds, about the Republican platform committee, that Dole wanted a tolerance plank, but the committee wouldn't hear of it. He moves to Jack Kemp, the new veep (!) nominee. It'll be "the first campaign where the running mates will have a debate."

Earlier, on NPR's weekend morning News show, Daniel Schorr quoted his wife, saying she reminded him that Kemp works well with blacks. He didn't add, as long as he's throwing them a pass.

Once Dole decided to become a born-again supply-sider, Kemp became inevitable. It is the same sort of pairing that Dole-McCain would have been had Dole decided to remain a deficit kind of guy and put the draft-dodging, pot-smoking character issue up front, billboarding two veterans of two wars; but instead, he chose pie in the sky over Maya Lin's wing-shaped (an open V) Vietnam Memorial.

Kemp has pluses and minuses. He is a national figure, or much more so than all those governors that have been mentioned, and the used cars of the Reagan and Bush's cabinet's (though I guess that includes Kemp, too), like Baker and Cheney. Forbes must be really smiling now: they've got the good-looking flat taxer, gold standard, flat-earth candidate now.

In Woodward's book, he quotes Kemp acknowledging "to friends that he probably was not smart enough to be president" (80). (When I tell this to my friends they immediately mention Reagan, so smarts doesn't seem to be a requirement.)

8/11   The couch takes a family visit to Milwaukee (Americans vacation in August). My brother-in-law, now married (that June trip to California), has moved with his new bride to Milwaukee to start medical school. He's in his mid-thirties, had a quick rise in the fire department, being one of the youngest captains, but is giving up a comfortable life in Santa Cruz to become a doctor. He did well on his MCATS, but it was hard to get into a medical school. His age was an added difficulty, but this year saw the largest pool of qualified applicants ever to attempt to enter medical school.

He prevailed, and he's now a student, having sold most of his belongings, including his home, the equity of which will pay for the first couple of years of medical school, though not much more.

Only in America. Midstream course corrections, though this is partly evolution. A lot of his fire fighting wasn't fighting fires, but showing up at sites of human destruction—car wrecks, explosions, etc.—and he was administering to the injured quite a bit already.

Milwaukee still appears to be the America of my youth, or, at least, Chicago of the 1950s, a strenuously preserved working-class (in culture) town, especially in West Milwaukee, where my brother-in-law and his wife have rented half of a duplex.

There's a time-capsule atmosphere here, because the neighborhoods we drive through don't have vast, closed factory wastelands and blasted buildings, such as South Bend has in its center, the silent and spectacular pyramids and sphinxes of a former glorious era of industrial pharaohs. Over the past year, Milwaukee has been the setting for two documentaries shown on PBS about the working poor. One was a Bill Moyers extravaganza. On the last segment, when Bill is talking to a black woman who just borrowed money on her son's new credit card to pay his college tuition and is selling her home (she's in real estate) when there's still a profit to be made on it, I am shouting at the screen, "Why don't you reach into your wallet and pay her, Bill, she's given you four hours of television!" The other was on Harley-Davidson (motorcycles), and Briggs and Stranton, the lawn-mower motor company, showing the effects of layoffs and downsizing. Poor but proud, the town's folk seemed there.

So many neighborhood taverns, so many small homes, so much thirties and forties–era fake brick tar siding. The home of the Milwaukee Brewers, its stadium a dingy triumph of fifties industrial corrugated sheetmetal style, with its wonderful patina of dirt, gathers the *volk* for a matinee under gray skies. (The Brewers, like the upstate football Packers, are among the very few professional sports teams that are named after their hometown's industries. Most are named after animals, or Native Americans. The Chicago Bulls are another exception—though animal, rather than human; the Bulls' old and new arenas [the site of the Democratic convention to come] are built in the old stockyard area of Chicago, now vanished. Perhaps, one could stretch it to the Mariners, but that might be going too far.) Milwaukee doesn't seem vibrant, but still it seems alive.

When one used to think Democrat, one would think Milwaukee (as well as Chicago), but Tommy Thompson, Wisconsin's current governor, was on the short list (he, too, being short, like most of the midwestern governors, except for Illinois') for the Dole-whatever ticket. Now that it is Dole-Kemp, the governors are a bit sour (the Dole campaign people have yet to get to them, it seems), especially Wisconsin's Tommy Thompson, who is quoted by the local news Channel 4 program *Insight* as being "upset" with the "process," and feeling "used."

I had risen late and only got to see the last six minutes of *Meet the Press,* which consisted of commercials and promos for NBC. Driving up to Milwaukee had not been smooth. The fuel line on our new-used '93 Taurus ruptured (alert Ralph Nader and the Green Party) outside of Kenosha, spewing gasoline while going sixty-five and the rest of the evening wasn't a lot of fun, but we finally got to Milwaukee via my brother-in-law, who drove down and picked us up, the Taurus resting in the lot of a Kenosha dealership. Breaking down late Saturday afternoon is the closest thing to discovering a black hole in the world of car repair.

After hearing about Tommy Thompson's disappointment (luckily the former tenant left the cable on), I fell into C-SPAN, and saw two familiar faces, Julie Nixon and David Eisenhower, talking about the difficulties of being a child of a president. For a moment I was wildly confused, since

I thought David, now aged (my age?!), looks like Nixon, and Julie looks like Mamie, but I finally straightened it out. They both still would recommend a political life, they say, for their own children.

On CNN there's the *Evans and Novak* show, not one I catch often in South Bend. Haley Barbour is their guest. (Hey, Haley, any islands off the coast of Honduras for sale to the Marcoses? I want to call out, having read about his concern for the Marcoses recently in the book *White House E-mail*.) Haley, chair of the RNC, wears a "15%" blue button on his lapel, not a Dole and/or Dole-Kemp button. Obviously, that's what's running, the tax freebies.

"They shouldn't put old men out in the sun," my wife comments, walking by. Evans and Novak and Barbour are sitting outside in the wind, with expensive boats slowly undulating in the background. Ah, San Diego. "Women's magazines tell you that on a first date, if you go to the beach, stand in the shade," she says, exiting.

It isn't a pretty sight. Every line on their faces is a shot of the Grand Canyon. Novak's distended belly in a three-piece suit contrasts badly with the yachts behind. A Wall Street caricature going sailing.

It becomes hard to hear for a moment. You know you are in a working-class neighborhood when you're also underneath the airport's flight path.

Barbour says something about respecting the "widely differing views on a subject" in the GOP platform. The slower he talks (and he's talking slowly now) the less likely what he says is true. Novak is indignant. He asks what he calls the "question": "From what they said in Russell, Kansas, they [Dole-Kemp] are not going to attack President Clinton on the character issue. Is that correct?"

Another incoming plane drowns out Barbour's fudging.

Happier with a cup of coffee, I watch Cokie on *This Week with* (out) *David Brinkley*. Looking like a flag, Ralph Reed is on. A blue suit and a red-and-white striped tie. The stars are in his eyes.

Cokie mentions how happy Reed, Bay Buchanan, and Phyllis Schlafly must be, given the platform was a victory for the Christian Coalition.

"I believe it's Bob Dole's victory," Reed says, the Cheshire cat Christian. Reed is the only person I know who can turn self-effacement into perjury.

Campaign America '96: The View From the Couch

Cokie is in ABC's convention skybox. A snappy set. The surface behind her looks like impasto; it, too, is a flag, but waving white stripes on blue. Jasper Johns by way of Macy's window. There's talk about the poll gap narrowing to 10 percent. Governor Wilson says he's enthusiastic about Jack Kemp and he says it most unenthusiastically. Governor Engler of Michigan says Kemp will appeal to blue-collar workers (I look out the window for sprouting "Kemp" or "15%" signs). Cokie pushes and Wilson has trouble defending Kemp beyond a sentence or two. His voice is still bad. A political career hinging on a voice box. Engler mentions that in a Lansing, Michigan, newspaper poll, they were 20 percent behind. He says, "We're not going to win this in August. We will win it in October and November."

The tax cut equals Kemp. Every individual is paired to an issue.

Sam Donaldson wants to know from Wilson why his invitation to speak at the convention was withdrawn. He balks. His own "private speculation"? Wilson says his own "private speculation is that you want me to speculate publicly."

But the governors end the interview on an upbeat note. "Bill Clinton, watch out!" Engler says. "You'll be as surprised by the election as you were surprised by the selection of Jack Kemp."

Cokie Roberts is turning into an upper-class Catholic Barbara Walters.

How-you-look standards have gotten looser and more reasonable, though it is not likely you will see a bald anchorperson too soon. Barbara Walters has her famous lisp, made more famous by Gilda Radner, and Cokie has, besides her eyes, her modified lockjaw voice, which only gets really arch once in a while, when her class biases flare up.

This campaign season has finally elevated Elizabeth Arnold from radio (NPR) to PBS and the networks. When this first occurred she was a blast from the past. That long, fuzzy hair, those Berkeley-student clothes! "And they're her best clothes, too," I heard more than once from interested viewers, other than myself. Somebody has stepped in, it appears, because-Arnold's now a bit more together appearance-wise on the tube.

Again, this elevation from voice to view is a tribute to the new power of radio, since it has been (stepping into the vacuum) an *intellectual* force, odd as that might seem. All that talk radio, in various guises, including NPR's various news programs, has been an over-the-airwaves seminar, much more so than even PBS's programs. A lot of radio news consists of miniessays, much more than equivalent newspaper stories. If there's an equivalent, it's the op-ed pages; on radio there is a voice, hence there is a point of view. The news stories in newspapers have an institutional voice, not a human voice. They are not bereft of point of view, but it is the reflection of the corporation that owns the papers. Radio is human beings and, though representative in some manner of their employers, it is still their voice.

Back to *This Week with Cokie Roberts*: George Will, commenting on Republican themes in the air at the convention—hope, growth, and opportunity—says, "Wasn't that the mantra of Steve Forbes?"

NASA's funded life-on-Mars research has just been hitting and smashing over the public windshield and Cokie wants to turn the last minutes of the show over to it. "When the history of this millennium is written, that will be the lead," she says, all excited. Lead: "Life on Mars! Can't Phone Home." Donaldson and Will hem and haw, aren't quite as enthusiastic. The implication of the discovery, especially from Cokie, is that, despite what Bob Dole and the rest of the Republicans are doing, we are remarkable human beings. All three of them look out admiringly onto the technological wonders of the convention arena, waiting for Life On Mars to be discovered tomorrow in that cold, sterile atmosphere.

8/12   The couch on the road. Back in Kenosha, doing my American thing, dealing with a broken-down car. The Ford dealership doesn't have the Ford part for this Ford car. Tomorrow, maybe. It's rent-a-car time, since the rest of the family has plans other than watching the Republican convention.

I'm eating alone at Denny's (wife and child ate earlier while I dealt with the dealer at the Auto Mall, an extravagant multidealership space-station-like colony arrangement, off the interstate). Another intact American family, though, does arrive at the booth across from me, a family of four, two boys, around eleven and eight, dressed identically (with tiny variations). Tight black jeans, heavy silver chains, attached to large wallets in the back right pockets of their jeans. Black T-shirts sporting Harley-Davidson logos, black baseball caps, the one facing me with a Hard Rock Cafe Nashville logo on its front. They are both small and thin and their outfits are so crisp they looked like they are wearing uniforms. Mom has short dark hair and Dad is compact, muscular, tidy. All are very tidy. They haven't logged five hundred miles on their hogs today, I take it. (They might be pulling them in trailers, since back up the road in old Milwaukee is the home of Harley-Davidson.)

The father orders four coffees. Four?! the waitress says, not disguising her surprise. The boys are small, not yet teens. Yes, three regular and Mom wants decaf. Later, a different waitress appears balancing a circular tray with four coffees. She gets to the table and stares.

"You don't want all these coffees, do you?" she asks, also incredulous.

Yes, yes. Down they go.

The table behind them is a guy with an eight-inch sneaker. One leg is shorter than the other and one sneaker has been built up. Professionally. That must be a two-hundred-dollar sneaker worth two hundred dollars. He isn't quite as tidy as the family-that-drinks-coffee-together-stays-together family. He's waiting for someone. She returns, a woman about his age (near forty), Asian, still a heavy accent. I can't guess which of them was the mail-order spouse and which one got the best bargain.

In the table directly in front of me are another couple. Both wear American-flag shirts, and the guy, in his forties, sports a long ponytail. And this isn't even San Diego! I think. The usual morning crowd at Denny's in Kenosha. What I don't see is any black folks.

Driving back to South Bend late afternoon in my rented Escort, I catch a little of NPR's *All Things Considered* in between blackout areas. I hear Lamar! Alexander, newly risen from the primary news graveyard, say, "Our task is to convince people Bob Dole is a better man than Bill Clinton." *The better man.* That phrase has popped up before: it is the GOP mantra, the moral charge implicit, and seems to be one that will be said a lot in the days ahead.

Christie Todd Whitman's voice comes on as the signal starts to fade around the steel town Portage, Indiana. She's been asked about the no-tolerance abortion plank. "I wish the entire platform . . . ," she starts to say, and stops, beginning again, ". . . the entire plank was out of there." She's in the yank-the-plank group, but now appears to want to yank the platform.

I'm watching the combined NBC/PBS coverage, catching the

NewsHour portion. A discussion of the veep selection is under way. Whether it helps or hinders, etc. One of the best things quoted in the Ed Rollins book (*Bare Knuckles and Back Rooms*) is about the selection of Dan Quayle. Evidently, according to Rollins, Bush wanted "someone smaller than life" (190).

Thomas Eagleton's name is mentioned in the discussion, one of many problems of George McGovern's campaign. I recall descriptions of Eagleton "sweating bullets," or some such, in the wings of the '72 convention before his acceptance speech, one of the few indications of the revelation yet to come of his "shock treatment" problems. Years later, when Eagleton was still senator from Missouri, I was in the Columbia, Missouri, airport when the senator arrived for a flight with an aide. No one approached him (and the terminal was small, full of people), and there he stood, rung by a doughnut of nervous silence, and he still looked anxious, haunted, but he wasn't sweating bullets.

Gore helping Clinton is commented on; indeed, the contrast transcends conventional wisdom, Bubba the good and Bubba the bad, the yin/yang of the New Democrats. One's virtues, the other's vices. More of the same, only Gore is more service, more suffering, more saintliness, more the scion.

The president unseated by Clinton-Gore, George Bush, is being interviewed by Lehrer. Bush doesn't intend to stay for the whole convention. He is flying in and out to give his speech tonight. He's only staying seven hours. Bush says, in a reflective moment, "I'm the past, my sons are the future." He pauses and in that pause he realizes he has revealed too much truth, especially its class aspects. The firm is restructuring, the old CEO is moving aside, the young blood is moving up and which one (Bush like old Joe Kennedy musing) will be president? Bush adds after the pause: "Dole-Kemp are the future."

NBC takes over. Tom Brokaw is giving his introduction and finds himself talking over "The Star-Spangled Banner." "Always an awkward moment," he says. "Let's take a moment . . ." The shot goes to a young black youth singing, "O say can you see . . ." It's clear from the get-go that the Republicans are going to be shameless.

Bill Bennett, the prince of smugness (Al Franken's joke at the White House Correspondents banquet about Bennett recognizing smugness as "a virtue" hit the mark—C-SPAN showed Bennett giving Franken a halfhearted salute [a disguised slap] from behind his dinner plate), is being interviewed by Maria Shriver Schwarzenegger, and he handles his awkward moment differently. She's holding up a clipboard with a big yellow tape M on it (so she knows which one to pick up, doubtless), and as Bennett is giving his answer a moment of silence is called for and Bennett whispers through it in reply. He's pleased as punch, smugness over the top, given Kemp's ascendance, Empower America empowered.

Brokaw is back on talking about how the Republican delegates are 2 to 1 white male, high-income folks. (You can see why there is a GOP Network. Any such facts stated, ipso facto, obviously drip with bias at this convention. Get rid of facts, please.)

Back to NPR: Paul Gigot gives a new definition of a party's "platform." "A summary of what the activists believe." And the candidate says forget all this. Dole hasn't read it, Haley Barbour will get to it later. Governor Wilson is asked why his invitation to speak has been rescinded. He seems somewhat mollified since yesterday. "I can't say because I don't know."

Then he adds: "Maybe they heard my voice." It's still bad after throat surgery, a scratch on vinyl.

To change the topic, Wilson latches on to the subject of illegitimacy, throwing out the statistic that one-third of children are born out of wedlock. This is also his wife's issue (he doesn't mention that).

Alfonse D'Amato, Clinton's chief primary opponent is on the screen. "Tonight, we begin our campaign to restore hope and opportunity for America's working families," he begins, showing that those focus-group findings are to be adhered to. Al's on message. Republicans believe in workfare instead of welfare, Alfonse tell us. "We will restore the American Dream for our children." Restoring the American Dream is the theme and the pitch. The American Dream is upward mobility, just what stopped under the twelve years of Reagan and Bush. A lot of blame, it seems, is going to be heaped on the short window of time the Clinton administration provides. Only four years, a narrow balance beam (to be Olympian, in the spirit of the month/times) on which to pile all the weight of the vanquished American Dream. Republicans, of course, would blame the Democratic Congress, overlooking all the Republican presidents since JFK and LBJ. They can have it either way, but not both ways.

"My immigrant grandparents—believing in the American dream—came to America seeking opportunity for their children and grandchildren. And now I have the honor of serving in the United States Senate and representing the people of the great state of New York—only in America." Only in America, indeed. The American Dream is the rise of the unlikely to the unusual, from low aspirations to high office. Of course, the low is often not so low. But D'Amato shows why it has been difficult for him to make any smooth transition to national-figure status; his eyes swimming behind his glasses betray too much looking for the sweet deal, the soft spot, the main chance. When he talks he often looks like he's trying to locate the nearest exit, in case bullets start to fly.

But it appears the bootstrap theme is to be laid on thick. In the past, Republicans haven't overindulged in this, though I would mark the announcement of Clarence Thomas as the former high moment of it: Bush and Thomas in the sunlight, Thomas breaking down with the thought of how far and how quickly he had come—and the memory of his grandparents. I don't blame Clarence Thomas for being so shocked and emotionally disturbed by his selection to the highest court in the land. A lot of folks were.

Michigan's Governor Engler, the non–number two on the ticket (partly, no doubt, for being twice two disqualifying pounds overweight for his Vietnam-era draft physicals back in the bad old good old days), comes next.

Engler, too, ratchets down the class focus. Bob Dole's going to win, he says, "because he's going to do for America what Republican governors are doing for families in their states." What's that? I wonder. ". . . strengthening local control of our schools . . . reforming welfare and requiring more work and personal responsibility. . . ."

The nonunion white working class is the new demographic that the Republicans are after. Not the Reagan Democrats, who were the disaffected unionized working class that was pissed off at their kids. It was a hard hat versus longhair culture war that Reagan profited from. This population that the Republicans are mining (along with Rush and the talk radio world) has different cultural fissions.

Earlier CNN did an interview with a young Republican delegate. Variously reported statistics claimed the delegates to be 2 percent minority and 36 percent female, but the lowest percentage was among young delegates: only 2 percent were under thirty. So CNN found one. A young entrepreneur the usual sort of young Republican—a go-getter, running a business, ambitious, focused, not the volatile swing-voter type, those more working-class in cultural outlook; but he was a swing voter in the Republican world: he had first supported Gramm, then considered Alexander, and then, in his state's primary, voted for Buchanan. "Dole wasn't my first choice," he says, not entirely sheepishly. But he's gung ho now. He runs a "telemarketing" firm with thirty-six employees, a medium-sized firm in America. Now telemarketing may be all that is wrong with our country, but it is the perfect young Republican business: intrusive selling to captured audiences; no production, just distribution, capturing his percentage from his low-wage workers. No new taxes! Go Bob Go.

The southernization of the Republican Party is referred to, the fact that so many who have degrees—either delegates or members of Congress—are graduates of Southern colleges (47 percent of males, 45 percent of females). I wonder if Georgetown would be considered a southern college. Harley Barbour and Christie Todd Whitman are proclaiming the party's diversity: "We are diverse," Barbour says. The camera lands on some of the 3 percent. Boy, those faces are going to get a workout the next few days.

Mary Fisher is at the podium. She has big hair. And she has AIDS, reportedly from her husband. A network voice says they are divorced. "Gay men and African American communities are brutalized by this disease," she says, and there is a shot of a black man in the audience looking uncomfortable.

"I mean to live and die a Republican," she says, to applause. Mary Fisher is the daughter of a wealthy Detroit financier, I am informed over her speech.

A smallish African American girl comes onto the stage. Fisher introduces her as "a member of the AIDS community." The youngster has a nose ring. She has not said whether or not she is a Republican, but she recites a poem: "I dream that there will be a cure for AIDS." The refrain is, "I am the future and I have AIDS." There is a shot of a black woman crying, brushing away a tear. That's the Republican policy for African Americans.

After the poem is over, Ms. Fisher finishes a sentence, "after my late husband Brian died." She does not refer to any divorce. "I may lose my own battle with AIDS." I wonder, unkindly, if she will be back in 2000 at the next Republican convention.

Mary Fisher is the reverse of D'Amato, downward bootstraps. The rich empathize with the oppressed, downtrodden, the poor, when disease has stamped them with its own lethal A, and they are forced to enter the pariah brother- and sisterhood.

I am back to Lehrer and PBS and he says Fisher and the young poet were "terribly moving." "Yes, absolutely," Mark Shields replies. No one points out that the only AIDS representatives allowed are the women who get it from men and children. (Later, clicking around, I see Jerry Falwell being unforgiving of the way most men get AIDS. Less sympathy from Jerry for the "preventable.") Paul Gigot says there's been a "conscious effort on the part of the Republicans to avoid the mistakes of Houston." I guess. The *Wall Street Journal*'s master of the obvious.

Much is made of Dole's announcing he hasn't read the platform. Gigot supplies, "Well, the most conservative Democratic platform was in 1932 and President Roosevelt didn't read that one either."

Some of this seems rather handy research. Those behind-the-scenes ventriloquists who are producing talking points are turning a lot of commentators into Charlie McCarthys of the electronic age.

CNN has found Abner Mason, a Massachusetts delegate, who is black and openly gay. "There are four of us," Abner says. He means, I take it, four gays, not four black gays, which would really put a remarkable dent in the 3 percent minority presence. He doesn't feel alone. "This convention is the polar opposite of ninety-two," Abner says, looking very gay yup—no chains and leather here. "Buchanan isn't allowed to speak."

Gramm, Alexander, and Lugar appear together, the happy losers. It is clear this is why Lugar ran, in order to earn this status at this convention for his 1 to 2 percent. Lamar! says, "It's a choir and Bob Dole is the conductor." They are asked about Buchanan. "We want him to join us," Lamar! says. Gramm boasts about the Republicans' cry for "less government and more freedom." How that fits with the antichoice position never is made clear.

Michael Deaver is rolled out. Reagan's crew let out of the tomb. He's asked if this is a convention or a TV extravaganza. He replies, "a little of both." That's where they (he means the people) get their information. "I'm not sure it's about controlling the message, but scripting it for television," he finishes. It's jobs, jobs, jobs candor from the elegant sleaze merchant.

Ronald Reagan has become canonized. He's dead but not dead, or rather not dead, but dead, a Neomort, since all talk is eulogy for the tardily acknowledged Alzheimer's victim. How did that happen? The Great Communicator. Tear down that wall! He has entered Republican heaven and it looks like San Diego and the common recreation room is the trade-show hall.

The folks at PBS are decrying the Deaver remarks. After listening to the high dudgeon, I start to sympathize with Nancy's favorite compos mentis guy.

John McCain is speaking. I see one reason he might not have become the veep nominee (other than being the fifth of the Keating Five). He's a bit stiff up there. "When our children are drawn to the antiheroes of Hollywood, Bob Dole is a rebuke to them." McCain introduces the famous bug eater, Scott O'Grady, our Bosnian hero. There is a shot of the former Secretary of State, George Schultz, in the crowd. It's Reagan's party, obviously, Southern California triumphant. Scott recalls being "alone and facing death." He might have been facing capture, too. Scott's calling for more men and women to be honored, "especially the POWs and MIAs who have defended this country . . . to guarantee the American Dream for all."

This harkening back to the Vietnam War produces a shot of Dan Quayle and his wife, the noted thriller author Marilyn. The POWs and MIAs function for the Republican Right the same way abortions do for the most ardent Christian Coalitionists—as symbols of lost innocence, of perfect things destroyed. There's a metaphysic here: purity found, located. All else might be faulted and flawed, but this alone is inviolate and is the site of belief born and restored.

The PBS coverage is shifting back and forth and falls into an odd, parallel rhythm. The convention's speeches are short, five minutes or so, and so are the discussion periods. Thus far, like the O. J. trial, we have talking heads, and television has become talk radio, or, more correctly, talk television. PBS cuts back to the convention: it is like going back to the O. J. trial after cutting away from the sidebar conferences. Though, in this case, the sidebar conferences involve Lehrer, Gigot, and Shields. Then we get Beschloss, Goodwin, Kristol, and Haynes Johnson. Who is the prosecution, who is the defense?

Haley Barbour turns up. "You might not have heard this from the media, but the Democratic Party is the liberal party and we are the conservative party." This comes up to counter the discussion that the televised convention, thus far, looks like a Democratic convention. Minorities everywhere, women everywhere, whatever. "If you believe Bill Clinton," Haley jokes, "then I'm the poster boy for Slim Fast."

Barbour does better one on one than as a public speaker. He gets broader and coarser before a large audience, his accent thickens. He calls Clinton a chameleon, always changing colors. "We'll put him on scotch plaid and make him sweat."

Following Barbour, Doris Kearns Goodwin comments that there is "too much" biography given—a strange remark for a biographer to make, especially one who supplied quite a bit on LBJ. Diane Sawyer followed Nixon to San Clemente, but Doris blazed the trail, following LBJ to his ranch in Texas. "FDR wouldn't be talking about his mother," she says. Given FDR's mother, I can see why. Gingrich is shown mentioning Colin Powell. "He's a best-selling author," Gingrich says with real animation and admiration. Gingrich's own book, *To Renew America,* the one he needed to reject Rupert Murdoch's proffered millions for, never, ah, took off.

Gerald Ford comes on. This is as close as we are to get to Nixon. No video tribute for Tricky Dick. Perhaps they could run the last few minutes of Oliver Stone's film, the funeral documentary montage. Ford reminds me, and some portion of the audience, of . . . himself. Aaaaggghhh! as Bob Dole would say. Ford's method of public speaking fits this smallish television studio set that Deaver has managed to turn this trade hall into not at all. Not a bull in a china shop, but bellowing in a closet.

Ford tells us we need "a commander in chief who has earned his salutes." Who's writing these speeches? Not Mark Helprin, quite yet. "The primary purpose of a political party is to win." The Republican Party welcomes "every American who believes in liberty and justice for all."

All great writing is anonymous, or so goes an old truism, but Joe Klein aside, all the writing here this evening does seem to spring from one source, or is, more likely, tied together out of one single committee, like a standing roast wrapped with string. "Ours is the Republican Party of Abraham Lincoln." Photos of Lincoln fill the multi-TV television screen, the video wall, the flattened-out fly's eye of the late twentieth century that is the stage's backdrop. "Ours is the Republican Party of . . ." And as the names are recited we get pictures: Eisenhower, Reagan, Bush, and . . . Bob Dole. No Nixon. Nixon's grave is the ugly chasm Ford leaps over. Only dead can Nixon safely be ignored; imagine what his fulminations would have been to the impressionable, young Monica Crowley, the author of *Nixon Off the Record*.

"I found Bob Dole fit to be president then," in '76 and "I find him even more qualified today," Ford claims, though Ford wasn't fit to be president when it fell to him, thanks to the man who goes unmentioned.

It's over, finally, after bringing up his "cliff-hanger" loss of '76, seemingly hours longer (that voice! those days!) than its actual few minutes. Betty Ford coming up to be with him unfortunately stumbles as she gets close to her husband, reminding the world instantaneously of all her pre–Betty Ford Clinic problems.

Young George Bush, cohost of the convention and governor of Texas, gets to introduce his dad. There's a shot of Quayle sitting with Liddy Dole. Then the former president appears, the vanquished patrician.

Bush the elder comes more to heap scorn on Caesar than to praise him. His "speech"—it's obvious that these short speeches are one long speech, crafted by the same team's many-fingered hand—touches on the White House as scandal central: "It breaks my heart," Bush intones, "when the White House is demeaned, the presidency diminished" by the occupants within. It's curious watching former presidents do this work. There seem to be more living ex-presidents kicking around at this time than ever before in human history (could this be true?), especially when Nixon was still alive—Nixon, Ford, Carter, Reagan, Bush—and the gang of five seem to want their number returned to five, with the addition of Clinton to replace the unlamented, at least in San Diego, Richard Nixon. Is there something wrong with a country when too many ex-presidents are dragging their chains like Dickensian Marleys, clanking on the ramparts, scaring the present-day chief executive? Another *Macbeth* parallel that besets the Clinton administration. *MacBird,* the Johnson-era satire, yoked *Macbeth* to LBJ's presidency, but it now seems more pertinent to Clinton's.

Bush gives a litany of Reagan-era triumphs, most notably the Soviet Union imploding, the Berlin Wall coming down, the Baltic states going free (that's Bosnia, the former Yugoslavia, folks, free to slaughter one another), "Latin America on the democratic move . . ." And "when Saddam Hussein attempted to take over another country . . . we saw the United States of America lead an historic international coalition to kick him out of Kuwait." Only "out of Kuwait," I say to the screen. Saddam rules on. "There is no substitute for personal sacrifice, for courage, for honorable service." The subtext—is "How could I have lost to this guy?" And the old CIA hand does want to believe (given his earlier list of "triumphs") that it was Ronald Reagan and his clandestine services (Ollie North!) pulling the strings that made it happen.

Bush then introduces "a woman who unquestionably upheld the honor of the White House," and Barbara Bush sails out of the wings, a patrician matriarch clipper ship, all lofted canvas swollen with rich air, brow jutting proudly forward. Bush manages to praise her and damn Hillary. Not WASP gallantry at its finest. He is still pissed off at losing. The hall is full of cheers, a twofer, lauding Barbara, bashing Hillary.

Since I'm watching PBS, I am startled for a second when it appears a commercial has come on. Maybe it's a promo for Archer Daniels Midland (ADM). Then I comprehend what it is: the Reagan video. Lee Iaccoca, the space shuttle, Kissinger, all saying Ronald Reagan won the cold war (except for Kissinger: "I won the cold war" is his translation). Jack Kemp appears—he must have been taped before being selected veep—and Scott O'Grady gushing, "The first person to write me was Ronald Reagan." I find that hard to believe. Puleeze. The Reverend Billy Graham, the assassination attempt (such a thing gives status, gravity, to a man), then the Gipper is in front of a Notre Dame banner throwing a football, shades of Kemp campaigning to come, doubtless. Nancy saying they stuck together "through thick and thin." When was the thin? I wonder. Only now, I suppose.

We're back live. Mrs. Reagan stands there wearing white. She is the transformative moment, the young starlet becoming her own version of elegance and taste. To the wealth Mrs. Bush was born to, Nancy climbed to, on the back of Ronald Reagan, the Great Communicator. The Fords, Betty and the ex-prez, have replaced Dan Quayle at Liddy's side.

Nancy gets the longest applause thus far. She starts to describe "a life we never thought we'd have," and I have to grant the truth of that. There's a shot of Maureen, one of the unsuccessful at winning an election by the political progeny on display.

Nancy mentions the ex-president's present condition: "each day brings another reminder of this very long good-bye." There is a real ambiguity in her voice; she does seem upset, wronged somehow, put upon. At least that emotion is mixed, ambiguous, not entirely fraudulent. A note of despair at Ronnie still being alive, and she having to suffer through it. It's human, at least.

"Ronnie's optimism, like America's, still shines brightly." Lots of women crying in the audience, a shot of a man crying. Nancy knows she would make a great widow, but it is being denied her. Will she have to do this four years from now, too, like Mary Fisher? Or will the Republicans have what they appear to want right now, Reagan as history, history as the Age of Reagan, their most celebratory moment always to be celebrated? Nancy is a premature widow; she's ready for the role, no more auditioning (those dreary degradatons of her youth), irritated it is being withheld from her.

She leaves and an announcer's voice intones: "Ladies and Gentleman, General Colin Powell." It's a spectacle-to-come voice, before the curtain is swept open on the one-of-a-kind attraction. "Ladies and Gentlemen, *King Kong*."

The general takes the podium. Lots of applause. Starts tapping his watch. The general does a lot of public speaking, but he's used to being obeyed, too. And the crowd is not obeying. Finally, he just talks through it: "My fellow Americans, my fellow Republicans." More applause. He quickly reprises his résumé by mentioning the former presidents. Ford saved us from "national despair" and brought "dignity and respect back to the presidency." That's about all the dead Nixon is getting here in San Diego. George Bush: "my boss"—now that's important—not Ronald Reagan, "who brought us through the end of the cold war and the defeat of Communism"—there's a shot of a black guy in a white hat. "Ronald Reagan . . . who restored the fighting strength and spirit of America's armed forces."

The general is talking fast: ". . . a fellow citizen who has lived the American Dream to the fullest." Lots of shots of women, a glimpse of the Wilsons, a shot of another black guy standing. "Values that must be lived and not just preached"—taking a swipe at his most recent boss— "The family, fueled by values, must be restored to the central place in American life if we are to keep the dream alive. Yet families cannot thrive and pass on these beliefs if parents cannot bring home a decent, living wage from a hard day's work . . . The free-enterprise system is unleashed to create wealth. . . . Government assistance is a poor substitute for good jobs . . . we fight for welfare reform [more shots of black faces]. . . . we fight for health care reform . . . not just to save money, but because we believe there are better ways to take care of Americans in need than the exhausted programs of the past." And what are those? I wonder. "It is the entitlement state that must be reformed, and not just the welfare state. . . . Ineffective government, excessive government, wasteful government are the enemy." The general wants it both ways. This is an old song, an old sellout. "The descendant of a slave, or a miner in Appalachia, must be as welcome—and find as much appeal—in our party an any other American," he tells us, though Appalachian miners wouldn't be happy with the comparison.

He, too, tells us that this is "the party of Lincoln." Who is he kidding? Why is he a Republican? Because the party espouses the principles of "freedom, opportunity, and limited government." The federal government is "too intrusive in our lives." This is all very odd from a man who has worked his whole life for a very unlimited arm of government, where he found a lot of opportunity, maybe even a little freedom, one that was certainly intrusive in his life.

There's a shot of Christie Todd Whitman looking distressed. The camera resumes its tight focus on Powell. "You all know that I believe in a

woman's right to choose and I strongly support affirmative action"—
speeding up his already rapid speech he runs over a surge of sound—
and he says something about "work together for our common goal," and
there is a huge cheer, topping other noise. I couldn't hear what the goal
is. Elect Bob Dole, perhaps, since he now extols Dole at length. Liddy
looks glum. Back to Powell; he's tapping his watch again. ". . . with the
absence of acrimony that the American people long for in our political
debate." He finishes by yelling out "America!"

It's over. He's used to giving pep talks to the troops and he grew more
confident as it went on, though he was still surprised by the . . . unruli-
ness.

Discussion follows. I'm looking at J. C. Watts, another Republican
quarterback congressman. He's African American. "We are a party of
inclusion." Gary Bauer, from the Family Research Council: "Any party
wants the door open." But "a party has to stand for something." He's
upset with pro-choice Powell. Bauer has helped make the Christian Right
male a physical stereotype, since he has this bland, strangely unformed
face, as if it at one point he stopped developing, ripening. So he looks
like an old child.

Michael Deaver had mentioned earlier in the day that seventy channels were available to viewers and that they had to meet that competition.
I begin to wonder what's on them. Mark Shields says that the Republicans had been "dour and dyspeptic" and now they've been given "an
injection of optimism."

I turn to C-SPAN. And get to see a smiling Vin Weber fulminating
against the Democrats: "To reduce politics to an argument about class
is close to reducing it to an argument about race." That's a problem? I
wonder. By declaring one of the GOP's vulnerabilities off limits, bad
taste, etc., Vin hopes it will go away. "Kemp has been the leading spokesman for expanding economic opportunity. . . . A political argument that
centers on class . . . is an ugly form of politics." Right on, Vin!

On C-SPAN there's discussion of the boos during Powell's speech,
though I didn't hear them. They must have come after the a-woman's-
right-to-choose remark, that momentary roughening of response that
Powell hurried on past, followed by the larger cheer.

I haven't seen Buchanan much, but I do so see, as C-SPAN pans around, Buchanan being interviewed, but not on C-SPAN. I did see Buchanan being interviewed yesterday. It might have been his wife's birthday. "I bought her a little shredder," Buchanan said. It was a small rally delegates attended, along with Ollie North, those wanting Buchanan to fight on. He was joking, about Clinton: "You shouldn't criticize a man when he is still on active duty in the armed forces." Pat does his dark chuckle.

CNN does a reprise of all the speeches. Ford: Clinton is "not a Ford or a Lincoln, but a convertible Dodge." As I thought, the excerpts become commercials almost instantaneously, since they were all sound-bite material.

There's a shot of Gingrich, a convention cohost. Newt sports a new haircut; his hair is smoother, thinner. The networks have been off for some time. I try to find *Nightline,* but our local affiliate is showing *M*A*S*H.*

Life on Mars, Part 2

8/13   In the morning as I awake I hear on NPR's *Morning Edition* someone screaming, "You are libertines! Get out of the Republican Party!" This turns out to be directed at the head of Republicans for Choice when a group of them were at the podium congratulating themselves for "leaving a footprint" for the first time on the platform of the Republican Party. That must be the footprint in the appendix to the platform. I am bestirred by the notion of "libertines," though; it does capture the cultural clash, nineteenth versus twentieth century, or thereabouts.

Christie Todd Whitman is quoted today saying she'd like to get rid of the "platform" entirely and have, instead, a "statement of principles." That notion, obviously, was the source of her slip yesterday.

There's a piece on Ralph Reed. He has a "war room" at the convention and has been applying for tax-exempt status for the last seven years, but hasn't yet been allowed it by the IRS. So much for his earlier pride when he claimed the CC wasn't a tax-exempt organization.

My old colleague Richard Moran comes on, giving one of his radio essays on crime—his usual beat for NPR. It's refreshing hearing his downscale Massachusetts accent, though he teaches at the upscale Mount Holyoke College, one of my former employers. Richard ties the resentment with welfare to the increasing costs of police, criminals, prisons, etc. It's an equation, though one not often expressed: the poor get money from the government and the poor commit crimes, costing the government yet more money. The double-dipping of the poor is resented.

In the *New York Times*'s letters section, there's a missive from Alice Goldfarb Marquis defending the culture of San Diego, which she thinks has been defamed in a *Times* op-ed piece of only three days ago (she must have the *Times*'s fax number). She highlights the town's cultural attractions, highlighting the fact that San Diego's theaters let her see " 'Tommy,' 'Damn Yankees' and 'How to Succeed in Business Without Really Trying' months before they reached Broadway." She must be talking about revivals. Perhaps that is the culture of the Republicans: those Broadway hits hit the mark. I have an aunt and uncle who live in La Jolla, along with Ms. Marquis, and it is, without a doubt, all that money can buy, and great fun to live there, but the *Times* does not take note, so I will, that Ms. Marquis wrote an informative (she's good on the culture of the rich—living in La Jolla, I would think so), but confused (terminally middlebrow when it comes to the actual arts—see *How to Succeed in Business Without Really Trying*, above) book, *Art Lessons*, calling for the demise of the National Endowment for the Arts. So says the champion of *Damn Yankees* as cultural boon, but it does appear everyone out there is spending too much time in the sun.

This is another aspect of the culture wars, just what culture individuals and groups participate in and feel comfortable with. I don't want to seem too Gramsci-ish about this, but it is a matter of "style," of what one reads, sees, surrounds oneself with, finds admirable, excellent, what the homes look like, their cultural comfort zone, Martha Stewart versus Sears Roebuck, Wall-to-wall WASP versus Wal-Mart. Class in America. And what is class betrayal in the late twentieth century, watching television? Going to demolition derbies? The opera? Championing *Tommy* as worthy of the citizens of San Diego?

Powell's speech is discussed on Diane Rehm's show. She brings up the boos. "The first boos I heard at this convention." A delicate moment for

Powell, the boos from the antiabortion stalwarts, that he rode roughshod over. I don't so much wonder why Powell "became" a Republican, but when. Eisenhower was a Democrat till he ran for president as a Republican. The military does what it's told.

I'm driving back to Kenosha to pick up the repaired Taurus. On the way I catch some of Rush. He's saying he was watching TV and didn't hear any boos for Colin Powell. (On the tube they were pretty well muffled.) He was watching CNN. What I heard was a roughening of response, an overall louder volume, and Powell speeding up, racing on. Rush is chortling that the Democratic fax machines are sending out responses. He's wowed by the optimism at the convention, since it is his own. Now it's up to you, you being all of us out here in Radio Land. Only you (ourselves, that is) stand in the way. Of success, etc. Rush is doing his snake-oil salesman pitch: Go, go, do, do, Dale Carnegie of the airwaves. He exults over the prime-time speeches, reminding us of "how one hour can make a difference—remember about dropping Dole from the ticket?" He's happy, happy. Rebuking the claims that the convention is "scripted," Rush says, "It needs to get scripted to get past the press."

Rush is over and the signals are breaking up and I hear a bit of a local Indiana talk show. A guy calls in to praise Clinton, yes sirree. "I'm a member of the American Communist Party and I am going to vote for Bill Clinton." The *Sound Off* talk show host asks a question about "the American Communist Party," "Does that exist?" and the caller says, "Oh, yeah," and hangs up. He doesn't sound like much of a Marxist scholar. A self-starter out there doing his bit for Dole-Kemp.

It does appear, from the variety of radio talk shows I have listened to over the year, that there are plants, small-time confederates, who are instructed to call in with the approved spin, to pose as the person in the street, like the guys in a crowd who play the shell game on the card table and win in order to lure the actual citizens into losing their pocket money. There are lobbyist telemarketing outfits that can salt a radio audience for a price. And there are those, like the member of the "American Communist Party" above, who just catch onto the game and want to play it themselves, like-minded freelancers who enjoy the thrill of being "under cover."

Watching the second night of the Republican convention, I remember my first television memories of conventions, black and white, grainy, the narrow state signs and candidate placards being raised up and down frantically like pikes and poles in some medieval battlefield. The harbinger of Buchanan's pitchfork brigades.

Another young memory: The sermons I would hear at church on Sundays were pitched at twelve-year-olds. Which was fine when I was younger than twelve. It is the nature of public rhetoric, perhaps, though it has been refined through focus groups, where the inner twelve-year-old of adults is isolated and appealed to.

Political campaigns and conventions are not necessarily aimed at "the lowest common denominator," as is often charged, unless one examines that cliché to see it is not an all-encompassing generalization, meaning "the base"—and not the mathematical sort. The "denominator" of what? A denominator shows how many parts the whole can be divided into. And the campaign does do that.

With all the "draft-dodging" charges thrown at Clinton (Ford's "a convertible Dodge"), what doesn't get discussed is the "draft" part.

The draft, the selective service system, was the largest government program of social eugenics ever foisted on the American public, and it was run by some of the same social-science whiz kids who gave us the Vietnam War, "winning hearts and minds," etc. As they say, I was there. So was Bill Clinton and a good bit of our generation. General Hershey bestrode this great experiment in tracking the newly hatched baby boom. The system of deferments was put in place to siphon the smart into college, the less smart into the military, to make enlistment attractive to the working class, and when trouble started to brew in the sixties, the invisible hand got a lot more visible, culminating, at least for me, when in 1965 there were tests given and, if you scored sufficiently high, you could retain your college deferment and then stay in school. Deferments for graduate school, marriage, etc., were phased out in the late sixties and this all coincided with the height of the antiwar movement, when a lot of boys were at risk for the draft and made their feelings known. A lot of this became a headache for the military and for President Nixon.

The institution of the lottery changed everything. Gone was generational solidarity. Only a certain number were at risk for being drafted. Those what weren't put it out of their mind. They were the majority.

And it was Bill Clinton's fork in the road. His high number led him to abandon this ROTC commitment. The antiwar movement did not end the war in Vietnam. The Vietnamese ended it. They won. We lost. It seems hard for the establishment, especially the military establishment, to accept that.

But second to the social-science scourge of the selective service system is the one of social-science polling, what was left for displaced academics when there wasn't any continuous ongoing (for over a decade!) war and draft to run. Polling works the same way the draft did; it channels behavior (through policies), not just reflects it. And the political dependency is as fervent as it was in regard to the draft. And the people who run it have the same hauteur as their forebears.

The campaign and conventions are directed at the "undecided" and "nervous" voter, the anti–health care ad duo, Harry and Louise (the new Dagwood and Blondie), the dumb and the dumber. There are roughly three constituencies (as I used to say long ago, in the McGovern era, 33 percent would vote for George, 33 percent for Nixon, 33 percent for Hitler—and 66 percent voted for Nixon); two of them are already certain of their decision, one is in play. What has happened is that as the two parties lose their "base"—watch, for instance, the Reagan Democrats vote for Reagan, or the Clinton Republicans (this year) vote for Clinton—they become less of what the "base" was, because they are chasing the fickle, the mercurial, those who seem to vote for reasons left to the pollsters, the "social" scientists, to decide.

First, my generation gets the draft, the selective service system, then we get the pollsters, the selectively serviced society system, the age of polling. No wonder we feel manipulated. General Hershey leads to Dick Morris, the other poll mavens.

The second night of the Republican convention makes the actual physical setting much clearer. They've turned the trade-show arena into a television studio. That light blue emanation from the tube might be *the* color of the advanced television era. I wonder if some of this could have been just chance. San Diego was "selected", for whatever payoff reasons, and the blue sky there just leaked into the interior of the building. Or the building was smallish, so shrinking the scale of the podium, etc., followed.

Campaign America '96: The View From the Couch

This is no Cow Palace, no Cathedral of the People, as I recall other convention sites, both Democratic and Republican, to have been. A Grand Canyon of space above the speakers' heads and often seemingly the same amount of space below. The speakers' platform, situated high up, like Lincoln at his memorial, eyes raised, heads raised in tribute, the people below, cheering. Il Duce! Il Duce!

But not in San Diego. The platform isn't much higher than a typical Broadway stage, a smallish podium, light blue everywhere, lots of light everywhere. The video wall behind. That is what the raised heads see. A television studio, though one larger than usual.

And the video wall shows videos to . . . us. Meaning, my set becomes one entire video wall, not just part of the grid, the crossword puzzle of images linked into one. The videos are for me, not the delegates, who are only the secondary audience. The delegates get still pictures, which act as applause cues.

The videos are actual commercials and a lot of money has been spent on them. They seem to function like the Super Bowl commercials, one shot (or first exposure) of something really special. Newt has one. His theme is Freedom. He's presented as a friend of the earth. He appears and brings on a recent gold medal winner, a member of the beach volleyball team. It's surreal, but at the same time it's not, and that is what presentation does. It's like the "makeover" shots magazines used to do (or still do); I remember a number of years ago *Esquire* found a few derelicts (as they were called then) down on the Bowery and cleaned them up and put them in spiffy clothes and made them appear as models. The surreal made real. So here we have Newt Gingrich, friend of the earth, the lover of real newts, having spent a night at the nearby zoo, bringing on Mr. Beach Volleyball, affirmative action at the Olympics gone wild. (Where is Buchanan? Can't there be a stop to this lowering of standards in sport? Where is Bill Bennett?) Newt is saying, "Ken is a good example of what freedom is all about." Let Us Now Praise Famous Beach Volleyballers. Newt has already called Martin Luther King "the greatest Georgian of the twentieth century" and now he quotes his "I Have a Dream" speech. Shameless, shameless, worse than the shameless hussies of the legal profession during the O. J. trial. The edge of Newt's suit coat is askew, so at least it was impossible to smooth him out entirely; some quirk popped up.

Then he introduces a woman who founded Canine Assistants, and her dog, her canine assistant, Nicholas. "Helping others help themselves" is the subtheme. "True compassion is measured by our own good works, not by how many tax dollars we spend to support a failed federal bureaucracy." There's no mention of the Contract with America.

Four of the nonveeps have been paraded past the podium, Governors Ridge, Engler, Thompson, and Rowland (the latter of Connecticut). They all look strangely alike, slightly (or more) overweight, no neck, fat faces, ethnic, but not WASP. You can be short and ethnic looking and be governor of a state, but it gets much harder to do that nationally, given the demands of television. It is easy to see how Clinton stood out in the crop of governors. Tall, but not patrician, one of the people, but above the people.

Christine Todd Whitman is talking to Maria "M" Shriver. Maria brings up the tax-cutting success Christine had in New Jersey. (Paid for by reducing contributions to the state workers pension funds.) This is a subject not without controversy, but Maria does not bring this up. Christine goes on in some double-talk, "we're well on our way" to more jobs (tax-cut promise) in New Jersey. A variety of numbers are offered, 400,000, or 150,000, or 100,000, or it should be 400,000 by the time her term is over. It is appalling to listen to this millionaire talk gobbledy gook about tax cuts. One of Whitman's biographers, Patricia Beard, an old friend of Christie's, writes in the prologue to *Growing Up Republican,* we "grew up in similar circumstances (comfortable)." That "(comfortable)" would gag most horses, thoroughbreds, even, but not Maria Shriver.

Predictably the pundits are attacking the plan, Christine tells Maria, feeling comfortable she is not insulting nonpundit Maria. There does seem to be orchestrated media bashing going on. The governor of New Jersey claims that the public will find "more money in their paychecks, for mortgages, braces,"—must have been a problem for Christine—"education."

They'll need it, I'm sure.

The video wall at the rear of the convention stage has been showing a variety of images, still photographs, during the speeches from the podium, but during Powell's speech I couldn't see any. He remained in a tight shot throughout on the channel I was watching, but flipping around I now see that some other cameras caught different angles. There were photos of Reagan saluting while Powell referred to him, a shot of Reagan saluting Powell.

But I do get to see the video wall during Kay Bailey Hutchison's remarks. She seems to be doing a Texas Gal Ann Richards impersonation, a payback for Ann's 1992 dumping on fellow "Texan" Bush. Hutchison's having fun attacking fellow good ol' boy Bill Clinton. She mentions "candidate" Clinton's pledge to restore ethics in government, adding, "President Clinton put a former bar bouncer in charge of confidential FBI files."

Hutchison is wearing Republican red, which Nancy Reagan must be given credit for, establishing better-dressed-in-red-than-Red red as the female GOP color. The video wall shows a montage of different years Bill Clinton mentions for a balanced budget: seven, nine, eight, ten. It's amusing, the same sort of thing Rush has been doing on his television show for quite some time. Oddly, it seems to be the only non-Reagan-era technique employed.

After that, Hutchison hits her stride, making use of the rousing rhetoric of the list, a long, hyphenated list; "It's time to wake up to President Clinton and his high-taxing, free-spending, promise-breaking, Social Security–taxing, health-care-socializing, drug-coddling, power-grabbing, business-busting, lawsuit-loving, UN-following, FBI-abusing, IRS-increasing, two-hundred-dollar-hair-cutting, gas-taxing, over-regulating, bureaucracy-trusting, class-baiting, privacy-violating, values-crushing, truth-dodging, Medicare-forsaking, property-rights-taking, job-destroying friends. And that's just in the White House!"

It's a mega–bumper sticker, fit for the back of the largest Republican retiree's palatial RV: "Honk If You Think Bill Clinton Is . . ." During the long peroration the crowd was yelling "Dole-Kemp," but at first I thought they were yelling, surreally, Bullshit, Bullshit. It's the syllables and accents.

There are shots of Jack Kemp and Liddy coming into the arena. Jack grabs the hand of a big blond woman dressed in an American-flag shirt.

He needs more of that. A little hetero scandal wouldn't hurt Kemp, the most touchy-feely Republican out there.

It is amazing how much football there is in the Republican party: J. C. Watts, Steve Largent, Kemp, the Gipper. Watts begins his American Dream story with, "Let me start by saying, I'm thrilled Bob Dole has chosen the second best quarterback in the Republican Party, Jack Kemp, as his running mate."

Last night was the highway of the presidents during prime time, Ford, Bush, leading to the I'm-taking-the-off-ramp of General Powell. But to-night we get some of the female scenic route.

The destination is Susan Molinari, the "keynoter." I was still amazed by the announcement, scripted as if it was news to her, but even I know how television works, since when I was ten I was a contestant (by phone) on a local TV show, a quiz-kid after-school show. You sent in a postcard with your name on it and the show "chose" one at random to call and ask a question. Right answer won a prize. We were called and told that we would be phoned during the show, so make sure we were ready. And we were. I won a model aircraft carrier, assembly required. So I presume Ms. Molinari knew the call was coming. She phoned Larry King—his show has replaced the smoky back rooms where the political deals were made—and I haven't heard such gushing giddiness on TV since Tiny Tim married Miss Vicky on the *Tonight Show*.

The Molinaris' new baby is being shown quite a bit tonight, Dad holding it as some foreign object, looking to pass it off to whomever, whatever. Grandfather ends up with the kid. Susan Molinari is the young American mom in the GOP parade of femaleness, another uplifting story of the American Dream, bootstrapping uber alles.

Molinari qualifies, not as another example of America's true bootstrap-ping, nepotism, and inheritance, but because she is as "working-class" as the Republicans can come up with, the most familiar type to their focus-group female family out there in flyover land. She's Italian with a bad borough accent, which, in Republicans' demographics, translates into working-class, despite however close to half a million dollars the Moli-naris bring in each year. Short, ethnic, with a regional voice qualifies as one of the people.

If a viewer just happened upon network prime time, he or she wouldn't know what s/he was looking at: Democrats, Republicans? Who knew? And who are Kay Bailey Hutchison and Susan Molinari?

If the viewer is watching C-SPAN s/he will get everything, but the networks and PBS are a bit more selective. Of course, this convention is advertising and the effect is achieved through small bits of repetition, but how many of the elusively fickle and profoundly uncommitted are tuning in at all?

Regardless, we all now get Susan Molinari, after J. C. Watts, doing the Clarence Thomas story, but with a good arm, after Kasich—does any "undecided" voter know who he is?—winds up, after saying the GOP is "sending a clear message to God that he is being invited back into American life," by quoting the Beatles! All of this is meant to reinforce the do-it-yourself generation's slogan (Bob Vila probably has had more to do with creating young Republicans than any political figure, even the newly neutered Newt): "People help themselves, not government." Kasich is wearing a rocket-ship-and-star tie.

Molinari's kid is now in the hands of a large black man. She's wearing what looks like a Century 21 gold jacket, without the logo. Dad has the kid back. There's a wisp of something—a slip?—above the gold jacket's top button. She has a frantic, isometric smile on her face.

She's shaky at the start. "We can help you spend more hours at home with your family." How is that? Somehow the tax cut is going to do that. I'm not sure Ms. Molinari's family hours, or her husband's, will grow very much over the next four years, but she does want to send people home. Fewer jobs, perhaps. "We simply can't go on like we have for the last four years." That notion has come up quite a bit. The Republicans are stuck with a problem. All the world's woes cannot be blamed on Bill Clinton or his administration. There were twelve years of Republicans in the White House previously. There's always the Democratic Congress, but it has been eliminated and what the convention seems to be avoiding is the Republican Congress that has replaced it. Molinari is in Congress, but she's not talking about that, she's talking about how her family lived the American Dream, whereas the Congress competes to be the American Nightmare. The speedup for the culture has a paradoxical effect (one of many, doubtless): four years does not seem such a long time, especially if we are not at war, or are not in a deep depression.

But everyone's sticking to the earlier announced script: restoring the American Dream. In Molinari's case, it is generational, since she is an example of not squandering the American Dream, since her father's seat in Congress was passed down to her.

"We must choose the better man for a better America and that man, we know, is Bob Dole." That "better man" is the character issue in their nutshell and that's getting as much play as the black faces in the audience. "Better man" is code for Gennifer Flowers, better man is thanks for getting me out of the draft, etc.

Earlier Molinari said, "Americans know that Bill Clinton's promises have the life span of a Big Mac on *Air Force One,*" adding, "While that may be funny, what's not funny is what he is doing to the promise of America." She is also telling us she didn't write the line. "While that may be funny" is absent of proprietary feeling.

The Republican image makers are the true dreamers, the true American dreamers, because this convention is obviously a dream of a Republican America, one that only exists in their dreams. And what is always troubling is that the image makers know the difference between what is and what they would pretend it to be. No mask is successful unless you know the true face it hides.

There's a shot on C-SPAN of the wonderful congresswoman from Utah, Enid Greene Waldholtz, yet another model of new Republican motherhood, other than Ms. Molinari. Molinari's husband (Enid's was sent to the land of the courts), now back with the kid on the platform, is the representative from Buffalo, whereas Molinari is representing Staten Island. Last I looked their districts were at different ends of the state. No wonder Susan hopes for more time at home, wherever home is.

The "it's not how many you have on welfare, it's how many you have in the workforce" line is getting more of a workout here than the joke about Clinton starting to date again since he has such a big lead. One small step for welfare, one large leap for Bill Clinton.

8/14 The *New York Times* reports today that Robin Dole is a former lobbyist for Century 21. That might explain Susan Molinari's keynoter outfit.

On Diane Rehm there's discussion of the "bump" in the polls, up 12 percent, down 9 percent. Bounce city. The "news" of the convention, other than Ted Koppel's walkout (no news! Ted says!), taking his ball back to Manhattan, is waiting for the polls, to see if the Republican "message" is getting through. But from my perspective, the bump in the polls is secondary to the bump the Republicans get from the media. The media get bumped from one rut (Dole is dead man walking) to another, smoother rut (Dole-Kemp has energized and tightened the race). The latter is more immediate and lasting than the former. The conversation in the media has already been largely redirected and it's beneficial to Dole-Kemp.

President Bush never managed to sell his "kinder, gentler" approach, but this convention does manage to project that. The kinder, gentler convention.

A woman calls in to Diane Rehm, saying she works, her son works in a McDonald's, and that she heard on C-SPAN that Susan Molinari makes three hundred thousand dollars. "If she doesn't have the American Dream, who does?" she asks. The caller's tearful. The reporters seem subdued by her emotion. "Even if I didn't pay any taxes I will be hurting." Silence, unusual from the radio. The commentators recover and we finally get tepid answers. About the caller, pollster Ed Goaz remarks, "If women define their work as a career, they're Republican. If it's a job, they are Democrats."

Rush says in the afternoon that the media "are flummoxed." His woman problem pops up again when he gets on a jag about breast-feeding, and all the shots of Susan Molinari's baby. He says if her husband, Bill Paxson, "could have breast-fed that baby, we would have picked up some electoral votes in California."

Rush is upset some network gave Stephanopoulos press credentials to troll the floor and cause trouble. The press wanted some action, someone to "beat up the little guy." He then can't resist his happy self-promotion—"I thought I was watching my own television show"—regarding the TV clips of Clinton on balanced-budget deadlines. Yes, indeed.

On a newsbreak during Rush's show, we're told that corn futures are going up. Yesterday, there was an NPR report on how corn has suffered, too much rain, not enough hot sun, etc. Yesterday I was driving by acres of cornfields, all high as an elephant's eye. Orville Redenbacher isn't going to buy this corn this far north. Doesn't seem to pop right, not fluffy enough. I'm looking at ethanol and feed or meal. It's August in the Midwest.

Rush is going on about how the three networks didn't show the J. C. Watts speech. I flipped the dial, he says, "and they flipped you off."

Rush's cultural moment has peaked. There is definitely a failing-mall atmosphere about it. The same low-end ads, something just not catching on, not fresh. *Saturday Night Live* a long time ago had a recurring skit on a fading mall, some down-at-the-heels Scotch tape store. It had the bad-dream atmosphere down just right.

A caller says the angry white men at the Republican convention are Ted Koppel, Tom Brokaw, Dan Rather, and Peter Jennings. We can be Democrats, too, the caller contends. We can show compassion. He compliments Rush.

The rumor that Dole will name his cabinet by Monday is aired. Is a cabinet position a career or a job? I wonder.

A career woman steals the show this evening. Liddy Dole, America's first nurse, leaves the podium equipped with a traveling microphone clipped to her yellow outfit and comes down among the folk. Not hard to do, since the platform and podium aren't very removed from them. It's not Moses coming down with the tablets, as it would have been in the old days. It's a chicken-and-egg question: Did they arrange this layout so this could happen, or is this happening because of the layout?

She's telling us about the man she loves, Bob Dole. I hear again echoes of Paul Manafort, the convention's manager, who, for all I know, might love Bob Dole, too, but this is to make Bob Dole known to the great public, and to all the Republicans who don't know him already.

It's difficult to arrange spontaneous encounters with people in wheelchairs, so someone must have mapped this out earlier. It's a *This is Your Life,* Bob Dole, done by the first nurse, Liddy Dole. She's taking care of her man, telling us of his lifelong travails, introducing us to his former caretakers, and the handicapped people the Doles have looked after themselves.

Her "invisible" mike has gone dead and she is handed the karaoke sort, the large ice-cream-cone version, and continues unflustered. That the Republican convention has now turned into afternoon television isn't strange, given that the "set" is made for it. Late in her stroll among the people Liddy's voice becomes strained. A thin, but intact, membrane of terror seems to vibrate at the back of her throat. Its timbre resonates every now and then. Reviewing the life has awakened some sort of dread.

From Liddy we go to the video wall and we're taken live to Russell, Kansas. The visuals are great. Two youngsters put Bob Dole's name in nomination. There are wonderful fireworks over what I take to be city hall (low camera angle, very dramatic), pom-pom girls in red. From one show to another, both without a hitch.

The schedule given out by the Republicans' Web site gave only one hint of what was actually in store. It gave Robin Dole a half hour of remarks, an unlikely prospect if one would have given any thought to it, since—I'll pick just one—Dan Quayle only got five minutes.

All the commentators seem wowed by Liddy. Boy, the conversation has changed. Paul Gigot says, "Bill Clinton steals their ideas, they take his style." The fact that one of the debates in '92 let Clinton roam with a mike is brought up. Doris Kearns Goodwin says people will "remember the body language, not the words," mentioning that Liddy has given this sort of speech a number of times in smaller venues. No one mentions that this is a smaller venue. But the point of living in an age of images is that you remember the images more than the words. I did like the fireworks over the stately building in Russell, Kansas, though the town did resemble the one on view in the happy part of *It's a Wonderful Life*. The image of Dole's hometown still living in the 1940s, on reflection, might not necessarily be the best image to project as we hurtle toward the twenty-first century. Dole ages, his hometown does not.

The roll call is starting and PBS goes to it, though the buzz is still Liddy's tiptoeing through the tulips. I do hear the boos the Alaska spokes-man gets for his long speech extolling our northern outpost. He finally casts sixteen votes for Bob Dole. The two secretaries record thirteen.

We then get an ambiguous moment of sadomasochism with Arkansas, "home of the newest Republican governor." Mrs. Janet Huckabee, the new governor's wife, tells us Arkansas is "the home of southern hospi-tality," a dubious claim all around, though interesting too for her stress on "southern," and that Arkansas is "the land of opportunity," which, given the career of Bill Clinton, no one would dare gainsay. She casts the seventeen votes the state has for the better man, Bob Dole. That *better man* refrain seems a bit hollow coming from Arkansas.

The District of Columbia gives us the sight of a nervous black guy saying D.C. is "where we know Bill Clinton has surrendered the war on drugs."

The first fellow with the microphone from Georgia keeps yelling out, "Mr. Chairman, Mr. Chairman," and is replaced by a second who says, "Madam Chairman."

We get to Illinois and there is a lot of cheering and Governor Edgar says a bit testily to the people surrounding him, "All right, all right, we only have a minute."

My Indiana has a corpulent fellow claim that Indiana will be "first in the column for Bob Dole for president of the United States," even though in '92 the first sign that evening that Clinton had it won was the fact that Dan Rather and CBS wouldn't immediately call Indiana for Bush-Quayle.

Louisiana is unruly. Ten votes for Pat Buchanan. Boos gust around them. Two votes for Phil Gramm, "our neighbor." One vote for Robert Bork, "in tribute," so that [the Congress's treatment of Bork?] "will never happen again." And, finally, "seventeen votes for an American hero and the next president of the United States, Bob Dole."

These moments are clearly the only potential chaos in this convention: that the local yokels will go wild and say something unapproved.

Michigan casts five votes for Pat Buchanan, said hurriedly, and, with emphasis, "fifty-two votes for Bob Dole."

Looking at the variety of state officials crowded around the microphones for their minute in the limelight reveals, given regional differences, the ubiquitous profession of well-dressed people standing up and saying the preposterous, the unbelievable, with conviction and a straight face. This profession has now grown into a mass phenomenon, where an entire party says preposterous things with a straight face. We are the party of Lincoln, we are the party of diversity, etc.

Mississippi says it "is best known for two things," and I try to guess what that is—strange fruit hanging from a poplar tree? the poverty rate?—and it turns out to be "hospitality and the ability to produce great political leaders," in this case, Haley Barbour, Trent Lott, the leaders of the southernized Republican Party.

Missouri (yeah!) votes twenty-four for "our neighbor, Bob Dole," eleven votes for Pat Buchanan, and one for Alan Keyes, the stealth candidate at this convention. He turned up briefly in the video shown earlier, along with Ralph Reed, edited and sweetened, but I haven't seen him in the flesh, so to speak, even during the first night, when cameras searched out every African American face, including a *Time* reporter's.

The first thing heard from Nebraska is "back-to-back national champions in football." The American Dream on parade, to be sure.

Nevada is touted as "the entertainment capital of the world."

New Hampshire tells us that "Pat Buchanan has graciously released his votes to Bob Dole—where taxes are low and will be lower."

The governor of Ohio shows that Mr. Freud is in attendance when he says how his state reveals a "great, great *specter* of diversity, race, gender." I suppose he was after "spectrum."

Puerto Rico: Viva Dole!

Rhode Island: "The smallest state that gave Bob Dole his largest margin of victory."

South Carolina: "The home of the legendary Strom Thurmond." Legendary, indeed. Interviewed by the rapper from Public Enemy for MTV, Thurmond claimed he's changing his legend.

The recurring device most used during the roll call is stating the amount of money the 15 percent tax cut will save the citizens of each state. There's something startling about a party actually trying to buy an election so baldly. Here's the bribe, come and get it. Sixteen hundred dollars eighteen hundred. Rhode Island claimed, "seventy-two million from the five-hundred-dollar tax deduction for children."

South Dakota mentions "a party divided against itself cannot stand," which is the first acknowledgment of strife and dissent I've heard. "Crazy Horse, a man who was willing to stand up and fight for his nation and his people," is praised. Everything's being stood on its head.

Tennessee praises its football team and women's basketball team.

Texas has Boone Pickens as spokesperson. The Reagan revolution continues. It's odd that the primaries turn out to be reality, and the convention is the fantasy.

Utah: "The average family will save two thousand dollars."

The lady from Vermont wears a spangly American-flag shirt, very popular in San Diego this week.

Virginia praises its governor: "He abolished parole, abolished outcome-based education." That must be bad, frightening words to the home-schooling crowd. But then Arthur Ashe and Colin Powell are extolled. Once again, the right hand must know what the left hand is doing.

"The sun will rise first on the Virgin Islands when Dole-Kemp are inaugurated" and for some reason (doubtless, the *Saturday Night Live* skit: baseball has been berry berry good to me) this reminds me of the photo in today's *New York Times* of a baseball player about to hit another with his clenched fist. He's coming right at the camera. The pugilist not at rest. Something too American about the scene, a ballplayer being violent.

Of the two women conducting the roll call, one is black; the other is a white woman who seems a quite familiar face from Republican conventions past, but the black woman appears to be a fresh face.

West Virginia, the average family, seventeen hundred dollars saved.

Wisconsin, where it all began—"a few individuals started the Republican Party in Rippon, Wisconsin"—that's the Rippon Society, I take it. Wisconsin, which produces "one-fourth of the cheese, one-third of the butter," and, they omit, half the heart attacks, in America.

Dole is referred to as "a plainspoken man," a phrase often to be employed, trying to make a virtue out of a vice, the Gary Cooper of the plains.

After Kansas puts him over, there's a shot of Dole giving out hugs in a hotel suite, first one, it appears, to his daughter. There's a shot of James Baker looking pleased. PBS continues its commentaries of O. J.–style experts. Michael Beschloss muses that this—meaning the images, technology, videos—will replace political rhetoric. There's a shot of James Baker now with his hands in his pockets. Lugar is clapping. Doris Kearns Goodwin comments on the state spokespersons: "Their sports teams have replaced politics." Mark Shields remarks, "Dole has spent more time in Russell, Kansas, the last two weeks than in the last ten years." Dole is being Lincolnized, insofar as the image makers are fashioning him a log cabin. An electronic log cabin.

Sander Vanocur reminds us that there has been no second ballot at a convention since 1952. This is in response to Lehrer's statement that the primaries changed the conventions.

Speaker Gingrich moves that the ballot be declared unanimous. Asks for nays, there are a few, and then he declares the motion passed.

"Going to Kansas City, Kansas City here I come" is playing over the loudspeakers. Of course the state is wrong. The state the song refers to is Missouri, but, like so much, accuracy is incidental to allusion.

It is commented on that none of the delegates seemed to care when Jeane Kirkpatrick and James Baker gave their foreign policy speeches.

The governor of New York, George Pataki, nominates Jack Kemp: "Mr. Clinton, next year Dole and Kemp will cut your taxes 15 percent percent." Pataki is stiff, but his body is moving nonetheless. A bad dancer's nongrace. Lynne Cheney seconds the nomination. She is a tireless proponent of altering history and she hints at that, saying, "Every election is important, but some change the course of history in fundamental ways." Like many members of former Republican administrations, Cheney bites the entity that has fed her, in her case, the National Endowment for the Humanities. After their time is over, these folk want to eliminate the agency they once headed.

The treasurer of Ohio, a black man named Blackwell, loses his way in his speech. His stumbling stands out since it is so unusual.

William Bennett comes on. After yet another football analogy, he says about Kemp: "He prays, he learns from suffering, and he walks with God." William Bennett is the '96 version of the Pat Buchanan of '92. And the incremental differences between Buchanan and Bennett are all that the GOP requires for this convention. He handles the secularized Wrath of God position. Bennett carries on the culture war from within (once an academic . . .); Buchanan, when it came to culture, was always outside the walls, in the popular culture, with the pitchfork crowd. But Bennett has made his way in: *The Book of Virtues,* indeed! "There is nothing like the moral power of example." Right on!

C-SPAN replayed Buchanan's '92 convention speech earlier today and it was remarkable to view the immediate contrast. It wasn't so much Buchanan's speech, which, for the most part, was a big endorsement of Bush, but the few paragraphs on the culture war near the end were seized upon. What was startling was the crowd and the place. Houston was the old model, an arena large enough for dirigibles, a cow palace, a Cathedral of the People. Buchanan high up on a very raised platform. And the crowd! So many angry white males, since, in '92, they were near their peak, the peak to be surmounted by Timothy McVeigh and the White House kamikaze pilot, the afternoon White House automatic-gunfire enthusiast, and Charles Murray and Rush Limbaugh, and on and on.

So this convention was not so much about muzzling Buchanan, as about changing everything else. The space, the people. That has the larger effect. No more Cathedral of the People, no more Albert Speer settings—not in the age of Martha Stewart. No more angry young men in white shirts looking like the punch-throwing ballplayer in today's *New York Times*. Moms and dads and kids and diversity, affirmative-action faces everywhere, small, intimate, everything bathed in light blue, the color of television heaven.

Lehrer says Paul Gigot predicted eight or nine months ago that Jack Kemp would be the veep. He certainly would be one of the few. Even the week before the convention, no one I heard on the Sunday shows chose Kemp.

C-SPAN shows some milling crowds and cleanup crews coming in to deal with the human harbor trash washing up on the screen. Ohio pineapple hats (for Dole), other after-event flotsam, bagged and dumped, cleaning the halls for mañana, the night of two speeches, Bob Dole's big moment.

For this moment, C-SPAN shows us Dole and Kemp are attending a fund-raiser on the waterfront, out in the fresh air. Money on the hoof, but except for the organizers on the stage, the money givers are in the shadows at tables, their privacy intact. Dole says once more, "We are the reform party, the party of change. . . . We can downsize the federal bureaucracy, the IRS, we can get it done, make America better. . . . That's what will happen in the next eighty-two days."

Dole welcomes "our Olympic athletes who are with us tonight," and a large wrestler (silver medalist) gives Dole an enthusiastic endorsement. Dole asks for further comments—"not on me," he says—and another wrestler says, talking about the Olympics, winning, competing, "It was an awesome feeling . . . impossible to describe . . . overwhelming." Awesome.

Ken Langone is the dinner chairman. He thanks a litany of funding-raising groups: Team 100, Republican Eagles, the Presidents Club, a lot of those alarming sort of inner-circle clubs. Though a number of years ago I got an invitation from Paul Laxalt to join the Republican Inner Circle, for a paltry thousand dollars. I deduced from the address that my name had been harvested from *Who's Who in America*.

Dole leaves "early," a privilege of being the nominee, he says. He shakes a lot of black musicians' hands as he exits, and then the San Diego night is filled with their lively music.

8/15 Diane Rehm's show has speechwriters talking about the speeches. "Narrative has high recall," I'm told. It's the consensus that the speeches themselves have been forgotten, but that Mrs. Dole's performance has not been.

Yes, the speeches seem to have their life only in memory, and that is the place their authors want, a foothold in memory, and their existence in the present is only accidental.

Rush is going on about Liddy's walk among the people. We've got to show we are compassionate, he says with some irony. He points out that not a word has been said about Whitewater at the Republican convention. (What may be correct is that the word "Whitewater" has not been mentioned—though I haven't seen every minute.) Every criticism of Hillary whispers its name. Do you think, Rush, ah, pontificates, the Democrats would go this long without mentioning Watergate? Then he says, not able to resist the obvious, "This convention reminds me a lot of this show." Right on, Rush. He says the press has raised the expectations for Dole's speech. The press is waiting for something to criticize in this convention. Rush is leery. He's also upset that the *Washington Post* has misquoted him today, about his Molinari remarks yesterday. The *Post,* according to Rush, wrote that if Susan Molinari breast-fed the baby, they'd get more California votes, etc. Yes, the columnist got it wrong, Rush, I'll testify. Rush wants to apologize to Molinari for the *Post*'s mistake.

The conventions are in many ways superfluous, given the revamped primary system (there has been no second ballot since '52, but having a nominee since March is a bit much), but the TV fantasy convention for the Republicans serves an important purpose: to give conservatism a human face. After the "bruising" primaries, cleaning up the mess is necessary. And the press is talking about the new conservatism with a human face, the first nurse, blacks and women everywhere, even the wheelchair bound. So what that the delegates were 97 percent white? Sour grapes.

The Republicans had nowhere to go but up. Getting rid of Dole had been discussed semiseriously before the convention began. So this convention is succeeding and tonight the only fear is that Dole will drop dead giving his speech, or stumble in some terrible way.

The Democrats, obviously, have the opposite problem. Before the convention bounce started, Clinton was at his highest in the polls. One reason he signed the welfare bill was to limit whatever the Republican bounce would be from the convention—a pollster-inspired couterbounce. Since there were no Democratic primary fights (other than those in the congressional hearing rooms), its upcoming convention is truly in danger of being a superfluous exercise. In fact, it stands a good chance of being harmful because it isn't there to wipe clean a muddy primary picture and, only obliquely, I presume, will it try to correct Whitewater, Paula Jones, Filegate, and the rest. The New Mourning Campaign deals with scandals past by keeping those coffins closed.

On PBS's *NewsHour* Mrs. Kemp is telling America that "for a time we collected Don Quixote statues." She is asked, almost rhetorically, "Are you a born-again Christian?" She responds, after deciding not to give a simple yes (or no), "That's like stuttering. I'm a Christian." It's clear she doesn't want to answer. There must be a track record on this, but who would find that strange? We learn that her father was a high school football coach. Don Quixote statues and the culture of football.

The other display of culture we get to see is "The Vocal Majority," the singing senators. Trent Lott and some other stooges singing "Elvira."

This isn't so much the rare example of kitsch, as something more pervasive and less odd and eccentric.

Jeff Kemp, late of the football field, gets to introduce the veep nominee. He tells us, "He's my dad." Jack, that is, and "All the kids are excited at the prospect of him holding down a steady job."

Laughter rolls up the edge of the platform, though not for the irony of a millionaire lacking employment. Or maybe so.

Kemp hugs his son appreciatively. He is a buoyant figure, the right Bill Clinton-ish silver hair. (Or as Rush has it, Kennedy hair.) Kemp begins, after taming the applause, "Mr. Lincoln believed, you serve your party best by serving your country first." It's a twofer, dragging in Lincoln, the Great Emancipator, and slamming Clinton, the great draft evader.

Reagan is paid the usual obeisances for his triumph in ending the cold war: "And when Communism came down, it wasn't because it fell. It was because he pushed it."

Yes, isn't it nice to think so. Whatever history's current verdict is, it doesn't disturb the San Diego version. I always thought Communism would "fall"—a generation that didn't fight World War II just needed to come of age. Communism falling and Clinton being elected are more connected than Reagan and the collapse of the Soviet Union, but it happened and for a lot of people in government (CIA, etc.), that fact absolved a lot of sins.

Martin Luther King is again raised from the dead. I'm sure he has been quoted more in the Republican convention of '96 than in the Democratic convention of '92. "Dr. King believed that we must see a sleeping hero in every soul."

Kemp does his own version of the American Dream. He chokes up over the story of his dad and his truck, mentions that he "saved"—must have been those Teamster wages—and "started his own trucking company." There probably is an interesting story there, but Kemp is not telling it.

Instead we learn that the Democratic Party is "not democratic." It is full of "elitists." It's interesting, the permutation of the conservative side of anti-intellectualism in the Republican Party. The singing-senator side, the Phyllis Schlafly side, the Ralph Reed side—once anti-intellectualism was only personified by the charge hurled at Adlai Stevenson, that he was an "egghead." Now it's "elitists." "They think they know better than the people." Warring populism here from Mr. Kemp, the former footballer, present millionaire, who wants to cut taxes. There's never enough for these guys. He and Dole will "scrap the current, fatally flawed Internal Revenue Code and replace it with a fairer, simpler, flatter system. We will end the IRS as we know it."

Steve Forbes may have lost most of his primary battles but he has won the war, and, if the Dole-Kemp ticket wins, the return on his thirty-something-million investment will pay off handsomely (even though it has already done wonders for him).

And, thank you TV Land, after—at last—a shot of Alan Keyes, sitting with a woman I presume is his wife, there is a shot of Steve Forbes, looking both immeasurably smug and immeasurably fierce.

Kemp is now, to my surprise, quoting Ted Hesburgh, "the former president of the University of Notre Dame" and, he doesn't add, current member of the Bill Clinton Pay the Lawyers fund. (Hesburgh, when asked why he agreed to sign on, was said to have replied, "If a president asks you to do something . . .") Kemp quotes him on immigration: "We must close the back door of illegal immigration, so we can keep open the front door of legal immigration—and keep the light of opportunity lifted beside the golden door." Mentioning Notre Dame does bring in the whiff of football and the Gipper once again.

It's clear Kemp is not to be a hatchet-man veep, as Dole was characterized when he ran with Ford against Carter, but a nice-cop veep, smoothing the prickly edges for blacks and immigrants, making GOP policies for both constituencies seem not so draconian, but merely common sense. Kemp's role is Mr. Tough Love.

Kemp finishes by calling Dole "the first lion of the twenty-first century." Ronald Reagan was "the last lion of the twentieth."

Over the applause Kemp's conclusion gets, as Kemp's family appears on stage, Lehrer's voice remarks, "Everybody's initials in that family are J. K."

There is a shot of Buchanan and Lugar, some lineup seating arrangement of the also-rans.

The Dole film begins. Dole is narrating. There's a picture of Dole as a teenager, bare chested, using his arms, holding someone on his shoulder. It is shocking. I realize I hadn't seen pictures of him active, athletic, before the war. The background, humble, etc. Dole gives his own American Dream line: At twenty-seven, healing up, "Who in their right mind would think that 46 years later I'd be talking about running for president?"

There are shots of Russell, Kansas, from Dole's youth and there is a black-and-white one of blacks and whites in a swimming pool and, of course, that would not have been taken in Dole's youth (or middle age), in Russell, Kansas, but as it is shuffled in with other older photos we are supposed to think all was well back there in John Brown territory after the war.

The video has Dole speaking in a house, windows behind, an open shirt collar. He does seem rested and at ease. It is more *It's a Wonderful Life* than *The Best Years of Our Lives*. (And for Dole's generation the "Best Years" were, terribly, World War II. For Bill Clinton's, alas, they were high school. Clinton is the boomers ultimate student council president.)

But those films are ignored. The theme music from *Rocky* is played. Dole walks up out of the audience ("Come on down!"), reminding the viewing audience of his wife's meandering. It is—to stay in the movie-world context this event keeps us in—like the trip an Oscar winner makes after the announcement. Dole's shaking hands, looking grateful.

There's a white piece of paper—a strip of tape?—on the shoulder of his dark suit jacket. As he walks up the few steps to the podium an aide snatches it off. There's applause still and he takes a sip of water. He's pretty wound up. He's giving a lot of his thumb-up gesture.

"Thank you, thank you . . . Thank you very much. What a night! The folks in Hollywood will be happy to know I finally found a movie I like!"

Movies movies movies. Dole seems a bit manic, both elated and uncomfortable. "This is a big night for me and I'm ready to go," he says aloud, though it seems like he's talking to himself. Then he moves to the biggest movie of them all: "By the way, I spoke to President Reagan this afternoon, and I made him a promise that we would win one more for the Gipper." Football football football. All this yoking of Dole to Reagan throughout the convention has a downside, of course. It keeps reminding us that Dole and Reagan are contemporaries and Reagan's "mental" problems are only a heartbeat away, more or less, in our aspiring septuagenarian candidate.

"It is for the people of America that I stand here tonight, and by their generous leave.

"And as my voice echoes across darkness and desert . . . as it is heard over car radios on coastal roads . . . and as it travels above farmland and suburb, deep into the heart of cities that, from space, look tonight like strings of sparkling diamonds, I can tell you that I know whose moment this is: it is yours."

Though it is clear the words are not his. Bob Dole is poetic only by accident. And the self-conscious poetry of all that is most likely Mark Helprin's, since they are Helprin's cadences, the same used in the Senate resignation speech ("echoes across darkness and desert"). Dole has said the long sentence quickly, with a bit of a slur, since the language isn't his own, the words don't have any glue, aren't really sticking to his consciousness, and are sliding off his tongue.

During applause pauses he's laughing, pointing. "Like most small towns on the plains, it is a place where no one grows up without an intimate knowledge of distance. And the first thing you learn on the prairie is the relative size of a man compared to the lay of the land." The slurring continues. When he mentions his mother and father ("Doran . . . Bina") the slurring sounds more like emotion. But the soil metaphors remain: "I stand, with my feet on the ground, just a man, at the mercy of God."

If Mark Helprin is Dole's Theodore Sorensen, what is the difference? Sorensen had Kennedy speak about America's relationship to the world, but Helprin has Dole speak about Dole's relationship to himself.

He's talking about the "gracious compensations of age," and "that greatness lies not in what office you hold, but in how honest you are, in how you face adversity, and in your willingness to stand fast in hard places.

"Age has its advantages. Let me be the bridge to an America that only the unknowing call myth." It's a strange remark. Who are those "unknowing" who are calling America's past a "myth"?

"Let me be the bridge to a time of tranquillity, faith, and confidence in action. To those who say it was never so, that America has not been better, I say, you're wrong, and I know, because I was there."

The sheer oddity of that hits me: it's a man of my generation describing a man of Dole's generation. It's how Helprin sees, or wants to see, Dole, but Dole can't believe it. Dole says it like some sort of secret language code; the grammatical construction remains foreign to him: "To those who say it was never so . . ."

It's going to be a long speech. "We have fought and prevailed on almost every continent and in almost every sea." Those qualifiers are strange; more than a whiff of Vietnam rolls over San Diego, and Cuba's tropical odors are not far behind. Still, the speech does not seem to be sticking to him. He finally stumbles. "We are founded upon a rock . . ." And he starts again, "The rock upon which this country was founded . . ." Then he steps on Hillary again, "It does not take a village to raise a child. It takes a family." It is . . . undignified . . . to have so many former presidents and men who want to be president dumping on Hillary. That they don't leave it entirely to their surrogates is one gauge of their desperation, I guess. The big applause that follows notwithstanding.

Bill Clinton's acceptance speech in '92, I recall, had the line "I never met my father. . . ." The family/village metaphor has now become the buzzwords of the late-twentieth-century culture war, replacing hawk and dove. And the metaphor reaches deeply, back to the initial dramatic fact of Clinton's paternity. Half an orphan. It is probably the most profound thing Clinton has ever uttered publicly: "I never met my father. . . ." Clinton really doesn't seem such a mysterious figure. It's as plain as the nose on his face.

Dole's speech continues to be an attempt to make silk purses out of sows' ears: "To those who believe that I am too combative . . ." "To those who believe that I live and breathe compromise . . ." He had dealt earlier with his age; "Let me be a bridge to the time . . ."

He moves on to sounder ground with Clinton bashing: "We have had a leadership that has been unwilling to risk the truth." That must be Helprin again. Always better for the cornered to fall back on the truth.

Dole brings up, "It is not, as was said by the victors four years ago, 'the economy, stupid.' " He doesn't mention the unsaid thing about that often said slogan, the "stupid" part—the insulting manner of address that became commonplace in the eighties. One polite step above "asshole."

Dole is still slipping and sliding on his words, their unfamiliarity gives him no traction. Sweat forms on his upper lip.

"It is demeaning to the nation that within the Clinton administration a corps of the elite who never grew up, never did anything real, never sacrificed, never suffered, and never learned, should have the power to fund with your earnings their dubious and self-serving schemes."

I am stunned. Part of the audience is too. There is some yelling and clapping, but others, the roving camera shows, are silent and somewhat shocked. Hard to believe those words are coming out of Bob Dole's mouth. It's one thing to be a bridge to the past; it's quite another to take on an entire generation.

Bob Dole, as Bob Dole would say, would never do that. Mark Helprin is doing that. That line is the battle cry of internecine warfare, one part of a generation taking on another part of the same generation. That is the song of the neocons of the baby-boom generation, the converts from "liberalism," radicalism, hippyism, whatever, like Ronald Rodash, Peter Collier, David Horowitz, like the members of the nepotism corps, Podhoretz, Kristol, etc., all the ideological kids—like Mark Helprin—who hated the rads who rose in the world, the symbol of which is Bill Clinton.

As used to be said about the working class ("one half could be paid to kill the other half"), one part of the baby boomers hates the other part. It's not quite half, but the 20 percent on either end really do not care for one another. (Though, if they are equally rich, they will get along just fine.)

Bob Dole doesn't believe that attack. He might get pissed off at someone lazy, shiftless, who gets ahead, but Dole's "charm" is his pragmatism, his midwestern-style laissez-faire, part cynicism, part enjoyment of human weakness.

The television screen shows Pat Robertson.

Dole is going on about his tax cuts. He seems happier now, talking numbers.

". . . balance the budget by the year 2002 . . . reduce taxes 15 percent across the board . . . a five-hundred-dollar-per-child tax credit . . . taxes for a family of four making thirty-five thousand dollars will be reduced by more than half—56 percent to be exact . . . reducing the capital-gains tax by 50 percent . . . end the IRS as we know it." The list goes on and becomes a bit absurd. "And I won't stop there."

The audience, as they say, is a study in contrast: some are clapping and frenzied, others are stoic, and some look terribly worried.

Dole tells a story of a "man who rode on a train from Kansas to Michigan to see his son, who was thought to be dying in an army hospital. When he arrived, his feet were swollen, and he could hardly walk, because he had to make the trip, from Kansas to Michigan, standing up most of the way. Who was that man? He was my father. My father was poor," Dole says, showing real emotion. He might not have written this part, but he had to have told it to someone, sometime, since his is the point of view, and the result is taking a toll on him. "And I loved my father. Do you imagine for one minute that as I sign the bills that will set the economy free I will not be faithful to Americans in need? You can be certain that I will, for to do otherwise would be to betray those whom I love and honor most, and I will betray nothing."

That's said with conviction and is, so far, the speech's best part. His wounds show he didn't betray his country, and that carries most of the weight, and Dole's other betrayals are more private, less public—or forgotten; but, nonetheless, it's the high point, thus far.

There's another shot of Pat Robertson, looking fierce, and a shot of Jerry Falwell, just looking.

Dole moves on to immigration with more World War II anecdotes. There is a little too much Remember Bataan in all this, a foxhole full of affirmative-action dead, but it is meant to show the human side of Dole, Dole on a stick, and it is doing that.

"We are not educating all of our children. . . . Not for nothing are we the biggest education spenders and among the lowest education achievers among the leading industrial nations." Dole then slams the "teachers unions" for supporting Bill Clinton: "They are running his reelection now, and they, his most reliable supporters, know he will retain the status quo. I say this not to teachers," Dole says, after throwing mud on their work up till now, "but to their unions: if education were a war, you would be losing it. . . . To the teachers unions I say, when I am president, I will disregard your political power."

I see the teachers union getting out its checkbook right now. Pay to the order of Bill Clinton. . . .

Is this another sop to the Christian Coalition, the voucher world, the no-evolution-in-the-school folks? Bad schools is a code word these days for racism. I liked the Kansas City, Missouri, solution—construct new magnet schools near the inner city that would by their excellence attract white students. Up until recently, when the state high court (with the Supreme Court declining to review) finally reversed the work of the judge who decided money could solve—or at least, help—the terrible segregated school situation there, the solution worked. Now they have beautiful new schools, but they will have to limp along with slashed budgets.

"There is no reason why those who live on any street in America should not have the same right as the person who lives at 1600 Pennsylvania Avenue—the right to send your child to the school of your choice." Poor Chelsea. Another twofer, smack the Clintons and give aid and comfort to the evangelicals.

Dole's list gets long: crime—he's lost the criminal vote, guns, terrorists, defense. He's on a roll since all this has to do with legislation, the subject he's truly comfortable with.

"My administration will zealously protect civil and constitutional rights, while never forgetting that our primary duty is protecting law-abiding citizens"—and then he says, seemingly spontaneously, "everybody in this hall"—which gives me a good chuckle, especially since the camera gives us a shot of a Charles Keating look-alike (it can't be him, the convicted banker, can it?). "I have no intention of ignoring violent—I said violent—criminals, understanding them, or buying them off."

A bit later he says, "And on my first day in office, I will put America on a course that will end our vulnerability to missile attack and rebuild our armed forces."

All this and his tax giveaways! A missile-attack gap?

It really is too much. First days in office can be dangerous, I guess. Carter, on his first day in office, signed his pardon for draft resisters, generating some discontent, enough so he never mentions the pardon in his presidential memoir, *Keeping Faith*.

Though not on his very first day, Bill Clinton stumbled around with his gays-with-guns initiative and managed to bungle it badly.

Dole is feeding California with this bit of federal pork in the sky. Newt praises beach volleyball, Dole gives huzzahs to the sun-bleached military-industrial folks. Conservatives believe in "free" enterprise, except in the case of our military and its businesses, which is the biggest trough for the fattest pigs imaginable. Don't get me wrong, I think my father-in-law should have worked for decades on military contracts. I enjoyed the tour of Teledyne and the exploding-bolt world, part modern research campus, part medieval craft workshop. But it does grow tiresome how the benefactors of all this largesse and these federal make-work projects complain about other government interventions in other people's lives. Cut those food stamps, Bob, even though they've been agricultural subsidies all along.

"In Vietnam the long gray line did not fail us, we failed it. . . . I will never commit the American soldier to an ordeal without the prospect of victory." Dole needs to wallow in the military, because it is the one place Clinton can't wallow in. "And when I am president, every man and woman in our armed forces will know the president is commander in chief—not Boutros Boutros-Ghali, or any other UN secretary-general."

This is for the black-helicopter crowd, the militia, New World Order devotees. Go get 'em Bob!

"We are obliged by history to keep the highest standard possibly." Possibly? He must be getting tired. Possible, I guess, possibly.

All the bellicose rhetoric is wearing him down. He fought those battles fifty years ago.

We're back to Reagan again. Winning the cold war.

"My friends, a presidential campaign is more than a contest of candidates, more than a clash of opposing philosophies. It is a mirror held up to America." Boy, you can say that again.

"Tonight, I stand before you tested by adversity, made sensitive by hardship, a fighter by principle, and the most optimistic man in America," he says, somewhat grimly. But he's happy it's over, the speech that is. The applause begins and so does the commentary.

We get William Safire's opinion, after it's been processed through the what's-in-it-for-me machinery of his mind: The speech "picked up steam when he began to sock the teachers union."

Michael Beschloss thinks it was "cobbled together by committee."

Doris Kearns Goodwin says it has "a literary quality."

Mark Shields doesn't think much of it, but later, prodded by Lehrer, he agrees with Beschloss that the Dole speech might best be seen as one of contrast, showing him to be an "un-Clinton."

Andy Kohut, of the Pew Research Center, reminds everyone that "most people will hear this on the eleven o'clock news in clips."

Safire concludes he liked "the meat and potatoes" of the speech.

Watching television has often been described as staring into a fire, but these days it's more like staring into a sparkling blue sea, where colorful, exotic fish flash by. An aquarium, full of personalities, at home in the buoyant media.

I catch the last moments of GOP TV. It does a great job on the closing tape clips: wonderful shot of Bob and Liddy and TV-friendly confetti. It's on the Family Channel, thanks to some conservative zealot, Amway having its way on the Family Channel. "The preceding was a paid political program" comes up on the screen. I realize I did miss the sight of credits, what my now six-year-old refers to as "up and downs," of the people who did produce the convention rolling by; and a long list it would be, too, if they dared, like those of the Oscars or Emmy award shows, "TelePrompTer technician," etc., since this is total TV. The credit here is always sotto voce, banished to résumés.

MTV closes its coverage with a fashion report and the tiny reporter-singer Jewel is full of trepidation. MTV shows a lot of wardrobe, none of which would meet the approval of any high school hipsters. Jewel finds a young white male Republican to interview. He will be going places in the GOP, down the road, for he puts a positive spin on the gaucherie displayed: "It's a big party, room enough for sequins and no sequins."

On C-SPAN, after the crowds have gone, I watch the people, the nonmillionaire class, the "workers," finally swarm the floor, tear up the carpet, take down the podium. Roadies, guys and gals who work in the theater, stagehands, the same sort of work I used to do. I feel momentarily nostalgic. One of their number, I read in *USA Today,* had been discovered with some illegal substance on his person during a security check and had been fired on the spot.

Graham Fraser, from the *Toronto Globe and Mail,* is being interviewed while the stage is being struck. He reports that the print journalists feel marginalized. He's not asked if he feels maginalized on C-SPAN.

C-SPAN's Susan Swain retains the company neutrality (though her poker face always looks like it is about to burst; her lips are set in a half smile, half smirk, but her expression doesn't change) however absurd the call.

"The Martians have landed!"

"Thanks for your call."

TWELVE

The Conventions of August II

Life on Venus, Part 1

8/16 On Diane Rehm's Friday journalist roundup show, featuring the usual suspects—Steve Roberts of *U.S. News & World Report,* Susan Page of *USA Today,* Doyle McManus of the *Los Angeles Times,* and Josette Shiner of the *Washington Times*—the last says she has an inside story. According to Josette, *New Yorker* reporter Sidney Blumenthal was pontificating at a convention hotel bar, saying the best thing that could happen would be that Dole would drop dead and Kemp would take over. A woman delegate to the convention overheard this and thought she was hearing an assassin (or wanted to give a journalist a hard time), and the Secret Service swooped down and hustled Blumenthal off. He was in a room for forty-five minutes, explaining. After he was let go he said it was "a real *X-Files* moment."

After the TV reality of the convention, everyone, including Blumenthal, still lives in a TV-reality world.

All of the journalists seem pumped up, excited, full of energy. And they complain there was no news! Hogwash. Only attending a power event transfers the kind of high they display. That, of course, is the real bounce of the convention.

Post-convention callers are anti-Dole. One quotes from the book *Senator for Sale* or other bios. They do seem planted or true believers.

A teacher calls in appalled at Dole's union attack. Another quotes an AP article that questioned the charge that Clinton was responsible for the largest tax increase, saying the largest was Reagan's. One day in eight is used to pay taxes, lower than other industrialized nations, the caller asserts. We should be happy with our taxation. Diane says, "Some people want to pay no taxes at all."

Later, a tax lawyer who worked for the Reagan administration calls. The Republican rapid-response team is also in action. (As talk shows become more pervasive and influential, calling in has become less stigmatized, and more upscale types do call, whereas a few years ago, such activity would have seemed too déclassé.) He contends it was not a tax hike in '82. What it did was prevent some of the tax cuts from coming on line from the '81 act. These were the famous "revenue enhancements." He claims it was "not the same as taking money out of someone's pocket." They just prevented further reductions from taking place. Diane is not about to take his analysis, though it sounds like accurate spin. She says there are competing points of view on the subject.

On a newsbreak at the hour, I hear a report about the master's thesis candidate killing three professors at San Diego State yesterday. The academy's industrial accidents.

There are comments about fewer people seeing the Republican convention. But the convention is a stone thrown into the media pond and its ripples radiate out everywhere.

In the *Chicago Tribune*'s "Inc." column there is a wan item about the Republican convention: "Four years ago ex-congressman Bob Michel literally ran the convention in Houston [in '92], but this year we spotted him standing in line for shuttle buses."

Rush is irate: You want nasty and dirty, Bernie, look to the Democrats. "Bernie" Shaw of CNN. Evidently Shaw made a remark that Rush takes exception to. It's been nasty and dirty for a year, kicking people off Medicare—Rush goes on in that vein. He quotes Tim Russert, who Rush caught on the *Today Show*: " 'Every time they talk about "trust" you know they're talking about Bill Clinton.' " Of course! Rush says. Anytime anyone hears of someone having an affair . . .

Rush's not happy with the coverage of Dole's speech. "Fast pace could turn off viewers," he offers by way of critique. Who is working at *USA Today*? he asks about a column not entirely favorable. "Timing is everything. They're just looking for anything to criticize. . . . You'll never see Bob Dole with a legal defense fund," Rush says darkly. Dole has said how things have gotten worse and "this is gutsy, folks."

A caller says he's sorry about Rush's TV show going off the air. Rush not going to the convention was a smart move on his part, I conclude. The convention came to him, more or less. He's still going on about the false charges of starving children and taking Medicare away. He plays highlights from Dole's speech. His "And I will betray nothing" rings out.

A woman caller says watching Dole at the convention was "just like looking at a Norman Rockwell painting." She is not being ironic. Rush says, slightly uneasy, "That's not the way I would put it." Rush brings up Michael Deaver, Ronald Reagan's PR person. His influence has been tremendous, Rush says.

Rush's first caller pointed out a contrast, Liddy and Bob praising each other, Bill and Hillary defending each other. Rush says he, too, was worried at the start of the speech, that Dole wasn't pronouncing syllables, usually a sign that the words are not your own. Rush does seem to know something about the art of talking.

The *CBS Evening News* estimates 25 million watched Dole's speech, 25 percent less than watched The Republicans in '92. Dole is shown talking to a crowd, telling them that the big push is beginning, money is at hand. "Think of it: we've been running on empty for ninety days." Though it wasn't for lack of money; it was just against the law for him to spend it on the campaign. Dole is "full of excitement, full of enthusiasm, full of confidence. . . . We can ask anybody and they will come forward if they love the United States."

The ratio of media to delegates at the convention, CBS reports, was five to one. The fourth engine of TWA 800 is plucked out of the sea. There are indictments in the black church fire burnings. There are more media links in the burnings than racist group links.

The PBS *NewsHour* shows "the other" convention. We see a "free-speech cage," a fenced-in area where protests were allowed to take place. They do a review of the convention's corporate sponsors and interview an African American *Wall Street Journal* reporter who has been covering this side. I contemplate how the word "corporate" has evolved in the culture: it now means ritzy, the most expensive, the money-is-no-object world of doing it right. They are the courtiers of Versailles, except they don't live off of the favor of the king; rather, the exchange goes the other way—the president lives off their favors and then reciprocates.

A decade ago a friend of mine had a short story accepted by a brand-new publication. It wanted a photograph, and she said she would send them a snapshot. The woman on the phone laughed and said, Oh no, they would send a photographer to her. On the appointed day, three people arrived—a makeup person, a photographer, and his assistant—with a great deal of equipment. Three hours later they had a few photographs. It turned out to be Whittle's Channel One empire (of Lamar!'s backyard) and his dentist-office magazine, *Special Report*—and a taste of corporate culture my friend hadn't hitherto encountered.

There is discussion of the Republicans. It is a family—no dirty laundry allowed to be aired is the judgment. David Gergen, who ought to know, brings up some statistics. The networks devoted one hundred hours to the conventions of 1980 and only sixteen hours this time. He says there was a one-third drop in the audience for Dole compared to the audience for George Bush.

During the day I heard these questions: "Am I going to have to vote?" and "Is it close enough that I need to vote?" That still seems to be Bill Clinton's biggest problem, the lack of enthusiasm. It's not the undecided voter, but the voter who has decided whom he or she would vote for, but is undecided about voting at all.

In the *South Bend Tribune*, I discover our cable company will cut out the Chicago PBS station and we will be left only with the local PBS outlet, which doesn't seem like a terrible loss, except the local PBS censors programming in a way the Chicago station does not. No homosexual or shows thought to be anti-Catholic get through here in South Bend on PBS. It's a company town, though the company is no longer Studebaker. Notre Dame is the largest employer in the area. It turns out that TCI, the cable company, is in corporate bed with Fox, and it is the new Fox news channel (future home to Rush?) which will bump the Chicago **PBS** station from our cable world. We don't get Comedy Central, which, given its coverage of the campaign, is a loss.

On *Washington Week in Review,* Elizabeth Arnold (looking good) quotes Dole saying this morning about his speech, "I always wanted to be the last one to speak." There are scenes of the Dole-Kemp Kickoff rally in San Diego. Kemp in his number 15 San Diego Chargers football jersey, with a football, getting ready to throw the football—hold that football, we're in for a long season. Pete Wilson is there, looking dour: "We need a president we can believe and respect."

Dole seems to have three gestures (when he is not speaking, but standing around): Hand out to stop traffic, pointing out a troublemaker (or friend), and his thumb-up.

Then Dole . . . speaks: "Let me say this to my friends—the press isn't listening." There's laughter. He retells his Elizabeth/FDR joke: She's so good FDR's trying to reach her. "There are no doors in the Republican Party." I wonder if he dropped a word, given the oddness of the remark. No closed doors, perhaps.

8/18   The prez is on *60 Minutes.* For only the second time since Gennifer Flowers? I wonder. Happy birthday to the prez. The setup looks oddly like Bob Dole's convention video. Clinton in front of windows, his shirt open. He is asked about the "learn nothing generation" quote from Dole's speech. He gives a soft answer, says it doesn't matter whether "the ideas are old or new," and avoids answering the heart of the charge. There is much conversation of this sort: you know what they are asking and there is no way I'm answering. But the evasions show how well they do understand the question.

Clinton is in his "Stand By Your Gal" mode of the State of the Union address. In his fifty years, he does know, he's "most grateful for the years I had with Hillary and with Chelsea." Though it is one way to put it, the past tense in this context is sort of strange.

Dole, he reminds viewers, after saying that he wants the election to be about ideas, not insults, has been called by Newt "the tax collector for the welfare state."

Dole, it is announced, has been asked to appear on *60 Minutes* after the Democratic convention. Mike Wallace says that "Bill Clinton is the first American president to take an antismoking stance." (I recall a photo of Clinton with a cigar.) Tobacco companies, which used to give liberally to both parties, we are told, now are giving heavily to the Dole campaign, hoping for more receptivity from Dole in the White House.

The visit with the prez is a birthday gift of sorts, whatever the Gennifer Flowers vibes that radiate from it. Later in the same show, Morley Safer does a piece on Britain's comic program *Spitting Image,* which is going off the air. We get the Muppets, the Brits get savage satire. Among the funny bits shown are lampoons of Clinton himself. "There's a woman to see you." "Hold on, I'm not dressed yet." Then his pants drop, revealing shiny American-flag boxer shorts.

On CNN we get Perot's Reform Party convention. There's yet another biographical film (keeping those documentary makers employed; the four-year cycle of campaigns keeps a lot of people employed: the work's hardly seasonal anymore). Perot's father was a cotton trader. "Sell it, you can't eat it," says a sign in his warehouse. Ross on a horse, Ross getting into Annapolis, married in '56, goes from the navy to IBM (the military-industrial complex at work, more or less, despite Ike's warnings); and then, though he's a wiz at sales, Ross reads in a '61 *Reader's Digest* the Thoreau line, "The mass of men lead lives of quiet desperation"; some-how he did not come upon it at Annapolis. It's disquieting to reflect in this age of generational typing how Ross is a product of the "silent" generation, the "organization" man, one of the "lonely crowd."

Digesting the Thoreau, Ross thinks, "That's me."

His response is not to get a divorce and head to California, but to found his own company, Perot Systems.

Since he is a part of the military-industrial complex, his government connections get him contracts, along with his tried-and-true Willy-Loman-with-an-Uzi approach. But it is more of Sammy Glick, Sammy Glick that makes him tick.

We see Ross heading into Laos for the POWs, we see Ross freeing his two EDS employees from Iran.

Then we hear a voice: "The next president of the United States . . ."

Ross walks out and CNN cuts to a commercial and I go to C-SPAN. It shows the audience. The Reform Party's convention space is no large-scale television studio, it appears to be a high school auditorium, badly lit, exhuding a fifty-year reunion senior prom atmosphere. There are a lot of spectacular American faces in attendance, many that compete with the earlier *60 Minutes* display of *Spitting Image* caricatures. These folk are a step beyond the mean, certainly beyond what we saw at the Republican convention, and they are absent entirely of the ditto quality of Rush's TV audience. These Reform Party people are individuals.

Ross is defending the Indians: "Look what happened to these great warriors and hunters and survivors" after we began "to take care of them." A backhanded compliment, of sorts. At the start, Ross complimented his troops for setting the agenda for '96. What's that? Tax cuts and antismoking legislation? Somewhere the balanced budget must lurk.

We're five trillion in debt, Ross says, and "all the currency we have won't add up to five trillion." He derides Dole—there goes the bounce—for embracing supply-side economics. We tried that in the eighties. "I said in 1992 that if we ever tried that again we'd be in deep voodoo. Well, here we are."

On education today: "My parents never read me my Miranda rights." Then Perot goes on a private jag: Blindfold a child for six months and he'll be blind for life. He seems convinced by this little tale of horror, a salesman's staple. It's like Ralph Reed saying with utter conviction that women who have abortions get cancer. It's a look into personal craziness, where the physical entwines with an idea in a thoroughly unwholesome way.

Now, I'm going to have to ask a doctor. And who does blindfold a child for six months? Ross and his sadistic truths.

We see the audience again and some are wearing bumper stickers on their hats (economies of a different kind of scale, multiple use): "In Perot We Trust."

Ross is going to take the feds' money (our money!), the twenty-nine million and change, and individual donations.

Ross does look like Harry Truman on Ritalin. At the close, Ross goes for poetry, resorts to popular song lyrics: "You are the wind beneath the wings of the Reform Party." He finishes with "Thank you." At least he doesn't say, "God bless America," but then he adds, "I got to run to get to Larry King." Maybe that is God bless America.

Campaign America '96: The View From the Couch

We see the stage set, cheap blue flats painted with stars and REFORM PARTY, and the audience, where I glimpse a handwritten sign: "There are more of us than you think!" A threat of sorts.

Sousa march music plays in the auditorium. Isn't that Steve Forbes's favorite?

Then I abandon C-SPAN to follow the Ross-ter to Larry King.

He's telling Larry "all they do is pass the mess on to the next person who goes into the office." Nothing happens for the first four years. Sounds like he's endorsing Clinton.

King asks about the Republican tax cut. "If I wanted to," Ross says, "it would play to me as a symphony." Who better would it help? he comments. "But I am not greedy."

Ross criticizes the fund-raiser held tonight for Clinton in New York City, Bill's birthday bash at Radio City. (Are the Rockettes safe?) The yachts in San Diego Harbor are alluded to. "These guys are controlled by special interests." Right on, power to the people. Ross, needless to say, is a special interest of one.

Larry King brings up the "Gore thing in his ear" story reported in the Posner book, a tiny "hidden" listening device from which Gore was getting NAFTA answers.

Ross is momentarily sheepish, which means he slows down a micro-beat. In Japan I saw film of the show, he contends, and saw something flashing in Gore's ear. The Washington cocktail circuit called me with the story and I laughingly repeated it. Ross gives it no credibility now. But this does unleash some paranoia from the Ross-ter. A lot of the big media have their own candidates, he says. They do manipulate. "I'm not complaining. That's just the way it is."

King, the sly old manipulator, goes to commercials. Office Depot. Guy in a wheelchair with his own computer business. Good-looking young people around. One older guy. I suppose the wheelchair is to make us feel Office Depot is a welcoming sort of place. Then there is an LCI phone company, an upstart competitor to the biggest carriers, commercial. One of the type where the actual CEO gives the pitch: "We don't round up to the next minute." Why doesn't he be Perot's veep? I wonder, since Perot seems to be having trouble finding one.

When we return, Ross is talking about health care: "One shoe doesn't fit every foot," he says. The health program that works for New York City won't work for a small town in Wyoming. He's against big government, or whatever he thinks that is, but he's for big government contracts. "Just passing laws creates stress." And Ross doesn't need more stress. He does admit affirmative-action laws did some good. (And their consequences required a lot of his company's software applications!) "These things are dynamic."

NAFTA comes up. "I love the Mexican people"—like Dole loves teachers—but "thirty-five families own half the country." About the same as ours, I figure.

Ross, like Dole, is comfortable with numbers. He tells us that Social Security and the IRS are numbers—you can really nail down the best system. . . . Use the computer as a wind tunnel. (Always the salesman.) Medicare and Medicaid are too complicated, too many factors. He means people.

During a commercial, I go to C-SPAN and see Bob Dole in Buffalo, New York, promising what Perot was just criticizing. "We can cut taxes and balance the budget by 2002. We will end the IRS as we know it." Dole introduces Jack Kemp and Kemp says ambiguously, "I'll be the quarterback for eighty days and then turn it over to him."

Back to Ross, who says, joking: I've got a "Road" scholar on the phone. I'm counting on hundreds of them. Ross the punster, praising a complimentary caller. Ross rails against "Now you see it, now you don't politics." Again he hits the untouchable—Ronnie, in this case—chastising "former presidents" who get "two million for two twenty-minute speeches in Asia. . . . This is so rotten," he concludes with conviction. It is interesting, billionaires who don't consider themselves greedy. Something similar in John D. Rockefeller handing out dimes to the needy.

Back on C-SPAN Kemp says, "I believe so much in NAFTA we exported Jimmy [another family footballer] to Canada [the league, that is]."

Kemp goes on his numerology kick again. He was the veep on August 15, the tax cut is 15 percent, his football number is 15, etc.

Alfonse D'Amato and a lot of Republican New York pols are on the makeshift platform. Kemp talks on, inspiring a lot of looks at wristwatches (Dole and Al). Kemp seems almost as stunned as Dan Quayle at being picked as veep. Grateful and stunned. ". . . on this stage, on this football field . . ." at the University of Buffalo. "I went to HUD in the Bush administration." He quotes Martin Luther King Jr. "I have an abiding faith in the United States and an audacious belief in the goodness of people."

Everyone's happy he's done speaking. There's some confusion about who follows up. Alfonse says to the taller Pataki, "You going to do it?" Pataki thanks Dole and Kemp, and the Republican New York attorney general (short, in the Bobby Abrams mode) gives them both Buffalo Bills jerseys. Kemp's former New York teammates lumber on, and I do mean lumber—the stage groans when these big guys (now considerably bigger) climb aboard. The Republicans have succeeded in dropping down in class connection. All the style of the Democrats is here; small state university, football field, ethnic state politicians, Buffalo—Buffalo! In the language of the moment, they have taken a page from the playbook of Clinton-Gore. Hut, hut, hut.

8/19   Rush is upset. *"60 Minutes* was an infomercial for Bill Clinton!" Rush plays the tape of Marilyn Monroe singing happy birthday to JFK, in tribute to the prez's fiftieth. "They're seething out there, folks," Rush gloats. *"Newsweek* poll—down to two points!"

He lampoons Perot. Everything that Perot proposed, the Republican Congress addressed. Where was Perot the last two years?

On the *CBS Evening News* there's a report on smoking. A spokesperson for tobacco complains about smokers being turned into "pariahs or freaks." That this is a Republican issue is more class downsizing on the GOP's part. I envision "I smoke and I Vote" bumper stickers. I see the little clots of smokers gathering at the outside doors of workplaces. Ah, yes, cancer-stick pariahs. There's news about convicted ex–Arkansas governor Jim Guy Tucker being under "house arrest"—no prison time, whereas Susan McDougal is going to the slammer. Susan McDougal, though, is not the once and former guv. It's hard to jail a governor—or, say, Dan Rostenkowski. Tucker has some hard-to-see liver ailment for which no sufficient medical care would be available in our federal gulag system.

On NPR's *Campaign Connection* Jesse Jackson is being interviewed.

Jesse has cut back on the rhymes. Rhymes are a young man's game. Jesse says, of the Republican Party, "It's a book; on the front cover is Dole and the back is Kemp and you open it up and inside there is Gingrich and Ralph Reed. . . . Both parties are suffering from a dream deficit disorder." Jesse has had his own election dreams deferred, permanently it appears, now that his son has been elected to congress.

Larry King comes on and he's interviewing Tony Robbins, one of the audio-and videocassette sultans of the self-help world, politics for the unpolitical. Over the years I've surfed by Robbins's infomercials and, at first, I put him in the alien category appealing to other aliens. A get-rich, positive-cash-flow kind of guy, or, rather, his infomercials blended in with the great eighties romance with real estate. But he has much too much jaw (Jay Leno–like), so he seems to be one of those wild DNA guys, one physical attribute a bit too exaggerated and he overcompensates like crazy. But the times have been kind to him. Success continued and he's become more and more polished as his assets have grown. He's been to the White House, part of the parade of thinkers sampled by the Clintons. I don't know if he's a Renaissance Weekend kind of guy. Maybe he'll be taking Donna Shalala's place in the cabinet in Clinton's likely second term. Tony says the secret of success is to look good, sound good, have congruency. "Congruency" means a lot of things to Tony: conviction, for one, and, I suppose, not seeming to be a lunatic at the same time.

But these past eight months have taken their toll on me. All this TV has done its insidious work. I must be getting dumber, since I find myself agreeing with Robbins: he and Larry conclude that Dole has no sexual spark, whereas Clinton, woweee. I watch one infomercial king on another King's show critiquing the infomercial convention. Tony gives us some numbers. It's 50 percent looks and 38 percent voice. What is? Who cares? I wonder who does Tony's very white teeth. Big jaw, lots of teeth. He's a guy who's overcome having too many teeth and a face drawn by Al Capp.

C-SPAN, getting ready for the Democratic convention, is replaying old Democratic conventions. Black and white, the early fifties, Adlai Stevenson from the podium reminds the American people there is "no gain without pain." He's echoing the yet to be crowned (born?) world muscle-building champion, Arnold Schwarzenegger, Maria's ("M" 's) husband, well-known Republican. And people think Carville-Matalin is strange.

It looks like Truman is sitting behind Stevenson. Or is it Ross Perot, in the new Hollywood special-technology manner? Try to name Stevenson's first veep candidate? I couldn't. (It was Sparkman of Alabama.)

"I say *trust the people*," Stevenson says. Is Dole running the Stevenson campaign of '56?

8/20   Rush sounds more upset than optimistic today. He's sympathetic to poor Richard Jewell. (I say: Jail anyone who fits the profile. Get him out of his mother's place; she may be in danger.) Rush wants the gorilla (Binti) who "rescued" the three-year-old (just how did the child fall in the gorilla pit, anyway?) to speak at the Democratic convention. Kevorkian is back with dead bodies (he's been dropping them off at emergency rooms). Kevorkian continues to keep his macabre spotlight on health care and Medicare-Medicaid every time he helps off another sufferer.

From CNN's *Headline News,* I learn Susan McDougal has been sentenced to two years. Her brother is appalled. No liver disease, I guess. And just how do you get liver disease? Too much Arkansas moonshine perhaps?

An anonymous message is left on my answering machine, apropos Dole's acceptance speech: "I have withstood adversity and struggled against perversity and believe in a party that stands for diversity and, today, if you ask me, I am the luckiest man alive, next to Lou Gehrig."

There's a Dole story on *Nightline* about Dave Owen, former lieutenant governor of Kansas, a guy who was with Dole on the campaign trail in 1980 in Russell, Kansas, now characterized as a "money collector, campaign manager." Koppel prefaces the program with the disclaimer, "Regular viewers know how many shows we've done on Whitewater, Travelgate, Filegate."

We get a tour of Kansas cronyism, à la Arkansas (different latitude, same longitude). One change is that Owen ran Liddy's blind trust and sold half an office building in Overland Park (a suburb of Kansas City, Missouri) that Liddy owned to John Palmer, who then got a lucrative federal contract via Dole. Owen is made out to be the McDougal of

Dole. "They weren't friends?" the reporter asks the Dole spokesperson. "That's Senator Dole's view." Dole was earlier quoted as saying, in the usual Dole doublespeak, "Dave Owen never worked for me and when we find anything wrong he's gone." Translation: Though he doesn't work for me, I fired him as soon as the scandal hit.

Shots of Liddy and Bob at the time of this dustup, Liddy's hairstyle helmetlike. It isn't the warm and fuzzy Liddy of the stroll among the wheelchairs.

Tipper Gore shows up on the *Tonight Show* with Jay Leno, ostensibly to promote *Picture This*, her book of photographs of the studly Al. Tipper jokes about the Secret Service on the family rafting trip (subject of many photographs). They wear "earpieces and sunglasses, that's as far as it goes." There's laughter, picturing nudes with earpieces.

Tipper is wearing a gray pin-striped suit and black turtleneck. She looks studly herself. There's more banter about the Secret Service and the camera shows one of them standing in the studio, an African American looking serious. But then he cracks a small smile and a partial wink.

Jay escorts Tipper off. These appearances (Clinton's *60 Minutes* turn) seem like preconvention promos, but Tipper looks like she's enjoying herself. A blond and zaftig Tipper in gray pinstripes projects the effect of costume (i.e., cheerleaders in pinstripes). Her pictures of Gore are full of desire—as much as admiration. I try to imagine what a collection of candid photos would look like of Bill taken by Hillary.

Thinking about women, given the Republican convention, I think again of the Woodward campaign book. There are women in *The Choice*, but they are Hillary's women. Clinton might have wanted to meet Marianne Williamson at Camp David in order to get the name and address of the buxom, seminude model on the cover of her book, *A Woman's Worth*. (He may have thought it was actually Williamson's picture!) It's his bubba, Sparta side. No wonder Dee Dee Myers is gone. Whereas Mike McCurry in the same job gets lots of Clinton's time and ear, Woodward shows.

Television ads have become op-ed pieces for the willfully uninformed. It's a time-and-space similarity. In the past, the time I spent with public figures revealed that part of their ability—like being ready for a press conference at the drop of a hat—comes from sheer conditioning, like an alcoholic's great tolerance for alcohol. It's a matter of tone.

One interesting cross-party phenomenon is becoming clear, how celebrities now become pundits. This is especially true on the Left. When Al Franken and Robin Williams are as likely to be quoted as anyone, one realizes how "Left" celebrities need to become pundits, since so few pundits on the Left ever become celebrities. Comics are the Left's pundit stable, because they are the only ones with credibility (since they are well-known) and experience tossing off impolite rhetoric. Name recognition is still the easiest way to get published these days (first the chicken then the egg), and what has been true there for some time (celebrities publishing books) has now moved to television, celebrities being authorized to give opinions. TV is the great leveler. It has only one way of showing you something. And if the "variables" are controlled (set, lighting, looks, clothes, etc.), everything can be made similar. Looking at the Christian news is close to looking at any kind of news. You can throw money at the problem and solve it.

In the primaries, you had something similar. Morry Taylor had money, but no intellectual cachet of any sort. No magazine was named *Morry*. If Michael Lewis hadn't latched on to him (and *The New Republic* hadn't run Lewis's funny pieces), Taylor would be known to practically no one, other than the folks he actually met on the campaign trail.

8/21 I am on the phone with a friend from Truro, Massachusetts, getting a report on the vacationing second family. There's been an article in the *New York Times* about the nude beach in Truro being beached, but the Gores have now left Cape Cod, and things have returned to normal. My friend knows people connected to the house the Gores stayed in and the big news, I am told, is, "The Gores don't recycle!"

Evidently, when folks showed up to reclaim the house, they found that the Gores' garbage had all been mixed together. When this was discovered, one indignant Cape Codder close to the scene wanted to write a letter in protest to the editor of the *Provincetown Advocate,* but second thoughts prevailed. I envision Recyclegate, followed by the coverup. Recycling is a big deal in the narrow neck of those precious woods.

The Gore girls spent most of their time trying to sneak away from their Secret Service protection. But my friend was worried about the Gores' safety. The house was left empty the night before the Gores arrived and Lord knows what terrorist devices could have been planted there. I suggested that the Secret Service must have done a sweep of it before the Gores arrived the next day. My friend said the "Secret Service screw things into the light fixtures. But they've told the Gores they can have privacy by turning the lights off." Do the Gores actually believe that? I wonder.

Though I do see Hillary's problem (and motive?), hurling lamps with listening devices across the room. Being governor of a small state gave the Clintons the illusion of privacy, but becoming the first family of the United States presented them with the reality of always being under surveillance by a "neutral" third party.

My friend had been surprised to see the Gores at the Olympics at the same time they had been vacationing down the beach, but they had flown down and flown back. No problem with reservations.

8/22 It remains old-home week, Massachusetts division, in the *New York Times*. There's a piece about two women racetrack employees, from the Raynham-Taunton dog track, fired for not working on Christmas. They said it was against their religion. Catholic. One priest says yes, their priest; the other side's priest says no. As long as they go to Mass. The story is that the state supreme court has struck down the law. The employees remain unemployed. This is a wonderful story, for what's underneath it. Ah, America. Where the dog track is open on Christmas Day! Ah, America, where any lawyer can get competing Catholic priests to testify against one another! Ah, America, where fired employees say it is their religion, not just their obvious and natural desire to be at home for Christmas, rather than at work, that prevents them from pleasing their employer!

USA Today is full of horror stories, macabre violence everywhere, and the horror-story graph of income distribution: poor getting poorer, rich getting richer, middle stagnating.

Rush is talking with a supporter of Harry Browne, the libertarian, who claims Rush for the libertarian persuasion. Rush, though, says he stands for "public betterment," a fallen libertarian who wants government controls over "drugs, alcohol," but not cigarettes. Rush explains cigarette effects take time, unlike drugs. Harry Browne's mantra—"Would you give up your favorite government program in order to have no income tax?"—would appeal, perhaps, to Steve Forbes, but not the folks on food stamps.

8/23   On Diane Rehm there's a call from a "nonvoter." More of the general lack of enthusiasm for Clinton coming to the surface. The man's going to vote for Congress, but not for president. That statistic, of those who don't vote for any presidential candidate, but do vote, must be tiny, but it will triple, at least, this election. Later, another caller, a fortyish woman, says she worked for Clinton in '92, but not this time. She feels it's the same with young people.

I contemplate Nixon in China. Will it be Clinton in America?

Another caller thinks Kemp is a one-night stand. He will vote for Clinton, not because he really wants to, but in atonement for voting for Anderson in 1980, throwing away his vote and helping elect Reagan.

It does seem clear that Perot will no longer be the protest vote. It will be the "nobody for president" vote that will be the protest slot.

It's becoming clearer to me that the Internet is the apotheosis of the model of press coverage that was spawned by the Pentagon Papers, the Watergate tapes, etc. The "press" will have to return to selection, synthesis, interpretation, where the gatekeepers, the Bill Gates gatekeepers, will have more power. It's not a Babel of languages, but a Babel of data, raw material. What will the Internet do to the word "media"? It won't be a synonym for the press much longer. The prevailing metaphors will lead us nowhere: the information highway—hah! The "net," yes. It will snag us, leave us trapped. The world wide web. The spiders talk to the flies.

8/25   The curious thing is how the Republicans managed not to mention Richard Nixon at their convention. He's doubtless spinning in his grave, but he'll extract revenge somehow, I'm sure. The *New York Times Book Review* critique of Ms. Crowley's book of Nixon speaking from beyond the grave makes that clear.

William O'Rourke

On *This Week with David Brinkley* I see Al Gore. He has a way of making time slow down. It's some sci-fi special effect. You expect the screen to soon fill up with mimes at rest.

CNN does a piece on old age and the rise of the aged. The old-olds have skyrocketed and that is just the top of the barrel, the bottomless barrel of the boomers to come. There are scenes of "older" women doing aerobics. "We'll have youthful bodies at ninety," it is claimed. A new kind of residential community is popping up around the country, "campus living." (It has been a standard joke of mine over the last two decades that my generation will end up back at college after the campuses are turned into old folks homes to accommodate us.) We see "Charlestown," outside of Baltimore, full of mainly single women. A seventy-six-year-old is interviewed: "I'm not anywhere near being old." "We are here for the duration of our lives," one man says, in order not to burden their children. A hundred-thousand-dollar deposit is required for a one-bedroom, but the deposit is "refundable."

These campuses are equipped for various rates of dying. The spirit of Dr. Kevorkian hovers over this issue, as well as the aged as generational scapegoat. The privatizing Social Security crowd, the Concord Coalition, and orbiting organizations engender this sort of generational class war. The believe-more-in-UFOs-than-Social-Security line promoted by such groups is aimed at everyone, young and old. Luckily, or unluckily, the aged are still somebody's parents, or grandparents, so it is hard to demonize the elderly completely, but it is easier to demonize the government programs that currently keep them out of the direst poverty. The crowd at "Charlestown" is the top of the barrel in any number of ways, mainly economic.

C-SPAN is showing the beginning of Clinton's train ride to Chicago. We're at Huntington, West Virginia, at an old C & O railroad station. The Clintons are there with West Virginia's Senator Jay Rockefeller, who says, about the Dole tax cut, "I don't need it." There are chuckles on the stage. He describes the Republican Congress's balanced-budget budget, which had $295 million tax cut proposed for the rich, along with the $270 million cut from Medicare. The conjunction of those two figures was a damning bit of symmetry. I've always been amazed at Jay (John D. IV) Rockefeller being a senator (and former governor) from one of our country's bits of the Third World. His relatives bought the mineral rights and he becomes king of what's left. Anyway, he doesn't need the tax cut, as he admits. He also wants to see how quickly we can take away the hammer (gavel, I trust he means) from "that fat GOP baby." Ah, some patrician Newt bashing, doubtless inspired by the patrician Bush bashing Hillary. He makes a dotty remark about his wife: "Sharon—she's in a very nice thing over there." The camera doesn't follow his remark, so it's hard to see if he means her dress or where she sits. It is easy to see why high WASP is not playing well nationally these days.

An African American woman, a success story from AmeriCorps, introduces Bill. He's very energetic, forceful, lively. He seems to be, as usual, enjoying himself. We're "on the right track," he says, which makes perfectly clear why he's taking a train. As the Republicans wanted to endlessly repeat (Buy us, buy us) in tiny sound bites, so, too, does the prez. Every stop, one can foresee, local and national audiences will be told "we're on the right track." "No U-turns," he says, which mixes the metaphor a bit, but trains do not do U-turns, in any case.

C-SPAN then immediately shows a Dole rally at Palos Park, Illinois. "I'm a Dole Man" is playing to the familiar tune. Dole is there, waiting to talk. The contrast is stunning between the vigorous Bill Clinton and the dry stick Bob Dole. Under what circumstances would that chasm, the portrait of vitality versus decline, ever become insignificant enough to allow Dole to be elected? Recession, depression? The CNN report on old folks never mentioned Dole, but he was there. All the age issues have become too hot for the Republicans to handle. Even when Dole pledges not to destroy Medicare and Medicaid, no one thinks he'll be there long enough to save them.

"Let's give it up for Bob Dole," the leader of the "Dole Man" band says.

Governor Edgar proclaims Illinois to be "Dole-Kemp territory." Dole is wearing a white shirt, no jacket. The rally is also some sort of picnic. There's a huge "15%" banner at the back of the stage. Standing in the sun, Dole, Liddy, and Haley Barbour all have the Munster family look.

Dole again tells his Liddy/Eleanor Roosevelt joke. The crowd is chanting what sounds like Kemp-Dole, Kemp-Dole. They just might have the rhythm wrong. I can't imagine it to be deliberate. My mind wanders to the Woodward book, where Dole is quoted, after Kemp declined to endorse him in New Hampshire (375): "Last time we're dealing with the Quarterback." The chant corrects itself; now it's "Dole-Kemp, Dole-Kemp."

Dole is going on about how "we're going to enjoy cutting the capital-gains tax in half."

Somehow the 15 percent tax cut is supposed to muffle the explosion of halving the capital-gains tax in the minds of the average working stiff. The speech, however, is a long laundry list of Clinton's cuts on the war on drugs.

This is Dole crashing the Democratic convention, payback for Stephanopoulos (or whatever) slogging around San Diego, since the rally is taking place on the outskirts of Chicago.

Dole's saying Clinton "replaced 'Just say no' with 'Just say nothing.' " Clinton's made 119 statements and mentioned drugs in just 2.

The McLaughlin show replayed the MTV clip of Clinton being asked if he would have inhaled way back when. Clinton replied awkwardly, "Sure, if I could—I tried." It's a clip that's getting a lot of action, on ABC, on Fox, in Republican ads.

There aren't many black faces in this picnic crowd. Haley Barbour says these are "better men for a better America." There are some fireworks at the end. A Dole-Kemp sign lights up and burns, a bit too much like a cross on the lawn.

Then C-SPAN shows Al Gore at a hall full of AFL-CIO delegates, along with its new leadership, Sweeney, Trumka, and Linda Chavez-Thompson, the Hispanic woman named to the newly created position of executive vice president of the AFL-CIO. Bill Clinton said he would make his cabinet look like America, and the leadership of the AFL-CIO now looks a bit more like its members. "America Needs a Raise" is the theme of the confab.

Gore is full of compliments. "I've never seen such leadership . . . as the American labor movement has received from John Sweeney." He talks about all the contact he's had with labor groups over the last few years. I met with "the Bricklayers"—and there is a microsecond of unease in the crowd, since it is the Bricklayers' president, John Joyce, who has broken ranks and is refusing to support Clinton, because of his ve- toing the partial-birth abortion bill—"or AFSCME"—there's a big cheer then. It's Chavez-Thompson's home union. "We're on your side" is Gore's message, and his voice gets distressingly more folksy as he talks to this crowd; it becomes the oral equivalent of Lamar!'s checked shirt, getting down with the people.

Gore makes the same point about the Republicans shutting down the government. They're there. It's a theme. The opening salvo of the cam- paign, the November-December management lockouts by Gingrich, Dole and Company. Unless there's a Democratic Congress elected in '96, it will happen again, Gore says solemnly. "That would test America as it hasn't been in a hundred years."

Gore speculates on the terror of a Dole presidency, a Republican Congress, and the resulting appointments on the Supreme Court. The end of the world as we know it. But, for now, everyone's happy, upbeat. Gore intends to be the nominee in 2000 and, oh, what a difference that will make.

8/26   Rush is quoting an editorial from *Investor's Business Daily* about the CBS *60 Minutes* Dan Rather interview of the president. And the *60 Minutes* post–Super Bowl XXVI appearance after Gennifer Flowers's revelations. The editorial quotes Don Hewitt, *60 Minutes'* producer, from the Germond and Witcover book on the '92 campaign, giving Clin- ton advice right before they started taping the show. "When he asks you if you committed adultery, say yes. It will be great television. I know. I know television. The last time I did something like this, Bill, it was the Kennedy-Nixon debates and it produced a president. This will produce a president, too." Rush's point is that this shows how much "the main- stream media" favor Bill Clinton and that *60 Minutes* is just doing the same old thing with the recent Clinton appearance. The point in the Germond/Witcover book is how outrageous the advice was. (Clinton managed to say . . . neither yes or no.) Oh, well. A caller asks what Rush's favorite conservative Web site is. Rush doesn't know any conservative Web sites, he says. He does sports, weather, news on the Internet. "I read you," he says, addressing "liberals." He doesn't need to consult conservative Web sites (none, obviously, has bought his endorsement).

Rush is piqued they are using his hometown, Cape Girardeau, Missouri, as a stop on the Clinton train ride. He brings up the health care express bus tour in unflattering comparison. "We had a large part to play in screwing up Hillary's health care bus tour," he boasts, which is the pointed revelation of Haynes Johnson's and David Broder's investigative book, *The System,* which covers "the battle" over universal health insurance for Americans.

The Nation reviews Woodward's *The Choice* in its September 9–16 issue. In the same issue there's a review of gays-in-politics books; the reviewer says that Jim Kolbe, a congressman from Arizona, has recently been "outed," doubtless the result of the presidential campaign. More rocks are turned over during a presidential campaign and a lot of things normally hidden are revealed.

Clinton's problem is the utter lack of enthusiasm. It's Dump the Hump revisited—since we are in Chicago, all the references are to '68. Democrats turning against themselves, letting Nixon be elected because of Humphrey's supposed transgressions, the scorn heaped upon him by the arrogance of youth. But in Clinton's case, it's a different kind of Hump involved.

Life on Venus, Part 2

The United Center is no television studio, it is an arena of the old style: a cow palace. But this one is the new home of the basketball-playing Bulls, a place where black men work. Charles Rangel, the African American congressman from New York, in a tribute to Ron Brown, calls Brown's parents "royalty of Harlem." Another sort of royalty usually runs up and down the hardwood floor of the United Center when it is empty and polished. Now it's filled with delegates. No small, controlled space here. It's huge, full of milling people, dark, not shadowless like the San Diego trade center, but thick with chiaroscuro. Clinton's on the train and this is the station, full of surging throngs, with an immensely high ceiling, the nexus, the center of things, an energy sink, charged with the promise of romance and adventure.

A cathedral of the people. The United Center. But this convention is full of danger, since it is to serve no direct purpose, only indirect ones: igniting the troops, raising money, showing the flag, pounding its collective chest.

Daley junior begins the festivities; an only half-interested audience mills around down below him. He talks about '68: the country at war, abroad and at home. Daley is sweating and he has an active tongue, searching out his cheeks and lips. His accented voice makes an odd slip. He calls Clinton a "successful president," but the word that emerges sounds like "sexsessful."

"America America" is sung by the Democratic Convention Mass Choir, a lot of African American faces, all wearing white, waving in front of the stage. Music from the film *2001*, good old Richard Strauss, *Thus Spake Zarathustra*, fills the huge arena. Green laser lights stab the darkness, a light show of sorts. The people staging this show have Las Vegas backgrounds and this does seem a bit too much Siegfried and Roy, the albino lion-tamers—it's a casino stage show of gargantuan proportions. At music's end, there's a hot white light on somebody who turns out to be Ernie Banks, but to anyone under forty-five he just looks like some elderly black man. When he's finally introduced, "Mr. Cubs" says something unclear about some other Chicagoan who wants to welcome everyone to the city, and then the show jumps outside and we see Hillary loitering in the street. Talk about Dole being badly lit for his State of the Union reply! Mrs. Clinton stands in some kind of lineup light. She starts to speak, but then stops, since someone is confusing her with cues. Is she on? Is she not on? Finally, it's decided she's on and she starts to speak again: "I too . . . want to welcome you to the great city of Chicago," said with an unhappy expression on her face. She's not at ease. Then the scene turns into pure C-SPAN, though C-SPAN is not controlling the cameras. She presumes she is off the air, but she's not, and we watch her desultorily hand off the mike and walk away alone. Not a successful moment. Not a Liddy Dole moment. Hillary should have been surrounded by excited Chicago faces and she should have appeared happy, just waving and smiling, in party mode. Instead, she did it as Bob would do it, alone, not like Liddy, in a crowd.

But then we are back inside listening to an injured Chicago cop, Mike Robbins, on stage telling us when he heard the head of the NRA calling law enforcement personnel jackbooted thugs, "I took it personally."

Then we get Todd Clancy of Toledo who was laid off in the Bush administration days and had no health care and ran out of unemployment, but got a job with Chrysler building Jeeps in '93. "Some people say it's a miracle; I say it's President Clinton."

Well, we can see where this is heading.

Then we have Marilyn Concepcion, of Puerto Rican background, a real firecracker, who dropped out of high school, but got into the AmeriCorps program, taught children, and got her high school equivalency degree, though her proudest moment came when one of her preschoolers pronounced the letter F (as in frog). Now she's at Brown, class of '99. "Thank you, President Clinton," she said, owing it all to AmeriCorps.

Well, these are American Dream stories, though not of the bootstrap variety. Here it takes a village (though I still wonder why Hillary was standing alone on a dark city street).

There are long gaps, since this is not happening with the crack precision of San Diego. (It takes a director.) Hillary enters and is seated with a longhaired youth, accompanied by a well-coiffed blonde with intricately put together hair.

We are seeing a video on Jim Brady, Reagan being shot by Hinckley, another lovelorn guy with a gun. Earlier there was a video on Ron Brown (source of Congressman Rangel's remark about royalty). Both are not as slickly done as the San Diego videos were. After some of the lights come back on, Sarah and Jim Brady are on the stage and Jim rises from a wheelchair and walks, slowly, to the podium with his wife.

"Jim," she says, "we must have made a wrong turn . . . this isn't San Diego." It is a *Wizard of Oz* moment, especially since it is entirely staged. We aren't in Kansas anymore. I figure the longhaired boy with Hillary must be a Brady.

Sarah is doing most of the talking. The NRA said no to a seven-day waiting period; in fact "seven hours was too long to wait to buy a handgun." Boos roll up to the podium. "We learned the value of having a president who is really committed to ending gun violence. . . . He understands the difference between a Remington rifle and an AK-47." A voice supplies that it is Scott Brady, now seventeen years old, who sits with Hillary. The NRA is writing another check to the Dole campaign. Jim says a few strained words and is lowered back into his wheelchair.

The Bradys are replaced by an African American, currently a Seattle school superintendent, a former army general, a double-dipper of sorts. "Keep America on the right track for America," he says, harkening to Clinton on the rails. The theme is "It takes a village." Individualism versus helping hands. Children. Education. The general says of teachers, "Give them a hug." The implication being that Dole gave them a slap.

The background behind the speaker's podium is full of darkness. Even the video wall's most constant blue is a darker shade than the lighter blue of San Diego. Some of the testimonies of "citizens" come from satellite podiums, surrounded by darkness. Light versus dark big-time. More Eros versus Thanatos, though, in this case, Thanatos (Dole) is in the white light at the end of the tunnel of the near-death experience and Eros (Clinton) is surrounded by the dancing shadows of the bacchanalian revel.

The voice from above intones, "On this night of American heroes, another American hero, Christopher Reeve!"

Reeve is in a circle of white light, surrounded by darkness, an unsettling funereal display. He's wearing a dark suit, his hair is raven black, his face flattened by the awkward position the wheelchair enforces. But he is a movie star, his is a famous face, somewhat less tortured than James Brady's, but distorted by his calamity nonetheless. He says, with effort, referring to Clinton, "I saw your train go by—I think I can beat it." It brings up his historic persona—Superman—and some Special Olympics undertone, the speedy wheelchair on which he sits. It's painful. We're feeling their pain, all of them, the Bradys, the shot-up cop, the dead Ron Brown, the high school dropout. They are all triumphing, cop, Brady, the new Brown student, Ron Brown's memory, all are overcoming their histories, but Bill has felt all our pain and now the convention is making us feel it, too. All of this seems to be some version of the conversion experience, popularized by the variety of religious channels: I was lost and now I'm found. However you cut it, it does have a bit more going for it than cut the capital-gains tax, or, I started with nothing and now I've got my millions. The Republicans, for all their infusion of Christian Coalition fervor, still can't get the secular out of their economics. The Democrats have found that religion isn't family, it is community. To have religion it does take a village, a church—not just a house.

Reeve talks about family values: "It means that we're all family and we all have value. . . . America cannot tolerate discrimination of any kind." Every word he says has a deathbed-speech quality, which does make it riveting. The *Time* magazine cover of Reeve last week was done with the same skillful promotion of any movie opening (where stars arrange to have themselves on covers of national magazines right before a film's release) and on PBS we have the author (Roger Rosenblatt) of the cover article commenting (how's that linkage, Time-Warner-PBS) and we have been informed by Rosenblatt that at any moment Reeve can go into spasm, so we wait, alerted.

Reeve mentions the Americans with Disabilities Act and how architectural attitudes have changed, and asks for "more funding for research."

Reeve quotes FDR and the camera cuts to Hillary, who does not appear to be channeling.

"America does not let its needy citizens fend for themselves." There's the welfare state in a nutshell. The Democrats versus the Republicans. Reeve says it with great—unfortunate—conviction. The camera is back to Hillary. It is clear now that the very together blonde is Reeve's wife.

The Bradys were Republicans and Reeve broke his neck show jumping and though the Republicans are dropping down in their class pitch (a result of the southernization of the party), Democrats are picking off the rich in need, the well-off who want to do good as well as get well.

Reeve sits in the hot white light surrounded by his darkness. His speech has ended and I watch amazed. What I am impressed by is how good an actor he is. I never thought Reeve was a particularly good actor. The last movie I saw him in before his accident was the 1992 British door-slamming farce *Noises Off,* and he played the romantic dolt rather stiffly. But all his training shines forth here. Who else could do what he did: give this composed, dramatic speech, from a wheelchair, without appearing completely ludicrous? His best role, his greatest performance.

Quickly, too quickly, we're in another cutaway, the bookend of Hillary's, I suppose: this time it's Bill, on his train, in Toledo, Ohio. In the crowd—and it's a boisterous, full-of-life throng, in high contrast to Hillary forlorn, alone, on a curb—there's a sign: "Chelsea in 2016."

"We're on the right track," Bill says, from the track, light shining on him, darkness surrounding. "Thank you for loving America."

The other contrast is startling, too. From the immobilized Reeve to the energetic Clinton. In theatrical parlance, the prez stepped on Reeve's moment. The ebullient Clinton following the mournful Reeve did create atonal music, which might have played well to the young, though—a real MTV moment, dissonance at the maximum.

We're back to the United Center. Ethnically mixed singers, singing something that sounds like off-Broadway. It must be the cast of *Rent,* the hot off-Broadway (Broadway bound) musical of the moment. The arena is back to shadows and darkness, beyond the lights on the singers, dark like the night surrounding Clinton in Toledo.

We're back to PBS commentary. Mark Shields doesn't like the Clinton cutaway, either. Didn't work, he says. Ruined the Reeve moment. Commentary, of course, would ruin the Reeve moment, too, but they are talking about literally a moment. The night had a lot of intervals, but not just then. Perhaps they were afraid that if they didn't cut to Clinton immediately, the networks would have broken away. Give them an inch, etc.

There's a black woman preacher giving the benediction. Her voice is at odds with her appearance, which is slick and youthful, whereas her voice is old, rough. An African American version of Bailey White. She's the Reverend Vashti McKenzie, of Payne Memorial AME Church of Baltimore.

I switch to CNN and catch *Capital Gang*'s show. There's a sign behind the standing commentators: "Republicans Lie." Bob Novak, referring to the blacks who spoke tonight: "At least Colin Powell is a political figure."

It has been an odd night. Except for Hillary and Bill, the speakers have been "citizens." Not so much American dreamers, as those who have awakened from various American nightmares.

Novak also supplies, "The last four Democratic nominees of Chicago have lost."

Larry King Live has part of the Clinton cabinet on his show. Rubin, Shalala, Cisneros, Kantor. Rubin says, "People think we are on the right path." We're going to be lashed to the train metaphor. King asks, but none will admit to resigning and/or staying on in the next Clinton administration. Laura Tyson, unannounced, is already moving back to Berkeley, California, enrolling her child in school there.

Then we get three old childhood friends of Hillary. They think she's swell. In an earlier Hillary/Judy Woodruff interview (recorded during the day), Hillary contended she didn't take Bush's insulting comments as an insult, so she had no comment on them. She said Bush was merely praising his wife.

It was not a helpful evasion since it was, at its core, similar to all the Whitewater prevarications. The public sees one reality; Hillary denies it exists. Even though, in this case, it is supposed to be polite lying, a matter of good manners.

Then King has Mary Matalin, whom he amusingly refers to as a "famous wife."

I hop to the *Tonight Show* and see it is a rerun of a March broadcast. Robin Williams, now one of the Left pundits—mostly comics, famous first—quotes Steve Forbes, "I'm a self-made man," and then Williams says, "Oh, yeah," and starts to make elongating nose gestures.

8/27 The *New York Times* runs a story on Richard Jewell's mom. "Now my son has no real life," she said at a news conference arranged by her son's lawyers. Real life. The accompanying photograph is straight *madre dolorosa,* with microphones.

On the next page of my edition there's a full-page photo by Helmut Newton (advertising underwear I presume) of a model in a black bra, etc, climbing (up, it appears) some industrial ladder, somewhere. Real life. She has strong, vaguely "German" buttocks, encased in black, that Helmut seems to favor.

Then there's an article about Hillary and her speech yesterday to a "women's caucus." In a discussion of all the criticism directed at her and her friend, Eleanor Roosevelt, "I won't say that they paled in comparison to what is said today, but they didn't have as wide a circulation."

Yes, indeed. With all the Hillary-inspired "village" talk, what I don't hear referred to is the older "global village" idea. And we do live in that global village. Just as the avant-grade has been eliminated today (if there are six people doing something no one else is doing, they will be appearing on daytime television telling the world about it and the exclusive cachet evaporates), every despicable crime, whatever the isolated hamlet it occurs in, will be shared by the nation at large. It's hard to leave the global village. What is always startling about survivalists (the recent Montana Freeman group will do as an example) is that they will nonetheless have a satellite dish next to their long cabin. It was a dream of my youth to leave the provinces (the Midwest) and go to the big city (New York City), though now the provinces are both everywhere and nowhere. It's not a matter of not being able to go home again. It's a village none of us can ever leave.

There's an article on Indiana's governor, Evan Bayh, one of the last Democratic midwestern governors, though when he first ran for governor in 1988 he seemed more Republican than his Republican opponent, John Mutz, who wanted to raise taxes to help Indiana public schools. Bayh's win was seen as a prefigurement of Clinton's "victory" in '92. The only similarity is the ability to out-Republican the Republicans on some social issues. If anything, he's Clinton lite.

Indiana's "balanced" budget ran a surplus last year and Bayh disposed of the surplus two ways: he put some of the money in the underfunded state employee pension system, and he rebated, very unprogressively, the state's car-registration fees. As a symbol, at the press conference, he took the tax bill for a Jeep Grand Cherokee and tore it in half. What was most galling was the model he chose. The yuppie tank, born of death-squad chic, now the vehicle of choice for soccer moms going on safari through the jungles of Indianapolis. The sport utility vehicle world is the white response to what whites consider the Africanization of the cities. The old Range Rover of legend was the imperial safari conveyance. In South Bend you have the ne plus ultra of this impulse, people driving around in Hummers (they are manufactured here), heading out to the wealthy subdivisions in their Humvees.

Bayh looks much too much like Gore to be his perfect running mate in 2000. It would be eerie, the similarities between the two couples, with the men's unremarkable good looks of the matchbook Draw Me man and their very blond, fleshy wives.

The *Times* today is a smorgasboard of slice-of-life stories. I skip from A6—Jewell's mom—to A9—besides the Hillary article, there's one of Francis X. Clines's picturesque pieces on the contrasts between the sixties and now; he quotes Rangel saying, "When I die I want to be buried in Chicago so I can stay active in politics"—to All—"Looking for the Passion" is the page's theme piece on the convention—to A12—Bayh and Katharine Q. Seelye (like Francis "X." Clines) who noticed, as I did (on C-SPAN), the sign "Ethnics 4 Dole" at the Illinois Dole picnic—to A13—the cost of the TWA disaster, considerable (similar, or on a much larger scale, to when the Coast Guard aids yachts, etc., gone astray—no one complains of that sort of welfare)—to A15 and a "Reefer Madness" piece (it's alcohol, stupid, when it comes to youthful drug abuse)—to A16, Boston University president (and almost governor of Massachusetts) John Silber's defense of half-million-dollar salaries for university presidents.

Diane Rehm has Dan Rather on, shouting, "No one is watching! No one is watching!" about the convention, echoing "The whole world is watching!" of Chicago 1968.

Rush is going on about "ultraliberals . . . the whiners . . . the victim parade."

Tonight at the United Center there are politicians. Citizens first last night, but these politicians are citizens, too, especially Mario Cuomo, more or less out of a job since he lost his radio show. Mario looks shrunken; it must be age, not just that political power has been sucked out of him. He's not exactly a husk, but giving this speech he does seem, excuse the expression, a shadow of himself.

Since he appears smaller he appears more ethnic, more Italian. His speech starts strangely: "The last time that we all came together, four years ago, this was a very different party. Many Americans, you'll recall, had lost faith in us, and frankly, many Democrats had as well." Four years ago, Mario seems to forget, the Democrats won the presidency for the first time in over a decade. Mario, though, had lost, lost big, in both

'92 and, terminally, in '94. I suppose that's what's playing in his mind. *It must be a different party because I'm no longer in office.*

But he starts rummaging through the past, where he might find what he's looking for: "The truth is that, beginning in the 1970s, the heart of our Democratic Party, America's strong, striving middle class, began drifting away from us."

Why am I not being renominated? is the subtext of Cuomo's historical remarks: "We allowed ourselves to be caricatured by our opponents . . . And those attacks proved to be effective. In 1980, in 1984, millions of middle-class Democrats became Reagan Democrats. And more of them drifted toward the Republicans with Bush in 1988."

And though there is not much logic on display, at least there are some facts, when he goes on, "And then came the stark failure of supply-side that was measured in crushing recession and debt. And by 1992, America decided on a new course and a new captain. And the captain was Bill Clinton."

Captain Bill. It's really hard for Mario to admit he blew it. America decided on a new captain. And that one happened to be that man from Arkansas. But things went to hell in a handbasket those first two years (I paraphrase). "He [B. C., aka "the captain"] fought for universal health care. But we did not succeed. And there followed a new political force. It ascended—the radical Right and the rabid revolutionaries led by Newt Gingrich. And in 1994 that force drove Democrats out of power all across this country, leaving the president standing virtually alone." How's that for taking personal responsibility? A "force" threw Mario out of office; he didn't have much to do with that. "It was a low point in our modern history as a party"—i.e., Mario's defeat—"and it was less than two years ago. Think about it. Now, less than two years later, most of America believes that Bill Clinton and his incomparable vice president, Al Gore, will win the election on November 5. How did things change so dramatically in less than twenty-four months?"

Yes, the Republicans are pondering the same question that plagues Mario. I get kicked out and that bastard Clinton is going to be reelected! How did that happen?!

"What is it? What happened?" Mario says obligingly. Then we get the list. "First, America came to understand and to reject the Republicans' new harshness—policies that would, in effect, punish the least fortunate of us for the sake of the luckiest of us. And at the same time that America was waking up to their harshness, President Clinton found a way to preserve our party's basic principles while erasing the stigmas that had been branded upon our reputation over the years. Who will say today that Democrats are in love with big government and big spending after Bill Clinton has cut the federal government dramatically and brought the deficit down by 60 percent? Who can argue today that Democrats are soft on crime"—or in 1992 when Bill Clinton left New Hampshire to oversee Arkansas's execution of the brain-damaged perp (on the eve of Gennifer Flowers's revelations) and Mario clung to no death penalty in New York till the electorate pulled the switch on him—"after President Clinton banned assault weapons, controlled handgun sales with the Brady law, and made possible one hundred thousand new police? Who will say it today? Who will say antifamily? Who will charge us with being anti–middle class?" And so on. On C-SPAN the camera has cut to a woman wearing a ludicrous cake hat. Then we get to see a woman wearing 1996 glasses, her nose sticking out between the two nines.

About signing the welfare bill: "I've spoken with him [B. C.] and with the vice president, and with Hillary; I know that they all understood and understand the risk. But the president is confident that he can avert this risk by further legislation before children are actually harmed." School uniforms, no smoking! "We need to help the president make this law better, as he has assured us that he will."

Mario is preaching now. Different though from Jesse Jackson earlier. Mario and Jesse could go around doing their own version of the Three Tenors, though they'd be just two. Different kinds of tenors, though operatic still. But Jesse is Pavarotti and Mario barely Carreras. Is it Jesse Jackson or Jessye Norman, of the Olympics? What does it matter. Jesse sings up there, as he did before Mario, but because of its virtuosity, the performance seemed to be from another world entirely. That was its chief oddity, the man of the people seemingly not of this world, otherworldly, as all opera seems. Jesse was great, but he flew above everyone in the auditorium the same way Michael Jordan flies above everyone in the same space.

Jackson was introduced by his son, Jesse Junior, now a congressman from Chicago's South Side (where I was born), having taken over from Mel Reynolds, an ousted corrupt congressman (easy to say, in Chicago, these, and former, days) in a special election. Earlier, Maria "M" Shriver interviewed Jackson large and small and it was eerily similar to the Bush interview. *My sons are the future.* Jesse senior does seem ready to hand over the mantle, and he joins the display of the higher nepotism evident at both conventions, keeping it in the family, the real lodestone of American political life. And his son's race helped keep Jesse on the presidential sidelines. Those of the Clinton sort (no family in public office to speak of) make up a portion of American political life, but just a portion. (Clinton did have a relative or two in Arkansas connected to local politics, but he forged his own national connections.)

Jackson's speech tonight wins the award for being the most different from the prepared remarks (the version printed in the *New York Times*). He sings. It is the vanished-jobs aria. Mixed in are other familiar strands: "The number one growth industry in America, jails. Half of all public housing built in the last decade, jails."

He makes fun of the Republicans, their beach volleyball and Trent Lott's singing group. He doesn't have this voice on his CNN television talk show, or when he's on the radio being interviewed. Only to a crowd. He absolves Clinton of the worst sins of his welfare slashing: "The fight was never about welfare. It was always about jobs and opportunity." He can say, about a number of subjects, "It's a moral obligation," and not sound entirely ridiculous.

"In 1932, Roosevelt did not run on the New Deal platform. . . . Workers at the plant gates, they were the answer." Workers act, the party responds—the old-fashioned way of doing things. Civil rights, the anti–Vietnam War protesters, the people act, LBJ responds.

Jackson talks about his son and his father, the anecdotes both personal and historical. He excoriates: "In your cynicism, don't you walk away from this vote. If you don't vote . . . you do not have the integrity, you are a coward."

He tells a story of his father coming home from the war, disembarking from Washington's Union Station, having had to "sit behind Nazi war criminals because they were white," and then seeing his son being sworn in, becoming a member of the U.S. Congress. "I had one eye on him and one eye on that station." The end is full of rhetorical music: "Stand with . . . Keep that . . . Stand with . . . Keep that," and, finally, "Stand tall, Mr. Clinton. We will win and deserve to win. Keep hope alive."

But Mario's much more down-to-earth. He's in deep sorrow-more-than-anger mode: "Keep your eye on the one big idea: The Republicans are the real threat to the most fundamental of all the ideas, the idea that this nation is at its best only when we see ourselves, all of us, as one family."

There is darkness all around Mario—his jowls are as dark as Nixon's ever were—he seems old, buffeted by circumstance, playing second banana in a way that is almost, it seems, physically painful to him. He concludes with poetry, of the Statue of Liberty sort: "The truth is ageless: Either we make it together, all of us of every faith and color, straight or gay, with or without disabilities, whatever our accent, whatever our past—wherever we are in this great land, whether we are rich, struggling, desperate, either we make it, all of us together, or there is no America worth the gift that God has given this blessed place."

"Four more years, what do you say?" he finishes, and the crowd begins to chant, "Four more years!" Maybe they think Mario does look like Nixon. Snafus follow. Who is running the cameras? I wonder. Rough transitions all around, unlike the practically hitchless San Diego show.

The Soul Children of Chicago, a kids choir full of African Americans, are singing. It's been a banner season, what with the Olympics, for showcasing black entertainers of every stripe all throughout August. Get the work while you can.

I'm now watching CNN and asking myself who these two young women are who are offering commentary. Friends of Chelsea? Their conversation and manner pegs them as two high school valedictorians. Maybe they're local, Chicago products. One's white, Kellyanne Fitzpatrick, and the other is black, Farai Chideya, and in both cases *nomen est omen,* or, at least, they look like their names, Kellyanne being Kellyanne through and through and Farai is the more *farai.* Or Ferrari, voom, voom. They're with David Broder and Jack Germond, who, by contrast, really look like old white guys. The two young women offer their bland conventional wisdom with the annoying, arrogant confidence of youth.

Campaign America '96: The View From the Couch

I learn from the old guys that Cuomo checked with Hillary before checking with Gore about mentioning the welfare bill in his speech.

(Flipping through magazines while I watch, I see the Sidney Blumenthal "arrest" story has made print. In *In These Times* [September 2, page 9].)

Gephardt is now speaking—"So many issues come before us in dry and categorical words, in numbing numbers"—and for a moment I think he is describing his own speaking style. However bad Gore is, Gephardt is worse. The slogan "Families First" keeps ringing through; that is the mantra, meant to counter "American Dream," and to play to the constituency. Why not "Corporations First," "Military First"? "Husband, father, son," is Gephardt's proudest title. In the throng, there are a lot of "America Needs a Raise" signs.

There's more dead space and then we get a parade of representatives and common citizens touting the Families First agenda, a long-planned-for PR campaign. We're hitting this evening's prime time and the national anthem is being sung. I guess the ball game is really going to start now. But it's not Roseanne singing, it's *Aretha!* Who else? She's all in white. A veteran in the crowd is saluting, faces are singing along in pleasure, "and the home . . . aw, wa, wa, wa . . . the brave. . . ."

Gephardt is back (he's convention cochair). He introduces "the incomparable Tipper Gore."

She's keyed up, about to fly off: "Hi, Tennessee. Hi there. My family. Thank you very much. Hello everybody." It's all those "Hi"'s. The effect is a balloon being held down, her nature restrained. Blondness rising. Brightness not falling. She's championing "a civil society," and recalls her fight to protect children from violence and obscenity. "We won voluntary labeling of records and CDs. . . . Then the battle was music." Yes, the early Tipper, scourge of the Mamas and the Papas, Frank Zappa, Quiet Riot. All her efforts—before rap! "But now, thanks to President Clinton and to Vice President Gore . . . the V-chip . . . gives the TV controls back to families." No one to my knowledge has a V-chip in a TV, but it is an odd victory, victory really at sea, or to see, or not to see: a device to curb the tube baby-sitter for absent parents (when not secretly taping an actual baby-sitter to see if she or he is abusing the kids).

We get to see the Gore children. Are they sneaking away from the hotel? Throwing their pop cans in with the paper trash? What about those lightbulb microphones? On or off?

Tipper is now introducing a "woman who . . . is building a more civil society for all of America's families." I'm wondering who is coming out, given the unabashedly laudatory tone. Another citizen with a sad story? ". . . an unwavering voice for those who haven't yet found their voices . . ." and it isn't till she says, a woman "who maintains her grace, dignity, and humor, even while being subjected to the most unimaginable incivility" that I realize she's introducing Hillary.

Hillary appears, and both women, the two blondes, wave, the beauty-queen-on-a-float wave, the hand swiveling from the wrist, the arms still. Hillary comes forward to the podium. She's wearing a lime sherbet outfit, with pearls, multistrand, linked to a medallion. The camera cuts to Ferraro (a delegate or a journalist?), one woman deserving another, seems to be the message.

There's lots of applause for the embattled Clinton, the hometown girl. After many thank-yous, she says, "I am overwhelmed by your warm welcome," delivering the line like Bob Dole saying he's the most optimistic man in America. Oh, yeah. Hillary does not appear overwhelmed. It is now a standing ovation and maybe if this does continue long enough she will be overwhelmed.

She pushes on. She makes jokes about Binti, "the child-saving gorilla. . . . Binti is a typical Chicagoan, tough on the outside but with a heart of gold" and about Dennis Rodman, the cross-dressing, basketball-playing Bull: "I should cut my hair and color it orange and then change my name to *Rodman* Clinton." Hillary telling jokes is a sobering experience.

"I wish we could be sitting around a kitchen table," she says, starting on her themes of children and family. The camera cuts to Chelsea. She has a big smile on her face and the lights bounce off it. Roger's there, too. It's family night all around. The recently published what-Tricky-Dick-told-me-as-I-was-typing book has more about Clinton parenting styles in it than I've found in the number of Clinton biographies I've read. Dick Nixon, who knew something about coldness, thought Hillary was a kindred spirit. I recall the funny Chelsea, "Don't call my mom, she's too busy, call my dad" story that surfaced early in the Clinton administration. I was on a tourist trolley in Washington in '94 with my then four-year-old and the driver/guide claimed he was the source of the story, that a friend of his worked at the Sidwell-Friends school and heard Chelsea say it and he passed it on to a reporter buddy. He seemed to be one of the many Washington underemployed, perhaps a political consultant between jobs, so who knows? Camille Paglia took a lot of heat for saying in March that Chelsea looked like a war orphan at the end of the '92 campaign, but she looks happy this evening.

Hillary's the mom tonight: "[I] was in the hospital as long as my doctor thought I needed to be there. . . . But today, too many new mothers are asked to get up and get out."

My wife and I went to the hospital at eleven at night and left the next day at three in the afternoon with our new son. It was "natural" childbirth, without drugs, in a hospital, but in a "birthing room" which looked like a Motel 6 down on its luck. Complete with a dead fly on the windowsill. Everything went OK, we left. As my wife's doctor said, first-time moms want out as soon as possible, second births they want to stay a week.

We hear about the family-leave bill, the "very first piece of legislation" her "husband" signed into law. As the speech goes on it's clear that Hillary has never before used the word "husband" so often in such a short space.

It's the Village People versus the Rugged Individualists (like rugged Rush). A few weeks ago, the actual Village People came to the local Elkhart County Fair, and even northern Indiana seemed accepting of them. (Our basketball cheerleaders at Notre Dame do their most popular cheer to the tune of "YMCA." It's always odd to watch the homophobic student body cheer along with this gay anthem.) Two men began to dance in the aisles of the Elkart grandstand and they weren't stoned to death.

"We all know that raising kids is a full-time job. . . . Just think what many parents are responsible for . . . lunches, dropping the kids off at school, going to work . . . shopping for groceries, making dinner, doing the laundry . . ."—I'm trying to picture Hillary doing all this—". . . bills . . ."—bills! How about billing records?—"and I didn't even mention taking the dog to the vet." Hillary again sounds like Bob Dole spouting alien ideas: one thing the Clintons haven't done is to buy a picturesque dog, like the Reagans did. Nixon, of course, pandered to the large dog vote.

Hillary's on to an "it takes" refrain. Then, finally, "Yes, it takes a village. . . . And it takes a president."

We see a shot of John Kerry and is it his missus, Teresa Heinz? It takes inheritance to own a village.

She describes watching Chelsea "doing her homework . . . talking to a friend on the phone," and "I think to myself, her life and the lives of millions of boys and girls will be better because of what all of us are doing together." That is what she thinks, what absolves her of—whatever: that the lives of millions of boys and girls will be better since she and Bill are in the White House. "They will face fewer obstacles and more possibilities. That is something we should all be proud of, and that is what this election is all about."

She's thanking us—them, the crowd is standing, the band is playing "Chicago," and it is a hell of a town.

Geraldine Ferraro is interviewed and says not much. Like many in public life, she has perfected a talk-but-don't-say-anything language. Of the five folks engaged in that long-ago New York Senate race and primary battle, three (D'Amato, Sharpton, and Holtzman) have produced recent autobiographies, and Ferraro is doing *Crossfire* not too crossly. Only Bob Abrams has retreated into "private life." And that aspect, the inclination to no longer be in the public eye, is, perhaps, one reason he did not win in '92. Everyone else involved is still jumping up and down, yelling, "Look at me! Look at me!"

Carolyn McCarthy, a candidate for the U.S. House from New York's Fourth District, speaks next. Her husband was killed in the Long Island Rail Road massacre of December 7, 1993. The lunatic who defended himself in court also shot her son: "My son Kevin was partially paralyzed. . . . He is back at work. . . . Kevin, I am very proud of you." More injured children, more wheelchairs, more triumphing with the it-takes-a-village people's help. "But he still spends many hours a day with rehabilitation."

Bob Dole knows about rehabilitation, which is why he is in the unfortunate position he is: the torturous embrace of so much personal contradiction. But what is also so clear from both conventions is the groaning smorgasbord out there in the country that allows both Democrats and Republicans to fill television's plate with whatever meal they want to serve up. Pick a theme: the metaphors and personnel will follow. The lines are long at the employment agencies.

Then we get Victor Morales, candidate for the U.S. Senate from Texas. Jim Lehrer's voice supplies, "He came out of nowhere" to win the primary, whereas the party bosses wanted someone else to be the nominee. He's trying to unseat Phil Gramm, a noble calling, Mr. Stuffed with Ready Cash, the best friend of politicians. Morales speaks in Spanish a bit, then thanks his mom and his teacher. But there's no thanks for Dad. It reminds me of college football and the many African American stars who mug for the camera, saying hi to Mom, never to Dad. "Y porqué no?"

Harvey Gantt is the African American out to defeat Jesse Helms. No thanking moms or dads here since it is a thankless task he's up to. "I will defeat Jesse Helms this November." Gantt isn't eager to trash tobacco, but lighting up will not fire up his race.

Then we get the keynoter, Evan Bayh (Birch Evans Bayh III), to much expectation, though the only expectation he fulfills is mine. It's the quality of his voice. It's the legatee's problem; he might be like Bill Clinton "ideologically," but he didn't have to come out of nowhere to become a backward state's governor.

"I come from here in the heartland . . . a place where the most important title a man can have isn't governor, but husband, father, son." The fruit-is-falling-(not)-far-from-the-tree theme at this convention is hit hard. "My parents didn't start with much, but they believed in the promise of America." Luckily, Evan started with quite enough. We get to see Birch, Susan, and the new twins, her fertility over the years being quite a story in Indiana. Yea, twins! Added to the quite natural desire to have children was the equally natural desire of a politician to have the right sort of publicity photos.

If it's Gore-Bayh in 2000, the physical resemblance will be just too strange. They are not identical, but fraternal twins. Gore better go gray and one of the wives should dye (stop dyeing?) her hair.

I notice that a large arena TV sports closed captioning. I wonder if it is for the hearing impaired, or just to be intelligible over the din. One problem Evan has on TV is his eyes. Is it contacts? But his upper eyelid seems partially shut, hardly any eye at all shows, and this gives him a very sleepy look, which his voice does not overcome.

He boasts of Clinton's record on education, and on Indiana's: "That's just what we did in Indiana. First we balanced the budget, and then passed the largest tax cut in history"—those Jeep Grand Cherokee drivers cheer—"and more support for education every single year," which, of course, is the hollowest vote, since Indiana ranks near the bottom in spending per child, and all it takes is an additional dollar a year to have "more support for education every single year." Indiana is one of the three states that still makes its schoolchildren buy their textbooks. Guess who is most likely not to buy them?

In the crowd the camera pans and I see a "Gore/Bayh 2000" sign. This speech is not going anywhere, but Bill Clinton's '88 convention speech was mocked everywhere, too. Clinton wasn't a national figure, either, in '88. (In one '88 campaign book, *The Quest for the Presidency*, Clinton has one tiny entry, and it is not for his speech.) In Bayh's case, it's not so much playing to the public as playing to the powers in the party—that is, the inner Clinton-Gore world. They owe him.

Susan and the twins are on stage. Susan Molinari, another legatee, only has the one (and, for that matter, a *girl*).

Paul Gigot, after PBS cuts from the family-in-ecstasy scene, says the speech was "a fact sheet from the Clinton-Gore campaign." That there are empty seats in the convention hall is commented on, some visible friction between the Daleys and the Clintons. Mark Shields says that Bayh's effort was a speech "crafted by the reelection committee."

Hadn't anyone ever watched Evan Bayh give a speech before? Even on tape? Could he deliver Indiana for Gore? Possibly. Is that enough? Maybe, quite likely, given his other desirable aspects.

Doris Kearns Goodwin says, commenting on the speech's folksy content, "Daily lives do not soar. . . . The attempt to make everything so personal takes the public out of public life."

Though public life, in a lot of quarters (the Bayh family, especially), is private life.

The young Kristol says Bayh's speech was "a bit flat," thinks the Democrats are "sitting on their lead."

Our historian Beschloss (he and Doris Kearns Goodwin are most clearly in the moonlighting O. J. lawyers mode) comments on the "ambiguity . . . between going left or remaining a New Democrat." That the speech is a "handout for the Clinton reelection committee" is mentioned again. Why is that not a surprise?

Lehrer says, "I want to thank Doris and you all, gentlemen." The white-guy atmosphere is still quite thick, though it tends to be acknowledged only in these last-minute thank-yous.

CNN's *Capital Gang* is doing its stand-up routine. (I'm waiting for Mark Shields, double-dipper extraordinaire, to run in breathless.) Novak is giving Bayh a "C minus, D," for his speech. (I'd stick with a gentleman's C.) Kate O'Beirne, as designated skirt, gets right on Hillary's "my husband, my husband." She points out that Hillary wants to be seen as being "the traditional first lady." Zell Miller from Georgia is the Democratic stooge for the evening, and he offers that exciting conventions make for bad politics, citing the excitement of the Democrats in Chicago of '68 and the Republicans in Houston in '92.

In all the commentary I've heard, nobody has referred to Tipper's performance, pro or con. The CNN wrap-up has edited Hillary's speech: It takes a family, it takes a village, it takes Bill Clinton.

Larry King Live has Evan on. He does better. He's not much of an arena person. Then we have the Jackson Five. Jesse's son Jonathan is wowed that his father was speaking in the House of Jordan, Michael's house. It's truly families first this evening. Jesse says, "In the absence of our enthusiasm what we will be left with is Dole, Gingrich, Trent Lott, Clarence Thomas, Scalia. We deserve better than that." And what does Jesse deserve for not contesting Clinton in the primaries? Then we get Hillary siblings. Tony Rodham says, "The way that we were raised you had to be tough." He allows that his father, Hugh Rodham, "was tough."

C-SPAN's Susan Swain is back with her neutral look, her half smile, half smirk plastered on her cute mug. "Thank you for calling."

8/28 On the *New York Times*'s op-ed page there's a piece on Carter's absence from the Democratic convention. It's good to have a biographer at the ready, full of facts. *The State of Americans: This Generation and the Next* is reviewed. It is a book of statistical tables and commentary,

Richard Bernstein, the reviewer, writes, "by five faculty members at Cornell University"; the book "takes a pessimistic view of the United States even though some other analysts, looking at the same picture, have found room for optimism." One of the optimistic has been Robert J. Samuelson, who has been popping up all year (the yellow smiley face on the cover of the January 8 *Newsweek* was for him) all over, taking on the "pessimists," being defensively the sour purveyor of good news, promoting his book, *The Good Life and Its Discontents*. The Freudian allusion of the title does seem to capture the source of Mr. Samuelson's pique at the gloomy reporting he finds all around him.

The authors of the book under review, according to Bernstein's reading, claim that "education . . . is the most important variable" in predicting economic success. Except when experts disagree, education doesn't seem to be the most important variable.

E. J. Dionne, on Diane Rehm, brings up the courageous Bricklayers' chief, Jack Joyce, calling him "as loyal a Democrat as there is," though obviously not "loyal" enough not to buck the president, since he refuses to back him because Clinton vetoed the partial-birth abortion bill. The discussion is hovering around abortion. It is mentioned that Tony Hall, an antichoice Democrat from Ohio, was allowed to make remarks at the convention. Pollster Jeff Garret says welfare is the divisive issue with Democrats, and abortion is the divisive issue with Republicans.

Rush is going on about taking the dog to the vet. "The real star was the nanny." The nannies Hillary had hired over the years, Rush says, to take care of Chelsea. Hillary had to ask her how it's done. That nanny we know has a dog, Rush says. We know they have a cat, not a dog. Rush is beside himself. It takes a president—there's lugubrious music and crying in the background—to have time to buy Pampers . . . to go to a veterinarian. . . .

A friend and I discuss Clinton's train trip to Chicago. He sees it as deep metaphor. The train, wending its way toward the convention, the egg, the new life of the new Democratic Party ready to explode, when the Clinton sperm train pierces its quivering convention egg membrane. I'm pretty sure we won't hear that imagery from the podium, just the usual we're on the right track, etc.

. On NBC/PBS's convention coverage, Barney Frank is being interviewed by Gwyn Ifill. "You're here with your lover, Herb Moses," she says. I presume that is a first, the first time at a Democratic convention a congressman and his male lover are introduced on the floor to the viewing public. Frank says there has been a backing off from gay issues, but both he and Herb have been with Clinton "physically" the last four years. It's an odd way to put it, but I suppose he means social events, large dinners.

It's reported that an MSNBC poll has Clinton's lead rising from 8 percent to 13 percent.

I catch the last of John Sweeney's speech on C-SPAN. Not even PBS is showing it. Sweeney does not have Lane Kirkland's ease with power, none of the arrogance of being one of the big players in Washington for decades, till the Democrats lost Congress, making it possible for Kirkland to lose the presidency of the AFL-CIO. Sweeney is saying that one's destiny should "not be determined by an accident of birth or by the selection of a partner," and he wants a society which takes care of its old, its disabled, its poor, and its working people, and "leaves the rich to fend for themselves." That word "fend" is showing up at this convention. "God bless American workers," he finishes.

The evening program has been a parade of "Remarks on . . .": Remarks on the environment, on health care, on the budget, on work, on crime, etc., and now we have Governor Roy Romer of Colorado remarking on education.

Maybe he was reading this morning's *Times* review. "What will make the most difference in a child's life?" he asks rhetorically. Education, comes the answer. There's a shot of Gerald McEntee, AFSCME president, and Richard Trumka, secretary-treasurer of the AFL-CIO, in the audience, the Sweeney side of the revolt that removed Kirkland.

Then there's the national anthem, announcing prime time again. "Bombs bursting in air." Billy Ray Cyrus, a white country-boy singer from Kentucky, I believe, is warbling. Not "Achy Breaky Heart," though. He's got a flattop and a retro bad attitude.

By night three I have become accustomed to the shadows, the darkness, the chiaroscuro in the United Center, but still marvel over the contrast with the sunny, shadowless world of San Diego's arena.

Judy Woodruff is hashing things out with three women, one of whom is Bella Abzug. There is also a parade of "the Democratic women of the U.S. Senate" on the platform, Senators Mikulski (Md.), Moseley-Braun (Ill.), Feinstein (Calif.), Murray (Wash.), and Boxer (Calif.). Abzug is wearing a colorful outfit, though she looks like a large bloom that has been drenched with rain. She's combative and dismissive. But no one mentions Carol Moseley-Braun's problems with Nigeria, seemingly brought upon her by Moseley-Braun's boyfriend, the same guy who took her off to Africa before she took her seat in the Senate, making her the last arrival in Washington for the '92 changeover. Man trouble. It's the feminization of the Democratic Party! The feminization of the news!

The empty-seats problem comes up again. They're up high. The camera shows them. The Daleys are upset. But the people are doing the Macarena, some Spanish-import semaphore dance.

I can't remember the Republicans dancing in the aisles in sunny San Diego. Politicians are performing artists, and like all artists they court acceptance and often find rejection. But now Clinton is a success. Everyone finds him important.

I flip over to *Rivera Live* and O.J. appears to be having his own convention. He's speaking to an audience full of friendly faces. Lesser mortals are surrounding him at a podium, fielding questions from the audience. O.J. is with a group of Muslims. Geraldo is aghast. O.J.'s supposed to be under a gag order. O.J. says, "If God is for you, who can be against you?" A woman says to O.J., "Praise the Lord, Brother O.J.."

"This is a small minority of African Americans," Melanie Lomax, a black lawyer, says to Geraldo. It's a church in Washington, D.C., and those on *Rivera Live* are watching it "live." The snake has its tail in its mouth.

I return to CNN, also "live," and find the Dukakises being interviewed by Bernie Shaw. Dukakis looks beat-up and Shaw asks for an explanation and none too gallantly, Dukakis says that Kitty fell asleep at the wheel, their daughter was in the front seat, and Dukakis was in the backseat "grading papers." (My heart goes out to him.) Ten minutes from their house the car runs off the road and crashes. The scent of pills drifts over Kitty.

That Dick Morris is on the cover of this week's *Time* (September 2) and the front page of *USA Today* is mentioned—the consultant as guru, Morris coming out of the shadows. "The Man Who Has Clinton's Ear," the *Time* cover proclaims, showing a tiny Morris leaning next to Clinton's large ear.

Rush said early today that he wasn't going to watch this evening's events. Well he misses Gore putting on a funny/serious face. The effect is weird. It's a version of Newt with newts and beach volleyball. Gore is attempting to counter his stiff image. "Tradition holds that this speech be delivered tomorrow night. . . . Clinton asked me to speak tonight, and you can probably guess the reason why. My reputation for excitement." Then we get the funny face. "This is some crowd. I've been watching you doing that Macarena on Television. . . . I would like to demonstrate for you the Al Gore version of the Macarena." Again, with the face. The crowd dutifully laughs. "Would you like to see it again?" Less laughter.

Everyone who is speaking for more than a couple of minutes starts with jokes. But Gore's speech becomes another extolling of the Clinton record. One in five of the delegates in San Diego was a millionaire; one in four of the delegates here is in a union. Unlike Reeve, Gore would not be able to give this speech from a wheelchair.

It's likely Gore will be the nominee in 2000. He's working at it. Though he is the good Bubba, he's learning from the bad, insofar as the public side of Bill Clinton is rubbing off. Gore's learning how to appeal, to be appealing.

The Democratic heir-apparent presents a major problem for the newly reconstituted Republican Party. The Christian Right and the southern absorption of the Republican Party has staked everything on this election, because if they do not prevail, Gore will be there in 2000 and all their rhetoric will evaporate in the light. It will have to retreat to its coffin. Its power will be gone. The attack on Bill Clinton is focused on character, and when Gore is the candidate the Christian Right will be bereft of language. Gore doesn't appear to be a serial adulterer; he didn't kill Vince Foster, or take money from Jim McDougal, or sire mixed-race children in Arkansas, or lie, or marry Hillary, or the whole long list of Bill Clinton's sins, supposed, or real. Al Gore leaves them speechless and the Republicans will have to find a new target. All they will have is abortion, tree hugging and whatever fund-raising skullduggery shows up later. A vacuum will be created in Republican rhetorical structures and they will collapse. Whether or not the Republicans lose the Congress will be important, because it is likely the presidency will be kept from them until 2008.

What else will be gone? The VFW will be dying out like orders of nuns. Old white guys, a few young ones. Maybe the budget deficit will be helped when that generation does kick off. Less veteran pensions to be paid. The only numerous VFW members will be Vietnam vets in 2008, and they will be in their sixties.

Gore is saying that he and Clinton, unlike Dole, will be a "bridge to the future," though he prefaced that with praise of his character ("a good and decent man"), mentioning his war wounds, praise one usually reserves for the elderly, retirement praise, somewhat backhanded compliments. And, he goes on, "the future lies with the party of hope and the man from Hope who leads it."

He then slams Dole's record: "Senator Dole was there. We remember that he voted against . . . the creation of Medicaid, against the Clean Air Act, against Head Start in the 1960s and AmeriCorps in the 1990s. He even voted against the funds to send a man to the moon. If he's the most optimistic man in America, I'd hate to see the pessimist."

That's what you get for attacking us, Gore's speech proclaims. Then he's on to the Republican Congress: "They passed their reckless plan [and] shut government down twice because they thought Bill Clinton would buckle, . . . cave into their demands. But they did not know the true measure of this man. He never flinched or went to their level, and, of course, he never attacked his opponent's wife."

Yeah, take that. Having all those men attack Hillary, ex-presidents and wanna-bes especially, doesn't play well and just stretches the gender gap.

Bill Clinton as the protector of Medicaid, as protector of a woman's right to choose via Supreme Court appointments—"the next three justices," Gore says, making me wonder if resignations have already been unofficially tendered. "They want someone in that Oval Office who will rubber-stamp. . . . But we won't let them." Gore pronounces "won't" "want," somewhat unsettlingly.

"You can judge a president by the enemies he is willing to make."

There's a silk purse/sow's ear argument: like the "liberals" he's willing to anger by signing the welfare bill.

Gore talks about children, absolving parents of "monitoring every second that child watches" TV, thanks to the V-chip (and so V-day becomes, at the end of the twentieth century, a chip), and then he begins to tell his personal story, about his sister Nancy. She started smoking at thirteen, Gore says. I try to picture that. A thirteen-year-old girl smoking back then (and like Bob Dole, I was there back then—at least with Nancy) would, ah, stand out. Did Mom and Dad complain? Was she smoking behind the schoolhouse with other fast girls? A lung is removed at forty-five. Gore is telling this story slowly. Dole might be poetic only by accident, but Gore needs to have emotion wrung out of him deliberately, and this story is told with some cost: between decorum and perceived necessity, to show he is human, to connect. Ah, connect. This public display of private ambivalence seems to set up more torture than the recollection of his sister's early death. He knows there's something terrible about his use of it. "Until I draw my last breath, I will pour my heart and soul into trying to protect young people from the dangers of smoking."

He commends Clinton: "It took courage for Bill Clinton to take on the tobacco companies." So much for the evil empire within; after the public banished smokers to the fringes of society, the loading docks of warehouses, the prez thinks it prudent to go after tobacco companies. And Gore supported them until his campaign conversion. And he exhumes his dead sister as the rationale.

Martin Luther King Jr. comes into the last paragraph. He's replaced Gandhi as icon, second only to Lincoln for allusion in speeches.

Gore's off, Tipper's on stage, and the kids. One daughter has a very short skirt on. I wonder if she was the one always attempting to elude the Secret Service on the Truro vacation.

Christopher Dodd nominates President Clinton, saying, along the way, "Stop attacking the president's family!" Families First is the convention's theme, but the irony is apparent.

Chelsea jumps up and claps, though her visage is somber—mom Hillary smiles as if surprised, then sits back.

The roll call of the states begins, with—Arkansas! An older woman with a lot of blond hair casts the first forty-seven votes for Bill Clinton. Roger is standing behind her. Could he possibly be a delegate, or does he just want to be on camera?

I visit MTV and they have been visiting Chicago's West Side and are camped outside of George's record store, where a "Choose or Lose" concert is in progress in the vacant lot next to George's store. Lots of vacant lots to choose from in the neighborhood. George is interviewed. A big African American, George likes being a father figure to a lot of young fatherless kids. A man in the street is asked what should—or does—the community give back to George for all his involvement with the community.

"Cash," the guy says. "Cash for the tapes you buy."

MTV's commercial breaks seem longer and the ads seem shorter and more numerous. Hard to tell if they are show or commercial, since MTV's styles are interchangeable.

Tabitha Soren is back, showing a lot of leg. She mentions the temporary sound tower collapsing on the crowd at Michigan City, Indiana, today (a local story, it seems, except for Tabitha taking note) at a rally at the end of Bill's excellent train ride. Our local stations have been playing it all evening. The crush of people toppled an unstable audio tower, causing some serious injuries, though it was put out that injuries were minor, which they weren't, so it wouldn't be too much cold water poured on Clinton's arrival (which had yet to happen). The campaign did get their good pictures: Clinton looking happy, shaking hands with the party faithful who got tickets to be near the rope line, kids up front. But afterward, the crowd grew surly. People weren't allowed to leave for an hour and a half and they realized they were the herded-cattle extras for the cowboy movie. "A Secret Service screwup," one Notre Dame professor I recognized in the crowd called it on our hometown news.

Back to the roll call. I notice each state has an upbeat statement on how many new jobs have been created, in contrast to the Republicans roll-call refrain of how much money each family would save by Dole's pie-in-the-sky tax cuts.

We're now looking at Clinton flying to a Chicago park in his helicopter. He gets off, giving a perfunctory salute to the soldier at the bottom of the steps. Oh, what history lives in that perfunctoriness! Clinton doesn't look happy now at all. I wonder what has transpired since he had his happy face on in all the Michigan City film I saw on the local news. Hillary and Chelsea have been brought to the landing site and he embraces them.

John Glenn casts Ohio's votes for Clinton, saying he "put us on track for the twenty-first century." Everything is metaphor and no one shies away from cliché. I was once in the company of rich Ohioans in Columbus and one made a crack about Glenn: "I'd like him to be my pilot." The implication was that was all that he was qualified for. Everyone laughed, except for me, since I didn't own a plane.

Larry King Live has McGovern and Dukakis, two losers separated by a lot of history. McGovern has been in the media world for the last few months because of his book, *Terry*, about his daughter who died frozen in the snow, after collapsing drunk in an alley after leaving a bar. It is the personal triumphing over the political, though McGovern is trying to make it political, or at least social, hoping to bring attention to the plight of alcoholics, not a subject left too obscure. It is odd though that McGovern uses his daughter's death as his own public resurrection. As if he wanted to say "I'm sorry" for a whole number of things.

Dukakis's injuries are commented on again, Kitty driving, etc. He talks about finding distasteful the wall between him as a candidate and the "people." He says it is worse for a president. He calls the White House "the crown jewel of the federal prison system." Hillary and Bill would consider Gary Aldrich (*Unlimited Access*) to be one of the snitches of that prison system.

8/29 I catch a few minutes of Rush today and he is sounding judicious, which means something really *bad* has happened to the Democrats, so bad Rush doesn't have to play it up. I hear Dick Morris's name. The *New York Post,* evidently, has run a scandal story. Morris on all fours. Morris letting a "hooker" listen in on his phone calls to the prez. Rush sounds sober. A sad moment for democracy. Morris told his call girl that Bill Clinton was "the Monster" and Hillary was "the Twister," and gave her Hillary's speech, Gore's speech, told her about life on Mars before it was released. Rush intones sardonically, "Character doesn't matter."

A caller thinks Gore's sister story was "phony." Rush says it shows how empty the Democrats campaign is. He complains that Gore went to more private schools than Newt has ever been in. The real class war rears up in Rushworld. He says Gore's sister died in '84, but in '88 Gore was still telling tobacco people, I'm one of you, I picked it, stacked it, etc.

A caller says the convention is "the best performance of *Les Misérables* I've seen." Rush calls it not McCarthyism but "Gephardtism." The Right is flexible in how it uses its past.

Rush is back to the Morris story. Even he seems to believe there are some sinister forces at work with the timing of the Morris story. Rush asks, "Why should Morris resign? I don't understand the hypocrisy here."

A caller is mad about John Sweeney—says Sweeney wants "class warfare." Sweeney is the most honest, Rush says, agreeing. It's hard to keep all the different classes of class warfare straight when listening to Rush: Newt versus Gore, labor versus management, the haves versus the have-nots.

Rush goes to an ad for Woodman chain saws, an ad he does himself. Fully assembled, a large muffler, good "if you want to use a chain saw for recreational purposes." Is this comedy? I suppose it is, being funny to sell to the happy-go-lucky chain-saw world.

By early evening the Morris story has spread throughout the media irrigation system and America is soaking with it: a forty-something (!) call girl Morris had been keeping busy for a year at the Hotel Jefferson (wild Sixteenth Street!), photographs (no denying it now), Morris denouncing "yellow journalism," which shows he doesn't know much journalistic history. (The phrase came about since the actual paper the jingoistic newspapers used was yellow.) He won't dignify the story with a reply. No wonder Clinton looked so unhappy coming off the helicopter last night. That was the news he must have gotten. Morris has resigned (I guess). Here's the rain on the Democrats' parade. The Macarena metastasized, the trail derailed.

No one likes Morris, so he's getting beat up everywhere. The sleazebag punching bag. Luckily, he has Trent Lott and other Republicans in his Rolodex, so he is being treated as a "consultant," a species of bottom feeder so low nothing can squeeze beneath it.

The Republican convention at least had a purpose: to try to resuscitate

Dole's campaign. The Democratic convention is without purpose. And any superfluous event is inviting disaster. Dole's polls were lowest and Clinton's were highest in early August. The Republicans had only one place to go: up. The Democrats had only one place to go: down. I was waiting for something bad to happen and Morris appears to be it.

Families First, indeed. The emperor's man wasn't wearing any clothes. And now everyone gets to notice. The bad news is that it ruins the convention; the good news is that there is only one day left. Clinton's speech tonight will be another "test" of his "character"—he only seems to be tested in his ability to spring back from personal troubles. It's not the Cuban missile crisis; it's Gennifer, or Paula Jones, or Dick Morris, that tests the mettle of the man from Hope. As a young man, his tests of character were personal: the curious thing about the draft as crucible for a generation (rather than the war itself as crucible) is that it was often a very private trail. Unless one chose to make it public, to burn one's draft card, to protest and go off to jail (and some, thankfully, did), it was private, alone, and alienating. Bill Clinton's clash with the draft was private (or, at best, semiprivate). The famous letter, one must remember, was, until it surfaced (and Clinton thought it destroyed), a private form of communication. Clinton dealt with individuals, though I wonder how many of his peers participated in discussions with him about it. Still a private circle, though, and Clinton did seem most involved with the one friend who did become a draft resister and who eventually committed suicide.

His public testings were running for office, winning and losing those battles, and then the biggest battle, the '92 run, showed him picking himself off the ground and continuing to battle, Rocky '92, enough to impress that other publicly embattled president, Richard Nixon.

Mayor Daley is being interviewed and asked about Morris and he is very uncomfortable. Families First at a holiday dinner and here's the black sheep throwing up on everyone. Daley's Irishness really seems pronounced, since he is so uncomfortable with the sexual content of the scandal.

On the convention floor we see Patrick Kennedy, the recently minted Rhode Island congressman, introducing his father. I recall the delightful PBS documentary, *Taking on the Kennedys* (May 28), on young Patrick's

'94 race, a counterpart to '92's documentary *The War Room,* except the filmmakers seem to have had more access to the Republican challenger than did *The War Room's* crew. (*The War Room* had access [limited] only to Carville and Stephanopoulos.) Tim Russert brings up the old quote, "Joe Kennedy said, 'I won't pay for a landslide,' " apropos of Patrick's victory.

Ted comes out and there's more embracing ("Want to go out for a drink later tonight?"), and Kennedy says, echoing the unadvertised (Family Ties First?) theme of the week but also his own thoughts, "In the great passages of my public life, on the great issues of our national life, I have spoken before to other Democratic conventions, but what I feel in my heart tonight can hardly be expressed. It is a father's sense of pride and joy and honor."

Both conventions have been displays of raging nepotism. I wonder if it's possible for Roger to run for governor of Arkansas.

"It seems like only yesterday that I was helping Patrick with his homework," Senator Kennedy says. Neglecting to add "and taking him to bars in Florida." "Now . . . he's writing the legislation." Yeah, it does give you pause.

"When I think of the attacks on [Hillary]," Teddy says, "from the likes of Newt Gingrich and Rush Limbaugh, I recall what was said of another great Democrat long ago. We love her for the enemies that she has made." That notion is getting a lot of play. "No one in this convention hall has to point to the exit signs to tell the prejudiced, the extremist, and the intolerant that they are not welcome here . . . We do not offer the illusion of inclusion"—sounding like Jesse Jackson of old—"while forcing a vice president nominee to betray his own conscience and endorse a law that would deny equal opportunity to women and minorities." Is that Clinton? No, Kemp. Then Kennedy does his own RV bumper sticker, à la Kay Bailey Hutchison, describing the Republican platform: "education-cutting, environmental-trashing, Medicare-slashing, choice-denying, tolerance-repudiating, gay-bashing, Social Security–threatening, assault rifle–coddling, government-closing, tax loophole–granting—there's more." And there is. The contrast, meant or not, was the same theme of individual (Bill Clinton bad) versus the collective (Republicans' Congress trashing groups) that has been the trope of both conventions.

During the long recitation the camera shows a sign: "Equal Rights for Newt Gingrich's Sister." Kennedy's hair is smoother this evening, so he looks less dissipated, not quite a banker, but not such a hell-raiser either.

Discussion ensues on PBS. Another Kennedy-era figure, Ted Sorensen (who does look like a banker), says, "On TV old-fashioned rhetoric seems too heated." On political rhetoric as a whole, he holds, "Frankly, I think the standard has declined." From an old speechwriter ("Ask not," etc.) the remark seems self-serving. It's odd in this electronic age how the name of Marshall McLuhan doesn't come up much or at all. The medium is the message. Cool and hot. So when Sorensen says his "too heated" remark, he is echoing what McLuhan had made a cliché a quarter of a century ago (Sorensen's heyday).

The Pew research and polling fellow, Andy Kohut, equates the brouhaha that followed the Dan Quayle selection for veep with the Morris story. Bush still got his postconvention bounce is his point.

Linda Bloodworth-Thomason is being interviewed wearing a black Chinese tunic. She produced the new Clinton video, to be unveiled shortly. She's definitely FOB and FOH. Her confidence is so substantial it's derisive. In her tunic she resembles Jean Houston of Eleanor Roosevelt fame. FOBs and FOHs were so important because after the provincialism of exile in Arkansas only old acquaintances could be trusted in Washington. Everyone new is suspect after you're famous, and being governor of Arkansas doesn't make you quite famous enough. But the presidency! New Agers like Jean Houston offer a simulacrum of deep thought. But they are essentially valets, spiritual advisers to the wealthy and powerful. Yet instead of seeing to the manners of the wellborn, they provide guidance in moral philosophy. They turn into soul valets.

Linda Bloodworth-Thomason isn't that sort of hanger-on. She's a hanger-on, been there, done that. She says she doesn't feel attacked by Washington or the press corps. If they were "any more loving . . . I would have to get a restraining order." However she did act offended when asked if she was being paid for her work. "I'm from Hollywood," she said, as if that explained why there was no need to take any money. "I don't get paid for the film." To the question "Will you do the inaugural again?" she replies, "My husband is involved in the campaign."

The strangest interview is with Bob Squier. It turns out he and Morris ran the "November 5" group, which did "strategy, polling, production" for the campaign. Squier has been all over the tube, bouncing from one show to another. He's effervescent in the Jack Kemp mode, an obvious charmer; the good cop of the November 5 group, doubtless. He and Mary Matalin appear often on CNN, more examples of the O. J.-ification of the news, people employed in the business being the commentators on the business. It's self-interest cubed.

Squier claims that if Clinton is elected his victory will be "a monument to the strategy he [Morris] laid out." And, by reflection, what Squier was part of laying out. Having the business partner of the disgraced be so buoyant is the disgraced's own life jacket. The sleaze factor is limited, the oil leak contained. It's Morris-centric and doesn't even splash on the upbeat Bob Squier.

Squier does seem like the Gotti of the recent HBO *Gotti* film. The behind-the-scenes guy who doesn't want to be behind the scenes. The old guys were out of the public eye and the Gotti or Squier sort can't get enough of it. Morris had resisted, since he didn't come off that well in public, unlike his more suitable partner. When she gets to sit with Squier, Mary Matalin calls the convention a "sobfest." Regarding Morris, she says she feels for "the wife."

Tom Brokaw on NBC says Linda Bloodworth-Thomason grew up in the same town as Rush Limbaugh (Cape Girardeau!). Their fathers were political rivals.

Joe Kennedy is nominating Al Gore. He reminds the throng that his father's (RFK's) last public words were "On to Chicago!" There's a shot of Ethel, looking older, smaller. "As we know, he never did get to Chicago." The Kennedys tonight are as ubiquitous as Reagan's entourage was at the Republican convention. JFK is still the president Clinton wants most to share the stage with.

Joe Kennedy quotes, or adapts, "Seamus"—no last name—Seamus Heaney, the new Nobel laureate. "In spite of all we sail beyond ourselves, and over and above the rafters aching in our shoulder blades the give and take of branches in our arms. Those lyrics always remind me of my dad." Ethnic pride thickens in the United Center.

The mayor of Atlanta, Bill Campbell, follows, claiming that in the old Fourth Ward of Atlanta, they are "now working to realize Dr. King's dream, and we did it with Al Gore's help," and that Gore is "a great Macarena dancer."

Another wheelchair is on the platform, filled with a pretty young woman, Michela Alioto. It's two for two in accidental paralysis: Reeve jumping horses, she, the former San Francisco mayor's granddaughter, from a skiing accident, two upper-class avocations bringing them down. She is effusive about Al Gore. "We really talked. He looked at me, not through me." Given her looks, not a difficult thing to do. "And soon someone told him he had to move on. Al Gore got up and said that he'd come back. . . . He did come back. And he listened." She is now a congressional candidate in California, more keep-it-in-the-family politics. Gore is, Michela says, "a very cool guy." Her ski accident happened when she was thirteen; she's now twenty-eight.

Kathleen Vick comes out again, an older woman with ageless hair, and Gore is quickly nominated the veep. Alabama forecasts the "American train of progress moving into the twenty-first century," and yields to Tennessee. "The ayes have it," Gephardt intones and the deed is done. The woman is gone. Now we hear the Macarena song and the camera shows the signers signing it: they actually dance the best, because these signers (all women—is signing a feminized profession?) really know how to gesture meaningfully. In a post-literate age, we all need signers.

Gore comes out to the tune. "Thank you very much," he says, and he makes his Macarena joke again: "Want to see me do it again?" He thanks his nominators: "Congressman Joe Kennedy of Massachusetts, a leader for today and a leader for tomorrow. Atlanta mayor Bill Campbell, who just hosted the best Olympics ever." Where is Richard Jewell? "And my former aide and friend, the next U.S. representative from the first district of California, Michela Alioto. And finally, to President Clinton, thank you for giving me the opportunity to serve our country. Working beside you is an inspiration. Tipper and I treasure our friendship with you and the first lady."

He's shortly off and the wave of gratitude ebbs. Then we get Linda Bloodworth-Thomason's video: *A Place Called America*. Clinton again looks oddly like Dole in his interview video (since so much of the convention is reactive, I wonder if this was shot after they saw the Dole video; but it appears to be the same setting *60 Minutes* used). Clinton's in an open shirt and looks like he's in a regular house. If it's the White House, it's not made obvious. Bill says there were "a lot more funerals to this job than I thought there would be." We see a montage of funerals, deaths, Oklahoma City. Mourning in America. It's a signal fact that Clinton's power of seduction is enhanced by grief. He has worked the combination of sex and death, of Eros and the skull, to his advantage. His vitality and his sympathy, each equally large.

We see in the video Hillary's mom taking an odd swipe at her late husband, while she praises Bill and Hillary's relationship, fixing on her daughter's good fortune: "I wish I had someone to bounce off these ideas." Hillary's bargain, a meeting of minds. We then get to Chelsea— "I was kind of bursting with pride when Chelsea went to Pakistan"— and see Tyler, Roger's boy, and then Bill talks of wanting "civility" in politics. "One of the things that I do not like about public life is that it is consistently too partisan and too personally harsh." He seems to be pleading his own self-interest. "You know, most of us my age anyway were raised in an environment where our parents would have whipped us," he says confidently—and strangely: isn't that "personally harsh"?

Clinton talks about Dole being "terribly wounded in World War II," thereby reminding everyone again of Dole's generation. We see more dead Israel's Prime Minister Rabin, fighting in Northern Ireland. Clinton speaks of a "little girl in Northern Ireland, I will never forget" (who we've heard saying, "My first daddy died in the Troubles. It was a sad day"); "she introduced me to two young men, one was Catholic, one was Protestant."

There are more Ireland scenes, then Ellis Island scenes. After those he says, "I am convinced more than ever in my life that the best days of this country are still ahead of us." Then he quotes Carl Sandburg: "Nothing happens without a dream." A voice from the video says: "America has always been not only a country, but a dream."

Yes, a dream. The American Dream is a dream. Sanctioned wishful thinking. And Ms. Bloodworth-Thomason's video has various presidents and candidates talking over pretty pictures. Iwo Jima. Michael Jordan. The Berlin Wall. Cal Ripken. ("Go, baby, go.") Statue of Liberty. We are back to a clip of Clinton, finishing, "And I still believe in a place called America."

The video ends. Muhammad Ali is sitting next to Hillary. No Elie Wiesel this time, though Muhammad Ali is the victorious battler, however poignantly impaired now. A voice (Lehrer's?) says Clinton will speak for about an hour. Oh, Bill, say it ain't so.

An announcer says: "Ladies and gentlemen, the president of the United States, William Jefferson Clinton."

My question, and others', has been how Clinton will get through this speech, cut through the sulfurous smoke that the Morris revelations have belched up. The coronation, the celebration, the curtain of conviviality has been torn down and behind it we have the Republicans' Clinton exposed, Kay Bailey Hutchison's bumper-sticker president, Paula Jones's president, the Wizard of Oz. And it all falls on him. No one in his administration, other than Hillary, is identified with Morris. Morris is Clinton's hunchback in the tower, is his Banquo's ghost, and there Morris is, taunting his king at the banquet.

Many thank-yous and much applause. He finally says, with just a trace of real impatience, "I can't shout over you." You feel that he wants to shout "Shut UP!" "Mr. Chairman, Mr. Chairman, Mr. Vice President, my fellow Americans, thank you for your nomination. I don't know if I can find a fancy way to say this, but I accept." We're going folksy, it seems. Fancy, though, equals Morris. We're not going that way. "So many, so many have contributed to the record we have made for the American people. But one above all, my partner, my friend"—I'm waiting for a shot of Hillary—"and the best vice president"—!—"in our history, Al Gore."

Well, well.

"I love Chicago for many reasons. For your powerful spirit, your sports teams,"—he was "watching football" when automatic-weapon fire raked the White House—"your lively politics, but most of all, for the love and light of my life, Chicago's daughter, Hillary. I love you," he finishes, and it isn't entirely clear if that is personal (Hillary) or public (Chicago).

"I began a train ride to make my way to Chicago through America's heartland." The train ride I recall is Bobby Kennedy's funeral train. Mourning in America. Earlier, when Linda Bloodworth-Thomason was interviewed, she boasted that the train ride was her husband Harry's idea, something to make up for the travel-office fiasco, doubtless (though he's still in the transportation area).

"We are on the right track to the twenty-first century. Look at the facts. Just look at the facts: 4.4 million Americans now living in a home of their own for the first time; four hundred thousand women have started their own new businesses." Yeah, and Dick Morris has been a big supporter of that.

"Look at what's happened." Yeah, look. "We have the lowest combined rates of unemployment, inflation, and home mortgages in twenty-eight years." And that will help him be reelected.

"We are making democracy work. . . . We have come a long way. We have got one more thing to do." We wait. "Will you help me get campaign finance reform in the next four years?"

The corporate skyboxes explode, shards of glass rain down. (No, not really.) The camera does cut to ABC's honcho Roone Arledge, though. He's not smiling. It's Clinton's last race and he wants to change the rules for those who come behind. Perhaps Morris suggested that line.

More right-track-to-the-twenty-first-century rhetoric chugs along, the little engine that could. Clinton seems tired but he intends to get through it. But there is no sparkle. Morris robbed him of that. Clinton's face is taut, muscles engaged; he's holding a whole lot in. He is rising to the occasion, but the occasion, alas, is just another speech.

We see Carl Lewis, Candice Bergen applauding. "On welfare, we worked with states to launch a quiet revolution." And it is quieter in the arena; some are sitting on their hands.

Clinton's voice is dry. He offers his tax cuts: "I propose a fifteen-hundred-dollar-a-year tuition tax credit a year for Americans, a Hope scholarship for the first two years of college to make the typical community college education available to every American." He drinks water during a period of applause. "Every working family ought also to be able to deduct up to ten thousand dollars in college tuition costs per year for education after that. . . . I want to say here before I go further that these tax cuts and every other one I mentioned tonight are all fully paid for in my balanced-budget plan, line by line, dime by dime, and they focus on education."

But Clinton introduces the saddest paradox, his version of JFK's sending a man to the moon, when he says, "Tonight let us set a clear national goal. All children should be able to read on their own by the third grade."

He must be thinking of Arkansas. All teachers should be able to read on their own. Middle-class tax cuts! The problem is the bottom, not the middle. Not the folks who get off welfare, but those who stay on. And what to do with children who can't read on "their own" by third grade. Tough love for the nation. If that's the national goal, everything is worse than we have dared admit.

"I know that Hillary and I still talk about the books we read to Chelsea when we were so tired we could hardly stay awake" I sympathize with that. There are many unionized delegate-teachers out in the arena and by these comments (40 percent of eight-year-olds "cannot read as well as they should") he's agreeing with Dole's charges ("losing the war"), yet he asks them—about having children learn to read by third grade—about sending "volunteers" into the schools, "Will you help us do that?" and still there is applause.

I think of O. J.'s semiliterate "suicide" note, Nicole's semiliterate letters to O. J., all the evidence there is of never learning, at whatever time, of whatever generation.

From schools to the budget, one that "preserves Medicare, Medicaid, education, the environment," to the government shutdown—"the blackmail threat of a shutdown of the federal government"—high point of the low point of 1995–96. Then it's violence, the Bradys, victims' rights, then "Drugs nearly killed my brother when he was a young man. And I hate them. He fought back. He's here tonight with his wife, his little boy's here, and I'm really proud of him." Roger, poster boy of the Betty Ford Clinic. It takes a president. Roger is to Billy Carter as Bill Clinton is to Jimmy Carter, at least in the PR sweepstakes. "Drugs are deadly. Drugs are wrong. Drugs can cost you your life." OK. "The very first person I ever saw fight that battle was here with me four years ago and tonight I miss her very, very much. My irrepressible, hardworking, always optimistic mother did the best she could for her brother and me, often against very stiff odds." I'm struck by his slip, "her" brother instead of "my" brother. Unless Virginia had some hell-raising brother she took under her wing. Clinton must be tired; he's still putting up his rigid front, but his eyes aren't happy.

He's on to families and smoking and health insurance (all the stops on this speech train), to abortion: "but believe as a matter of law that this decision should be left to a woman, her conscience, her doctor, and her God." The environment stop: "Our children should grow up next to parks, not poison." Haiti, Bosnia, Israelis and Palestinians, Europe, Latin America, North Korea, and on and on the train chugs. Terrorism and airport security. Back to Bosnia, the Middle East, Northern Ireland, Northern Ireland—he does say it twice—Burundi. "What do these places have in common? People are killing each other and butchering children because they are different from one another. . . . They hate their tribe, their ethnic group, their religion. We have seen the terrible, terrible price that people pay when they insist on fighting and killing their neighbors over their differences."

His face has slowly been softening during the speech's second half. He's getting through it and that realization relaxes him. "We still have too many Americans who give in to their fears of those who are different from them. Not so long ago, swastikas were painted on the doors of some African American members of our Specials Forces at Fort Bragg."

Ah, yes, white supremacists in the armed forces, Timothy McVeigh, etc. It's a curious yoking of symbols. Not that the Special Forces are Nazis, but neo-Nazis are using anti-Semitic symbols to taunt blacks. Confusion everywhere.

"So, look around here. Look around here. Old or young, healthy as a horse or a person with a disability that hasn't kept you down, man or woman, native American native born, immigrant, straight or gay, whatever,"—a reference to Bob Dole, that whatever—"the test ought to be I believe in the Constitution, the Bill of Rights, and the Declaration of Independence."

Home stretch appears to be in the air (it's been at least an hour), and I find it appropriate that the event that repositioned Clinton's Presidency, and the mood of the country, as much as, if not more than, Hinckley's shooting of Reagan, the bombing of the Oklahoma federal building, should be permeating the air.

"The real choice is whether we will build a bridge to the future or a bridge to the past," he says, hammering the metaphoric last nail in Dole's career coffin. Too old, too much of some other time. There's no going back. I've seen the future, and it is me.

"Let us in short do the work that is before us. So that when our time here is over, we will all watch the sun go down as we all must, and say truly, we have prepared our children for the dawn."

He still believes in a place called Hope and a place called America. I am still reeling from the all the death imagery in the sentence before: mourning in America again, except it is linked to Dole, Dole in the grave, dawn approaching, the vampire at rest. Our children prepared. Weird stuff.

"Thank you. God bless you." The politician as priest. "And good night."

There are chants of "Four more years" and the band Chicago singing its hit, "Only the Beginning." One hour and six minutes, Lehrer reports and the fact that 1,400 pounds of Mylar confetti are dropping from the heights of the United Center. Mylar looks best on television, glinting in the lights.

Commentators comment: Haynes Johnson calls the speech, "safe," "modest," emphasizing Clinton is "the bridge to the future." The boy Kristol says Clinton lost the audience in the middle of the speech, but at two-thirds through, regaining it at the "straight or gay" portion. Beschloss thought it a "missed opportunity."

The cast of Les Misérables is singing tonight (not Kristol, Beschloss, etc.) down on the stage. No one says anything about Clinton's demeanor. He got through it, which seemed its high moment. Gergen calls it "prose not poetry," and thought it "lasted to the twenty-first century." Another speechwriter appraising the competition. The politics of children filled the speech, it's decided. Gigot says it had a lot of "we feel your pain." Kristol thinks the convention was successful for Clinton, but not the Democrats. Doris Kearns Goodwin, the lone woman among the white guys, says something genderized: It was a "portrait of a marriage, not a presidency." Mark Shields adds the second quarter's 4.8 percent GDP growth is "the best news of the week."

On the platform everyone is now doing the Macarena. The dancing signers continue to be eloquent. Gergen does bring up the disappearance of Dick Morris, but PBS is not going to rehash that material; however, others take up the slack. On the *Capital Gang* at CNN, it's mentioned that NBC showed Gennifer Flowers's picture during the Clinton video.

And on the *Tonight Show*, Jay Leno makes cracks about the White House being Mustang Ranch East. Jay imagines Morris's hooker listening in on the president's conversation, and she interrupts, saying, "Bill?" And the president says, "Sherry, is that you?"

Leno contends that Sherry charged more than two hundred dollars an hour when she had to listen to Al Gore's speeches. Leno holds up a doctored book: *It Takes the Village People,* picturing that happy crew of singers.

Back to CNN. Larry King has George Stephanopoulos. He doesn't look too sad discussing Morris. It's a human tragedy, feels for the family, etc. Stephanopoulos can't keep from smiling, but he finally gets on message. How moving the president's speech was, the usual blah blah blah.

Chicago's not burning, but everyone's doing the Macarena. The auditorium isn't clearing out as fast as it did in San Diego (out there it was as if someone had yelled "Fire!" or "Free Drinks!"), but it's over and only Dick Morris had been lashed to the train tracks, but it did run over him. The Republicans are doubtless from Mars and the Democrats are definitely from Venus.

8/30 Rush is going on about the convention being a video on marriage. Mary Matalin had made that point, too, last night, as did Doris Kearns Goodwin. As an attack point, it doesn't do much. Both conventions, the whole campaign, seem like enormous make-work projects that keep a lot of overeducated (and some undereducated) people employed. All those taxpayer matching funds, those corporate "donations," the Keynesian engine of Phil Gramm's ready cash, buying TV time, hundreds of technicians, consultants, carpenters, painters, real estate, on and on, every four years it heats up the economy and simmers the rest of the time, the nonpartisan Big Engine That Does, a happy combination of the private and public sectors even the Republicans don't seem to complain about.

Morris and Clinton compete for space in the news, Morris being Hyde and Clinton being Jekyll. Luckily, the "revelations" didn't come at the beginning of the convention. Its momentum carried it through.

All news is equal insofar as it shares the same space and time. If Morris gets as much space in print and time on the air it is equal to Clinton and the convention, if they get the same amount. It's a bit different from form over content; it's space and time over content.

I was struck by a line Norman Mailer used about the first Apollo moon landing, which turned up in the 1969 *Life* magazine articles he did, and not, I think, in the book he finally wrote, *Of a Fire on the Moon*. It was the sort of language that stuck with me back in 1969: Mailer was talking about the Herculean accomplishment of sending men to the moon and the public's rather nonchalant response to it. His equation was: "the magnitude of the event and the paucity of the response."

Given the changes in information dispersal, media in general, since then, the phenomenon has reversed itself. It is now a matter of the paucity of the event and the magnitude of the response.

I have always thought that the sixties (and early seventies, through Nixon's resignation) made hypocrisy harder to achieve in the culture. But the Reagan years certainly restored it to its honored place in the culture. Miss Manners achieved the social version of this. Yuppies wanted a certain facade to be maintained, so it was brought back. Clinton is not immune to hypocrisy's charms. He never forsook it. No one who was actually in the world did. Hypocritical was still the most potent charge left over from the sixties. The election of Clintion in '92 did signal what I thought was a healthy acknowledgment, the end of a certain kind of hypocrisy. Both things could be known simultaneously and not cause breakdown. F. Scott Fitzgerald's old test of a first-rate intelligence is the ability to hold two opposed ideas in the mind at the same time and still retain the ability to function. The country was growing up. Cynicism became a new charge thrown by those who long for the old way of doing things. When I hear that the country has grown too cynical I take it as praise for us all. It means the country-at-large can be critical and see things for how they are. It is the legacy of the sixties. It is Bill Clinton's

America. Bill Clinton's successful juggling of his generational baggage is no mean feat (Clinton was anti-war, but he was never anti-capital). But it doesn't mean the power holders aren't any less fond of decorum. Clinton wants it, Martha Stewart wants it, the rich and powerful always want it. Dick Morris wants it, too. He won't "dignify" the *Star* with a reply. Who is dignified? Where has it gone, Joe DiMaggio?

8/31 I talk with a friend who does large, convention-style video walls. I ask why the Democrats had an L-shaped portio of their video wall that was monochromatic, stationary, not part of the larger image shown. I learn that the video wall at the Republican convention used contrasting still pictures, cued with the speeches. (I recall those, but they were not much seen by the home viewer. Pictures of Powell and Reagan together, Reagan saluting.) The Republicans have to stick to speeches and not deviate from the script. In '92 the Democrats were not under control, and no one could coordinate, or really be sure the person scheduled to speak would be speaking. There would be backup images for the video wall prepared to fill in, but after using them once, it was chaos.

The Republican setup was more expensive. This time the Democrats decided to show the speakers speaking. They went to the L shape because there is a lag time, less than a second, between images moving on the large multi-screen screen and reality, and it is distracting, since the wall is showing what is happening on the podium. So they put in the "static" L-shaped screens, so they could shoot those behind the speaker's head and have an unwavy backdrop.

Their tight shots ended with the top of the speaker's head so there wouldn't be a band of motion jumping around above it. During Clinton's speech it was just Stars and Stripes on the video wall behind him, though they still shot him tight.

The Republican convention, it appears, is the future. San Diego was a light blue TV studio, the color of television heaven. No longer will conventions be held in the Cathedrals of the People. More like chapels of the media.

The biggest difference, it is clear, is that the Republicans do have more control over their troops. The platform was the Christian Coalition victory, and for that they agreed to go along with the show. The show was not for the people in the San Diego convention center, it was for me, us, the people in the television audience. The Democrats still had to play to the people in their arena.

The platform story wasn't as portrayed. Those folks are disciplined. They got what they wanted—no tolerance, a right-to-life veep, all the red meat they could handle, so they were ready to go along. The convention didn't ignore them, as was often reported. They were an integral part of the show. They were as scripted as the speeches themselves. The paradox was best shown when Liddy went "down" among them. That was a staged event, showing that the audience was merely props, but willing props, completely tamed. She wasn't going into a lions' den.

The Republicans are indeed the future. Every consultant for every small election in every small state will be after that same shade of light blue. Of course, the television people criticized it. The conventions were no longer "news" to cover, the conventions were the competition. As if ABC had to cover CBS's evening news show. Oh, we do it so much better. How tacky. Our cutaways are so much sharper, etc.

Hey, it's TV. A friend was once called by a local television station to provide an expert on-camera quote. She said she didn't know anything about the subject. Hey, it's TV, the man said, we just need someone saying something. Television, my television. It is no wonder that there was GOP TV. You can buy the technology and the talent. It continues to be the Jim and Tammy Bakker influence, since evengelicals led the way in this television universe. Send in that money. Praise the Lord. And they did. Lunatics with surplus capital can build these great fantasy empires, huge glass houses of worship and with Pat Robertson and company their biggest edifice of their imagination is the Republican Party '96.

The Democrats aren't yet as disciplined. They're still sloppy. The United Center was full of shadows, the high darkness of Chicago versus the low, clean well-lightedness of San Diego, though the symbols were inverted. The light was Thanatos (the Whiteness of the Whale, etc.), whereas the dark was Eros (bacchanalian, all that Macarena, all that Dick Morris). The pro-life party still reeks of death, whereas the prochoice party is the vital one, full of energy. Part of that is the standard bearer of each party: Bob Dole (Dracula, the living dead) as portrayed by Christopher Lee, Bill Clinton (Superman, defeating death) by Christopher Reeve. Both presidential candidates still set the tone, but underneath them is a large orchestra playing its own tune. Venus and Mars, Eros and the skull.

THIRTEEN

September, September

9/1   Before I sit on the couch today, I notice it has taken on a new bodily indentation, like Anthony Perkins's mother's bed in *Psycho,* because of the last month of conventions. But still I sit. Donald Rumsfeld, now a "top" official in the Dole camp, is on *Meet the Press*. He's a guy with a lot of no opinions: he has no opinion on Dick Morris, no opinions on Clinton's team of loose cannons, no opinions on the upcoming debates. He's taking the high road, he thinks. Since Dole has been around for so long Dole can open any number of long-closed doors and who knows who will pop out: Donald Rumsfeld, for one. He is a great survivor, a Ford administration jack-of-all-trades, who had the honor of offering Ronald Reagan (in 1975) the secretary of commerce job (Reagan turned it down). It is always interesting to watch the spectacle, often played out, of men and women of accomplishment claiming they know nothing about something. Hillary does this a lot; most public figures do. *I know nothing about it.* Of course, they are hired, paid, kept on, put near power, only because of what they do know, but they are often called upon to claim no knowledge of a great many things, and Rumsfeld is carrying on in that tradition. No opinion. I don't know.

Half of ABC's *This Week with Cokie* is on Iraq. Yesterday, the whole *Inside Politics* show was an interview with Gore about Iraq. Saddam's latest dustup is helping bury the Morris story in sand, at least for the weekend.

There's less coverage of the Democratic convention in any case, since it is the second one and so much coverage has already been devoted to the first, the Republican show in San Diego. It's old news, at least for, as Rush would say, the "mainstream" media.

Clips are shown. Clinton thanking Chicago. He says "convention," but it comes out sounding oddly like "conviction." Whose conviction? I wonder. There's a shot of Daley the younger, looking like the shot of his father in '68 calling Senator Abraham Ribicoff names.

9/02   There are a lot of sad Labor Day shows on Labor Day. Ray Suarez has the prolabor Bishop Eagen on *Talk of the Nation* along with a Catholic businessman. Unions bad, the businessman thinks. The *New York Times* runs three "labor" poems. *NewsHour* does a bit. "It wasn't FDR who thought of the New Deal, it was the workers in the factories," my wife, watching momentarily, says.

Derek McGinty, the African American talk show host who is having a good year, does a show about the Internet as I stare at my computer screen. And now I know very few writers who are not staring into a screen. How can they ever complain when people no longer want to pick up a book, want only to watch images flitting across a screen?

Clinton was quoted today on NPR about the fact he feels Arkansas' pain. He was back visiting. Some might see Clinton as a mythic figure out of some Faulkner novel, who brought to his home state not wealth and patronage but death and pestilence, and he seems willing to take the blame. He talks to the hometown crowd about how people made fun of a small southern state and how it held up under the criticism. He thanks them, he loves them. A dark cloud of locusts rises up on the horizon.

There's a Dole-Kemp rally in St. Louis on C-SPAN. Kemp calls out: The quarterback for the next century, Bob Dole. As the *New Yorker* used to say in its newsbreaks, Block that metaphor. Now that the football season has started we might get a break from all this, but I doubt it. Dole's line is that one parent works and the other parent works to pay taxes. It's an odd strategy, since its point is to keep mom at home, go back to the fifties (that bridge to the past), the old by-and-by, gender-gap gulch. When the Christian Right speaks of "family" it means Dad at work, Mom at home, and the kids in school. "It won't be that way when Jack Kemp and I are in charge," Dole says, meaning, I suppose, Mom will have to work 15 percent less. If he wants to claim women are at work because of "high federal taxes," let him. I'm sure Liddy agrees, since she could be home with what Bob is pulling down. Though both Liddy and Hillary have been ostensibly the big moneymakers in the family, since their men have been sacrificing fortune for their selfless public service.

Whenever Kemp is around the nonghost of Forbes looms up. Forbes is the Perot of the '96 race, insofar as he set the wedge issue, shaped the Republicans' economic rhetoric, even though they are now in the position to have to wade through the balancing-the-briar-patch-budget rhetoric of the last four years that Perot in '92, and the deficit hawks of the party (Dole among them), had turned into the conventional wisdom.

Dole makes an odd remark about the Dole-Kemp ticket. Their names are "two four-letter words you can teach your children." Maybe when Dole hears the chant he hears, at first, what I have: Bull-Shit Bull-Shit.

Dole hammers the pot smoker Clinton for cutting the drug office 83 percent. I recall Leon Panetta saying on a Sunday show that the White House drug policy office was the dumping ground for political appointments. I can attest to that, since Notre Dame's former basketball coach, Digger Phelps, finally got an appointment from the Bush administration to the "Weed and Seed" program out of the Office of National Drug Control Policy, a post Digger lost when Clinton won. Phelps wanted to be kept on, saying, after all, he was a Democrat. Phelps had been a local Democrat for Reagan and a Democrat for Bush, but Digger had been digging his own partisan grave. Though, last year, he did announce that he was thinking of running for president.

Dole is now telling us we won't be a country "defenseless against incoming ballistic missiles." Dole seems at sea with this missile defense gap. But he does say that after he is elected, "men and women who wear the uniform will be welcome again in their White House." He compliments the "Oak Ridge Mountain Boys"—who earlier had sung the national anthem—and looks forward to having them sing in the White House.

The rally ends; there are some sort of weird red, white, and blue tubular balloons behind the stage. The theme from *Rocky* is piped out over the crowd.

Clinton gets to launch cruise missiles against Saddam and sign the welfare bill within a few weeks of each other. The cruise-missile makers are happy. Perhaps they can open up some jobs for the welfare-evicted folks.

PBS airs a show, *The People and the Power Game*. We're back to the highlights of '92s and '93. And it's not even the History Channel. ABC's Jim Wooten claims Gennifer Flowers was no story for them, but an ABC affiliate ran the tape (off satellites), so ABC went with it the next day. All of this rehash seems pertinent in the light of the Dick Morris story. Wooten is saying that now the Clinton marriage was strong. But the tabloids drove the Flowers story. The Ruth Bader Ginsburg appointment to the Supreme Court is announced by Clinton and the first question by Brit Hume is off the subject, and on the subject of Clinton's inconstancy, the wavering of his opinions. Clinton's angry objection ends the news conference. The haircut story (costly stylings on the Tarmac) of May 23, 1993, is redone. Gingrich ethics problems of early December 1995 are aired.

You can train yourself to read more quickly, though you can't train yourself to watch television more quickly, since you are locked into real time (though it is odd what you notice when you fast-forward with no sound). The Internet, too, happens in real time, which will always curb its use, no matter how efficient the watcher becomes with the medium. That computers and television are the two parallel lines that have met at the end of the twentieth century bespeaks a twenty-first century where the television consciousness will be elevated into the so-called literate consciousness (the Internet as reference, research library) in a most insidious way, the fear of cross-species organ transplants, where unknown viruses may be passed which the host, the literate consciousness, will not be able to defend itself against.

The Harry and Louise anti–health care ad campaign wrung concessions out of Dan Rostenkowski, but as soon as Rostenkowski was indicted, the ads went back on. Steve Largent, another Republican athlete, be-moans the fact that $1.5 billion will be spent on "this election cycle." Why am I not surprised?

We see the Republican congressman John Boehner, who passed out the checks on the House floor from lobbyists, say he wouldn't do it again and "we should stop" such practices. The height of hypocrisy, but Boehner delivers it with a straight face (and slightly askew eyes). He's fourth in the Republican hierarchy. Lobbyist groups are able to do talk show rapid responses, one practitioner boasts. Labor is outspent by business 7 to 1 and environmentalists are outspent by energy folks 10 to 1.

9/3 It's Saddam versus the Kurds in the news, which brings up Bosnia. One effect of Bosnia's ethnic cleansing was how it highlighted Northern Ireland, made what is going on there more of an embarrassment, because the religious and nationalist foes in the former Yugoslavia have been taking their differences to the edge of "civilization." One would have thought that the soil of Europe had seen enough of mass graves, etc., but here they are again, and it does make everyone feel a bit bad. It has increased the shame factor, if any shame exists anymore. So Northern Ireland has a cease-fire of a sort, but no NATO troops, though it might need them yet.

John Sweeney is on Diane Rehm. He has a book (*America Needs a Raise*), too, which allows him access to the public square, FM public-radio division. On a day other than Labor Day.

9/4 Some movies of the moment: *Jack*. Is there any mystery why there is a movie about a forty-year-old man who is really only eight? I finally get to see Altman's *Kansas City*. It seems really static. He does have the characters' teeth right (bad). Altman and the movie spend a lot of time at Union Station, one of the great Pendergast monuments to concrete and construction. I spent a lot of time at Union Station, too; there was a little theater there in the sixties, established when the station began to fall into disuse. And I worked one Christmas season unloading mailbags from frozen boxcars down on the tracks below it. Now it can be a movie soundstage. Altman manages to reinforce every cliché there is regarding race, gender, and class. He does assemble some shots of his jazz musicians to look just like the paintings Thomas Hart Benton did of them: same light, color, and composition.

From a spate of previews I sit through, it appears that Whoopi Goldberg is in every movie that will be released in the next few months, except for one to be released right after the election, *Ransom,* which stars Mel Gibson as a real rich guy whose son is kidnapped. And Mel, full of tough love, offers all the "ransom" money to the person who gets the kidnapper. It appears this is a Clinton allegory of sorts, a twist on the welfare/workfare bill, where the chief dad has to be tough to save the child (the nation, the poor). Family values at a cost. It looks like it will be a big hit.

There's more O.J.-ification of the news going on, this time with Saddam and the Kurds. We have more moonlighting professionals telling us what is going on: generals talking about Saddam, historians talking about presidents. The *NewsHour* is at one end of the continuum, *Rivera Live* at the other.

9/5   There's more Morris news. He evidently got *Time* magazine to change its initial cover (September 2), according to Sherry and the *Star,* so his picture wouldn't be bigger than the president's. *Time* and its covers: Morris and his wife, Eileen McGann, are on this week's (September 9), one of the grimmer Families First portraits I've seen. One thinks of other fun couples, the Ceaușescus, the Slobodan Milosevices. One wonders why Morris is so cozy with *Time.* Escort services everywhere.

I'm discussing Morris with a feminist theorist. We are both lost in the idea of forty-something call girls. Following Dole's example, age holds no bonds. I contend that Morris held two contradictory views of Sherry. My friend agrees with my first one, which is that Morris thought Sherry didn't exist. She wasn't there, so he felt free to open up to her, Morris-style. She was an employee and hence invisible, the shoeshine boy, the paper seller in the kiosk, the guy that opens the door, the taxi driver, the maid, a sex maid, but a maid nonetheless. My second view my friend considers more ambivalently: Morris, even though Sherry didn't actually exist, thought Sherry liked him, so she'd never turn him in. His cash wooing of her, with whatever fiscal promises to come down the road were to carry her over at least till after the election.

The *Star* has finally hit the newsstands out here in the provinces: world exclusive "White House Call Girl Scandal." Brooke Shields in white on the cover. A smaller picture of Sherry Rowlands with her legs in the air. There is some yellow, journalism here: the color scheme of the *Star*'s cover is yellow, red, and black, with just a tiny touch of blue: "I thought Jan Michael was trying to kill me"—gal pal's own story. That collection of colors is a mixture of stop signs, fallout-shelter symbols, and black-cat caricatures, slightly nightmarish pulp paper hues achieving a poster effect, a nice collage done by the least brain-damaged artist in the rehab unit.

The *Star* knows its audience, including me. The ad for Virginia Slims on the back is more typical advertising-agency work, aimed at a more upward-mobility mentality, with a large dollop of fantasy, not the flat-out exuberance of the We're One of You cover art.

There are the "candid" photographs of Morris and Sherry, and posed shots of Sherry in front of the White House, her single strand of pearls slightly askew. The *Star* seems to be protesting a bit much in a sidebar article, "How *Star* Checks Out This Story," seemingly stung by all the bad-mouthing tabloids have received in the past. I believe every word of Sherry's account: ah, the exciting life of Washington, where even the powerful are power-crazed. Morris seems to be bitten by the I-can't-believe-I'm-so-close-to-the-hot-center-of-the-universe bug and gets really buzzed about it. Send in the call girls!

Morris has to pay, Bill doesn't, seems to be the moral of this sad story. Or, Bill doesn't expect to pay. Send in Paula Jones! But Morris isn't going to be elected to anything, not even the governorship of Arkansas. Looking back at the *Star*'s February 4, 1992, Gennifer Flowers issue after four years is a strange experience. Everyone involved looks younger. The *Star* captioned one picture of Clinton: "Bill Clinton often jogged from the governor's mansion to her apartment," though the photograph shows Clinton putting on bowling shoes, not jogging shoes. But there are no pictures of Bill with Gennifer then; now we do have Morris and Sherry locked in a fleeting embrace.

9/6 Art Buchwald on the *Diane Rehm Show* makes the comic point: with twenty thousand FBI and satellites, why doesn't the president know what's going on? The subject is Morris. It's more of the no-opinion world, people who are groomed to know everything claiming to know nothing.

The *New Yorker* of September 9 has a short piece (page 32) on the two valedictorians of CNN. The article is on the African American. There's also convention coverage, but after that there is an article about the Hutus and Tutsis. One would hope that such a macabre spectacle of neighborly slaughter would be a sobering lesson and we could act less vicious and more reasonable to one another, but our real condition is that we're afraid the machetes will come out here next.

If the Republicans were really optimists, they'd grant that life is better in '96 than it was in '56. A prochoice activist at Notre Dame says, regarding Ralph Reed, Gary Bauer, etc.: "The pro–life leadership like their men to look like fetuses."

9/7 C-SPAN is showing a lecture, the "Role of the Military in American Society," given to the military at the Air Force Judge Advocate School in Montgomery, Alabama, on August 21 by Charles Moskos, of Northwestern University, a sociology professor who seems to have spent his life courting and covering the military. Some statistics are launched: 61 percent in the Senate are veterans, 40 percent in the House. It is this high because of World War II, and the percentage will really drop in the next eight years. I wonder if these stats were compiled before Dole resigned. Moskos claims there are no novels of the all-volunteer army. I wonder about that, though the point is clear. The Vietnam War was novelized largely by journalists turned novelists, though some of the best-known, and most well regarded, novels were written by actual soldiers: Tim O'Brien, Larry Heinemann. I wonder about proportions: the bibliography of literature on the Vietnam War is extensive and doubtless that war has a higher ratio of novelists per square foot than World War II. It is generational, though some (most) critics only grant Vietnam-War–writer status to those who actually set foot in country.

Moskos is claiming an absence of elites in the all-volunteer army, though novelists don't necessarily come from elites (though they do need an education: some grim day ahead "elite" might equal "literate"); what they also need is story and conflict, and battle serves that up on a platter. For this era, there still is that, and I'm sure the Persian Gulf, Somalia, and Bosnia are going to show up in novels. I'm especially certain that the other sort of battles, gays in the military, Tailhook follies, will show up too.

Moskos says popular culture markers have changed: films like *The Caine Mutiny* showed the military as good, *A Few Good Men* showed it as bad. Captain Queeg (Humphrey Bogart) as the exception, the Jack Nicholson character in *A Few Good Men* as the rule. He brings up the summer movie *The Rock,* the spectacle of an errant officer with loyal troops. The point he's after is that the whole is now corrupt, rather than the part—at least, in his view, as viewed by Hollywood. In 1956 he says two-thirds of the Princeton class served in the military. This year only thirteen graduates did. Elvis served. "Could you imagine Michael Jackson in today's military?" he asks, and some of the officers in attendance probably can. Now that's marching. Moskos would like to see a "service only benefit" for college. Isn't that ROTC, aren't there benefits already for service? He would, it appears, eliminate the benefits for those who don't serve. He says academics are against it. Especially the notion that only veterans should get tenure.

C-SPAN is working its magic again here: what they provide is a version of how the inside talks to itself. Such speeches are not usually seen by outsiders, and though the speakers know they are being filmed for the "larger" public, there still is enough insider atmosphere left to color their speech. There is a we're-all-being-taped consciousness at large at the end of the twentieth century, but even that guard gets let down: Dick Morris hoist with his own petard. Writing down his "private" conversations with the prez, not thinking that Sherry, the hooker, is writing down his.

Moskos holds that the underclass began with the fall of conscription. He doesn't say that the military began downsizing slightly ahead of private industry. Given the Dole generation versus the Clinton generation, the sea change in the military culture is large and looming. We've gone, generationally, from the counterculture to subcultures. The military was a screen through which the whole culture passed, some being picked up, some not. Now it's a tributary, like so many others. There used to be "mainstream" religious; now there are many sects and cults. There used to be (and, according to Rush, still are) the mainstream media; now there is every creek and stream available. There used to be three networks;

now there are hundreds of channels—and the new Internet interactive television. Screens everywhere. There are militias, Amway, Odd Fellows, and baseball-card conventions. Subcultures everywhere, no longer the simple counterweight of the "counter" culture.

Moskos fields a question, hostile to gays, referring to Judeo-Christian values, Sodom and Gomorrah. Moskos says it's a matter of the "lifestyle Left versus the religious Right," and tells the officer to stay away from the "moral" argument. "Don't seek, don't flaunt," he says, echoing his infamous Don't ask, don't tell. If you stay the course in the military, he says, there is usually a reward; not so true in civilian life, he holds. The draft allows for casualties, but in the volunteer army, it isn't tolerated. If elite youth are not dying, he concludes, the conflict is not in the national interest.

9/8   Bill Bennett is on *Fox News Sunday*. They were doing the Kurds earlier. Bennett is thumping his chest for "moral authority." It's the most important thing. Teddy Roosevelt is held up as an exemplar. No San Juan Hills in Bennett's background, but he does like to trash wherever he's walked: the Department of Education, the NEH. The bull artist in the china shop.

Robert Novak is on *Meet the Press*. "The election is almost over," he says gloomily.

My son is doing the Macarena, trying to teach it to me. He learned it in "gym." He's a first-grader.

Watching the Sunday shows, it is clear that journalism is working just fine. The problem lies elsewhere. I watch the replay of *Washington Week in Review*. They're talking about the firing of Dole's ad makers, the same subject that gave Novak the blues. Alex Castellanos, one of the many C-SPAN faces, is taking over Dole's media. He's out of the Jesse Helms school, I'm told. On *Wall Street Week,* Ruykeser goes over movie grosses. *Independence Day* is in the $269 million range, *Twister* somewhat behind. *Mission Impossible* is a moneymaker, too. He says Disney is "a global consumer franchise company," like Coca-Cola, I add.

He says the biggest problem out there in the entertainment world is the "continuing demise of network ratings," 5 percent each year. But the good news is that large companies own networks (Disney! GE! Murdoch!), so the networks don't drive their stock. While all this is being discussed, the studio lights are going on and off because of the hurricane going up the East Coast on Friday. It's a nice touch—television's hard times illuminated by flickering storm light.

We are approaching a Babel situation, not of languages, but of ideological and cultural comfort zones. The television is the sacristy lamp in the chapel of the people and it now can go to whatever storefront church it chooses.

It isn't so much the content of Clinton's character that disturbs me, but the content of his résumé. What has he ever done except be president of the United States? Be governor of Arkansas? That's what is at the center of the charges of hollowness. Right out of school to Arkansas: run lose, run win, run lose, run win win win win. Of course, the central fact of my and Clinton's generation is its opposition to the Vietnam War, but that was what it was: opposition. Managing to do nothing, other than protest. Getting out. Not going. That negative experience lies at the heart of the generation, except for those who went or who did something decisive. Jail, Canada. But most slid by, found a way around it. It is a hole in the generation and Clinton could have filled it by holding it up as admirable, something he was proud of, but, like many of the generation, his ambivalence is still so strong, he sidestepped his way past it throughout his political career, the only career he's had.

The McLaughlin Group is rebroadcast on Sundays. Laura Ingraham, Clarence Thomas's former clerk, here identified as representing the Independent Women's Forum, who goes on her safaris in Washington behind the wheel of her Range Rover, is sitting in, replacing, I presume, another conservative voice—Kondracke is absent. She's been hired, it is mentioned, to replace Joe Klein at CBS. A different primary color for the bloodshot eye. The show's last bit is McLaughlin fulminating about poor police sergeant Jenkins who stopped his daughter from "having sex" with a boyfriend and was temporarily demoted in Stillwater, Oklahoma, but the city has backed down on the cut in rank, though it still holds out for a week without pay.

9/9 Rush says Dole-Kemp should "go negative." He's the tough guy today, going on about Iran, unhappy at the cover it's providing Bill. Rush has got war fever himself, decrying the "pansies" who didn't want to take Saddam out. Exasperated, he says that even if Bill Clinton wins, it will only be a blip of the screen of this country's move to the right. It does appear that the only thing that's holding the bounce it got out of the conventions is the Macarena.

9/10   There's a picture of "Susan McDougal Sent to Jail" in the *New York Times* this morning. It looks like an S and M shot, shiny handcuffs around her black nyloned ankles, a chain accessory around her waist, more handcuffs. This photo is above a "Tale of Love" murder story, two military academy cadets, boy and girlfriend and the dead girl they allegedly killed. Perhaps she should have applied to the Citadel: Hell Week wouldn't have fazed her. The cliché used to be, in a literate age, that everyone had one novel inside him or her. Now it is clear in a postliterate age that each of us has at least one TV movie inside. These two are *Natural Born Service Academy Kids*.

Dole is running around talking to "real people" audiences, which turn out to be handpicked groups of supporters. Morris says he was talking about polling data when he said Hillary was responsible for Filegate, etc. Which is worse?

Rush is defending Dole on tobacco. If cocaine is addictive . . . if nicotine is addictive . . . some aren't hooked, is Rush's point, which was Dole's point. Some quit, some don't, appealing to Dole's view that there are winners and losers in life. Rush says "kids are smart" and they'll sort it out. Right on, Rush. A caller tells him they took the radio out of the "Rush room" in the Green Bay Packers' locker room before the presidential entourage got there. But it'll be back, he assures Rush. And Rush goes on about Rosie O'Donnell saying "Dole sucks" on her TV show. Whoopi Goldberg defended her by saying, "I don't think anybody complained about Rush." I get all sorts of grief, Rush says; they can say whatever they want. . . . There's a lack of proportion . . . a bias in the liberal media. No conservatives could hold on to their contracts, he complains, if they made such ad hominem attacks. Rush plays a tape from Rosie's show. Below these complaints is the unspoken upscale envy of Whoopi doing prime-time phone commercials and Rush hawking chain saws.

Rush still wants to go negative. "It's out there waiting." On Morris, he says, "I want to know what this amoral creep was doing in the White House." The fact that Bill and Hillary called Morris is trotted out. For sympathy? To keep him on the reservation. We all know why, Rush makes clear.

Paul Manafort, another Dole C-SPAN face, gets some print in *Newsweek*'s September 16 issue. Morris should take note of its cover story: Testosterone, just what the world needs more of.

On PBS in the evening there's a program on the budget battle. This redoes the world of Woodward's *The Agenda,* but with pictures. Former senator David Boren (D-Okla.), now president of the University of Oklahoma, says that the party didn't do anything for him; it only raised one-half of 1 percent of his campaign funds. Boren changed his mind on the budget, even though he got concessions on the BTU tax: "Take it out or lose my support." The prez was shocked at Boren's offer of a bipartisan budget. We get definitions of yellow-dog Democrats and blue-dog democrats, by the blue dog Mike Barber (Miss.), who finally became a Republican, one of the gender-benders of the period. A yellow dog will vote for a yellow dog if he is on the ticket, whereas a blue dog has a better sense of smell and will bite you.

Leslie Byrne wants to discipline the blue dogs. That sends Mr. Mike of Mississippi over to the Republicans. Marjorie Margolis Mezvinsky (now former member of Congress) gets her arm twisted and Gore gets to vote to pass the budget. Then we have a reprise of more hard times of the Clinton administration. From the budget battle to the health care war. In February 1994, business backed the Cooper plan, the Democratic "alternative." Cooper ends up losing his Senate bid in Tennessee. Newt and Bill's only nongovernment job is in "academia," though not quite the private sector. Of the seventy-three Republican freshmen elected in '94, half had never held office. The Congress had become an oligarchy. The Senate manages to slow Newt's one-hundred-day blitzkrieg down. Cohen of Maine says the "mandate is not to sack Washington as if it was Imperial Rome." On November 30, 1995, the balanced-budget bill was sent up. Then there were twenty-one more days of shutdown of "nonessential" government services. Then there was the "Crybaby" story on Newt in New York's *Daily News*. On January 3 Dole and the Senate voted to open the government. Fifty-one House Republicans wanted to follow Dole, but fifteen Republicans were hanging tough and voted no. In April came the budget, seven months late. The show managed to be a before-and-after picture. Why Clinton looked vulnerable, how the Republicans lost their beachhead.

On C-SPAN I watch Perot's infomercial. It's a mind-numbing experience. He's got charts. His puzzle of the government is like the maps of the world that aren't made to scale. There's defense and Social Security and Medicare, all the same size. Then tax base, job base, ethics. Ross's solution for abolishing the IRS relies on computers. Surprise, surprise. He's going to enlist the best minds. Warren Rudman, Pete Peterson. Ross is doing Dale Carnegie, a sales pitch with video graphics. Ross has the salesman's aspect of being willing to look absurd as testament to his sincerity. The computer is our wind tunnel, Ross says. His set is stupefying: on the left there are bookshelves with encyclopedias, on the right, Washington crossing the Delaware. There will be a national referendum on the new tax system. "Both in writing and on television," he says, which at least shows an appreciation of the difference. Ross says he shakes the special interest groups. Willy Loman with a gun.

Then we have an older African American man praising Ross, comparing him to Martin Luther King. The same fire burning from within. . . . Is this guy Ross's veep, to be announced shortly?

No, it appears not. It's back to Ross sitting down and he's introducing "Dr. Choate," sitting next to him. Pat, Ross tells us, was in charge of public policy at TRW. His views are your views. Choate is a fat guy with a beard. He wrote a book with Ross. Now it is a bit clearer. He's an employee, or a former employee, or someone who had a previous financial relationship with Mr. Perot. "I know Washington and I know it can't be changed from the inside," Pat says. That would leave him out, too. This ends with a crying baby, crying at how much taxes she will have to pay. 1-800-96-Party for the truly deluded, and for surfers, www.perot.org. Do either of the other candidates give you this straight talk? Ross snaps at the camera and at us. Say yes and I will knock your block off.

9/11   *USA Today* stories of note. Walter Shapiro's column says it is a closer race than it appears. Nobody's paying attention yet. But when? is the question. There's a Clarence Thomas article next to one about VMI. The pope gets some news, election '96 pieces, and on the op-ed page the always amusing Linda Chavez.

I'm still thinking about the Clinton/Gingrich connection via the academic jobs they briefly held. The academy let baby boomers jump class. Thomas's son is at VMI, not to jump class, but to insert himself into the other dominant culture, the military culture. The two cultures of the baby-boom generation are the military and the academic. If you don't have a mix of the two, you remain at odds with the power structures. Clinton's opposition to the war announced his absence from the military culture, whereas Dan Quayle didn't lose his ticket by guarding Indiana golf courses. Quayle isn't given enough credit for preparing the country for Bill Clinton. Quayle did pave the way for a baby-boom president (had someone else been Bush's veep, someone of the Korean War generation, the ground wouldn't have been softened up at all). Quayle's own draft experience was so shoddy that Clinton's history didn't look that bad. Dan Quayle, Mr. National Guard, vice president, a heartbeat away.

Rush is reading a poll of Miss America candidates' presidential picks: Dole received twenty-two votes, Clinton nine, and nineteen were either undecided or won't say. Dole, Rush reports, says he's humbled by their support. (And he wants to thank Bert Parks, too.)

Rush goes on about Morris. Lots to go on about there.

USA Today has the same picture of Susan McDougal as the *Times,* but it is in color, which makes it lose some of its dark oomph.

Given the Susan McDougal picture, I imagine Jay Leno jokesters writing, "Did you see the picture of Susan McDougal today in chains. She looked like she was on her way to Dick Morris's hotel room." I don't know if I'll get to check if he actually makes that sort of joke tonight.

Given all the sludge the Morris story brings up—he's got another woman and a child by her back in Texas, it is now reported, a working girl not working, the mother of Morris's only child—I muse again over the Christian Coalition's looming problem: 2000 and Gore. Gore, of course, didn't have to jump class to run for president; he is not in the line of Truman, Nixon, Johnson, Carter, Clinton. He's more in the line of Kennedy and Bush, born to rule. There will be a rhetorical vacuum created in 2000 without Bill Clinton to kick around, and what will fill it? Fifteen percent? Abolishing the IRS as we know it?

Jack Kemp is on C-SPAN talking to the House and Senate Republican conference. "Thank you, guys," Kemp says, momentarily oblivious of the women in the room. Kemp is off on his numerology kick again. Fifteen percent, add nine and six and what do you get? Yeah, yeah. Call Nostradamus. Four children and eleven grandchildren. Wives names add up to fifteen. Jack Kemp and Bob Dole add up to fifteen. Stop already. He's got the Ouija board vote. "Numerology has a lot to do with politics," he says, and I think he means counting votes. "I believe that Bob Dole's whole life had led to this moment," he says—rather, I suppose, than not leading to this moment. But what it really leads to is the introduction of Bob Dole. Bob thanks Kemp, saying with the economy on the front burner there's "no better salesman than Jack Kemp," and continues: "Fifty-four days is a long time in politics as we all know," and I realize what this speech is all about. He's trying to raise morale. "But the candidate can't be pessimistic." He slams the National Education Association again. "I see Ross Perot has picked up on it . . . a lot of me-too candidates in this election." Dole and Kemp have a book, too. *Trust the People,* published by HarperCollins, the Bobster announces. What's the deal here, Rupert? I wonder. Drug use: "Just say nothing." "House of Shame" in the judiciary. Stop the partial-birth abortion. "All they have is fear." Trust. Dole has the letter to his father about Dole being in the hospital. Emotional tough spots, ups and downs. "We're going to win." Down in the crowd are D'Amato, Connie Mack, Coats, and Gingrich, and I think of Nixon's final speech to his people in the White House. Despite the rhetoric, there's the air of the concession speech about it.

Pat Choate is on, at a press conference, saying there is a "disconnect" between the "elites" and the great mass of people. Most of the nonelite, Choate says, "get their information from talk radio," which is where he plans to do a lot of campaigning, free campaigning. His name might be a setback for appealing to the nonelites, since it brings to mind the fanciest of private prep schools. "The main thing is not where you are," Choate says, but how you deal with the media. He presumes he will soon be widely known by the public at large. Radio, television, and those "long-form programs," aka infomercials, are planned, one upcoming on Social Security. Choate expects the race to tighten up between Perot and Clinton by October. Voting for Dole will be "the throwaway vote."

If Choate is a sensible man, does it do his credibility any good to say such senseless things?

9/14 Ralph Reed is on Tim Russert's CNBC show. He's upset that Clinton won't come to the Christian Coalition convention. The spider accusing the fly of cowardice. They wouldn't accept a surrogate. Dole wasn't going to appear, but will now. Russert mentions a poll, where 46 percent to 33 percent of evangelicals preferred Clinton. Ralph wants to know what it would be for "churchgoers," not just people who identified themselves as evangelicals.

Ralph doesn't look good today; he's sporting a Nixon-like five o'clock shadow. The small-town mortician look. Russert asks if they were wrong to stress economic issues. "If I were running a campaign," Ralph says, in good economic times, "I would hit crime and drugs."

Ralph talks about abortion polls. Only 9 percent would allow it for "any reason." And 56 percent would allow it for what Reed strangely calls "hard cases." Health of mother, rape and incest, etc. Seems to be a chink in his no-abortion position. Reed cites a Battleground poll, where 55 percent claim to be conservative, 34 percent liberal. I'm surprised it's that high on the liberal side. Speaking of conservatives, he says "in our analysis of this constituency," which does reveal that he at times stands outside of it: "this" constituency, rather than "our" constituency. Ralph does show signs of hearing the siren song of the Russert media world, which is still another crowd than the *700 Club*. Sixteen percent of Christian Coalition members are Catholic, Reed claims. When it comes to "the gambling issue . . . our natural allies were on the Left," Ralph says. He seems beset by contradictions, hard cases, allies on the Left. He does see life ahead without Bob Dole in the picture.

In the *New York Observer* (September 16) there is an article about Richard Gooding, the *Star*'s man on the balcony, Sherry's (Deep Throat) Bob Woodward. It's another generational saga. A former draft fugitive who wrote about it for *Look* back then, with a checkered career in straight journalism after he surfaced and went unprosecuted for draft evasion. Woodward and Bernstein were young and hungry and got to collide with an older, corrupt president. The generational game of Jack and the Beanstalk was at play. Gooding's intersection with his president came late, after both men had peaked at midcentury, and the connection was Dick Morris and Sherry had to come to him. The *Observer*'s take on him is its usual one, suffused with being so much in the know (Gooding is a familiar figure—and type—in the New York journalism world) that it manages to devalue *knowing* itself, which reveals why only money and looks count in our time. (The same issue of the *Observer* has a fashion ad, a woman sporting handcuffs, but it isn't an homage to Susan McDougal.)

Rivera Live is rerunning a Friday show which I catch. Howard Fineman of *Newsweek* says Newt at Dole headquarters says to go after Morris/Hillary via Klinger's committee. Forty-eight hours later Klinger gets a ridiculous letter from Morris, confirming most of the *Star*'s article, except for Morris's spin on Hillary: poll data show people *think* she's responsible for Filegate. Yeah, yeah, yeah. Morris is a tar baby and everyone it seems is leery of getting too close.

I watch *The War Room* again, the '92 Clinton campaign documentary, the first time in a couple of years. I wonder why the Family Channel, or GOP TV, isn't playing this every night. It starts with Gennifer Flowers, goes to the draft letter, Hillary as copresident ("my Valentine's Day girl," Bill calls her, leaving a lot of other days open), all the usual right-wing wish list. Pat Robertson's Christian Broadcasting Network could sell this rather than the Who Murdered Vince Foster? video. *The War Room* isn't investigative. It's the Loud Family as campaigners, though Mr. and Mrs. are Carville and George. Hillary and Bill are the kids who run in and out and are glimpsed fleetingly. It does capture the frisson of winning, the change in atmosphere of victory night in Little Rock. Everything becomes darker, though it hardly cuts the elation. Clinton the long shot has come in by a nose and has paid a fortune.

9/16 Martin Walker, the author of *The President We Deserve*, is on Diane Rehm, one more Brit who met Clinton at Oxford, and who is now Washington bureau chief of *The Guardian*. He sounds a lot like Christopher Hitchens, but has less malice in his voice. A caller says,

"Thank God he [B. C.] didn't go to Vietnam, he had a higher calling." Walker is happy that Clinton likes his book and recommends it. "The president we deserve" has always been a truism—I'm trying to think of a president we didn't deserve. None leaps to mind. Walker doesn't mention that Clinton has the electorate he deserves.

Rush is reading a letter from a fan which is a real downer. Moral life awful, everything going to hell, it's all Clinton's fault. A call comes from Dole and it's a little hard for Rush to switch gears; he'd been preparing for a jeremiad against the cultural evils afoot, resisted through the power of positive thinking. "Thinking negative is easy, thinking positive is hard." Rush is deferential and asks Dole about the economy. Dole starts to attack the "liberal" media and then pulls back as if it dawns on him what he is doing—sailing out to America on the medium of radio waves.

9/17 Today Diane Rehm has Paul Hendrickson, the author of *The Living and the Dead,* a book about Robert McNamara and a few other individuals affected by the Vietnam War. There's a pro-McNamara, anti-Clinton caller, offering a denunciation of Clinton as "the most untruthful president now" and forever. The caller has a hillbilly voice, a twang of real hate. There's a lot of emotion today. Hendrickson is also heated: McNamara really bothers him. One of the subjects in *The Living and the Dead* is a man on a Cape Cod ferry who wanted to (but didn't) push McNamara overboard because of the Vietnam War, and Hendrickson doesn't seem too far from that, either. Diane adds that when McNamara came on her show, he wouldn't agree to take phone calls. She let him come on, anyway. His arrogance was persuasive, the best and the brightest chutzpah still prevailing. McNamara's own book (*In Retrospect*) seems to be a ploy in the if-history-won't-absolve-me-I'll-absolve-myself sweepstakes. As any number of folks said or thought back then, the sight of all the commanders, the desk generals, who ran the Vietnam War, leaving government one by one as the war continued, the rats abandoning the sinking ship, was disgusting. No one was sticking around for the duration. They'd come and go and McNamara went to the World Bank, where he could fail on an even larger scale. Such men are used to having their way and McNamara certainly is, and continues to.

Rush leads with Perot being ejected from the debates. "I agree with

the decision. . . . Obviously some entertainment value will be missing."
Of course, the large question is not why Perot is not let in the upcoming
debates, but why he was let in the '92 debates. No candidate looked
more lunatic. He had quit the race, but letting himself back in, they let
him into the debates. The phenomenon explanation may suffice: It was
new, it was different, it was Ross, it had gotten to double digits in the
polls. But his presence was shattering for the Bush campaign. By the
third '92 debate the damage had already been done to him, but Perot
was there, each one of his answers a bucket of cold water thrown on
Bush. Take that, take that, take that. Even now, it's hard to believe. But
no Perot this time, at least for the moment.

Rush, joining the keep-Perot-off forces, is acknowledging the devastating effect Perot had in '92, though Rush doesn't articulate it. Dole, he
says, is "up" in the ABC poll to 8 percent. Eight percent behind, that
is.

Listening to Rush's callers today I conclude talk radio has mutated,
because all the callers seem suspect. A woman caller named Shirley is
going on about Dole shooting himself in the foot. Bad for the congressional races. It's wrong not to want Perot. His people are organized. All
the callers seem professionalized. It doesn't take long for that to happen
even innocently. This is mass education in communications. Listeners
learn, or mimic, appropriate caller behavior. They have notes, they are
rehearsed. It happens on television, too, but the TV gatekeepers are still
a bit more stringent and there isn't such immediate access to getting your
face on the screen. Someday, perhaps. Even C-SPAN just gets their
voices, which is a version of talk radio. When it's truly "interactive,"
meaning television equalizes performer and . . . performer, the media will
be equal.

9/18 Rush is claiming that the debate commission is quoting his show
from yesterday, that their reasoning and language are the same as his:
baseball, the World Series, only the best left to compete, etc. Yes, great
minds work alike, and those piercing sports metaphors cover most everything.

Ross, though, on PBS's *NewsHour,* is fuming at the half-Republican, half-Democratic, lobbyist-for-gambling-corporations-with-an-interest-in-this-debate commission membership.

Later, I see Ross on C-SPAN at the Commonwealth Club of California in San Francisco, saying in reaction to being banned from the debates, "Registered puppies don't like to be around cur dogs."

But the news for me is Spiro Agnew is dead. The old clips reel by. The Pentagon Papers were published on June 13, 1971. Who would want to claim authorship of "nattering nabobs of negativism"? Safire, Buchanan? I recall reading an article long ago describing how, when Agnew used the term "Spock-marked generation," both of those speechwriters turned to each other and realized that Spiro had made that one up himself. Maybe. Again, what is most poignant about the Spock-marked generation is that Spock's book didn't unleash an era of permissiveness; it was only suggesting that there were other ways to discipline kids than beating them.

The Watergate break-in was June 17, 1972. One of the first crashes of a 737 had Dorothy Hunt aboard with her suitcase of cash. Woodward turns up in the retrospective. He's in the Gore mode of speech, positively eerie. What would Woodward's spontaneous speech sound like? Does he ever have any? Woodward was and is the guardian of the establishment. That's his role, self-proclaimed, or programmed, whichever. We have Nixon saying "I'm not a crook," rather than the president is not a crook. He talked of himself in the third person quite a bit, too, though it was mainly "the president," not "Dick Nixon." That's where Dole probably picked the habit up. In emulation of Nixon. The dates roll on. October 12, 1973—Ford replaces Agnew. On October 20 the Saturday Night Massacre happens. Busy times. Rose Mary Woods "erasing" eighteen minutes (like the former Rose law firm secretary "finding" the Whitewater billing records in the White House book room). Nixon saying, "I've earned everything I have done," a remarkable Freudian slip, since he meant to say, "everything I have."

Nixon's resignation under threat of impeachment brings to mind a former local U.S. attorney's opinion that Hillary will be indicted before November 5. I don't think so.

We see the Judiciary Committee voting on July 27. Trent Lott casting one of the few no votes.

Nixon said in his departure speech: "I'm not educated, but I do read books." There the modern root of the Republican hatred of "elites." Nixon did go to college, to law school, and yet he claims he's not educated. What a spectacle of self-pity. What he is saying is, "I'm not liked." That remark might have engendered some sympathy, since it was true.

In September he gets pardoned by Ford.

C-SPAN reruns a May 24, 1995, event, the unveiling of a bust of Spiro Agnew in the halls of Congress. What I first saw was a shroud over a bust and I thought it was today's programming. The ceremony is full of affection and dignitaries. Dole is there, Moynihan. It's been twenty-two years since Agnew left "in disgrace," but no one mentions that, until Agnew himself speaks. He brings it up, saying that some will object to what is occurring today, though placing the bust in public view is not so much honoring him as history (I paraphrase). He receives a standing ovation. There are warm, sentimental looks on most of the faces of the people applauding, the attitude being, So what did he do? Took a little money. What's that? Congressman John Boehner was passing money out from lobbyists on the floor of the Congress, so what's the difference? Agnew looks to be in good health. When the bust is revealed its classicism is overwhelming. Agnew is Greek and it does look like the most Greco-Roman bust in the place. Marble absolves everyone.

9/19   Rush points out that the university in Chico, California, was a *Playboy* favorite party school. Chico is the city of Dole's platform fall. What's interesting is Rush's keeping up with *Playboy* party schools (Chico first appeared on the list more than a decade ago). Dole is quoted on a newsbreak as saying the fall was the result of "trying to do that Democratic dance, the Macarena."

The Living and the Dead, the McNamara book, was reviewed today in *USA Today.* Saturation is required to bubble up on the surface of the culture. You need to appear many places in a short period of time. Then you can pop in the American consciousness.

9/20   Bork is on Rush today and Rush is treating him with Rushian deference. Bork's book: *Slouching toward Gomorrah,* a truly bad title. He quotes Learned Hand from the book. The court responds to the ruling class in the country. Hand, it is clear, was speaking about the business class. Bork holds it is now the "intellectual" class. They're not really intellectuals, they are merely, Bork says, those "who use words and symbols." That would be Rush, I suppose, even Bork himself. "Egalitarianism triumphs over individualism," Bork barks. He has it down. Egalitarians, equality of outcomes, bad. Individualism, maybe good. Bork admits to writing a depressing book. His next, he says, "will be called *Little Mary Sunshine*."

The problem with Bork is that he has no wit. He is an intellectual, just not a popular one. It is clear his rejection from a possible seat on the Supreme Court still gnaws at him, is the bitter cud he chews. He says the legislature is bad, but courts are worse. He wants decisions reversed by the legislature. Bork's original sin is, doubtless, his firing of Archibald Cox. But he is certainly out of paradise and his photos show that, a howler outside the walls. Feminists, he says, have ruined college education; now they're going to ruin the military by putting women in combat. The Supreme Court should be overturned by a two-thirds vote in Congress.

A young attorney calls in (Rush's program has been hijacked; it's now Diane Rehm–like) and asks about some famous cases, which restricted police abuse. Bork reluctantly agrees that some abuses have been lessened, but he says, "We have to find another way to improve the court." The young lawyer sounds reasonable, Bork flip.

I have a conversation with a friend by the Coke machine about Dole's fall: it's the first human thing that happened in the Dole campaign, the first thing that makes us connect with Dole. He's human, we feel some sympathy; first warm moment. Commentators saying Bob is a trouper. We can put aside politics for a moment and relate to him as a human being. (He didn't collapse, pass out, he fell—a big difference.) I say it is a "Felix culpa." "A what?" "Felix culpa, a fortunate fall." "In contrast," my friend says, "to all of Bill Clinton's mea culpas."

Right.

9/21 Michael Feldman's show *Whad'Ya Know?* is coming from Little Rock. A reporter from the local paper is talking about Kenneth Starr (they're broadcasting from the famous Central High School); big applause after saying a million dollars a month is spent on small-time political contributors and a gubernatorial election seven to eight years ago. He does more boosterism for Little Rock. Touchy? Feldman implies. I guess so.

9/22 On *Meet the Press,* Perot slams Dole. Dole "poisons the atmosphere" by kicking him out of the debates. He blames Dole, and Dole alone, big-time. Ross says Dole's action will alienate independent voters who "moved the earth and won their Congress." Perot's pissed. Afterward, when Haley Barbour appears to be interviewed, even he looks crestfallen, so sharp was the attack on Dole.

Chris Dodd is partnered with Barbour. Dodd's going on about Newt's ethics report. "You should get this out and beyond you . . . why isn't it released?" James Wright's was out after a year; this is two years later. Barbour retorts with Clinton signing the same-sex marriage bill after midnight. And the fact Hillary wants to work on welfare reform.

Meet the Press ends with praise for the photojournalist in Chico who dropped his camera (forgoing a great picture) and "caught" Dole's head before it hit the ground.

Ross is on *Fox News.* He's still snapping at Dole. Dole disappeared at a critical time during the balanced-budget battle, he complains, which was lost by one vote. Now he's on to the Gulf War. A one-hundred-day war, some "PR" man saying it has a nice ring—we gave him (Saddam) nuclear capability. That should be investigated and laid out for the American people.

Ross is being Banquo's ghost again, haunting the Republicans. Tony Snow is not happy with the points Ross is scoring. He tries to bring Perot to Mena, Arkansas, and Clinton drug stories. I don't know about Mena, Ross says, going back to the contras, saying the CIA treats them like "Dixie cup people ready to be discarded."

On ABC's *This Week,* Clinton's drug general calls the flap about drugs and Clinton "election-year twaddle." His military disdain for politics, in this case, is on Clinton's side. ABC shows the Dole ad that features Clinton's MTV response to the would-you-inhale question. "Sure . . ." Then we see a clip from the Barbara Walters (ABC) interview. It was wrong, Bill says. Cocaine use is down. Roger doesn't use it anymore, doubtless. William Bennett, Mr. Morals, is interviewed. George Will points out that the recent upsurge started in '92 under Bush and it had gone up under Nixon. Isn't it the culture? Will asks. Yes, Bennett admits, but he's all for the countervailing power of the "bully pulpit." He's for bullies everywhere. Then Bennett says, "Culture is the water these fish swim in," sounding like Mao's *Little Red Book*. Perhaps Mao's in Bennett's *Book of Virtues*. I should check. (He isn't.) Bennett is on a satellite hookup from Aspen, Colorado. Enjoy Colorado, Brinkley says, signing off. I intend to, Bennett replies, the sybarite scold. Brinkley says that coming up there will be a "discussion among ourselves, no outsiders, no experts." That's for sure. We go to a commercial for Merrill Lynch, praising privatization, lots of shots of brilliantly clean foreign public buildings, all palatial.

Donaldson at the end criticizes the *Washington Post*'s use of a front-page picture of Dole down on the ground. The picture "lies." Donaldson praised how Dole jumped up, made jokes. It was a "kind of triumph" he says. He doesn't get his brain around to the notion of *felix culpa*, but he does see the tumble as a plus—though not as portrayed by (he didn't use the words) the mainstream media. He also adds that "Bill Clinton will owe his reelection to Alan Greenspan." Yes, Greenspan and Bob Dole and Newt Gingrich and . . . and . . .

On *McLaughlin,* Father John plays some of Dole's fall jokes: "I just earned my third purple heart." He turned a negative into a political plus, McLaughlin exults (faintly). Since he's a "former" Jesuit, he's trying to put whatever good spin he can on crucifixion imagery (see *The Washinton Post*'s picture, above). Eleanor Clift adds the fact that the Secret Service didn't want the railing nailed down, lest someone use it to climb onto the platform. The SS on the ball again. McLaughlin still is pushing the wonderfulness of it all. "Television has exposed the bias in the print press!" (Maybe Donaldson saw the *McLaughlin* show on Friday night.) Dole's Nomo/Brooklyn Dodgers slip is aired. No one thinks that's a plus. Dole was trying to be one of the guys, talking about Hideo Nomo, the Japanese pitcher for the Los Angeles Dodgers, but he called them the "Brooklyn" Dodgers, which they were and will always be to Dole.

The *Indianapolis Star,* which I happen to see today, is running the *Philadelphia Inquirer*'s series on income disparity and other bad news for the have-not-muches. It is actually shocking to see those melancholy graphs in that Republican rag, which is owned by the Pulliams, a branch of the Quayle family, one of whom is married to the mayor, Steve Goldsmith, the Republican candidate for governor in Indiana.

There's an article in my local paper, the *South Bend Tribune*: "Michiana welcomes James Carville and Mary Matalin" at the Economic Club of Southwestern Michigan. Where there's a buck to be made someone will be making it.

9/23 The tabloids have been having a run. The *Star*'s September 17 issue published the love diaries full of wonderful things about Dick and Sherry and Hillary and Bill. The *National Enquirer* and the *Star* both chimed in (in their September 24 issues) with more about Sherry's revelations: "Dick Morris Plotted Gay Smear on Jack Kemp." It seems Morris is related to Roy Cohn, late of the Rosenberg case, late of the gay closet, and now, thankfully, just late. But a Republican story is out and about, too, in the *National Enquirer*. "Top Dole Aide in Sex Orgies Scandal." Roger Stone, a "political strategist," is a man-about-town: swinger magazines, World Wide Web pages, a very large-breasted wife, a "former lingerie" model. Cha cha cha.

I had caught a bit of Roger Stone on the CNBC show *After Hours* a couple nights ago, though I didn't know who he was, not yet having seen a photograph of him. I did wonder who was that strange-looking guy sitting next to the host as some tangled story was being discussed. He (Stone) looked like John Dean after taking a lot of steroids, with a *café con leche* tan that might have been applied with a paintbrush. The show was ending, and the host was thanking Roger for appearing. One odd dude. But here is Roger Stone again, on *Hard Copy*. There's a video of what looks like Roger with his shirt off at what is called "an exhibitionists' party" in San Diego, during the Republican convention. His wife, it is alleged, was the winner of a party prize in 1993. Stone denies, denies. Stone stonewalls. Some mysterious person has created all this material on him and his buxom bride. OK, sure. There's film of Stone with Reagan, Bush. El supremo tacky, but Stone certainly does exude the same sweaty aura of Reagan's Southern California kitchen cabinet swinger set, the Alfred Bloomingdale and Vicki Morgan world of too much sun and wanna-be sex among the hardbodies.

The October *Esquire* arrived and they have my Joe Klein/Oleg Cassini scoop. Boo hoo. Who next will have the Gores don't recycle? *Vanity Fair*? Oh, well.

9/24 Rush is going on about the "arousal gap," his personalized version of the gender gap. Rush can't suppress this side of himself. He's talking about how Clinton is the perfect second husband, enough of a "screwup" to satisfy the normal female tendency "to fix, repair, and make up."

Rush discusses a *Washington Times* article on the Dole, Clinton, Barbara Walters interview. He says Leon Panetta humiliated Barbara by mocking her speech impediment. Rush's umbrage in this case is a little hard to take. He's now championing his "pick the pardon pool" that he's got under way. And then he begins to spout his own version of the Borkian rhetoric of the other day, the country slouching once more toward Gomorrah.

9/25 Rush is still on women. This time, it's the kissing-boy story out of North Carolina, a six year old suspended from first grade. Feminists up in arms. Rush is appalled. (Here it is, the paucity of the event and the magnitude of the response.) A caller tells Rush his local "AFL-CIO" radio station has been bashing Rush. No surprise to Rush, though it is a surprise to me the AFL-CIO has radio stations.

Rush is now onto partial-birth abortion. It's done for "convenience," according to Rush. "The vast majority" are not done to save the life of the mother. Though Clinton was surrounded by these women, he was misled.

A friend on the phone tells me of Clinton's recent visit to New Jersey. He was at the UN signing a nuclear test ban treaty and helicoptered down for a rally for a close local congressional race. Low on the agenda, but the people got to see the power of the incumbency. The cult of celebrityhood. Snipers on the high school roof, Chevy Suburbans with six guys in black jumpsuits. Clinton's speech wasn't good, but his charisma was still high.

We talk about the Massachusetts senate race. During a campaign event, Governor Weld jumped in the Charles River fully clothed. It was successful, furthering Weld's image as a wacky WASP. If Kerry had done it, it would have appeared ridiculous. Weld had thought of lowering flags to half-mast for Jerry Garcia's death, but didn't, yet got the bounce anyway. Kerry should be the symbol for that generation, but isn't.

We discuss the Macarena. He, too, learned it—a year ago—from his child, who learned it at day care a year ago, day care being ahead of the curve. Talking about Dole's World War II generation, he recounted a conversation he had with World War II veteran, a bombardier. My friend asked, Did you think about the effect of dropping the bombs? Yeah, the man said, if you got two close together, it was a good run. He hadn't realized my friend was asking a moral question. He would have said, they were trying to kill us and we were trying to kill more of them. They were the enemy. It is a job, not an ideology. Dole's often said to be a pragmatist, not an ideologue. They were so busy, there was no time for ideology; oddly, it was a generation without ideology (though they were surrounded by it on all sides, but not the young soldiers themselves). That came later for all the kids in World War II, a variety of ill-fitting suits. The sweet, long-gone by-and-by.

The Brooklyn Dodgers, Dole's world. That flap still waves in the air. Eight million World War II veterans are still alive, eight million out of sixteen million. Not for much longer, though.

Dole's presidential campaign doesn't seem superfluous, at least for them. But, as bad as it's going, it allows Dole to decompress from public life. If all he had was one day in the sun (as his Senate resignation would have been and was, handled the way it was in the summer), private life would have been a rude shock, indeed. The campaign is a long decompression chamber for Dole, allowing him to be bends-free when he surfaces after November. A one-day story would never have been enough. That's why Dole still seems happy, even though things are going badly, why he still lives in the world of the Brooklyn Dodgers.

A retirement tour, my friend says, commenting. Like Kareem Abdul-Jabbar's last year as a pro. A farewell tour. Like Julius Erving's. A celebration, a tribute, at every arena he played at for the last time his final year. Cheers and thanks and regard. Senator Dole! Senator Dole!

One day would never have been enough.

9/26 CBS's *48 Hours* is doing the sentencing of Polly Klaas murderer, Richard Allen Davis. Mr. Murderer is permitted a statement and he attacks Polly Klaas's father, saying he, the killer, committed no "lewd act," because as he was walking Polly through the gully she said, "Just don't do me like my dad," prompting Dad, sitting in the courtroom, to jump up and scream at him, followed by the sight of the father being restrained and hustled out as the murderer smirks, yet another foul deed successfully accomplished. Richard Allen Davis manages to make capital punishment seem as American—and desirable—as apple pie. Where's that *Dead Man Walking* nun? She's got her work cut out for her.

48 Hours follows this with a story of LeAnn Rimes, a fourteen-year-old country singer (a little older now than Polly Klaas was, but, in effect, her exact contemporary). LeAnn's fourteen, but looks like she's going on forty; she favors sultry country songs. They show a clip from her appearance on *Letterman*. During a commercial break later for *48 Hours,* there's a promo for CBS doing the Country Music Awards show later in the week. Self-promotion is going on all around. The fourteen-year-old has been singing forever. High school's on hold. Her best-selling album (CD) is called *Blue*. Rimes does Patsy Cline covers. She's interviewed about the Patsy Cline connection and replies, haltingly, that folks tell her, "Even though I haven't [lived the life of the music and lyrics] I make them feel like I have." She, evidently, has the Clinton touch, the Clinton magic.

While I watch all this I'm reading Katha Pollitt's column in the October 7 *Nation*. She's not going to vote for Clinton—lack of enthusiasm, division of the Left—and among the reasons, she mentions Rickey Ray Rector, the brain-damaged guy Clinton fried in Arkansas during the '92 campaign, right before the Gennifer Flowers story broke. Given Polly Klaas's killer's remark, frying does look a lot more reasonable tonight. What is curious about the killer's line of dialogue—Davis's fiction hurled at Polly's father— is that he made Polly sound like him: "Just don't do me" is certainly Richard Allen Davis's world and speech, not the dead twelve-year-old's.

9/28 On Diane Rehm, Susan Page of *USA Today* is guest host. A caller, a musician, asks why no one is supporting the NEA, the National Endowment for the Arts—which has survived, barely, in the budget that was finally passed. Our high art, he says, isn't being supported. Orchestras, ballets, and symphonies are what he considers high art. Yellow-dog Democrats are calling in. And no-enthusiasm-for-Clinton callers. One is going to do a write-in vote for Paul Wellstone. My own private rebellion and protest, she says. I recall a joke someone told me yesterday, purportedly heard on Garrison Keillor's *Woebegone* show. Does Dole wear boxers or briefs? A takeoff on Clinton's '92 *MTV* question. Dole scratches his head and replies, "Depends."

I'm on the phone with a friend who holds that it was more surprising that Dukakis was the nominee in 1988 than that McGovern was in 1972. McGovern was the result of a great movement within the party. Now we get governors who gain the national spotlight for some reason, usually voodoo economics. Like the rising fortunes of Christine Todd Whitman. We agree it's an odd television phenomenon; that's what makes them national figures so quickly. Property taxes are skyrocketing in New Jersey to pay for Whitman's income-tax cuts. He wonders why no one catches on.

9/29 *Capital Gang Sunday.* How well does Mona Charen know Dick Morris? I wonder. The six-year-old kid "kissing story" out of North Carolina is batted around. Jonathan Prevette is getting a lot of ink and air for his inappropriate touching, his smooch. A new pun has been invented: school bussing. Some outlandish feminist plot, according to Mona. "Anytime you want a kiss, Mona, just ask," the moderator says, doubtless infected by dark Mona desire (it's her death-alluding last name: Charen = Charon). Juan Williams, the show's resident African American, says to Mona, "Sue. I'm a witness!" In the "Hall of Fame" segment, Mona praises Richard Cohen, the *Washington Post* columnist Rush is always quoting, for reversing himself this week on partial-birth abortions. She says he got his earlier information from proabortion people. "Bravo," Mona crows.

I catch a little of *Crossfire Sunday:* Charles Rangel, Susan Molinari, Lynne Cheney, and the "liberal" co-host, Bob Beckel. They're all yelling.

Some figures emerge: 1.4 billion, twenty-seven days of doing nothing. Rangel is talking about the government shutdown. Molinari continues to yell. "What?" Cheney asks. "I want to get in the mood here," Susan says, all full of Staten Island spunk.

A commercial break comes on: partial-birth abortion. Pictures of premature babies in incubators. There's no sponsorship of the ad disclosed. Just an 800 number. It is followed by commercial with Elton John singing "Georgia." (Actually, it's a Georgia commercial featuring Elton John.) On one hand there are partial-birth abortions, on the other there is Elton John.

9/30 Rush is railing against Clinton stealing the glories of the Contract with America. As I listen to Rush after all these months I realize I am experiencing the often-remarked twist on Marx's line. First we have history as tragedy—bigoted radio fascists of the past, Father Coughlin, etc.—then history repeats itself as farce: Rush himself.

FOURTEEN

It's Debatable

10/1   Rush is reading the papers and he's got a story from the *Houston Chronicle* about Clinton's appearance at a $1.5 million Democratic fundraiser in Texas. "The arousal gap documented!" Rush exults. He reads a quote from the story, a woman's reaction after seeing Clinton. "That good-looking! All that power! Just think of it!" Rush doesn't bring up the Kissinger line, power being an "aphrodisiac," though, in Kissinger's case, one would have to drop out "That good-looking!" from the list.

Rush is now reading Jeff Jacoby's column from the *Boston Globe*. Forty more reasons to say no to Bill Clinton. The list is one of the oldest rhetorical devices and it hasn't lost any of its power. Letterman's ten reasons, the Top 40, sixty ways to leave your lover—lists are both narrative and concrete, a ladder logic, a story of facts. Rush reads: number fourty-four: Ira Magaziner . . . Forty-seven: The Clintons donate their used underwear to charity and deduct it on their tax returns . . . Fifty-one: a historic first: The first lady is called before a grand jury. Fifty-two: another historic first: White House reporters ask if the president has a sexually transmitted disease. . . . Fifty-nine: shameless exploitation I: "I have vivid and painful memories of black churches being burned in my own state when I was a child." (No black churches were burned in Arkansas when Clinton was a child.) Sixty-five: triangulation . . . Seventy-nine: He wants more money for the National Endowment for the Arts.

I wonder about those black churches burning in Arkansas, post-1946. Crosses burned in front of them? None burned? By accident? Old, badly wired churches. Oh, well. Jacoby's list energizes Rush. He gives the *Boston Globe*'s Web site address: www.Boston.com. It takes my computer two hours to make a connection. America responds to Rush!

A caller says that, regardless of his faults, Clinton is a "good father." Rush tells the Chelsea-Sidwell-Friends story ("Don't call my mom . . ."), my trolley driver's leak.

Another caller mentions Rush's words yesterday about the four hundred richest people list and says Rush was so kind since he's "four hundred one."

Rush starts reliving his past, saying that when he lived in Kansas City (one of our slim connections) he wanted to knock on the homes of the rich (he lived in some modest place "across the street") and ask them what they did for a living. He was never envious, he says, he was curious. Rush as everyman, stunned by wealth, the magic of money: how is the trick done?

After memory lane—Rush's bottom line, his bedrock, is if I can do it anyone can—he's on to, Who's paying Craig Livingstone's legal fees? He's defying a subpoena to tell who is helping him afford $350-an-hour attorneys. Rush still wants to knock on doors and ask the people how they do it.

Bill Maher, I see later in Barnes & Noble, has just published a book: *Does Anybody Have a Problem with That?* (Villard), a collection of his remarks from his Comedy Central show, *Politically Incorrect*. Speaking of historic firsts, he's got one: three author photos (all in color). Front, back, and back flap. Modesty, doubtless, left one flap unadorned. He calls his prose (tinkered with by many hands) "TelePrompter Ready." That, too, is a first, a new genre. Soon to be taught at your local university.

And at my university, E. J. Dionne is speaking. He reprises a lot of material from his book on the Democrats, *They Only Look Dead*. The public is presented with a lot of "false choices," he says, equal rights versus family life, welfare versus work, big government versus no government. He says the large unease in the country is the result of globalization of the economy, not the Reagan tax cuts. That there isn't the small townnation division, so much as a big cityglobal contest. College-educated, high-skills people do well in the global environment. E. J. is certainly in a global environment himself: Harvard, Oxford, a Rhodes Scholar, Catholic, he covered the Vatican for the *New York Times* and now is a columnist for the *Washington Post*. Newt's attitude about the counterculture is, "Nice try. You failed. You're wrong." The moral crisis is not the result of the counterculture, but because of the long hours at work. E. J. quotes Lamar! as saying that no one describes the country better than Bill Clinton. The midterm election was about Democratic failure, not Republican victory. The Contract with America was anti-government, but was taken as making government accountable. It wasn't just angry white men, but women, too. People with no college (though he's overlooking the "some college" category, which is also quite volatile). Big government has now entered the maternity ward. The Republican Congress at the end was carrying out the Kennedy Contract with America. "A lot of Democrats are petrified at taking over Congress again," he says. Ignore what they say the next three weeks on the shows; "no one has a clue" who will win the house. Newt has united the Democratic Party, but for one election only. Divisions will reappear. Barney Frank wants to lead the charge against the military budget. *(!—ask and yell?)* He says the commercial impetus for an "objective" press is more customers. Talk radio is the reappearance of the partisan press. The Supreme Court scotched campaign reform—by allowing millionaires like Perot, Forbes, and Huffington (and Morry Taylor?) to finance their own campaigns. *(Attention Robert Bork!)* E. J. on the '92 Perot voters: They were an odd coalition—Volvo-driving New England Tsongas supporters, truck-driving militia men from Montana, Buick-driving anti-NAFTA people from Michigan.

It's nice to publish books, but sometimes it's even better to pick up a few thousand for an hour of orality.

On *CNBC* there's Gerald Posner, the JFK conspiracy squasher, now Perot biographer *(Citizen Perot)*, along with a pro-Perot fellow, discussing the "No Debate for Ross" decision. Posner says Perot hated Bush. Why?

Bush was the one who brought Perot the news, threw him out of the Reagan administration, ended his officially sanctioned POW work.

Nightline does a summit show on Arafat and Netanyahu. One fact that comes out is Arafat and his men were sitting in their hotel room eating cheeseburgers and French fries. Ancient tunnels, helicopter gunships, the Wailing Wall, cheeseburgers and fries.

10/2 The campaign is winding down. If you have a permanent campaign, the last few weeks of it become less, not more, important. We've been in denouement mode for some time now. One bit of proof of this is that my local news, at least the NBC affiliate I watch this evening, did no campaign news at all, no national news, nothing on the Middle East, even.

10/3 Rush is making fun of Clinton. "I didn't part the waters but I silenced their voices," he quotes Bill saying, when Arafat and Netanyahu didn't want to talk at the White House news conference. Rush is mad. "This is life and death." Not a joke. He's mad that Bill made a crack, "I didn't part the waters . . ." Lampoons southern charm. Rush, though, jokes Clinton should have said, "Pardon the waters." It's the anniversary of the O.J. verdict and to "celebrate," Johnnie Cochran is on *Larry King Live* puffing his book, *Journey to Justice*. A commercial break gives us a Harry Browne ad, plugging an 800 number and promising to "abolish the IRS and replace it with nothing." Then there is a Ross Perot commercial objecting to not being in the debates. Bill Clinton in black and white (black and white bad—old TV, old print; color good, new TV, etc.). Ross Perot, the commercial says, made balancing the budget an issue. Then there is a CNN promo on an upcoming show: "Cynicism Has Become the American Way of Life." Yes, right on!

Back to Larry King and Johnnie Cochran. Jeffery Toobin (author of *The Run of His Life: The People v. O.J. Simpson*) is a liar, according to Johnnie. He never thought O.J. was guilty, as Toobin reports. No sirree. King makes a strange slip. He says "Clinton bashing" when he means "O.J. bashing," talking about before the trial began, all the mean things that were said about O.J. on talk radio, etc. In King's world, the two are not far apart.

Johnnie is very upbeat. And why not? He's a winner. It's a sweetheart interview. King is not anything but humoring and agreeable, but he has a grim profile when he listens.

More commercials: Save the Children. Sally Struthers looking like an ad for a welfare mother says, "For eighteen years things haven't gotten any better," and she's not talking about herself, just the years she's been working for Save the Children. A Dole commercial follows: Clinton's "a real tax-and-spend liberal."

I catch a little of *48 Hours*. The last fifteen years (see Sally Struthers, above), the number of women in prison has risen 400 percent. Seventy-five percent of them are mothers. We get to see the kids visiting. American gothic at its finest. Things haven't gotten any better.

10/4 There's an obituary of Peter Brennan in the *New York Times*. He is the labor guy (secretary of labor from 1973–75) who is credited with organizing the hard hat protest against the young during the Vietnam War, thereby alienating a portion of the generation against labor forever. He was president of the Building and Construction Trades Council in New York, and it was his rally in 1970 that produced the often-reproduced photograph of hard hats clashing with young antiwar protestors. The anticommunist American labor movement didn't understand the protests against the Vietnam War any better than Nixon. The obituary quotes a Long Island Republican representative: "The concept of 'Reagan Democrats' would not have existed if not for Peter Brennan."

Rush is calling the front page of the *New York Times* a "Clinton campaign poster." The pictures of Dole and Clinton the *Times* printed there today do buttress his point: there's one of Dole using the head of a little boy as a footrest, though it's Dole's head that's resting on top of the boy's head. Dole's eyes are closed; he looks asleep, or lost in a reverie so private it shouldn't be on the front page of a newspaper. Next to Dole's photograph is one of Clinton upright, smiling, left arm cocked in a fist, charging ahead through a crowd, enjoying himself. It's a real dead and/or alive contrast.

I'm on the phone discussing New Jersey politics with a resident of New Jersey. Malcolm Forbes ran for governor of New Jersey, I am reminded. We talk over Christie Todd Whitman's agricultural tax break for her spread. You might find this hard to believe, she was quoted as saying in her campaign, but five hundred dollars is a lot of money to some people. That's our "comfortable" Christine. The wrestler at the Dole rally after his acceptance speech in San Diego was a silver medalist. The Nike ad applies: You don't win silver, you lose the gold.

10/6 C-SPAN has done its usual yeoman work, showing the preparations for the first presidential debate in Hartford, Connecticut. One continues to marvel at how the campaign functions as an unacknowledged quadrennial WPA project. Millions are provided by the government, more millions in matching funds by corporations and common citizens. This jobs program favors the well-educated, though: technicians, consultants, high-skilled labor is employed, the biggest circus ever coming to town, outdoing Barnum and Bailey. C-SPAN shows us the Connecticut senators and other politicos wandering around the auditorium, marveling at the transformation taking place, awestruck by the balcony installations for the networks. And they don't even have to lavish any tax abatements like they usually do on the foreign corporations they want to lure to town. When people speak glibly of the "O. J. industry," they are at least noticing the phenomenon. This is the campaign industry. The multiplier effect is large. The permanent campaign just acknowledges it is cheaper to keep the operation running year-round than restarting it from scratch.

After the first eight minutes of the debate it seems over. What else is on? I see remote controls aimed at sets all over America. The expectations for this debate have been lowered (and raised) so much that even the expectations of the expectations are flat. The public could be surprised by only two things: Dole dropping dead on stage and/or Clinton jumping on the prettiest young woman in the front row.

We have Jim Lehrer giving everyone instructions, including the two candidates (one being the president), waiting for "the networks" to come on. Fifteen seconds to silence.

There's a logo behind them, which reminds me of the one on the Buchanan Web page, though this one is an eagle, with a hard-to-read motto on a ribbon. But there's blackness behind them. And two strips of darker blackness, glass through which cameras point, two strips like those put over the eyes in old-fashioned tabloid photos to make a person "un-recognizable."

The "format" of these joint appearances (hard to call them debates) was said to be a triumph of the Clinton team. Dole lost everything. Two debates only, compared to the three of '92, one of the two "town hall" style, Bill Clinton's favorite venue. But as the debate gets under way, it's clear that the Dole camp won at least one concession: the ninety-sixty-, thirty-second time limits. I can't think of a more nightmarish situation for Dole then to have to speak extemporaneously for, say, five, seven, nine minutes. The two-minute opening statement made this clear. Clinton compliments Dole for his "record of pubic service," which translates into "long"—as in old—record, and says, "I will try to make this campaign and this debate one of ideas, not insults," daring Dole not to do the same, at least for tonight; and then Clinton reels off a speech of his accomplishments: "10.5 million more jobs, rising incomes, falling crime rates and welfare rolls," etc., finishing up with "let's make education our highest priority so that every eight-year-old will be able to read," the saddest sow's ear/silk purse pledge I've heard.

Then we get Dole. "Thank you. Thank you, Mr. President, for those kind words, and thank the people of Hartford, the commission, and all those out there who may be listening or watching." It's not just the grammar, but the way Dole's saying it. He may want Mr. President to thank the people of Hartford, but I think he wants to, too. And the commission. Thank them for not letting old Ross in. And all those out there who may be (or may not be) listening or watching. It's one thing for Bob Dole to talk about Bob Dole in the third person, but it's quite another to talk about the audience which is hearing you in the third person, too. How about: and I want to thank the people of Hartford, and all of you who are listening and watching. . . .

Then he says, "It's a great honor for me to be here, standing here as the Republican nominee. I'm very proud to be the Republican nominee reaching out to Democrats and Independents." As Clinton planned to run in '92, regardless if he won or lost (it was time), so Dole winning the nomination and being the nominee, because it was his time, is enough. "I'm very proud to be the Republican nominee." Yes, he is.

But Dole may or may not be reaching out to Republicans. Then Dole goes personal: "I have three very special people with me. My wife, Elizabeth, my daughter, Robin, who's never let me down, and a fellow named Frank Carafa who, from New York, who along with Ollie Manninen, helped me out in the mountains of Italy a few years back. I've learned from them that people do have tough times." Well, Robin never let him down, but has her dad ever let her down? Frank Carafa didn't let him down. He seems to be the thoughtless hero who pulled a number of wounded men back out of harm's way, including Dole, with no thought to his own safety. A few years back, though, is fifty years back, not quite a few. "I've learned from them that people do have tough times." That remark is really strange. He has learned that he's had tough times, but he didn't learn it from them, unless Robin has had tough times, and Elizabeth has had tough times, and perhaps, Mr. Carafa has had tough times. But we know what he means, and once Dole gets rolling one better know what he means.

If he goes on about the personal too long he starts to choke up and over the months of the campaign, he's shed a number of tears, which might be to show he's warm not cold, but it also seems to be the thick skin of Dole getting thinner with age, and the emotions flowing quicker and more concentratedly. "I've tried to give something back to my country, to the people who are watching us tonight." Tears, by themselves, don't eliminate you as a candidate in our more sensitive times, as they did in Senator Ed Muskie's day.

Dole finally abandons the third person and gets to the second: "Now, I know millions of you still have anxieties. You work harder and harder to make ends meet and put food on the table. You worry about the quality and the safety of your children and the quality of education. But even more importantly, you worry about the future, and will they have the same opportunities that you and I have had. And Jack Kemp and I want to share with you some ideas tonight. Jack Kemp is my running mate, doing an outstanding job." People may worry about the "quality" of their children, but not often publicly. And when you worry about your children you are worrying about the future and you might not think the "future" is more important than your children. Jack Kemp is not, to my knowledge, going to be sharing ideas with us tonight, but I'm glad to know he's Dole's running mate, doing an outstanding job. Now all of this is just Dole-speak and it isn't just his confusions of subject and predicate that are notable; again, we do know what he means, sort of. This is how powerful men speak. People are ready to do whatever interpreting it takes. People who aren't powerful who talk like this usually become figures of amusement. Dole hasn't had to become more articulate over the years, but less, since he has consistently gained power, not lost it. Other than his 1974 race, he's had no real challenge to his Senate seat. And that was a few years back. It's hard to shuck off the habits of a lifetime in power, especially if they haven't been injurious to your health in office. He did badly in the primaries because he needed to win votes from people who were listening to him for the first time, or, at least, listening closely for the first time. His run as veep with Ford was a few years back too long ago.

"Now, I'm a plain-speaking man, and I learned long ago that your word was your bond. And I promise you tonight that I'll try to address your concerns and not try to exploit them. It's a tall order, but I've been running against the odds for a long time. And again, I'm honored to be here this evening."

Mark Helprin might think Dole's a plain-speaking man, but he is truly a laconic-speaking man, an elliptical-speaking man, something a bit different. Loquacious no. And I presume that that promise is a line recalled, since a promise is usually prepared. *I've been running against the odds for a long time*. Yes, he has. That's his bond with so many and his bond with his predecessor of note, Richard Nixon.

Lehrer starts off the "debate" with a slow, fat pitch to Clinton, the difference in how "the role of the federal government" is viewed by him and Dole. "Well, Jim, I believe that the federal government should give people the tools and try to establish the conditions in which they can make the most of their own lives." We now know what Clinton is: He's head of the Toolmaker Party!

Dole, on the other hand, says, surprise, "I trust the people. The president trusts the government." It took a few sentences to get those two out. He runs through some numbers. Talks about the BTU tax. Refers to his "little card" in his pocket (the Tenth Amendment). And ends with "That's my difference for the present. We'll have specific differences later. He noted a few, but there are others." This is going to be nothing but Dole-speak and Clinton-speak it appears. In Clinton's thirty-second response to Dole's one-minute response, he mentions "ending those drive-by deliveries," which has got to be one of the most ah, infelicitous conjunctions ever uttered by a public figure. Drive-through maybe, but drive-by, as in shootings? Just what we all want to associate with childbirth.

Lehrer asks, "Senator Dole, the president said in his opening statement we are better off today than we were four years ago. Do you agree?"

"Well, he's better off than he was four years ago," Dole says, getting off his first joke. Clinton tries to step on the laughter: "I agree with that. That's right." Dole continues, "And I may be better off four years from now, but I don't know," which sounds more than vaguely metaphysical. But he's on to stagnant wages, more Perot/Buchanan/Democrat talk. "Saddam Hussein is probably better off then he was four years ago." Which manages to attack Bush and remind folks of why Clinton is president. "Réne Préval is probably better off than he was four years ago." How many millions of Americans are asking their televisions now, "Who?" For those who aren't, Dole reminds us that Haiti is in the Clinton plus column.

If this goes on like this too much longer no one is going to be watching the second debate. What we continue to hear is a rehash of speech snippets, from both Dole and Clinton. Clinton has the better memory and does them smoothly whereas Dole lunges toward them, like toward passing driftwood in a flood. Clinton seems more and more relaxed as he realizes this is a walk in the park. He is now talking mainly to Lehrer, not to Dole.

Clinton manages to have Dole explain why he voted against Medicare (Dole: "We had a program called Elder Care"), the Brady bill, etc. In between explanations Dole stumbles into the briar patch of "trial lawyers": "The trial lawyers, I don't—you know, my wife's a lawyer. We're the only two lawyers in Washington that trust each other. But we're lawyers. I like lawyers. I don't dislike trial lawyers." He had already retold his trial lawyer joke ("before I hit the ground I had a call on my cell phone from a trial lawyer") and now he is doing a Bob Dole parody, a comic turn. It has pathos.

Clinton is wearing a black-and-white tie and a dark suit and against the black background he looks well composed, some contemporary fashion shot, all black-and-white tones (shiny handcuffs would not be out of place), whereas Dole is wearing a tie that is a slash of red. His makeup and tan give his face a nutty shade; his hair is dark with a few strands of silver, and the effect is not modern fashion (Clinton's hair white, paler face, low contrast), but the portrait of the founder of the bank, hung high in the shadows. Some networks are split-screening the debate and the contrast again is extreme.

It's clear that Dole has made a mistake in eliminating Perot from the debates, if for no other reason than that the age difference wouldn't have appeared so acute. With Perot it would have been at least a stairway, three generations. As it is, it's a cliff.

Lehrer asks Dole: "If elected president, would you seek to repeal the Brady bill and the ban on assault weapons?" Dole replies, looking downward, "Not if I didn't have a better idea. But I've got a better idea. It's something that I worked on for fifteen years. It's called the automated check or the instant check." Dole on the defensive is not a pretty sight. He ends his answer with a plea: "Let's get together on this instant check because that will really make a difference." It isn't Rodney King he's echoing, but Bob Dole the Senate majority leader, the deal maker extraordinaire.

Dole does a halting tour through the world: "I've supported the president on Bosnia," thereby undercutting what follows: Somalia, Haiti, Bosnia, Northern Ireland, Bosnia again, "Americans shouldn't have gone there in the first place," contradicting his support. It's a mess, Dole explains, letting Clinton then take credit for the relative calm in Haiti and Bosnia. Lehrer asks Dole, "What criteria would you use to decide when to send U.S. troops into harm's way?" Dole reaches back, and back. "We, it—after World War I, we had, you know, a policy of disengagement." The implication is that Dole was there. "Then from World War I to World War II, we had sort of a compulsory-engagement policy. Now I think we have to have a selective-engagement policy."

It's Dole being Dole, Clinton being Clinton.

Earlier today on the Sunday shows, former veeps got some airtime. Like the floats in the Thanksgiving Day parades, Quayle and Kemp and clips from old debates were paraded by, occasioned by the debate season.

It was odd seeing Quayle, though he did make clear once again it was he that softened up the electorate for Bill Clinton's draft history. When Quayle was elected a heartbeat away from the presidency the country began the generational shift Clinton represents and carried through—a permanent one, it is likely.

Obviously, my mind is wandering from the debate at hand like Dole's seemingly is. They're on health, the Kennedy-Kassebaum bill, Dole droning, "Another way you can do is to expand Medicaid. In America, no one will go without health care. No one will go without food—" Lehrer attempts to interrupt, to call time, but Dole's last remark ("without food") comes out like such a non sequitur it seems that Lehrer is trying to help him, quiet him, lead him away from his foolishness. The audience responds to the subtlety of the intervention and laughs somewhat uneasily and Lehrer attempts to paper over it with, "Senator, go ahead and finish your sentence. Sorry," which is the worst thing Lehrer could have said, since Dole never seems to finish his sentences, or thoughts, and Lehrer says it so kindly and deferentially that he seems to be talking to some doddering old man. Dole looks confused, lost, but then says: "Food." Lehrer repeats it dumbfoundedly, "Food."

It's time to bring on the nets and take everyone away, but Lehrer continues, "Back to foreign affairs for a moment . . ."

But when Dole isn't saying he's supporting the president ("I have supported the president when I thought he was right on Bosnia; I supported him on NAFTA and GATT"), he's explaining why he didn't vote for Head Start, or why he would be for eliminating the Department of Education. On the school-choice question Clinton makes an odd slip; "I support school choice. I have abdicated expansions of public school choice alternatives."

Doubtless, he meant advocated, not abdicated. But I do consider all that Clinton has abdicated: his signing of the welfare bill, his signing of the silly Defense of Marriage Act, all the other "liberal" positions from which he has truly resigned, abdicated.

Lehrer asks Dole about the "core of the elite" remarks in his acceptance speech. "Whom precisely did you have in mind?" Dole says, repeating Lehrer's language, "I had precisely in mind a lot of the people who were in the White House and other agencies who've never been—

had any experience, who came to Washington without any experience. They're all very liberal, of course, they wouldn't be in the administration. And their idea was that they knew what was best for the America [*sic*] people." That's not precisely what Mark Helprin had in mind, though after about seventy minutes, it is the first time the term "liberal" is used in the debate—and Helprin did have in mind, as discussed earlier, an entire generation of "liberals" he's happy to detest. Things have gone on long enough and Dole is getting tired, making more slips, more than Clinton: "This is the administration gave you the big tax cut." Dole's private brownouts are occurring more frequently and there are still around ten minutes to go.

Lehrer lobs Dole a juicy one: "Are there also significant differences in the more personal area that are relevant to this election?" There it sits. The character issue. Gennifer, Paula, the mummy, etc. Dole says, "Let me say first on the president's promise for another tax cut. I mean, I've told people as I travel around, all of you've got the tax cut he promised last time, vote for him in '96, and not many hands go up."

It's safe to say everyone is stunned. Dole's still meandering about tax cuts, and asks rhetorically (or for help), "Are there personal differences?" Lehrer steps in: "That are relevant to this here."

"Well," Dole says, "my blood pressure's lower and my weight, my cholesterol. But I will not make health an issue in this campaign." He appears very out to lunch, especially since he's parroting Reagan's line, though reminding everyone at the same time that Reagan's health (i.e., age) is not what one hopes for in a chief executive. "I mean, I don't like to get into personal matters. As far as I'm concerned, this is a campaign about issues."

I hear the rumble of disgruntled Republican stalwarts, the bleats of the Christian Coalition, the collective *oh no* ripple across—how did Mark Helprin put it?—the star-flecked plains of trailers and wheat (or some such). What skeletons does Dole hear rattling?

But Whitewater finally gets out of Dole's mouth. "I know you talked about it on the Jim Lehrer, on a PBS show, and I've never discussed Whitewater, as I've told you personally, I'm discussing Whitewater now, but I am discussing a power of the president has to grant pardons."

One could consider it a first: the reason not to reelect someone is because of fear of the pardon privilege. Dole's essential character, his ability to find compromise, to work out something, leads him once again to shoot himself in the foot. He starts giving Clinton counterarguments about the subject of pardons, finishing with, "But as the president of the United States, when somebody asks you about pardons, you say no comment, period." There are not enough periods in Dole's speech. He goes on, caroming from D'Amato to Kennedy, ending with an anecdote wholly private, "And I remember one day on the floor I said, 'Now gentlemen, let me tax your memories,' and Kennedy jumped up and said, 'Why haven't we thought of that before?' So, one of your liberal friends." In a car, it's called dieseling, when the motor still runs after the key is turned off. Dole has a bad case of dieseling.

Lehrer turns to Clinton. "Mr. President, thirty seconds."

"No comment," Clinton says, low laughter from the audience in response.

"What's the subject matter?" Dole says during the chuckling, and the pity is, it is not clear whether it's a jab, or an inquiry. A jab, I suppose. For a second he seems as lost as Perot's old veep candidate, Admiral Stockdale. And it seems painful, these last minutes, Dole speaking about his past, the country's past, lost, ah, lost. "Well, I'd say, you know the first homeless bill in the Senate was the Dole-Byrd bill, part of the Dole-Byrd bill—I can't remember who was in control then. I remember working with Senator Ribicoff from Connecticut on the hospice program, and now twenty-five hundred hospices. As I said, I remember—I've worked all my life while I was in the Congress. I left on June eleventh because I wanted the American people to know that I was willing to give up something. . . . So I rolled the dice. I put my career on the line because I really believe the future of America is on the line. We can give you all these numbers. They don't mean a thing if you're out of work, you have nothing to eat or you can't have medical care or you're holding a crack baby in your arms right now, and what do you do next?

"You know, America's best days are ahead of us. I've seen the tough times. I know they can be better." His voice has been getting shakier and now it really wavers. "And I'll lead America to a brighter future."

Dole doubtless believes he "put his career on the line," though most Americans are not shocked when a seventy-three-year-old retires. Careers are over then—not on the line. Quitting the Senate, rather than dying in office (Hello, Fidel!) was hard for Dole since he is using this campaign as a decompression tour, his farewell tour, gathering applause in all the cities he's played in before. When Dole said, "I've seen the tough times. I know they can be better," he seems to conflate the public and the personal in a particular way. He knows *he* can be better, *knows* it, if only he'd be given the chance. To be president. But it doesn't look like he's going to get the chance, since this debate is over and whatever it was supposed to do for him it hasn't. If anything it has hurt, or just deeply confirmed whatever misgivings both supporters and detractors carried around.

It's been too real, but then the actual end becomes surreal. Dole says, "If you really want to get involved, just tap into my home page: www.dolekemp96.org. Thank you. God bless America."

God bless my home page.

PBS cuts to its commentators. They, too, look stunned, abashed. But I'm waiting for the first comment, since that will set a level and everyone will go to it. Gigot is asked his opinion first. He's kind. Shields is kind. Kristol moves off the mild compliments by saying there was "nothing really memorable." Haynes Johnson says we saw "the authentic Bob Dole." Doris Kearns Goodwin says there were "no gaffes." Michael Beschloss tries to retain some intellectual status by calling it one of the "grimmer" debates in history.

Kay Bailey Hutchison attempts fake optimistic pirouettes and Barbara Boxer (D-Calif.) delivers her one-two message: "We know Bob Dole wants to cut the Department of Education." Hutchison's smile is especially forced: no mega–bumper stickers tonight.

But Gigot is pushing the happy line and it does appear to be his most unctuous performance, akin to George Will praising Reagan after he had coached him; it is Gigot's most partisan moment.

Mark Shields says the most memorable moment was "the mirror image picture" at the end, when the families came up on stage. Dole and Clinton and the two wives and two daughters. Not exactly mirror image, but we know what he means.

Switching channels I see Kevin Phillips being interviewed and his dour countenance is at least reassuring, and he judges there were no gains made by Bob Dole and Clinton's lead freezes.

Dan Rather signs off saying that Dole made a strong close. And ABC's Peter Jennings holds up a Clinton-Gore '96 rebuttal fax, marveling himself at how quick is their response.

Ross Perot is yapping on Larry King: "Eighty-nine percent can't pass the history standards. The good news is the only way is up." Schools as close to the homes as possible are the answer, Ross says.

King asks, "Schools at birth?"

I try to picture that.

Ross replies, "Yes."

C-SPAN has separate phone numbers to call if you are a Dole supporter or a Clinton supporter.

I come across Tony Robbins, the take-charge hustler, being interviewed. "How does it feel to have the president call you and say, 'Come to Camp David'?" some info babe (as Rush might say) asks him. Well, I can only imagine. But Tony says, self-deprecatingly, little old me, the "guy with the big teeth." Ain't it grand. This is selling something called "Mastery University" in Hawaii. Enroll Dole. He's ready for a career change.

Back to Ross. He's worried about a "stock market meltdown." Who's going to buy the stock, save those pensions? he asks darkly, rhetorically. China, I darkly reply to the tube; recalling the answer my wife had given to the same question. "We are going to have one," Ross reiterates, a financial meltdown, that is. "We created a party for you." And you better like it. "No one can kick us around."

C-SPAN is showing discussion groups of students at George Washington University. "Questions were asked and never answered," one student mildly complains. It is mentioned that the football game being broadcast on TNT was really exciting (tied in the last quarter) and a lot of viewers probably switched to it. Another student says, "By the time he [Dole] answered the question I forgot what the question was." The students are majority African American, at least in the discussion groups.

Ross is off Larry King. Now it is the also-rans, Natural Law, Green, Libertarian, Taxpayers Party. The last is an antiabortion party. John

Hagelin is a mild-mannered transcendental-meditation guy into very natural law. Ralph Nader wants to dismantle government, too, but does attack "corporate Democrats." Harry Browne, The Libertarian, attacks Ross.

C-SPAN—I almost typed C-SPIN—has Ann Lewis spinning in Spin Alley: "The Dole campaign will be rethinking how they can talk about education." Haley Barbour: "Bob Dole trusts the people, that's the best synopsis of the whole debate." Dole, according to Haley (who better to judge?), is "a witty, warm, comfortable guy." He says, "I've got to do a live shot," and hustles off, seemingly unaware of what he was doing. A dead shot? Barbour ends a lot of conversations that way. It is clear: Spin is propaganda in a hurry.

Trusty C-SPAN callers follow. The Clinton number must be getting a lot of calls. "Dole's campaign is on its last straw," a guy says, on his last leg. A lot of seemingly fake calls are coming in, of the I'm-a-Clinton-supporter-but variety. Telemarketing takeover. Are these people being paid above minimum wage? I wonder.

It appears that final statements are being given on Larry King. Harry Browne, Mr. Libertarian, recites his ad: "Would you give up your favorite federal program? We can repeal the IRS and replace it with nothing." The Natural Law guy says, "We're going to infect the political process." That gives me pause. Infect? Probably. Ralph—Mr. Green—Nader says: Vote for us, so corporate Democrats can't say you got nowhere else to go.

Back to C-SPAN. Donald Rumsfeld is there, morphing more and more into a nineties version of a slightly younger Robert McNamara, appealing to the youth vote. "He gave a very nice ending—contact our Web site. . . . I don't know how you could have done a better job than Jim Lehrer. After an hour and a half," people understand who Bob Dole is. They're still introducing Bob Dole to America. Yes, they probably do know who he is. He's the old guy.

More callers, this time from the Dole number. A woman exercised about abortion (unmentioned in the "debate"), homosexual rights, lesbian issues. Another, "I was a Clinton supporter . . ." One from Indiana sounds like she's reading a prepared statement.

Both the *USA Today* and AP home pages are shown. Each uses "vigorously" in its lead. Such leads are usually focus-group tested (the other print reporters in the room are the focus group) and one slant becomes preapproved, dominant. Ask people twenty words that come to mind about the debate they just witnessed: "vigorously" would not be one. But in deadline-land, it seems safe.

More planted callers. "Bob Dole is getting my vote." Standing in Spin Alley is a portion of the Clinton administration—Reich, Shalala, Panetta, and McCurry—looking happy, really pleased, talking to each other, not the press. Jesse Jackson is talking to the press, though. "I would have liked Ross Perot to be in the debate. . . . There was no talk of downsizing. . . . Most poor people aren't on welfare, they're working every day." On Dole, Jesse says, "He is a man tonight experiencing a sinking feeling."

It's eleven o'clock my time (midnight in New York)—we're always on EST and everything's about over. Because of the long *Larry King Live* show, CNN is just doing its *Inside Politics*. Polls are in. CNN/*USA Today*/Gallup. Who did the better job? 51 percent Clinton, 32 percent Dole. Are you better off from four years ago? 52 percent yea, 34 percent nay.

Dole is at a postdebate rally. It's an historic night tonight, he's saying. "We turned it around tonight." What has he not been inhaling?

Judy Woodruff interviews Gore. "I'm partisan," Al tells us. Clinton, he says, "tried to lift up the tone" of the dialogue. Bernie Shaw talks to Kemp. "He had to show his humor," Jack tells us about Bob. "This may be the start of the campaign." One wonders when it is going to start. It's Pascalian: an ending which is nowhere and a beginning which is everywhere. "It leaves it up to the second debate." The caravan is already moving on to the next New Beginning. Kemp can't stay on message though. "We want to repeal the tax code." Maybe he'll run with Harry Browne next time.

Ed Rollins, Mr. I Could Have Been a Contender, is telling Americans "this race will close up." He's upbeat. I guess he's looking for a job. He's identified as a "GOP strategist." "Republicans will be energized," he says. Bob Barnett, identified as Clinton's '92 debate coach, says it was a "most clear exchange of views. . . . The voters won tonight."

Back to polls. Does Bill Clinton exaggerate the truth? 51 percent yes, 47 percent no. (It looks like Clinton's hard core is 47 percent.) Three quarters of the voters said no-Perot was OK. My mind wanders back to the debate, Dole saying that Cuba is a haven for drug smugglers. Since I'm lost in time with Brooklyn Bob I had wondered if he was talking about the good old days when the Mafia ran the island. "It is not midnight in America," Clinton had said, but it's midnight now in my America.

10/7 Some callers to Diane Rehm wonder if they watched the same debate as the commentators. It appears to be an example of low expectations: Dole was human, he was funny, he didn't lie down in his coffin and close the lid. One caller quotes a Dole student supporter at George Washington University (people watching the same C-SPAN coverage I did) saying Dole needed to appear "old and wise and he just looked old."

Rush is despairing. "Damn that stupid tube!" he says, in his most Shakespearean mode. He's unhappy that people are calling in, demonstrating that Dole can't even hold his own base, people saying Dole should have done this, he didn't look good, etc.

On a newsbreak, it is said that the TV audience was off 20 percent from past debates.

I hear the sharpest critique of Dole's performance on Rush, whereas the other programs I've heard or seen today (the usual) seem to have watched some other debate.

Robert Bork is on Pat Robertson's program/network. (A colleague mentioned that she heard on Pat Robertson's program that the "cyst" on Clinton's neck [health-records-unreleased news division] comes from Clinton mainlining drugs.) Bork is talking about the politics of meaning, that it gives meaning to their lives, and utopian visions have replaced the transcendental. Robertson, the non-anti-Semite, says darkly that the originator of "the politics of meaning" was "a rabbi who was a leader of SDS in Berkeley." Should I send Pat a gift subscription to *Tikkun*, I wonder. Yes, Pat, it all links up, especially Clinton shooting up in the neck. Bork is making clear that "egalitarianism is equality of outcomes, not opportunity." Bork fits right in on the Christian Broadcasting Network: he's on the hot side of the weird spectrum. Something about his face, his facial hair and jowls, gives it a melted-candle look, recalling the drippings on the side of a straw-covered Chianti bottle, coffeehouses, circa 1965.

10/8 Rush is reading a news story on his interview with Dole and balks at the characterization "under sympathetic questioning." Who are these people kidding? Why don't you guys get tough on Clinton! he says. "It was designed to give Dole a forum," Rush says, for whatever he wanted to say. He turns to a video wherein Hillary is supposed to have said to an audience of "fat cat" fund-raisers, "When Al [Gore] and I feel totally at ease to be our real selves" after the election, all the liberal horrors will be unleashed. Rush is still fuming about after-debate coverage: "Mainstream guys said it was a slam dunk for Clinton and Dole was rotten." Rush seems to be making the charges worse in order to smear the "mainstream guys," but he ends up exaggerating the slanders he objects to. To my ears the "mainstream" still seems inordinately kind, except, maybe, for Rush. How could 21 million listeners not be the "mainstream"?

He's then onto soccer moms, which unzips his women problem, and he calls them "sucker moms," since they are supposedly supporting Clinton.

Rush runs a fake ad: "SOB, Save Our Bill, Send More Than You Can Afford." The humor is a relief. Rush then quotes his "Zagbe" poll: 5.3 percent race. "The gap is narrowing." Rush talked to the pollster yesterday. "Dole's real problem was his base." He's then on to making fun of Mary McGrory, imagining Tim Russert asking her about the "arousal gap."

A local commercial comes on for our congressional race. Joe Zakas, the Republican challenger, is running a pro–death penalty radio ad, saying how important the death penalty is in deterring crime. Tim Roemer, the Democratic incumbent, is, according to Zakas, against the death penalty. Joe seems to think that's the cutting-edge issue up here near the Michigan border, but I don't think so. The National Republican Congressional Committee is funding his campaign and Zakas, for doing its bidding, reaps the dubious reward of three scare mailings sent to area voters: Beware! Extremists! Congressman Tim Roemer's Sex Survey. I saw on C-SPAN actors filming generic scare ads (car jackings, wife beating, drug taking) and they show up in the Beware! mailing's stills.

Rush is now talking about *Fox News,* up and running. His buddy Roger Ailes (unmentioned) is running the show (and used to produce

Rush's television program). Rush says everybody's on TV now (but not Rush). It's no big deal. "There's so much more sifting required," Rush says, and I couldn't agree more.

Speaking of sifting, *Frontline* does a Dole/Clinton show. It begins with photographers and caricaturists. Roger Morris finally turns up on my television screen, but here he is identified as *Nixon's* biographer. We see Bob Dole's Kansas. It's actually Truman Capote's Kansas, real *In Cold Blood* territory, but *Frontline* doesn't mention that (I'm doing my own sifting here). Murderous windy plains. Holcomb (scene of the *In Cold Blood* killings) is southwest of Russell. *Frontline* has old Dole friends in a coffee shop talking about silence, laconism. Another old geezer says Dole's mother "waxed the inside of the wastebaskets."

Then we see Arkansas, the kudzu growing everywhere, humid, fertile, primordial even. Marshall Frady is interviewed and he says Clinton is Jimmy Carter and Billy Carter morphed. (There needs to be another ingredient. Maybe Marshall Frady?) A local prosecutor, after we see randy Hot Springs, says "you lived a lie" in the town. In order to get along, you went along.

Back to Dole. He's quoted saying, about his war wounds, "I still don't look in the mirror." We know what he means, but even he realizes it isn't true. "Except when I shave," he adds. But the not-looking-in-the-mirror remark hangs in the air, its truth more figurative than literal.

He tells the same Dad-swollen-ankles story from his acceptance speech and breaks down again. This must have been taped before the convention. Michael Kelly of *The New Yorker* is saying Dole's "as if it mattered" attitude is a result of his World War II service. *I've been through worse* could be the real Dole mantra. It's Richard Ben Cramer's point, too.

Dole is breaking down giving his eulogy at the Nixon funeral (Oliver Stone time again). Clinton does remain dry-eyed.

My wife comes in from her office, where's she's working, notices what I'm watching, and says, "Unfortunately, the presidency is now middle management and you don't get the best people for those jobs anymore." She returns to her work.

Dole is a Methodist and we look at a gruesomely plain church on yet another windswept horizon. Bill is a Baptist and we see humanity swaying, hand clapping, hot bodies in loud prayer.

In one of the still photographs of Dole, whom do we see but Roger Stone standing next to Dole, though Stone is not identified. Not a photo you would use in swinger magazines. Dole's difficult 1974 race (the last difficult Kansas race) is pawed over. Dole playing the abortion card, foreshadowing the attacks on Clinton's second African American nominee, Henry W. Foster, Jr., to be surgeon general (not mentioned by *Frontline*), leaflets put on cars with pictures of "dead babies." By coincidence (which is what the world of TV is; everything is coincidence), Jocelyn Elders, Clinton's first African American surgeon general, was on Diane Rehm saying she's sure Clinton will "fix" the welfare bill. As is the fashion these days, it is claimed on the *Frontline* program how similar Bob Dole and Bill Clinton are. Ha. Yes, they are both politicians. Others claim Hillary and Liddy are much the same. No they're not. The biggest difference is they come from different generations and that difference alone is a chasm.

10/9   It's veep day. Vice presidents often become president (Nixon, Bush), and some do not (Mondale, Quayle), and Dan Quayle has been visible these days, and the clip of Lloyd Bentsen's "You're no John Kennedy" crack to Dan has been played over and over, another brief, frenetic, seasonal news-life-cycle video moment. Quayle still carries forward the generational mantle for the right wing. Quayle quickly became a figure of fun in the Bush administration. Not because of his arduous service in the National Guard, but his intellectual, ah, reach. Trouble passing the bar. Potatoe. His Freudian mangling of the NAACP motto, "A mind is a terrible thing to waste": "What a waste it is to lose one's mind. Or not to have one. How true that is." Brains aren't everything, but Dan did appear to be what he was, a rich kid from Indiana who hadn't ever been overly taxed by life, a Hoosier with a talent for golf. Given the differences apparent in '92, the clearest one, which no one would dispute (except perhaps Quayle's novelist wife) was that Clinton was smarter. One of Bush's handicaps was having Quayle a heartbeat away (and had Bush gotten a second term the actuarial possibilities went up), and Americans do seem, at times, rational.

Clinton/Gore was a helpful pairing, whereas Bush/Quayle was not. Clinton/Gore was a successful generational couple, given their offsetting virtues and vices. Usually, it is countergenerational; the same generation can lose. Mondale/Ferraro. Dukakis was not helped by Bentsen. Younger/Older is going backward. Clinton couldn't have gone younger and he realized older might be fatal. The two-for-one he talked about was not Bill/Hillary, but turned out to be Bill/Al.

Dole had no trouble finding a younger running mate, but picking Kemp highlights a number of things, one being energy versus stamina. Having throw-one-deep-for-the-Gipper at Dole's side does, again, offer a continuing contrast. Kemp might be a lightweight, but he's bouncy. He's Empower America, but he's also out to Empower Kemp.

The interest in the veep debate has been slightly increased by the first presidential "debate"—will Kemp KO Gore? Will anyone watch? Here are the men in waiting, waiting.

On C-SPAN we wait for the networks. Lehrer is counting down the time. One minute and a half. Thirty seconds. The sartorial look is reversed tonight. Kemp looks more like Clinton, more black-and-white contrast, dark tie, silver hair. Gore is being Dole, dark hair, red tie. There's the same logo hanging behind, and for some reason (depth of the stage?), the banner is easier to read: "The Union and Constitution Forever." The stage isn't as dark as it was for the presidential debate. The background is a dark blue rather than gray-black.

"Here we go," Lehrer says, bringing to mind Gary Gilmore (Let's do it) once again.

"Good evening from the McAfrey Center. . . ."

Lehrer seems to want some good TV, so his first question pleads for fireworks: "Some supporters of Senator Dole have expressed disappointment over his unwillingness in Hartford Sunday night to draw personal and ethical differences between him and President Clinton. How do you feel about it?"

Lehrer's presumption is that veeps are supposed to do the dirty work; this is how they become made men. I recall the old ass-kicker George Bush, gloating after he was done mopping the floor with that Ferraro woman.

"Bob Dole and myself do not see Al Gore and Bill Clinton as our enemy. We seem them as our opponents." Kemp doesn't seem to be into parallel construction, giving Al pride of place. And he doesn't, it seems, want to take the bait. He wants, it appears, to make an opening statement. He's on to Bob Dole, "one of those men who's served in the United States Senate." There's a ringing endorsement. "His public life is a public record. He fought on the battlefield. He has worked with Democrats and Republicans." Kemp seems to be confusing battlefields. "In my opinion, it is beneath Bob Dole to go after anyone personally."

Yes, but is it beneath Jack Kemp? Everyone hopes not.

But, it appears, it is. "Clearly, Abraham Lincoln put it best . . ." Once Lincoln's name comes out all hope flees.

He rambles on, Mr. Nice Guy.

Gore says, unsurprisingly, "I would like to thank Jack Kemp for the answer that he just gave." I guess. One question rises in a lot of viewers' minds: Isn't there a ball game on? "I think we have an opportunity tonight to have a positive debate about this country's future. I'd like to start by offering you a deal, Jack. If you won't use any football stories, I won't tell any of my warm and humorous stories about chlorofluorocarbon abatement."

The bad joke is rewarded with nervous laughter from the audience. This show is going nowhere.

In response to a question about taxes, Kemp says, "Jim, this economy is overtaxed, overregulated." Kemp is comfortable talking with reporters. His "Jim" makes this all too cozy. Kemp says, "Our biggest debate with this administration on domestic policy is that they think we're at our fullest capacity." Wow, news here. I thought it was drugs, abortion, big government, etc. Taxes, even. "That we've reached our potential, and that two and a half percent growth is enough for America."

Kemp defends trickle-down, stays on his economic theories to no discernible benefit, and keeps coming back to it. "And by cutting and eliminating the capital gains, by cutting and eliminating the estate tax, by bringing the top tax rate down to something reasonable—here he goes again." All this is so bald, so clearly beneficial to the rich, even Kemp seems to have lost his way. Is he talking about himself in the third person? Who knows? He continues: "I think in peacetime it shouldn't be higher. Bob and I don't think it should be higher than 25 percent—be phased in." It does seem like he's let out a secret. We're eliminating capital-gains and estate taxes and cutting the top rate to less than 25 percent.

He's blown a hole in something. "The capital would flow out into the economy." Oh, yeah. "Trickle-down" has become as hot a phrase as "liberal Democrat," but Kemp doesn't seem to notice it. He doesn't seem to realize he's talking to the American people, not business groups that have paid him twenty thousand dollars to speak.

Everyone's into personalizing the electorate and Kemp brings in another citizen's name. "Dana Crist of Lancaster said the day the tax bill is passed in the Congress she will open a new factory with forty, or fifty, or sixty employees in Lancaster, Pennsylvania. He'll call that trickle-down. I call it Niagara Falls."

Gore says, "The problem with this version of Niagara Falls is that Senator Dole and Mr. Kemp would put the American economy in a barrel and send it over the falls," Gore says, well prepared.

Even I want to turn on the ball game. I keep wondering what Gore's normal speaking voice would sound like. How similar to this stilted, mannered, solidifying, plodding drone? Too bad he never lived in New York. Say it Al, get it out.

Since abortion went undiscussed in the presidential debate, Lehrer asks directly, "What . . . would a Dole-Kemp administration do to change the current legal status of abortion in this country?"

Like Dole before him, Kemp sidesteps the question at the beginning, talking about a letter from "*Money* magazine suggesting that Bill Clinton wanted and did lower the cost-of-living allowance for senior citizens as a way of reducing Social Security."

Kemp finally gives a very middle-of-the-road reply: "This country should not be torn asunder over this debate. It has to be carried out with civility and respect. And Bob and I believe it can be." At the end, he does say, "We have a president who vetoed a congressional ban on the ugly and gruesome practice of snatching life away from a child just moments before he or she enters the world. That is unacceptable." By inference, a lot else is acceptable. So much for the pro-life veep. Kemp sounds more like his buddy Forbes than any of the Ralph Reed legion.

Gore says, "President Clinton has made it clear that he will sign legislation outlawing procedures such as this, if there is an exception to protect the health of the mother." Then he returns Kemp's soft blow with a harder one: "Mr. Kemp has voted forty-seven out of forty-seven times to have such amendment [outlawing all abortion] and to restrict this completely no matter what the circumstances, even where rape and incest is involved. We will never allow a woman's right to choose to be taken away."

Kemp's speech patterns are falling into a quarterback's cadences: hut hut hut.

Once more to foreign climes: Kemp responds to Lehrer's question about Dole's criticism of Clinton's handling of Haiti, and Kemp veers to "We caused problems in the first place by denying Caribbean countries and Third World countries a chance to trade freely in the United States. . . . And then we have to turn around, as we did in Mexico, having to bail them out." It's all south of the border to Kemp. The exchange is ended oddly by Kemp: "Diplomacy first, and don't bomb before breakfast."

Gore's in protection-and-puffery mode: "When there was a crisis involving the Mexican peso, again President Bill Clinton showed bold and dynamic leadership. . . . You know, people said it was a big risk at that time. We've ended up making a five-hundred-million-dollar profit. All of the loans have been paid back."

Kemp sounds, all of a sudden, like Ralph Nader (Go Greens Go): "It's unbelievable that we could cause a drop in the standard of living of a friendly country like Mexico by nearly 40 to 50 percent. Unemployment goes up. We send U.S. tax dollars and IMF moneys to Mexico and we make a profit. At that level, that gives new meaning to the word profitability for U.S. foreign policy. The pain, the suffering, the unemployment, the bankruptcies, the loss of the standard of living, the people who have had to come across the border of California, Arizona, New Mexico, Texas . . ." Republicans must have their fingers in their ears as this Democratic tirade issues from Kemp's mouth.

Lehrer asks Kemp about his *Meet the Press* appearance last Sunday where he said "that the federal government engages in 'regulation reign of terror.' What exactly do you mean?"

Kemp says, "Well, exactly just what I said." Kemp has been so used to using the rhetorical exaggerations of the gadfly he was (and is) that he seems to be tone-deaf to how it sounds coming from a vice presidential candidate.

Gore accuses Kemp of voting against the Clean Water Act and the renewal of the Superfund Act. Then he extols the Clinton administration's environmental record. Kemp replies, "When I went to Congress from Buffalo in 1970, you could almost walk across Lake Erie because of the pollution. Today, thanks to the secondary and tertiary treatment plants which many of us voted for on both sides of the aisle—which actually started under Richard Nixon, a Republican president—our water is cleaner in the Great Lakes." Thereby making Gore's point. The environment is cleaner thanks to legislation. I feel the pain of the Republicans who are watching this.

Gore says, "I think, Mr. Lehrer, that throughout much of his career, Jack Kemp has been a powerful and needed voice against the kind of coarseness and incivility that you referred to in the question," not just damning Kemp with faint praise but condemning Republicans with clear inference. Gore *does* attack baseball's famous spitter, Roberto Alomar: "I won't hesitate to tell you what I think. I think he should have been severely disciplined, suspended perhaps, immediately." Kemp, in jock solidarity, had refrained from commenting on Alomar in his response to Lehrer's direct question about the incident. But Gore's voice still sounds like voice-recognition software.

Kemp compounds the insult by saying, "Well, I thank you, Al." A smattering of nervous laughter. "I mean that very, very sincerely." Too bad there's not a camera on Dole now, wherever he's watching this from. The good news is this is just about over.

Gore attacks Dole: Bob wants "to abolish the Department of Education. He voted against the creation of Head Start. He vigorously opposed the Family and Medical Leave Act." And it is a reminder of how seldom Kemp attacked Clinton.

Mercifully, it's over. There is no double family posing this time. Kemp leaves the stage rather quickly.

I turn to PBS. The younger Kristol is saying if folks came down from outer space they would have thought Gore is the Republican and Kemp the Democrat. No, they would have thought they witnessed some bizarre ritual of a dark-suited sect hoping to pacify unknown deities. Mark Shields says there was "no indictment delivered." Shields quotes Michael Deaver, Nancy Reagan's friend, that the performance may change numbers a "little bit." Shields says that is a most cautious endorsement from the Spinmeister. I catch Dan Rather saying the end of the Yankees-Orioles game was much more exciting.

Larry King on CNN is talking to Senator Judd Gregg (R-N.H), who played Gore in practice debates. "Were you a good Al Gore?" King asks. "No, I might have been too lively," the senator replies. (Maybe he should have played Kemp.)

Ed Rollins, still looking for a job, says on *Inside Politics* that he thought Kemp has "had better nights." Tom Downey, the former Democratic New York congressman, calls it a "high-minded debate," one absent of "mudslinging." He played Kemp for Gore in debate rehearsals. He adds, "I wanted to answer some of the question for" Kemp.

Bill Schneider comes on with a *CNN/USA Today* poll. Fifty-seven percent say Gore won, 28 percent Kemp. But asked who's more "exciting," Kemp scored 53 percent, Gore only 31 percent. But 53 percent thought Gore "better informed." Aren't polls wonderful? Regarding 2000, would people be satisfied with them as opponents? 78 percent yea, 19 percent nay.

Schneider says Gore "showed a command," and compliments King: "His debate with Ross Perot on your show" prepared him. Schneider adds that there have been over "two hundred polls published this year and Bob Dole hasn't led in one of them."

King says the Orioles were "robbed." I search for a sports news channel.

10/10 The subjects of the Diane Rehm show are kids kissing, (sexual harassment division), mutual funds. There is no mention of the previous night's debate, which, of course, is mention enough.

Rush is upset. "I'm surprised AlGore [he says it as one word] didn't call for a bathroom break . . . and point out what the bathroom looked like." Rush tends to go for infantile analogies. He's upset at Gore's tone. "The arrogance!" He seems to be talking to himself. "Here I am, getting off message already." Back to Gore: Here's how "liberals think of all of us. . . . We're morons, we're second and third graders. . . . We get talked down to." Democrats are "most afraid of taxes," Rush says. "They're scared to death of tax cuts, tax relief."

But he's unhappy with Kemp, too. "In my mind, it was not refuted," referring to Gore's charges. "It was a big letdown." So much could have been done, Rush holds. "AlGore was a hanging curveball." The mainstream press (said with Rushian sarcasm) says, "It was civil, it was polite."

Rush leads me to the conclusion that for Republicans the One Hundred and Fourth Congress was '96's Buchanan of '92.

Rush is still dismayed. "When we have to wait for Dan Blather to do our bidding," he says, we've reached the end. He then becomes personally positive. He takes the credit for Al Gore saying there were only twenty thousand new cops on the street, not the one hundred thousand Clinton always claimed.

Kevorkian has notched another MS victim and Rush calls him "Jack the Dripper."

10/11 The *New York Times* has a graph today showing that the viewers of the vice presidential debate dropped almost by half from 1992, from around 37 percent to 21 percent, though fewer watched the baseball game on Fox.

Rush is still going on about the pardon problem.

But the question is not whether Clinton will pardon anyone, but whether the country will pardon Clinton by reelecting him. Unlike Watergate, which hadn't developed before the election beyond a second-rate burglary, the sins of the Clintons have been examined extensively, if not exhaustively, and the public is aware of much more than the tip of the iceberg. So it isn't the Watergate analogy that holds. The referendum in '92 was on Clinton's girl and draft (sex and death) problems. This election's referendum will be more general, since so many other legal issues have been uncovered. Sex and death are not problems this time around, they are persons. The ghost of O. J. looms again. People won't be voting on November 5, they'll be rendering a verdict.

Yesterday, the *Wall Street Journal* ran an article on Dole's money machine. His grunts and groans on the lecture circuit, his "talks," fetch thousands of dollars a pop. What will his fees be now?

10/12 Charles Keating, I read in the *New York Times,* has been released from jail (though not in time, it appears, to have shown up at the

San Diego convention). O. J.'s main man, Judge Ito, screwed up Keating's state case (improper jury instructions) and that was overturned and now Keating is flirting with bail because his federal case might also be overturned. Some jurors, it appears, talked about the state conviction. Maybe Bill Clinton could pardon Keating too, declare amnesty for all savings and loan crimes, heal the Wall Street generation (rather than the Vietnam generation). The sons of George Bush would be relieved. Those who opposed the Vietnam-era amnesty would most likely be for this one, though those who wanted amnesty for draft dodgers, etc., might be against it. But it would be a perfect Clinton swap. Charles Keating also turns up in the *Times*'s review of the movie *The People vs. Larry Flynt,* shown at a film festival. Keating, like Ed Meese and other doyens of Reagan's own seamy southern rim, was a righteous firebrand against low-rent smut peddlers like Larry Flynt, rather than the puffed-up, pneumatic interest-rate flesh peddlers like himself. Life is grand. The film resurrects Jimmy Carter's sister, Ruth Carter Stapleton, of Jesus-saves fame, and displays the ubiquitous Jerry Falwell. Where's the Keating Five these days?

10/14 A friend calls from California to report a *San Francisco Chronicle* story on Dole's campaigning there. A subhead on a story reads: " 'He's too old,' say the residents of Leisure City." They ought to know.

Steve Roberts is again hosting the Diane Rehm show. He has a lot more time on his hands since being fired by James Fallows at *U.S. News & World Report*. Everyone lives on the head of a pin in the Washington media world. Fallows, after being especially hard on the revolving door of press/government hacks, has set aside the role of press critic. Mort Zuckerman's millions have lured Fallows to the helm of *U.S. News*.

Roberts and his wife, Cokie, had become too promiscuous on the corporate talk circuit and since Fallows had already slammed them in print it was no surprise Roberts was let go. Though that is not the fate of David Gergen, the ur-example of journalist/government fl/hack, who is practically the social equal of Mort Zuckerman.

Regardless, the show Roberts hosts today does nothing much about the election.

Rush replays, acceding to popular demand, his fifteen-minute rap on the "great lie," which is that Republicans wanted to cut Medicare.

Rivera Live, on CNBC, has Darden and Dershowitz doing their odd-couple routine. Who's the schmuck here? Darden the sour loser or Dershowitz the smug winner? Charles Grodin does have an election show.

The talk is now of financing the campaign rather than the campaign itself. There's the spectacle of ADM, the agribusiness giant, paying a huge fine for past improprieties, and Indonesian money flowing to the Clinton campaign. This year's Nobel (Peace) Prize winners (a Catholic bishop and an exiled leader of the Timorese independence movement) have helped to locate Indonesia on the globe for the readers of the *New York Times*. East Timor was "annexed" by Indonesia in 1975 and things have gone from bad to worse there. The late Ron Brown's job ladder from head of the DNC to the Department of Commerce linked campaign fund-raising rather closely with encouraging global trade. Indonesia, from what is coming out in the papers, might become (or be) Clinton's Philippines (the Marcoses never made Reagan look good) and the Riady folks Clinton's version of too many shoes. Margaret Carlson, who's usually on the *Capital Gang* show, is here saying all people think politicians and money are suspect, so it's a wash.

CNBC goes to an ad, paid for by Prudential Securities. It's a series: "If I Were President." This time it's . . . Peter Fonda. Peter wants to abolish everything but the Supreme Court and have it be in session constantly. Or, as Peter Fonda said a long time ago in *Easy Rider,* "We blew it."

I've seen Dave Thomas, of Wendy's, do the same ad: he wants to have homes for every foster child. Homelessness recalls last week's *Whad'Ya Know?* show. Michael Feldman had Benton Harbor as the "Town of the Week" and cited its lowering homicide rate as one of the reasons for taking note of it. For the unknowing, Benton Harbor is a "town" right next to St. Joseph's, in Michigan, right above the Indiana boarder, on Lake Michigan. St. Joseph's is the "white" town, Benton Harbor is black and as poor and burned out as you can get. Northern segregation at its worst and as St. Joe (as it's called in these parts) gets gentrified, its beachfront spiffed up, downtown revitalized, Benton Harbor continues to be ground down. The woman they called for a "spontaneous" on-the-air interview sounded like a middle-aged, working-class African American, one with a job at one of the more stable factories in the area. But Feldman's jauntiness and the wacky humor generated by inappropriate answers weren't flowing from the phone line. We were way beyond irony here. Asked about the crime rate, the woman attempted to be positive, saying it had gone down, but she sounded overwhelmed by the enormity of it. The African American actor Sinbad came from Benton Harbor and she said she knew his family, but not him. Her favorite restaurants were Bill Knapp's and one other chain. This woman was struggling, very depressed, and the picture she painted was so bleak and true that finally even Feldman realized it wasn't funny. The only thing that was funny was that his show was going to send her a selection of gourmet coffees and the like for her time. Graveyard humor. Some things just don't inspire yuppie yuks. Irony doesn't always save the day.

Back to Charles Grodin. The head of Coca-Cola's salary is mentioned. One billion (?!) in seven years. Five percent taxes. Margaret Carlson says the obvious, 15 percent tax cuts help the rich. The big mistake is that the Republicans think they can squeeze the poor while letting the rich get richer. John Fund of the *Wall Street Journal* says perkily, "That's why there should be a flat tax." The bad news, of course, is that there already is a flat tax. Except for the very rich, who can always find ways to dip below the 26 percent most people pay in federal taxes.

On CNN's *Inside Politics,* Kathleen Hall Jameison claims that TV coverage of the campaign is down 60 percent. (She must be referring to the networks, or, given all the TV time available on cable [the QVC world, etc.], a smaller percentage of total hours is given over to politics.) It is poignant to think back to precable days ("Stop Pay TV" on movie theater marquees). Three networks and PBS, most not even on twenty-four hours. The Stone Age. Print coverage (what's on the front page), Jameison says, is down 50 percent from 1992.

10/15   Rush is ruminating. We've spent the whole time trying to convince people we're not like that, we're polite. (He's objecting to the new civility—he wants Dole to go negative.) We've fallen prey to the stereotype images fashioned for us. It's a focus-group con, he says. I don't know if it's too late, Rush intones. There has been fraud, he says, in these focus groups, the networks wired-up guys and gals. The president doesn't think it's over, Rush says. Clinton has a radio ad aimed at the Christian Coalition praising the Defense of Marriage Act. He wants a complete ban on partial-birth abortions, except when the mother's life is in danger. It's the height of how-we-can-fool-them-today, Rush complains. But only 24 percent are paying any attention to this election, he says, taking comfort. On to "Lippo suction," the Indonesians, the Riadys. If Clinton is reelected, it will come crashing down on him in a year or so. He seems to be taking Clinton's reelection for granted. I recall the Reagan ten-million-dollar contribution in Ed Rollins's book (215). From the Marcoses, though Rollins claims the campaign person who accepted it just kept the money for himself. A caller says the conservatives aren't fired up because the Republicans ran their most liberal candidate. A woman caller says the press is setting Dole up to be negative. Rush demurs. He reaches for poetry—focus groups are a scam designed to make us go gentle—somewhat tripping over his Dylan Thomas.

Look at the numbers, Rush says, attacking the veracity of the polls. I don't watch WWF wrestling. Look at the numbers. I don't read the *National Enquirer*. Look at the numbers. Meaning, they have big audiences, someone must look at them, though they deny it, as they deny Dole. A caller says he's going to vote for Clinton so Americans feel the pain of runaway spending. Rush says, I can't go on with this.

10/16 Rush is having a ball today replaying the call of "Rita X," a black woman from Detroit, a "Calypso Louie" (Farrakhan) follower, which is full of wild malapropisms. He's reacting to last night's Ted Koppel interview of Farrakhan on *Nightline*. Rita X is talking about the "chiefs of joint"—I loved that one—and the spaceship hovering over the earth, a notion that Farrakhan seems to embrace, as he did last night with Koppel. Farrakhan invoked Jimmy Carter as a fellow spaceship maven. Rush is running his own version of *Amos and Andy*. After he calms down he quotes Dick Armey saying that in the privacy of the voting booth people will pull the R lever. He congratulates a Republican candidate (Robert Braden) for morphing a picture of Richard Allen Davis,

Polly Klaas's killer, into the face of his Democratic opponent (Vic Fazio) in an attack ad.

The last debate. We're back in San Diego, at the auditorium of a local college. And it is an auditorium, though this is supposed to be the "town hall" debate. On the stage they've set up bleachers for the "audience," the citizens. Podiums are downstage, at the front. The candidates' backs are the view for the large audience that is seated in the auditorium. It's like *Equus* on Broadway. The folks in the auditorium seats are watching a play. The theatricality of all this is now overt. It's a show of a "town hall" event. Why couldn't they find a true theater in the round, where the artificiality wouldn't be as apparent? What lock does San Diego have on the "commission"? The Republicans? What is ITT paying this time? Frank Fahrenkopf, co chair of the Commission on the Presidential Debates, reads out a list of production people to the C-SPAN crowd. We hear about the national sponsors: Phillip Morris, Sara Lee, Sprint, and others. He introduces Alice Hayes, president of the University of San Diego. She's a large woman in a red dress, sporting a flag scarf around her neck. She introduces her boss, the chairman of the board of trustees, Peter Hughes. "President Alice," he calls her. It's a Catholic university, apparently. We're in the Shilaey Theater and he introduces (his boss?) Darlene Shilaey. She's even larger than President Alice, wearing green. Darlene brings on the Presidential Debate Host Committee, which emerges from the back of the stage. It's civic pride night in the Shilaey.

Lehrer is talking, putting everyone at further ease. President Ford is in attendance, sitting front row center in the auditorium. Lehrer banters, asks Ford to be "hall monitor," to help keep everyone quiet. Liddy Dole and Robin come on and sit on the bleachers. So does Hillary, accompanied by George Mitchell. (A job in the second Clinton administration?The Supreme Court? He can't get the baseball commissioner job, so he'll settle for second best, now.) Liddy's in her among-the-people yellow and Hillary is in white, her politics-of-virture look.

The candidates come onto the stage.

Lehrer says, "This is what's called 'the awkward time.' "

The theater audience is in the dark, and a quick look at the people in the bleachers reveals about a 96 percent white crowd and a red rug beneath the candidates' feet.

"Thirty seconds to silence," Lehrer says, and the president reacts. Ha ha.

"Forty-five seconds to real."

Both Dole and Clinton now look like they're waiting for the firing squad.

"Here we go."

The Gallup organization has picked this crowd and it doesn't look like a cross section of anything, though it might resemble a cross section of San Diego—except for the half of San Diego which is from south of the border.

Bob goes first and gives a sports update: "Braves one, Cardinals nothing—early on."

Clinton, in his opening remarks, says, hopefully, "Again, I will say I'll do my best to make this a discussion of ideas and issues, not insults."

The first audience member rises for a question. She is young, a "beginning educator," and is holding a book and papers in her hand and she's determined to ask a long, confused question, bad class planning demonstrated by the "beginning educator." She could read at eight, four probably, but that's not the problem.

She's heading toward a question, but everyone is getting impatient (except, perhaps, Bill Clinton). She quotes from her book, a sentiment of a sixth grader (hard to tell the difference): " 'If I were president I would think about Abraham Lincoln and George Washington and what they did to make our country great. We should unite the white and black people. . . . ' " Finally, after more grammar-school platitudes, she gets to a question: "How will you begin to practice what we are preaching to our children, the future of our nation?"

"Well," Dole says, "I'd like to say first of all, I think it's a very good question. I appreciate the quote from the young man." Why Dole thinks the sixth grader is a young man is not clear—it could be a young girl playing "If I were president." He's in Brooklyn Dodgers mode. "There's no doubt about it that many American people have lost their faith in government. They see scandals almost on a daily basis. They see ethical problems in the White House today. They see nine hundred FBI files, private person, being gathered up by somebody in the White House. Nobody knows who hired this man. So, there's a great deal of cynicism out there."

Nothing, it appears, was going to keep Dole from giving that speech, whatever the question.

Clinton's reply jumps over Dole to the questioner. "One of the reasons that I ran for president, Sandy"—*Sandy!*—"is because not just children, a lot of grown-ups felt that way. And if you remember four years ago we had not only rising unemployment, but a lot of rising cynicism. . . . You mentioned Washington and Lincoln. They were presidents at historic times. This is a historic time. It's important that we go beyond those old partisan arguments and focus on people and their future. When we do that, instead of shutting the government down over a partisan fight on the budget, we're a better country and that's why we're making progress now."

Dole is not disarmed (I see that's a bad pun), but he's thrown off. "Well, bringing people together again is obviously a responsibility we all have. I know you do it. Everybody here does it. You do a lot of things nobody knows about. I have a little foundation for the disabled called the Dole Foundation. We've raised about ten million dollars. We don't talk about it."

Except in these last two debates. But Dole's reply is better than his first answer, since he's had second thoughts, it appears. Dole does have second thoughts; almost immediately, usually. He qualifies almost every sentence, which is why he could legislate. "So it seems to me that there's also a public trust. When you're the president of the United States you have a public trust. . . . And I think now that trust is being violated, and it seems to me we ought to face up to it. And the president ought to say tonight that he's not going to pardon anybody that he was involved in business with who might implicate him later on." Dole seems satisfied he's got that in.

But Lehrer goes to the next questioner, a cardiologist. San Diego's cross section. He wants to know in a "substantive fashion" how Clinton plans to deal with health care.

Clinton serves up the list. Competition. Medicaid. Kennedy-Kassebaum. Drive-by deliveries. Children covered.

"Well, first let me say, there you go again, Mr. President," Dole says, "talking about a Medicare cut. Now I've heard you say this time after time. And I've heard you say on TV appearances, the media made me do it. You're trying to defend your cut, which was not a cut either—reduction in the growth of spending."

Dole does it again. He's running out of feet to shoot.

Clinton looks tired, which might be how he's processing anger. Dole just looks tired. He really doesn't have the heart for this. Clinton stares at him, the old mojo working. Not many easy smiles tonight. The third cross-section person identifies himself as "active-duty military and small business owner." I thought these folks were the great "undecided." Who can believe he's undecided? He wants the "gap" closed between military and civilian pay. Though, it appears, he's able to own his "small business" while being "active-duty military." Dole wades in: "You know, we have seventeen thousand men and women today wearing our uniform that receive food stamps. It shouldn't happen in America." What about the PXs? I wonder. But Bob should know about food stamps. Do commissaries accept food stamps?

Dole is trying to turn this into an attack on Clinton, but thus far it appears to be general carpet bombing, a lot of government feeling the heat. "And it's time we take a look at the pay scales. You did get a 3 percent increase this year but that's not enough. If we're going to ask young men and young women to protect us and defend us around the world—and we've had more deployments under this administration than any time in history. Fifty times we deployed troops around the world," Dole says, though if that number surprises anyone, the surprise would be that so little tragedy has resulted from it. Bush "deployed" the troops to Somalia. Scott O'Grady came back. "But I think anybody who wears the uniform is a great American," Dole says, only being able to get close to an inference. His elliptical style seems to possess him. He continues to use his private shorthand when addressing the nation, but the nation hasn't been taking his dictation for years and it remains dreamlike, eerie: "Remember Vietnam? Remember when people almost used to walk across the street rather than have contact with somebody who was in Vietnam?" No, I don't remember that, Senator Dole; that was a right-wing fantasy, often expressed. But it does seem personalized, how the young man Dole himself might have felt recovering from his war wounds, battling a kind of pity and self-hatred.

Clinton, as commander in chief, asks what branch of service the questioner is in. "I'm in the United States Navy, sir," the man replies, uneasily, to his boss, and Clinton, as friend of business, asks what kind of business he owns. "I have an Amway business," he again uneasily answers. Well, we are getting America on stage: the beginning educator rambling on, a cardiologist, Amway. Clinton says he "got through Congress" an increase in pay "above the rate of inflation." And he speaks of military families, since he is still more comfortable with the idea of families than the idea of the military.

Other than Dole grousing and Clinton smiling less (he was too happy too early in the last debate, after seeing what a cakewalk it was going to be), this is more of the same. The questioners (like so much else) put me in mind of the O.J. jury, or juries in general. They are taken up by their sense of civic responsibility, become their role, want to share in the majesty of the law. The ritual elevates. If it goes on too long, like the O.J. jury did, the reverse happens: civilization crumbles, anger replaces honor, it becomes tawdry rather than elevated, it becomes all too human. We're outta here.

But these questioners are taking their "responsibility" seriously: earnest questions come about the Middle East, smoking, welfare. I wonder about all the folks Lehrer isn't calling on. The alternates, they turn out to be. Some of them look a bit wilder than the ones Lehrer selects. There's a high percentage of military personnel, a couple of "Hispanics," and one large black woman who asks, "Do you feel that America has grown enough and has educated itself enough to totally cut out affirmative action?" One side of her face looks slightly impaired, as if she's had a stroke—during the debate?—but Clinton leaps at the question. "No ma'am"—that's our boy from Arkansas—"I don't. I am against quotas. I'm against giving anybody any kind of preference for something they're not qualified for. But, because I still believe that there is some discrimination and that not everybody has an opportunity to prove they're qualified, I favor the right kind of affirmative action." Clinton's kinder, gentler affirmative action. Our whole generation, Clinton's, mine, of white males from Nowhereville has been the beneficiary of "affirmative action," probably more or as much as any minority directly affected. It was the atmosphere of the times. Bright kids from Arkansas got to go to Georgetown, Oxford, Yale: the "meritocracy" was affirmative action. You needn't be cut from the usual cloth to taste what the elites always feasted upon.

Dole says grumpily, "It seems to me that we ought to support the California Civil Rights Initiative." That must be 209. "It ought to be not based on gender or ethnicity or color or disability. I'm disability," he says, in his fashion, "and I shouldn't have a preference."

That ignites his humor (he does have medieval humors): "I would like to have one in this race, come to think of it. But I don't get one. Maybe we can work that out. I get a ten-point spot." He's back to telegraphese: "This is America. No discrimination . . . Equal opportunity. But we cannot guarantee equal results in America." It's the Borkian line. Another right-wing fantasy: those Vietnam vets walking alone down one side of the street and equal results equals socialism.

Clinton responds, mentioning Colin Powell, the Martin Luther King of the technocratic age. "Colin Powell . . . fears that the initiative [209] would take away the extra effort programs."

Another slice of San Diego, a mechanical engineer, asks Dole, "How do you reduce taxes and balance the budget?"

Dole says, "Oh, I'm glad you asked."

"So am I," Clinton butts in.

But Dole then returns to quotas: the "Piscataway case up in New Jersey. It's pretty clear that was a quota case. And just because one teacher was white and one teacher was black and they had the same qualifications, you know they decided who would stay there. It shouldn't be that way."

And Dole shouldn't have been wounded. The price of history.

Dole gets to the "economic package." A constitutional amendment to balance the budget is the answer.

I'm forgetting Dole is supposed to be ripping Clinton's "face" off, according to Scott Reed, his campaign manager (and when one sees Scott Reed, one realizes how good James Carville was). Dole seems more petulant, but he does come back after Clinton's response about his "targeted tax cuts." "Your targeted tax cut, Mr. President," Dole says, "never hits anybody. That's the problem with it. Nobody ever gets it." That is true; a lot of "tax cuts" are the phantom sort, though you get to advertise them a lot. For instance, the proposed capital-gains cut for houses: most everyone buys up, so they don't pay much capital gains on houses, anyway, so there's little decrease in revenue: It's a perfect "tax cut." Only overly ambitious trophy-house developers lose. "But I—I must say I'm a little offended by this word scheme. You talked about it last time. You talked about a risky scheme and then Vice President Gore repeated about ten times in St. Petersburg. If I have anything in politics, it's my word. . . . Bob Dole kept his word. I'm going to keep my word to you. I'm going to keep my word to the American—we going to cut taxes and balance the budget. We're not going to touch Medicare."

Dole seems to be shorting out. His language multiplies his age problem, since it seems to be part physical. Neurons misfiring, insufficient grammar a result.

Another slice of cross section, "I'm a martial arts instructor and a father"—a stimulating juxtaposition, that—asks Clinton a gift-horse question: "any plans you have to expand the Family Leave Act?" and Clinton replies, "Thank you," and gets two minutes on his Big Brother act: then Dole assumes the sour numbers duty: "Well, 88 percent of the people, the president claims, eleven million are already covered. And only 5 percent, keep in mind, 5 percent, of the employers are even affected by the Family Leave Act."

Then we get an apparently gay guy, a larger slice of San Diego, asking a question. "I'm a travel agent. Can you please explain how your policy on the employment nondiscrimination act would have prohibited discrimination, would have prohibited people from being fired from their jobs simply for being gay or lesbian."

Clinton says, "I'm for it." He then goes on to the economy, saying, "I have a little time left, so let me just say that I get attacked so many times on these questions it's hard to answer all those things. In February—Senator Dole just said we had the worst economy in a century. In February he said we had the best economy in thirty years. In February. And I don't want to respond in kind to all of these things. I could. I could answer a lot of these things tit for tat, but I hope we can talk about what we're going to do in the future. No attack ever created a job or educated a job or helped a family make ends meet. No insults ever cleaned up a toxic waste dump or helped an elderly person." I'm sure that second "job" was supposed to be "child," but I'm also sure that will become a snippet of tape shown and shown again.

Dole's in swampland in his reply: "I am opposed to discrimination in any form, but I don't favor creating special rights for any group. That would be my answer to this question." But, he goes on. "And I'm— there would be special rights for different groups in America—but I'm totally opposed to discrimination. Don't have any policy against hiring anyone, whether it's lifestyle, or whatever." Whatever has come a little earlier in this debate, Dole is now tired—he's been blinking a lot—the bleacher people seem tired. Everyone is stuck on this small stage, doing a show for the audience in the dark, and there are no refreshments. In another sort of auditorium the people asking the questions would still be spectators, the candidates being the focus, the show. Here they're all performers together.

Clinton asks for a show of hands—he's taking his own poll!—during a managed-care question. "How many of you are under managed care?" There aren't many hands. Dole injects: "There aren't many young people here." Clinton goes on: "How many of you like it?" "Two," Dole supplies. A little less than half, from the tiny show of hands, but Clinton says he hoped that everyone would have at least three choices of managed-care plans to choose from.

A questioner announces, "I'm Iris Seifert and I'm unemployed." What's San Diego's unemployment rate? Shouldn't there be more than one? Iris doesn't look too disturbed about being jobless; in fact, she seems more concerned about savings and retirement. She wants to know from Dole, "Are you planning any incentives to encourage us to take care of ourselves rather to rely on the government and on Social Security when we retire?"

Dole's for IRAs. "We think it will encourage savings. You could also use those accounts for health care or education or a first home." It also seems to encourage spending, rather than retirement income. Clinton says, "This is one where we have some agreement, I think. . . . And I think it's [my plan] almost identical to what's in Senator Dole's plan." Dole displays his humor in his reply: "Did you say you're unemployed?

You see, the first thing we got to do is get you a job." After that, he cements his and Clinton's "identicalness": "Obviously, Social Security is a very important program. It'll be preserved. Democrats or Republicans, it'll be preserved. . . . Just as we did back in 1983. And we did it on a bipartisan basis. We took it out of politics. People get so tired of politics." Yes, tonight especially. The hard core is left watching, but barely. "Maybe, we can make a deal there tonight," Dole says, the old deal maker, forgetting he's no longer in the Senate.

Another questioner arises: "Ron Kite, minister," he says curtly. Dole responds, "Hi, Ron." Ron ascends his pulpit: "This great nation has been established by the Founding Fathers who possessed a very strong Christian beliefs and godly principles. If elected president of the United States, what could you do to return this nation to these basic principles? And also, do you feel that the president, the office of the president, has the responsibility to set the role example to inspire our young people?" This is the closest we've gotten to the Christian Coalition, and the all-exclusionist shades of its narrow rainbow are displayed. Not even a nod to "Judeo-Christian" values, etc., which the more polished advocates employ.

Here's a chance for the last/first twentieth/twenty-first century lion to seize the diversity prize.

"Well, no doubt about it, our Founding Fathers had a great deal of wisdom." At this point, one wonders. And near the end of his answer, Dole gets to ethics. "And as when it comes to public ethics, he has a responsibility. And you have thirty-some in your administration who have either left or being investigated or in jail or whatever, and you've got an ethical problem."

Dole has made "whatever" his signature word. It will last a long time as a word-association game. Whatever. Bob Dole.

"It's public ethics. I'm not talking about private, we're talking about public ethics. When you have nine hundred files gathered up by some guy who was a bouncer in a bar and hired as a security officer to collect files—in Watergate, I know a person who went to jail for looking at one file. One FBI file."

Who is that? I wonder. I review the names of the jailed. Must have been more than just one file.

"There are nine hundred sequestered in the White House—nine hundred. People like you." He must mean the folks in the dark, not the bleacher people.

Clinton has caught the us-against-them flavor of the minister's question. "This is the most religious—great country in history. And yet, interestingly enough, we have the most religious freedom of any country in the world, including the freedom not to believe. And now we have all these people—just up the road in Los Angeles County, we've got people from one hundred fifty different racial and ethnic groups, and they've got tons of different religions."

Finally, the last question: the Gallup organization has fallen down again. "I, too, am a minister," a woman with short pepper-and-salt hair says, but it is clear she's not from the narrowest band of the spectrum. It, too, is a gay rights question, explicitly criticizing Dole: "And when he [Dole] was asked if he would support equal rights in employment for gay and lesbian people, you said that you favored that. And he [Dole] said that he did not believe in special rights. And I thought the question was, equal rights for all people. And I don't understand why people are using the term 'special rights' when the question is equal rights. Can you help me in understanding that?"

This New Age entreaty is a spoonful of sugar for Clinton. "I want to answer your question, but let me say one other thing. We don't need a constitutional amendment [Dole had just proposed one] for kids to pray. And what I did was to have the Justice Department and the Education Department, for the first time ever, issue a set of guidelines that we gave to every school in America, saying that children could not be interfered with in religious advocacy when they were praying." Then he starts to say something. "Now, I think I have to let Senator Dole speak for himself. It wouldn't be fair for me to do that. I would wind up—I mean, it's the last question. I'd mischaracterize it to try to make you happy." It is the last question and Clinton has answered it. There is laughter: he has said something too true. He heads for the darker consequences of mischaracterization and finishes up with "Bosnia, the Middle East, Northern Ireland, Rwanda, Burundi. . . . We still have some of that hatred inside us. You see it in the church burnings. . . . We're stronger when we unite around shared values instead of being divided by our differences." Dole stumbles through a reply in Dole-speak: "No discrimination in America. We've made that clear. . . . We shouldn't discriminate—race, color, whatever." He veers to a final charge: "There's really no foreign policy in this administration."

Their closing statements reflect the eighty-odd earlier minutes. Dole looks at the floor, not at the camera, the same well-of-the-Senate look he's long used to. "So we have our differences. We should have our differences. You mentioned other parties, they have their differences. If we all agreed, it would be a pretty dull place. We should have more debates. I think we'll have another debate on the economy." No one thinks there should be more debates—even Dole says it with hesitancy: but it does seem he now regrets kicking Perot off the stage. He turns personal: "This is the highest honor that I've ever had in my life, to think that somebody from Russell, Kansas, somebody who grew up in a basement apartment, somebody whose parents didn't finish high schools, somebody who spent about thirty-nine months in hospitals after World War II, somebody who uses a buttonhook every day to get dressed. . . ." He goes out protecting the flag ("with a constitutional amendment"), perhaps remembering Bush's '92 campaign. Dole wants Americans to be proud of their vote.

Not to be outdone, Clinton invokes Hope, Arkansas, his widowed mother. He has a bit more energy. "Your responsibility is to show up on November fifth," he stresses. Perhaps he's seen some worrisome poll data.

I contemplate Dole's asides about having a third debate. He said it somewhat halfheartedly, but no one wants to see another debate of this sort. Clinton, in his many shows of not directly responding, never acknowledged the demi-offer. Ross might take Dole up, though.

Clinton is finishing with his defeat-announcing goals and hopes: ". . . Whether we're going to give our children world-class education where every eight-year-old can read, every twelve-year-old can log in on the Internet, every eighteen-year-old can go to college."

That bridge to the twenty-first century. It's so sad. In the 1960s education was booming. From 1960 to 1971 the number of people in higher education almost tripled, after not even doubling from 1920 to 1960. Children could read at eight. The promise of the baby boom and the

Great Society was that eighteen-year-olds could go to college. Clinton went to Yale and Oxford, for God's sake; now, Clinton wants for the twenty-first century what we as a generation took for granted in the late sixties. It's so sad. But at least the debate is over.

On stage the wives extract themselves from the bleachers. The scene is a greenroom now, all the performers mingling. The questioners are now bonded with the two stars. Clinton chats them up. C-SPAN shows this, but no sound comes forth. I do catch Dole avoiding the travel agent who asked the gay-bashing question.

On PBS Mark Shields is saying that in the three hours of debate, the word "sacrifice" has never been mentioned. The conjunction of the word "sacrifice" and the presidency makes me think of Carter, the only president who seemed to embrace that idea, and where is he? Rehabbing houses and the world.

Paul Gigot says Clinton showed more empathy than a convention of funeral directors. Abortion never came up in a question and that disappointed him.

Shields invokes Clinton's defense of himself, the obviously planned response to Dole's forecasted attacks—"No insult ever cleaned up a toxic waste dump."

Bob Shrum and Mike Murphy are point/counterpoint, two campaign operatives doubling as commentators. More creatures of the event. Shrum, the Democrat, says Dole has two options: defeat with honor, or defeat with dishonor. Murphy is blond, sleek, whereas Shrum is older, worn. Murphy "resigned" from the Dole campaign two months ago. He complains, "I'm kind of a grump about this format. But I think what Clinton was trying to do was kill the clock." Shrum is generally pleased (and why not!). Mike lashes out at the people on stage, says the Gallup organization "kidnapped a bowling alley." Hardly—cardiologists, travel agents, military people, beginning educators, ministers. What he doesn't want to say is that the citizens of San Diego let his old boss down.

Doris Kearns Goodwin says Dole's attacks on the "character issue" were "ineffective jabs."

Kristol the younger says Dole did not land a knockout punch. He quotes Dole's lugubrious remark toward the end, "all the people who may still be watching," as an acknowledgment that the election is over.

Michael Beschloss thinks for Dole this debate was better than the first one. In this TV age, Beschloss says, Dole is handicapped. Though if Dole had been running seventy, eighty years ago, he wouldn't be doing so bad. It's surreal, that idea. Dole versus Wilson?

Haynes Johnson says Dole appeared "snappish and peevish," whereas Clinton walked right up to the person, stayed focused, honed his skills in the television age (though it is Reagan who literally honed his skills in the television age).

Kristol adds there was "no dramatic" moment. But he adds later that Dole didn't look at his watch. None of this bunch talks about the questioners.

Gigot says Clinton didn't say, "If we get a Democratic Congress" we can do a lot for this country.

Shields brings up Bruce Babbitt and offers Babbitt's analogy: Pandas mating at a zoo, great commotion, no result.

Back to C-SPAN. Haley Barbour is saying, "Nothing we could have improved on. Got to do a live shot."

Callers are Dole supporters: "This man [Clinton] doesn't tell the truth." "God bless you Senator Dole." "I'm a soccer mom and I'm voting for Bob Dole." Asked what a "soccer mom" is, the caller gets legalistic, doesn't want to be misquoted, though it appears she's repeating something, rather than just speaking.

Hillary is signing autographs on stage. The crowd isn't gone yet, but I can't see Dole.

More callers: "I'm fifteen years old. Why would anyone vote for Bill Clinton?" "Dole didn't hit Clinton enough." A fax from Walnut Creek, California, is held up. Clinton "reprised his bandsmen youth . . . tooting his horn. . . . Dole slammed into the line . . . had new plays . . . threw deep." A real Walnut Creek wordsmith at work.

CNN faithfully has Ross Perot yapping: They tell you what you want to hear, everything's wonderful, but, he reminds America, the standard of living is down for three out of four people.

C-SPAN's phones throw up a Clinton supporter: "Hey, I could convict Billy Graham for rape with all that money," one says, referring to Special Prosecutor Starr.

There's a string of Dole callers, the last saying this country is great only "with right men."

Back to CNN and Ross: he's onto how children's brains develop. When he delves into biology, Ross appears even stranger, quirkier. Ross's left eye looks wide-open, whereas the right is more shut, slanted. It gives him a pirate look.

Back to C-SPAN. "I really like the form [of the debate]," a caller says. (it's just like him calling in to C-SPAN.) A caller from Kansas says, "I'm for Bob Dole. I'm for keeping jobs in our country." Another caller, a Perot supporter, says he really likes "the form."

CNN now has Harry Browne. The government doesn't work, doesn't deliver mail on time. (Hey, I get my mail.) Reduce government to the absolute minimum, Browne says. Kill the brutes! Kill the brutes!

Caller: Great format!

The Natural Law Party's Hagelin oozes along. Even Perot won't appear with these guys. Ralph Nader has skipped this evening, it appears. Since there are only the three of them, Hagelin, Browne, and Howard Phillips of the U.S. Taxpayers Party, they do look like—the Three Stooges. Phillips says that in New York his party is the Right to Life Party. He's against abortion, legalizing drugs, etc. He was director of the EOC in the seventies. He wants the United States to withdraw from the UN, the World Bank, etc. Phillips has withdrawn from the world. Larry King is broadcasting from Atlanta's Omni Center, across the street from the Olympic grounds. This assemblage recalls a show King did from the desert Southwest on UFOs, near the secret air force base where the "alien bodies" are kept.

An ad comes on, high style, high fashion, a reprise of history, exotic images, juxtaposed on top of one another: the space shuttle taking off behind a cityscape, colorful "native" children next to a car on Park Avenue in New York City. It turns out to be a Boeing advertisement. Whoever made it should be doing campaign commercials. Boeing is messing with our minds.

CNN finally sends off the lunatic fringe and we get William Schneider's report from the instant polls: who won? 59 percent for Clinton, 29 percent for Dole. Who has the better vision: 58 percent Clinton, 37 percent Dole. Performance trumps character, Schneider says.

Gore is interviewed: he says "the live audience" wasn't interested in Dole's attacks. They didn't ask any similar questions. He says there are "theological" differences between personal and public attacks. Bernie Shaw asks about nine hundred FBI files. If this is what Senator Dole wants to talk about, Gore says, instead of education, the environment, the economy, it's OK with him. I thought it was an excellent debate, Al concludes.

Judy Woodruff is with Kemp. He is saying it's a "narrow little bridge" to the twenty-first century, with "taxes and tolls" along the way. Asked if he's not disappointed that there was no personal question from the audience, Kemp says, "No, no for the third time."

Bernie and Judy are back. "That's all the time we have," Bernie says. Judy announces, *Showbiz Today* is next."

10/17   Diane Rehm's show is hosted today by Susan Page of *USA Today*. The word getting used the most regarding Dole is "sad." More debate poll results, a 30-point spread in Clinton's favor, 55–25. The conventional wisdom has now solidified: It was a mistake for Dole to stress economic issues. The economy is too good, the Ray Fair effect holds.

Rush says, "I wasn't sure how I felt about it." He quotes George Will saying that never was so little done with so much ammunition. Rush sounds lost. He brings up Clinton's "mischaracterize it to try to make you happy" line. Bill Clinton in a nutshell, Rush says, no dumb-bunny he. He disputes Clinton's claim that seven hundred hospitals were poised to be closed.

A local ad comes on, sponsored by a local right-to-life group. Infanticide. Vote against Bill Clinton.

Rush is back attacking the mainstream media, lamenting, "They all make fun of what conservatives believe." It is the culture war again. But Dole comes on the line. He seems like a regular these days. Rush snaps into his I'm-talking-to-an-important-person voice, slightly higher, a tinge of nervousness, not faked, organic. Dole says of the bleacher crowd, "I'm surprised the questions were that good." But Rush doesn't want to let them off the hook. Dole goes on, saying that after the debate one person asked a question on Indonesia, one on Vietnam. "We'd like to have one additional debate," though even Rush can't work up too much enthusiasm for that. "We're going to win!" Dole exclaims, joining the earth-is-flat society.

USA Today reports that the "town hall" questioners were sequestered during the day, à la the O. J. jurors.

Larry King Live has Newt on: "I don't think they'll get into it until after the World Series," Newt is saying, meaning the public and the election. He's still putting off the start of the campaign.

There's a commercial. The LCI CEO is back, urging us to vote—for his long-distance company, his Baby Bell. He does want to run.

And Newt is back. He holds that the elite media are liberal and talk radio is middle America, which is antiliberal. He brings up monks giving $5,000 campaign contributions to the DNC, the "gardener" who gave $450,000. King asks about abortion and Newt says you have to change the culture. People have to change in the heart. He is now parroting the Forbes line.

On C-SPAN Ross Perot is speaking down the road at Purdue University. He's on to campaign financing, too. The Gandhi guy, Ross is explaining, who gave Clinton the Gandhi Foundation Award, is not related to Gandhi. He gave $350,000 in soft money to the DNC. Another recipient of the Gandhi Award, Ross tells the Boilermakers and us all, was a Class A Japanese war criminal. That's where the $350,000 came from. NAFTA is a bust. Ross is throwing figures around. Seventy billion in the deficit hole. Doesn't count the $120 billion of illegal drugs. Crack babies. Forty-two days in the hospital at the cost of $140,000. After three days, the mothers disappear.

There's a storm here in Indiana and hail is hitting the metal roof of the auditorium where Perot is speaking; the tintinnabulation quite loud. "Can you hear me?" he asks the students. Ross is picking hail off his podium, but he doesn't look up or stop.

On CNBC, Chris Matthews, late of the Carter administration, has on Susan Estrich (he introduces her as a "former prosecutor"—shades of O. J.) and Mary Matalin. When she ran the Dukakis campaign, Estrich was known by her enemies as Susan Estrogen. Mary Matalin is spinning like mad. "Everything is the character issue." Estrich quotes what she thinks Clinton was thinking the night of the debate: If nothing happens tonight, I win. Mary is in a denim vest and Susan's wearing pearls. Mary explains why Dole isn't an effective attacker: You have a man from the Midwest who's lived a life of civility.

CNN does a news story on money from the California Buddhist temple in April after Gore's visit. The monks and "nuns" hold a vow of poverty, we're told. I'm holding that thought.

10/18 *Nightline*'s a first lady/first nurse show: Liddy Dole is shown doing her floor talk, giving the same line three times in a row in three different rooms. "This campaign is about . . . ." She's now holding up the little red toy Clinton rocker once more. It rocks sideways, left to right. Madame DeFarge playing with the guillotine.

Then we get to see Hillary with kids, with older Americans, at colleges, on soft news shows, on *Regis & Kathy Lee*. She's doing the Dan Quayle circuit, more or less. No potato(e) goofs, though.

10/20 The speedup is now so extreme that the *New York Times* is running on the front page a campaign postmortem two weeks before it's over. CNN runs a show with clips from Dole's '74 Senate race, his last tough campaign, because of Nixon and Watergate. Dole plays the abortion card, etc. We see the usual suspects, such as Gary Bauer of the Family Research Council. Partial-birth abortion, Clinton scandals. Dole's family life is touched on, first wife, marriage to Liddy. Everyone seems to have a fascination with Hillary and Bill's sex life (*The Seduction of Hillary Rodham,* by *The American Spectator*'s gay reporter David Brock, has been out for a while), but Liddy and Bob's is one most Americans do not want to contemplate. Speaking of books, CNN has a former aide of Dole saying, "Bob Dole does not read books." And, speaking of Brock, I recalled a poignant scene from the period when he was promoting his *The Real Anita Hill* back in 1994. He was on William Buckley's show and Buckley couldn't mask his distaste for Brock during the interview. It was apparent that Buckley, though doing his part to spread Brock's line on Anita Hill (a little nutty, a bit slutty, etc.), realized this young conservative journalist was a long way from Buckley's earlier protégés, Garry Wills and George Will.

10/21   There's desperation in the air. Diane Rehm is doing a show on the medical histories of presidents. A woman caller says, "It is known that Clinton is a daily cocaine user." Diane asks, not absolutely incredulously, "Do you have any information about that?" Lawrence K. Altman of the *Times* and Michael Beschloss of PBS give reasonable answers, which, since they didn't attack the woman's assertion, leave the charge floating in the realm of the reasonable. Perhaps she gets her info from the *700 Club*.

10/22   Rush is back on Lippo suction and the Indonesian money. A caller says, I don't think this is going to change anyone's mind; after the election, hunting season will begin for the Pulitzer Prize to nail the Clintons down. Rush is unhappy with that. I'm not just going to sit here, he says, with two weeks left to go and not believe it doesn't make any difference. . . . I'm not going to cave. He mentions getting a fax from Bob Tyrrell about Clinton ransacking an Arkansas state pension fund and the Lippo people plugging the hole for him at the last minute. Rush is also spreading the news about a September 1995 *American Spectator* story that's redone in Tyrrell's book, *Boy Clinton*. A BCCI-engendered brush with one global wheeler-dealer, Machtar Riady, kindled their (the Arkansas Stephenses) ambitions to become global wheeler-dealers themselves. . . . Stephens became Riady's partner in banking closer to home . . . creating the Worthen Banking Corporation, "Arkansas's largest bank holding company." Tyrrell identifies Riady as "a central member of the ethnic Chinese clique that controls much of Indonesia's economy" (105). It takes a global village, again. It must have been picturesque down in Little Rock.

   Hillary trying to earn money in this atmosphere always seemed poignant—if she thought a divorce was possible back then, she'd need her own money to get divorced—though it always seemed absurd that they would have money worries. But a vignette in the 1995 David Maraniss book, *First in His Class,* does offer a counterexample, an anecdote from Diane Blair (a FOH) about the day Clinton announced his candidacy for the presidency. "There on the sidewalk in front of her stood Orval Faubus, symbol of the Old South, an ancient and lonely man, reduced to a sideshow, hawking one of his books. A television crew swept past, oblivious of the old governor's presence. History rises, Blair thought, and history rejects" (462). So being governor of Arkansas doesn't always mean a golden future awaits.

A reviewer of *The President We Deserve* in the *Philadelphia Inquirer* of October 6 marveled at how many Clinton books have been published, and at the absence of Bush books (even Reagan books, he could have added). Not that the Clintons will inspire as many books as Hitler, but the profusion of books—friendly, vicious, intellectual, imbecilic—does show how the Clintons exemplify the culture. And all this in just one term! (And I should know.) Clinton can put one foot comfortably in the trailer-camp world and one in Oxford Yard. He covers the culture's entire spectrum. Bush was only a tiny slice, high WASP, which even television could never convert into a popular show. (*Dallas* was about the vulgar rich.) The popular culture has a hard time warming to the nonvulgar rich.) Bill and Hillary do mimic the Kennedys in popular fascination but with, obviously, a difference. Jackie O naked on a beach in Greece was as vulgar as she got, but Paula! Gennifer!, the rest. It wasn't out of place for the *Star* to accompany Clinton's rise to power, for just as Rush rightly complains that the *New York Times* is part of the Clinton campaign, so too is the world of the *Star*: he fits on its pages, and the stories are all too familiar to the tabloid readers everywhere. It's their world. All the Clinton books have flowed forth since everyone is *looking*. They have captured the country's gaze. Clinton wants to shake everyone's hand and everyone, it turn, knows Bill Clinton, feels connected. Hillary, too. It is contemporary soap opera, but the television public finds it almost comforting, to have the country domesticated. Carter, because of his ministerial aspects, never seemed truly populist. Clinton does. He roams high and low. Reagan is a model, except he was never real, three-dimensional. He was iconic on the screen, revered, but removed. Clinton is among us all.

It is also the *Paradise Lost* effect. Bad angels are more complicated than good angels, Satan more compelling than God. The right wing has made the Clintons even more interesting to the American people. The Miltons of the Right have been getting the vivid and gaudy news out and out, saving us from the drab, pious do-goodisms the Clintons often clothe themselves with.

Frontline on PBS airs "Why America Hates the Press." It has amusing clips of the people at the Republican convention yelling "Jump Sam jump!" at Sam Donaldson, standing above them. Christopher Hitchens lets them film him talking to *The McLaughlin Group*'s man telling him the subjects (*The $64,000 Question!*) to be discussed. Gave him the time to come up with the pun the "Bleating of the Lamm." Hitchens compares it to pro wrestling. *Frontline* is making the point about the revolving door between government and the "press." We have Fallows, we have Russert, but not *Fox*'s Tony Snow, nor the guy on *Crossfire Sunday* who worked for McGovern, nor Matalin, nor Meyers (most of the CNBC crew for that matter), and on and on, all the creatures of the events, of the black lagoons. Russert gives a variation of the once-a-philosopher-twice-a-pervert excuse. You can do it once, you just can't keep doing it. Using Fallows as their thesis's linchpin is an example of the problem, not a critique of it. We see Fallows defending the indefensible (given his stance), that Gergen is not one and the same (as Steve Roberts, who Fallows fired, or worse), he's "writing the editorial" with Mort Zuckerman. The program could be, should be, called "Why the Press Hates the Press."

The *New York Times* alerts the nation to the fact that Steve Goldsmith, the Republican candidate for Indiana governor, is married to one of the Pulliams (Dan Quayle's family), a power in Indiana (most notably, Indianapolis) as well as Arizona. It takes a family. It drives home the irony of Senator Lugar's endorsement of Goldsmith (in Goldsmith's best TV ad: "I saw a man who could do anything he wanted in this world"). Ah, yes.

I suppose Clinton did learn the lesson of the 1990s when he lost the governorship in the late seventies: it's a winner-take-all society and politicians learn that young. *Can you send me some money? Can you help me out?*

10/23   The *Indianapolis Star* (Goldsmith's wife's family paper) has a front-page section E story with a big headline: "Prozac Breathes Life into Lilly Profits." The Lilly drug company is a big Indiana business. The article reports, "Rebounding sales of its bestselling product, Prozac . . . helped boost Eli Lilly and Company's third quarter results" ($415.6 million versus $310.5 million last year). Prozac nation lives! Is this surge of Prozac swallowing correlated with Clinton or the campaign? Doubtless, both.

Rush is back on the Richard Allen Davis (Polly Klaas's killer) ad in the Vic Fazio/Robert Braden campaign in California. Davis's picture ends up being the one on the screen. Rush says, "I like the ad . . . even if it is sleazy." It's come up again since the Democrats have an ad featuring the father of Polly Klaas saying Clinton has character. Dueling child killer/killed endorsements. Rush is now on to the arousal gap. He wants us to recall his calls for Dole to replicate the Clinton way. "Arrange to have women pop up" and claim affairs, Rush has recommended, he says. "Get some bimbos." There must be something coming up, or Rush wouldn't be laying down this line. Aha, as they say in cartoons, here it comes: Rush heard a KNBC (in Kansas City) report quoting a newsletter called *Probe* that Dole had brought some woman to a KU Medical Center for an abortion. A doctor is mentioned. Dole denies. Not true. Never happened. Rush says, it looks like somebody was listening to his calls for a Dole bimbo eruption. Rush says the story has been looked into for a year. It is odd over the course of a year to see how Rush blossoms into both a leak and a plant.

"Can someone explain to me the psychology of women who think Bill Clinton respects them?" Rush asks, baffled.

CNN reports on *Inside Politics* that Scott Reed, Dole's campaign manager, is off to Dallas to get Perot out of the race. And to endorse Dole. Dole, whom Perot blames for his debate ouster! Bill Schneider says it appears "an act of desperation." Especially if nothing comes of it.

The first nurse is on *Larry King Live*. She says Bob is like Harry Truman. He will come from behind. Larry, as an aside, says Dole "holds the record for guest appearances on this show." Liddy has her little red rocker, again playing Madame DeFarge. A caller says he's quoting Haley Barbour from the *New York Times* saying it's all right for congressional candidates to cut from Dole. Liddy says, "That's not true!" Her face settles into anger, becomes frozen for a moment, a glimpse of another Liddy. This after about forty minutes of good cheer. Recovering a bit she says, "The pundits are going to be wrong."

10/24 *Nickelodeon*'s vote (cast by kids) for president is reported in *USA Today*. Clinton 45 percent, Dole 37 percent Perot 15 percent. My six-year-old had seen some of Nickelodeon's promotions. He wants Dole. Why? "I like what he said about stopping crime," he says. Being six, he is the one most affected by campaign ads. His mother is trying to convince him to vote for Clinton (because he will raise taxes) and not to watch TV like his dad.

Paging further through *USA Today* I discover that Al Gore has been visiting the entertainers with animals Siegfried and Roy in Las Vagas. Why weren't they in Chicago? I wonder. Any soft money there? Heads in the mouths of lions?

10/25 The front page of the *Chicago Tribune* has the Perot story, headlined: "Dole's Gambit Backfires." Perot criticizes the press for concentrating on the weird and inconsequential Scott Reed trip. Ross is quoted saying, "Do I intend to campaign to the bitter end? Yes." Bitter end, indeed.

Rush is on Jorge Cabrera, the cocaine smuggler and Democratic contributor. He was moaning about Reed's trip yesterday to Perot, "waving the white flag," etc. Today he's on an *American Lawyer* (November) story about Paula Jones, concluding she has more corroboration than Anita Hill had. Who doubts Paula Jones? I wonder. Rush is the parallel campaign, but he's not closing the poll gap for Dole, either. "Anita Hill had nothing," Rush says vehemently, defending the man who officiated at Rush's (second? third? fourth?) marriage. Coke cans, X-rated videos.

On a radio newsbreak an announcer is describing the O. J. civil trial, the Akita barking, Heidstra hearing Goldman's "Hey hey hey," the white truck speeding away.

Back to Rush. A caller says, "The Democrats aren't going to turn out to vote." Rush cuts him off, saying, Shhh, shhh, I'm not going any further with this. This, evidently, is Rush's hope. Turnout low, Democratic turnout even lower.

Moses—Charlton Heston—is doing a local radio commercial for Steve Goldsmith's campaign for governor. "Don't believe the smear campaign of his opponent." It ends, "Marilyn Quayle, campaign chairman." There's one woman who isn't afraid of being called a man. I keep thinking that Marilyn and Dan's respective book titles, *Embrace the Serpent* and *Standing Firm,* must be some sort of family joke.

10/27 *Fox News* has Newt going on about the Yankees winning the World Series, a great comeback, just like Dole's to come. A poll reports that 60 percent of the people think Newt hurts the Dole campaign. Newt gives his victim-of-thousands-of-attack-ads defense. First thing in a Dole administration–Republican-controlled Congress would be term limits, Newt says. There's something so fatuous about that I think that Newt is on Jay Leno's show, or cracking ironies with Dave. He follows that with other things, among them a mandatory death penalty for major drug dealers. Limit and kill, a positive agenda. Newt's exercised about Jorge Cabrera's invitation to the White House. Jerry Zeifman's October 25 *Wall Street Journal* article claiming the Clintons are "likely to be indicted after November 5" is trotted out. Newt then imagines a Democratic Congress paying off the unions and the trial lawyers. Newt says the country doesn't realize how hard the wind blows from the Left when they watch the evening news. This, on Fox TV, the newest "free" network.

Beleaguered Scott Reed is on *Meet the Press.* He looks to be under a great strain. He sits chin up, bushy mustache flaring, eyes a bit too bright. Reed looks like he's expecting to be hit, and he is. George Stephanopoulos is the other side. He's happy, holding his head level, looking into the camera. Ross Perot said it best, George says, weird and inconsequential. John Huang, Jorge Cabrera, Scott brings up. What about education? George (the future, what, journalist?) spins. Zeifman's *Wall Street Journal* piece again is brought up. Russert plays Dole saying, "I wonder if the American people are thinking at all." Wake up, wake up, wake up. Russert asks, Isn't that condescending? Stephanopoulos steps up to the plate (recently vacated by the Yankees and Braves): Dole was negative on Clinton, negative on the press, now he's negative on the people. George goes on about how Newt OK'd the don't-let-Clinton-have-a-Democratic-Congress "blank check" ads of the Republican congressional campaign committee. It's selective outrage, he says of Dole. Jesse Helms has taken hundreds of thousands from foreign countries, George adds.

Reed's face remains tilted upward and his eyes continue to be almost teary. The Yankees and Braves come up again. The "school-skipping truant," the young man with a big glove, robbed the Orioles, is claimed once again.

Jack Kemp's on *Face the Nation,* and he does distance himself from the Scott Reed–Perot trip. Jack was on a plane when that was decided. Is this a sinking ship? Is this rat time?

On ABC's *This Week* Sam Donaldson asks the pollster Rothenberg, could anything except an act of God win this for Dole. "Nothing, nothing, nothing," Rothenberg says, in Lear-like fashion. But Haley Barbour says it's not over. He brings up the Braves being up 2–0, 6–0 in the third game, etc.

Steve Forbes is the guest on *Wall Street Week,* rebroadcast from Friday. Forbes the big winner of '96, Wall Street the big winner of '96. A mere $37 million for Forbes's Oedipal hit—Steve is now the famous Forbes. Dear old Dad is assigned to the dustbin of history. Forbes is gloating, telling Rukeyser that the "biggest villain is the tax code. . . . The IRS has got to go. . . . The status quo might be indefensible. . . . It's not a recession, but sluggish." The status quo might be indefensible but it's an Oscar Wildean moment on *Wall Street Week*: the pursuit of the inedible by the unspeakable.

Forbes can now pontificate, since he's been tested in the arena. On Newt: "He shouldn't have played as much with the animals on the shows." It's not completely clear if he means real animals or the TV people. "He can't shed a tear on cue as Bill Clinton can." Forbes still seems the awkward preppy who grins and mugs at the wrong time with inappropriate glee.

On the "unrehearsed" *McLaughlin Group* we have the blond speechwriter-Laura Ingraham back, even though Morton Kondracke is too. It's all conservatives now. No Germond. We have the baronial-Michael Barone. They think Kerry will win Massachusetts. The show ends with a "discussion" of California's Proposition 215, legal marijuana for medical uses. Joking about the video they used of drug addicts, shooting up, etc. Where did we get that video? The White House.

10/28   Rush is talking about seeing Morton Kondracke on C-SPAN being asked by Brian Lamb whom he's going to vote for. Kondracke said Clinton. I like his agenda, Rush quotes Kondracke as saying. Though he added, but there's all these scandals, and Kondracke is worried about what will happen in the second term after the pack—Washington journalists, Rush glosses for us—gets to him. Rush says it's "the craziest logic I've ever heard." He's amazed Kondracke could vote for Clinton as long as he isn't "nailed" down. "I'm not convinced Bill Clinton will win this election," Rush says.

Arianna Huffington is denouncing Bob Dole on CNBC's Charles Grodin show. It's been "over ever since he was nominated." He's terrible, terrible. She makes me want to vote for Dole. *Newsweek*'s Howard Fineman says it reminds him of the Mondale campaign, though Mondale took to the high ground at the end. Susan Estrich recalls her old boss, saying Dukakis finally embraced a populist message at the end of his campaign, but to little effect. Bob Dole, she says, is doing immigrant bashing, affirmative action bashing.

Arianna continues her undiluted spite: "Scott Reed has been a disastrous campaign manager" and "Bob Dole is a disastrous candidate." How about Ed Rollins, Arianna? How about your husband? Maybe the realization of her own failings is where her venom comes from. "This country is disintegrating and falling apart." I wonder if her redundancy is a translation problem. "No one is pointing this out," she pouts. Where is Al Franken? Where is the bed?

The newsbreak carries more about Richard Jewell no longer being a "target" of an investigation by the FBI. Is our diamond in the rough on his way to exoneration? But it appears Jewell has been wolfing down a lot of Big Macs during this hellish period. If he wants to continue in law enforcement he will have to lose some weight. Jewell does look like he's ready to join the Tonya Harding gang. Look out when you want to be famous, you often get your wish. The Dow has dropped below 6000.

Back on Grodin, Arianna raves on. "The problem with the media is not that it is liberal, but that it is cynical." There's the pot calling the kettle cynical.

On my local news Jewell is saying, "The FBI trampled on my rights." Ah, yes. Thus far, in the Indiana governor's race, Goldsmith has raised $8.7 million and his Democratic opponent O'Bannon $5.7 million. There's a teaser for the upcoming *Tonight Show,* a headline proclaiming

"Clinton Takes Credit for Drop in Teenage Birthrate." Leno jokes: He's been out campaigning. He doesn't have the time.

10/29 Diane Rehm does a show on campaign financing. Lippo, Riady, soft money. The DNC is refusing to file an election report, but will release a list. News of *O. J. 2* elides time.

A friend says she saw Letterman and Dave said Dole's so desperate about the gender gap he's going to come out as a lesbian. We talk about Gore in 2000. I reiterate how the spokespeople for the religious Right will have all their rhetoric pulled out from under them. She thinks that Gore might be a relief after eight years of warm, enveloping Bill. Gore's such a technocrat, dull in a solid way, that he might be desirable. Gore is spinproof, she says, which might be his strength.

Rush is talking to a woman caller who saw Dan Rather's report last night on Clinton and golf. They give him a mulligan on every hole, she says. "The guy cheats," Rush says. That this is news to Dan Rather is news to me, he says. He agrees with the caller that to pick on the golf issue is to downplay the honesty/character issue, but, "I still think it is relevant."

A radio ad comes on denouncing Clinton and I expect it to end with Elect Dole, but it ends with "I'm not taking any chances with a Democratic Congress."

Rush gets a call from "Lake Airhead, California." Is that a real place? Fifty-five years old: If I had paid for an insurance-type investment fund I'd have $2.5 million. Instead of "contributing" to Social Security, that is. Very optimistic figures there. Is he counting his employer's contribution? What investments? What if he had been injured or downsized fifteen years ago, what would he have now?

Rush says the thought of all that money lost makes you want to throw up. If this guy was such a potential saver, I wonder, why didn't he invest some money in an investment fund? If no one had made him "save" for the future, when would he have started to do it? It makes me want to throw up.

Rush says he's calling Scott Reed. He says he has him on the phone. "Call Clinton a socialist," he tells "Reed." Reed seems to doubt the efficacy of the attack. They've done that already. "I'm just passing it along," Rush says; it was some caller's suggestion. I have no idea if the call is bogus or real.

I read in the *New York Observer* that Joe Klein has been hired by Tina Brown at *The New Yorker*. Rick Hertzberg, former Carter speechwriter who's back at *The New Yorker*, defends the hire. Flocking birds of the fanciest feathers nesting at *The New Yorker*.

On *Equal Time* on CNBC, Bay-at-the-Moon Buchanan and Dee Dee Myers are now the sparring females. Richard Jewell is the topic. His complaints against the media at his press conference sound a lot like Dole's. The Atlanta office of the FBI must be filled with a lot of Klan holdovers. They attempted to "trick" Jewell into making a "training" film and, along the way, waving his Miranda rights. Maybe Jewell should campaign with Dole. End the FBI as we know it.

In other news the pope says that evolution is OK. A Bob Dole thumb-up for the Pope. Or, make that an opposable-thumb-up for the pope.

10/30   Rush says, "I lost it the last hour yesterday," over the lack of defense of our leader Newt. He's reading a piece by Ben Stein, the former Nixon speechwriter, comparing Nixon and Clinton and their various crimes. Nixon "was as bold as Clinton." But "Nixon had shame." According to Stein and Rush, there's "nothing to stop us but our own sense of shame." My recollection is a bit different. Nixon might have been riddled with a sense of shame; it might have been the psychological engine that ran him; but he only had shame at his civic crimes when he was caught and had to resign the presidency. Of that he was ashamed. But Rush sees shame as salubrious and Clinton lacking once again.

This election is being run in more than two mythic time zones. The first is the sixties generation against the World War II generation. The counterculture against the culture. When those terms were current, the country was more of a piece, or at least perceived to be so (precable, a different sort of PC). Two large forces at odds. Bill Clinton versus Bob Dole. But the "culture" became the counterculture. It was subsumed, helped by the huge marketing bulge of the baby boom. Now we don't have a counterculture. Not even the phrase is used. We have "subcultures." That is the word one hears. Subcultures are isolated shafts dug straight down through the culture, not interconnecting, and thereby anticommunity. They are their own communities. The Christian Coalition is the one attempt to organize some subcultures into an oppositional one, but the CC just want to run the show, give the orders, make everyone conform, but Reed's folks are only successful when they appeal to their subculture roots. The grass roots.

Subcultures are self-sustaining, and in the marketing world they are played to: niche marketing, niche employment, niche interests. The campaign "special interests" are subcultures and as they become ever more special they resemble the purest forms of subcultures: the NRA who show up at gun shows, the fetishizers. At Notre Dame during the summer, there is a parade of subcultures that rent the large facilities available: tiny baton twirlers, people who live in identical silver trailers, specialized religious groups. They are happy to be among their fellows. One can be nostalgic for the older, simpler split: culture and counterculture. The sky above is a sunny corporate monoculture, the mud below is a Babel of messy subcultures. Luckily for Bill Clinton, he has sampled a lot of them.

On C-SPAN there's a Perot rally. Ross says, "I never thought I'd live long enough to see a convicted drug dealer invited to the White House." The implication is that Ross wouldn't invite such people if he was president.

10/31 Safire's column in the *Times* today offers my notion that Clinton will claim, if he wins, he is "acquitted" by the electorate. Great minds, once again.

Diane Rehm takes callers. One male goes on about Dole's "ugly" and "hideous" face, says Dole has a mean streak. Then he announces, "We are breeding ourselves into extinction," thereby revealing more than partisanship. Diane says, "Listen to your own comments," regarding the caller's charge of Dole having a mean streak. A caller rehashes the liberal-press charge. Diane mentions that 111 daily papers have endorsed Dole and 65 have endorsed Clinton, according to *Editor & Publisher* magazine. It's a free press as long as you own one, etc.

Rush is saying he was on the phone with William Bennett, who asked if he had read the Safire column. Clinton will say people have pardoned him. Rush is agog at all the wisdom at his fingertips. But he's even more excited that Anita Hill has quit the University of Oklahoma. He reads her letter of resignation. "Pure gobbedlygook," Rush says. "What it says is nobody likes her." Then, "Let's Asian-bash some more," he says, regarding Lippo suction, etc. "I'm only kidding." Chinese-born Democratic fund-raiser John Huang had sixty-five visits to the White House, Rush reports. "Last visit on October third," less than a week after the *Los Angeles Times*'s exposé. Huang was in the White House for two hours. "He did not undergo a background check," Rush says, appalled.

Rush is sure Clinton is losing it. He quotes Clinton saying to and about the hecklers he's run into: A dog needs fleas. Rush thinks the whole thing was staged so Clinton could appear tough.

On NPR I hear that Ross Perot wants to debate Bill Clinton the night before the election on "ethics." I suspect infomercials will be on instead. Ross is just doing some bait-and-switch advertising.

Other news: Dole is saying whatever happens is "God's will."

Yesterday, Dole was talking to Abraham Lincoln, à la Nixon and his conversations with portraits in the last days at the White House. When God and Lincoln are mentioned in close proximity, the end is near.

FIFTEEN

The Verdict

11/2   On the *Whad'Ya Know?* show broadcast from Birmingham, Alabama, Michael Feldamn is making fun of the current Republican governor, Fog James, Jr., who evidently does not believe in evolution. He made his fortune pouring concrete into plastic forms, according to Feldman. Barbells, I presume. Feldman jokes about gorillas never being able to think of pouring concrete into plastic forms. The governor, unlike the pope, believes only in creationism. Feldman asks for presidential preferences from the Birmingham audience. Dole gets a large round of clapping. Clinton, to my surprise, gets a larger one. Perot gets a smattering of applause. Feldman says the audience more or less mirrors "the national average."

11/3   Gwen Ifill, on *Meet the Press,* predicts Clinton won't reach 50 percent. The program closes showing a tape of Dole saying to a midday "crowd" in Denver that his people have to get the plane back to Washington by 10:20 "or they send us to Dulles." A fate worse than death for Washington power people. "The ultimate insider's concern," Tim Russert supplies for the noninsider portion of the show's audience. All personnel on deck predict a Clinton victory and a Republican Congress. Christopher Dodd and Haley Barbour, respective heads of their parties, are blathering on about campaign reform. Dodd proposes they both agree here and now not to accept foreign money and soft money. Barbour has a real problem with that and begins minutes of equivocating and backing off, which does take some of the sting out of all his earlier barbs. One wonders why he just didn't say an equivocal yes and then just fudge it down the road, another version of the Clinton/Gingrich handshake on the same going-nowhere subject (everybody for it, nothing to be done, bureaucrats' and politicians' happiest equation). As it is, Barbour just looks weaselly.

On a newsbreak it is announced that 98 percent of the TWA 800 airplane has been recovered. The dives have been called off. (On the phone my father-in-law remarked, "At least Clinton didn't go down to the Long Island shore and hold up a body part for a photo op.")

On *Face the Nation* Tom Daschle, the Senate minority leader, talking about the economy and budget battles to come, is saying he "doesn't want the government shut down," and the campaign seems to be ending where it began in January. One of the effects of the blanket coverage of the O. J. trial was to discredit "expert" witnesses. The public now views economic experts as hired guns, the same sort of bought testimony. Whose side are you on? becomes the question, not Where do you get your authority?

On *This Week,* we have David Brinkley interviewing Dole, two old white guys talking. Brinkley is barely older than Dole, but does seem to lack Dole's nutty color. All that time in the sun. Dole's vow of a final ninety-six hours of campaigning is brought up. They shoot presidential candidates, don't they? Dole's last filibuster. To Brinkley's question, Dole says giving up his Senate seat and majority leader job showed the American public he was "serious" and therefore the people would take a serious look at him. Dole does seem delusional. He's said the same before in other venues, that he was giving up his career to show he was willing to sacrifice something more for the office. No one thinks a seventy-three-year-old man is giving up a "career." The career part has long ended. People see a man retiring after a very, very long career. It isn't a sacrifice, it's the realization that one must let go. Brinkley not kindly points out that most of the legislation now talked about was passed after Dole left. Brinkley's own imminent retirement hovers around Dole not so much as an omen as a curse.

On *The McLaughlin Group,* which was first aired Friday and I see Sunday, the consensus is that Clinton will get more than 50 percent of the vote. What a difference two days of Perot can make. On the live Sunday shows everyone is down to under 50. Perot is responsible for that, though no one says so. Perot's tilting the "undecideds" with his attacks on Clinton to himself and Dole, which will probably cost Clinton 1 or 2 percent. McLaughlin does do a turn on the Indonesians, resurrecting film of Clinton's visit there, wearing one of those wonderful shirts, a combination of the Mexican wedding sort that hangs outside the pants, and covered with a tropical, Hawaiian-inspired print, on shiny Asian fabric combining the worst of all the couture cultures.

On *Wall Street Week,* Rukeyser is merry as usual, making Halloween jokes, saying those scary characters out there are the presidential candidates. The Dow closed at 6021. Merry, merry. The Mexican peso plunged to a historic low against the greenback, he announces jauntily. Rukeyser led the way twenty-five years ago, presenting economics as entertainment on television. Now, for a certain class, it's a leisure-time activity. Rukeyser, Julia Child, Bob Vila, and their many spawn have championed work as relaxation. In his roundtable today, Mort Zuckerman admits a wee bit sheepishly (Rukeyser forced him into it) that his New York *Daily News* has endorsed Bill Clinton. William O'Neil, of *Investor's Business Daily,* likes Dole. Michael Bloomberg, a "registered Democrat" who runs the *Bloomberg News,* wants Bill. Is this a fair program, or what? Rukeyser says. They talk about the liberal press, Zuckerman saying that reporters are Democrats, but editors are Republicans (he doesn't mention the owners). O'Neil says a Roper poll, one of Rush's favorites, claims 89 percent of Washington reporters voted for Bill Clinton. Bloomberg says there's no evidence. Rukeyser asks O'Neil about his reporters. He said when he started his rag (he didn't say rag), he had twenty-two reporters, twenty-one of whom were Democrats. He makes Zuckerman's point. (But has O'Neil ever looked at the salary of the average, noncelebrity reporter? It's economics, not ideology.) Though none of them suggests, as a friend of mine has, that reporters' politics may be influenced by their on-the-job experiences and/or their bosses' views.

At night CNN does some news and shows Dole at a truck stop, trying to use up time in his ninety-six-hour (for '96!) filibustering finish. Go Bob Go. He's sitting in an eighteen-wheeler's cab, playing with an avocado-size CB microphone. "This is Marathon Man, Marathon Man," he's saying over and over into it, somewhere beyond parody. CNN puts up a CNN/USA Today/Gallup poll showing the race 50 percent Clinton, 37 percent Dole, 7 percent Perot, the rest undecided, which will be going to Dole and Perot, I expect. Bill Schneider puts up a map of the United States with the states Dukakis won in 1988 illuminated. There they are, the Democratic strongholds. Pacific Coast, upper Midwest, some of the Northeast. He shows the states Clinton won in '92, which expand the Dukakis base. Not that many more, but enough. New York, Ohio, California. Looking at the map one sees Clinton losing a landmass majority, having won with a landmass minority. Some film from early in the year is shown, uncommented upon. There's William Bennett standing with Lamar!. There's Kemp with Forbes. The old days. Before "Marathon Man" sat in trucks.

On CNBC there's Tony Blankley, Newt's chief of staff, and James Carville. Carville is going off on Kenneth Starr, a "right-wing partisan politico." James is in high serpent mode. Blankley seems bemused; he'll have a job after the fifth.

11/4 Rush is quoting a *New York Post* columnist saying "Where's Hillary?" Last seen with Bill on a stage together, not making eye contact. Imputations of marital discord.

I pick up the November 5 *National Enquirer* since it has the Rush-forecasted Dole bimbo eruption in it. The story doesn't rate a cover headline. It concerns some hot Australian Washington number Dole knew when he was a congressman in 1968, when his first marriage was "in trouble." The *Enquirer* reports: "The Australian-born secretary's apartment in Arlington, VA., featured an enormous $1,000 bed on a swivel base."

What that sentence carried with it was a bygone odor, the nonyouth, the adult part of the sexual revolution. The sixties were sex, drugs, and rock 'n' roll, but there was a high-end side to what the low-rent kids were up to—free love!—which was, more or less, personified by JFK, the Rat Pack, Las Vegas of the late fifties and early sixties, James Bond, and Bob Dole's contemporary, Hugh Hefner (now age seventy)—expensive love. There's a picture of the young woman in question from the late sixties, wearing white toreador pants, and you can see how she'd turn the head of our boy from Kansas. I stand in line in the grocery store marveling over that thousand-dollar (1968 dollars!) *swivel* bed.

Ross's infomercial is on our local CBS outlet. Who's profiting? Ross asks. Our CBS outlet, I reply. But Ross says, Not us, or you all out in Television Land. The standard of living is down for four out of five of us, he says. "Meanwhile, Democrats and Republicans are selling out your country to big foreign contributors." But most of it is dump-on-Bill time. "Why would you even think about voting for" that scoundrel Clinton? We're in for Watergate II, Ross assures us, if Clinton is reelected. Along with Ross's jeremiad, there's some biofilm interspersed. Ross, it turns out, purchased the Magna Carta, or at least a copy that England would part with. Then we get to see Ross's collection of Norman Rockwell paintings. Ross culture, it's grand. We're back to Ross. "Don't waste your vote!" and "You got what you voted for," he reminds us, meaning we have Bill Clinton. Can we watch our government grind to a halt while we engage in Watergate II? Ross reiterates. Ross mentions the little naked girl he's been featuring in these programs and intones, I don't want her to grow up in a country run "by corrupt power-driven people." Right on, Ross. He wants her to grow up in a country run by uncorrupt power-driven people. Ross is pulling no punches. If you don't vote for Ross, he says to those who don't vote, you'll be "selling your futures to corrupt foreign interests." There are shots of little naked Amanda, Ross appealing to any pedophiles lurking in the Reform Party. There's a painting of George Washington behind him. Ross is crossing his Delaware. I think he will be picking up votes—or driving them away from Clinton to Dole, at least. So he is a "protest" vote, after all.

On *Fox News* there's Ralph Reed, offering a premortem postmortem: It's a lost opportunity. The perception is that the economy is doing well . . . but Dole should have hit on crime, on partial-birth abortion. He mentions that a poll once showed that there was a fifty-fifty split among evangelicals on Clinton, but now they're coming home and Ralph is happy for that. *Fox News* tries something new. Instead of putting a tiny LIVE in the corner of the screen, it beams NOW. NOW is to LIVE as Clinton is to Dole. Then comes Matthew Freeman, a vice president of People for the American Way. Balance on *Fox News*! Murdoch putting his best foot forward. It's very *now*. Matthew complains about the Christian Coalition's voter guides, says there are forty-six million of them. They wouldn't be dumping them in the churches at the last moment, he says, if they were true. The two guys on *Fox* asking questions are Hannity ("conservative") and Colmes ("liberal"), and I wonder what dead campaigns they crawled out of. The PAW person is still complaining about the voter guides. They just ain't true. They are full of "bad facts." Then we get the John Zogby poll: it puts the spread at seven points. There is also Warren Mitofsky, father of exit polls. After a bit of conversation Zogby says, "Dole has no chance." but the House is too close to call (the Reuters/Zogby poll has it 43 percent to 41 percent).

C-SPAN has Dole in Knoxville, Tennessee. Lamar! is in the background, not wearing red-and-black check. "I believe in redemption," Dole is saying hoarsely, "and if some of you voted for Bill Clinton in '92 you can redeem yourself tomorrow." He spits out 15 percent! Five hundred dollars per child! Halve the capital gains! Protect-the-flag amendment! Voluntary prayer! God bless America! The Oak Ridge Boys sing "God Bless America" and Dole joins in sporadically, like a man popping in and out of consciousness. They're at something called the Cotton Eye Joe restaurant. The one Oak Ridge Boy with the very long white-silver hair and beard is crooning into Dole's ear.

Charles Grodin sent cameras to Democratic Clinton headquarters in New York City and was granted interviews with staffers there. They go to Dole Republican headquarters and have the door slammed in their faces. Finally, a woman comes out and tells them no one has been authorized to speak for them. It's real bunker stuff, people rummaging around for suicide pills. Grodin is in a reverie (he's the most reverie-prone television host). All these shows on O.J. and the election, he's saying, and I'm waiting for him to make my point, but he only says, all the lies, lies, from everybody, the exaggerations, lies. Bob Beckel, the *Crossfire Sunday* liberal, is there with Charles. Beckel says he managed "the biggest loss in American history," and a lot of other campaigns. McGovern, I suppose. He joins Grodin in mutual reverie.

I turn to the Christian Broadcasting Network looking for reality. Pat Robertson is saying the "Christian Coalition is geared up in Texas," and Newt has told him they will "pick up five seats." Robertson has a pollster, too. John Waage. He sees Congress as 235 to 197 for the Republicans. "And the voter guides have made an impact," Robertson says gleefully. Where's the PAW person? Put that on *Fox News*. The Senate will be 53 to 47, up 4 for the Republicans. "Your votes are crucial!" Robertson says to us all. Waage says the White House will still be the same. Robertson says the miracle scenario is still possible, though not likely. Coming up is the *700 Club,* and he says we will be seeing "an atheist who demanded evidence and found a verdict." Who's that? I wonder. Dick Morris? Bill Clinton?

On CNBC Mike Murphy, former Dole employee, is saying, regarding the Clintons, it's "looking like a bridge to the penitentiary to me." He's beside himself enough to bite the hand that's feeding him (currently). He's incensed that they call exit polls "news." If they say it's news, "they know at three-thirty. Why don't they put it out then?" The answer is so obvious that the question becomes rhetorical. "It's toxic," Murphy concludes, how the media colludes.

11/5   The sky is clear, the temperature mild for early November. Before heading to school for class, I stop by my polling place to vote. My neighborhood is called "urban," a euphemism used to mean black folks live in it. It's on the fringe of South Bend's no longer thriving downtown (malls, etc.), but the downtown has been fighting back with the College Football Hall of Fame, the Century Center—for conventions, a new Marriott, and the neighborhood has been fighting back, but losing to absentee landlords and the like. But it is an area of old, substantial homes, right along the river, then it falls off to what were workers' homes (when there was work at the now defunct Studebaker plant). So there's a lot of poverty around: 20 percent in my census track. But by some fluke of the area's more stable past, there are a set of quasi-public supervised (locked) tennis courts, with a building next to them which functions as the local polling place. Up a ways is a YWCA, now home to battered and single mothers and their children, who fill up the playground in Leeper Park down the street. There, playing with my son, I've watched ballets of childhood and gothic scenes of neglect and courtship on the part of the mothers (the boyfriends and/or husbands show up and fraternize with the women, white, black, Hispanic, etc.). One black boy of about seven was once playing with a plastic handgun, making a variety of moves to rival Fred Astaire with his cane, holding the gun out flat, parallel to the ground, the position favored in what passes for gangland popular culture in film and life. But he was dancing, though without Ginger Rogers. In a nearby grammar school, a first grader brought a real gun to school for show-and-tell and was suspended for a bit, and on our block a thirteen-year-old held up eight-year-olds with a loaded gun for candy on Hallow-een. But the tennis courts are kept clean (and locked—reservations required). Their building's circumference is stuck with the politicians-for-sale signs, and I walk in and find only the precinct workers, the usual handful of old men and women. Who's going to take these jobs when these old folks drop dead within the next four (or two) years? A whole generation of poll watchers wiped out. I decide to play reporter and ask, "Has it been busy today?" "Oh, yes," the blue-haired lady responds enthusiastically, "all morning." Though I'm the only voter around I still want to believe her. Turnout, turnout, turnout. This end of Indiana is the remnant of Democratic power in the state and our mayor is on the ticket as lieutenant governor with O'Bannon. They're hoping for big numbers from up here. I go into the booth. Pulling the long lever that shuts the curtain around me, I'm now in what appears to be the cab of an old steam locomotive, staring at the control panel. In this part of the world, you can still vote a straight ticket by moving one big lever, which I do. All the little levers drop down over the Xs. Four more years. I yank back the large lever that opens the curtain. I step out and there is no one there to follow me in.

Later, Rush says Clinton has rented an entire hotel in Bangkok for a vacation after the election. Rush is taken with the idea of Bangkok, doubtless for the pun issues. The implication of this vacation stop, Rush makes clear, is in the realm of the senses.

I'm chatting with a friend and we discuss our local congressman Tim Roemer's last television ad. It's the "click-click" ad described in *Primary*

Colors (226) brought to the tube. Life replicating art, or art, etc. Who knows, Klein might have seen it used some time ago. In the novel (and on our local TV screens) a candidate (in this case, Roemer) is watching a TV; his opponent's ad is on the screen, attacking him, and he clicks it off with a remote control and turns to viewers (the camera) and says, Ain't that too much, etc. In *Primary Colors* the ad is criticized because it's "too complicated." Well, not to whoever put it on for the Roemer campaign. We speculate whether or not Roemer knows the reference.

At the end of the workday I'm in Notre Dame's faculty/staff exercise room in the JACC, doing cardiac rehab on the treadmill. The faculty/staff exercise room at Notre Dame gets hand-me-downs from the football team. There's a television set hanging from the ceiling, broadcasting CNN's *Headline News*. It's almost five, and the room, coincidentally, is full of Roemers: the congressman, his brother, and their dad. He has been a longtime fixture at Notre Dame in university relations and the congressman got his Ph.D. here. About the brother I know nothing, though he's bigger than Tim (but not as big as their father), but they're all working out strenuously. It feels distinctly odd spending the last hour the polls are open in Indiana with the candidate. He appears happy. They are all enjoying themselves. Their own polls must have given his a comfy margin. (Though two years ago his winning margin was only 5 percent.) It will be a long night, though, many hands to shake, so he's keeping in shape. (Roemer's Republican opponent, Joe Zakas, has a Notre Dame connection, too. His wife works here as a secretary. That tells a tale, too.) The country's weather map appears on the television screen: gentle undulating waves of color cross our great continent, our sweet land. Only in the Rockies is the temperature in the thirties. Everywhere else it's forties, fifties, sixties, seventies, eighties. No storms. Wonderful weather across the country. Turnout, turnout, turnout. And the economic weather comes on: the Dow closed at 6081. Great weather! No exit-poll numbers on the news yet, though. Shots of Dole and Liddy voting. Shots of Chelsea and Bill going to vote together. Russell and Little Rock. Our congressman is not looking. He's doing ab crunches.

I get home and contacts in Washington have faxed us the 3:00 P.M. exit polls. Clinton 49, Dole 42. Florida is 47 for Clinton, 45 for Dole. CNN is not putting these on the air, though they doubtless have them, if I had them at 3:30. Torricelli (N.J.), Kerry (MA.) Durbin (IL.) Well-stone (MN.), and Levin (MI.) are winning. The Dems who are up 2 points are Johnson (S.D.), Bruggere (OR.), Harkin (Iowa), and Sweat (N.H.); even are Gantt (S.C.) Landrieu (LA.), and Clelland (GA.). Down are Brennan (ME.), Karpan (WY.), and Strickland (CO.).

There are also the results of an hour later. Clinton 52, Dole 41, Perot 7. I add that up and it appears the "others" haven't gotten any votes. I don't believe Clinton's 52. He's losing Texas, Indiana (oh, surprise), and Nevada (lots of unions, there), but he's winning many states, some in the South. Florida, too.

We're off to a couple of parties, joining in the communal spirit of Election Day for a while at least. CNN's first call is at 6:40 my time and it is *O'Bannon wins the governor's race in Indiana!* How about that. I thought there was a fair chance (the outgoing Bayh left coattails behind), but not one that could be called so early. First returns usually come from the Indianapolis area. Goldsmith must not have done well there, so much so that the computer projection gives it to O'Bannon. Those Marion County Republicans really don't like him. Broadripple backlash! Indiana polls have been closed ten minutes.

CBS is on for a moment. Its poll person is reporting the results of a question: Did you learn anything from the campaign? Twenty-three percent say yes, 75 percent say no.

CNN comes back, reporting white voters in Texas are voting 30 percent for Clinton, 60 percent for Dole. The *Capital Gang* comes on for a couple of minutes. Novak is ranting about how Dole was an "absolutely terrible candidate." Perhaps he's been lunching with Arianna Huffington.

On *Larry King Live* we are treated to Roger Clinton. He thinks his sister-in-law should run for "high political office." He thinks brother Bill should be her campaign manager. Bob Woodward has succumbed to television's siren song and is cohosting with Larry King. Woodward asks Roger a solemn question solemnly, his assessment of his brother, as if Roger Clinton is going to confide in Woodward, be confidential, spill the beans over this remote hookup. The Woodward style. In a quiet confessional room. Woodward hasn't yet reformatted his brain to TV. Bob, bless him, is not a TV kind of guy.

Roger answers that Bill "stayed the course." Roger's a happy guy.

The next drug czar in the second term? CNN's recurring picture of Bill Clinton in their computer poll graphic is a bad one, uncomplimentary, whereas CBS's photo is a good one, an attractive one.

CNN's *Inside Politics* says Republicans have won the Senate seat in Arkansas. Bernie Shaw says no Republican has won a Senate seat in Arkansas for a hundred years, until now. It appears some Arkansans haven't forgiven Bill for the attention his presidency has cast upon that benighted state. But be prepared for the Clinton Library. Arkansas, not all is lost.

CBS reads a statement by Nelson Warfield, Dole's top guy, saying that "even in defeat" Bob Dole has much to be proud of, which appears to be a very early (though obvious) concession.

Back home on the couch after one other brief party moment, watching CNN; Tony Bennett is in Little Rock singing "America, America, God shed His light on thee," in distinct contrast to the Oak Ridge Boys' rendition in Knoxville yesterday for Dole. There's the culture war: Vegas high-end lounge singer versus white boys in juke joints.

C-SPAN has Susan Swain fielding calls. One is irate: I am a female and am ashamed to be a woman. . . . people who voted for Bill Clinton will be ashamed. . . . I'm looking forward to Bill Clinton's two terms, one in the penitentiary, and his wife, too.

Thank you, caller.

All the networks have a kaleidoscope of familiar faces, switching around, keeping busy, having a show to put on, all the usual "journalists," pols, Mario, etc. On ABC Peter Jennings reads Warfield statement number two, which says the first was released "prematurely." "Even in defeat" is now inoperative; Bob Dole has conceded nothing. Even in defeat the Dole campaign is screwed up.

Fred Barnes and Ben Wattenberg are on CBN with Pat Robertson (not in the same studio, though). No shame, no shame. Barnes is saying that Democratic senators are going to blame Clinton for losing the Senate again. Robertson is gloating that Clinton has "not yet received the 50 percent" he wanted. Wattenberg at least looks a wee bit embarrassed, but he's touting his own virtue book. The *700 Club* rolls on. Send in your tithe.

I watch a bit of line dancing on TNN, the happy nineties version of the polka, nothing too wild for the cowboy-booted masses.

William Weld loses the Senate race in Massachusetts. Kerry remains. Weld concedes graciously, saying the people of his state want him to remain governor. My collapse theory holds. Dole fell, he didn't collapse.

ABC has more creatures-from-the-black-lagoon people. Mary Matalin is on, saying "they're going to attack Ken Starr." Who's they? Her husband. Is he nearby? George Will says sourly, Dole "could have won it." A real spoil sport. If Dole had followed all my wife's advice, Will implies. There's a real weird husband-and-wife scene going on here: Carville *is* on the set. He's says you have to give the president credit for winning, not Morris, Newt, and Greenspan. Mari Will, George's wife, should be here, then we would complete the bizarre picture. The small, small world.

Newt's winning speech from Georgia is on, a victor in one of the most expensive congressional campaigns—or, at least, he *raised* the most money. The crowd is shouting: No more Clinton, No more Clinton!

CNN has Kellyanne Fitzpatrick and Farai Chideya, who is wearing a whole lot of citified cornrows. Kellyanne is identified as a Republican pollster and Farai as a CNN political analyst. Their conversation recalls the Natural Law Party member who called Rush today and said he voted for Dole, convinced by Perot to do so.

There's tape of Dole saying that on his way down in the elevator today, he realized, "Tomorrow will be the first time in my life I don't have anything to do."

Yes, perhaps. So much for his foundation, wife, etc. It has finally dawned on him that he is now officially retired.

Kemp is in California, Dole in Washington. I'm struck again, as I was in the gym earlier watching *Headline News,* by the fact that there are no more campaign commercials on the tube. Hooray.

Dole is giving a concession speech. Liddy is in violet and is wearing a formidable necklace. Gold? Pearls? Gold and pearls?

The crowd is cheering. Dole wants them to pipe down. He wants to get this over with. "You're not going to get that tax cut if you're not quiet," he says, in his unstrange strange way. CNN cuts away from him, the unkindest cut of all. Boy, is he history. They begin to exchange more commentary, but then, as if they just realized what they did, they go back to Dole's speech. "I'm still the most optimistic man in America." I'm still out to lunch. He thanks his "faithful and loyal team." He tries to thank some of the party faithful, but he seems not to recall the name of the cochair of the Republican Party, an African American standing on the stage with him. Dole gives 1951 as the date for the beginning of his political life. This, by implication, is the end, I guess. CNN's folks start talking over the end of his speech. Dole finishes, "And God bless America."

Perot is being interviewed. It is mentioned that he drew votes away from both candidates equally in '92; this time, he drew more from Clinton. Ross says you can't keep people from repeating myths. He means Clinton and Dole drew votes away from him. Kemp is now giving his concession speech, saying it's been the "greatest experience of my life." Yes, a free ride for the rootless Kemp. Bigger fees for Empower America, more empowerment for Kemp. CNN leaves Kemp's speech and this time doesn't return. The Long Island housewife, Carolyn McCarthy, whose husband was shot on the Long Island Rail Road commuter train, wins a seat in congress.

On ABC we see Little Rock, the same scene as election night '92. Clinton walks out of the interior of the state house with Hillary and Chelsea. He favors these long entrances down empty corridors. Then the Gore family comes out. Bill and Al eventually step forward. Brit Hume says, in a voice full of genuine male success envy, "Can you imagine how it feels?"

Al gives a laudatory speech, praising Bill. Peter Jennings interrupts the veep's "concession speech," pauses, and says, "Did I say concession?" Yes. He reports that it appears to be the lowest voter turnout since 1924, 49 percent. I wonder what it would have been if the weather had been bad.

Gore is back, saying only thirteen presidents have been elected to two terms. Will this be the unlucky thirteenth?

Clinton gives his speech. My fellow Americans, we have work to do. He thanks his mom, "smiling up there," imagining her saying, "I never had a doubt." He thanks Ron Brown, similarly. Mourning becomes him.

He thanks his pastor for praying with him before he came out to give this speech. And unnamed ministers who have prayed with him in the White House. Of late he's been brought closer to God and eternal wisdom, he says. Thanks to Dole, I suppose. Perhaps Pat Robertson was going to do "Clinton saved" on the *700 Club*. He's born again. Dole's victory wasn't the miracle scenario, it was Clinton's. Bill thinks it's miracle. Born again, born anew, borne on high.

Copland's "Common Man" music thunders from unseen speakers. The baby boomers' Wagner, played loud. Then we get *Annie's*—good old Daddy Warbucks—song, "Tomorrow, Tomorrow." There, are fireworks (shades of Russell, Kansas, and its old government building on Dole's one triumphant San Diego night), great bursts from behind the Arkansas statehouse. Bill, Hillary, and Chelsea turn away from the crowd to stare up at the fireworks, a camera pointed right at them, the first family. For a second, Hillary's face starts to dissolve with emotion. An incipient sob, a look of overwhelming sorrow and terror begins to overtake her visage, but in yet another blink of time she stops it. Her expression settles, like Bill's and Chelsea's, into a stable gaze at the ephemeral beauty bursting so high in the air.

C-SPAN has a woman caller, appalled by Clinton's reelection, saying, "I'm in shock. You can't understand what I'm feeling." The country still appears to want to know, Who shot Vince Foster? Who killed Ron and Nicole? Who shot J. R.?

I turn to ABC, more tired than I realize, and see its Gang of Five standing up alongside Jennings and Brinkley. Lynn, Jeff, Cokie, Sam, Hal (Bruno). They're adding their two cents to the night's proceedings. Jennings will leave a last word to Brinkley, who proceeds to praise his colleagues, saying how creative they are. His remarks are thick with retirement-night hyperbole, gold-watch-time rhetoric, his accolades swollen with sentiment. Then he speaks of Clinton: "He has not a creative bone in his body, therefore he is a bore and will always be a bore." There's an audible intake of air from his unseen colleagues and Jennings interrupts him, thanking him. Donaldson's voice intrudes: "Strong letter to follow." Brinkley makes what looks like some drunk's gesture when Jennings reaches toward him, a half-flinching, half-testy rebuff.

So much for the liberal media. And I suppose it does show why the

American people decided not to elect a seventy-three-year-old man to the presidency. What seems odd about Brinkley's truculent comment is its freshness. No one, hitherto, has ever called Clinton a bore, uncreative—not that I've heard. It seems counterintuitive, but I see what Brinkley means. Clinton, though he represents the baby boom through and through, has become president again not for his rarefied subtleties, his Oxford-going side, but for his common side, his middle-America side, his boring side, his lack of "creativity" side, as Brinkley sees it. Golf, broads, the guys, the glad-hander, the charmer, the man who makes everyone feel good. Clinton's utter lack of true eccentricity is what has made him ultimately so very acceptable to the American public, its viewing public especially. The theme for the "Common Man," the bore beatified.

It is over, I think, and I decide to call my father and ask him whom he voted for.

Afterword

My father voted for Clinton, as did an interesting array of Americans: black Americans overwhelmingly (83 percent to 12 percent), women substantially (54 percent to 38 percent) *Newsweek* reported. The *New York Times* ran a table of exit polling that compared '94 House votes with '96. Here's what interested me: Under $15,000 of income voted largely for Democrats (62 to 38); under $30,000 still favored Democrats, but not by much (51 to 49); then it began to favor Republicans, 45 to 55, till income rises to over $75,000 (40 to 60); then it really jumped when you hit $100,000, 37 to 63.

The AFL-CIO money ($35 million) won 3 percent of "union households" back from '94's results: it was now 63 percent Democrat to 37 percent Republican, rather than the 60 to 40 vote in '94. Jack Kemp and the Republicans gained 10 percent of the black vote for the House; from 92 percent Democrat to 8 percent Republican in '94, it rose to 18 percent Republican and lowered to 82 percent for Democrat in '96.

Education is roughly similar to income, though with important differences. Less than high school education went Democratic (58 percent to 42 percent). After that it stays majority Republican (by about 10 points, more or less) until you hit the most-educated Americans, those with postgraduate education. There it reverses itself and the spread is in favor of the Democrats by 2 percent, 51 to 49. That is the source of all the right-wing charges against the "elite," the "liberal media," all the cultural apparatuses they find so intolerable, the NEA (artists and writers and whatnot), the NEH (liberal academics controlling academia), on and on. The people who make Rush mad, who Rush thinks looks down on him and his dittoheads. The source of the culture war, that tiny 2 percent. But that gap is closing, since in '94 it was 14 percent, 57 to 43. This presidential election did bring out a higher percentage, 2 percent higher, of over $100,000 voters, and that accounts for some of it, but nonetheless, the gap is narrowing. (And someday it will close.)

One poll in March had Dole getting 41 percent of the vote and Clinton getting 49 percent, and those are the percentage they got on November 5. Perot's endgame attacks on Clinton, I'm sure, cost Bill his magical 50 percent, and perhaps gained Dole a point or two. The "undecideds" stayed at home, or went for Dole or Perot.

B-1 Bob Dornan lost out in California, the only presidential contender from the Congress to lose his seat (too much exposure for B-1 Bob?), though he blames motor-voter registration and "illegals."

If you look at a map of the United States, Clinton country is the West Coast and a bit of the lower Southwest. Dole has Texas, and states directly north, following the slightly jagged straight line the eastern edges of Texas, Oklahoma, Kansas, Nebraska, South Dakota, and North Dakota fashion across the heart of the country. With the exception of Indiana (oh, Indiana!), Clinton has the upper and lower Midwest, through New England. The South (Mississippi, Alabama, Georgia, the Carolinas and Virginia) is Dole country, though without dangling Florida (the elderly abandoned the elderly) and happy (Carville's Cajuns!) Louisiana. It looks like one of those science fiction or futuristic maps that imagine our country no longer one of separate states, but four regions with odd names: Pacific Rim and Goodviews; Plains, Mountains, and Empty Deserts; Breadbasket and Headcheese; Dixieland minus Beachville.

Is the permanent campaign over? Now that Bill can't run again what will he do? The same as he has done, I suppose. Ken Starr gets to be the disloyal opposition, but he has no John Dean. (The opposition does have Paula Jones, summoned once to a Little Rock hotel room, and now summoning herself equally compliant lawyers to the Supreme Court to hear motions on her case, *Paula Corbin Jones v. William Jefferson Clinton*.)

For the past year or more, those who have written about Whitewater have wondered why the American public is not more exercised over it. Or, for that matter, over Travelgate, the Indonesians, etc. To quote Bob Dole's marathon mantra, "Where's the outrage?"

It was said early and often that Whitewater and attendant issues were "too complicated" for the poor, distracted public to comprehend. Far from it. No American thinks it too complicated that politicians get and extend favors that end up enriching the few at the expense of the many. The ubiquity of that circumstance makes it rather toothless as a charge. But, most importantly, unlike Watergate, Whitewater is not the culminating episode of more than a decade of a calamitous, divisive war. If anything, it is an extension of the savings-and-loan debacle, and a demonstration of the management (and personal) style of the two young people from Arkansas who became president and first lady.

All the desperate linking of Watergate and Whitewater has always missed the point. Richard Nixon wasn't drummed from office because of the break-ins his people carried out, not even because of Nixon's own attempts to cover up his involvement. He was taken to the edge of impeachment because the country was still involved in the Vietnam War. All the Watergate-related shenanigans were seen, rightly, as part of the overall conduct of the war, part of the long history of duplicity, malice, ineptness, the waste, the lack of accountability, the crimes and misdemeanors, the body count and the body bags. The country was sick at heart by then and when the president of the United States revealed himself to be—through testimony and the release of his tapes—such a half-baked schemer and liar, it was just too much to swallow. He was gone, he was history.

Nixon's departure from office (and, I suppose, it was fitting I saw it once more on film in *Nixon* the night this book began), was the Pyrrhic victory of the antiwar movement, just as the fall of the Berlin Wall is claimed to be the vindication of all the legal and illegal excesses of the most virulent anticommunist conservatives, however illogical that logic may be. Nixon leaving the presidency, the Vietnam War finally concluding, was the end of "our long national nightmare," as Gerald Ford put it. Ford was primarily speaking of Nixon's constitutional problems, but it was truly the nightmare-ending that was paramount.

Watergate is inseparable from the Vietnam War. When Nixon resigned on August 9, 1974, he had already signed into law a $1 billion ceiling on military aid available to South Vietnam. Congress, on the heels of Nixon's departure, cut it to $700 million. That led to the war's end, which came less than a year later.

Whitewater is connected to what? Arkansas? Naïveté?

I've always felt a bit of sympathy for Nixon, that he had his own counsel turn on him, his own lawyer rat him out. H. R. Haldeman and John Ehrlichman went to the mat for him, but not John W. Dean III. Clinton's John Dean is Hillary Rodham Clinton, and she is not going to sell him out, for whatever tinhorn business as usual they may have been involved in back in Arkansas.

John Dean was supposed to buffer Nixon, be his fire wall of deniability. Hillary is Clinton's fire wall and she is not going to cut a deal with Ken Starr. And the public will continue to be unpersuaded that Whitewater is the end of democracy as we know it.

Americans do not take lightly the impeachment of a president (or an indictment of a first lady). Nixon's disgrace and departure came about because of the terrible weight and momentum generated by the dark consequences of the Vietnam War. There is no such wretched wind behind Whitewater.

The campaign of '96 was more than adequately covered by the press. The problem is the silver-bullet question. Everyone seems to want the press to do one thing simply: Give the public the truth, in an easily digestible form. Sorry, corporate America has a limited interest in truth, especially in an easily digestible form. What's to sell if it's too fast and easy? Other interests are involved. Information is out there for the folks to discover, but it does take effort, and it's not likely to hit your front door early every morning, and less likely to turn up on your TV, though it does here and there, in odd times and places.

As the rich get richer and the poor get poorer, so too will the information-rich get even richer and the information-deprived become more deprived. A media homelessness will set in for those without access to the Internet, cable, or satellite dishes. (Though many Americans are without health insurance, most have VCRs.) American towns, by and large, are one-newspaper towns, and magazines supplement that, but you need a semipermanent address and the money and curiosity to subscribe. Network news will continue to be entertainment-driven, C-SPAN will continue to be viewed by retirees and shut-ins, and the Internet will be plied by data-crazed and demanding elites and Tolkien-styled permanent adolescents. Books will exist and be read by a small slice of the population. The messenger can be blamed, but only for the message, not the medium. It's all out there. Individuals just have to go get it. And the great majority of us, of course, will watch TV and listen to the radio. In the "old days," prose style and publications used to be time-oriented. The shorthand was that the roughest prose was in the daily press, slightly more polished prose was in the weeklies, very polished prose was in the monthlies, and the absolute best was in books, prose's final resting place. That may no longer hold, but the progression does: there's a lot of horizontal information out there, and going vertical doesn't always make you wise, but the more time you spend, the more you will know.

To indulge in the rhetoric I have been listening to all year, Campaign '96 was not the last presidential campaign of the twentieth century, but, actually, the first campaign of the twenty-first. Unfortunately, whatever shortcomings it has had, the next one, Campaign 2000, will be worse. Good luck to us all.

Acknowledgements

I owe thanks to a number of people, not least of all the members of the press who actually covered the campaign out in the trenches. I watched on and off: ABC, NBC, CBS, CNN, PBS, C-SPAN, Fox, and the thirty-odd cable stations my local cable company (TCI of Michiana) dispenses (not, alas, *Comedy Central*). I listened to, primarily, two radio stations: our NPR outlet, WVPE FM and the all talk and sports WSBT AM. I subscribed to many magazines (the list sounds like one from a dedicated door-to-door salesperson), and I read others in libraries. Most are mentioned in the text. Since the book has a diary structure, sources are dated when they are used, in lieu of notes. But it's largely an oral-aural-visual world out there and I was awash in it. When you have so many people writing and commenting on a single subject (the "campaign"), you encounter a variation of the monkeys-at-a-typewriter notion: If enough monkeys are typing, eventually more than one will make the same pithy remark. The standard I employed is that if I wrote it before I saw it in print, or heard it, I left it in. It wasn't a big problem. I also attempted to credit anyone I quoted and I apologize in advance if something slipped by—and for misspelling anyone's name. At times it was only an oral world out there and though I tracked things down, something might have eluded me. I'll be happy to correct future editions. A brief portion of the Afterword appeared, in different form, in the *Chicago Tribune*, December 10, 1996. There are a number of individuals who played a role in this effort whom I want to acknowledge by name: David Black, Corinne

Campaign America '96: The View From the Couch

Bliss, Clair Brown, David Chalfant, Nick Cinglia, Jennifer Combs, Kevin Coyne, Mary Craypo, Charles DeFanti, Richard Elman, Judy Fox, H. Bruce Franklin, Jerome Frese, David and Sally Ghilarducci, Harry and Ruth Ghilarducci, Marion Ghilarducci, Adam Goldberger, David Hoppe, Chris Jara, Patricia Ledesma Liebana, Mark Marino, Dan O'Connor, all the O'Rourkes, Eileen and Ernie Sandeen, Irini Spanidou, Chris Tiedemann, John Weber, Ed Zuckerman, my colleagues at Notre Dame, especially Matt Benedict, Doug Bradley, Charles Craypo, Chris Fox, Dolores Frese, Robert Frishman, Sonia Gernes, Jill Godmilow, Barbara Green, Gene Halton, Graham Hammill, Glenn Hendler, Marjorie and Doug Kinsey, Gloria-Jean Masciarotte, John and Diana Matthias, Steve Moriarty, Erskine Peters, Valerie Sayers, Betty and Michael Signer, Patrick Sullivan, C.S.C, Jay Walton, and, of course, my wife Teresa Ghilarducci and my son Joseph Ghilarducci O'Rourke, who put up with a lot during the year.

Bibliography

Abu-Jamal, Mumia. *Live From Death Row*. New York: Avon Books, 1996.

Agronsky, Jonathon I. Z. *Marion Barry: the Politics of Race*. Albany, N.Y.: British American Publishing, 1991.

Aldrich, Gary. *Unlimited Access: An FBI Agent inside the Clinton White House*. Washington, D.C.: Regnery Publishing, 1996.

Alinsky, Saul D. *Reveille for Radicals*. New York: Vintage Books, 1969.

Alterman, Eric. *Sound and Fury: The Washington Punditocracy and the Collapse of American Politics*. New York: Harper Perennial, 1993.

Bailey, Brad, and Bob Darden. *Mad Man in Waco*. Waco, Tex: WRS Publishing, 1993.

Barlett, Donald L., and James B. Steele. *America: Who Really Pays the Taxes?* New York: Simon and Schuster, 1994.

Bates, Tom. *RADS: The 1970 Bombing of the Army Math Research Center at the University of Wisconsin and Its Aftermath*. New York: HarperCollins, 1992.

Beard, Patricia. *Growing Up Republican: Christie Whitman: The Politics of Character*. New York: HarperCollins, 1996.

Bennett, William. *Body Count: Moral Poverty—and How to Win America's War against Crime and Drugs*. New York: Simon and Schuster, 1996.

———. *The Book of Virtues: A Treasury of Great Moral Stories*. New York: Simon and Schuster, 1993.

Bentley, P. F. *Clinton: Portrait of Victory*. Sausalito, Calif.: Warner Books, Epicenter Communications Books, 1993.

Bergmann, Barbara R. *In Defense of Affirmative Action*. New York: Basic Books, 1996.

Bibb, Porter. *It Ain't As Easy as It Looks: Ted Turner's Amazing Story*. New York: Virgin Books, 1994.

Campaign America '96: The View From the Couch

Blanton, Tom, ed. *White House E-mail: The Top Secret Computer Messages the Reagan/Bush White House Tried to Destroy.* New York: The New Press, 1995.

Blitzer, Wolf. *Between Washington and Jerusalem: A Reporter's Notebook.* Oxford and New York: Oxford University Press, 1985.

Bloom, Harold. *The American Religion: The Emergence of the Post-Christian Nation.* New York: Simon and Schuster, 1992.

Bolick, Clint. *The Affirmative Action Fraud: Can We Restore the American Civil Rights Vision?* Washington, D.C.: Cato Institute, 1996.

Boorstin, Daniel J. *The Image: A Guide to Pseudo-Events in America.* New York: Antheneum, 1961.

Bork, Robert H. *Slouching towards Gomorrah: Modern Liberalism and American Decline.* New York: Regan Books, 1996.

Bradlee, Ben. *A Good Life: Newspapering and Other Adventures.* New York: Simon and Schuster, 1995.

Bradley, Bill. *Time Present, Time Past: A Memoir.* New York: Alfred A. Knopf, 1996.

Brock, David. *The Real Anita Hill: The Untold Story.* New York: Free Press, 1994.

———. *The Seduction of Hillary Rodham.* New York: Free Press, 1996.

Broder, David S., and Haynes Johnson. *The System: The American Way of Politics at the Breaking Point.* New York: Little, Brown, and Co., 1996.

Broyard, Anatole. *Kafka Was the Rage: A Greenwich Village Memoir.* New York: Carl Souther Books, 1993.

Brummett, John. *Highwire: From the Back Roads to the Beltway.* New York: Hyperion, 1994.

Buchanan, Patrick J. *Right from the Beginning.* Washington, D.C.: Regnery Gateway, 1990.

Burgheim, Richard, ed. People Weekly, *Yearbook: The Year in Review: 1995.* People Weekly Books, 1996.

Bush, Barbara. *A Memoir.* New York: Charles Scribner's Sons, 1994.

Capote, Truman. *In Cold Blood: A True Account of a Multiple Murder and Its Consequences.* New York: Random House, 1965.

Caro, Robert A. *The Years of Lyndon Johnson: Means of Ascent.* New York: Alfred A. Knopf, 1990.

Carpozi, George, Jr. *Clinton Confidential, The Climb to Power: The Unauthorized Biography of Bill and Hillary Clinton.* Del Mar, Calif.: Emery Dalton Books, 1995.

Carter, Jimmy. *Keeping Faith: Memoirs of a President.* New York: Bantam Books, 1982.

Carville, James. *We're Right. They're Wrong: A Handbook for Spirited Progressives.* New York: Random House, 1996.

Caute, David. *The Great Fear: The Anti-Communist Purge under Truman and Eisenhower*. New York: Simon and Schuster, 1979.

Chopra, Deepak. *The Seven Spiritual Laws of Success: A Practical Guide to the Fulfillment of Your Dreams*. San Rafael, Calif.: Amber-Allen Publishing; New World Library, 1994.

Clifford, Clark, with Richard Holbrooke. *Counsel to the President: A Memoir*. New York: Random House, 1991.

Clinton, Bill and Al Gore. *Putting People First: How We Can All Change America*. New York: Times Books, 1992.

Clinton, Hillary Rodham. *It Takes a Village: And Other Lessons Children Teach Us*. New York: Simon and Schuster, 1996.

Cochran, Johnnie L. *Journey to Justice*. New York: Ballantine Books, 1996.

Cockburn, Alexander, and Ken Silverstein. *Washington Babylon*. New York: Verso, 1996.

Cohen, Richard M., and Jules Witcover. *A Heartbeat Away: The Investigation and Resignation of Vice President Spiro T. Agnew*. New York: Viking Press, 1974.

Colborn, Theo. *Our Stolen Future: Are We Threatening Our Fertility, Intelligence, and Survival?—A Scientific Detective Story*. New York: Dutton, 1996.

Colfax, S. Thomas, ed. *"Deng Xiaoping is a Chain-Smoking Communist Dwarf": The Sayings of Pat Buchanan*. New York: Ballantine Books, 1996.

Collier, Peter, and David Horowitz. *The Kennedys: An America Drama*. New York: Summit Books, 1984.

Corry, John. *My Times: Adventures in the News Trade*. New York: G. P. Putnam's Sons, 1994.

Covey, Stephen R. *The Seven Habits of Highly Effective People: Restoring the Character Ethic*. New York: Simon and Schuster, 1990.

Coyne, Kevin. *Domers: A Year at Notre Dame*. New York: Viking, 1995.

Cramer, Richard Ben. *What It Takes: The Way to the White House*. New York: Vintage Books, 1993.

Crowley, Monica. *Nixon Off the Record*. Random House, 1996.

D'Amato, Alfonse. *Power, Pasta and Politics: The World According to Senator Al D'Amato*. New York: Hyperion, 1995.

Damore, Leo. *Senatorial Privilege: The Chappaquiddick Cover-up*. Washington, D.C.: Regnery Gateway, 1988.

David, Lester. *Good Ted, Bad Ted: The Two Faces of Edward M. Kennedy*. New York: Carol Publishing, Birch Lane Press, 1993.

Davis, Patti (with Maureen Strange Foster). *Home Front*. New York: Crown Publishers, 1986.

Day, James. *The Vanishing Vision: The Inside Story of Public Television*. Berkeley, Calif. University of California Press, 1995.

Dealy, Francis X., Jr. *The Power and the Money: Inside the* Wall Street Journal. New York: Carol Publishing, Birch Lane Press, 1993.

Dean, John W. *Blind Ambition: The White House Years*. New York: Simon and Schuster, 1976.

Dees, Morris. *Gathering Storm: America's Militia Threat*. New York: HarperCollins 1996.

de Grazia, Edward. *Girls Lean Back Everywhere: The Law of Obscenity and the Assault on Genius*. New York: Random House, 1992.

Dershowitz, Alan M. *The Best Defense*. New York: Vintage Books, 1983.

Dionne, E. J. *They Only Look Dead: Why Progressives Will Dominate the Next Political Era*. New York: Simon and Schuster, 1996.

Dole, Bob, and Elizabeth Dole, with Richard Norton Smith and Kerry Tymchuk. *Unlimited Partners: Our American Story*. New York: Simon and Schuster, 1996.

Donovan, Robert J., and Ray Scherer. *Unsilent Revolution: Television and American Public Life*. New York: Cambridge University Press, 1992.

The Downsizing of America. By the reporters of *the* New York Times. New York: Times Books, 1996.

Draper, Theodore. *A Very Thin Line: The Iron-Contra Affairs*. New York: Hill and Wang, 1991.

Duffy, Michael, and Dan Goodgame. *Marching in Place: The Status Quo Presidency of George Bush*. New York: Simon and Schuster, 1992.

Eastland, Terry. *Ending Affirmative Action: The Case for Colorblind Justice*. New York: Basic Books, 1996.

Ehrendhalt, Alan. *The United States of Ambition: Politicians, Power, and the Pursuit of Office*. New York: Times Books, 1991.

Eisner, Robert. *The Misunderstood Economy: What Counts and How to Count It*. Boston, Mass.: Harvard Business School Press, 1994.

Ervin, Sam J., Jr. *The Whole Truth: The Watergate Conspiracy*. New York: Random House, 1980.

Fallows, James M. *Breaking the News: How the Media Undermine American Democracy*. New York: Pantheon Books, 1996.

Faludi, Susan. *Backlash: The Undeclared War against American Women*. New York: Crown Publishers, 1991.

Faux, Jeff. *The Party's Not Over: A New Vision of Democrats*. New York: Basic Books, 1996.

Ferraro, Geraldine. *Ferraro: My Story*. New York: Bantam Books, 1985.

Fisher, Mary. *I'll Not Go Quietly*. New York: Charles Scribner's Sons, 1995.

Flowers, Gennifer, with Jacquelyn Dapper. *Gennifer Flowers: Passion and Betrayal*. Del Mar, Calif.: Emery Dalton Books, 1995.

Fonzi, Gaeton. *The Last Investigation*. New York: Thunder's Mouth Press, 1993.

Ford, Richard. *Independence Day*. New York: Alfred A. Knopf, 1995.

Franken, Al. *Rush Limbaugh Is a Big Fat Idiot and Other Observations*. New York: Delacorte Press, 1996.

Frantzich, Stephen and John Sullivan. *The C-SPAN Revolution*. Norman and London: University of Oklahoma Press, 1996.

Friday, Nancy. *The Power of Beauty*. New York: HarperCollins, 1996.

Friedman, Thomas L. *From Beirut to Jerusalem*. New York: Farrar, Straus, and Giroux, 1989.

Frohnmayer, John. *Leaving Town Alive: Confessions of an Arts Warrior*. New York: Houghton Mifflin Co., 1993.

Frum, David. *What's Right: The New Conservative Majority and the Remaking of America*. New York: Basic Books, 1996.

Gentry, Curt. *J. Edgar Hoover: The Man and His Secrets*. New York: W. W. Norton and Co., 1991.

Germond, Jack W., and Jules Witcover. *Mad as Hell: Revolt at the Ballot Box, 1992*. New York: Warner Books, 1993.

————. *Whose Broad Stripes and Bright Stars? The Trivial Pursuit of the Presidency 1988*. New York: Warner Books, 1989.

Ghilarducci, Teresa. *Labor's Capital: The Economics and Politics of Private Pensions*. Cambridge, Mass.: MIT Press, 1992.

Gibson, James William. *Warrior Dreams: Paramilitary Culture in Post-Vietnam America*. New York: Hill and Wang, 1994.

Gingrich, Candace, with Chris Bull. *The Accidental Activist: A Personal and Political Memoir*. New York: Simon and Schuster, 1996.

Gingrich, Newt. *To Renew America*. New York: HarperCollins, 1995.

Gingrich, Newt, with David Drake and Marianne Gingrich. *Window of Opportunity: A Blueprint for the Future*. New York: Tor Books, 1984.

Gitlin, Todd. *The Sixties: Years of Hope, Days of Rage*. New York: Bantam Books, 1987.

Glazer, Nathan, and Daniel P. Moynihan. *Beyond the Melting Pot: The Negroes, Puerto Ricans, Jews, Italians, and Irish of New York City*. Cambridge, Mass.: MIT Press, 1970.

Goddard, Donald and Lester Coleman. *Trail of the Octopus: The DEA-CIA Coverup at Lockerbie*. New York: Argonaut Press, 1995.

Goldhagen, Daniel Jonah. *Hitler's Willing Executioners: Ordinary Germans and the Holocaust*. New York: Alfred A. Knopf, 1996.

Goldman, Peter, and Tom Mathews. *The Quest for the Presidency*. New York: Simon and Schuster, 1989.

Goodwin, Doris Kearns. *Lyndon Johnson and the American Dream*. New York: Harper and Row, 1976.

Gore, Tipper. *Picture This: A Visual Diary*. New York: Broadway Books, 1996.

Goulden, Joseph C. *Fit to Print: A. M. Rosenthal and His Times*. Secaucus, N.J.: Lyle Stuart, 1988.

Haig, Alexander M., Jr., with Charles McCarry. *Inner Circles: How America Changed the World: A Memoir*. New York: Warner Books, 1992.

Haldeman, H. R. *The Haldeman Diaries: Inside the Nixon White House*. New York: G. P. Putnam's Sons, 1994.

Harr, Jonathan. *A Civil Action*. New York: Random House, 1995.

Harrington, Michael. *The Other America: Poverty in the United States*. New York: Macmillan, 1962.

Helprin, Mark. *Refiner's Fire: The Life and Adventures of Marshall Pearl, a Foundling*. New York: Alfred A. Knopf, 1977.

Hendrickson, Paul. *The Living and the Dead: Robert McNamara and Five Lives of a Lost War*. New York: Alfred A. Knopf, 1996.

Herman Edward S., and Noam Chomsky. *Manufacturing Consent: The Political Economy of the Mass Media*. New York: Pantheon Books, 1988.

Hernnstein, Richard, and Charles Murray. *The Bell Curve: Intelligence and Class Structure in American Life*. New York: Free Press, 1994.

Hersh, Seymour M. *The Price of Power: Kissinger in the Nixon White House*. New York: Summit Books, 1983.

Hillin, Hank. *Al Gore Jr.: His Life and Career*. New York: Carol Publishing, Birch Lane Press, 1992.

Hilton, Stanley G. *Senator for Sale: An Unauthorized Biography of Bob Dole*. New York: St. Martin's Press, 1996.

Holtzman, Elizabeth, with Cynthia Cooper. *Who Said It Would Be Easy?* New York: Arcade Publishers, 1996.

Huffington, Arianna Stassinopoulos. *Picasso: Creator and Destroyer*. New York: Simon and Schuster, 1988.

Ireland, Patricia. *What Women Want*. New York: Dutton, 1996.

Jackson, Charles. *The Lost Weekend*. New York: Farrar and Rinehart, 1944.

Jaspersohn, William. *Senator: A Profile of Bill Bradley in the U.S. Senate*. New York: Harcourt Brace Jovanovich, 1992.

Johnson, Haynes. *Divided We Fall: Gambling with History in the Nineties*. New York: W. W. Norton and Co., 1994.

Karnow, Stanley. *Vietnam: A History*. New York: Viking Press, 1983.

Kelly, Charles M. *The Great Limbaugh Con: And Other Right-wing Assaults on Common Sense*. Santa Barbara Calif.: Fithian Press, 1994.

Kelley, Kitty. *Nancy Reagan: The Unauthorized Biography*. New York: Simon and Schuster, 1991.

Kiihl, Stefan. *The Nazi Connection: Eugenics, American Racism, and German National Socialism*. New York: Oxford University Press, 1994.

[Klein, Joe]. *Primary Colors: A Novel of Politics*. New York: Random House, 1996.

William O'Rourke

Knox, Michael. *The Private Diary of an O. J. Juror*. Beverly Hills, Calif.: Dove Books, 1995.

Koch, Edward I., with Daniel Paisner. *Citizen Koch: An Autobiography*. New York: St. Martin's Press, 1992.

Kurtz, Howard. *Media Circus: The Trouble with America's Newspapers*. New York: Times Books, 1994.

————. *Hot Air: All Talk, All the Time*. New York: Random House, 1996.

Lapham, Lewis H. *The Wish for Kings: Democracy at Bay*. New York: Grove Press, 1993.

Leapman, Michael. *Arrogant Aussie: The Rupert Murdoch Story*. Secaucus, N.J.: Lyle Stuart, 1985.

Lehman, David. *Signs of the Times: Deconstruction and the Fall of Paul de Man*. New York: Poseidon Press, 1992.

Lesher, Stephan. *George Wallace: American Populist*. New York: Addison-Wesley Publishing, 1994.

Lewis, Charles, Alejandro Benes, and Meredith O'Brien. *The Buying of the President*. New York: Avon Books, 1996.

Limbaugh, Rush. *See, I Told You So*. New York: Pocket Books, 1993.

————. *The Way Things Ought to Be*. New York: Pocket Books, 1992.

Lind, Michael. *The Next American Nation: The New Nationalism and the Fourth American Revolution*. New York: Free Press, 1995.

————. *Up from Conservatism: Why the Right is Wrong for America*. New York: Free Press, 1996.

Litchfield, Michael. *It's a Conspiracy! The National Insecurity Council*. Berkeley, Calif.: Earth Works Press, 1992.

Lowry, Malcolm. *Under the Volcano*. 1947. New York: New American Library, 1971.

Macdonald, Andrew. *The Turner Diaries*. New York: Barricade Books, 1996.

Mailer, Norman. *Of a Fire on the Moon*. Boston: Little, Brown, and Co., 1970.

Maraniss, David, *First in His Class: The Biography of Bill Clinton*. New York: Simon and Schuster, Touchstone, 1996.

Maraniss, David, and Michael Weisskopf. *"Tell Newt to Shut Up!": Prizewinning Washington Post Journalists Reveal How Reality Gagged the Gingrich Revolution*. New York: Simon and Schuster, Touchstone, 1996.

Marc, David *Bonfire of the Humanities: Television, Subliteracy and Long-Term Memory Loss*. Syracuse, N.Y.: Syracuse University Press, 1995.

Margolis, Jon. *The Quotable Bob Dole: Witty, Wise and Otherwise*. New York: Avon Books, 1996.

Markusen, Ann. *Dismantling the Cold War Economy*. New York: Basic Books, 1992.

Marquis, Alice Goldfarb. *Art Lessons: Learning from the Rise and Fall of Public Arts Funding*. New York: Basic Books, 1995.

500

Mason, Todd. *Perot: An Unauthorized Biography*. Homewood, Ill.: Business One Irwin, 1990.

Matalin, Mary, and James Carville, with Peter Knobler. *All's Fair: Love, War, and Running for President*. New York: Random House, 1994.

Mayer, Jane, and Jill Abramson. *Strange Justice: The Selling of Clarence Thomas*. New York: Plume, 1996.

McFadden, Robert D., Joseph B. Treaster, and Maurice Carroll. *No Hiding Place: An Inside Report on the Hostage Crises*. New York: Times Books, 1981.

McGinnis, Joe. *The Last Brother*. New York: Simon and Schuster, 1993.

McGovern, George. *Terry: My Daughter's Life-and-Death Struggle with Alcoholism*. New York: Villard Books, 1996.

McKeever, Porter. *Adlai Stevenson: His Life and Legacy*. New York: William Morrow, 1989.

McLuhan, Marshall. *The Mechanical Bride: Folklore of Industrial Man*. Boston: Beacon Press, 1951.

McMillan, Terry. *How Stella Got Her Groove Back*. New York: Viking, 1996.

McNamara, Robert S., with Brian Van De Mark. *In Retrospect: The Tragedy and Lessons of Vietnam*. New York: Times Books, 1995.

Medved, Michael. *Hollywood vs. America: Popular Culture and the War on Traditional Values*. New York: HarperCollins, 1992.

Meese, Edwin III. *With Reagan: The Inside Story*. Washington, D.C.: Regnery Gateway, 1992.

Mervin, David. *George Bush and the Guardianship Presidency*. New York: St. Martin's Press, 1996.

Metz, Robert. *CBS: Reflections in a Bloodshot Eye*. Chicago: Playboy Press, 1975.

Miles, Michael W. *The Odyssey of the American Right*. New York: Oxford University Press, 1980.

Miller, Judith. *God Has Ninety Faces: Reporting From a Militant Middle East*. New York: Simon and Schuster, 1996.

Milton, Joyce, and Ann Louise Bardach. *Vicki: The True Story of Vicki Morgan and Alfred Bloomingdale and the Affair That Shook the Highest Levels of Government and Society*. New York: St. Martin's Press, 1986.

Moore, Michael. *Downsize This!* New York: Crown Publishers, 1996.

Morris, Roger. *Partners in Power: The Clintons and Their America*. New York: Henry Holt and Co., 1996.

———. *Richard Milhous Nixon: The Rise of an American Politician*. New York: Henry Holt and Co., 1990.

Morris, Willie. *New York Days*. New York: Little, Brown, and Co., 1993.

Munson, Richard. *The Cardinals of Capitol Hill: The Men and Women Who Control Government Spending*. New York: Grove Press, 1993.

Murray, Charles A. *Losing Ground: American Social Policy, 1950–1980*. New York: Basic Books, 1984.

Nelson, Rex, and Philip Martin. *The Hillary Factor: The Story of America's First Lady*. New York: Gallen Publishing, 1993.

The New Republic *Guide to the Candidates, 1996*. New York: HarperCollins, A New Republic Book, 1996.

North, Oliver. *Under Fire: An American Story*. New York: HarperCollins; Grand Rapids, Mich.: Zondervan, 1991.

Oakley, Meredith L. *On the Make: The Rise of Bill Clinton*. Washington, D.C.: Regnery Publishing, 1994.

O'Rourke, P. J. *All the Trouble in the World*. New York: Atlantic Monthly Press, 1994.

——, comp. *The Enemies List*. New York: Atlantic Monthly Press, 1996.

O'Rourke, William. *The Harrisburg 7 and the New Catholic Left*. New York: T. Y. Crowell, 1972.

——. *The Meekness of Isaac*. New York: T. Y. Crowell, 1974.

Page, Clarence. *Showing My Color: Impolite Arguments on Race and Gender in America*. New York: Harper Collins, 1996.

Paglia, Camille. *Sex, Art, and American Culture*. New York: Random House, Vintage Books, 1992.

——. *Sexual Personae: Art and Decadence from Nefertiti to Emily Dickinson*. New Haven, Conn.: Yale University Press, 1990.

Patterson, Thomas E. *Out of Order*. New York: Random House, Vintage Books, 1994.

Phillips, Kevin. *Arrogant Capital: Washington, Wall Street and the Frustration of American Politics*. New York: Little, Brown, and Co., 1995.

Polsby, Nelson W., and Aaron Wildausky. *Presidential Elections: Contemporary Strategies of American Electoral Politics*. New York: Free Press, 1991.

Posner, Gerald L. *Case Closed: Lee Harvey Oswald and the Assassination of JFK*. New York: Random House, 1993.

——. *Citizen Perot: His Life and Times*. New York: Random House, 1996.

Powell, Colin, with Joseph E. Persico. *An American Journey*. New York: Ballantine Books, 1995.

Quayle, Dan. *The American Family: Discovering the Values That Make Us Strong*. New York: HarperCollins, 1996.

——. *Standing Firm: A Vice-Presidential Memoir*. New York: HarperCollins, 1994.

Quayle, Marilyn T. *Embrace the Serpent*. New York: Crown Publishers, 1992.

Queenan, Joe. *Imperial Caddy: The Rise of Dan Quayle in America and the Decline and Fall of Practically Everything Else*. New York: Hyperion, 1992.

Radosh, Ronald, and Joyce Milton. *The Rosenberg File: A Search for the Truth*. New York: Holt, Rinehart, and Winston, 1983.

Reed, Ralph. *Active Faith: How Christians Are Changing the Soul of American Politics*. New York: Free Press, 1996.

Reeves, Richard. *Running in Place: How Bill Clinton Disappointed America*. Kansas City: Andrews and McMeel, 1996.

Regan, Donald T. *For the Record: from Wall Street to Washington*. New York: Harcourt Brace Jovanovich, 1988.

Rendall, Steven, Jim Naureckas, and Jeff Cohen. *The Way Things Aren't: Rush Limbaugh's Reign of Error*. New York: New Press, 1995.

Resnick, Faye D., with Mike Walker. *Nicole Brown Simpson: The Private Diary of a Life Interrupted*. Beverly Hills, Calif.: Dove Books, 1994.

Richardson, Eliot. *Reflections of a Radical Moderate*. New York: Pantheon Books, 1996.

Robertson, Pat. *The New World Order*. Dallas, Texas: Word Publishing, 1991.

Rollins, Ed, with Tom Defrank. *Bare Knuckles and Back Rooms: My Life in American Politics*. New York: Broadway Books, 1996.

Rosentiel, Tom. *Strange Bedfellows: How Television and the Presidential Candidates Changed American Politics, 1992*. New York: Hyperion, 1993.

Roth, David. *Sacred Honor: A Biography of Colin Powell*. Grand Rapids, Mich.: Zondervan Publishing, 1993.

Rubin, Joan Shelley. *The Making of Middlebrow Culture*. Chapel Hill: University of North Carolina Press, 1992.

Sabato, Larry J., and Glenn R. Simpson. *Dirty Little Secrets: The Persistence of Corruption in American Politics*. New York: Random House, Times Books, 1996.

Samuelson, Robert J. *The Good Life and Its Discontents: The American Dream in the Age of Entitlement, 1945–1955*. New York: Times Books, 1995.

Schlafly, Phyllis. *The Gravediggers*. Alton, Ill: Pere Marquette Press, 1964.

———. *Strike from Space: How the Russians May Destroy Us*. New York: Devin-Adair Co., 1965.

Schmuhl, Robert. *Statecraft and Stagecraft: American Political Life in the Age of Personality*. Notre Dame, Ind.: University of Notre Dame Press, 1992.

The Senate Ethics Counsel. *The Packwood Report*. New York: Random House, Times Books, 1995.

Sharpton, Al, and Anthony Walton. *Go and Tell Pharaoh: The Autobiography of the Reverend Al Sharpton*. New York: Doubleday, 1996.

Shaw, Randy. *The Activist's Handbook: A Primer for the 1990s and Beyond*. Berkeley, Calif.: University of California Press, 1996.

Shawcross, William. *Murdoch*. New York: Simon and Schuster, 1993.

Sheehan, Neil. *A Bright Shining Lie: John Paul Vann and America in Vietnam*. New York: Random House, 1988.

Simon, Paul. *Winners and Losers: The 1988 Race for the Presidency, One Candidate's Perspective*. New York: Continuum Books, 1989.

William O'Rourke

Sirica, John J. *To Set the Record Straight: The Break-in, the Tapes, the Conspirators, the Pardon*. New York: W. W. Norton and Co., 1979.

Slansky, Paul, Steve Radlauer, and Dan Quayle. *The Airhead Apparent: A Fair Unbiased Look at Our Nation's Most Dangerous Dimwit*. Berkeley, Calif.: Potatoe Press, 1992.

Squires, James D. *Read All About It! The Corporate Takeover of America's Newspapers*. New York: Random House, Times Books, 1993.

Srodes, James L., and Arthur Jones. *Campaign 1996: Who's Who in the Race for the White House*. New York: Harper Paperbooks, 1996.

Staggenborg, Suzanne. *The Pro-Choice Movement: Organization and Activism in the Abortion Conflict*. New York: Oxford University Press, 1991.

Stern, Kenneth S. *A Force upon the Plain: The American Militia Movement and the Politics of Hate*. New York: Simon and Schuster, 1996.

Stewart, James B. *Blood Sport: The President and His Adversaries*. New York: Simon and Schuster, 1996.

———. *Den of Theives*. New York: Simon and Schuster, Touchstone, 1992.

Stockman, David A. *The Triumph of Politics*. New York: Harper and Row, 1986.

Stone, Deborah J., and Christopher Manion. *"Slick Willie" II: Why America Still Cannot Trust Bill Clinton*. Annapolis, Md.: Annapolis-Washington Book Publishers, 1994.

Summers, Anthony. *Official and Confidential: The Secret Life of J. Edgar Hoover*. New York: Pocket Books, 1994.

Sweeney, John J. *America Needs a Raise: Fighting for Economic Security and Social Justice*. Boston: Houghton Mifflin Co., 1996.

Thomas, Bill. *Capital Confidential: One Hundred Years of Sex, Scandal, and Secrets in Washington, D.C.* New York: Pocket Books, 1996.

Thompson, Hunter S. *Better than Sex: Confessions of a Political Junkie. Gonzo Papers Vol. 4*. New York: Ballantine Books, 1995.

———. *Fear and Loathing: On the Campaign Trail '72*. San Francisco: Straight Arrow Books, 1973.

Thurber, James A., and Candice J. Nelson, eds. *Campaigns and Elections American Style*. Boulder, Col.: Westview Press, 1995.

Thurow, Lester C. *The Future of Capitalism: How Today's Economic Forces Shape Tomorrow's World*. New York: W. Morrow and Co., 1996.

Toffler, Alan. *Creating a New Civilization: The Politics of the Third Wave*. Atlanta, Georgia: Turner Publishing, 1995.

Toobin, Jeffrey. *The Run of His Life: The People vs. O. J. Simpson*. New York: Random House, 1996.

Troy, Gil. *See How They Ran: The Changing Role of the Presidential Candidate*. New York: Free Press, 1991.

Tyrrell, R. Emmett, Jr. *Boy Clinton: The Political Biography*. Washington, D.C.: Regnery Publishing, 1996.

Virga, Vincent. *The Eighties: Images of America*. New York: HarperCollins, 1992.

Von Hoffman, Nicholas. *Capitalist Fools: Tales of American Business from Carnegie to Malcolm Forbes*. London: Chatto and Windus, 1993.

————. *Citizen Cohn: The Life and Times of Roy Cohn*. New York: Doubleday, 1988.

Waldman, Steven. *The Bill: How Legislation Really Becomes Law: A Case Study of the National Service Bill*. New York: Penguin Books, 1996.

Walker, Martin. *The President We Deserve: Bill Clinton, His Rise, Falls and Comebacks*. New York: Crown Publishers, 1996.

Warner, Judith. *Hillary Clinton: The Inside Story*. New York: Signet, 1993.

Warner, Judith, and Max Berley. *Newt Gringrich: Speaker to America*. New York: Signet, 1995.

Warren, Donald. *Radio Priest: Charles Coughlin, the Father of Hate Radio*. New York: Free Press, 1996.

Wattenberg, Ben J. *Values Matter Most: How Republicans or Democrats or a Third Party Can Win and Renew the American Way of Life*. New York: Free Press, 1995.

Weissman, Art. *Christine Todd Whitman: The Making of a National Political Player*. Secaucus, N.J.: Asbury Park Press, 1996.

Wharton, William. *A Midnight Clear*. New York: Alfred A. Knopf. 1982.

White House Domestic Policy Council. *Health Security: The President's Report to the American People.* New York: Simon and Schuster, 1993.

White, Theodore, H. *The Making of the President, 1972*. New York: Atheneum 1973.

Whittemore, Hank. *CNN: The Inside Story*. Boston: Little, Brown and Company, 1990.

Williamson, Marianne. *A Woman's Worth*. New York: Random House, 1993.

Wills, Garry. *Lincoln at Gettysburg: The Words That Remade America*. New York: Simon and Schuster, 1992.

Witcover, Jules, *Marathon: The Pursuit of the Presidency 1972–1976*. New York: Viking Press, 1977.

Woodward, Bob. *The Agenda: Inside the Clinton White House*. New York: Pocket Books, 1995.

Woodward, Bob, and Scott Armstrong. *The Brethren: Inside the Supreme Court*. New York: Simon and Schuster, 1979.

————. *The Choice*. New York: Simon and Schuster, 1996.

————. *The Commanders*. New York: Simon and Schuster, 1991.

————. *Veil: The Secret Wars of the CIA 1981–1987*. New York: Simon and Schuster, 1987.

Woodward, Bob, and Carl Bernstein. *All the President's Men*. New York: Warner Books, 1975.

————. *The Final Days*. New York: Simon and Schuster, 1976.

Wong, Jan. *Red China Blues: My Long March from Mao to Now*. New York: Doubleday/Anchor Books, 1996.

Zeifman, Jerry. *Without Honor: Crimes of Camelot and the Impeachment of President Nixon*. New York: Thunder's Mouth Press, 1995.

Index

Index

Index

Index

Index

Index

Levin, Carl
on Gingrich and entitlement issues, 123
Levy Institute, 232
Lewis, Ann
on Dole campaign, 426
Lewis, Michael
Bob Dornan story, 80
on Morry Taylor, 79–80
Libertarian Party, 233–234
Liddy, G. Gordon
on the Unabomber, 156–157
Limbaugh, Rush, 104, 174, 390
AFL-CIO dues issue, 136–137
on Al Gore, 171, 437
on Alan Sokal article, 186
on all-news cable stations, 237
on Anthony Marceca, 229
on Ben Stein story, 469
on Bill Clinton, 413
on class envy, 210
on Clinton's *60 Minutes* appearance, 333–334
on Colin Powell, 106
on coverage of Dole's speech, 316
on Dan Rostenkowski, 145
on David Denkins, 118
on Dick Morris story, 361–362
on excluding Perot from debates, 397–398
on the FBI, 247
on Filegate, 211
Frontline bio, 147–148
on Jack Kemp, 262
on Jack Kevorkian, 115–116
on Jeff Jacoby's column, 410–411
on Joe Klein, 246
on John Huang, 471
on John Sweeney and AFL-CIO, 133
on Kennedy/Kassebaum health bill, 163
on liberal bias in press, 46
on Liddy Dole, 301
on Maya Angelou, 174, 182
on minimum wage, 136–138, 145, 161
on Morton Kondracke, 466–467
on Newt Gingrich, 245
Our Stolen Future and, 133
on partial-birth abortion, 405
on Pat Buchanan's real estate dealings, 110
on "Rita X", 442
Robert Bork interview, 400–401
on Robin Williams, 174
on Ross Perot, 130–131
on Social Security, 118
on Susan Molinari, 301–302
on Unabomber, 140
Lind, Michael
Diane Rehm interview, 249
Livingstone, Craig
testifying in congress, 210–211
lobbyists
John Boehner on, 383, 400

Louisiana caucus results
Nightline coverage, 83
Lowry, Malcom, 219
Lugar, Richard, 89, 93
Lyons, Gene
on *Blood Sport*, 207
review of *Partners in Crime*, 237

M

Maher, Bill, 143, 411
Mailer, Norman
quote from *Life* article, 375
Manafort, Paul
on Republican convention, 250–251
Maraniss, David, 460
Marceca, Anthony, 229
Markusen, Ann
at ASSA conference, 32
Marquis, Alice Goldfarb, 283
Maslin, Janet
review of Virginia campaign documentary, 204–205
Mason, Abner, 274
Matalin, Mary
Chris Matthews interview, 458–459
McCain, John, 275
McCarthy, Carolyn, 350
McCormack, Lisa, 223–224
McCurry, Mike
on Bill Clinton, 227
McDougal, Susan, 323, 390
McGovern, George, 408
Larry King Live interview, 361
McLarty, Mack, 172
McLaughlin Group, 77
on crucifixion imagery in media, 403
on culture of business, 75–76
feminization of cabinet positions, 76
on Perot factor, 474
McLaughlin, John
on airline safety, 239–240
McNamara, Robert, 397
McVeigh, Timothy, 9
Medved, Michael
on trash television, 242
Meet the Press
Christopher Dodd interview, 402
Donald Rumsfeld interview, 379
Haley Barbour interview, 402
James Carville on Perot, 117
Ross Perot on Dole, 402
Scott Reed interview, 465
Miller, Dennis
on Pat Buchanan, 117
Milosz, Czeslaw
comparison of Russians and Americans, 7
minimum wage, 157, 164
David Card story, 175
Kennedy/Nickles interview, 133
1935 Fair Labor Standards Act, 261–262

512

Index

Index

Index

Index